Cast of Characters

Grandchildren and secretary of Grandpa Multree ("the Boss"):

BILL Vice President of Sales: ex-retailer (shoe store). New to the company.

BOB Vice President of Manufacturing: engineer. Worked for the company a long time.

DORIS Grandpa Multree's secretary for 25 years.

JACKIE Controller, CPA: financial accountant. Already worked for the company.

JULIE Chief Financial Officer, CMA: management accountant (15 years banking experience). New to the company.

NANCY Vice President of Strategic Planning: just graduated from college with a philosophy degree. Very practical, but inexperienced. New to the company.

SID President: traditional manager. Has worked for the company the longest of the grandchildren.

TOMMY Manager of Human Resources: grew up with the people who now work in factory; very ethical. New to the company.

Acronym List

Acronym	Meaning
ABC	activity-based costing
ABM	activity-based management
CMU	contribution margin per unit
CVP	cost-volume-profit
COQ	costs of quality
EDI	electronic data interchange
EVA	economic value added
GAAP	generally accepted accounting principles
IMA	Institute of Management Accountants
JIT	just-in-time
LTE	lead time efficiency ratio
POR	predetermined overhead rate
QFD	quality function deployment
ROI	return on investment
TOC	theory of constraints
TQM	total quality management
WIP	work-in-process

Management Accounting

James T. Mackey
California State University–Sacramento

Michael F. Thomas
University of Nevada–Reno

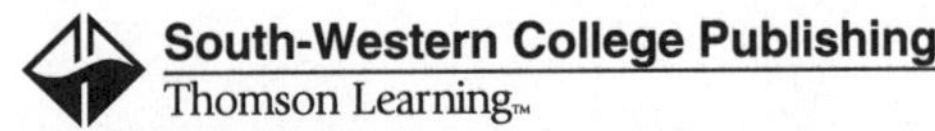

South-Western College Publishing
Thomson Learning™

Australia • Canada • Denmark • Japan • Mexico • New Zealand • Philippines
Puerto Rico • Singapore • South Africa • Spain • United Kingdom • United States

Management Accounting: A Road of Discovery, by Mackey and Thomas

Acquisitions Editor: Sharon Oblinger
Developmental Editor: Sara Wilson
Marketing Manager: Matthew Filimonov
Production Editor: Rebecca Glaab
Manufacturing Coordinator: Doug Wilke
Cover Design and Internal Design: Meighan Depke Design, Chicago, Illinois
Cover Photographer: ©Rob Matheson/The Stock Market
Photo Researcher: Cary Benbow
Production House: Cover to Cover Publishing, Inc.
Printer: R.R. Donnelley

Printed in the United States of America
1 2 3 4 5 02 01 00 99

For more information contact South-Western College Publishing, 5101 Madison Road, Cincinnati, Ohio, 45227 or find us on the Internet at http://www.swcollege.com

For permission to use material from this text or product, contact us by
- **telephone: 1-800-730-2214**
- **fax: 1-800-730-2215**
- **web: http://www.thomsonrights.com**

Library of Congress Cataloging-in-Publication Data
Mackey, James T.
Management accounting : a road of discovery / James T. Mackey, Michael F. Thomas.
p. cm.
Includes bibliographical references and index.
ISBN: 0-538-87189-X; 0-324-02708-7
1. Managerial accounting. 2. Accounting--Decision making.
I. Thomas, Michael F., II. Title.
HF5657.4M274 1999
658.15'11--dc21 99-24166

This book is printed on acid-free paper.

PREFACE

"In the beginning, before computers, before paper, even before man painted on cave walls, hunters sat around camp fires telling stories about the hunt. This is how the old taught the young. Even today, people love a good story. It is still our easiest way to learn."

Management Accounting: A Road of Discovery provides an overview of how management accounting information supports traditional and modern management strategies. It also can be used as a case study supplement, or background reading, for intermediate, advanced, or masters-level management accounting courses.

Philosophy

This book introduces readers to the uses of accounting information in managing an organization. *Management's purpose is to create and maintain value. Accounting systems support value-creating activities by providing decision-relevant information and motivating management to exercise good judgment.* In particular, we identify conditions in which traditional accounting systems work and conditions requiring changes in the accounting system. The appropriateness of the accounting system is then a function of both the use of the information and the firm's operating conditions. Consequently, a critical aspect of good management (and a critical success factor for this book) is the ability to identify when the circumstances are such that the accounting system fails to support management's value creating strategies.

How we learn

Our book is written in a "brain-friendly" manner. The brain is constantly bombarded with large amounts of data. One way it economizes data processing is by grouping concepts into common categories, thus reducing the number of unique concepts to store. Low variety makes it easier for the brain to assimilate new ideas. Therefore, we introduce heuristics commonly found in practice, like *"costs versus benefits," "functional silos," "if it isn't broken don't fix it,"* and moving from *"black boxes to glass boxes."* Heuristics need not be correct in all aspects, nor all of the time, but they must capture sufficient critical aspects to trigger recall of the most important ideas.

The more new concepts can be linked to existing frames of reference, the easier it is to retain them. To capitalize on the readers' experiences, we use vivid personal examples, such as *dog training, parent-child relationships, a student's college budget, baseball, cooking,* and *weekly food shopping.* These analogies evoke concrete physical memories of similar events in a reader's life. While formulas are soon forgotten, the underlying concepts will stay with readers much longer. If sufficiently vivid and relevant, the example should serve as an anchor readers can use to recall and apply concepts. In distinguishing between effectiveness and efficiency, the following story serves as an example. Two people are playing darts. One is demonstrative, making many gestures and taking a long time to throw the darts. The other just steps up to the line and throws. Both are very effective, hitting the bulls-eye regularly. The latter is much more efficient, though.

Because of the brain's tendency to connect new ideas with existing ones and its need to economize, we use a story line connecting earlier ideas with later ones in a logically sequential manner. For example, scientific management leads to standard costing. Activities are designed in the *one best way*. This is *learning from above* (engineering). This is later connected to continuous improvement, or *learning from below* (the shop floor). Readers see how *functional silos* promote efficiency under scientific management but are sources of inefficiency for JIT. The story line allows our characters to refer back to earlier episodes, highlighting the differences in environments, information needs, and management accounting concepts.

To sustain interest and increase the vividness of the ideas, our characters were developed so readers can easily identify with them. We believe this writing style enhances reader interest and involvement. Readers visualize the context and concerns of the individuals running the organization.

Differentiating features

- *One company's management team travels "a road of discovery" from traditional to new management strategies, discovering the accounting information needed to support them.* Our characters inherit and must learn how to manage the business. Each chapter is a meeting in which the new owners answer their next question in learning how to run their company. Each character plays a specific role [i.e., a CPA, CMA, traditional boss, production manager (engineer), behaviorist, marketer, and secretary]. During these meetings, our characters express many of the same questions and anxieties a reader would have in these situations. Thus, readers can easily internalize and identify with them, enhancing reading enjoyment while moving away from the too often heard complaint of books that focus on "dry procedures written to cure insomnia." Readers repeatedly tell us the dialogue format makes the environment and concerns of the people running it come alive. This unique transition, based on their managerial evolution, allows the importance of changing conditions to drive our pedagogy. It is critically important that readers understand the conditions creating a need for changes in management accounting systems.

- *Emphasis is on the big picture: management exists to create value.* Readers can relate topics across chapters to this theme because we use one common example throughout the book. This is unlike other situations where readers too often fail to integrate ideas because chapters tend to stand alone, like *functional silos*, with weak formal linkages that fail to exploit earlier lessons. In this book, chapters and concepts are knit together. Because the chapters build off of each other, as the company's environment changes, readers can recognize this. By experiencing these changes, readers can develop the ego to question accounting information relevance when environments and management strategies change.

- *The dialogue format stresses strategic management* rather than just "decision making" as in most books. A critical element of management is control. By introducing personalities and investigating their thoughts and values and how they are shaped by differing operating environments, this book stresses management issues rather than "data-bound" issues.

- *Simplicity.* Using one company and a few key characters reduces the cognitive processing so often causing reader frustration. Jargon and terminology are limited to minimize cognitive processing. Concepts are stressed over detailed calculations that will be performed by the accountants. Rather than spending chapters on FIFO and weighted average process costing calculations and standard cost system journal entries, for example, we use chapters to introduce new environments and management coping strategies and identify the relevant accounting information supporting these strategies.

- *Complete coverage* of traditional and new technologies, corresponding management methods, and accounting systems to support them is provided. Yet, the depth of coverage is kept at an appropriate level for this audience. Readers do not need to be able to design and implement a detailed standard costing system. However, they should be able to realize the need to modify it in support of a continuous improvement strategy (i.e., evolve into a kaizen costing system) and the new meaning and usefulness of cost variances in this environment.
- *Simple analogies to everyday reader experiences* introduce new ideas. This is important so readers can identify, relate to, and remember key concepts.

Pedagogical features

- Virtually all books present overly complicated accounting procedures requiring up to 20 chapters. Our book is limited to 14 chapters, providing complete coverage at an appropriate level within one semester or quarter.
- Each chapter begins with a list of key objectives and ends with a summary organized by objective. The summary includes reinforcing demonstration problems for each calculation-related objective.
- To reinforce management accounting's applicability in all economic sectors, specific chapter sections illustrate nonmanufacturing applications. Demonstration problems also are presented in nonmanufacturing settings.
- Easy-to-locate notes in the margins identify key objectives and terms.
- At the end of each chapter, a Reality 101 section provides real-world examples to drive home and expand the chapter's main points. This is accompanied by a list of articles readers can understand.

Our objectives in writing this book

1. *Accounting systems are useful to management when they help create value. Accounting information can be misleading, though, when it is created for one purpose but then used in other situations.* The book provides a managerial emphasis stressing value creation over accounting techniques. In Chapter 2, we set the stage by discussing the meaning of value, how it is created, and the limitations of financial accounting information in measuring value.
2. *The book presents accounting systems as a tool embedded in good management practice.* Readers need critical analysis skills. Too often, though, they only memorize specific, unrelated calculations as they move from chapter to chapter. Our book is divided into two parts. Traditional environments, management practices, and accounting systems comprise Part One. After readers understand this "world," Part Two introduces environmental crises, new management techniques, and the accounting information needed to support good management in these new situations. We have found when new techniques are introduced too early, readers fail to appreciate when different situations require different accounting systems. Management accounting systems differ from firm to firm because of the strategies used to cope with the situations each faces.

3. *Our goal is to demonstrate how accounting systems evolve to satisfy ever-evolving information needs.* The changing environmental conditions an organization must deal with are easily identified as readers progress through the chapters. Readers see how "the numbers" were developed for certain uses and how they may be inappropriate in new situations. By using the same company and financial data throughout the book, readers can integrate topics and ideas without the cognitive overloads often experienced by introducing new, unrelated scenarios as they move from chapter to chapter.

   The inability to link concepts across chapters in a simple, understandable, and entertaining way is one of the most serious pedagogical limitations of some books. Too often it is claimed that being able to select, skip, or reorganize chapters is an asset called "flexibility." The independence of each chapter is really a liability. It inhibits readers from seeing the big picture.

4. *Critical thinking is encouraged* by allowing readers to consider different views and positions on the same issue. Readers should realize the importance of different assumptions and conditions on the adequacy of the information systems used. For example, the standard costing chapter includes discussions showing the varied influence of these systems from the boardroom to the shop floor. A system may be very appropriate for boardroom planning but may be a disaster if not applied correctly on the shop floor! This also allows us to identify ethical issues highlighted by the different values, personalities, and positions of power our characters exhibit during the course of each meeting.

5. *Readers should be able to apply management accounting information in service, non-profit, and governmental sectors, and in international situations.* In addition to real-world examples throughout the text, assignment problems allow readers to apply concepts and calculations to these varied environments. This is how we believe the concept of flexibility is beneficial. You can vary the environmental applications to best suit the cognitive complexity and interests of the readers. "Flexibility" that inhibits readers integrating ideas and forming good management judgment is counterproductive.

6. *A customer focus for accounting information is stressed.* This book is equally useful for accountants and non-accountants by emphasizing management information needs. In fact, it is extremely useful for accountants as they are exposed first to their customers' information needs. This customer focus is the fundamental building block for TQM, both in business and education.

7. *Readers should be able to deal with changing management environments.* Coping with different value-adding management philosophies will be the challenge faced by our graduates. These philosophies will define accounting system relevance. Our transitional approach from traditional to continuous improvement and learning organizations allows readers to understand and expect change in a manner impossible to communicate using a traditional topical approach. By mixing traditional and new approaches in the same chapters, the influence of changing management philosophies is too easily masked.

Organization

We identify fourteen questions management asks in learning how to run the business. In order, each becomes a chapter providing an integrated survey of management and management accounting's evolution from traditional to modern worlds.

Chapter 1 establishes the goals for financial accounting and compares them to management accounting's goals. Readers can anchor on learning heuristics such as *hard versus soft data, financial versus nonfinancial information,* and *decision-based versus rule-based systems.* The management issue is stewardship. Accounting systems are artifacts created by man for specific purposes. Thus, the users determine the value of different accounting systems in satisfying their information needs. Financial accounting standards are set by the needs of external users, while management accounting information relevance is determined by the needs of internal users.

Chapter 2 introduces the fundamental management philosophy: *good management maintains and creates value.* As a cash machine, value is determined by a firm's customers. Cashflows from the goods or services provided to customers measure the firm's success in creating long-term value. The cashflow value model is contrasted with the profits measured by the financial accounting system. The justification for strategic planning then is seen in the need to maintain long-run cashflows. This chapter ends with considering management accounting's role in the strategic planning process.

Chapter 3 considers traditional cost behaviors, the contribution margin income statement, and cost-volume-profit analysis. By focusing on the relevant range and the volume-based nature of short-term CVP analysis, we promote the idea that managers must *know their business* in order to *manage by the numbers.* The management philosophy is that cost behaviors sufficiently represent cause-effect relationships to plan short-run business activity. CVP supports the strategic plan by responding to changing environments through manipulating only price, cost, and volume. This sets the stage for later considering how organizations differ by changing their strategies to strategic cost management and ABM in response to dynamic environments.

Chapter 4 views cash budgeting as part of the planning and control system needed to support the strategic plan and CVP analysis. The budgeting process translates strategic plans into operational activities and measures the cashflows from these value-creating activities. It also allows organizations to adjust for contingencies and change as necessary. Finally, budgets form the basis for control. As well as teaching cash planning techniques, the conceptual focus demonstrates the power of prior planning to manage scarce resources, like money. *Scarce resources require prior planning and control.* The chapter begins with a *student's school budget,* which is shown to be the basis for management by exception. This example also links to responsibility accounting by showing how the budget frees our student to exercise discretion within his plan.

Chapter 5 moves from planning to organizing work into *functional silos.* Scientific management is introduced as a strategy to efficiently deal with operating uncertainties. Its philosophy is based on separately optimizing each process to maximize the value of the company as a whole through specialization and engineered task design. Cost accounting systems assigning full absorptive costs to products are explained within this context. Believing in independent silos, it makes sense to assign overhead using capacity, or volume-based cost drivers, rather than individual product characteristics (the ABC logic).

Chapter 6 considers how to evaluate the efficiency (productivity) of these *functional silos* with variances. Using scientific management, each activity is engineered in the *one best way* leading accountants to develop standard costs. The critical learning objective is realizing how scientific management drove accounting system design. As long as unfavorable variances are avoided, the functional silos are "under control." The management-by-exception evaluation strategy supports the *if it isn't broken don't fix it* management belief.

Chapter 7 introduces relevant decision analysis using incremental CVP to aid short-term decisions when unforeseen threats and opportunities develop during the year. Traditional strategies, such as cost-plus pricing, are juxtaposed with the *incremental cashflows—opportunity cost-benefit* model. We also consider how the functional silo strategy creates a need to specifically consider *externalities*.

Chapter 8 examines the behavioral side of control. By this chapter the family is nervous. While the new owners have followed good management practices, variances abound. Because they believe the accounting numbers must be right, if something is wrong, it has to be with how the people are behaving. *Motivating good judgment* then becomes the issue. After exploring various motivational strategies, they begin to challenge the appropriateness of using financial measures for performance evaluation. The adverse behavioral effects from emphasizing a single financial measure in performance evaluation leads them to consider *multiple measures*.

Chapter 9 is the turning point in our book. The concerns from the previous chapter have advanced to a crisis stage. This chapter begins with identifying operating conditions that violate scientific management beliefs and justify abandoning volume-based costing. Through an ABC analysis of specific activities, the logic behind volume-based cost-plus pricing is challenged and the family's management errors are exposed. A new management philosophy evolves which focuses on activities or processes rather than each functional department's capacity. The new focus becomes *activities, not departments or volume, drive resource usage.*

Chapter 10 turns the owners' focus to the management of change, which is necessitated by increasingly competitive environments. The new management philosophy is to *maximize value through managing the value chain*. In this chapter, the owners begin by considering supplier and customer value chain relationships. Strategic cost management, using ABC, identifies how these relationships can be improved. Then, they develop financial and nonfinancial ABM performance measures to manage these relationships.

Chapter 11 moves inside the organization, introducing TQM, process value analysis (PVA), and continuous improvement. Scientific management's *one best way* allowing for an acceptable level of quality failures is challenged in a *quality is free* debate. Costs of quality reporting then is used to justify change. The new quality strategy becomes *do it right the first time*.

Chapter 12 considers what to improve next through a step-wise continuous improvement strategy focusing on constraint activities. By identifying and eliminating the constraint most limiting value, theory of constraints (TOC) management focuses on the *throughput world*, rather than on cost management in every department (the *cost world*). The owners then realize TOC is a short-run, decision-focused strategy for profit maximization. Thus, they also develop performance measures to assess TOC's effect on long-term value.

Chapter 13 introduces business process reengineering (BPR) through a JIT application, and contrasts BPR (a *big step* strategy) and TOC (a *small step* strategy). The JIT philosophy is to create low-volume production systems that are as economical as high-volume production lines. JIT reduces variety (reducing setups through group technology), reengineers into cells (reducing moves), uses *pull versus push* scheduling (reducing wait time), and employs TQM (reducing inventory and quality costs). Once reengineered, kanban management for JIT continuous improvement is compared with the TOC continuous improvement approach.

Chapter 14 addresses how the change process can be strategically controlled through capital budgeting and balanced scorecards. Capital budgeting, as a component of strategic planning, is forward looking. Balanced scorecards, in contrast, are backward looking, combining *nonfinancial and financial measures* to focus on the success of the firm's continuous improvement plans. Balanced scorecards include critical success factors, goals, and measures developed in the strategic plan. Thus, readers are left with an understanding of how planning, control, and evaluation are (and should be) linked together into a continuous improvement philosophy.

Learning approach and logic

We believe this book is a radical departure from the "norm" in two ways. First, its organizational logic follows a management, and management information, evolution from traditional to modern strategies and needs. We believe this approach promotes a better understanding of the problems faced by organizations in transition, their management strategies, and the accounting information needed to support those strategies. Thus, separate chapters are devoted to ABC, value chain analysis and strategic cost management, TQM and ABM, TOC, JIT, and balanced scorecards. Secondly, its writing style specifically addresses problems we see in information processing and retention, and in creating subject interest.

We also believe our pedagogical elements differ from the norm. These differences are highlighted next.

Included within each chapter

Materials	Comments
1. *Key objectives summary* 2. *Demonstration problems*	Logic: Usually these are separated, and many books do not include a demonstration problem for each major calculation introduced within a chapter. Thus, readers fail to link calculations to the concepts learning objectives seek to reinforce. By placing demonstration problems within the key objectives summaries, readers can better relate concepts and calculations. To further emphasize management accounting's applicability in other economic sectors, each objective requiring a calculation is demonstrated in a nonmanufacturing setting.
3. *Reality 101*	One- to two-page real-world company examples. Logic: In many books ¼- or ½-page inserts are placed throughout each chapter. As with exhibits, though, they are often placed at the top of the nearest, most convenient page. This often interrupts the flow of ideas as readers are forced to stop reading, locate a special insert, and then find where they originally were. This makes reading more difficult and time-consuming. We have heard comments like, "I read the inserts about real companies at the beginning of the chapters. But, as I get further along, I start skipping them. By the end of the chapter, I completely ignore them." Some books use one example at the beginning of the chapter "to set the stage." Student feedback suggests these are not very insightful because the chapter material is unknown. Thus, we place a real company example at the end of the chapter. Throughout the chapters, we seamlessly insert brief real-

world references to authenticate concepts. Our goal is to not break the book's flow.

4. *Reading list* — Each chapter ends with a list of usable and readable references to the companies cited within the chapter and used to authenticate concepts. The reading list is organized by company cited. Students do not have to reference another source to obtain bibliographic lists.

Web site. Both professors and students have access to our Web site. Among the resources available are references to new articles, a FAQ (frequently asked questions) section with answers provided by the authors, and links to our email addresses to promote dialogue with adopters and students. Our Web site address is www.mackey.swcollege.com

ABOUT THE AUTHORS

James T. Mackey is a professor of cost and management accounting at California State University, Sacramento. He earned a B.A. in economics and mathematics from the University of Guelph, an M.B.A. from McMaster University in accounting and finance, and a Ph.D. in accounting, with a minor in industrial engineering, from the University of Illinois. His professional designations include both a CPA (Illinois) and CMA (Ontario). As a management accounting educator for over twenty years, his assignments have included graduate and undergraduate instruction at the Universities of Illinois, Wisconsin, Michigan, and York and Wilfred Laurier Universities in Canada. He has taught shorter courses at UC Davis, Nankai University in the Peoples' Republic of China, and at the Helsinki School of Economics and Business Administration in Finland.

Continuing scholarly activity has led Dr. Mackey to contribute numerous articles to *Management Accounting*, the *Journal of Management Accounting Research*, *CMA Magazine*, *Advances in Accounting*, *Information and Management*, *Issues in Management Accounting*, *Issues in Accounting Education*, and the *International Accounting Review*. He has contributed to several books and edited a case series on the Theory of Constraints for the Institute of Management Accountants. He also co-authored the book *The Theory of Constraints and Its Implications for Management Accounting* which sells internationally. Throughout his career he has served as a learned reviewer for such journals as the *Journal of Accounting Education*, *Management and Information Technologies*, *Omega*, the *International Journal of Management Science*, *Accounting Horizons*, and the *Journal of Business and Management*.

Pursuing his passion for applied managerial practice, Dr. Mackey has particular pride in serving as a consultant for the Society of Management Accountants in Canada, the Institute of Management Accountants in the United States, and the Consortium for Advanced Manufacturing-International (CAM-I). In addition, he has worked for and with numerous companies and the Canadian government.

Michael F. Thomas currently teaches at the University of Nevada—Reno. His expertise also is in management and cost accounting. Dr. Thomas brings over twenty years of teaching experience to this project. He previously has taught at Oklahoma State University, California Polytechnic State University—San Luis Obispo, the University of Wisconsin, and San Jose State University. He has won an outstanding teaching award and been nominated for many others.

Dr. Thomas' research accomplishments include three international awards for his developments of second generation activity-based cost systems and transfer pricing systems. He has published in the *Journal of Accounting Research*, the *Journal of Management Accounting Research*, the *Journal of Accounting and Finance Research*, the *Academy of Accounting and Financial Studies Journal*, *Issues in Management Accounting*, the *Journal of Accounting Education*, *Management Accounting*, the *Internal Auditor*, and other outlets. Dr. Thomas also has made numerous presentations at AAA and IMA conferences, as well as at other international research and practitioner conferences. Additionally, he contributed many chapters to Dr. John Burch's *Cost and Management Accounting: A Modern Approach*, as well as co-authoring its Instructors Manual and Solutions Manual. Outside of accounting, his award winning research in applying ABC to healthcare management has been published in *Behavior Therapy* and *Prescription Privileges for Psychologists: A Critical Analysis*.

Active in practice and consulting, Dr. Thomas brings years of practical experience to this project. He has held virtually all types of accounting positions from a bookkeeper (where he claims he learned how to type by preparing checks) to controller. He also was co-owner of a construction company in the Bay area and Lake Tahoe. Currently, Dr. Thomas serves as the Reno area chapter president of the IMA. He continues to regularly make IMA presentations and authored an IMA monograph on using second generation ABC with a JIT conversion project.

ACKNOWLEDGMENTS

As this project evolved, we received a great deal of helpful suggestions and guidance from many people. We first thank the hundreds of students at California State University—Sacramento, and the University of Nevada—Reno, Paul Jensen's students at the University of Central Arkansas, and Marc Massoud's students at Claremont McKenna College for their straightforward, constructive feedback. These students span the introductory undergraduate course required of all business majors, through the junior level cost course, a senior level management accounting seminar, MBAs, and business executives. Without their overwhelming support, this project would not have been completed!

We want to specially acknowledge Silvercrest Western Homes Corporation, which generously allowed us to use photographs of its manufacturing process so students can better understand the manufactured home industry. We wish to make clear the fact that the story in this text is fictional, and all characters and Multree Homes referenced or used in the text are fictitious. Any similarities to real people or organizations is merely coincidental.

The following individuals reviewed the chapters in the development stage. We thank these professors for their timely and constructive remarks:

Surendra P. Agrawal, University of Memphis
Roderick S. Barclay, University of Texas—Dallas
Wayne G. Bremser, Villanova University
Carroll I. Buck, University of Nevada—Reno
James M. Emig, Villanova University
Margaret Gagne, University of Colorado—Colorado Springs
Paul Jensen, University of Central Arkansas
Paul Krause, California State University—Chico
Leslie Kren, University of Wisconsin—Milwaukee
Gina Lord, Santa Rosa Junior College
Paige Paulsen, Salt Lake City Community College
Roy W. Regel, University of Montana
Bin Srinidhi, The State University of New Jersey—Rutgers
M. Cathy Sullivan, James Madison University
David N. Wiest, Bentley College
Jack Zeller, Kirkwood Community College

To the ladies in my life,
Teresa, Carrie Ann, and Kathryn
JTM

To Dr. John G. Burch, a visionary,
collegue, mentor, and good friend
MFT

BRIEF CONTENTS

CONTENTS

Part 1: Traditional Roles for Management and Cost Accounting Systems

PART 1

Traditional Roles for Management and Cost Accounting Systems

CHAPTER 1

What is Management Accounting?

Accounting for Planning, Control, and Evaluation

KEY OBJECTIVES:

1	*Explain stewardship and why the dominant goal of accounting systems historically has been financial reporting.*
2	*Describe eight modern management trends changing the role of accounting in organizations.*
3	*Define the four types of accounting systems and relate them to their four organizational roles.*
4	*Discuss the differences between financial and management accounting information.*
5	*Contrast the four accounting certifications and discuss the role of ethics in management accounting.*

It was one of those days Nancy would rather forget. Actually, she'd like to make the whole week go away. Grandfather Multree had died, and today was the funeral. Of course, it rained and the clammy October cold still hung in the air. She shivered as she sat in the stuffed reading chair by the side of the fireplace. The whole town showed up for the funeral, but that was expected. Grandfather founded Multree Homes; it was the reason for the town's existence. She hoped for a little solitude in the library, but couldn't find it as his portrait seemed to ominously stare down upon her. Doris, a close family friend and Grandfather's personal secretary for as long as everyone could remember, almost went unnoticed as she sat in the corner quietly reflecting on how he built up Multree Homes, the town, and its now uncertain fate. "The Boss," as everyone called Grandfather, always included her in all his executive meetings. Many thought she knew as much about Multree Homes as he did.

Two months ago at her college graduation, Nancy pondered her fate. Her philosophy degree, even with a minor in logic, hadn't prompted a single job offer. Now her fate was clear. The Boss left the company to his seven grandchildren. Just the prospect of being a businesswoman was amazing! The thought of starting as vice president of strategic planning was overwhelming. The closest thing she had to a business suit were her new jeans, a cotton blouse, a leather vest, and her old cowboy boots. Life had been good in college, but that was about to quickly change. Within a week, the grandchildren must meet and decide how to run the business.

As Nancy reached for the lamp switch on the reading table, she shivered again. This time, however, it was more like an ice-cold knife stabbing through her heart. She gasped, but couldn't catch her breath. She knew the papers on the table were meant for her, and she knew she didn't want them. A tear ran down her face. Her hand seemed frozen. No matter what Nancy did, she couldn't pull it back to her lap. All she could think about was trying to hide underneath the chair's soft cushion.

KEY OBJECTIVE 1

Explain stewardship and why the dominant goal of accounting systems historically has been financial reporting.

History's Changing Role for Accounting Information

THAT was not practical! She was a survivor. She could overcome this. Even though full of remorse, her grimace strengthened. She thought her teeth would break as she crushed her jaws together. Then, she picked it up. Last year's income statement and balance sheet beckoned. Surprisingly, Multree's financial statements were easy to discard, though, as her attention focused on what lay below, *The Historical Development of Management Accounting*.

Stewardship and the opening of the American West

She began reading. Chapter 1 started with the following story:

Slim was a tall man with big hands and leathery skin from days in the sun and in the saddle. He'd fought Indians and cattle rustlers, endured blizzards and droughts and faced angry grizzly bears and rabid wolves to make the Lazy K the largest ranch in the new territory. What he faced today made his hands tremble and his brow sweat. As he walked to the hotel, Slim involuntarily brushed his hand past his hip. He was instinctively reaching for his gun. Slim's hand came up empty, though. He was not wearing a holster. This was a different kind of challenge; one he wasn't ready for. He cursed the day he brought in those British investors. Slim wished he had his shooting iron. Still, he wouldn't have a ranch today without their invested capital.

A small bearded man in a clean eastern-style suit stepped out of the hotel. He seemed to know Slim. Quickly he raised his hand. It was high noon on Main Street. Slim winced as he again reached to his side. "No gun," Slim cursed to himself. A shoot-out would have been preferable to what was going to happen next. "Good day, Mr. Jorgersen!" the man said, with what Slim interpreted as a menacing grin. "I am Randel Cummings of Price Waterhouse. I'm here as a representative of your British investors to audit your book of accounts and swindle sheet."

Slim gulped. He preferred to call them a balance sheet and income statement. The term "swindle sheet," left over from the days of the Mayflower, always raised fears that his European investors would sell the ranch if they didn't like his management. Truly, the auditor's pen is mightier than the sword (or the six-gun)!

So this is how accountants opened the American West, mused Nancy. She put down the book as Jackie walked into the library. Jackie was one of the grandchildren inheriting Multree Homes. She already worked for the Boss, though, as Multree's controller. Glancing apprehensively at Multree's financial statements which still lay in her lap, Nancy wished she was a CPA [certified public accountant] like Jackie.

JACKIE

"I see you're reading the Boss's favorite book! While the story is perhaps a slight exaggeration, many historians acknowledge the important role played by European investors in developing the American frontier. Along with these investors came their accountants. Properly managing these investments, or **stewardship** as it is called in financial accounting, became a major concern for foreign owners. Price Waterhouse, for example, originally was a British auditing firm. Coming to America, the firm developed an immense network of partners in what is still one of the largest auditing firms in the world today. Public accounting firms evaluate management's stewardship of the company's assets. Because Slim kept books and had them audited, investors thousands of miles away could feel secure enough to invest in the Lazy K ranch. Audited financial statements increased the security of investing with strangers. *Accounting systems had two powerful uses in the opening of the American West:*

> **Stewardship** *is (1) developing records and controls to safeguard assets and (2) reporting on the firm's financial condition and how it has changed.*

- Creating records and internal controls to safeguard the company's assets, and
- Preparing financial statements that:
  - Reported the firm's assets, liabilities, and equity [a balance sheet], and

- Provided an objective measurement of period-to-period performance [an income statement]."

Jackie was interrupted by the squeaking library doors as they slowly opened. Julie peeked into the room. She, too, was one of the inheriting grandchildren. Julie was to be Multree's chief financial officer [CFO]. Nancy wondered why Jackie, a CPA, was not chosen for that position. Jackie already worked for Multree. Julie, like Nancy, was new to the company. Maybe it was due to Julie's 15 years of banking experience and her cashflow orientation. But, that thought would have to wait.

The Industrial Revolution and the need for product cost information

JULIE

"I see you guys are having a history lesson! While stewardship is not the only goal of accounting information, it was the dominant one at that time. The only 'books of record' Slim had was a general ledger. When only one set of books is kept by a company, its dominant goal determines what is recorded, how it is measured, and the form in which this information is reported. *When settling the West, accounting's dominant goal did not include supporting management decisions.* This historical background influences the role of financial accounting in society to this day. However, within organizations, the role of accounting quickly changed with the advent of the Industrial Revolution.

"Around the beginning of the 20th century, American manufacturers wanted information about the costs and profits of specific products. Complex, multiproduct giants, such as DuPont, developed separate internal accounting systems to support management decision making. Carnegie Steel's system provided daily production cost information for materials, labor, and energy. It was used for product pricing, day-to-day operating control, and managerial performance evaluation. Textile mills developed costs per yard for cotton weaving. The railroads calculated cost per ton-mile for different types of shipped goods and for different geographic areas. Around 1920, when Alfred Sloan took over General Motors, a new 'management accounting' system was installed that included annual operating budgets and divisional performance reports. Budgets were revised on a monthly basis to reflect changes in the newly required weekly sales reports. During that time, industry emphasized the development of new internal accounting systems for costing products and managing the business."

JACKIE

"After the 1929 stock market crash, accounting's emphasis changed back to stewardship, which lasted for the next sixty years. Also following the stock market crash, the Securities and Exchange Commission [SEC] was established. Companies trading stock on the major U.S. stock markets had to maintain rigid standards for financial reporting, and have their financial accounting systems audited by CPA firms. The professional body governing the CPA profession is the American Institute of Certified Public Accountants [AICPA]. It works closely with the SEC and the Financial Accounting Standards Board [FASB] to ensure FASB's generally accepted accounting principles [GAAP] meet the SEC's standards."

JULIE

"In the economic prosperity following World War II, many firms expanded into new product lines and markets. These businesses incorporated and publicly sold stock to raise the capital they needed. Meeting SEC rules was more important than developing and maintaining detailed internal accounting information for costing products and managing the business. Without serious competitive pressures, management found it difficult to justify the extra cost of these internal accounting systems. It was easier to try to adapt the financial accounting system information."

Making cars, yesterday and today

Julie was interrupted by a chuckling from the hall. Bob had been standing in the doorway. Another of the grandchildren, Bob had been working at Multree Homes for many years. He was an engineer and the vice president of manufacturing.

"I remember manual cost accounting systems. What a pain! Just about everything in our society and economy has completely changed since then, including our accounting systems.

"During the advent of our Industrial Revolution, Henry Ford became one of the wealthiest men in America, and helped the United States become a premier world power with his West Rouge manufacturing plant. Automobile costs were driven so low cars became accessible to most people.

"To do this, Ford built next to the river so he could use cheap transportation for iron ore. Then, he built a railway to carry his coal. The West Rouge plant went from raw materials to finished product in one cycle and in one complex of buildings. A new car was made every thirty seconds. Ford virtually invented the modern assembly line, which was copied throughout American industry. Assembly-line manufacturing helped to create the wealthy country we have today.

"This was the era of engineering methods and the scientific management approach to manufacturing. These ideas drove down the costs of consumer goods and created an affluent middle class. Scientific management used engineers to design the 'one best way' for performing each task. Accounting systems were shaped by these events. Work standards for materials and labor, translated into dollars, established expected performance levels in terms of financial income. Using this system, variances [deviations] from expected performance could be related to the difference between actual and projected profits. To hold the organization accountable to its owners/investors, individual department reports were developed. Financial measures, such as return on investment [ROI], became management's critical success factors.

"Today, Ford builds a 'world' car. Over 70% of the components for most of its cars come from other companies and countries. Components are made and shipped from all over the world. No longer is everything done at one location. What has allowed this dramatic change to occur? What makes this approach more efficient than the earlier approach? I think the answer is in what many economic historians call the second industrial revolution. Computers, new information and transportation economies, and radically different standards of living have created a new global economy and competition. *While accounting's stewardship role will always be important, modern managers need new and different information to cope with this new economic environment."*

At that point, Sid walked into the library holding a recent Toyota annual report. Sid also had been working for the Boss a long time. He was to become the president. As usual, a half-smoked, unlit cigar hung from the corner of his mouth. All of the other grandchildren liked his gruff style. His favorite expression was, "This is the way the Boss always did it!"

"Good, you're both here!" Sid glanced up at Julie and Jackie. "Of all the well-run companies, many consider Toyota the best in the world. But, I just don't understand what Toyota's saying in its Management Letter. It goes something like this: 'Just as quality management and just-in-time [JIT] was our competitive advantage in the 1980s, cost management will become our competitive advantage in the 1990s. Value is measured in dollars. Cost management is essentially applying a value criterion to every decision we make, every activity we perform, and every process we complete. As we enter the 21st century, this is still true.'

"Why are they changing their philosophy? Will we have to change ours? Why can't we just continue to do things the way the Boss did them? It seems Multree has always been very profitable."

Overhearing Sid's question, Bill stepped into the library looking somewhat perplexed. He was the grandchild who was to become the vice president of marketing. As with Julie and Nancy, though, he never had worked for Multree. Bill had a lot of experience in retail sales.

BILL

"The answer is simple, Sid. If we add value to the houses we make, and manage the costs of what we do, I can sell them for a profit. As long as customers value our houses more than the houses cost us, the sales price will exceed cost, and we will make a profit.

"We have many ways to create value. But, because 'value,' as defined by our customers, changes over time, we, too, must change. Remember the first Volkswagen? It was so ugly, it was called a 'bug.' However, the Volkswagen bug revolutionized the automobile industry. Why did everyone buy one? It got great gas mileage [cheap to operate], and it never broke down [high reliability]. Obviously, the market changed to valuing reliability more than beauty! Toyota also differentiated its cars on reliability and operating cost until everyone else recognized how valuable these qualities are to consumers."

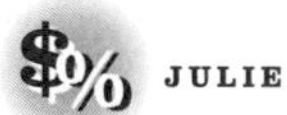

JULIE

"Toyota is just an example of how Japanese management views stewardship differently from most American firms. *Their guiding principle is simple: success results from creating long-term value.* A good 'steward' of an investor's assets adds value to them, resulting in profits to the owners now and in the future. This is often different from maximizing short-term [annual] profits reported on an income statement. Toyota's value came from building unique, desirable cars. Now, as other automobile manufacturers are emphasizing these attributes, Toyota will create value through a different approach. They want to focus on strategic and activity-based cost management."

NANCY

"Sid, you said we should have a series of weekly meetings to learn how to manage our business. I hope our first meeting can address what value is, and how to create it. We also should consider what kind of accounting information is needed to create, sustain, and measure it."

BILL

"We are also in a rapidly changing competitive world. Total quality management [TQM], enhanced electronic communication, cheap reliable transportation, and the elimination of trade barriers—for example, GATT and NAFTA—have created worldwide competition. Over 75% of the firms responding to a 1997 survey I saw plan to increase exports. Increasing 4% over 1996, 59% already regularly export their goods and services. And, 64% report their greatest competition comes from Mexico and Canada, followed by Europe and Asia. The Japanese and Germans may have done the best job capitalizing on global competition to date. Although, it'll be very interesting to see how the new European common currency [the euro] changes their competitive abilities. Multree Homes has been very successful in our local markets and against our local competition. We have to be careful, however, because tomorrow our competition may come from the other side of the world!"

KEY OBJECTIVE 2

Describe eight modern management trends changing the role of accounting in organizations.

Modern Management Demands for Accounting Information

"The economic, technological, and societal changes Bob and Bill mentioned require new management strategies and techniques. To be a successful 'world-class' organization, new information is needed to support these strategies. Accounting systems have been the major business information systems for literally thousands of years. *Now, management is redefining accounting's dominant goal from stewardship to decision support and organizational control.* The argument for change is simple; external investors have no need for financial reports if the company is no longer in business!"

JULIE

"You're right! I've seen this change in all of the national CPA firms. Auditing is no longer the largest revenue source. Instead, it's now management consulting. In fact, I just saw a report showing that three of the top four consulting firms are CPA firms." Jackie remembered how hard it was to get a job with a CPA firm upon graduation. The need for entry-level auditors has radically declined from the 1980–1990 levels.

JACKIE

"In addition to the need for new management methods to survive global competition, computer technology has created new business and information systems changing the way accounting is used. What are these new business and technology trends, and what is their impact on management?"

Customer focus

BILL

"Many movements combined in the late 20th century to create a new competitive world and new management techniques to survive within it. **Total quality management [TQM]** introduces a customer focus. TQM's objective is to provide a product or service at least meeting, and hopefully exceeding, the customer's needs. 'Customer delight' is TQM's credo. This may not be practical in all circumstances, but by focusing on what the customer values, we can make cost-benefit trade-offs when designing our products and services. *The underlying idea is the customer [marketplace], not the company, sets the value of goods and services. The company only controls the cost.* The value [benefit] of our products to our customers determines which costs are justified. Cost management is all about developing accounting systems supporting this philosophy."

> **Total quality management (TQM)** *is simply knowing how to delight customers, and then doing it.*

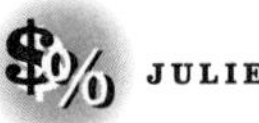

JULIE

"Cost-value information gives management a competitive advantage. It justifies examining the things we do [activities] that add value to the customer. To support TQM, accounting's focus shifts from the traditional reporting of revenues and expenses, and assets and liabilities, to costing our activities. *Simply stated, we need information about which activities create value, and what they cost.*"

Quality focus

BOB

"Numerous definitions of quality exist. The most popular relates to meeting customer needs. This is a lofty goal that should drive strategy. It becomes workable when simplified to mean *meeting product and process specifications.* For example, consider this hypothetical situation. Which is the quality product, a Geo or a Mercedes? I expect the wheels to fall off the Geo in 50,000 miles. I expect the Mercedes' wheels to fall off after 250,000 miles. The Geo's wheels actually fall off at 60,000 miles. The Mercedes' wheels fall off at 200,000 miles. Which is the quality product in the eyes of the two car owners? The Geo! It delivered more than it promised [customer delight]."

At that point, the last of the grandchildren stormed into the library. Tommy grew up with the people now working in the factory. Tommy had not worked for the Boss before, but the Boss knew him to be a people person, a behaviorist. Tommy was going to be the manager of human resources.

TOMMY

"Wait a minute! I own a Geo. It's not a top quality car, but I didn't pay much for it. I'd much rather have the Mercedes!"

NANCY

"Yes, but why didn't you buy a Mercedes? You weren't willing to pay for that much quality. I see where the phrase 'You get what you pay for' comes from! Quality is not an absolute concept. While the Mercedes has higher quality, it also has a higher sales price. The value the market places on different products is based on differing levels of quality. Quality is really a relative concept. How much do I want? What am I willing to pay for that much quality?"

TOMMY

"I guess I see your point. I am happy with my Geo, and I'd buy another. It's delivered more quality and value than I expected. If I valued the extra quality of a Mercedes high enough, I would have bought it instead."

SID

"O.K. Quality, then, is meeting customer expectations in a manner that increases value in the customer's mind. Thus, we must expand our definition of quality to include how much value the market is willing to pay for, that is, how much value the market expects for a given price. The Geo improves quality by delivering increasing value to the customer. That is, the wheels don't fall off until 50,000 miles or more, while the cost remains low."

BILL

"Using a customer quality focus, many airlines have changed their in-flight meals. Delta discovered a lettuce garnish didn't add value for their customers, so Delta dropped it and is saving millions of dollars. Many 'low cost, no frills' airlines have discovered their customers don't even want meals. Learning customer desires and then providing for them has significantly changed that industry, too."

BOB

"We've also done this at Multree. Different customers want different types of houses. That's why we added custom cedar log homes to our standard line of prefabricated houses. Quality also drove our decision to make trusses [the beams supporting the roof]. We used to buy them from another manufacturer, but the quality wasn't good enough for the snowy winters at Lake Tahoe."

NANCY

"Let's see if I understand. Quality is defined many different ways. For a customer, quality means getting what she wants. For a company, quality means delivering what it promises. Often these are not identical ideas. However, generally speaking, an organization always delivering or exceeding what it promises usually is considered a 'high-quality' firm."

JULIE

"What are the implications for accounting, though? *Our system will have to tell us about the costs of quality.* We'll need to know failure rates, warranty repair costs by product, inspection costs, and a host of other costs related to the quality of our homes."

Delivery focus

BOB

"If quality means you get what you expect, delivery means you get it when you expect it. Florists are selling roses from South America in New York City. Manufacturing plants making automobile components in Osaka, Japan, and assembling them in Fremont, California, operate with only a few hours of parts available in Fremont. The Fremont plant expects quality parts delivered on time. When delivery and quality are uncertain, though, companies must keep extra inventories to avoid costly production shutdowns and lost sales. However, when quality is perfect and on-time deliveries are guaranteed, these very expensive excess inventories are not needed. **Just-in-time [JIT]** means manufacture and delivery as needed, not before, and cer-

> **Just-in-time (JIT)** *is a management system that eliminates inventories while delivering materials, manufactured components, and finished products only when needed. This is done by emphasizing total quality management and doing only those activities that create value.*

tainly not after! Reliable parts delivery adds value to the customer by eliminating the need for 'safety stocks' [extra materials inventories] and all the costs they incur."

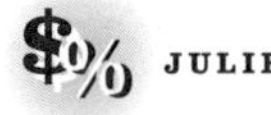

"So, the accounting system needs to tell us the cost of buying, receiving, inspecting, storing, insuring, and moving all that inventory, along with the costs of recording everything and reporting it. We then can compare this cost to the costs of JIT delivery. Overall, if the total cost with JIT is lower, we can significantly reduce our inventories, save money, and provide the same quality product to our customers at a lower price, thus increasing our value."

"Yes, but Bob was talking just about raw materials inventories. What about finished product inventories? Customers ordering from the JCPenney's catalog want JIT delivery, too. This means large regional distribution centers and huge inventories! *I want the accounting system to tell me about activities affecting on-time delivery rates and complete order filling."*

Outsourcing and the virtual company

"Some activities costing more than the value they add may be **outsourced**—contracted to other companies. To illustrate, I know of a Canadian manufacturer making hydraulic air brakes for railroad cars. It converted to JIT manufacturing. However, the hose-making process involved a lot of labor, and was expensive and difficult to fit into the system. What to do? They took the process of making, installing, and testing the hose to another company that specialized in hoses. The other company now delivers hose assemblies to the brake manufacturer on a JIT schedule. Reliable delivery and quality allows parts to be made anywhere in the world. Outsourcing is not limited to manufacturing, though.

BOB

Outsourcing *is having certain activities performed by another company.* **Virtual companies** *are created by sharing information between them so they behave as one large organization.*

"Many governments are outsourcing activities. For example, my youngest son no longer goes to the city's after-school childcare program. It has been terminated because the YMCA can do just as good a job and at a lower cost than the city. My daughter doesn't play in a city baseball program any more. The city also canceled this because the national Little League offers the same program. Pressures to balance budgets and cut taxes have forced many governments to re-evaluate their services and outsource [privatize] those not justified in terms of customer value. Government–private firm partnerships are forming, such as the one to revitalize Boston's Charlestown Navy Yard. California wants to privatize road maintenance and outsource its $7.3 billion workmen's compensation fund."

"Outsourcing also happens with service organizations. Two law firms, one in London, England, and the other in Vancouver, Canada, work closely together. As the English law firm closes for the day, unfinished work is telecommunicated to the Canadian firm starting its work day. The quality is comparable and delivery is just-in-time. These companies use fast turn-around time as a competitive advantage."

"Automobiles manufactured in the Tennessee Saturn plant are another good example of the **virtual company** idea. Parts suppliers actually have offices right in the Saturn plant. Virtual companies are created through outsourcing and maintaining extremely close links with the different companies involved. In effect, all of the companies 'virtually' become one huge organization."

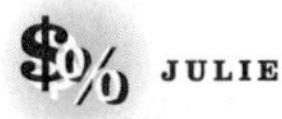

"Before we can consider outsourcing some of our activities, we need to know what they cost. We also need to know 'best practices' costs, that is, who is doing it better and less expensively. We also will need an accounting system that can share information within a virtual company environment."

Communication

"Yes! Communication is a key prerequisite for the tight coordination virtual companies need. Products, parts, and changing customer preferences must be communicated in a timely, efficient manner to coordinate worldwide activities. *The accounting system will have to support electronic communication between our 'partners'—for example, electronic data interchange—and cheap data entry—for example, bar coding—to accomplish these objectives.*

"Once quality and delivery are guaranteed, only cost is left to control. This, of course, is overly simplified since other types of required communication, cultures, and national laws may slow the process. But, as these obstacles are removed, negotiation and international outsourcing will become more prevalent. In this global environment, the importance of good cost management increases."

"That reminds me of a problem we encountered in the plant last year. Remember when we outsourced electric switches to that Japanese firm? We specified defects could not exceed 1% of the total number delivered. The Japanese firm, though, had a zero defects policy. They didn't understand our 1% clause in the first order. Not wanting to offend us, they shipped 500 good switches in one box, and 5 broken switches in another!"

"I've heard a lot of complaints from the workers concerning communication and accounting information availability. As we install more equipment, computers, and software like computer-aided design and computer-aided manufacturing packages [CAD/CAM software], they can't get the accounting information they need. The drafting staff is complaining the loudest. *So, we also have to share information within Multree between different computer systems.*"

Shortening product life cycles

"Technology, competition, and changing customer preferences are causing us to redesign products more frequently, and to introduce new products more quickly. Products just don't last as long as they used to. This is not a quality issue. Consider the life cycle of computer processing chips. The 486 chip was only on the market a year or two before the Pentium chip replaced it. I've gone through six computers in the last ten years: an original IBM-PC with two floppy disk drives and no hard disk drive, a 286, 386, 486, a Pentium, and a Pentium II. I can only wonder how long it will be until new software forces me to get another better and faster PC!"

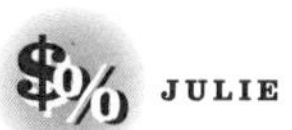

"This really places a new demand for accounting information about the total costs and revenues projected over the entire life cycle of new products. With financial accounting, we think in time periods of a month—we close the books and prepare income statements monthly—or a year—for balance sheets. Now, we have to create accounting information for longer time periods. I sure wouldn't want to be projecting the sales price for Pentium chips and personal computers for the next few years!"

"It seems Multree Homes will have to reconsider how we look at new products and design them. Increasing competition, fast-changing technologies, customer and quality focuses, and the like mean we will have to become more flexible. We will need to adapt quickly to changes in our environment so we can maintain our competitiveness. And, we'll need information to identify when these changes happen and how we can change."

"Nissan does a good job being flexible. For American car manufacturers, changing the machine that makes steel parts can easily take a day. Nissan now does this in about 15 minutes! They also can change paint colors in 15 seconds."

Team development

"One major upcoming change in the way Multree Homes is managed hasn't been talked about yet. We still have a very traditional manager-worker, line-staff way of organizing work. As Multree grew over time, we hired many specialists in staff positions. We also hired a lot of middle management types. I suppose this was just an outcome of scientific management. Of course, it has created problems. Personnel costs are continually rising, coordination is more difficult—we hired even more middle line managers, information sharing is basically nonexistent, and nobody ever sees the 'big picture.'

"Spurred by the customer focus, quality, JIT, outsourcing, and shortened life cycle movements, many organizations are redesigning how people work. They call it **employee empowerment**. Cross-functional teams and quality circles are replacing staff specialists and middle management. These 'world-class' approaches train people to do many tasks, rather than specializing in only one task, like welding or painting, as in the scientific management approach. Teams build products from start to finish, and are responsible for the product's ultimate quality. Some teams even move around the plant, and to other companies, selling their services where needed."

> **Employee empowerment** *is giving traditional management decision-making responsibility to workers. For this to succeed, employees need to be properly trained and provided with good accounting information.*

"The implications for accounting systems are staggering! *Accounting won't be providing information just to managers. Everyone in the company will need access to the accounting information. The way accounting information will be presented is going to be radically different, too.* Charts and graphs already are replacing formal reports. Even factory workers now have PCs, and they use databases to download information into spreadsheet programs with very sophisticated graphics."

Deregulation in the service sector

"These trends are not merely manufacturing or international phenomena. Service and public organizations face outsourcing and privatization movements due to deregulation and its ensuing competition. Historically, the need for accounting information has not been as strong here as in the manufacturing and merchandising sectors. Often prices are fixed by regulatory boards, or taxpayer dollars are arbitrarily allocated to governmental agencies. Accounting has been pretty simple; budgeting costs by department and tracking actual spending against the budget.

"Few governmental and service organizations have traditionally measured the costs of specific services or different customer groups. Their noncompetitive, monopolistic markets probably are the reason why this kind of accounting information hasn't been needed. Deregulation, downsizing, and outsourcing are changing the need for accounting in the service and governmental sectors. Also, more attention is being drawn to the service sector as it employs about 80% of U.S. workers."

"Everyone seems to be competing now. Hospitals in the same community are specializing based on which ones can provide specific services at the lowest cost. County Hospital handles all the emergencies in its new Trauma Center. If we need heart treatment, though, we have to go to Saint Mary's.

"Have you seen the new U.S. Postal Service advertisement? They're in some serious competition with Federal Express, UPS, Emery Freight, and many other private firms. Who knows what effect electronic mail will have on these firms! Do you think our children will even know what a post office or a mailbox were?"

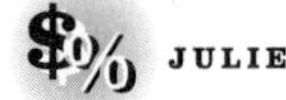

"What are the implications for accounting? Manufacturers need to know the costs of making and delivering each of their different products. Merchandisers need accounting information about the costs of obtaining and selling each of their product lines. *Now, the service and governmental sector organizations will need both kinds of information.* Some think costing services will be harder than costing tangible products—like treating a heart attack in a hospital's Trauma Center as compared to the houses we make as a manufacturer. I don't think so, though. Whether our product is a house or a welfare case, social security claim, letter delivery, or sick patient in a hospital, all types of organizations take resources, do something to them [conversion], and then sell them."

When it comes to providing accounting information for management needs, it should not make any difference whether the firm is in the merchandising, manufacturing, service, or governmental sector!

KEY OBJECTIVE 3

Define the four types of accounting systems and relate them to their four organizational roles.

The Roles for Accounting Systems in Organizations

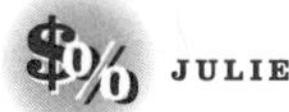

"Accounting systems can be defined by the way the information is used. I see four roles [uses] for our accounting systems:

- Regulatory compliance, such as financial reporting for investors and other outsiders,
- Protecting the firm's assets,
- Providing information for decisions [decision support], and
- Getting people to do what we want them to do [behavioral control].

Financial and tax accounting systems satisfy the first two roles. Management accounting systems exist for the last two roles. Additionally, all four roles require information about product and service costs. This is provided by the cost accounting system." [Exhibit 1-1 summarizes the four types of accounting systems and the topics they cover.]

Types of Accounting Systems			
Financial Accounting	**Management Accounting**	**Cost Accounting**	**Tax Accounting**
Rules and procedures	Decision support	Product costing	Individuals
Accounting information systems and internal controls	Organizational control	Activity-based costing	Partnerships and corporations
Auditing	Cost management		Estates and trusts
	Profit management		International taxation
	Investment management		Special tax issues and topics

Exhibit 1-1

Financial accounting systems

"We've already talked about financial accounting. Its primary use is for stewardship. This involves the first two organizational roles. Financial accounting is governed by GAAP. Companies use the same measurement practices and reporting formats so investors—external owners and creditors—can compare one firm's performance with other companies. Specialty firms, called CPAs, developed to assure these rules are followed. This is the audit role of financial accounting. When successfully audited, investors are assured the financial statements meet GAAP standards."

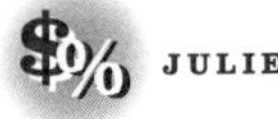

JULIE

"Financial accounting systems also serve another role. Upper management too often is evaluated and rewarded based on the firm's financial performance as reported in the external financial statements. Bonuses and employment contracts frequently are tied to earnings targets and stock market values. Therefore, senior level managers are very interested in how the financial statements look. Managers may be motivated to manipulate financial statements so they receive bigger bonuses, even though they have not really increased the firm's value. This is called 'window dressing.' Rewarding managers based on the financial statements is much debated, as you might expect. It raises some interesting ethical dilemmas I'd like to talk about in a later meeting."

Management accounting systems

SID

"All organizational members should be interested in increasing value by achieving the firm's goals and objectives. At the Lazy K, Slim had clear goals: raise cattle, feed them, protect them, drive them to market, and sell them for the best price he could get. No matter which activity Slim was doing, he continually asked four questions." [Exhibit 1-2 relates these to the three generic management functions.]

The Three Management Functions

Questions asked:	Management functions:
What do I want to do?	Planning for the future (strategic)
How can I do it?	Planning for the future (operational)
Am I getting it done?	Monitoring and controlling the present
How well did I do it?	Evaluating the past

Exhibit 1-2

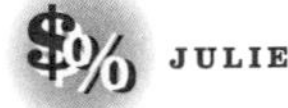

JULIE

The decision support role. *"Management accounting systems exist to provide three kinds of information:*

- Information to help people better plan,
- Information to help manage day-to-day operations, and
- Information to help evaluate performance.

This is the **decision support role** for a management accounting system. People at all levels must exercise their judgment to develop goals and strategies, make operating decisions, and evaluate performance. The management accounting system adds value when better decisions result from using its information.

In its **decision support role**, *management accounting information is used in long-run strategic planning, short-run operational planning, monitoring and controlling operations, and evaluating performance.*

"I see three aspects to planning decisions. We strategically plan for the long run. We plan how to accomplish long-run objectives and short-run goals. And, we operationally plan for daily activities. As we engage in each aspect of our planning decisions, different information demands will be placed on the management accounting system. In our second function, day-to-day operational management, we will need more and different types of accounting information about what is happening, what is going wrong, how it can be fixed, and what the cost is. Finally, when evaluating performance, we will have to combine planning and control information. Looking at the differences between our plans and actual outcomes will help us better understand what happened, whether we achieved our goals, and where we went wrong. Management accounting systems exist to support all three managerial decision-making functions."

TOMMY

The control role. "We also need to control behavior, or simply, *get people to do what we want them to do.* This is the management accounting system's **control role**. Really, 'control' is the wrong word. We want to motivate them to make decisions accomplishing our goals and objectives. This is called **goal congruent behavior**. *Management accounting information influences people's behavior because it is used to evaluate and reward them.* Organizations have many different ways to assure goal congruence. We can hire people who think like us. We are all family. Or, we can take on partners. They may not think like us, and often will not work like us, but they will be motivated to act in the best interests of the company. Finding people who act and think like us may be difficult, though. Giving people partial ownership may be too expensive. So, other options are often considered, and accounting data is useful here. However, accounting's role changes at different organizational levels.

Management accounting is used to motivate **goal congruent behavior**. *In other words, management accounting's* **control role** *involves promoting decisions in the best interest of the organization.*

"For routine tasks, simple rules are used. These are specific procedures and ways for individuals to perform their tasks. A typical example is hourly workers in a McDonald's fast food restaurant. Scientific management is applied. Tasks are designed in the 'one best way' by skilled engineers. Every hamburger is made the same way all over the world. This consistency is part of the quality customers value. No judgment is required by the workers; they are simply told, 'This is how it is done.'

"The information needed from the management accounting system is fairly simple. Once the process is designed, management's primary function is daily monitoring. For example, it should provide information to answer:

- How much material and labor is needed today?
- Are we using the correct amounts?
- Are we getting things done on time?
- What was the cost of our work today, and was it within budget?

"But what happens when the job becomes complex and more uncertain, when the 'one best way' is unknown? Under these circumstances, with sufficient training and motivation, workers can contribute significantly to our productivity and success. Worker empowerment and motivation are important. Accounting information can help these people identify changes adding value. From a control perspective, though, how do we motivate our workers to search for and make improvements? Is the same accounting system used to support decision making as well as control behavior? What is the role of accounting in these situations?

"My point is simple. We must be careful in developing management accounting information because it will be used to both support decisions and motivate employees. As a Chinese philosopher, Kung Fu, once said:

What gets measured gets done.

If we measure the wrong things, or don't measure all of the right things, bad decisions may result! I think designing a management accounting system for both decision support and organizational control [motivating proper behavior] is going to be a very difficult undertaking! I hope we have the right people for this job."

"I think we do! I remember reading about Ford. Upon purchasing Mazda, Ford discovered dramatic differences in accounting staffing levels. Four thousand accountants worked in Ford, while Mazda had only five or six doing the same things. Ford has since massively reduced the number of accountants in payroll, purchasing, and the like, and plans on continuing this reduction. Many old financial accounting roles were changed to new management support roles. We can do this at Multree Homes."

JACKIE

"All right. Let's see if I understand the relationship between managing an organization's activities and the role of management accounting. *Management accounting information informs decision makers. It also influences the decisions they make. The informing role supports better decisions. The influencing role motivates the right decisions.*"

NANCY

Suitable control motivates good judgment and good judgment requires good information.

Cost accounting systems

JACKIE

"**Cost accounting systems** exist to provide the costs of making products, or at least this has been their traditional role. As Julie mentioned earlier, management's need for product cost information around the time of the Industrial Revolution marked cost accounting's renaissance. Different types of companies make different products under different conditions, so cost accounting systems tended to be unique. With the capital expansion movement, though, financial accountants developed standardized rules for all manufacturers to use in reporting product costs. Consistent external reporting became the dominant goal."

> **Cost accounting systems** *measure a product's manufacturing costs for financial reporting. To support decision making and motivation, the cost accounting system also should provide information on all aspects of a firm's product or service.*

JULIE

"Financial reporting rules have inhibited the evolution of cost systems to satisfy new management information needs. These needs arise as companies diversify into new product lines, automate production processes, and globally compete. Now, as we are entering management accounting's renaissance, cost systems are evolving to do more as management needs better information. Cost accounting is no longer restricted to manufacturers. I've seen some very sophisticated cost systems in the service sector, such as railroads and hospitals, and in merchandising, especially in logistics management of distribution centers. I've also seen systems go beyond just the costs of manufacturing. Some modern systems also include sales and marketing, warehousing and distribution, and even accounting costs in the product's 'cost.'

"Cost accounting provides information to both the financial accounting and management accounting systems. For financial accounting, we need to know production costs in order to value inventories for the balance sheet and to cost products that have been sold [cost of goods sold for the income statement]. For management accounting, costs incurred in product or service design, production, distribution, and customer service are needed to support decisions and control operations."

Tax accounting systems

JACKIE

"Tax reporting also is necessary as part of the first organizational role, regulatory reporting. Tax accounting rules seem to change yearly, though, as our federal and state governments create new laws and regulations. The Internal Revenue Service and state tax agencies also continuously produce rulings and interpretations affecting tax law. As more firms become 'global,' international tax issues will grow in importance and complexity. This is why I really became a CPA, to practice tax accounting! Little did I know that I didn't have to be a CPA to do taxes for a living."

JULIE

"The tax accounting system needs financial and cost accounting information. Financial accounting uses information from cost accounting. Management accounting uses cost, financial, and tax information. Whether each accounting system is independent or linked together through a computer system, the different information has an important role to play in organizations. While we will be mainly talking about our management accounting system in future meetings, we should remember that all four accounting systems are intimately related."

KEY OBJECTIVE 4

Discuss the differences between financial and management accounting information.

Characteristics of Management Accounting Systems

NANCY

"Wow! No wonder accounting is so complex. Accounting systems have to provide different types of information for different uses by people both inside and outside the organization. It seems we must have all these different accounting systems. That has to be very costly! Do all organizations really have four separate accounting systems? How much accounting information do we really need?"

The costs and benefits of better decisions

JULIE

"Gee, you ask good questions, Nancy! The answer to both is, 'It depends.' Firms that have investors and creditors must have financial accounting systems. From a manager's perspective, the financial accounting system is a free management tool. Management accounting systems, though, are optional. We can get management information manually through special analyses, or we can develop computer programs for each system. These systems can be independent of each other, or they can be linked together through accessing a central computerized database. The types of accounting systems within a particular organization, and their sophistication, is a management choice based on its needs. Thus, these systems can be different for each organization. Since we must already have a financial accounting system, it doesn't cost us much extra to use it for management, cost, and/or tax needs. Whenever financial accounting provides the information we need, we will use it.

"Financial accounting systems don't always provide us with the right information, however. Let me illustrate. Suppose we want to sell the property behind our factory. What information do we need? The financial accounts recorded the original purchase price when we bought it twenty years ago. That value may or may not approximate today's market value. Knowing the market value allows us to receive a better price for it. The financial accounting records don't tell us how much has been spent over time on this property's taxes, loan interest, insurance, and the like. We need this information, too.

"Generally speaking, if better information improves value, we should be willing to spend more money for it. Thus, the *cost* we are willing to incur for added information is determined by its *benefit* [improved decisions]. This is the 'cost-benefit' decision for management accounting. *The money invested in other accounting systems, beyond the money already spent on the financial accounting system, must be justified by improved decisions.*"

One set of books for many different uses

“That’s a very nice conceptual answer, Julie, but it doesn’t always work in reality! You just can’t go to the grocery store and buy some information when you need it. In other words, the costs of additional information are not easily known before a decision is made. How many times have you said, ‘If I had only known X before I did Y, I would not have done Y!’ My point is we often do not know the benefit from additional information [X] until it’s too late, that is, until after we have already decided to do Y. So, where does this leave us?

1. We use financial accounting information first.
2. If it is not sufficient, we will conduct a special study and modify the information.
3. If this isn’t good enough, we will search for new and better information.
4. The next time, we will repeat this process,
5. Until we realize we need a new formal information system.”

“It is extremely difficult to design one accounting system that is excellent for all purposes or companies. Companies have unique needs requiring different amounts of detail. Since greater detail costs more, firms tend to buy only what they need. Family members working together are motivated to support the company, but strangers may not be. Management control systems in family businesses need not be as complex and expensive as in large corporations. Highly trained and skilled managers may need less information to make good decisions than do new employees. Companies not selling stock or having outside investors may not need expensive auditing services. Consequently, accounting systems can vary widely from company to company. Our biggest problem, which is very common, is we exploit one set of books [the financial accounting system] for many different uses. This is the simplest solution to our information problem.”

“So, what you’re saying is we should always consider the costs and benefits of additional accounting information and systems, but it’s not always possible to measure this in ‘dollars and cents.’ And, I surely cannot make any generalizations about how many accounting systems a company should have. If true, how can I know when the financial accounting system won’t work for my immediate needs?”

Comparing financial and management accounting information

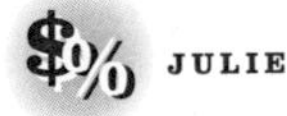

“Well, consider the kinds of information you need and the kinds of information you have. For example, let’s compare the information characteristics of management and financial accounting systems.”

Reliability versus relevance. “Financial accounting numbers are like the umpires in a baseball game. They are objective measures of performance. To be objective, they are based on ‘hard’ data. Hard data is factual, and not subject to bias or distortion. It can be verified. If data is verifiable, and the rules for reporting it are followed, external users of financial accounting information can rely on it.

“The other extreme is ‘soft’ data. It is subjective and based upon estimates and opinions. Consider again selling the property behind our factory. Would you rather know the original purchase price—the hard data—or an estimate of the current value—the soft data—when setting our sales price? Information improving a decision is called **relevant information**.

> **Relevant information** *improves decisions. It helps people do their jobs better.*

Historical costs used in financial statements are hard data. People generally prefer hard data to soft data for evaluation because everyone can agree on its accuracy. This makes financial accounting systems very useful to managers, but its usefulness is limited. For example, in reporting how the company is affecting its environment and community, the financial accounting system may not be very useful.

"To summarize, *financial accounting requires hard data to satisfy its reliability role in reporting to outsiders. Management accounting requires both hard and soft data to satisfy its relevance role.* For example:

- *Planning decisions:* Hard data about historical sales may improve the quality of future sales projections—soft data. The soft data then is used to plan activities, such as production quotas and labor needs.
- *Monitoring and control decisions:* To understand where things are going wrong on a day-to-day basis, we need hard information about what is currently happening. Understanding why it happened, though, as well as its significance, requires soft data. To illustrate this, consider the cost of building window frames and installing windows in our houses. We need soft budgeted costs to compare with the hard, actual costs. A large difference signals a problem. Before we can fix the problem, though, we need soft information about its cause.
- *Performance evaluation decisions:* Obviously, to evaluate someone's performance, we need hard data about what he has done. However, we need to compare performance against goals. Goal and budget information are soft data."

TOMMY

"But, isn't reliability also important for internal information? We've had a lot of problems in the plant with incorrect material usage reports, and with labor being charged to the wrong operations. How can we know if a problem exists when we cannot rely on the correctness of our information?"

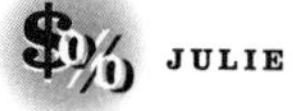

JULIE

"You're right, Tommy! Reliability is important in a management accounting system. It just is not the most important characteristic. Relevant information may not have to be extremely accurate to improve management's judgment. Who cares if the information is incorrect, though, if it's not relevant?"

Decision-based versus rule-based information. "In its decision support role, management accounting information is needed to direct decisions, that is, to inform people about where some action is required. We need to focus on activities improving our value the most, now and in the future. For a McDonald's restaurant, some of these critical success factors are product quality, fast service, and cleanliness. Quality means a consistent product. You get the same hamburger every time, no matter where you are in the world. One of McDonald's most important performance measures is customer waiting time, which is a 'delivery' factor. Cleanliness is another critical success factor. Their interiors are usually white, as with hospitals, to emphasize how clean they are. Everyone must be directed to focus on these factors and make decisions based on their judgment about when and where changes may be needed.

"Financial accounting systems may support this focus by examining the overall past profitability of a company. Financial statements may eventually indicate a problem, but they may not be able to direct attention to the particular problem or identify what caused it. When we have a problem, we want detailed information about that particular problem now. Often, an employee simply downloads current data into a PC's spreadsheet program and creates graphs to provide the information in a usable format. *Financial accounting is a rule-based system to provide hard, summary information in a particular format outsiders can rely upon. Management account-*

ing information must be more decision-focused, which requires hard and soft detailed information about the firm's critical success factors."

Financial versus nonfinancial information. "I see a third difference between financial and management accounting information. I want to invest in General Motors. The first information I want is its sales forecast for next year. As an outsider, the only information I have comes from the financial statements, which won't give me this nonfinancial information. As an insider, though, I can access this budget information through the management accounting system.

"Think about the performance evaluation information for McDonald's again. You mentioned quality, delivery, and cleanliness. Quality performance measures include the weight of the meat, the type of bun, the amount of catsup, mustard, pickles, and the like. The average time a customer waits in line and at the counter are delivery measures. The number of dirty tables is one measure of cleanliness. But, none of these are financial numbers! *My point is much of the relevant information we need to run the business is nonfinancial. This type of information has to be an integral component of the management accounting system."*

"O.K. It seems to me we do need separate management and financial accounting systems. Financial accounting systems must emphasize reliability through specific rules for recording and reporting hard financial information used by investors and creditors outside the company. Management accounting systems can be as flexible as we want. While reliability is always important, relevance is the most important attribute. Relevance means the management accounting system must collect and report both soft and hard data, in both detailed and summary formats, including financial and nonfinancial information." [Exhibit 1-3 summarizes these differences.]

Differences Between Financial and Management Accounting Information

Differentiating factors	**Financial accounting attributes**	**Management accounting attributes**
Users:	External creditors and investors	Internal organizational members
Primary use:	Financial performance evaluation	Decision support and behavioral control
Primary system attribute:	Reliability	Relevance
Primary outputs:	General-purpose financial statements	Special-purpose information on demand, and not limited to formal reports
Information attributes:	• Rule-based recording and reporting for all firms (GAAP)	• Every organization can have a different system based on its needs
	• Hard data about the past	• Hard and soft data about the past, present, and future
	• Summary information about the whole company	• Summary and detailed information about the company, its segments, and particular activities
	• Financial	• Financial and nonfinancial

Exhibit 1-3

"Companies get into the most trouble with their information systems when they try to use one system [financial accounting] for many different purposes. The recording rules and reporting formats for financial accounting may not support our decision and behavior control needs. Financial accounting systems may not provide relevant information, on a timely basis, in the most usable formats. So, accountants are beginning to read articles about the need for new accounting systems which capture relevant information about the events a firm engages in. For each event, we need to

answer, 'What happened? When did it happen? Who was involved? What resources were used? and Where did the event occur?'"

KEY OBJECTIVE 5

Contrast the four accounting certifications and discuss the role of ethics in management accounting.

The Professional Management Accountant

"When I was growing up, I wanted to be an accountant, a CPA. Accountant and CPA were synonyms. Life was simpler then. Go to college, study financial accounting, get a degree, and go to work for a CPA firm. Julie, you're not a CPA, though. You're a CMA. Accounting now has many specializations, much like lawyers, engineers, and doctors. In fact, 70% of all CPAs no longer work for CPA firms. Instead, they work for companies and governments, just like I do now."

Professional certifications

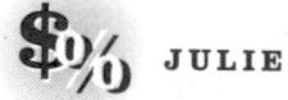

"Yes! Accounting is highly specialized now. It demands considerable training. An accountant can be certified through several professional accounting societies, which require rigorous educational training and experience in specific aspects of accounting. The oldest, and most widely known, professional designation is the CPA. The examinations are administered by the American Institute of Certified Public Accountants [AICPA]. Each state society administers its exams, licenses CPAs to practice in that state, and sets its own requirements for experience, though. Some don't require any. Some allow college teaching to substitute for experience. Some require one or more years of external financial accounting system auditing.

"Most CPAs are qualified to audit and offer a professional opinion on how well the financial statements meet GAAP. The SEC requires publicly traded companies to be audited by a CPA firm. Many other legal requirements—for example, state and city governments—also require CPA audits.

"External audits are expensive, though, so many companies have created internal audit departments to perform the internal control functions and evaluations GAAP requires. Internal audit departments also assure a company it has the financial accounting system expertise in-house when needed. In addition to financial system audits, many internal audit departments conduct operational audits. Operational auditing overlaps management accounting because it concerns auditing operations to improve their performance. In recognition of the specific knowledge requirements for internal auditing, The Institute of Internal Auditors provides a professional certification, the certified internal auditor [CIA].

The **Institute of Management Accountants** *is the worldwide professional organization for management and cost accountants. It offers professional certifications as a* **certified management accountant (CMA)** *and certified in financial management (CFM).*

"Management accountants also have their own professional organization and certification programs, the **Institute of Management Accountants [IMA]** and the **certified management accountant [CMA]**. Because the CMA has to be part of the management team and knowledgeable in all areas of management, the CMA qualifying exam consists of four interdisciplinary parts:

- Economics, finance, and management,
- Financial reporting,
- Management reporting, analysis, and behavioral issues, and
- Decision analysis and information systems.

The CMA is relatively new, beginning in 1972. In Canada, the official management accounting organization is the Society of Management Accountants. It, too, administers a CMA certification program. Japan has two management accounting organizations. The Enterprise Management Association is the Japanese chapter of the United States' IMA. The Japanese Industrial Management and Accounting Association is its oldest and most authoritative organization. The United Kingdom's professional management accounting certification program is run by the Chartered Institute of Management Accountants.

"The IMA has many formal partnerships with industry and local communities. Many of the best-run companies in the United States are IMA 'Corporate Sponsors.' These firms offer in-house CMA training, sponsor employees for the CMA exam, and support the local business community in many other ways, representing the management accounting profession. Virtually every city and locality has an IMA chapter with open membership. Most college campuses also have IMA student chapters, and are involved in national competitions based on their professional, community, and college activities.

"As a member of our city's IMA chapter, I've worked with many student IMA members from our local college. I've advised them on job seeking, interviewing, and résumé writing. As part of our corporate sponsorship program, student IMA members work with me for a day to see how 'real-world accounting' functions. We even have three student interns working for us in the Accounting Department. I always enjoy meeting student members at the monthly IMA dinner meetings. And, I know how valuable their IMA memberships have been in becoming CMAs, finding industry jobs, and getting jobs with CPA firms.

"The CMA is fast becoming a respected member of the management team. For example, at 3M [Minnesota Mining and Manufacturing] divisional controllers are no longer considered 'bean counters.' Coors Brewing Company's controller participates in all major decisions, not only to show how the decision will affect its financial statements, but more importantly to provide relevant information improving the decision. At the Caterpillar plant in Aurora, Illinois, management accountants are welcome on the shop floor, and actually have put on safety helmets and done the work!

"Many surveys have shown CEOs [chief executive officers] most often started as accountants [versus any other profession], probably due to accountants being most familiar with all aspects of the business. This reflects the metamorphosis accountants are experiencing, both in CPA firms as well as in organizations. No longer a number cruncher, the modern accountant is expected to be a high-level business strategist and decision support expert. In other words, organizations are looking for management accountants to lead them into the 21st century. This may explain why controllers' salaries averaged over \$80,000 in 1997 [up from \$70,000 in 1996], with 14% average bonuses, and why accounting department size has increased in 35% of organizations. Another survey showed IMA member 1997 average compensation was \$74,000 [an increase of 8% over 1996], with CMAs averaging \$13,000 more than non-CMAs.

"The IMA also offers a second professional certification. Management accountants can become certified in financial management [a CFM]. Similar to finance majors, many management accountants specialize in financial management. In recognition of this, and to provide expertise in this area, the IMA began this new professional certification program in 1996."

Ethical responsibilities of the CMA

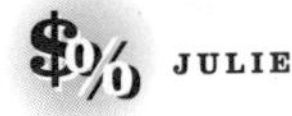

"Whether a CMA or not, all members of the IMA are bound by its code of ethics. We believe all organizational members, as well as society, can benefit from its use."

TOMMY

"Don't I know it! I've worked with too many people over time who I wish could be held accountable for their ethical conduct. In many organizations, upper management officers also can use a code of ethics. How about in government? Would this mean we have to come up with a different term to replace 'politician'?" Much tension was released as everyone laughed aloud.

JULIE

"I wish everyone lived by a code of ethics similar to ours, but alas, the IMA's Code of Ethical Conduct only applies to its members. The best we can do is try to convince everyone else we cannot participate in their actions if we consider them unethical. We have four ethical standards, which are detailed on a card I carry in my wallet. The IMA even has a toll-free phone service for ethical issues." [Exhibit 1-4 lists the IMA's standards of ethical conduct.]

The IMA's Standards of Ethical Conduct	
Competence	• Maintain professional knowledge and skills
	• Follow laws and regulations
	• Analyze all relevant data and provide complete information
Objectivity	• Communicate all information fairly
	• Fully disclose all relevant information
Integrity	• Communicate favorable as well as unfavorable information, including limitations about the information
	• Avoid apparent or actual conflicts of interest
	• Support attaining the legitimate goals of the organization
	• Avoid activities that will discredit the profession
Confidentiality	• Do not disclose confidential information, unless legally obligated to do so
	• Do not allow subordinates to disclose confidential information

Exhibit 1-4

TOMMY

"Too often, people do things right, but they may not be doing the right things. Some have called this problem 'finding the ethical forest in the trees.' I think General Motors has the right idea. It defines ethics as never doing something you'd be ashamed to explain to your family or see on the newspaper's front page."

JULIE

"I agree with you, Tommy. And, I believe ethical conduct is simple. What I don't understand is why companies with ethics policies are decreasing [51% in 1998 vs. 55% in 1997, 61% in 1996, and 66% in 1995]. Maybe it's because people are beginning to believe policies do not stop unethical behavior. Rather, it's the 'corporate culture.' If organizations want ethical conduct, their managements must practice what they preach! Let's make sure we do this as we learn how to run this business."

Professional characteristics of the modern management accountant

NANCY

"Wow! You guys are really serious about this ethics stuff. What other professional characteristics of management accountants should we expect?"

JULIE

"I just read an IMA report in its monthly magazine, *Management Accounting*. Generally speaking, the modern management accountant is no longer seen as a 'bean counter' or 'corporate cop.' About half work as members of cross-functional teams. Thus, we're expected to have excellent communication, problem-solving, and spreadsheet skills. Instead of spending our time preparing financial statements, we're expected to be able to identify relevant financial and nonfinancial information, analyze it, and present it clearly and effectively to others in the organization." [Exhibits 1-5 and 1-6 summarize the most important knowledge, skills, and abilities required of management accountants.]

Management Accountants—Skills and Abilities

Most important:

1. Work ethic
2. Analytical and problem-solving skills
3. Interpersonal skills
4. Listening
5. Spreadsheet abilities
6. Understanding the business
7. Understanding "bottom-line" implications of management decisions
8. Writing
9. Familiarity with business processes

Least important:

- Interpreting or analyzing financial statements
- Measuring and reporting revenues and expenses
- Accruals, deferrals, and adjusting journal entries

Source: Siegel and Kulesza, "The Practice Analysis of Management Accounting," *Management Accounting*, April 1996. © The Institute of Management Accountants.

Exhibit 1-5

Core Competencies for the 21st Century

- Professional conduct
- Work commitment
- Personal development
- Interpersonal skills (team leadership, teamwork, coaching, listening, persuasion and negotiation, presentation skills)
- Proactive skills
- Internal consulting
- Performance measurement and incentives
- Information systems knowledge

Sources: Woolfe, "IMA's Self-Assessment Survey Identifies Competencies for the 21st Century," *Management Accounting*, June 1998. "Controllers Give Their Opinions on the Core Competencies for Management Accountants," *Controllers Update*, January 1998. © Institute of Management Accountants.

Exhibit 1-6

"In addition to all this, the report listed areas that will increase in importance. The top six include:

- Customer and product profitability analyses.
- Process improvements.
- Performance evaluation.
- Long-term strategic planning.

- Computer systems support and development.
- Cost accounting systems.

This is what I call the 'joy of management accounting' and this is why I became a CMA." Nancy now understood why the Boss chose Julie to be the new CFO.

"Well, we've talked about a lot tonight. Doris, can you summarize for us, please? I think we'll need a series of formal meetings to discuss what we should be doing as the new management team of Multree Homes. We will discuss each idea in turn. The first, and most important question concerns how we can add value to the firm. This will be the topic of our first formal meeting, which will be first thing next week!"

KEY OBJECTIVES SUMMARY

"Here is what I remember about our discussion today. Five key ideas were stressed.

1. Explain stewardship and why the dominant goal of accounting systems historically has been financial reporting.

"Stewardship is safeguarding and managing a company's assets, and reporting on its financial performance to external creditors and investors. Accounting systems were first developed to provide this protection to financiers not physically close to the operations they financed. Examples such as the Mayflower and other exploratory and settling voyages come to mind. The auditing profession quickly developed to provide an objective, independent appraisal of the financial reports. Thus, accounting's historical emphasis has been financial reporting. Standardized rules for recording and reporting financial information to outsiders developed, providing them with further protection. Without financial accounting systems, venture capitalism would have been significantly more difficult.

2. Describe eight modern management trends changing the role of accounting in organizations.

- "*Customer focus.* To compete in our global economy, first we must be concerned with customer desires. Managers must ensure their accountants provide customer information and monitoring systems when designing new products or services, and when improving existing operations.
- *Quality focus.* Both external and internal customers demand quality. Without it, we will lose customers to our competition. The management accounting system must include information about the costs of quality and how we are assuring it in our products and services.
- *Delivery focus.* Having the right, high-quality products and services is not sufficient, though. We must be able to get our products and services to customers when they want it. We need information such as on-time deliveries and complete order filling.

- *Outsourcing and the virtual company.* As organizations become 'lean,' many activities, not part of their core competencies, are being outsourced. However, we have to maintain control over their quality, too. Thus, virtual companies are developing. Linking the information needed between companies so the final consumer gets a high-quality product on time is yet another role for the modern management accounting system.
- *Communication.* With customers, between companies, and within the firm, the management accounting system must provide relevant information available when needed.
- *Shortening product life cycles.* As products become obsolete sooner, management accounting systems need to provide information about activities, their costs, and product revenues for entire product life cycles. Monthly and annual reporting no longer is the 'correct' time period if we are going to remain competitive. The modern management accountant has to be intimately involved in planned costs and revenues over the entire life cycle of new products and services.
- *Team development.* As Julie discussed, management accountants no longer work in isolation, hiding in the dark recesses of an accounting department, located far away from the rest of the organization. Modern management accountants have to be excellent communicators, teachers, coaches, and team players.
- *Deregulation in the service sector.* Some of the most serious downsizing and outsourcing is happening in the governmental and service sectors. Deregulation has brought competition where monopolies used to dominate. All the needs of profit-making firms are now applicable to service and non-profit organizations.

3. Define the four types of accounting systems and relate them to their four organizational roles.

- "*Financial and tax accounting systems* support the regulatory reporting requirements [role 1] required of most organizations. Financial accounting also exists to protect the firm's assets [role 2].
- *Management accounting systems* serve the decision support and behavioral control needs of the organization [roles 3 and 4].
- *Cost accounting systems* ultimately exist to support all four roles. They provide product cost information to the financial and tax accounting systems for external reporting requirements. Product cost information also is needed for the management accounting system to support the organization's decision-making and motivation-control needs.

4. Discuss the differences between financial and management accounting information.

"I can see five basic differences [summarized in Exhibit 1-3].

- *Users.* Financial accounting is primarily for external users. Management accounting is for internal users.
- *Use.* Financial accounting is a reporting system about what we have, what we owe, and how that has changed. Standardized reports are required. Management

accounting provides all kinds of relevant information in many formats and media as needed to run the business.

- *Goals.* Financial accounting needs to produce reliable information. Management accounting information first must be relevant.
- *Outputs.* Financial accounting reports are standardized across companies and industries. Management accounting information is accessed in many ways.
- *Information characteristics.* Financial accounting systems are rule-based [GAAP], providing hard, historical, financial information in a common summary format. Management accounting systems are different for every firm, based on each firm's unique needs. They provide hard and soft, financial and nonfinancial data about the past, present, and future, in detailed and summary forms.

5. Contrast the four accounting certifications and discuss the role of ethics in management accounting.

"Accountants can become professionally certified in public accounting [CPA], internal auditing [CIA], management accounting [CMA], and in financial management [CFM]. All are equally valuable to society. CPAs have an expertise in external financial accounting system audits. CIAs have expertise in financial and operational audits within organizations. CMAs have expertise in providing information to support organizational decisions and control. CFMs specialize in financial management.

In supporting the management needs of all organizations, ethical conduct is absolutely critical. The IMA has developed four standards of ethical conduct for its members. These include competence, objectivity, integrity, and confidentiality."

"Good job, Doris! Let's get back to our guests. I'll see you all at our next meeting, Monday morning, 8:00 a.m.!"

REALITY 101

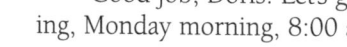

An Interview with Microsoft's Corporate Controller, John Connors:

How is the accountant's role at Microsoft changing?

Two years ago, Microsoft had no consolidated sales information. It took 13 days to close the books and issue income statements. While created by each division, the income statements were not centrally accessible (by corporate management). Today, we're close to having one of the best integrated financial systems in the world.

Most companies are focusing on the Internet for selling their products. Our accounting group, though, realized how to use it to cut accounting costs through more effective and efficient communications. For example, in 1994 we produced 350,000 reports. Now electronic income statements are a standard management tool. These 350,000 reports have been replaced with 12 workbooks. Within 15 minutes of closing our books, they are updated and available worldwide. Our Microsoft Finance Home Page allows someone to get financial information without having to know spreadsheet file names or locations.

All of our external financial accounting information is published on our Web site. Five years from now, it will be very unlikely that anyone will call a company to get a hard copy of its annual report.

Finance and information systems roles were well defined but significantly different 5 to 10 years ago. Now, the tools and technology are easier for non-computer system personnel to learn and use. Five years from now these separate roles will disappear. We are not traditional accountants in the way a lot of people think about accountants. We were in an industrial age 20 years ago. Now, we are in an information age. Those who have learned to use technology have gained huge global market shares.

How is this changing the controller's role in organizations?

The controller's new role is providing information managers need to make good decisions. Within that context, you have to have a certain amount of internal control and GAAP. But, our real purpose is getting the information that managers need to do their jobs better. I probably spend 50 to 60% of my time on processes, new information systems, or enhancements to existing systems.

The controller's role is shifting more toward a broad generalist and business person, as opposed to a numbers person. The controller has to be a guide, getting things done through influence, not control. Our goal is to have the fewest number of management layers possible. The accountants who do the work make decisions about what should be done. Our group is highly assertive, removing the obstacles that get in their way. They don't wait around for a manager to do it. They understand how to use the file server, spreadsheets, and the programs that link together different types of computer programs (e.g., Visual Basic).

What problems are on the horizon?

As with many companies, we grew so rapidly that we couldn't slow down enough to see what was happening internally. You should learn Microsoft's lesson. Companies and controllers who buy into the new technologies, harness their creative energies, and transform numbers into strategies are the ones who are going to reach the top. As we grow and get more complex, the only way we'll be efficient and effective is if we continue to improve our communications.

The rate of innovation, the rate of research and development spent, and the rate at which competitors take over entrenched companies that don't stay current is phenomenal. If you are slow moving and bureaucratic, the rate at which you fall will be much faster than 15 or 20 years ago.

Focus on communication. Learn what information people need to run the business in a world-class way, and provide it effectively and efficiently. Finally, identify your star performers and place them in the right jobs. Rounding out their generalist skills is something I owe them.

Source: Kathy Williams and James Hart, "Microsoft: Tooling the Information Age," *Management Accounting*, May 1996. © The Institute of Management Accountants.

READING LIST*

3M: Williams, "The Magic of 3M, Management Accounting Excellence," *Management Accounting*, February 1986.

Caterpillar: Hendricks and Rose, "Accountants On The Line," *Management Accounting*, June 1998.

Coors Brewing Company (Adolph Coors Company): Walker, "Coors, Brewing a Better Controllership," *Management Accounting*, January 1988.

Ethics: *Statement on Management Accounting 1C: Standards of Ethical Conduct for Practitioners of Management Accounting and Financial Management*, Institute of Management Accountants, revised April 30, 1997.

——: "IMA Revises SMA 1C, Standards of Ethical Conduct," *Management Accounting*, July 1997.

——: See also *Management Accounting: Special Issue on Ethics in Corporate America*, June 1990.

——: Driscoll and Hoffman, "Finding the Ethical Forest in the Trees," *Management Issues*, KPMG, September 1997.

Ethics policies survey: "Fewer Companies Have Ethics Policies, Controllers Report," *Controllers Update*, Institute of Management Accountants, July–August 1998.

Euro: Fiumara and Baldoni, "Will You Be Ready When The Euro Arrives?" *Ernst & Young's Business Upshot*, July–August 1998.

——: Estrada, Martin, and Wechsler, "All Aboard for the Euro," *Management Accounting*, August 1998.

History of management accounting: Johnson and Kaplan, *Relevance Lost: The Rise and Fall of Management Accounting*, Harvard Business School Press, 1987.

New accounting systems are needed: Aldridge and Colbert, "We Need Better Financial Reporting," *Management Accounting*, July 1997.

——: Walker and Denna, "A New Accounting System Is Emerging," *Management Accounting*, July 1997.

Privatizing government programs: "Privatization Grows and Grows. So Do Opportunities For Business," *Ernst & Young's Executive UpSide*, December 1996.

Role of accountants in organizations: Hrisak, "The Controller as Business Strategist," *Management Accounting*, December 1996.

——: Piturro, *Solutions in Finance*, supplement to *Management Accounting*, January 1998.

Salaries: Reichardt and Schroeder, "Salaries 1997," *Management Accounting*, June 1998.

——: "Controllers' Salaries Show Major Increase: West Coast Continues to Pay Best," *Controllers Update*, Institute of Management Accountants, February 1998.

Survey on global competition: "More Companies Target Foreign Markets Than Ever Before," *Controllers Update*, Institute of Management Accountants, October 1997.

*Alphabetic by topic, idea, or company referenced.

CHAPTER 2

How Do Companies Create Value?

Why We Can't Use Financial Accounting Alone to Manage the Firm

KEY OBJECTIVES:

1	*Define economic value and explain the factors that influence it.*
2	*Demonstrate how value chains, product differentiation, and cost management are used to create value.*
3	*Explain why financial accounting does not report economic value.*
4	*Give examples of the three manufacturing inventories.*
5	*Describe the three traditional manufacturing resources and prepare a cost of goods manufactured schedule.*
6	*List the six steps in strategic planning and discuss the role of management accounting in this process.*

It had finally come to pass. Grandfather Multree's affairs were settled. It was time to take over the business. His will was clear—learn how to run the company and increase its value within a year or Multree Homes will be sold. The seven grandchildren gathered for their first formal meeting. Some were at best apprehensive, and at worst downright scared. Doris could see it in the eyes of Bill, Julie, Nancy, and Tommy. They were new to the company. They didn't know how "the Boss" ran the company, and why it was so successful.

Of course, Doris saw a different type of concern in Bob, Jackie, and Sid. They had helped manage the business for some time now. However, they knew competition was growing fast and new technologies were threatening old, proven manufacturing methods. Profits were declining with decreasing sales and increasing costs. They did not want the business sold. They remembered when the Boss had to sell company stock to raise some quick cash. But increasing Multree's value, as mandated in Grandfather's will, seemed elusive. Especially after last week's discussion at the mansion.

While everyone felt they now had a better understanding of the need for a management accounting system, they had no sense of direction. Where do we begin? How can we get organized? What do we need to know? What information do we need? These, and a myriad of other questions, plagued them all. Sid, now the new president, took charge.

KEY OBJECTIVE 1

Define economic value and explain the factors that influence it.

What Is Economic Value?

SID

"Grandfather's will is brutally clear; we have to increase the company's value or we lose it! The will didn't tell us what he meant by 'value,' though. We have to define value, figure out how to measure it, and then decide how to increase it. It seems to me the first question we should ask is, 'What is value?'"

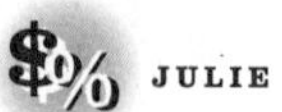

JULIE

"Things we want have value. What do we want? This may be just my banking background, but I want to *make as much money as possible, now and in the future.*"

SID

"All right then, let's get down to it and talk about making money! That's why the Boss wanted you to be our new chief financial officer [CFO], Julie. You're always thinking about cash and cashflows. You are interested in investments and their returns [cashflows]. To you, as an owner of the business, **economic value** is simply money-making potential."

> **Economic value** *is the ability to make more money, now and in the future, subject to acceptable risk and effort.*

Making money now and in the future, with tolerable risk and effort

"I guess Grandfather wanted me to run the Human Resources Management Department because I grew up with most of our factory workers. Even though I'm not an accountant, I agree with Julie. Anything making more money for me has value. However, I'm not willing to drill oil wells in our backyard or rob banks! I value money-making activities more if their risk is acceptable and they are ethical. I am not going to work 90 hours a week, either. So, value to me is money now and in the future, subject to tolerable risk and effort."

Risk is uncertainty of cashflows

"We all know what money is, but do all cashflows have the same value? Grandfather wanted me to be vice president of marketing because I've been in retail sales for 14 years. One lesson I've learned is I'd rather have a $1,000 government bond than be owed $1,000 from some of our customers!"

"Yes, some of our customers are less reliable than others. As controller, I've seen instances where it has cost as much to collect a receivable as we got out of it!"

"So two $1,000 cashflows are valued differently because of the uncertainty attached to receiving one of them? Yes, that makes sense to me. Risk influences value. Aunt Harriet chose to make less retirement income by investing in government bonds because their interest was virtually guaranteed. Of course, she isn't driving the fancy sports car Uncle Dave now owns. He invested in riskier companies promising higher returns if they were successful. Of course, not all of them were. I remember a time when he had to declare bankruptcy and move in with Aunt Harriet!"

The risk and return trade-off

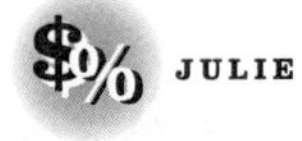

"O.K., I guess we can easily extend this relationship between value and uncertainty. *The more uncertain a cashflow is, the less its value.* In banking, we always looked at sources of income before lending money. When applying for a car loan, someone with a steady job was considered less risky than someone just starting a business. Given a choice, we'd rather lend to the steady worker. We would, however, lend to the new businessperson if she was willing to pay us a higher interest rate on the loan. In other words, we had a 'risk-return' trade-off in lending: *the greater the risk, the more money we had to make [the greater the return] from the investment."*

"Right! I had the same idea when selling my car. I knew my friend George would buy it for $2,500. I could accept his offer or try to sell it by advertising in the newspaper. I was willing to risk giving up his offer because I thought I could get more money if I advertised. To me, uncertainty is the ability to forecast the future. Since I believed the risk of getting less than $2,500 was pretty low, I turned down the original offer and advertised in the paper."

"Given the same expected cashflows, the one with more uncertainty will be less valuable. This makes sense to me, too. This is generally how the stock market values companies. When earnings change a lot from year to year, a company will be valued less [discounted] by the market. To be valued the same as more stable companies, riskier companies have to offer a higher return [e.g., higher dividends]."

The trade-off between returns and effort

"Nancy, I remember all the extra work you had to do, though, answering the phone, showing the car, placing the advertisement in the newspaper, renewing it, paying for it, and finally canceling it after the car was sold. How many times did you have to wash your car during those two weeks when all it did was rain?"

"You're right—it wasn't worth all the extra effort. I wish I had accepted the original offer. The extra effort was not worth the extra money. *I guess I'm willing to take less money now and give up the potential for more money, if the extra money involves too much effort.*"

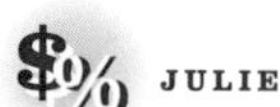

"We see this with credit card companies all the time. Better customers have little risk of not paying their charges. These customers have lower credit card interest rates. Riskier customers pay a higher interest rate. Some people are so risky, higher interest rates cannot compensate the credit card company for the extra effort needed to collect from them. These people are required to have a savings account or deposit with the company in order to get a credit card."

Nancy again thought of Aunt Harriet and Uncle Dave. She always had been jealous of the low interest rate Aunt Harriet had on her credit card. Nancy's was much higher because of some past problems she had in paying student loans. Uncle Dave, on the other hand, couldn't even get a credit card for many years after he declared bankruptcy.

Value is future-oriented

"We should look at value, risk, and effort in the same way when running this business. We know the cash we made today. *A company's value, though, is based on its expected future cashflows.* If Multree Homes has larger and more reliable expected cashflows than our competition, our company should be valued more highly. So, if we want to increase value, we need to do things to increase expected future cashflows and/or make them more reliable."

"Or receive the cash sooner! Just like with our customers. The sooner we get the cash, the more valuable the customer is to us! This idea has nothing to do with the uncertainty of being paid. I'm talking about the 'time value of money.' Sid, I owe you $100. Would you rather receive it today or in a year?" Everybody laughed.

SID

"Since your job depends on paying me back and I sign all the paychecks, I'm not worried about it!" Everyone laughed again. "I see no risk of you not paying me. If you pay me today, though, I can take the $100 and invest it. In a year, I'll have more than $100. Thus, a dollar today is more valuable than a dollar in the future because I can invest it and earn more money [interest]."

Value is relative

"Wait a minute, economic value is also a relative concept. An investment's value is related to my other investment options. If I can buy a government bond paying as well as a company's stock, I'll take the government bond or demand a premium [greater return] from the company."

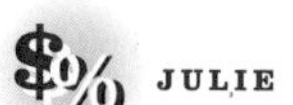

"You mean the company will have to agree to pay you more money? Of course! I understand. If I can invest in a bond with a guaranteed 5% interest rate, the company's dividend rate will have to be greater than 5% or I will not accept the risk. The company's dividend is not guaranteed."

JULIE

"Yes! Now consider the opposite situation. If I cannot buy a government bond with a 5% interest rate, I'm willing to accept a lower dividend rate on the company's stock. *The value of a particular cashflow to an investor depends on the other investment opportunities available.*"

"O.K., we now can say what economic value is. Value is determined by:

- Our expected cashflows,
- The risk of these cashflows,
- Their timing [when we project to receive them], and
- The availability and nature of competing investments.

Multree Homes, like all other companies and investments, is just a 'money-making machine.' Making more money, now and in the future, is our objective." [Exhibit 2-1 summarizes the factors influencing value.]

Factors that Influence Value

Economic value: Making money now and in the future, or money-making potential.

Value is influenced by	Which means	Its effect on value
Risk	The likelihood of receiving cash.	• The greater the risk of not receiving cash, the less its value. • If two investments have different risks, the riskier one will have to offer a greater return to be as valuable as the other.
Effort	How easy or hard it is to collect the cash.	• The greater the effort needed to collect cash, the less valuable it is. • If two investments require different amounts of effort to collect them, the one requiring the most effort will have to offer a greater return to be as valuable as the other.
Time	How long it takes to collect the cash.	• The longer it takes to collect the cash, the less its value. • If two investments have different time periods for collecting them, the one taking longer will have to offer a greater return to be as valuable as the other.
Opportunities	Other investments we can make instead of this one.	The value of an investment decreases as other investments with the same or greater returns become available.

Exhibit 2-1

KEY OBJECTIVE 2

Demonstrate how value chains, product differentiation, and cost management are used to create value.

How Do We Create Value?

"How does a company make money? As vice president of manufacturing, the answer seems easy. You buy something, do something to it, and then sell it. Look at this simple picture [Exhibit 2-2]. I call it our 'dollars-to-dollars' business cycle."

"It's not quite that simple. We have to buy something, *then do things that increase its value, so we can sell it for more money than we spent.* We also have to create conditions allowing Multree Homes to continue doing this in the future."

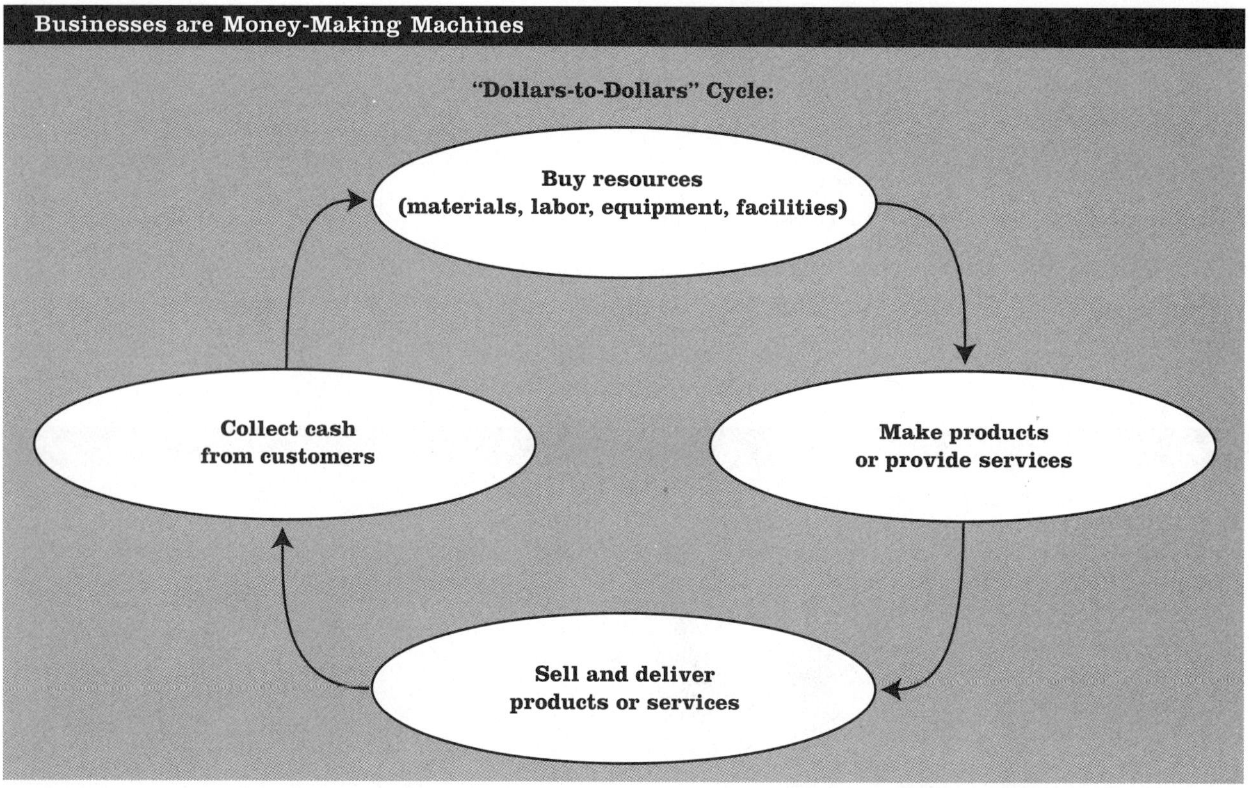

Businesses are Money-Making Machines

"Dollars-to-Dollars" Cycle:

Buy resources (materials, labor, equipment, facilities)

Make products or provide services

Sell and deliver products or services

Collect cash from customers

Exhibit 2-2

Positioning ourselves on the industry value chain

TOMMY

"Bob's diagram seems straightforward, but is this what our company looks like? I never thought of it in this way. I doubt any of our factory workers have either!"

BOB

"Well, basically this is how it looks to owners and investors. But, to be more specific, let's look at what we do. We buy materials. We hire employees. We use equipment and facilities to perform activities increasing the value of the materials to our customers. We can look at the business as a series of activities adding value to inputs. Activities are performed in a certain order, allowing us to group them together into processes. The chain of processes creating value to our consumers from converting inputs into outputs is called a **value chain**. Value chains are created for industries as well as for companies. Let's look at the home building industry's value chain first. Once we see how this analysis helps us create value, then we'll look at our company's value chain." [Exhibit 2-3 is a picture of the industry's value chain. Multree Homes performs the last four activities, which are highlighted.]

*A **value chain** is a listing of the processes involved in providing goods and services. Activities performed within each process are often listed below the process.*

SID

"Each of the different activities [businesses or services] in the industry's value chain creates unique opportunities. First, we identify which aspects provide the best opportunity for us. Then, we must provide those goods or services better and cheaper than our competition. If we can do this, our customers will value us more than our competition."

Creating value through product differentiation

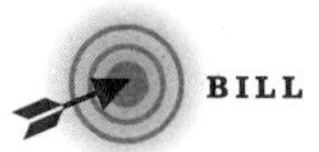

BILL

"By understanding the industry's value chain, our competition, our costs, and our customers, we can strategically position our company within the industry's value

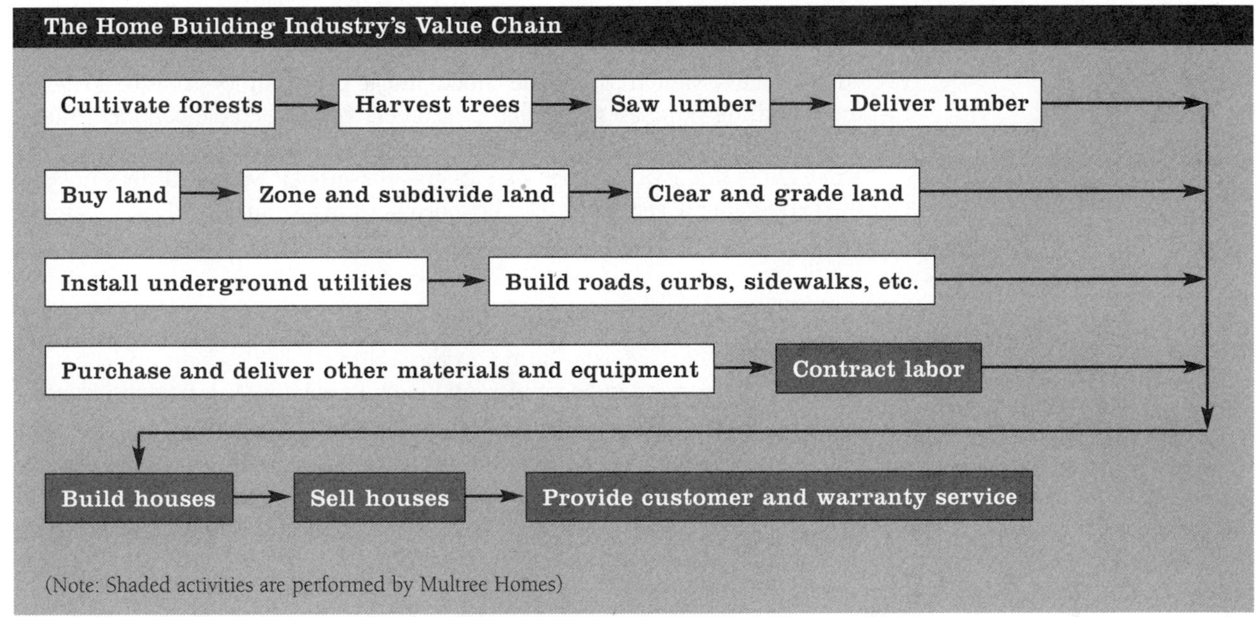

Exhibit 2-3

chain so we can maximize our value. *If our customers believe our product is different from the competition, it will have value.* This is called product differentiation. We have many ways to differentiate products:

- *Uniqueness.* We may be the only provider of a good or service. For example, we might be one of many manufactured home builders, but the only one in a specific geographic market. Or we may be the only one providing custom-designed log homes.
- *Image.* In our market, we have intense competition from other home builders. We need to differentiate our products based on image, such as brand name, product features, customer service, and/or technological leadership. Many companies are very successful with image differentiation. [Exhibit 2-4 lists examples of companies using image differentiation.]

Using Image to Differentiate Products and Companies

Brand name image	Product features	Customer service	Technological leadership
Band Aid	Cadillac	Federal Express	IBM
Xerox	Burger King	Sears	Hewlett-Packard
Ben & Jerry's Ice Cream	Karsten Mfg. (Ping golf clubs)	State Farm Insurance	Maytag
Coca-Cola	Canon cameras	Hilton Hotels	Intel

Exhibit 2-4

"We use the industry value chain to identify where we believe our company will have the greatest economic value. Our expertise is in building manufactured homes. We then differentiate our products in three ways: high-quality standard homes, custom-designed homes, and excellent customer service.

"Many firms use value chains to identify profitable complementary product opportunities. For example, Nintendo is probably best known for its video games.

Most of its profits do not come from the game players, but rather from selling the game cartridges. Victoria's Secret, a well-known retailer of women's apparel, discovered customers wanted to buy the 'mood' music played in its stores to go along with their clothing purchases. CDs have become a very profitable complementary product line for that company!"

JULIE

"True! These are good strategies, so long as the money we spend does not exceed the extra value it generates. The key idea is to make sure we always increase the value of our products, in our customers' eyes, by more than our costs."

Creating value through cost management

JULIE

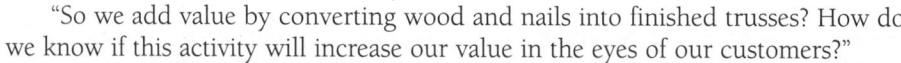

"Once we decide where we want to be on the industry's value chain, we can analyze our specific processes and activities. *Our ultimate objective is to minimize the cost of each process.* To achieve this objective, we must accomplish two goals:

- Identify and eliminate activities that do not create value, and
- For value-adding activities, perform them in the most effective and efficient way possible.

Cost management looks at the money we spend to acquire, convert, and deliver goods and services. At the beginning of the 20th century, Carnegie made a fortune practicing good cost management. Carnegie Steel's strategy was to keep operating costs below its competition. When times were good, it charged competitive prices, making more profit than other steel producers. But, when times were hard, it could cut prices to levels that drove out its competition but still made a profit for the company. Today, Wal-Mart and Southwest Airlines are examples of companies practicing good cost management. If we can save money, the company's value increases."

BOB

"Rather than drawing a diagram as I did for the industry-wide value chain [Exhibit 2-3], here's a simple list of our major processes and their activities [see Exhibit 2-5].

"We have six processes in our value chain. As an example of our value chain strategy, consider Activity 3.6, roof construction. Each activity can have many sequential steps. Let's focus on making the trusses, which are the support beams for the roof. First, we buy materials. Then we saw the lumber. We assemble trusses using clamps and nails into a variety of sizes as we need them."

NANCY

"So we add value by converting wood and nails into finished trusses? How do we know if this activity will increase our value in the eyes of our customers?"

BOB

"Good question! Remember, we can buy premade trusses from truss makers. So, we have a good measure of whether this is a value-adding process or not. If it costs us less to make equally good or better trusses, as compared to buying them, we can provide a home for our customers at a lower cost."

SID

"Just as we can buy trusses, our customers can buy houses from our competition. From the customer's perspective, all home building companies acquire the same resources. Customers buy the house adding the most value to those resources for the lowest cost. *Our job is to manage our value chain activities so we [and not our competitors] provide the greatest value at the lowest cost.*"

Economic value and the service sector

BILL

"I sure wish this idea of creating value applied equally to governmental and regulated services! It takes forever to get plans approved through local government

Multree Homes Value Chain

1. Customer order-taking
    1.1. Sales
    1.2. Credit check (Finance)
2. Materials acquisition (inbound logistics)
    2.1. Scheduling
    2.2. Purchasing
    2.3. Receiving, inspecting, and storage
    2.4. Delivery to factory
3. Manufacturing
    3.1. Lumber sawing
    3.2. Wall assembly (framing)
    3.3. Rough wiring
    3.4. Rough plumbing
    3.5. Wall finishing (including insulation, windows, and door hanging)
    3.6. Roof construction
    3.7. Finish carpentry
    3.8. Top-off plumbing
    3.9. Finish electric
    3.10. Carpeting
    3.11. Inspection
4. Shipping (outbound logistics)
    4.1. Packing
    4.2. Shipping
    4.3. Set up at retail dealer, customer lot
5. Close sales
    5.1. Customer walk-through and inspection
    5.2. Bill customer (customer's bank)
    5.3. Collect and deposit cash
6. After-sale customer services
    6.1. Provide warranty work
    6.2. Survey customer satisfaction
    6.3. New product and service advertising

Exhibit 2-5

agencies. Inspectors work on their own clocks. And, getting a house sold can take months dealing with the banks, title companies, and the local government recorder's office."

$% JULIE

"Historically, regulators just set customer rates to cover the costs of operations, regardless of how efficient [or inefficient] service providers were. Efficiency and cost management were not important as laws prevented private firms from competing. Similarly, taxpayers subsidized governmental agencies with little opportunity to challenge their value. Hopefully, this is changing, though. We can see it now in many services. Remember our discussion last week at the funeral? Competition drives the need to seriously consider value. It is happening in the service and government sectors with governmental downsizing and outsourcing [privatization], and deregulation. New competition in postal services, health care, transportation, communications, and banking will force those organizations to assess their industry value chains and how they can sustain value."

KEY OBJECTIVE 3

Explain why financial accounting does not report economic value.

Financial Accounting Measures of Value

NANCY

"Apparently, we have value creation and management under control. The value chain provides a good picture of our company. But I don't see how our accounting reports support, or agree with, this picture."

JACKIE

"They really don't. Financial accounting reports present a different picture of the firm: as bundles of value-creating assets [the balance sheet] and how they have changed over time [the income statement]. For financial accounting, we don't look at value the same way managers, owners, and investors do. We only recognize changes in value when 'arm's-length' transactions occur. Arm's-length transactions are sales to, or purchases from, outsiders. In other words, our financial accounting system only records and reports financial transactions with other firms. Arm's-length transactions provide objective, verifiable measures of past value that can be audited. The problem, of course, is these transactions have already occurred. It is past [historical] information."

NANCY

"So future cashflows are not considered? How do balance sheets and income statements measure value then? Why do we use these accounting numbers? Why are they so important?"

Historical costs: The need to look backwards

JULIE

"We look at our business in a completely different way than they do. Bankers and investors want to know how we spend our money, and how we compare with other companies. From their point of view, we are just another investment. Remember, value is relative. Value depends on the other investment opportunities available to them. Thus, comparability with other investments is very important to them."

NANCY

"O.K., that's fine, but don't they want to compare future values? Financial statements report past values. In other words, the balance sheet reports the historical costs of the resources we own, not their future values. Why do they want past data?"

JACKIE

"It is 'hard data.' The advantage of financial accounting data is its objectivity. Objective measures of value, and how value has changed, are needed for financial statements. Remember our discussion at Grandfather's funeral [Chapter 1]? Financial statements have to provide *reliable* information to outsiders. Past transactions can be audited [verified]. *Estimates* of *future* cashflows cannot! Our estimate of future cashflows may be completely different from our bankers' estimates!"

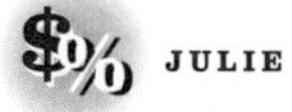
NANCY

"I see. The real strength of financial accounting is not that the numbers accurately measure value. Rather, they are reliable numbers not easily manipulated."

JULIE

"Exactly! Future cashflows create value, and creditors and stockholders want estimates of those cashflows. A company's management may be able to provide the most accurate estimates. Then again, management may be motivated not to! Management wants the investor's and banker's money, so it may give overly optimistic estimates to them."

TOMMY

"Wait a minute! That's not ethical! Are you saying management will try to deceive outsiders in an attempt to get their money?"

JULIE

"No, no. Don't misunderstand me. I'm only saying the possibility exists. Remember the IMA's code of ethics? One of its standards is integrity, that is, maintaining our professionalism. Another ethics standard is objectivity, including full disclosure. Yet a third standard is competency, which requires appropriate skills and knowledge, along with appropriate analyses. Purposefully misleading the public violates three of the four IMA standards of ethical conduct. Of course, most managers are not CMAs! Most, then, are not bound by my code of ethics. Without their own professional code of ethics, I'm just saying the possibility of knowingly misleading the public exists. Obviously, many firms and their managements are very ethically committed. Of course . . . "

JACKIE

"This is why we have CPAs. The CPA's role is to assure outsiders the information they are receiving is reliable. Therefore, accounting reports are based on objective information about value-making activities that have already occurred."

What does financial accounting information tell us about value?

JULIE

"Investors can be confident about receiving financial reports on different investment opportunities [companies] that have been prepared in the same way. They know the reports are based on verifiable, objective transactions. With this information, they can evaluate the company's past performance and compare it with other companies. By comparing companies' 'track records,' investors are in a better position to judge their future cash-making potentials, and choose among investment opportunities."

JACKIE

Balance sheet information. "In making these comparisons, investors want all companies' assets and liabilities reported in the same way, in order of liquidity. This means in order of cash now and in the future. The balance sheet is organized in terms of how fast we can get cash. Here, let me write the balance sheet equation on the board [see Exhibit 2-6].

The Balance Sheet Equation

Assets	=	Liabilities	+	Equity
Resources we have		How much we owe outsiders for the resources we have		Owners' residual accounting value (how much the owners invested in the resources we have)
Current Assets: • Cash • Promises for cash (accounts receivable) • The cost of products we own that will be sold for cash in the near future (inventories)		*Current Liabilities:* • How much we owe now (accounts payable)		*Contributed Capital:* • How much the owners invested in the business
Long-Term Assets: • The cost of resources we own that will make cash in the future		*Long-Term Liabilities:* • How much we owe in the future		*Retained Earnings:* • The profits not yet given back to the owners

Exhibit 2-6

"The balance sheet is a different picture of the business from the value chain picture. The balance sheet presents 'dollars and cents.' This is what we received from the activities we performed, and what we owe. The value chain shows the activities we do, and helps us determine how to create value now and in the future. The balance sheet reports on the value we created in the past."

"Wait a minute, Jackie. Not all balance sheets look the same! The balance sheet for the shoe store where I used to work was different from ours, especially in reporting inventory values."

"That's true. I used to work for a law firm. Its balance sheet didn't include any inventories. Multree has three different inventories on its balance sheet. What's going on?"

"Reporting the costs of inventories in the current assets section is probably the biggest difference in balance sheets. This is due to the different types of organizations being reported. In business, three types of organizations exist:

- *Services.* CPA firms, law firms, and taxicab companies provide labor-based services to customers. Because they do not sell products, they do not have inventories to report on their balance sheets. Value is created when customers are willing to pay more for the service than the cost to provide it.

  "Value has a slightly different meaning in the governmental and nonprofit sectors of our economy, but it is based on the same principle. Value is created when customers [taxpayers] are willing to pay [with taxes] for these types of services. Here, the profit goal is zero because the customers are also the owners.

  "Think of the relationship between taxpayers and the city bus system, or between a church and its congregation. As owners, we invest in the bus system [with taxes]. We also purchase this service [bus fares]. If bus revenues are greater than cost, we have a profit. The profit can be returned to us [similar to dividends on stock] or reinvested in the system [similar to retained earnings in a corporation]. In either event, this lowers our taxes. Instead of going through all this, the bus system sets fares so that when these revenues are added to tax revenues, costs are covered. A church operates in a similar way. We want this service and we're willing to pay for its cost.

- *Merchandisers.* Wholesalers and retailers purchase products and then resell them. The difference between sales price and cost of the products is the value these businesses add to society. Value is created by making products and services easier to get, or less expensive for their customers. Until products are sold, though, they represent value-creating assets. The cost of the unsold merchandise inventory is reported as a current asset.

KEY OBJECTIVE 4

Give examples of the three manufacturing inventories.

- *Manufacturers.* As with merchandisers, manufacturers create value by selling final products for more than their costs. These businesses differ from merchandisers, though, because manufacturers purchase materials, labor, equipment, and facilities specifically to produce goods. Using labor, equipment, and facilities, the materials are transformed into a final product. As with merchandise firms, the cost of the unsold product inventory is reported as a current asset. Similarly, the cost of raw materials not yet used is inventoried and reported as a current asset. From looking at our value chain, our activities are making houses. The cost of houses under construction is yet another current asset waiting to be finished and sold. So, manufacturers have three types of inventories to report on the balance sheet:

Raw materials inventory *is the cost of materials waiting to be used in making a product.* **Work-in-process inventory** *is the cost of making the product while it is being manufactured.* **Finished goods inventory** *is the cost of completed products waiting to be sold.*

- **Raw materials inventory** is the cost of the materials purchased but not yet used in production. We stockpile nails, paint, and plumbing and electrical supplies in the storeroom. We stockpile lumber in the yard behind the factory.
- **Work-in-process (WIP) inventory** is the cost of houses we have started but have not yet finished. As we use resources [materials,

labor, and the factory] in making a product, these resource costs are accumulated in WIP until the product is finished.

- **Finished goods inventory** is the cost of completed houses not yet sold. It is the same as the retailer's merchandise inventory."

Income statement information. "Our product's sales price is the value our customers place on what we do."

"Assuming they buy our houses!" quipped Nancy. Not everyone laughed this time, though.

"Income statements measure the increase in value we have created by comparing sales price to the cost of providing a product or service. At the law firm where Sid used to work, the income statement is simple: revenues minus expenses equals profit."

"Yes, but at my retail shoe store, we had to account for product inventories. Our income statement identified the gross profit on sales [revenues minus cost of goods sold]. Cost of goods sold is simply what it cost us for the inventory we sold. Gross profit is the money available to cover operating costs and generate profits."

"Less taxes of course," moaned Jackie, to the general laughter of the rest.

"Well it's a little more complex for a manufacturing company like ours. We convert raw materials into products. Although I sometimes think we just make inventories!"

"O.K., so sometimes we need a 'fire sale' at the end of the year, but let's stay on the topic. Let's compare the different income statement formats for these three different types of organizations. [Exhibit 2-7 illustrates income statements for a service firm, retailer, and manufacturer.]

"Retailers and wholesalers purchase finished products and resell them. The net delivered purchase price determines their cost. The total cost of all products sold equals the beginning retail inventory cost, plus the products purchased [the sum of these is what could be sold], less what wasn't sold [the ending retail inventory].

"With a manufacturing firm, products are not purchased, they are built. Thus, the retailer's purchases are replaced with **cost of goods manufactured**. [These two lines are highlighted in Exhibit 2-7.] Conceptually, though, they are the same thing. You either buy products for resale [a merchandiser] or you make products [a manufacturer]. *Purchases and cost of goods manufactured are the costs of getting your products* [the products bought or made this year]. Because manufacturers track resource usage more closely, their income statements include a detailed cost of goods manufactured schedule. [Exhibit 2-8 on p. 45 illustrates a cost of goods manufactured schedule.]

> **Cost of goods manufactured** *is the cost of completed products made by a manufacturer.*

"Service firms aren't very different from manufacturers. Both make something out of resources. They do differ, though, in one respect. Manufacturers use a lot of materials and have an expensive factory to make products. Some of the products still in the factory are not yet complete at year end [ending WIP]. Some of the products are complete, but not yet sold [ending finished goods inventory]. Because we have to value these ending inventories and report them on the balance sheet, the costs of making these products are separated from the other costs of running the business.

"Service providers also make a 'product' [a service], but they don't use a lot of materials [perhaps file folders, paper, and the like]. Nor do they have a big factory. Most importantly, services are not inventoried for future sale. Thus, the costs of providing services usually are included with the other expenses of the service firm."

Income Statement Comparisons

LAW FIRM (service firm)		SHOE STORE (retailer)			MULTREE (manufacturer)		
Revenues	$1,000	Revenues		$1,000	Revenues		$1,000
		Less: Cost of goods sold			Less: Cost of goods sold		
		Beginning inventory	$100		Beginning finished goods inventory	$100	
		Add: Purchases	550		***Add: Cost of goods manufactured***	550	
		Less: Ending inventory	(50)		Less: Ending finished goods inventory	(50)	
		Cost of goods sold		(600)	Cost of goods sold		(600)
		Gross profit		$ 400	Gross profit		$ 400
Less: Expenses	(900)	Less: Expenses		(300)	Less: Expenses		(300)
Net income	**$ 100**	**Net income**		**$ 100**	**Net income**		**$ 100**

Exhibit 2-7

Cost of Goods Manufactured Schedule

Cost of goods manufactured schedule			
Direct materials inventory:			
Beginning inventory	$ 75		
Add: Purchases	150		
Less: Ending inventory	(25)		
Direct materials used:		$200	
Direct labor		150	
Manufacturing overhead		300	
Manufacturing costs incurred			$ 650
Add: Beginning WIP inventory costs			100
Less: Ending WIP inventory costs			(200)
Cost of goods manufactured			**$ 550**

Manufacturer's income statement (from Exhibit 2-7)		
Revenues		$1,000
Less: Cost of goods sold		
Beginning finished goods inventory	$100	
Add: Cost of goods manufactured	550	
Less: Ending finished goods inventory	(50)	
Cost of goods sold		(600)
Gross profit		$ 400
Less: Expenses		(300)
Net income		**$ 100**

Exhibit 2-8

NANCY

Traditional resource categories. "O.K. I understand manufacturing inventories and cost of goods manufactured, but why do you label materials and labor as 'direct' in the cost of goods manufactured schedule? What is 'manufacturing overhead?' Where are the costs of the factory?"

BOB

"I can explain this.

- **Direct materials** are the raw materials physically and easily traced to our product, a house. Examples include lumber, appliances, carpeting, windows, and the like.
- **Direct labor** is also physically and easily traced to individual houses. We ask our carpenters, for example, to record on their time cards how much time they needed to frame each house. In this way, we can assign labor cost directly to the product.
- **Manufacturing overhead** includes all the other manufacturing costs we can't trace directly to a house. Let me give you some examples of these costs.
  - ➤ Indirect materials are factory supplies, like nails, tape, glue, saw blades, drill bits, et cetera. I could hire someone to actually count the number of nails used in each house, but that would be pretty expensive for such a minor item."

KEY OBJECTIVE 5

Describe the three traditional manufacturing resources and prepare a cost of goods manufactured schedule.

"Ha!" laughed Tommy. "You'd never get an accurate count either! It's just not worth the effort."

BOB

- ➤ "Similarly, indirect labor represents workers whose activities can't be traced directly to a house. Forklift drivers, stockroom workers, foremen and supervisors, and maintenance personnel are all needed to make a house, but can any of their time be traced directly to any particular house?
- ➤ Most of the factory costs you asked about cannot be traced directly to a house. How much factory or equipment depreciation are used in a house? How much electricity, heat, light, property taxes, and insurance go into making an individual house?"

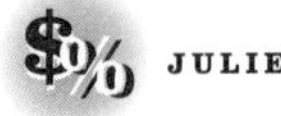
JULIE

"The point is some resources, and their costs, can be assigned to a product by tracing those resources directly to it. Many manufacturing costs, though, are indi-

Product costs include **direct materials**, **direct labor**, *and* **manufacturing overhead**. *Overhead includes all those manufacturing costs that cannot be directly traced to a particular product, such as indirect materials, indirect labor, as well as other factory operating and support costs. Overhead needs to be* **allocated** *(arbitrarily divided up) to be included in each product's cost.*

rect. In other words, because they cannot be traced directly to a product, they have to be arbitrarily divided up in order to be included in the product cost. Nails are a good example. Last week we spent $100 on nails and built four houses. I charged each house $25 for nails. Dividing up indirect manufacturing costs [overhead] so they can be included in each house's cost is called **cost allocation**. *In cost accounting, costs are assigned by direct tracing and through allocating overhead.* Finding the best way to allocate overhead so we have the most accurate product cost is what I call the 'joy of cost accounting!' But, we'll talk more about product costing in a future meeting [Chapter 5]."

JACKIE

"Financial accounting requires one more distinction from management accounting. Which resource costs should be included in our product's cost? For financial accounting, **product costs** are defined as the costs of getting our products. Product costs are inventoried [as raw materials, WIP, and finished goods] until the product is sold. Then product costs become the cost of goods sold when products are sold. On the income statement, product costs are matched against sales price, and the difference reported as the time period's gross profit. **Period costs** are operating expenses, that is, the costs of getting rid of our products [selling expenses] and running the business [administrative expenses]. Period costs are reported at the bottom of the income statement as a deduction from gross profit in determining net income."

Product costs *are assigned to specific products through direct tracing (direct materials and direct labor) or through allocation (of overhead).* **Period costs** *are assigned to time periods as expenses, but not to individual products.*

NANCY

"Now I'm confused! Many of our value chain activities [Exhibit 2-5] represent costs which must be expensed as period costs for financial reporting. But these costs can be traced directly to specific products. For example, shipping costs are unique to each specific house. So are sales commissions. Shouldn't these costs be included as direct costs of the product? Shouldn't we have a 'cost of goods sold' value that includes all of the product's direct costs, regardless of whether they are manufacturing, distribution, or selling costs?"

JACKIE

"You have a valid argument, Nancy. Financial reporting, however, requires costs to be organized by the type of activity they represent [i.e., the costs of getting a product versus costs of getting rid of it and running the business]. Costs are not reported according to whether they are traceable directly to specific products."

TOMMY

"It seems to me financial accounting reports make measuring value creation harder than it should be! Is this ethical?"

Good question! Jackie thought to herself. As she didn't have a good answer, though, she just remained silent. Quiet fell over the room.

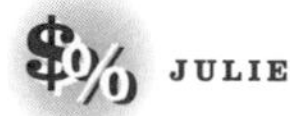

JULIE

"Let me explain. In financial accounting, costs must be separated into product versus period costs. It would be unethical to report costs in any other way, then, on the financial statements. Financial accounting is not designed to measure economic value! This is one reason why we need a management accounting system, as we discussed last week [Chapter 1]."

The relationship between accounting and economic value

NANCY

"Time out, time out [motioning with her best basketball hand signals]! I'm getting a little buried here. Something doesn't make sense. You started by explaining how value is created by making our company a more efficient and reliable cash-making machine. Right?" A general murmuring of agreement echoed throughout the room. "So now I'm confused. On our balance sheet, the owner's equity section shows $10 million. Isn't this Multree's value? Isn't this the amount we should be paid for this company, Jackie?"

"Well, ah . . . no, not actually. I mean it could happen, but it's not likely."

"Then I have two questions for you. First, why isn't this the value of the company? Second, if the accounting value isn't the real value, why are we bothering with accounting at all?"

"O.K. O.K." Jackie quieted the murmuring with her hands. "We have two measures of value, accounting value and economic value. Accounting value is the amount on the balance sheet. Economic value is what we can sell the company for, probably best thought of as the stock market value. Stock market prices are a good approximation of economic value."

"As CEO, that's what I'm concerned with! Just like Roberto Goizieta when he became CEO at Coca-Cola. At the time, Coke was losing market share, profits, and economic value to Pepsi. Goizieta took Coke's market value from $4 million in 1981 to $180 million in 1997, when he died. He believed a publicly traded company exists for only one purpose, increasing shareholder value. Using a stock option–based incentive plan, he focused everyone at Coke on building economic value."

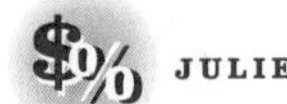

"*Accounting value and economic value just don't measure the same things. The accounting system measures the results of past transactions* These are hard, auditable transactions, and do not represent estimates of current or future economic value."

"O.K. If this is true, why bother with accounting value at all? Our objective is to increase the economic value of the company, right?"

"Well, recall the primary use of financial accounting from the very beginning was stewardship, not measuring economic value. However, accounting values help us understand economic value. Financial reports provide hard evidence of past value. We can compare this with our estimates of economic value for that time period. The comparison can be used to validate our past estimates and refine our future estimates. This is how accounting numbers influence economic value."

"I understand how financial statements can help us validate our estimating abilities, but why do we need to rely on this inaccurate measure of economic value? Can't we just use better measures?"

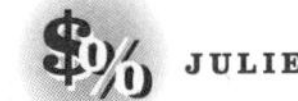

"Yes, we can. Remember, though, we've already paid for the financial measures, so we can use them without incurring any additional accounting system cost. We have to pay more for an accounting system that provides different measures of economic value."

"That's the trick! We need to know when to invest in better information systems. And that will be when better measures put more money in our pockets through making better decisions. Well, this becomes clear now. We must understand enough about the financial measures and their relationship to economic value to know when we need more information."

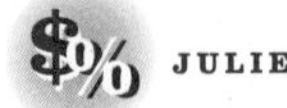

"Yes! We also need to know how our actions will be reported in the financial accounting system, because this is the information used by investors and creditors. Here's an example. Consider a computer company's investment in research and development [R&D]. If it stops investing in R&D, expenses decrease. This leads to an increase in accounting income. Accounting value increases, but will economic value? Probably not! Computer companies must invest heavily in R&D to keep their product lines current. If they don't, their future cashflows will be less. Here's a case where increasing accounting value does not increase economic value!"

"So, accounting measures are useful for estimating economic value in some cases, but not in others. As managers, we have to understand what causes economic value to in-

crease for our company and how these activities are measured by financial accounting systems."

SID

"Well, where does this leave us? To estimate future value, people outside our company only have financial accounting information about the past. As internal users of accounting information, we have all the company's information available. Instead of estimating value, we create it. We use all available information in determining the activities we do and their costs. And we will pay for better information when it improves our decisions and economic value.

"The income statement reflects how well we did this in the past. This may be a good starting point for creating future value. But, it's not sufficient! What we need is a plan. However, we cannot ignore financial accounting reports. That's the information used by the market to value our firm. If the market values Multree Homes too low, we could be subject to a hostile takeover!"

Strategic Planning to Create Value

SID

"I read strategic planning is the art of creating value. Our plan needs to identify where we create value within the industry's value chain. It also must direct our activities within our internal value chain. Finally, it must culminate in financial accounting reports allowing the market to see the value we're adding. When our plans are logically linked together, from the statement of our vision for the company all the way through our operating activities, we will have a **strategic plan** for the year."

A ***strategic plan*** *begins with a firm's vision statement: what it ultimately wants to be. The vision statement identifies critical success factors that include objectives [where it wants to be for each factor]. Measurable goals are attached to each objective. To accomplish each goal, the environment is evaluated, specific plans are made, and performance measures are created.*

Steps in strategic planning

"I see six steps in creating our strategic plan. We won't be able to complete all of them in this meeting, but we can make a good start." [Exhibit 2-9 lists the six steps in the strategic planning process.]

Multree's vision statement. "Grandfather had a vision we all share: make more money now and in the future. To do this, though, we need a more specific vision [mission] statement. The vision statement should be able to answer, 'Why will we be able to continue to create value in the long run?' Long-run value creation comes from identifying and man-

KEY OBJECTIVE 6

List the six steps in strategic planning and discuss the role of management accounting in this process.

The Strategic Planning Process

1. Create a vision or mission statement.
2. Identify objectives to be accomplished that will ultimately lead us to realize our vision.
3. Translate our objectives into measurable goals for the year.
4. Analyze our external and internal environments to see how we can accomplish our goals.
5. Determine what we need to do to accomplish our goals.
6. Develop measures of performance telling us if we have achieved our goals and added value to the company.

Exhibit 2-9

aging our critical success factors. These are the things we do that create long-run value. They should be clearly stated in our vision statement. Then, if we keep focused each year on achieving our vision through our annual strategic planning process, we should continue to make money and keep ownership of the company. I have an idea about what our critical success factors should be, and how they can be incorporated into our vision statement." [Exhibit 2-10 presents Multree's vision statement.]

Multree's Vision Statement

Multree Manufacturing will be the industry leader in:

Sales	Both in our standard home and custom home lines, no competitor will sell more homes than us.
Quality	We will offer the highest quality homes available in our market.
Service	No competitor will be able to satisfy the needs of our market better than we can. Nor will they be able to provide customer service faster than we do.
Cost	We will provide the highest quality homes at the lowest costs within our market.
Technological leadership	We will lead the industry in new technology development and use.

Exhibit 2-10

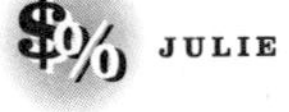

Objectives and goals. "Objectives are statements about where we want to be with respect to our critical success factors. I've seen a lot of vision statements in my 15 years of banking and lending experience. They all seem to be different. The important point is a vision statement provides a philosophy for doing business. For example, I remember the British Cooperative Bank Group's vision statement. Social value was more important than profit maximization. They would not invest in countries or companies engaging in illegal finances, repression, or manufactured products harmful to people or animals. I like the idea of incorporating our long-run objectives within the vision statement. This gives us a little more direction in our strategic planning.

"Goals, on the other hand, are short-run accomplishments. They differ from objectives in that goals are measurable and limited to a time period, usually a year. If we accomplish our annual goals, ultimately we will achieve our objectives. Thus, goals need to be developed for each objective and critical success factor."

"Our first objective is to make more money. Grandfather always set a profit goal first. For next year, I want our profits to increase 20% over last year. Our profit goal will be $1 million."

"To be the industry leader in sales, we should start by increasing sales volume 10% over last year. I propose we establish a sales forecast of 100 standard homes and 10 custom homes for next year. We should be able to sell standard homes at an average price of $50,000. Custom home prices should average $100,000 each."

"Yes, we can make that many in the factory. Our goal for quality should be a 50% reduction in scrap costs from last year. A second quality goal should be a 20% reduction in warranty costs from last year.

"Tommy and I have been investigating some new framing machinery coming onto the market. We believe this new technology will reduce lumber scrap, the cost of nails, and labor time. However, if we purchase this new equipment, we will have to rearrange some of our shopfloor operations. Let's set a goal of installing this new equipment next year.

"I also think we can reduce inventory costs by 15% from last year if we can develop better delivery schedules and quality from our suppliers. More frequent deliveries will reduce our costs of storing and moving materials, as well as warehousing, taxes, and insurance. Better quality also will reduce scrap costs."

"For customer service, let's set a goal of reducing the time to process a new house order from 20 days to 10 days. We also can try to reduce the time to respond to and complete a warranty work request from an average of 10 days to 2 days."

"Let's not forget our ethical commitment to the environment and the community. I'll create some goals for reducing pollution, stabilizing employment throughout the county, and initiating community improvement programs."

Environmental analyses. "These are all good goals for next year, but are they achievable? A lot is going on in the economy, making me believe we can't accomplish all of them, especially our higher sales goal and better supplier relationships. We need to look at our external environment for threats and opportunities. We also should analyze our internal environment for strengths and weaknesses. Our strategic plan should guard against threats and weaknesses. It also should include strategies to capitalize on opportunities and strengths. Our long-run success depends on identifying and attempting to control the environmental forces influencing us. Let's be proactive, instead of just constantly reacting to our environment."

"Well, one external opportunity is international sales. I read a study in which 38% of the firms responding said their highest priority foreign investments will be in China and Asia. Another 25% said their top priority is Latin America. E-commerce [electronic commerce over the internet] is another opportunity. About one-half of all retail and manufacturing Web sites serve international customers. Barnes and Noble projects international sales will boost internet sales to 30% of its total sales."

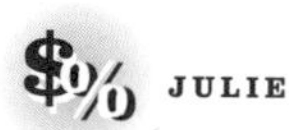

"Yes, but one external threat is the Federal Reserve Bank [FRB] raising interest rates. If this happens, we should have some long-term lending agreement with the banks so sales are not hurt."

"I disagree, Julie. I think we have an opportunity here. Next year is a Presidential election year. The president will want to be re-elected, so she will be pressuring the FRB to reduce rates. I'm more concerned about the threat of that new environmental protection act passing Congress. If it does, logging will decline and lumber prices will rise. We'll also have to install new pollution control equipment!"

"We better consider some internal strengths and weaknesses impacting goal achievement. If we don't give our workers a raise next year, they may go on strike! On the other hand, if we let them go to those new training programs, their skills will increase and they will be more satisfied with their work. They'll also be able to perform more quality control activities. They are highly motivated and loyal to Multree. Most of them have been with the company for many years. We might want to consider the Japanese PDCA [plan, do, check, action] system as part of our strategic plan."

"Good! I see we're all thinking about how we can achieve our goals. This is how Harley-Davidson saved its business back in the 1980s. The Japanese were threatening to take over the American market. But the new owner-managers saw an opportunity in that we wanted high-powered American motorcycles. The major internal weaknesses were finances and old production processes. Their major strengths included the company's image and loyal employees. They used their image and employees to obtain outside financing and rebuild the plant to make a high-quality motorcycle at a much lower cost."

"Yes! This is even going on in the federal government. Each agency has to submit a formal strategic plan that includes a mission statement, objectives and goals, environmental analyses, and performance measures. The 1993 Government Performance and Results Act also requires each aspect be linked to the others, just as we are doing now."

Management accounting's role in strategic planning

"Before we end this meeting, I'd like to be clear about what role I should play in our strategic planning and value-creation process. It seems the management accountant should have a significant role here."

"Of course. The Boss always used the accounting staff to take all this information and develop a projected income statement for the upcoming year. That will be your job, Julie. We probably will need another meeting to review it, and make changes. Let's schedule that meeting for next week. Once we have our projected income statement, with a satisfactory profit, we will be done with the strategic plan."

"Wait a minute, Sid. We are never going to accomplish the plan without our employees' commitment to it! We need to involve them in the entire process so they internalize our goals and feel the goals are theirs. Remember, they are the people who will accomplish Multree's goals, not us!"

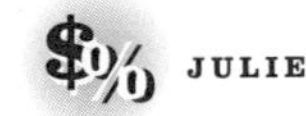

"O.K. I see three roles in strategic planning. First, I need to be a 'process controller.'

- By this I mean the management accountant should assure we follow a rational, logical process. The vision statement should be linked to critical success factors, objectives, goals, an environmental analysis, plans, and measures.
- And, I agree with Tommy. Everyone has to be part of the process. This should not be limited just to upper management. So, I must make sure that our vision statement, objectives, and goals are communicated to all employees. They have to accept our values as their own, or our goals may not be realized.

"Second, the management accounting system should provide information for the strategic planning process.

- This begins with financial accounting reports on past performance.
- While much of the strategic planning information is nonfinancial in nature, I have to make sure the relevant information is available, the right people have it, and it is timely.
- One of the major outputs from this process is a projected income statement for next year. One of my responsibilities, then, is the compilation of all this planning information into its financial results [i.e., the projected income statement]. We will review this at our next meeting.

"Third, I'm the 'cop on the block.' The sixth step in strategic planning is developing performance measures.

- Performance measures need to be developed for each goal. For example, I'll create reports on time-to-completion warranty work and time-to-approval of sales contracts for our customer service goals.

- The performance indicators must be consistently and accurately measurable.
- Finally, performance measures must be motivationally appropriate. Last night I stopped at McBurger-in-the-Box. I didn't get what I ordered! I remember working there as a high school student. We were evaluated on how fast an order was filled. First and foremost, it was a 'fast food' service. We were not evaluated on whether the order was complete or correct!"

TOMMY

"You know, Julie, our workers' perceptions about accountants as 'the police of the company' come from not involving our employees in the process. A fundamental performance evaluation axiom is, 'What gets measured gets done.' When grandfather was in charge, company employees saw accountants only when something was wrong. Remember all the houses we had to rebuild two years ago? Purchasing was blamed for not controlling their costs. To create favorable performance evaluations, they started buying the cheapest nails they could find. Of course, after six months the nails started coming out of the walls! They weren't responsible for quality, just cost. What I'm suggesting is if we involve the people being evaluated in setting goals and developing appropriate performance measures, we will have a better chance of achieving our goals. Management accountants have to work closely with all the employees. Remember, we are your customers!

"Southwire Company in Carrollton, Georgia, the world's leading wire maker, recognized its employees as its number one critical success factor. It measured employee involvement with its 'STAR' system [suggestions, thoughts, and recommendations]."

SID

"You're right. The organization's members are the users of management accounting information. We've discovered what economic value is, how financial accounting reports are not designed to measure future value, and the role of management accounting systems in strategic planning. I think we have done enough in this meeting. We will analyze the financial side of our planning process in next week's meeting. Later, we will look at the performance evaluation system."

KEY OBJECTIVES SUMMARY

DORIS

"Before we leave, I want to make sure I have good notes about what we have learned today. We discussed six topics in this meeting.

1. Define economic value and explain the factors that influence it.

"We need to make things [goods or services] people want and are willing to pay more for than our cost of providing those products. Economic value is simply money-making potential. Assets, investments, and/or companies have value when they can make more money now and in the future. How valuable something is depends on a number of factors:

- *Risk.* This is the uncertainty of its future cashflows. Investors have a risk-return trade-off, though. The greater the risk of not receiving the cashflows, the greater the return will have to be in order for an investor to be indifferent between this opportunity and one less risky.

- *Effort.* Value also depends on the effort involved in getting future cashflows. The greater the effort needed, the higher the return [cashflows, profits] will have to be.
- *Time.* Value is in expected future cashflows. The more reliable these future cashflows are, the more valuable they are. Additionally, the sooner we receive them, the more valuable they become because we can invest the returns and earn even more money.
- *Other investment opportunities.* Value is relative. It depends on what other investments we can make.

2. Demonstrate how value chains, product differentiation, and cost management are used to create value.

"A value chain is a picture of the processes and activities involved in a system. We use industry value chains to determine where we want to be within the industry. We choose what we want to do based on what will create the most value. We create value by differentiating our products or services from the competition's. We can do this by providing a unique product or service, or based on our image. Often name recognition, quality, product features, customer service, and/or technological leadership are means to establish that high-quality image.

"We create value chains of the processes and activities we do [an internal value chain of our company] so we can identify areas for improvement. We do this by:

- Identifying and eliminating activities not creating value, and
- Performing value-added activities in the most effective and efficient way possible.

"Cost management is concerned with effectiveness and efficiency. Consider my value chain for grocery shopping [see Exhibit 2-11].

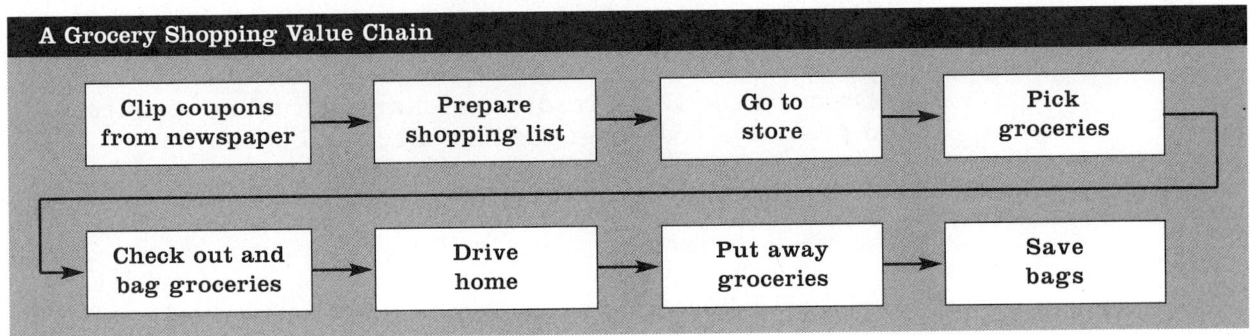

Exhibit 2-11

"Clipping coupons from the Sunday newspaper is much more efficient if I have scissors handy! Also, having a filing system to organize and store coupons increases their effectiveness. Preparing a grocery list, like the one I have here [because I have to go to the store after this meeting], allows me to get all the things I need more efficiently. I bag my own groceries because I don't like the eggs and bread underneath a three-pound coffee can! I can go on, but I think you get the idea.

3. Explain why financial accounting does not report economic value.

"Financial accounting systems are designed to provide objective, reliable information to people outside the company. Objectivity means we can verify the information's correctness. Reliability means users can be assured the information is processed and reported in the same way [following the same set of rules] for all companies. Only when transactions occur are they recorded in the financial accounting system. Thus, reports from it are based on past information.

"While investors might prefer information about future cashflows, this information is, by its nature, subjective. We all have different views of the future. Financial reports are not designed to verify the correctness or accuracy of subjective projections into the future. That is not their role. Investors must make their own projections of value. Financial accounting reports can only aid the process by providing information on past performance.

4. Give examples of the three manufacturing inventories.

- "Raw materials inventory contains direct and indirect materials. Direct materials can be physically traced to specific products. Examples include the lumber used in a house, its appliances, carpet, plants, and other landscaping. Indirect materials cannot be easily traced to specific products. Examples include nails, sheetrock tape, electric wire, paint, and other items too small to justify direct tracing.
- Work-in-process inventory contains all the costs of making a product, from the time we begin manufacturing it until it is completed. When I think of WIP, I think of the factory. All costs incurred inside the factory are included in WIP. Examples include direct materials, direct labor, factory equipment depreciation, factory supervision salaries, payroll taxes, and fringe benefits.
- Finished goods inventory is the cost of completed products waiting to be sold. Examples depend upon the products made by a particular company. A computer mail order firm will have product inventories that include CPUs, monitors, keyboards, printers, and the like.

5. Describe the three traditional manufacturing resources and prepare a cost of goods manufactured schedule.

- "Direct materials can be seen going into individual products. In other words, these costs can be assigned to specific products. They differ from indirect materials, which are factory supplies too small and inexpensive to be traced directly to products. We cannot [or choose not to] trace the costs of nails, glue, saw blades, and drill bits to each house. Only the materials easily traced to each product are considered direct costs.
- People working directly on making a product are usually considered direct laborers. Assemblers and machinery operators are good examples. People not working directly on the products—for example, warehouse workers, supervisors, janitors, and maintenance personnel—are considered indirect labor. Attempting to trace their time to individual products is too costly.
- Manufacturing overhead includes all the indirect production costs, such as indirect materials and labor, utilities, factory and equipment depreciation, factory in-

surance and taxes, and the like. Overhead costs have to be allocated in order to be included in the cost of a product.

To demonstrate, this is how I'd classify the following resource costs:

Resources	**Direct materials**	**Direct labor**	**Manufacturing overhead**
Assemblers		Work directly on the product	
Lumber for a saw mill	The major material resource		
Electricity for machinery			We have only one electric meter for the factory, so we cannot trace electricity to individual machines, even though we may be able to trace machine time to specific products.
Heat and light for factory			We have no way of measuring how much of the factory, including these costs, is used in making each specific product.
Materials handlers			These people move many products at the same time. Their time cannot be attributed uniquely to individual products. They are classified as indirect labor costs.
Paper stock for a publisher	The major material resource		
Machine operators		Work directly on the product	
Factory depreciation			We have no way of measuring how much of the factory is used in making each specific product.
Factory supplies			These are classified as indirect material costs because it is too hard to try to trace them to specific products.

"Different types of businesses need different income statement formats. We identified three types of businesses:

- With service organizations, profit equals revenues minus costs. Service firms usually do not have major inventories to account for, so all costs are treated as expenses.
- In retail and wholesale operations, inventories are bought and sold. Costs are separated into the costs of getting the inventory [cost of goods sold], versus the costs of getting rid of it [sales expenses] and running the business [administrative expenses]. Cost of goods sold is calculated by adding inventory purchases to the beginning merchandise inventory, and then subtracting what wasn't sold [ending inventory] to yield the cost of the goods sold.
- Manufacturing firms do not purchase merchandise for resale. Instead, they build the product from resources. The retailer's 'purchases' account is replaced with 'cost of goods manufactured.' This requires an inventory account [work-in-process] to accumulate these costs while the product is being made. WIP contains the resource costs used in making the product. Just as a retailer can have merchandise on the shelf at the beginning and end of the year [beginning and end-

ing finished goods inventory], a manufacturer can have partially completed products in the factory at the beginning and end of the year [beginning and ending WIP]. Cost of goods manufactured is beginning WIP cost plus the costs of resources used less the cost of ending WIP. To demonstrate, assume the following revenues, costs, and inventory balances:

Revenues	$100	Finished Goods Inventory:	
Expenses	10	Beginning balance	$20
Direct materials purchases	50	Ending balance	30
Direct labor	25	Work-in-Process Inventory:	
Manufacturing overhead	40	Beginning balance	50
		Ending balance	75
		Direct Materials Inventory:	
		Beginning balance	10
		Ending balance	25

The cost of goods manufactured schedule and income statement would appear as follows [see Exhibit 2-12]:

Cost of Goods Manufactured Schedule

Sample cost of goods manufactured schedule

Direct materials inventory:			
Beginning inventory	$ 10		
Add: Purchases	50		
Less: Ending inventory	(25)		
Direct materials used:		$35	
Direct labor		25	
Manufacturing overhead		40	
Manufacturing costs incurred			$100
Add: Beginning WIP inventory costs			50
Less: Ending WIP inventory costs			(75)
Cost of goods manufactured			$ 75

Sample manufacturer's income statement

Revenues		$100
Less: Cost of goods sold		
Beginning finished goods inventory	$ 20	
Add: Cost of goods manufactured	75	
Less: Ending finished goods inventory	(30)	
Cost of goods sold		(65)
Gross profit		$ 35
Less: Expenses		(10)
Net income		$ 25

Exhibit 2-12

6. List the six steps in strategic planning and discuss the role of management accounting in this process.

a) "Create a vision, or mission statement.

b) Identify objectives to be accomplished that will ultimately lead us to realize our vision.

c) Translate our objectives into measurable goals for the year.

d) Analyze our external and internal environments to see how we can accomplish our goals.

e) Determine what we need to do to accomplish our goals.

f) Develop measures of performance telling us if we have achieved our goals and added value to the company.

"Management accounting has three roles in strategic planning:

- The management accountant is a process controller. She should monitor the process to ensure each of the six steps are performed effectively and efficiently.
- Information is needed. Financial statements on past performance are a starting point for strategic planning. Information about environments, sales forecasts, anticipated costs, and the like also are needed to project future profits and cashflows.
- Finally, the management accounting system needs to provide relevant performance measures to assess whether the organization's goals are being accomplished."

"Good job, Doris. I think we're done with this meeting. We'll get together again soon."

SID

The **Institute of Management Accountants vision statement** is simple, bold, and far-reaching: "Global leadership in education, certification, and practice of management accounting and financial management." Achieving this vision will mean harnessing the power of the massive changes taking place in our world, such as the

Changing role of management accountants and financial management,

Highly diverse population,

Advances in technology,

New and changing organizational dynamics,

Global village, and

Economies based on information and service.

Based on these fundamental change forces, the IMA's vision will become reality as we

Identify our future customers and members, define our future markets and services and aggressively pursue membership acquisition and retention, including global opportunities;

Maximize our partnering with academia to improve accounting education to better prepare students for the demands of future practice and continue to build student membership;

Assume a leadership role in defining, education, and certifying the new skill sets and literacies necessary for professional success;

Vigorously pursue successful alliances with organizations having complementary strengths and skills, to more effectively improve and extend our services;

Implement the Certified in Financial Management (CFM) designation to recognize the changing member certification needs in management accounting and financial management;

Strengthen and support the continued growth of the CMA;

Identify structural and organizational changes needed to allow greater effectiveness, improved communication, member support and member input;

Offer education to members and other organizations, through Continuing Professional Education (CPE), the Continuous Improvement Center (CIC), Foundation for Applied Research (FAR), and Member Interest Groups (MIGs) for global compliance with varying professional standards and practice; and

Navigate towards enabling our members to be ahead of the curve of technological change and its impact on our profession.

Source: The Institute of Management Accountants, June 1996.

READING LIST*

Capacity management: McNair and Vangermeersch, *Total Capacity Management, Optimizing at the Operational, Tactical, and Strategic Levels*, IMA Foundation for Applied Research, 1998.

Carnegie Steel: Johnson and Kaplan, *Relevance Lost: The Rise and Fall of Management Accounting*, Harvard Business School Press, 1987.

Coca-Cola: Huey, "In Search of Roberto's Secret Formula," *Fortune*, December 29, 1997.

E-commerce and internet sales: Shern, "E-Commerce Makes It Easy to Go Global," *Business UpShot*, Ernst & Young LLP, April 1998.

Environmental analysis in the strategic plan: Brown, "How U.S. Firms Conduct Strategic Planning," *Management Accounting*, February 1986.

International investments: "Global Gold Rush," *Business UpShot*, Ernst & Young LLP, February 1998.

Managing growth through supply chain integration, international expansion, e-commerce, and strategic planning: *The Eighth Annual Grant Thornton Survey of American Manufacturers*, Grant Thornton LLP, 1997.

Mission statements and performance measures: Bailey, "Measuring Your Mission," *Management Accounting*, December 1996.

Nintendo: Gross and Coy, "The Technology Paradox," *Business Week*, March 6, 1995.

PDCA (plan, do, check, action): Martin, et al., "Comparing U.S. and Japanese Companies: Implications for Management Accounting," *Journal of Cost Management for the Manufacturing Industry*, Spring 1992.

Southwire Company: Agacer, Baker, and Miles, "Implementing the Quality Process at Southwire Company," *Management Accounting*, November 1994.

Strategic cost management: Shank and Govindarajan, *Strategic Cost Analysis, The Evolution from Managerial to Strategic Accounting*, Richard D. Irwin, 1989.

Strategic planning is an art: Normann and Ramirez, "From Value Chain to Value Constellation: Designing Interactive Strategy," *Harvard Business Review*, July–August 1993.

Victoria's Secret: Gross and Coy, "The Technology Paradox," *Business Week*, March 6, 1995.

*Alphabetic by topic, idea, or company referenced.

CHAPTER 3

How Much Profit Can We Make?

Proforma Income Statements and Cost-Volume-Profit Analysis

KEY OBJECTIVES:

1	*Explain the four cost behavior patterns.*
2	*Create a contribution margin-based income statement and compare it to a functional format.*
3	*Develop a profit equation and use it in cost-volume-profit analysis.*
4	*Perform "what-if" analysis with the profit equation.*
5	*(Appendix A) Describe three statistical techniques to break down a mixed cost into its variable and fixed components.*
6	*(Appendix B) Modify the profit equation to include income taxes.*
7	*(Appendix C) Apply CVP analysis to multiple product lines.*

The conference room was large and old. Grandfather Multree's picture hung ominously on the wall at one end, while the other walls were covered with numerous pictures of buildings, workers, and staff surrounding various family members. Seated around the large oak table were the seven family members replicating another of the Boss's famous Monday morning planning meetings. Doris, the Boss's secretary for the last 25 years, provisioned the room as usual with strong coffee, orange juice, and assorted pastries. Some of the grandchildren were blurry-eyed and more ruffled than others, but ready or not, Sid began the meeting.

SID

"Okay, we've determined where we add value on our industry's value chain, defined our vision, and developed our strategic plan for the year. Now let's get down to making money. Given our current mix of products and market strategy, let's make a financial plan for next year."

Everyone started talking at once. "Yes, what's our target profit?" "How much cash can we take?" "What should our salaries be?" "Do we need to change our product mix or strategy?"

BOB

"All right, all right." Bob projected his voice across the room as he attempted to quiet the din. "Let's not get chaotic. Let's be methodical about this. What is the goal? Where do we start?"

JACKIE

"How about at the beginning? Here's the **proforma income statement** I created from our strategic plan. Proforma just means projected. Since our last meeting, I analyzed last year's income statement, discussed our sales projection with Bill, worked with Bob on cost revisions, and reviewed our personnel requirements with Tommy. Julie believes it is consistent with our strategic plan. While overseeing the entire process, Nancy has approved it. Sid has been studying it over the weekend. Based on our sales and costs projections, we should make about a $1 million profit [see Exhibit 3-1]."

A **proforma income statement** *is a projected, or budgeted, income statement for next year (or some other future time period).*

Understanding Cost Behavior Patterns

SID

"We first need to discuss the issue of profit planning. The proforma income statement is the traditional report the Boss always received. How can we use it to plan for that $1 million profit we want?"

Multree's Proforma Income Statement

Manufacturing costs

Direct materials inventory:			
Beginning inventory	$ 10,000		
Add: Purchases	1,827,500		
Less: Ending inventory	(25,000)		
Direct materials used:		$1,812,500	
Direct labor		1,250,000	
Manufacturing overhead		592,500	
Manufacturing costs incurred			$ 3,655,000
Add: Beginning WIP inventory costs*			0
Less: Ending WIP inventory costs*			0
Cost of goods manufactured			$3,655,000

Multree's income statement

Revenues		$ 6,000,000
Less: Cost of goods sold		
Beginning finished goods inventory*	$ 0	
Add: Cost of goods manufactured	3,655,000	
Less: Ending finished goods inventory*	0	
Cost of goods sold		(3,655,000)
Gross profit		**$ 2,345,000**
Less: Expenses		(1,345,000)
Net income		**$ 1,000,000**

*NOTE: We want no WIP or finished goods inventories at the beginning or end of the year.

Exhibit 3-1

KEY OBJECTIVE 1
Explain the four cost behavior patterns.

JULIE

"Well, we really can't. We need a different income statement format to support our profit-planning decisions. You see, this format is designed for external reporting to stockholders, creditors, and financial analysts. It is organized according to the rules for financial statements, which are based on generally accepted accounting principles [GAAP]. *The real issue for profit planning is how costs should be categorized.* In financial reporting, the costs of obtaining products [making products if a manufacturer or buying products if a merchandiser] are shown in the top half of the income statement as cost of goods sold [product costs]. The costs of selling our products and running the business are reported in the bottom half as sales and administration expenses [period costs].

"Exhibit 3-1 is called a **functional form income statement** because it groups similar costs together, allowing comparisons among different companies. We also can compare the efficient management of each function. For example, shoe stores have administrative costs we can compare. We also can answer questions such as 'Which store has the greater sales margin [gross profit]?' This functional approach is used in the balance sheet as well, where assets and liabilities are grouped by function-related characteristics. Inventories and plant and equipment are examples.

A ***functional form income statement*** *used for financial reporting organizes costs according to the functions they serve. Product costs (cost of goods sold) are reported before gross profit. Period costs (expenses) follow gross profit.*

"Another GAAP-caused classification is the inclusion of distribution and shipping costs in sales expenses. These often can be traced directly to products, providing a more accurate total product cost. Many managers prefer this and think of it as a 'cost of manufacturing and sale.' However, GAAP requires costs to be reported by function and doesn't allow this type of cost organization.

"Many management accounting systems use GAAP classifications as a starting point, and then subdivide functional cost categories. For example, all of our salaries and wages are grouped together for financial reporting. We also subdivide them by department. Similarly, advertising is subdivided by product line and then by sales territory. A law firm may separate revenues into billable and nonbillable hours, and then by type of service [family practice, bankruptcy, personal injury, etc.]. This can be used in bonus contracts or as performance measures. The point is external financial statements must satisfy GAAP requirements. For internal information, though, I can organize our costs in different ways for the different decisions we have to make. The extra cost of classifying data in this way is minimal. But if salary costs were not already recorded, the costs of changing the accounting system would be much greater."

Variable and fixed costs

TOMMY

"Yes! For profit planning, we need to organize our costs by how they 'behave.' Let me explain what I mean. The more houses we make, the more lumber and nails we'll need, increasing these total costs. However, salaries are the same every month regardless of how many houses we make. Understanding how costs change with volume is important because as we project different production volumes, some costs will change and others will not. Ray Brown tells me standard home direct materials are budgeted at $15,500 per house. His salary is $50,000 per year. If these were the only costs, we'd budget $65,500 to make one house next year, or $205,000 for ten houses [$15,500 per house × 10 houses, plus $50,000 for his salary]."

JULIE

"In profit planning, we organize costs into their **cost behavior patterns**. These patterns show us how costs change as volume changes. Here, as in most business situations, we're interested in the budgeted cost of a home. This is our product. Thus, we measure how costs change as production volume changes. Selling homes generates our sales revenues. But, what are the 'revenue generators' for other organizations? With hospitals, it's patient-days. For hotels, it's room-days. A university generates revenues per student credit-hour. Law firms and accounting firms have billable hours.

"Traditionally, engineers and accountants budget costs as either variable or fixed:

- **Variable costs** change *in total* with production volume changes. As we make more houses, we use more direct materials and direct labor *in total*. For profit planning, the important relationship is *variable costs are* assumed to be *constant per product*. The cost of direct materials—$15,500—and direct labor—$10,000—are the same *per house* for all standard homes we make. This stable relationship can be used to budget total variable costs. Tell me the variable cost per product and how many products we will make, and I can calculate the total variable cost. For example, if we plan on making two houses, we will budget $31,000 for direct materials and $20,000 for direct labor.

Cost behavior patterns *identify how costs change with changes in volume. Costs usually are classified as* **variable** *(constant per unit) or* **fixed** *(constant in total).*

- **Fixed costs** do not change *in total* with changes in volume. To calculate the fixed cost per product, it must be averaged over the total houses built. Every time we add one more house, the average fixed cost per house goes down. Remember Ray's salary? $50,000 per year averages $25,000 per house if only two houses are built. It's $5,000 per house if 10 houses are built. *In budgeting, the important relationship for a fixed cost is to know what it is in total.* Expressing a fixed cost on a per-product basis provides an unstable number as soon as we change the volume."

BILL

"Oh! I remember. In economics, that's called 'economies of scale.' The more products made, the less the fixed cost per product." Everyone moaned at the thought of trying to recall economic theory. "*In budgeting, though, we need to know the stable relationships; variable costs per product, and fixed costs in total.*"

Nancy thought to herself about last night's ice cream. She only had a pint. Sharing it with Julie, each expected a large, satisfying serving. But, when Sid and Tommy unexpectedly arrived and wanted some, everyone got a lot less! The pint is a fixed amount, like a fixed cost. As it's spread over more products, the fixed cost per unit decreases. Similarly, the more people wanting some of the pint of ice cream, the less each gets. Her thoughts then changed to overhead.

NANCY

"Wait a minute, I'm confused. Do you mean all overhead is a fixed cost? Aren't nails, factory supplies, and electricity to run the machines really variable costs? And, what about foremen salaries? If we want to make more of our standard homes line, we'll need to hire another foreman. This salary cost isn't really fixed. It changes!"

BOB

"Well, you're right about the overhead. We need to break down overhead into its variable and fixed costs. A cost which is part variable and part fixed is called a **mixed cost**. I talked to Ray Brown yesterday about the standard homes line. He gave me the overhead breakdown [see Exhibit 3-2].

In addition to variable and fixed costs, **mixed** *and* **step costs** *exist. Mixed costs are divided into their variable and fixed portions. Small step costs usually are budgeted as variable costs. Large step costs usually are budgeted as fixed costs.*

"You're also correct about the salaries. Salaries are fixed over only a limited production volume range. This is called a **step cost**. To make budgeting easier, small steps [narrow ranges] usually are treated as variable costs, and large steps as fixed. Ray Brown did this with the indirect labor and supervision [his salary]. Since we are planning to make only 100 standard homes this year, we need only

Cost Estimates for the Standard Home Line

Overhead costs	Variable costs			Fixed costs	
Indirect materials	$ 1,000	per house			
Indirect labor	500	per house			
Power	500	per house			
Architectural				$ 10,000	per year
Supervision				100,000	per year
Total overhead costs	**$ 2,000**	per house	+	**$110,000**	per year
Other costs					
Direct materials	$15,500	per house			
Direct labor	10,000	per house			
Sales commissions	2,500	per house			
Advertising				50,000	per year
Total other costs	$28,000				
Total product line costs	**$30,000**	per house	+	**$160,000**	per year

Exhibit 3-2

two salaried factory foremen. If we increase our volume much past 120, though, we will need a second shift to work nights. Because we do not plan to do this, we do not expect supervision cost to change. At production volumes up to 120 houses per year, supervision is budgeted as a fixed cost of $100,000 [2 foremen at $50,000 each]. Since this production volume range is so big, it is considered a large step cost.

"Indirect labor, however, is a different issue! Ray budgeted this as a variable cost of $500 per house. Most of the indirect labor is needed to set up certain pieces of equipment, like the table saw. Once set up, the saw can be used to cut lumber for more than one house. After cutting the lumber for five houses, it needs to be readjusted. The setup cost is really a $2,500 step cost averaged over five houses. Because the production volume range is so small before another setup is needed, Ray treats it as a variable cost per house [$2,500 ÷ 5 houses = $500 per house]."

Graphical analysis of cost behaviors

"I'm having a hard time visualizing all this. I'll use my laptop's spreadsheet program and try to graph variable, fixed, mixed, and step costs using some simple numbers [see Exhibit 3-3]. I'm graphing total costs [the Y-axis] based on production volume [the X-axis]. Let's see if I get it right.

- Variable costs [the VC line in Exhibit 3-3's top graph] have a positive, constant slope and a zero intercept. The variable cost per unit is the slope because each product needs the same amount of that resource. Because each product consumes the same amount of a variable cost, total variable costs increase at the same rate for each additional product. So, a variable cost increases *in total* with increasing volume, but is the same *per unit*.

- Fixed costs are horizontal lines [a positive intercept and a zero slope]. Total fixed costs *do not change* as volume changes. [This is the FC line in the top graph of Exhibit 3-3.]

- Mixed costs are part variable and part fixed, so they have a positive slope and a positive intercept. The intercept represents its fixed cost component, and the

Graphing Cost Behavior Patterns

DATA SECTION

Volume	VC	FC	MC
0	$0	$100	$100
10	$100	$100	$200
20	$200	$100	$300
30	$300	$100	$400
40	$400	$100	$500
50	$500	$100	$600

VC = Variable cost per product @ $10 each
FC = Fixed cost @ $100 per time period
MC = Mixed cost @ $100 + $10 per product

GRAPHIC VIEW

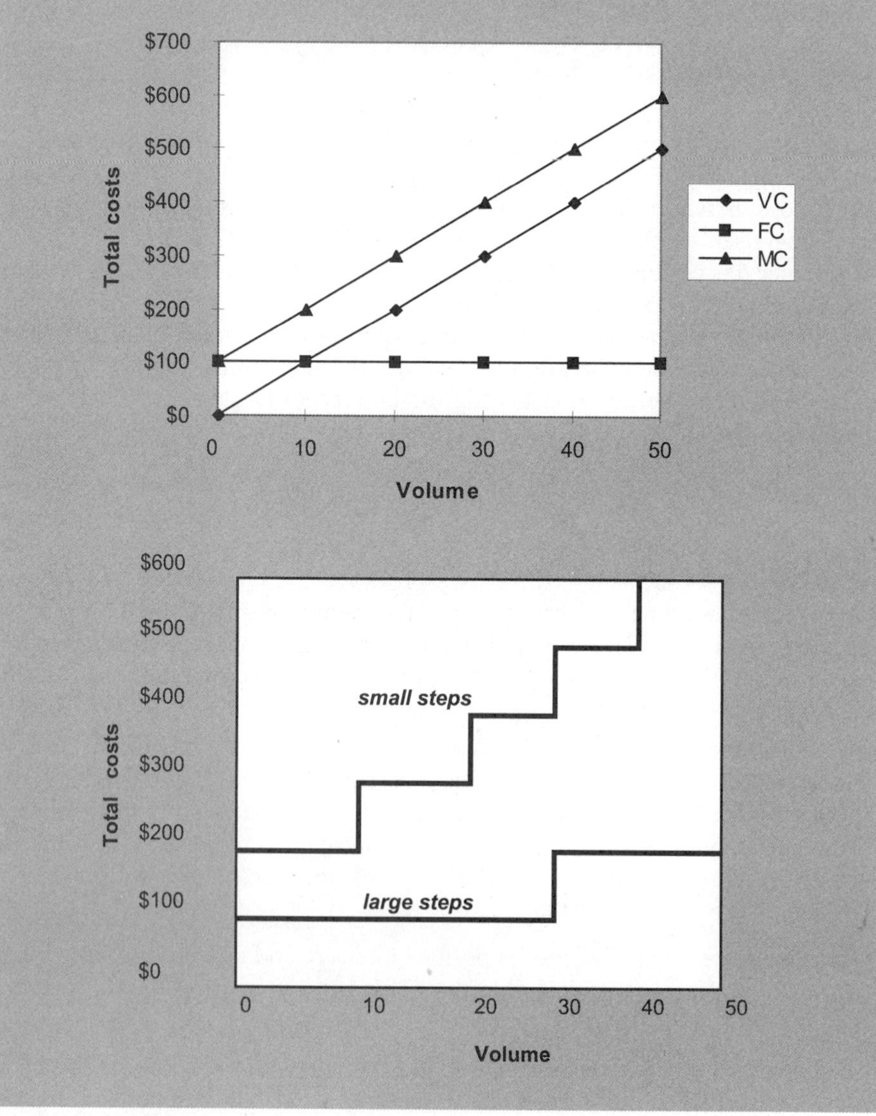

Exhibit 3-3

slope is the variable cost per unit. Using our data, the mixed cost [MC] line starts at $100. This is its fixed cost component. Every time volume increases by one product, the mixed cost increases $10. This is the slope which represents the variable cost component per unit.

- To illustrate a small step cost [the bottom graph of Exhibit 3-3], each time volume increases by 10 products, the cost increases $100.
- To illustrate a large step cost [the bottom graph in Exhibit 3-3], volume has to increase by 30 units before the cost changes."

Assumptions about cost behavior analysis

"I also want to understand the assumptions we're making with this analysis:

1. *We treat all costs as variable or fixed.* Mixed costs [like overhead] are broken down into their variable components [i.e., variable overhead] and fixed components [i.e., fixed overhead]. Step costs are usually assumed to be variable when the steps are very narrow and fixed when the steps are wide.
2. *Variable costs are constant per product.*
3. *Fixed costs are constant in total.*"

Julie knew other assumptions also were needed concerning inventory levels, product mix, and tax rates. But, she thought they could wait for a more sophisticated presentation. These three assumptions about how costs behave were the critical ones to understand now.

"So far you are correct, Nancy. Be careful, though, and ask yourself, 'Costs are either variable or fixed when compared to what, the weather?'" Everyone but Jackie laughed. She understood the importance of this question.

"Wait a minute. Not so fast. Tommy has a point. Our heating bills went through the roof last January and air conditioning costs in August were sky high. It seems our heating and air conditioning costs vary with the weather. Telephone bills vary with the number of long-distance calls. It's important to remember *this analysis depends on what we are trying to cost.* If you want to budget costs on a monthly basis, salaries are variable [they are constant per month and increase in total as the number of months increases]. If you are trying to cost a product, though, salaries are fixed. The total salaries cost is the same every month, so it does not change as production volume changes from month-to-month. *Usually, in business, we define variable and fixed costs as they relate to the product's volume.* Which costs remain the same for each product? Which costs don't change as production volume increases or decreases?"

Budgeting college costs: Tuition often varies with the number of credits, as do fees, books, and supplies. Rent is the same every month. Utilities vary with the weather. Phone calls to home depend on how much money you have left over!

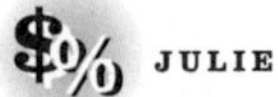

"To make this planning system work, we assume operations will be within some expected production volume range. Outside this range, variable costs may not remain the same for each product, and total fixed costs may change. For example, our total sales forecast is 110 homes [100 standard homes and 10 custom homes]. We believe our per-unit variable costs and total fixed costs are stable between 80 and 120 homes per year. Our cost behavior patterns are only 'relevant' within this range. Hence, we call this our **relevant range**.

The range of production volumes where variable costs are constant per product and total fixed costs do not change is called the **relevant range**.

"If we double production, many direct material costs per house will decrease due to quantity purchase discounts. Of course, electricity costs for our equipment will skyrocket. The more of this resource we use, the greater the cost per unit. This results from the fact that electric cost per kilowatt hour increases with increasing usage."

"If we increase production too much, we need unplanned overtime. What this means is within our relevant range, labor cost per unit is stable, but outside the range it isn't. Fixed costs have the same flexibility. We could have one, two, or three shifts, each with its own unique fixed costs. If sales decline too much, we may have to let some of our salaried staff go. As long as fixed costs don't change, our planning model works well. Since we're not concerned with sales outside this range, why waste our time and energy worrying about things not likely to happen?" Everyone nodded their heads vigorously in agreement!

"What I'm really concerned about is labor cost. Isn't it really fixed? I mean we don't expect to lay off any of our hourly workers, do we? For a long time, the Japanese had a tradition of 'forever employment.' In many families, the grandparents, parents, and children all worked for the same company. While about 86% of U.S. firms treat production labor as a variable cost, only 52% of Japanese firms do. For quality control labor, 75% of Japanese firms treat it as a fixed cost. In the United States, only 30% treat it as a fixed cost. In Australia, by comparison, 70% treat production labor as variable and 52% treat quality control labor as fixed.

"My point is a variable cost to one firm may be a fixed cost to another. This is a management choice! At Multree Homes, the Boss didn't believe in laying off and rehiring workers as sales demand changed. The whole town is built around our factory! Why treat hourly labor as a variable cost?"

"Good point!!" Doris muttered a little too loudly from the back of the room.

"Well, I can think of two reasons. First, in the early days of our company, no work meant the workers went home without pay. Direct labor really was a variable cost. Although the Boss stopped that policy after World War II, we still consider labor a variable cost in profit planning. Tradition dies hard. He felt it was his responsibility to get the work and the workers' responsibility to do a good job. He felt the owners, not the employees, should bear the business risk! So, you're right, Tommy. Even though we follow the traditional management accounting practice of treating labor as a variable cost, the Boss changed our real management practice to making labor a fixed cost."

"This is not uncommon. For years, the United Auto Workers union negotiated contracts with the 'big three' automobile manufacturers containing provisions for laborers to be paid even if they had no work. Back in the 1970s, Chrysler guaranteed its workers a minimum 35 hours of pay per week. In the early 1990s, General Motors guaranteed $3.3 billion for pay protection within its 3-year contract with the UAW. Even now, Saturn negotiated its contract with the UAW to greatly reduce the number of job categories so workers could be trained to work in other areas, rather than being laid off when demand declines."

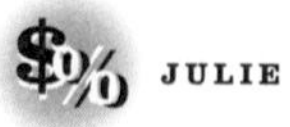

"Direct labor isn't the only fixed cost treated as a variable cost. Consider the credit card industry. Advertising, finance, and accounting budgets are all fixed costs. But in determining how much of these costs should be incurred, they are often treated as variable costs. For example, back in the 1990s companies spent $51 on average to obtain a new credit card customer and set up the account. We'll do the same thing when budgeting how many people we need for obtaining new customers, credit checking, setting up accounts, billing, and accounts receivable."

"This is the second reason for treating fixed costs as variable costs. Classifying direct labor as a variable cost helps us understand how much is needed for each house and how much to budget in total for the year. In addition to the planning benefit, this also facilitates control and evaluation of labor usage. For example, we are budgeting $10,000 per standard home for direct labor [see Exhibit 3-2]. If we end up spending a lot more, we will not achieve our profit goal due to a problem with labor. We need to know this kind of information to identify and correct problems, prevent them in the future, and budget our labor costs next year."

Contribution Margin-Based Income Statements

KEY OBJECTIVE 2

Create a contribution margin-based income statement and compare it to a functional format.

"Good! Now I'm more comfortable with the idea of identifying how costs behave with changes in volume. Julie, can you show me an income statement with costs reclassified as variable and fixed? Can this really help us better plan how much profit we can make?"

While this conversation was going on, Julie was working feverishly on her laptop computer.

Comparison with functional form income statements

JULIE

"Okay, here it is [see Exhibit 3-4]. I've formatted the proforma income statement both ways. On the left is the functional approach for external reporting. Our banker expects this. The statement on the right is formatted according to how our costs behave. This is called a **contribution margin-based income statement**. Both formats report the same revenues, costs, and profit. The only change I've made is costs are now organized as variable and fixed. I highlighted the fixed overhead costs moving from the top half of the functional format to the bottom half of the contribution margin format. I also highlighted the variable expense [commissions] moving from the lower half of the functional format to the upper half of the contribution margin format."

A **contribution margin-based income statement** *organizes costs as variable and fixed to aid in management decision making. For external reporting, the income statement organizes costs by the functions they serve (a functional format).*

"All you've done is move some costs around. I don't see the advantage in the new approach. Look at the net income on the functional format. Every time we sell another house, we make another $9,091, which is a 17% profit."

The need for contribution margin per unit (CMU)

"Well, actually no. You've identified the problem, though. Let me explain. When we sell more homes, our *total* variable costs increase, both manufacturing and marketing [sales commissions]. On the contribution margin-based format, you can see selling one more house increases our variable costs by $32,727. After paying for these variable costs from the sales price, we have $21,818 remaining. Since selling one more house will not increase the total fixed costs, this $21,818 is new, extra profit.

"Try that with the functional format on the left! All variable and fixed costs are shown as per-unit amounts. It is very easy to be misled. Apparently, selling one more house will create $9,091 in extra profit. Instead, it really provides $21,818. The problem is with averaging fixed costs over volume, and including this average per house with the variable costs per house. I've prepared another income statement comparison showing the mistake [see Exhibit 3-5 on p. 71].

"I highlighted the fixed costs per house shown in the functional format on the left, and then moved them into the per-unit column of the contribution margin

Multree Homes Proforma Income Statement: Comparing Formats

Functional format

	COMPANY TOTALS		
	Per unit	**%**	**Totals**
Revenues	$ 54,545	100%	$ 6,000,000
Less: COGS			
Direct materials	16,477	30%	1,812,500
Direct labor	11,364	21%	1,250,000
Indirect materials	1,045	2%	115,000
Indirect labor	727	1%	80,000
Power	568	1%	62,500
Architectural costs	1,000	2%	**110,000**
Depreciation	136	0%	**15,000**
Supervision	1,818	3%	**200,000**
Heat and light	91	0%	**10,000**
Total COGS	$(33,227)	(61%)	$(3,655,000)
Gross profit	**$ 21,318**	**39%**	**$ 2,345,000**
Less: Expenses			
Sales commissions	2,545	5%	280,000
Advertising	591	1%	65,000
Administration	9,091	17%	1,000,000
Total expenses	$(12,227)	(22%)	$(1,345,000)
Net income	**$ 9,091**	**17%**	**$ 1,000,000**

Contribution margin-based format

	COMPANY TOTALS		
	Per unit	**%**	**Totals**
Revenues	$ 54,545	100%	$ 6,000,000
Less: Variable costs			
Direct materials	16,477	30%	1,812,500
Direct labor	11,364	21%	1,250,000
Indirect materials	1,045	2%	115,000
Indirect labor	727	1%	80,000
Power	568	1%	62,500
Sales commissions	2,545	5%	280,000
Total variable costs	$(32,727)	(60%)	$(3,600,000)
Contribution margin	$ 21,818	40%	$ 2,400,000
Less: Fixed costs			
Architectural costs			**110,000**
Depreciation			**15,000**
Supervision			**200,000**
Heat and light			**10,000**
Advertising			65,000
Administration			1,000,000
Total fixed costs			$(1,400,000)
Net income			**$ 1,000,000**

FORMATTING NOTE: Many times zero decimal formatting creates apparent addition errors, such as in the per unit and percentage columns above. For example, 1.6 + 1.6 = 3.2. But, when the three cells are formatted to zero decimal places, they appear as 2 + 2 = 3. You can expand the per unit and percentage columns to one or two decimal places to see this. Formatting also affects all subsequent subtotal and total cells.

Exhibit 3-4

Multree Homes Proforma Income Statement: The Fallacy of Fixed Costs per Unit
(Fixed costs per product are unstable, so don't report them!)

Functional format

	COMPANY TOTALS		
	Per unit	**%**	**Totals**
Revenues	$ 54,545	100%	$ 6,000,000
Less: COGS			
Direct materials	16,477	30%	1,812,500
Direct labor	11,364	21%	1,250,000
Indirect materials	1,045	2%	115,000
Indirect labor	727	1%	80,000
Power	568	1%	62,500
Architectural costs	**1,000**	2%	**110,000**
Depreciation	**136**	0%	**15,000**
Supervision	**1,818**	3%	**200,000**
Heat and light	**91**	0%	**10,000**
Total COGS	$(33,227)	(61%)	$(3,655,000)
Gross profit	**$ 21,318**	**39%**	**$ 2,345,000**
Less: Expenses			
Sales commissions	2,545	5%	280,000
Advertising	**591**	1%	65,000
Administration	**9,091**	17%	1,000,000
Total expenses	$(12,227)	(22%)	$(1,345,000)
Net income	**$ 9,091**	**17%**	**$ 1,000,000**

Contribution margin-based format

	COMPANY TOTALS		
	Per unit	**%**	**Totals**
Revenues	$ 54,545	100%	$ 6,000,000
Less: Variable costs			
Direct materials	16,477	30%	1,812,500
Direct labor	11,364	21%	1,250,000
Indirect materials	1,045	2%	115,000
Indirect labor	727	1%	80,000
Power	568	1%	62,500
Sales commissions	2,545	5%	280,000
Total variable costs	$(32,727)	(60%)	$(3,600,000)
Contribution margin	**$ 21,818**	**40%**	**$ 2,400,000**
Less: Fixed costs			
Architectural costs	**1,000**		110,000
Depreciation	**136**		15,000
Supervision	**1,818**		200,000
Heat and light	**91**		10,000
Advertising	**591**		65,000
Administration	**9,091**		1,000,000
Total fixed costs	$(12,727)		$(1,400,000)
Net income	**$ 9,091**		**$ 1,000,000**

Exhibit 3-5

format on the right. You can see if these per-unit fixed costs are subtracted from the contribution margin per unit, the same *average* net income per house results.

"Remember, the functional format is for reporting year-end results to people outside the company. It is not designed for internal management decisions such as profit planning. On the external financial statements, accountants are taught to express the total revenues and costs as averages per unit and as percentages of revenues.

"But, by combining the per-unit variable and fixed costs, you might think selling one more house will cause another $12,727 in fixed costs [the sum of the fixed costs per unit shown in the boxed areas of Exhibit 3-5]. This is only the total fixed costs averaged over our volume. Believing if another house is sold, fixed costs will increase by $12,727 just is not true because we will not incur any extra fixed costs when sales volume changes within the relevant range [i.e., fixed costs do not change in total with changes in volume]. The point is you cannot think about fixed costs on a per-product or percentage basis. This is an unstable relationship that will change every time volume changes. For example, if we increase or decrease volume by only one product, the fixed costs per unit and as a percentage of revenues will change. To correctly project profits for any sales volume you want to consider, we must know and use the total fixed costs, not the per-unit or percentage amounts. Therefore, *we can't use the functional format to predict profits because it combines variable and fixed costs.*

"Look again at Exhibit 3-4. The contribution margin format separates variable and fixed costs. Notice fixed costs are expressed in total and not as per-unit amounts, so you will not be misled. If we sell one more house, what new costs will we really incur? Just the variable costs! After we pay for them, each house contributes $21,818 toward our fixed costs and profits. If the total contribution margin from previous home sales already has covered all of our fixed costs, the $21,818 is extra profit for us! If we haven't yet covered all of our fixed costs, selling one more house will give us another $21,818 to use in paying our fixed costs. The point is regardless of what we use this contribution margin for, every time we sell another house, we have another $21,818!"

NANCY

"Oh, I see now! *The contribution margin format supports our profitability analyses. It helps us to see the effects on revenues, costs, and profits from changes in volume.* This is an example of where the extra cost of a management accounting system is justified by the better decisions we now are able to make. We need accounting systems to support our decision needs. When the functional format from the financial accounting system can't do this, we need another formal system. We need an income statement showing us our contribution margin. Contribution margin is the extra profit from one more product!"

JULIE

"Not really, but you're close. Contribution margin is the total amount left over from all sales, which is used to cover fixed costs and provide profits. *This concept is really most useful when we think about it in terms of an individual product.* This is called **contribution margin per unit [CMU]**. A house isn't a house to me. It's another $21,818 in my pocket! Every time we sell another one, we have another $21,818 to pay for our fixed costs, or to keep as extra profit if all our fixed costs have been paid from previous sales. You are right, though, about the need for a formal management accounting system to generate this information. Some companies have gone so far as to change their chart of accounts in the financial accounting system so costs are organized by behavior. Elgin Sweeper, the maker of those large street sweeping machines, did this as part of its new strategic focus on cost management."

"O.K., I get it. But, why do you also express contribution margin as a percentage in the middle column?"

The need for contribution margin ratio

"The 40% is called the **contribution margin ratio**. For each sales dollar, on average, we will have another 40¢ in extra profit. We sell two product lines, custom homes and standard homes. The 40% is the weighted-average contribution margin ratio of the two product lines given our sales mix. Pretend we are a major department or grocery store. The grocery store's management doesn't ever know exactly what mix of products will be in a customer's shopping cart. But it does know, on average, every dollar of sales will generate 40¢ in contribution margin."

> **Contribution margin per unit (CMU)** *is the extra profit from selling one more product.* **Contribution margin ratio** *is the percentage of a sales dollar that is extra profit.*

"Got it!

- *Use contribution margin per unit when dealing with a particular product.*
- *Use contribution margin ratio when dealing with a lot of different products at the same time."*

SID

"Let's carry on then! Because almost all of our sales are standard and not custom homes, let's focus on that product line first [Exhibit 3-6]."

Multree Homes Standard Homes Proforma Income Statement

	STANDARD HOMES		
	Per unit	**%**	**Totals @ 100**
Revenues	$ 50,000	100%	$ 5,000,000
Less: Variable costs			
Direct materials	15,500	31%	1,550,000
Direct labor	10,000	20%	1,000,000
Indirect materials	1,000	2%	100,000
Indirect labor	500	1%	50,000
Power	500	1%	50,000
Sales commissions	2,500	5%	250,000
Total	$(30,000)	(60%)	$(3,000,000)
Contribution margin	**$ 20,000**	**40%**	**$ 2,000,000**
Less: Direct fixed costs			
Advertising			50,000
Architectural costs			10,000
Supervision			100,000
Total			$ (160,000)
Product line margin			**$ 1,840,000**

Exhibit 3-6

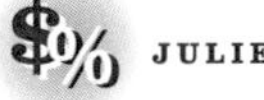

"Earlier we looked at projections for the entire company [Exhibits 3-1, 3-4, and 3-5]. We make both standard and custom homes. Therefore, the $21,818 CMU and 40% contribution margin ratio are weighted averages of both product lines. Custom homes are specially designed for customers desiring them. We're planning to make only ten during the year. Standard homes are the vast bulk of our business. We're projecting 100. As shown in Exhibit 3-6, standard homes generate a $20,000

CMU. They create $2 million [$20,000 per house × 100 houses] of the annual $2.4 million total contribution margin [Exhibits 3-4 and 3-5]."

BILL

"The other $400,000 of total contribution margin we are projecting for the year comes from custom homes. This product line is currently a small part of our business. We design custom homes for a unique market niche. In this way, we add value by differentiating ourselves from the competition. I see this as a growing part of our business, though, over the upcoming years."

JULIE

"Our projection is $1.4 million for total fixed costs [Exhibit 3-5]. Of this amount, three costs are specifically for standard homes: advertising, architectural costs, and supervision. I call these 'direct fixed costs' because they are traceable directly to this product line. By subtracting these direct fixed costs from contribution margin, I can calculate the profit directly contributed by this product line. The standard homes product line margin of $1,840,000 is used to pay for the other fixed costs of the company and contribute to our overall net income. I'll say more about this during our meeting on control and evaluation [Chapter 8]. Right now, though, let's just focus on our standard homes."

KEY OBJECTIVE 3

Develop a profit equation and use it in cost-volume-profit analysis.

Cost-Volume-Profit Analysis

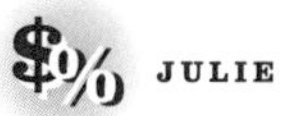

JULIE

"This income statement idea really works best, though, if we turn it into a profit equation. Let me show you."

Building the profit equation

"Sales must pay for all costs before any profits result.

The Profit Equation

Profit = Revenues − Costs

Revenues = Sales price × Volume

Costs = (Variable costs per unit × Volume) + Fixed costs

Substituting and factoring:

Profit = [(Sales price − Variable costs per unit) × Volume] − Fixed costs

or:

Profit = (CMU × Volume) − Fixed costs

"Subtracting the variable costs of a house from its sales price creates contribution margin per unit [CMU]. To do this, we have to assume the sales price is constant per house [the same for all houses] over our relevant range. This is an assumption for the profit equation. It's just the same assumption, though, we made for variable costs. Our profit equation for standard homes is:

Standard homes product line margin (*profit*) =
($20,000 *CMU* × Standard homes *sales volume*) − $160,000 *Fixed costs*

"Projecting 100 homes sold:

Standard homes product line margin = *$1,840,000* =
($20,000 CMU × *100* Standard homes sales volume) − $160,000 Fixed costs

Solving for volume and revenues

"Now we can see how this equation helps us plan profits for our standard homes product line. I've prepared the profit equation and solved it for some interesting numbers [Exhibit 3-7]. The top of this exhibit shows selling 100 standard homes at the budgeted sales price, given the budgeted costs and volume, should create a $1,840,000 product line profit margin.

JULIE

The Profit Equation

(CMU × Volume) – Fixed costs = Profit

For the standard homes product line:

($20,000 × 100) – $160,000 = $1,840,000

How many houses must we sell (volume) for our target profit?

$$\textbf{Volume} = \frac{\text{Fixed cost + Profit}}{\text{CMU}} = \frac{\$160{,}000 + \$1{,}840{,}000}{\$20{,}000} = \underline{\underline{\text{100 houses per year}}}$$

Revenues needed to achieve target profit:

$$\textbf{Revenues} = \frac{\text{Fixed cost + Profit}}{\text{CM ratio}} = \frac{\$160{,}000 + \$1{,}840{,}000}{.40} = \underline{\underline{\$5{,}000{,}000 \text{ per year}}}$$

What is our break-even point? (volume where revenues just equal costs)

$$\textbf{Volume} = \frac{\text{Fixed cost + Profit}}{\text{CMU}} = \frac{\$160{,}000 + \$0}{\$20{,}000} = \underline{\underline{\text{8 houses per year}}}$$

Break-even revenues:

$$\textbf{Revenues} = \frac{\text{Fixed cost + Profit}}{\text{CM ratio}} = \frac{\$160{,}000 + \$0}{.40} = \underline{\underline{\$400{,}000 \text{ per year}}}$$

Exhibit 3-7

"Look at the left side of the exhibit. When solving for a target sales volume, use CMU in the denominator. This emphasizes its importance in profit planning. If we have $160,000 in fixed costs and wish a $1,840,000 profit, we must sell 100 homes [we'll need the $20,000 CMU 100 times]. Remember, CMU is the extra profit from selling one more product. If we sell one more standard home, we make another $20,000. If we sell 10 more, we make another $200,000. If we sell one less, we make $20,000 less.

"We also can solve for the target revenues [instead of volume] to achieve this profit goal. Look at the equation in the lower left corner of the exhibit. In the denominator, substitute contribution margin ratio for contribution margin per unit [which is used in the equation above to solve for volume]. For a $1,840,000 profit from standard homes, we will need revenues of $5 million. This is just 100 homes multiplied by their $50,000 sales price."

Break-even volume and revenues. "Another important use for cost-volume-profit [CVP] analysis is solving for the sales volume and revenues needed to just cover our costs. The sales volume we must achieve to cover the costs of this product line is called its **break-even volume** [often called the **break-even point**]. Sales

> *The volume for zero profit is called the* **break-even volume (break-even point)**. *The revenues yielding zero profit are called* **break-even revenues**.

revenues to break-even are called **break-even revenues**. If we just cover our costs, profit is zero. Obviously, this is the minimum sales we must achieve to avoid losing money on this product line. On the right side of the exhibit, we have to sell eight homes [$400,000 in revenues] to cover the costs of this product line.

"On both the right and left sides of the exhibit, I factored the profit equation to solve for either volume or revenues. On the left side, we solved for the volume and revenues necessary to achieve a profit goal of $1,840,000. On the right side, we did the same thing, except the profit goal is zero. Using the profit equation in this format is a very powerful tool to determine how much we have to sell given any profit goal, whether it is zero, the break-even point, or some other amount."

Nonprofit and governmental applications. "This makes a lot of sense for profit-making businesses, but does it have any applications for non-profit organizations, like governmental agencies?"

TOMMY

"Sure it does! Think about the city's new drug rehabilitation program we worked with last weekend as volunteers. I was talking to its director during a break. She was complaining about the inadequate funding the city gave her. Treatment costs, like medication and counseling, average $500 per person [a variable cost]. The fixed costs of the rehabilitation center are $100,000 per year. She projected 100 people need treatment right now. The total funding she needs [break-even revenues] is $150,000, or $1,500 per person. Total funding needed is ($500 per person × 100 people) + $100,000. We also can use the profit equation to solve for the average cost [or funds needed] per patient:

$$\text{Break-even volume} = \frac{\text{Fixed costs} + \$0 \text{ Profit}}{\text{CMU}}$$

$$\text{100 people} = \frac{\$100{,}000 + \$0}{\text{CMU}}$$

"She needs $1,000 per person CMU to treat 100 people. If variable costs are $500 per person, she needs funding [a sales price] of $1,500 per person [which is $150,000 in total revenues for 100 people]. Remember, CMU is sales price minus variable cost per unit.

"She only received $125,000 from the city, however. She used the profit equation in its original format to calculate how many people she could treat with this funding:

$$\text{Revenues} - \text{Total variable costs} - \text{Total fixed costs} = \text{Profit}$$

$$\$125{,}000 - (\$500 \text{ per person} \times \text{Volume}) - \$100{,}000 = \$0$$

"Solving for volume, she can treat only 50 people with this level of funding. She plans to go back to the city and ask for an additional $50,000. With her knowledge of CVP relationships, her argument will go like this, 'It costs only $500 more to treat another patient. This is the variable cost per person. To treat the remaining 50 people in need, I need only $25,000 more. In other words, I can double the rehabilitation center's efficiency with another $25,000. Or, to double its productivity [the number of people treated], I need only a 20% increase in funding.' I think she will be quite successful with this logic!

"In the nonprofit sector, we're often asking two questions:

- How much funding do we need?
- Given the funding we have, how many people can we serve?"

"I remember a somewhat similar situation with the Pittsburgh Pirates. Back in the late 1980s they were having financial problems due to insufficient ticket sales and rising player salaries. Here's a case where direct labor is a fixed cost. Their payroll was about \$6 million. Broadcast revenues reduced administrative fixed costs to about \$2 million. Projecting an average CMU of \$6 per ticket, management figured they would have to sell around 1.4 million tickets to break even and avoid selling the team."

Using the proforma for "what-if" analysis

KEY OBJECTIVE 4

Perform "what-if" analysis with the profit equation.

"We also can use CVP analysis to ask 'what-if' questions, both in the service sector and our own business. To demonstrate how this works with our standard homes product line, consider the following illustrations.

- *What if* we want another \$100,000 in profit? How many more homes do we have to sell? The easiest way to answer this question is by looking at the contribution margin per unit. Each home generates a \$20,000 CMU, so we must sell another 5 homes [\$20,000 per house × 5 houses = \$100,000]. We can always use the equation to solve for this new volume, but it isn't as fast:

$$\text{Volume} = \frac{\text{Fixed costs + Profit}}{\text{CMU}}$$

$$= \frac{\$160{,}000 + (\$1{,}840{,}000 + \textit{\$100,000})}{\$20{,}000}$$

$$= \underline{\underline{\text{105 houses per year}}}$$

To make a \$1,840,000 profit, we need to sell 100 homes. To make another \$100,000, we have to sell another 5 homes [105 houses total].

- *What if* we just want a \$100,000 profit? This is \$100,000 more than the break-even volume's profit [\$0]:

$$\text{Volume} = \frac{\text{Fixed cost + Profit}}{\text{CMU}}$$

$$= \frac{\$160{,}000 + (\$0 + \textit{\$100,000})}{\$20{,}000}$$

$$= \underline{\underline{\text{13 houses per year}}}$$

Our break-even volume is 8 homes. If we want a \$100,000 profit, we need to sell another 5 homes [13 in total], or 5 homes each providing a \$20,000 CMU. Whether we use our original sales forecast of 100 homes or our break-even volume, we have to sell 5 more to make another \$100,000 in profits. Really, we could have used any volume and profit in the equation. The volume and profit we start with is not important. *The important point to remember is the product's worth to us is its CMU.* A standard home is worth \$20,000 to us. If we want another \$100,000 in profits, we have to sell 5 more houses. It makes no difference what our current volume and profit are, *as long as we still are within the relevant range!*

- *What if* we spend another $100,000 on advertising? How many more homes must be sold to make it worthwhile? Five homes will generate another $100,000 in profits. We'll have to sell 6 homes from this advertising before it increases our profits. Selling only 5 standard homes will just recover the extra advertising costs, which is the break-even point for this option.
- *What if* we want $1,500,000 in profits? What can we spend on fixed costs if we believe 100 standard homes can be sold? Solve the equation for fixed costs, given all the other values. We can spend $500,000 on fixed costs:

$$\textbf{Volume} = \frac{\textbf{Fixed cost + Profit}}{\textbf{CMU}}$$

$$\textbf{100 houses} = \frac{\textbf{Fixed cost + \$1,500,000}}{\textbf{\$20,000}}$$

$$\textbf{Fixed cost} = \textbf{\$500,000 per year}$$

- *What if* we can't hit our target sales volume? For example, assume Bill believes we can sell only 80 standard homes. If we want the same $1,840,000 profit goal, our CMU will have to increase. But, by how much?

$$\textbf{Volume} = \frac{\textbf{Fixed cost + Profit}}{\textbf{CMU}}$$

$$\textbf{80 houses} = \frac{\textbf{\$160,000 + \$1,840,000}}{\textbf{CMU}}$$

$$\textbf{CMU} = \textbf{\$25,000 per house}$$

This is what cost-volume-profit (CVP) analysis is all about! It's an equation-based technique to estimate profits. It's also used to solve for the sales volume needed to achieve a target profit, and to assess the profitability of different combinations of CMU and fixed costs.

If we can sell only 80 homes and we want the same profit, the contribution margin per home will have to increase $5,000 [from $20,000 to $25,000]. We need to raise the sales price $5,000. If this is not possible, we need to lower variable costs per house by $5,000. More likely, we will try to raise the sales price and lower variable costs in some combination resulting in another $5,000 in CMU."

"CVP analysis really helps us see how profits will change with strategic changes. For example, I remember when Apple Computers wanted to lower its prices on the Power Macintosh. Management felt it was necessary because of competitive pressures. Their CVP analysis showed that even though volume would increase, the tradeoff of sales price for more volume lowered its contribution margin and profits."

"Couldn't they just spend more on advertising," Nancy wondered aloud.

"Not really. Its CMU wasn't large enough. The companies I've seen spending a lot on advertising all have high CMU products, like cosmetics companies, cigarette companies, and airlines. For each advertising dollar spent, the return in terms of another sale [i.e., getting another CMU] is very high, thus justifying the advertising."

"In addition to controlling our CMUs, its important to control our fixed costs. I remember Seagate's problems from increasing competition by other computer hard disk manufacturers in the early 1990s. Companies like Conner and Maxtor controlled the design and development processes, but outsourced production. As demand declined, they could more easily cut back on orders to save costs. Production costs were variable costs. Seagate, however, owned its production facilities [fixed costs] and had a harder time maintaining profitability. It could not simply shut down some of the plant to save fixed costs. By the mid-1990s, Seagate's strategy changed and it began outsourcing about 40% of its production.

"My point is we must utilize our capacity [fixed costs] to maintain profitability. For example, with hospitals, all that special equipment is extremely expensive. They have to set very high charges for MRI [magnetic resonance imaging] scans or have very high usage rates [volume]. This is why we are seeing so much specialization in services among hospitals in the same geographic areas [i.e., product differentiation as a strategic choice]."

Graphical CVP analysis

NANCY

"While I understand the profit equation, I'm more of a 'picture person.' Can you show CVP analysis graphically?"

JULIE

"Sure. I easily can prepare a CVP graph using my spreadsheet program. [See Exhibit 3-8.]

"The top graph includes three lines: total revenues, total costs, and profit. Total costs include both variable and fixed costs. Because fixed costs are $160,000 per year, the total costs line begins at that point on the Y-axis. Its slope is equal to the variable costs per unit [$30,000 per house from Exhibit 3-6]. The point where total

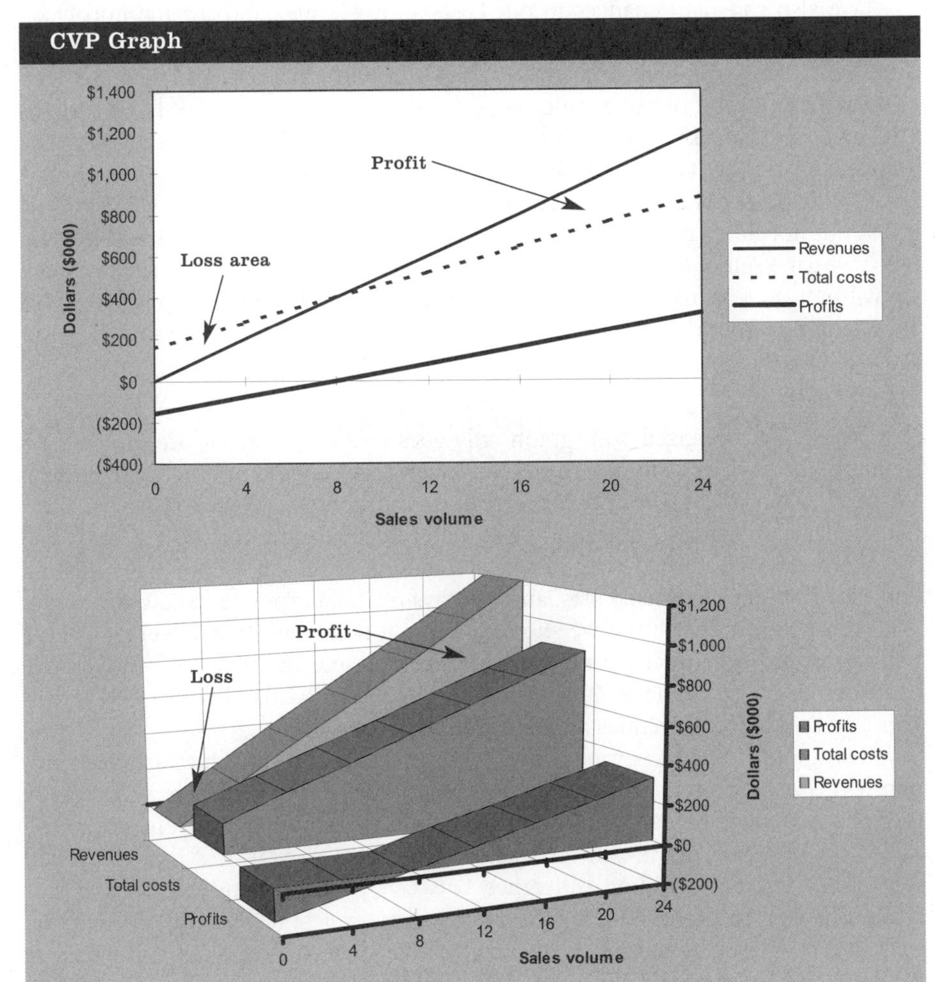

Exhibit 3-8

costs and total revenues cross is the break-even point [eight houses and $400,000 in revenues].

"The area between the total revenues and total costs lines is the profit we earn. To the left of the break-even point we have a loss [profit is negative as sales volume is less than the break-even point]. To the right of the break-even point we have a profit. Profit increases $20,000 per house sold, which is the contribution margin per unit.

"The CMU also is the slope of the profit line, which is the heavy black line in the top graph. The profit line begins at a sales volume of zero. At this volume, we have no revenues to cover our fixed costs. So, when no houses are sold, we have a loss of $160,000 [the fixed costs]. Every time we sell one house, we gain $20,000 in profit. I suppose you could say we reduce our loss by $20,000 until the eighth house is sold. When we sell 8 houses, profit equals zero [this is the break-even point]. Every house after the eighth creates another $20,000 in profit. But remember, it really doesn't make any difference which side of the break-even point we are on. Every time we sell another house, we make another $20,000.

"Since you're such a multi-dimensional person, Nancy, the bottom graph is the same as the top graph, only in three dimensions." Everyone chuckled, but they also noticed prettier, [three dimensional] graphs sometimes don't convey the information as well as two-dimensional graphs.

"We also can plan changes in our costs and revenues and see the impact on profits at different volume levels [what-if analysis]. Let me show you [see Exhibit 3-9]. Let's change the sales price to $45,000 [a $5,000 decrease] and increase fixed costs to $200,000. If our sales price goes down, so does our CMU. If fixed costs simultaneously increase, our break-even point should go up. We can see this on the graph. It looks like it's about 14 houses."

NANCY

"You're right, Julie! Our new contribution margin per unit is $15,000. Dividing it into our new fixed costs of $200,000 gives us a break-even point of 13.33 houses. Since we can't sell one-third of a house, we better round up to 14. If I round down, we will not quite make enough money to break even." Everyone then realized we always have to round up a break-even point.

Margin of safety

NANCY

"You know, I just realized your graph only goes to 24 houses. We are projecting a standard homes sales volume of 100. Not much chance we're going to lose money! We need to sell only eight houses to break even, but we're projecting sales of 100. Our actual sales can be significantly less than forecast before we show a loss."

SID

"Remember Nancy, this is just our standard homes line. We have custom homes with their own fixed costs, and we have overall corporate fixed costs to pay. With multiple product lines, we should look at total revenues and average contribution margin ratio. Going back to our earlier example [Exhibit 3-4], the average contribution margin ratio is 40%. Dividing this into total fixed costs of $1.4 million, our break-even revenues are $3.5 million."

JULIE

"Now, let's take a closer look at your idea. Break-even revenues are $2.5 million less than our projected revenues of $6 million. I think you are still correct, though. Actual sales can be significantly less than our projection before we lose money. In fact, actual sales can be 42% less than projected [$2.5 million difference between projected and break-even revenues, divided by the projected revenues]. This is called our **margin of safety.** It also can be calculated using volume instead of revenues.

The difference between the sales forecast and break-even point is called a **margin of safety**, *which is usually expressed as a percentage of the sales forecast.*

The CVP Graph and What-If Analysis

DATA SECTION

Volume	100	houses
Sales price	$45	per house
Variable costs	$30	per house
Fixed costs	$200	per year

SOLUTION SECTION

Sales volume	Revenues	Total costs	Profits
0	$ 0	$200	$(200)
4	180	320	(140)
8	360	440	(80)
12	540	560	(20)
16	720	680	40
20	900	800	100
24	1,080	920	160

GRAPHIC VIEW

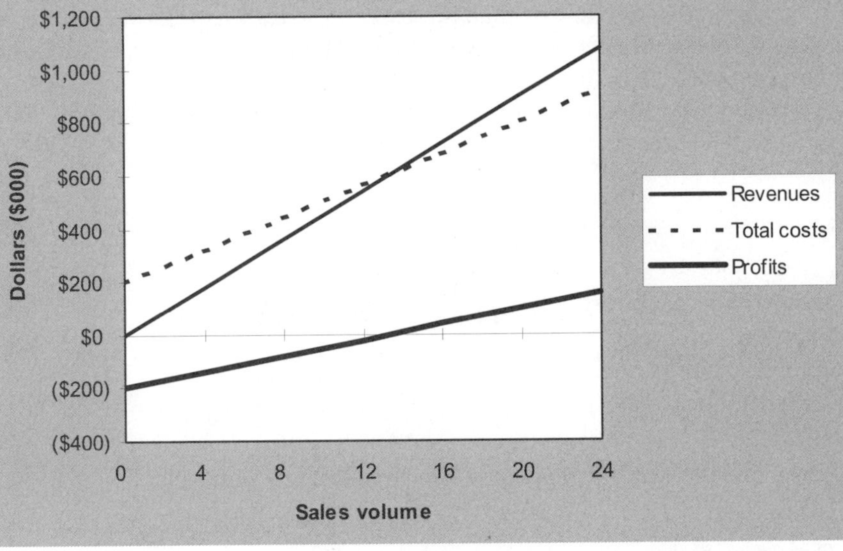

$1,200
$1,000
$800
$600
$400
$200
$0
($200)
($400)
Dollars ($000)
0 4 8 12 16 20 24
Sales volume
Revenues
Total costs
Profits

Exhibit 3-9

As you can see below, a 42% margin of safety means actual sales can be 42% lower than our forecast before we start to lose money."

Margin of Safety

$$\text{Margin of safety} = \frac{\text{Sales forecast} - \text{Break-even revenues}}{\text{Sales forecast}}$$

$$42\% = \frac{\$6{,}000{,}000 - \$3{,}500{,}000}{\$6{,}000{,}000}$$

BILL

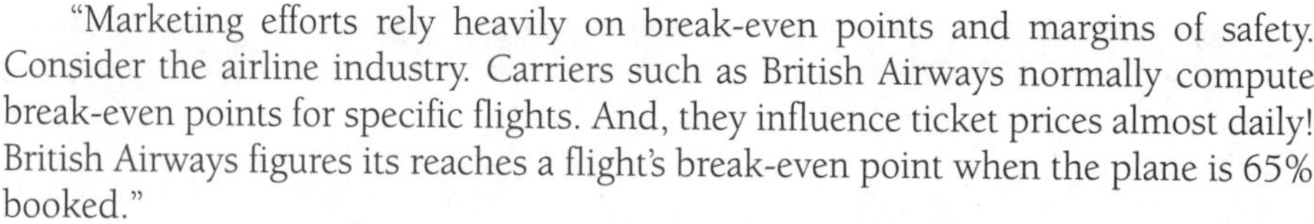

"Marketing efforts rely heavily on break-even points and margins of safety. Consider the airline industry. Carriers such as British Airways normally compute break-even points for specific flights. And, they influence ticket prices almost daily! British Airways figures its reaches a flight's break-even point when the plane is 65% booked."

BOB

"In managing break-even point and margin of safety, some companies trade off fixed costs for variable costs. This means they have lower CMUs, but they also may end up with lower break-even points, too. This is especially likely with start-up companies. Logue, the dog biscuit company, did this by outsourcing its manufacturing operations. By managing its fixed costs, Naxos, the classic CD producer, can sell digital CDs for $6 versus the competition's $18. With high fixed costs, the automobile industry constantly is looking for ways to reduce break-even points. For example, Chrysler reduced its break-even point 16% to 1.6 million cars a year in the early 1990s. Ford decided not to build new plants for its increasing demand, and instead had Mazda build some of its Probes. Jaguar cut its break-even point in half to 30,000 per year. Rolls-Royce dropped its break-even point from 3,300 to 1,300 cars in the same time period. And, Saab went from 125,000 to 83,000.

"Outsourcing computer operations is another common way to trade fixed costs for variable costs. EDS, the Dallas-based computer services firm, paid Enron about $6 million for its computer systems and hired around 550 of Enron's computer personnel. By outsourcing its computer processing, Enron saved $200 million."

NANCY

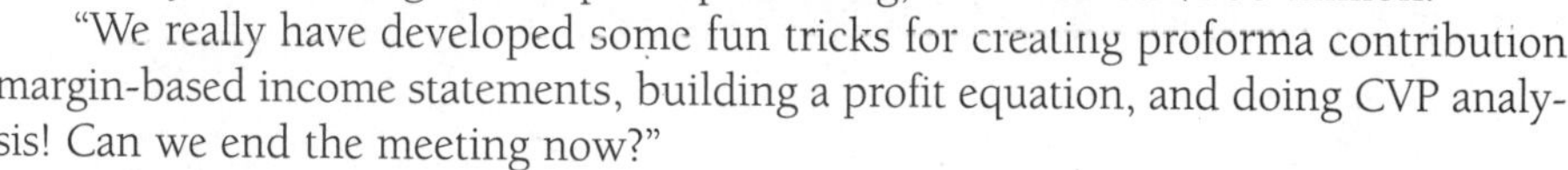

"We really have developed some fun tricks for creating proforma contribution margin-based income statements, building a profit equation, and doing CVP analysis! Can we end the meeting now?"

SID

"I think we have a satisfactory proforma. We've done our CVP analyses. We can go home now! Doris, do you have good notes on this meeting?"

KEY OBJECTIVES SUMMARY

DORIS

"I think I understand. We've covered four topics in this profit-planning meeting.

1. Explain the four cost behavior patterns.

"For profit planning, we need to know how our costs behave as volume changes. Costs need to be classified as variable and fixed so they can be used in a contribution margin income statement. This format allows us to see the effects on projected profits from changing sales and/or costs. Knowing cost behaviors also allows us to create a profit equation to use in CVP analysis. The four cost behavior patterns are:

a) *Variable costs* are constant per unit [usually a unit is a product] and vary in total with changes in volume. Knowing variable costs per unit allows us to budget their total costs for any given volume within the relevant range. When graphed, they have a positive, constant slope and a zero intercept. Examples include direct materials and labor, variable overhead, and sales commissions.

b) *Fixed costs* are constant in total over the time period we are budgeting. When expressed as a per-unit amount, they vary inversely with volume. We need to know total fixed costs in order to accurately budget. Graphically, fixed costs are a horizontal line [zero slope, positive intercept]. Examples include fixed overhead [factory rent, heat and light, property taxes and insurance, salaries, straight-line depreciation] and many administrative costs.

c) *Mixed costs* are part variable and part fixed. Manufacturing overhead, sales and marketing expenses, and some administrative costs are examples. These costs need to be broken down into their variable and fixed components. [Statistical methods to do this are discussed in Appendix A.]

d) *Step costs* are fixed, but only over a very specific volume range. When step costs change over very narrow ranges, they usually are treated as variable costs for profit-planning purposes. Step costs that change only over a wide range usually are treated as fixed costs. Examples include the extra fixed costs from a second or third production shift [additional foreman's salary, extra heat and light], setup costs for a production run, and duty fees on international shipments.

"We assume variable costs per unit and total fixed costs are stable over some range of volumes, called the relevant range. We also have to remember we are classifying costs as variable or fixed based on volume. All costs vary with some factor. We are interested in how costs change with volume, though. I wrote down the costs we talked about, what really causes them to change, and how we budget for them [see Exhibit 3-10].

Cost Behaviors

Cost item	Varies with	How budgeted within our relevant range of production volumes
Direct materials	Production volume	Variable cost
Direct labor	Maybe with production volume, depending on management's philosophy	Variable or fixed (depending on management's philosophy)
Heat and light	Weather	Fixed cost
Salaries	Number of people working	Fixed cost
Water	Usage per 1,000 gallons	Fixed cost
Telephone bill	Long-distance time	Fixed cost

Exhibit 3-10

2. Create a contribution margin-based income statement and compare it to a functional format.

"Once we know how our costs behave, we can reformat the income statement to make it more useful in profit planning. To demonstrate, assume the following:

Sales price:	**$10**
Sales volume:	**100 units a month**
Variable cost per unit:	**$8**
Fixed cost per month:	**$150**

The income statement shows a profit of $50 at this volume [see Exhibit 3-11].

Contribution Margin-Based Income Statement

INCOME STATEMENT

	Per unit	%	Totals @ 100
Revenues	$10	100%	$1,000
Less: Variable costs	(8)	(80%)	(800)
Contribution margin	$ 2	20%	$ 200
Less: Fixed costs			(150)
Profit			$ 50
Break-even point:	75 units		
Break-even revenues:	$750		
Margin of safety:	25%		

Exhibit 3-11

"The $2 contribution margin per unit [CMU] represents how much profit results from selling one more product. This is most useful when analyzing an individual product line's profitability. The 20% contribution margin ratio means for every dollar of sales, 20¢ is created to pay for fixed costs and generate profits. Contribution margin ratio is most useful when dealing with multiple product lines. I also have included the break-even point, break-even revenues, and margin of safety. These are discussed in the next summary point.

"Using the same sales volume, the contribution margin income statement and the functional income statement show the same total revenues, total costs, and profit. The difference in the two formats is how costs are organized. The contribution margin format separates variable and fixed costs. This format supports internal decision making. The functional format organizes costs by the functions they serve [product costs are included in cost of goods sold; selling and administrative costs are recorded as expenses]. The functional format is required for external, financial reporting.

3. Develop a profit equation and use it in cost-volume-profit analysis.

"We next transform this income statement into a profit equation used to solve for a target volume or revenues, given a profit goal. To demonstrate, let's use the same data as above to solve for a $100 monthly profit and for the break-even point [a zero profit goal]. [See Exhibit 3-12.]

"Focusing on the contribution margin per unit, each product is worth $2 to us. With monthly fixed costs of $150, we need to sell 75 products per month to break even. Selling another 50 earns a $100 monthly profit. Compare the profits at volumes of 100 [from the last summary point] and 125 products. The difference in profits is $50. This is the 25-unit difference in volume multiplied by the $2 CMU. The originally projected volume of 100 units is 25 greater than the break-even point. That is a 25% margin of safety. [Subtract break-even volume from projected volume and then divide by projected volume.]

The Profit Equation

$$(\text{CMU} \times \text{Volume}) - \text{Fixed costs} = \text{Profit}$$

$$(\$2 \times 125) - \$150 = \$100$$

How many products must we sell (volume) for our target profit?

$$\text{Volume} = \frac{\text{Fixed cost} + \text{Profit}}{\text{CMU}}$$

$$= \frac{\$150 + \$100}{\$2}$$

$$= \underline{\underline{\text{125 products per month}}}$$

Revenues needed to achieve target profit:

$$\text{Revenues} = \frac{\text{Fixed cost} + \text{Profit}}{\text{CM ratio}}$$

$$= \frac{\$150 + \$100}{.20}$$

$$= \underline{\underline{\$1{,}250 \text{ per month}}}$$

What is our break-even point? (volume where revenues just equal costs)

$$\text{Volume} = \frac{\text{Fixed cost} + \text{Profit}}{\text{CMU}}$$

$$= \frac{\$150 + \$0}{\$2}$$

$$= \underline{\underline{\text{75 products per month}}}$$

Break-even revenues:

$$\text{Revenues} = \frac{\text{Fixed cost} + \text{Profit}}{\text{CM ratio}}$$

$$= \frac{\$150 + \$0}{.20}$$

$$= \underline{\underline{\$750 \text{ per month}}}$$

Exhibit 3-12

4. Perform "what-if" analysis with the profit equation.

"With this income statement and profit equation, we can 'play games' with our profit projection by asking 'what-if' questions. For example:

a) What if we want to break even; how many products need to be sold? Using the above amounts, each product is worth $2 [a two-dollar bill]. How many two-dollar bills do we need to cover $150 in fixed costs? The break-even point is 75 products.

b) What if we want another $100 in profits; how many more products do we sell? This is the same as asking how many more two-dollar bills we need to get another $100. We need to sell another 50 products.

c) What if direct materials cost increases 50¢ per product; what happens to our profit? Contribution margin per unit will go down 50¢ to $1.50. If we sell 100 products, we will generate $150 in contribution margin which will just cover our fixed costs, yielding no profit. Selling 125 products will result in a profit of $37.50. This is equal to 25 more products [compared to 100 units] multiplied by the $1.50 CMU. The extra $37.50 contribution margin is added to the previous profit [$0] to yield the new profit.

We also can portray these CVP relationships graphically, as Julie showed us earlier [see Exhibits 3-8 and 3-9]."

"Thank you, Doris. I think we're finally done! Good night."

SID

Spreadsheet Programs and CVP Analysis

Julie created a spreadsheet program to do different types of CVP analyses. Spreadsheet programs provide a powerful and sophisticated tool for developing contribution margin income statements, performing CVP analyses, graphing CVP relationships, and asking "what-if" questions. Her program is presented in Exhibit 3-A1.

CVP and What-If Analyses Worksheet

DATA SECTION

Standard homes		**Variable cost**	**Fixed cost**
Sales price	$45,000		
Volume	100		
Direct materials	$15,500	$15,500	
Direct labor	$10,000	10,000	
Indirect materials	$1,000	1,000	
Indirect labor	$500	500	
Power	$500	500	
Supervision	$100,000		$100,000
Sales commissions	$2,500	2,500	
Advertising	$50,000		50,000
Architectural costs	$10,000		10,000
Sums		$30,000	$160,000

SOLUTION SECTION

	STANDARD HOMES		
	Per unit	**%**	**Totals @ 100**
Revenues	$ 45,000	100%	$ 4,500,000
Less: Variable costs	(30,000)	(67%)	(3,000,000)
Contribution margin	**$ 15,000**	**33%**	**$ 1,500,000**
Less: Fixed costs			(160,000)
Net income			**$ 1,340,000**
Break-even point:	**10.67 units**		
Break-even revenues:	**$480,000**		
Margin of safety:	**89%**		

Exhibit 3-A1

Using spreadsheets to do "what-if" analyses

This program allows us to quickly change amounts in the Data Section and see the results in the Solution Section. The program works because the Solution Section cells contain formulas and cell references referring to Data Section cells. You may have heard the word "template" used with this type of program.

To demonstrate how the program works, Julie used the proforma data for standard homes given in Exhibit 3-6, but changed the sales price from $50,000 to $45,000. Since the quality of the standard homes isn't being changed, the variable costs per house won't change. However, the variable cost percentages change since they are based on the sales price. As expected, if we lower the sales price, the contribution margin per unit will decrease by that same amount. This will change the contribution margin ratio as well. What is the effect on profit? CMU decreases $5,000 due to the lowering of the sales price. Selling 100 houses for $5,000 less results in lower profits of $500,000. The profit in Exhibit 3-A1 is $500,000 less than the original proforma profit for the standard homes product line shown in Exhibit 3-6.

Current versions of all three major spreadsheet programs also have menu commands to do what-if analysis. These are a little harder to work with as compared to just changing a Data Section cell value. It's well worth the effort, though, if we want to save various scenarios and compare them within a report the spreadsheet program automatically creates.

Goal-seeking with spreadsheets

Spreadsheets will also do goal-seeking. Basically, goal-seeking says, "Tell me your goal (e.g., a profit of $2 million), and what you want to change to achieve it (e.g., change the sales price). I'll solve for the variable's new value (the new sales price)!" This is a very handy trick in profit-planning meetings like the one in this chapter!

Set a profit goal of $2 million and ask the program to solve for a new sales price. It's really simple. Just click the mouse on the goal-seeking menu command, then click on the profit cell (the cell that is the goal), input $2 million (the value of the goal), click on the sales price cell in the Data Section (the value to be changed), and finally on the Solve button. To earn $2 million from standard home sales, the sales price will have to be $51,600. The program automatically placed this new value in the sales price Data Section cell and updated the Solution Section to verify it. A printout is shown in Exhibit 3-A2.

CVP and What-If Analyses Worksheet—Goal-Seeking Example

DATA SECTION

Sales price	$51,600	Power	$500
Volume	100	Supervision	$100,000
Direct materials	$15,500	Sales commissions	$2,500
Direct labor	$10,000	Advertising	$50,000
Indirect materials	$1,000	Architectural costs	$10,000
Indirect labor	$500		

SOLUTION SECTION

	Per unit	%	Totals @ 100
Revenues	$ 51,600	100%	$ 5,160,000
Less: Variable costs	(30,000)	(58%)	(3,000,000)
Contribution margin	**$ 21,600**	**42%**	**$ 2,160,000**
Less: Fixed costs			(160,000)
Net income			**$ 2,000,000**
Break-even point:	**7.41 units**		
Break-even revenues:	**$382,222**		
Margin of safety:	**93%**		

Exhibit 3-A2

Spreadsheet graphics

Julie also experimented with different graphic options for the CVP graph. Exhibits 3-8 and 3-9 demonstrate traditional two-dimensional graphs. Sometimes information can be displayed in a format easier to understand by using different types of graphs. Modern spreadsheet programs provide many options for modifying the appearance of graphs. To demonstrate this, Exhibit 3-A3 displays a three-dimensional format using the numbers from Exhibit 3-A1. This graph is rotated about 180 degrees from the bottom graph in Exhibit 3-8. Sometimes three-dimensional graphs are easier to interpret than are two-dimensional graphs. A lot can be done by rotating and tilting. Normally, however, two-dimensional graphs better portray information. Many options are available to help the management accountant prepare graphical displays.

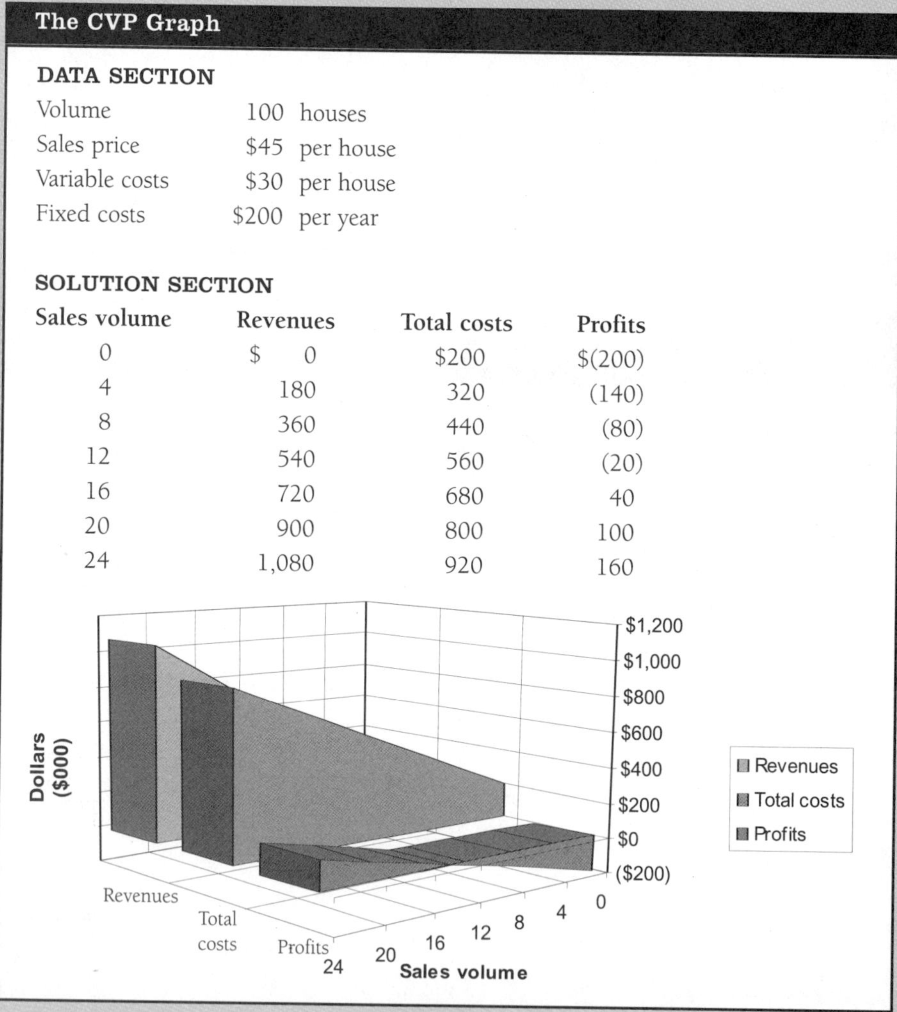

The CVP Graph

DATA SECTION

Volume	100	houses
Sales price	$45	per house
Variable costs	$30	per house
Fixed costs	$200	per year

SOLUTION SECTION

Sales volume	Revenues	Total costs	Profits
0	$ 0	$200	$(200)
4	180	320	(140)
8	360	440	(80)
12	540	560	(20)
16	720	680	40
20	900	800	100
24	1,080	920	160

Exhibit 3-A3

ESTIMATING COST BEHAVIOR PATTERNS

"I have another concern. How can we know how much of our overhead is variable and fixed? Overhead is a mixed cost. To properly budget, we have to separate the variable overhead from the fixed overhead."

"Traditionally, the Boss's accountant did this using some statistical techniques. I remember three. Our goal is to create an overhead cost equation. A cost equation represents costs as variable and fixed. For example:

Cost Equation

Total cost = Fixed costs in total + (Variable cost per unit × Volume)

"That's just the slope-intercept form of an equation for a straight line we learned in grade school!" Bob just smiled to himself, thinking this is also just a regression equation.

"As our first step with all three techniques, we need to determine what causes overhead. What causes a particular cost is called a cost driver. If we understand this cause-effect relationship [i.e., the overhead cost driver], we can predict variable, fixed, and total overhead cost."

Julie thought to herself about the nature of overhead. It's a potpourri of many different indirect costs. Each can have a different cost driver! She thought about discussing this, but decided it should wait until a future meeting [Chapter 9].

"Before we modernized the factory, we were very labor intensive. Labor usage caused overhead because most of the overhead resources were supplies and tools used by our workers. The more labor hours worked, the more overhead costs incurred. Thus, we always have used direct labor to predict our overhead.

"Now, some departments are very machinery intensive. Machine usage [hours] is a better cost driver for them. Other types of overhead can be caused by other drivers, though. For example, the overhead in a warehouse may be caused by its size. Square footage might be a good cost driver for it. The point is we can have many different cost drivers for different overhead items and departments. We have a very traditional accounting system in which all overhead is allocated to products using direct labor hours. We will use this as our cost driver."

Julie just smiled to herself. She was happy Bob realized the need for many cost drivers in budgeting and controlling overhead costs. She also realized everyone first must understand how the traditional cost accounting system works before they can understand what it's deficiencies are. Definitely topics for future meetings!

"The second step involves gathering historical data about labor hours and overhead cost. That information comes from our accounting system, which is why our accountant always did the calculations. Third, by using this information, an equation is derived to predict overhead based on direct labor hours. I've made up another simple example [Exhibit 3-A4]. Jackie supplied me with the total overhead costs and direct labor hours worked for the last six years."

The scattergraph approach

"This is a graphical approach. In statistics, I was taught always to graph our data first. Remember, we assume variable costs are constant per unit [e.g., variable over-

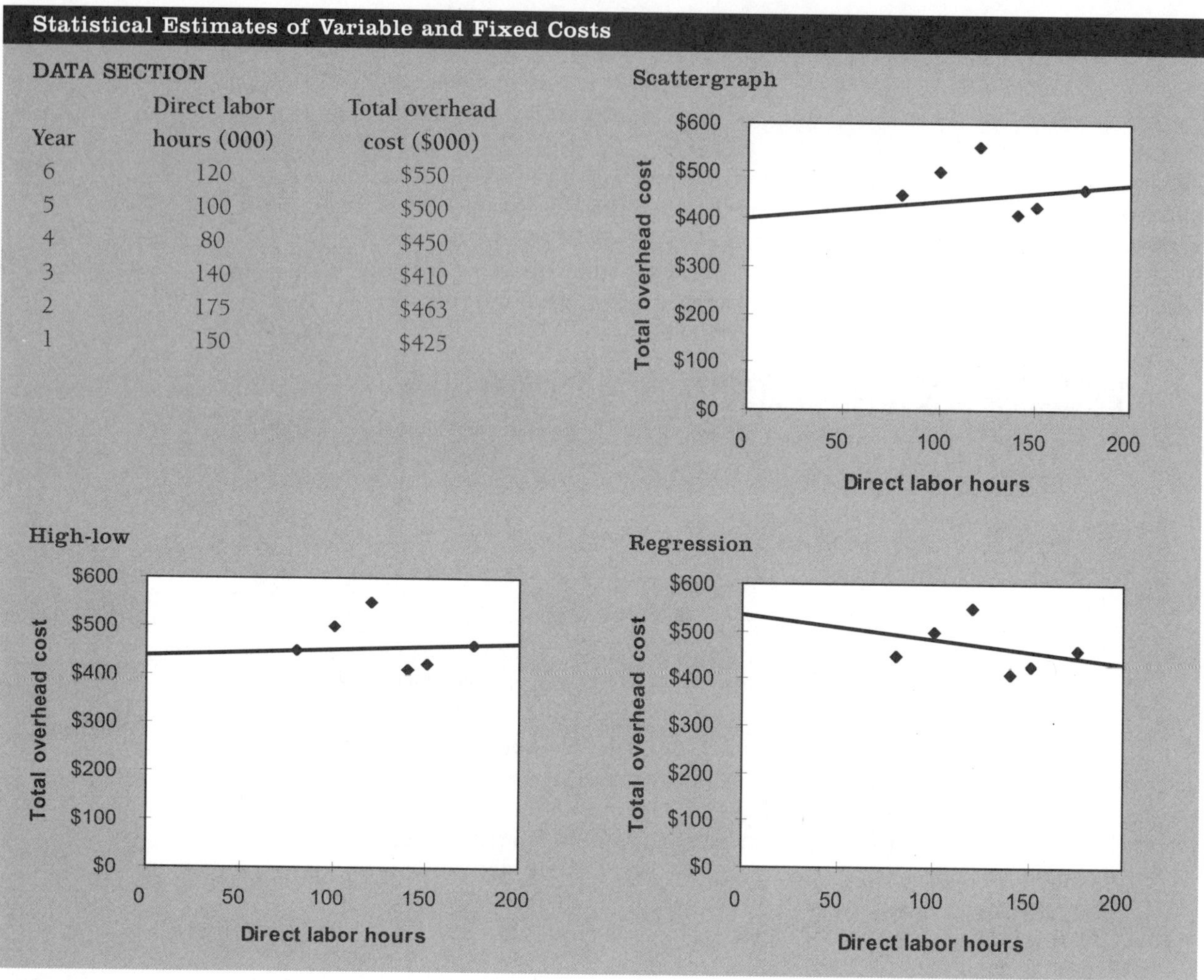

Statistical Estimates of Variable and Fixed Costs

DATA SECTION

Year	Direct labor hours (000)	Total overhead cost ($000)
6	120	$550
5	100	$500
4	80	$450
3	140	$410
2	175	$463
1	150	$425

Exhibit 3-A4

KEY OBJECTIVE 5

Describe three statistical techniques to break down a mixed cost into its variable and fixed components.

head is constant per direct labor hour]. This means a graph of total overhead cost will produce a straight line. With this approach, just draw a straight line best fitting the data. From the graph, create an equation for this line.

- The intercept is at $400,000. Since the intercept is the fixed cost component of a mixed cost, this is the total fixed overhead.
- Next, select a labor volume and read its corresponding cost. On this line, the total overhead cost at 200,000 direct labor hours is $450,000.
- If $400,000 of the $450,000 is fixed overhead, the remaining $50,000 must be variable overhead. Thus, the slope is 25¢ per direct labor hour [$50,000 ÷ 200,000 hours].

The equation for total overhead is:

Total annual overhead cost = $400,000/year + $0.25 per direct labor hour

The high-low approach

"This approach derives the overhead cost equation from using two of the points, the high and low observations. Always use the predictor variable [labor predicts overhead] to determine the high and low points. Looking at the Data Section, the high point is 175,000 hours. The low point is 80,000 hours.

- First calculate the slope [variable overhead per direct labor hour]. This is the change in cost divided by the change in hours, [sometimes called 'the rise over the run'].

$$\textbf{Variable overhead} = \frac{\$463{,}000 - \$450{,}000}{175{,}000 - 80{,}000}$$

$$= \frac{\$13{,}000}{95{,}000 \text{ hours}}$$

$$= \underline{\underline{13.7¢ \text{ per direct labor hour}}}$$

- Using either the high or the low point with the slope, calculate the total variable overhead cost. Subtract it from the total overhead to compute the fixed overhead. Using the high point:

Total overhead – Total variable overhead
= Fixed overhead

\$463,000 – (\$0.137 per DLhr × 175,000 hours) = \$439,025

- The equation for total overhead is:

Total annual overhead cost = \$439,025/year
+ \$0.137 per direct labor hour

The regression approach

"Regression analysis uses all the data to statistically create a 'line of best fit.' Manually solving the equations involved in this approach requires a lot of work. Statistics courses cover these calculations in detail. Calculators and spreadsheet programs do this automatically. My spreadsheet program calculated the following intercept and slope:

Total annual overhead cost = \$521,482/year
– \$0.433 per direct labor hour

Problems with statistical estimation

"I don't like any of these techniques! Here's my thinking:

- The scattergraph method is too subjective. Each person can draw a different line given the same observations. I mean the slope and intercept will be different, so no one will agree on the variable and fixed overhead.

- The high-low method is objective, so everyone will calculate the same equation. However, it uses the two most unrepresentative points [the highest and lowest], which means the equation may not be very accurate.
- While regression uses all the data to objectively derive an overhead equation, overcoming both of the above objections, all three methods assume we can predict the future from the past.

"It's the last point that bothers me the most. In Year 3, we modernized many of the plant's departments. The new equipment replaced many labor operations, and our labor force does a lot of other things. Now we are capital intensive, not labor intensive. Labor no longer causes our overhead, machine usage does. The other point I want you to consider is the intense inflation during that six-year period. While costs have returned to 'normal' now, all three overhead equations are based on past inflated costs. We can't use the past to predict the future if the future may be radically different! Tecnol Medical Products discovered that problem. Traditionally, medical face masks were hand stitched. By automating its production processes, Tecnol drove its costs below 3M and Johnson & Johnson. This allowed them to expand into new product lines and European markets. Thus, the historical data no longer could be used to predict the future.

"I went to school with most of our workers. They're well educated, and they know their jobs. Why can't we just ask them to explain the overhead they need? Nobody knows their jobs better than they do!"

BOB

"I agree with you! Prior to Year 3, we could pretty accurately predict overhead using $200,000 for fixed overhead and $1.50 per direct labor hour for variable overhead. After we automated, fixed overhead increased while direct labor hours decreased. This significantly changed our equation to about $250,000 in fixed overhead and $2.50 per direct labor hour. Remembering our statistics, this historical data should be sample observations from a homogeneous population. We really have costs from two different worlds, the pre-Year 3 labor-oriented world and the post-Year 3 machine-oriented world. *Statistical techniques using historical cost data work best when everything stays the same.* Then, the past can predict the future! We are, however, in a dynamic environment, not a stable one. Costs change radically from year to year, and the activities causing overhead have changed from labor-based to machine-oriented."

NANCY

"O.K., these techniques are really rough estimates. They must be used with caution. Let's look at our processes and talk with our people in identifying variable and fixed overhead. Nobody knows their jobs better than they do!" And, she thought to herself, they spend way too much time in this stuffy meeting room. To understand our costs, we need to understand our operations. The only way to do this is to get out of the office and go to where the work is done!

"By the way, how can we have a negative slope with the regression equation? Does this mean we subtract variable overhead? Don't you have to add variable and fixed overhead together to get the total?"

JULIE

"The problems Tommy and Bob mentioned are evident in the regression equation. You can't have a negative slope! The negative slope means every time one hour is worked, someone pays us 43.3¢ for variable overhead! This simply is impossible. Working with the shop floor people, Bob put together our overhead budget at $592,500. This includes $335,000 in fixed overhead + $2.48 per direct labor hour for variable overhead [total variable overhead of $257,500 divided by 125,000 budgeted hours]. This is the equation we should use."

CVP ANALYSIS AND INCOME TAXES

KEY OBJECTIVE 6

Modify the profit equation to include income taxes.

NANCY

"I've been looking at our proforma income statement again. Exhibit 3-1 shows a projected profit of $1 million. Can we keep the entire $1 million? I thought we only wanted about $100,000 in profits for each of us. What am I missing here?"

JULIE

"Nothing too serious, just income taxes!" Everyone groaned again, this time long and loudly. "Given our 25% income tax rate, one out of every four dollars we make goes to the government." Now the group was getting downright surly. Julie didn't want to continue, but knew she must. She tried to muster the courage of Slim the cowboy when he had to meet the auditor [Chapter 1]. She continued hesitantly. "If we want $750,000 after taxes, we'll need to make $1 million before taxes. We really should modify our profit equation to consider income taxes."

NANCY

"I guess I will have to remember *the profit equation only solves for pretax profit.* To convert the formula into after-tax profit, which is what we are really concerned with, let's fix it."

JULIE

"It isn't too hard once you realize after-tax profit is just pretax profit minus income taxes:

Converting After-Tax to Pretax Profit

After-tax profit = Pretax profit − Income taxes

= Pretax profit − (Pretax profit × Income tax rate)

= Pretax profit × (1 − Income tax rate)

Solving for pretax profit:

Pretax profit = After-tax profit ÷ (1 − Income tax rate)

Using Multree Company totals:

$1,000,000 = $750,000 ÷ (1 − 25%)

"We can adjust the profit equation to include income taxes using the pretax profit equation [see Exhibit 3-A5]."

The Profit Equation and Income Taxes

Original profit equation (solves for pretax profit)

$$\text{Revenues} = \frac{\text{Fixed cost} + \textit{Pretax profit}}{\text{CM Ratio}}$$

$$= \frac{\$1{,}400{,}000 + \$1{,}000{,}000}{0.40}$$

$$= \$6{,}000{,}000 \text{ per year}$$

Modified profit equation (solves for after-tax profit)

$$\text{Revenues} = \frac{\text{Fixed cost} + \dfrac{\textit{After-tax profit}}{(1 - \textit{tax rate})}}{\text{CM Ratio}}$$

$$= \frac{\$1{,}400{,}000 + \dfrac{\$750{,}000}{(1 - 25\%)}}{0.40}$$

$$= \$6{,}000{,}000 \text{ per year}$$

Exhibit 3-A5

KEY OBJECTIVE 7

Apply CVP analysis to multiple product lines.

CVP WITH MULTIPLE PRODUCT LINES

NANCY

"Throughout most of our discussion of CVP analysis, we considered only the standard homes product line. We have two product lines, though. How do we set up a profit equation for both? Can we just add their revenues and costs together? Can we still do break-even analysis with two or more product lines?"

JULIE

"Sure. With multiple products [as products 1 and 2]:

Multiple Products Profit Equation

$$(\text{CMU}_1 \times \text{Volume}_1) + (\text{CMU}_2 \times \text{Volume}_2) - \text{Fixed costs} = \text{Profits}$$

Solving for volume and revenues

JULIE

"The basic equation never changes. To solve for break-even volume and revenues, though, we have to make a very limiting assumption: the sales mix must remain constant. Our current sales projection is for 100 standard homes and 10 custom homes. Expressing this as a sales mix, we sell 10 standard homes for every 1 custom home. Our sales mix ratio is 10/11 standard homes and 1/11 custom homes. As long as this sales mix does not change, we can:

1. Calculate a weighted-average CMU for the two product lines using our sales mix ratio.
2. Compute the break-even point based on the weighted-average CMU.
3. Determine how many of the break-even units come from each product line using the sales mix ratio.

These three steps and an income statement 'proof' are presented next [Exhibit 3-A6]."

Multiple Product Break-Even Analysis

Product line	CMUs		Sales mix		Weighted-average CMU
Standard homes	$20,000	×	0.9091	=	$18,182
Custom homes	$40,000	×	0.0909	=	3,636
					$21,818

Break-even calculation:

$$\frac{\text{Fixed costs}}{\text{Weighted-average CMU}} \quad \frac{\$1{,}400{,}000}{\$21{,}818} = 64.2 \text{ homes}$$

Break-even sales mix calculation:

Standard homes	64.2	×	0.9091	=	58.3 homes
Custom homes	64.2	×	0.0909	=	5.8 homes

Contribution margin-based income statement:

Contribution margin on standard homes	$20,000	×	58.3	=	$ 1,166,667
Contribution margin on custom homes	$40,000	×	5.8	=	233,333
Total contribution margin					$ 1,400,000
Less: Fixed costs					(1,400,000)
Net income					$ 0

Exhibit 3-A6

READING LIST*

Break-even points are critical for start-ups: Thompson, "Planning for Profit," *Black Enterprise*, April 1993.

Chrysler break-even points: "Lots of Companies Are Lean, But Which Are Mean?" *Business Week*, February 3, 1992. Bennet, "Chrysler Chief's World View: Place to Sell, Not Build, Cars," *New York Times*, September 30, 1994, p. D1.

Credit card costs per customer: Reichheld and Sasser, "Zero Defections: Quality Comes to Services," *Harvard Business Review*, September–October 1990.

EDS and Enron: Kirkpatrick, "Why Not Farm Out Your Computing?" *Fortune*, September 23, 1991.

Elgin Sweeper: Callan, Tredup, and Wissinger, "Elgin Sweeper Company's Journey Toward Cost Management," *Management Accounting*, July 1991.

Jaguar break-even points: Eisenstein, "Jaguar Ledgers to Feature Black, Not Red, Ink Next Year," *The Washington Times*, September 16, 1994, p. D3.

Labor cost behavior in Australia: Joye and Blayney, "Cost and Management Accounting Practices in Australian Manufacturing Companies: Survey Results," Accounting Research Centre, University of Sidney, 1991.

Labor cost behavior in Japan: IMA Tokyo Affiliate, "Management Accounting in the Advanced Manufacturing Surrounding: Comparative Study on Survey in Japan and USA," Tokyo, 1988.

Logue: Murphy, "The Start-Up of the 90's," *Inc.*, March 1992.

Naxos: Tanzer, "All the Music Without the Trimming," *Forbes*, February 14, 1994.

Pittsburgh Pirates: Wucinich, "Profit Is the Name of the Game," *Management Accounting*, February 1991.

Rolls-Royce break-even points: Jedlicka, "Rebounding Rolls Needs a Partner," *Chicago Sun-Times*, October 17, 1994, p. 47.

Saab break-even points: "GM's Saab Unit Climbs Into Black," *Investor's Business Daily*, September 27, 1994, p. A4.

Seagate: Drtina, "The Outsourcing Decision," *Management Accounting*, March 1994.

Tecnol: Forest, "Who's Afraid of J&J and 3M?" *Business Week*, December 5, 1994.

*Alphabetic by topic, idea, or company referenced.

CHAPTER 4

How Much Cash Can We Take?

Developing Cash Budgets from Proformas

KEY OBJECTIVES:

1	*Explain why proforma income statements and CVP analysis have to be translated into a cash budget.*
2	*Discuss the usefulness of budgets when cash inflows are known.*
3	*Prepare a schedule for cash collections from sales.*
4	*Develop operating budgets (schedules for purchases, labor, overhead, and operating expenses).*
5	*Create a monthly cash budget.*
6	*Describe how cash budgeting can affect motivation and control.*
7	*[Appendix A] Comment on spreadsheet usefulness in budgeting.*

It was time for the next meeting. The grandchildren had gone over the profit plan again and again. Everyone felt comfortable with the proforma income statement and budgeted profits. Some were beginning to count their money. Nancy talked about the new car she was going to buy. Ways to spend the $1 million projected profit seemed to dominate the boardroom.

Cash Budgeting and Solvency

NANCY

"Well, Tommy, since I'm buying this car, you should buy lunch! I have to save enough for the down payment, insurance, license plates, and registration."

TOMMY

"Ha! You've got the same problem I do; lots of profit, but no cash! The problem with our proforma income statement is we can't take it to the restaurant and use it to pay for lunch. People want to be paid in cash."

Profit and cashflow are not the same thing!

KEY OBJECTIVE 1

Explain why proforma income statements and CVP analysis have to be translated into a cash budget.

JULIE

Julie entered the room with a handful of computer printouts. Her hard-headed banking experience showed through her troubled expression.

"Well, it looks like we're going to make our million dollars. But I'm worried. Profit is only one of our objectives. I've seen profitable companies that can't pay their bills. Grandmother Calendar Company was so successful it went bankrupt. It made custom calendars. Sales grew to 1,000 per day, but it only had the production capacity for 300 per day. Customers didn't pay for the calendars until received, but Grandmother had to buy all the materials and pay the labor, overhead, and operating costs before and while making the calendars. Its inability to meet demand in a timely fashion drove the company to bankruptcy. Because it couldn't deliver calendars on a timely basis, the company could not get the cash it needed to pay bills.

"Remember, long-term value results from becoming a cash machine. It's cashflow, not profit, which will keep us in business or drive us to bankruptcy. **Cashflows** are money coming into (**cash inflows**) and going out of (**cash outflows**) our bank account. While our $1 million projected profit looks good on paper, we need

> **Cashflows** *are the deposits made* (**cash inflows** *or "cash-ins") and withdrawals from* (**cash outflows** *or "cash-outs") a bank account.*

cash to run the business. You and I have the same problems any organization has; Multree Homes needs a positive cashflow in its checking account in order to pay bills on time. As is becoming more common with investors and creditors, our bankers don't trust our proforma income statement and balance sheet. Even though our financial statements are prepared according to GAAP, they can be manipulated."

JACKIE

"Of course they can! But, it's not illegal or unethical to choose one depreciation method over another or make some decisions resulting in our financial statement looking good at the end of the year. What am I really worth if I can't make the financial statements 'sing the song management wants to hear'?"

JULIE

"Yes, you're right. The heart of financial accounting is the accrual concept. It's driven by the matching principle. An income statement matches revenues to the expenses they require, as well as to a certain time period, like a year. It answers the question, 'What are the revenues, costs, and profit from sales this year?' However, the cashflows don't happen at the same time a product is sold or resources are used. *Our bankers think financial control should focus on cashflows and cash management.*

"Look at the balance sheet. We can own a lot of assets and still not be able to pay our bills. Assets include more than cash. In my meeting with them, the bankers weren't too interested in our long-term assets. Instead, they focused on our short-term liquid assets like cash, accounts receivable, and inventory. They were concerned with our bill-paying ability. Too often, customers and businesses alike want credit because they cannot pay their bills immediately. When the bankers looked at our cash budget, the amount of credit I asked for caused more than a little concern. It will surprise you!"

NANCY

"I don't understand. We've done our strategic plan, cost-volume-profit [CVP] analysis, and played our 'what-if' games. Why do we need a cash budget?"

The timing of cashflows is what's really important

JULIE

"Cash management is much more complex than CVP analysis. In our last meeting, changing an assumption, like increasing sales, affected a few lines on our proforma income statement [i.e., revenues, variable costs, contribution margin, and profit]. But, what are the 'ripple effects' on cash? When Bill sells a house, our customers give us only 40% of the sales price. We have to wait three months until the house is completed and delivered before we get another 50%, and then another month for the last 10%. Meanwhile, we have to pay for all the labor and overhead. We also purchase the materials right away and pay for them four months before we finally get paid.

"Our problem is not profits. It's the timing of our cashflows. The longer it takes to get the cash, the greater our bill-paying problems. Surprisingly, when sales increase, we need to borrow more and more cash because of the four-month lag between our cash inflows and outflows."

BILL

"In the home building industry, seasonal sales create another problem. We sell 75% of our homes within the four months between March and June. It's like being a farmer. Farmers need cash in the spring for seed and planting costs. They don't get any cash until the crops are harvested and sold in the late summer or early fall."

JULIE

"Farmers who pay their bills on time are 'solvent.' Those who cannot are insolvent. We need to worry because it looks like Multree Homes must borrow almost $800,000 in the first half of the year. As I see it, we have three choices: start carrying a whole lot of cash all the time, establish a huge line of credit [short-term loans] with the bank, and/or start some serious cash management. Fortunately, working closely with our bankers, we can combine these alternatives.

"First, I've prepared a **cash budget**. It's a report showing our projected timing of cash inflows and outflows based on the proforma income statement we prepared in our last meeting [Chapter 3]. With it, I've documented our plan for spending priorities. This covers only the first two cash management steps, though." [See Exhibit 4-1 for the four steps in the cash management process.]

*The **cash budget** is the output from the cash management planning stage. It presents the cashflows expected for a future time period (e.g., a year) and their timing within that period (e.g., each month).*

Steps in the Cash Management Process

1. Estimate cash inflows.
2. Plan expenditures (cash outflows).
3. Limit spending to budget (cash control).
4. Compare budgeted to actual cashflows (evaluation).

Exhibit 4-1

NANCY

"O.K. I understand the need for a cash budget, but we can't control what happens. There's just too much uncertainty in the world! This idea of performance evaluation also doesn't sound too appealing to me. Do we use budgets to evaluate and reward performance?"

TOMMY

"Of course we do. If we achieve our target profit and generate lots of cash due to good cash planning and control, we reward ourselves. You're going to buy a new car. I'm going skiing at Lake Tahoe for the whole month of December!"

SID

"And I'm going to buy season baseball tickets—a sky box above the dugout, with a wet bar, TV, couch, microwave, and hot tub—if it doesn't get too expensive. Our baseball team also is having cash management problems. You know, the major league teams make about $2 billion in annual revenues. But with player salaries running around 60% of revenues, they average only about a 10% net income. Our team needs around two million ticket sales to break even. With a profit of only $1 million last year, management is concerned about cashflows. A number of teams have lost money, been sold, and moved out of the area.

"Consider the uncertainties. Player salaries are a fixed cost. Ticket sales depend on how well the team is doing, the weather, and competition from other sports. [Should I go to the Toronto Blue Jays or Maple Leafs game tonight? Or worse, the Chicago White Sox, Cubs, Blackhawks, and Bears are all playing at the same time.] Concession sales depend on convention specials or Fathers' days [a lot of beer and brats sold] versus kids days [sell a lot of hot dogs, pennants, hats, and other soft goods] versus family days [sell less, but get a lot of parking revenues]. My point is professional sports have a great deal of uncertainty concerning solvency. Good cash management is critical. In deciding whether we need a cash budget, I think we should ask three questions:

1. How can we achieve our profit goal without a good cash plan?
2. How can we control operations without a cash plan to guide us on a month-to-month basis?
3. How can we evaluate our success without a budget to compare against actual performance?"

JULIE

"Sid's right. About 5% of the staff in large companies is involved in budgeting because of the uncertainties faced in increasingly dynamic, competitive, and international markets. Budgeting is not just an accountant's task. It's an organizational process involving all three management functions: planning, operational control, and performance evaluation. Here's my summary of the relationship between budgeting and the three management functions [see Exhibit 4-2]."

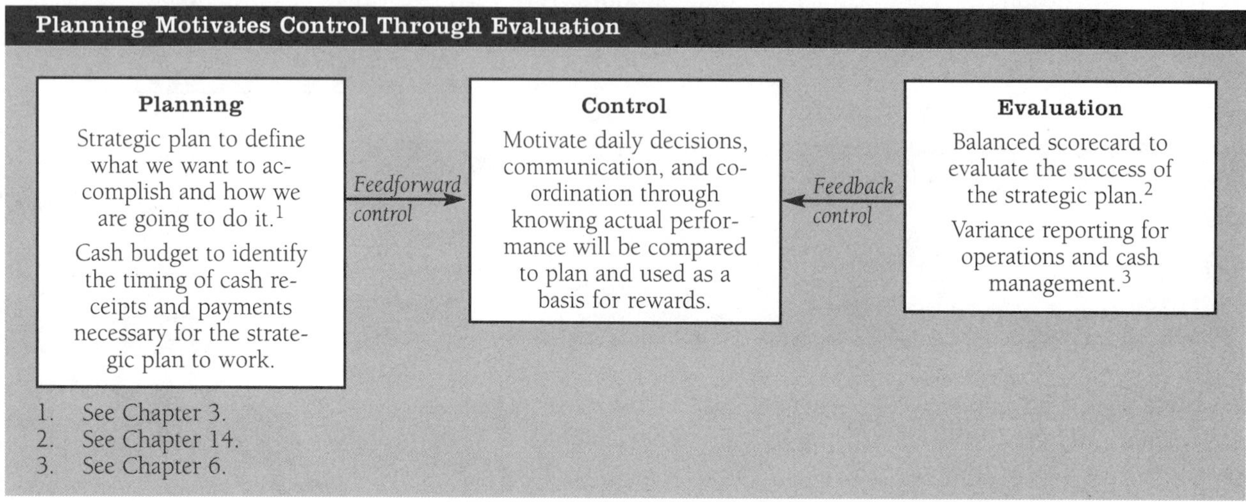

Planning Motivates Control Through Evaluation
Planning
Strategic plan to define what we want to accomplish and how we are going to do it.1
Cash budget to identify the timing of cash receipts and payments necessary for the strategic plan to work.
Feedforward control
Control
Motivate daily decisions, communication, and coordination through knowing actual performance will be compared to plan and used as a basis for rewards.
Feedback control
Evaluation
Balanced scorecard to evaluate the success of the strategic plan.2
Variance reporting for operations and cash management.3
1. See Chapter 3.
2. See Chapter 14.
3. See Chapter 6.

Exhibit 4-2

Budgeting in a Certain World: Brian's College Dilemma

NANCY

"So, are you saying the more uncertainties we face, the greater the need for cash management? I'm not sure I agree! While in college, managing money was hard enough. Having enough cash was almost impossible. My cashflows were very certain, so I had little uncertainty but a strong need for good cash management."

JULIE

"You're right. *While cash budgeting is still necessary, its role is more in control than planning and evaluation.* The government sector is very similar to your college situation. Let's see how cash budgeting works for a college student. I'll use my son's situation as an example [this is a real example and a real budget!]."

"Dear Mom, send cash, hurry!"

JULIE

"Is this a familiar telephone call? Not any more. My son is an undergraduate senior, and I haven't had a phone call like this since he was a freshman. He's a computer science major, so he knows something about spreadsheets. Spreadsheet programs make budgeting a whole lot easier, and allow us to do some of the financial analyses we looked at with CVP in the last meeting [Chapter 3]. Later, I'll show you some games we can play [Appendix A]. Here's Brian's budget for this year [see Exhibit 4-3].

"As soon as Brian receives his financial aid notification, these cash inflows are known with certainty. His first problem is not the amount, but rather the timing, of the cash-ins. School starts in August. financial aid money isn't available until September. His solution is to pay for tuition and books in August with his credit card. He won't have to pay the credit card bill until September. So we decided September will be the first month of his school year for budgeting purposes.

"In budgeting his costs, my first question is, 'What do you spend your money on?' Second, 'How much?' Third, 'When [how often]?' Let's begin with his school costs. Tuition includes per-credit course registration charges [a variable cost] plus

First Draft of Brian's College Budget

	September	October	November	December	January	February	March	April	May	June	July	August	TOTALS
Cash-ins:													
Pell grant	$1,300				$1,300								$2,600
State university grant	800				800								1,600
Scholarships	500												500
Student loans	1,700				3,600								5,300
Total financial aids	$4,300	$0	$0	$0	$5,700	$0	$0	$0	$0	$0	$0	$0	$10,000
Mom and Dad													0
Cash-outs:													
Tuition	(1,200)				(1,200)					(550)			(2,950)
Books	(500)				(500)					(50)			(1,050)
School fees	(100)				(100)					(35)			(235)
Miscellaneous exps	(71)	(71)	(71)	(71)	(71)	(71)	(71)	(71)	(71)	(71)	(71)	(71)	(850)
Living expenses	(1,150)	(1,150)	(1,150)	(1,150)	(1,150)	(1,150)	(1,150)	(1,150)	(1,150)	(1,150)	(1,150)	(1,150)	(13,800)
Beginning cash balance	0	1,279	58	(1,163)	(2,383)	296	(925)	(2,146)	(3,367)	(4,588)	(6,443)	(7,664)	0
Ending cash balance	$1,279	$58	($1,163)	($2,383)	$296	($925)	($2,146)	($3,367)	($4,588)	($6,443)	($7,664)	($8,885)	($8,885)

Notes:

School fees = $35 per semester lab pass + $65 per semester parking + $35 summer parking

Miscellaneous exps = Birthdays 5 @ $50, Christmas 5 @ $50, other 3 @ $50, clothes @ $200

Living expenses:	
Rent	$580
Utilities	45
Cable TV	25
Phone & modem	25
Food	300
Gasoline	30
Car insurance	55
Renter's insurance	20
License plates	8
Miscellaneous exps	62
Total per month	***$1,150***

Exhibit 4-3

fixed costs charged to all students each semester regardless of the number of credits taken. He also has a step cost, the health center fee, which is $60 per semester if enrolled for 15 or less credits, but $100 if more than 15 credits."

"So tuition is really a mixed cost, part fixed and part variable? It looks like you budgeted it as a fixed cost of $1,200 per semester, and $550 for summer. Am I confused?"

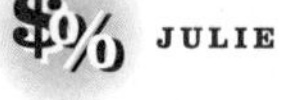

"Of course not. Brian is taking 14 credits per semester and two summer classes, so we know his total course fees [total variable costs]. His relevant range is less than 15 credits, so his health center fee is $60. Adding the other fixed costs, his total tuition bill is $1,200 each semester. The full amount is due the Friday before classes begin. Fortunately, the university takes VISA, MasterCard, and Discover, but not American Express. Sounds like a commercial, huh!

"The next cost is books and supplies. This is variable based on the number of courses, but we have no relevant range, like in business, where books cost the same per credit or class. Each class is different. Based on past experience, we estimated $500 per semester for four classes. The other school fees are fixed costs [the same amount each semester regardless of the number of credits taken]. They are itemized in the Notes section.

"It occurred to me if I want any birthday, anniversary, or Mother's Day presents, I better budget for them! Including postage and a card, we decided $50 per person for birthdays and Christmas was reasonable. We called these 'Miscellaneous expenses.' The 'other 3 @ $50' in the Notes section is Mother's and Father's Days, and our anniversary. I'm only giving him $200 a year for clothes, reminding him he's 'on a budget.' These miscellaneous expenses totaled $850 for the year. [This is a $71 per month average. Notice all amounts are formatted to the nearest dollar in the spreadsheet, so don't expect $71 × 12 months will equal exactly $850. This is not an error in the program. We could have formatted the cells to 10 decimal places, but do you prefer to see $70.8333333333, or $71?]

"Now let's look at Brian's living expenses. As with his school costs, I first thought about which are variable costs and which are fixed costs. I discovered a problem, however. The school costs were classified as variable or fixed based on the number of credits taken. His living expenses were all fixed costs from this perspective, that is, they do not increase or decrease if the number of credits changes. Monthly living expenses do change, though, due to other causes. Consider Brian's utilities bill. Heat is included in his rent. In the summer, his utility bill skyrockets because of air conditioning. His telephone bill is a mixed cost. He pays $15 a month for a student rate with modem. His long-distance charges vary with the number of minutes talked. Gasoline varies with the miles driven. Food is the same every day, but the total cost per month depends on the number of days in each month, and how many days he comes home! Each of these costs change somewhat from month to month. My point is *understanding what causes a cost to change is critical to budgeting. We need a good knowledge of cost behaviors [variable, fixed, mixed, step]*. However, let's be practical. We just budgeted average amounts for the month. Remember the "relevancy" attribute of quality information:

> **"It's more important to be approximately right than precisely wrong."**

"Some of Brian's living expenses are monthly, but some are semiannual or annual. For example, insurance is a semiannual bill, and license plates are an annual bill. If we don't budget for them monthly and actually put that money in his savings account every month, it will not be there when these bills are due. This is an example of the budget's role in operational control. It's Brian's responsibility to save this money every month and be able to pay those bills when due.

"His monthly living costs average $1,088. Remembering 'Murphy's Law' ['What can go wrong, will' or 'If you see a light at the end of the tunnel, it's really a freight train!'], some unbudgeted event always will happen. While he didn't think of this line item, I made it $62, making the monthly total costs equal $1,150. Sure enough, his car needed new brakes in October. Again, we were just being practical in allowing some money for fun and contingencies.

"You've probably noticed the last line in cash-ins, 'Mom and Dad,' is blank. Looking at his ending cash balance in the Totals column, Brian will need $8,885 for the year, in addition to his $10,000 in financial aid, just to break even. The second draft of his cash budget [Exhibit 4-4] has the cash-in from Mom and Dad filled in.

"As painful as this is, it's a simple calculation. We just input $8,885 ÷ 12 months into the September cell and copied it across for all 12 months. Now Brian's ending cash balance is zero. All of his costs are paid for on time throughout the year. We prepared this budget in a couple of hours over a pizza and drinks, which he bought out of his new $62 a month miscellaneous living expenses budget. When I saw the $740 per month he needs from me, I immediately felt the need for many stomach acid pills—of course, it may have been the anchovies, but I doubt it. Then, I realized he can work. If I give him only $500 a month, he will have to earn $240 a month to break even.

"He successfully argued against this, though. In some months he can work more hours but in others he cannot, like November when all his mid-term exams are scheduled, along with a few term papers and computer projects. Adding a new row for work income and inputting the hours, it looked like he would run out of money in December. Besides, a couple of other considerations convinced me he should not work while going to school. I always told my kids I have a responsibility as a parent to put them through school. Second, the better his grades, the more he gets in financial aid and the less I will have to contribute. Third, while the world is different now, those college years were a lot of fun for me. They should be for Brian, too. As it is, all the poor kid does is go to school and study. I remember my university ethic: work hard and party hard—in that order. Brian should have the same responsibility and reward. As long as he gets good grades and practices good cash management, I'll keep writing the checks. His strategic plan has an objective of graduating with a 3.5 cumulative GPA. In the long run, good jobs depend on it! In the short run, good grades get more financial aid."

What do you mean, I have to manage my checkbook?

KEY OBJECTIVE 2

Discuss the usefulness of budgets when cash inflows are known.

"Yes, we could have changed the budget or its assumptions, like eliminate the $62 monthly miscellaneous expenses, or find a cheaper place to live [the dorms or with 5 other 'party animals' in a house], but it would make studying harder and grades lower. Instead, he has to control expenditures. For this to work, he needs a reasonable budget—one he participated in creating and believes to be adequate. *If the budget is not reasonable, controlling costs and evaluating how well he did won't be valid.*

"It's his responsibility to live within this budget, and for two years he's been able to do it. I don't balance his checkbook, or have him give me a formal report comparing budget to actual costs. As long as he lives within the budget, gets good grades, graduates on time, and gets a good job, I see no need to evaluate his performance. His rewards? He can concentrate on his primary objective, a high-

Second Draft of Brian's College Budget

	September	October	November	December	January	February	March	April	May	June	July	August	TOTALS
<u>Cash-ins:</u>													
Pell grant	$1,300				$1,300								$2,600
State university grant	800				800								1,600
Scholarships	500												500
Student loans	1,700				3,600								5,300
Total financial aids	$4,300	$0	$0	$0	$5,700	$0	$0	$0	$0	$0	$0	$0	$10,000
Mom and Dad	740	740	740	740	740	740	740	740	740	740	740	740	8,885
<u>Cash-outs:</u>													
Tuition	(1,200)				(1,200)					(550)			(2,950)
Books	(500)				(500)					(50)			(1,050)
School fees	(100)				(100)					(35)			(235)
Miscellaneous exps	(71)	(71)	(71)	(71)	(71)	(71)	(71)	(71)	(71)	(71)	(71)	(71)	(850)
Living expenses	(1,150)	(1,150)	(1,150)	(1,150)	(1,150)	(1,150)	(1,150)	(1,150)	(1,150)	(1,150)	(1,150)	(1,150)	(13,800)
Beginning cash balance	0	2,020	1,539	1,059	578	3,998	3,518	3,037	2,557	2,076	961	480	0
Ending cash balance	$2,020	$1,539	$1,059	$578	$3,998	$3,518	$3,037	$2,557	$2,076	$961	$480	($0)	$0

<u>Notes:</u>

School fees = $35 per semester lab pass + $65 per semester parking + $35 summer parking

Miscellaneous exps = Birthdays 5 @ $50, Christmas 5 @ $50, other 3 @ $50, clothes @ $200

Living expenses:	
Rent	$580
Utilities	45
Cable TV	25
Phone & modem	25
Food	300
Gasoline	30
Car insurance	55
Renter's insurance	20
License plates	8
Miscellaneous exps	62
Total per month	***$1,150***

Exhibit 4-4

quality education leading to a good job. He had some extra money at the end of the fall semester allowing him and his girlfriend to go skiing at Lake Tahoe for a few days over Christmas break. I didn't ask for the surplus. My rewards? I don't receive any phone calls like, 'Dear Mom, please send money—I haven't eaten in a week!' And I get birthday presents, Christmas presents, and the like."

> **Good cash planning makes operational control easier,**
> **and**
> **good day-to-day control makes performance evaluation easier.**

Budgeting for school is like budgeting for government and nonprofits

"In many respects, Brian's college budget is similar to governmental and nonprofit budgets.

$% JULIE

- For municipalities, a major revenue source is property taxes. As with Brian's financial aid, these types of taxes are pretty well known in advance.
- Often, revenues [cash-ins] do not cause costs. In our business, selling a house causes costs for materials, labor, variable overhead, and selling expenses [the other variable costs, like sales commissions and shipping].
- Governmental and nonprofit organizations often receive a budget allowance based on what can be afforded by the granting authority. The amount received is a resource allocation. A city has to decide how much to spend on police, fire department, garbage collection, parks, and streets. Just like Brian, the receiving organizations have a fiscal responsibility to live within the funds provided, assume certain responsibilities, and achieve their goals.
- Similar to Brian, revenues can be earned from other activities. Brian can get a job. A nonprofit can sell other goods and services. For example, universities generate money from sports ticket sales and concessions.
- Brian's budget process has a similarity to the service sector, too. Brian decided which courses, and how many, to take each year. The courses and their costs drive the revenue needs. In a hospital, the mix of services and their costs drive the charges for those services. It's interesting to see the competition that's developing between hospitals in the same area. They are beginning to specialize based on the cost advantages each can offer for certain services [e.g., cancer treatment, trauma center, and rehabilitation]. Similarly, some universities are beginning to compete for students based on the cost of attending college. Our local university's enrollment is suffering because residents can take courses at home over the television or Internet that are offered by schools in other states.

"Brian's situation, though, differs in some very significant ways from governmental budgets:

- Some governmental entities do not have managerial accountability. They do not have to assess whether the programs the money was spent on actually achieved their objectives. Brian's budget is tied to his grades. Each year he revisits his strategic plan, sets his educational goals for the year, and achieves them. As long as he achieves his annual *quality* goals, I keep writing the monthly checks!
- Some governmental budgets provide a certain amount of money for specific activities. Here's an example. I was asked to make a budgeting presentation to our local college's accounting class last week. I arrived with my computer disk

> planning on a very professional, multimedia presentation. No computer was in the classroom. O.K.—I had a contingency plan. I got out my overhead transparencies, but the bulb was burned out in the projector. It was a night class and no one was available to help me. I was ready, though! I decided I'd just write on the chalkboard. But the chalk tray was empty. A week later I talked to the accounting professor. I had to wait that long because she was in Hawaii at a convention. Evidently, the school had no money for supplies but a lot of money for travel. If they didn't spend the money, they'd lose it. Worse yet, any surplus in the travel budget could not be spent on something else, like classroom supplies. It was then I realized I didn't need to talk to the students. Rather, I needed to make a budgeting presentation to the university administration and state government! Brian's budget is different. If he needs a little more money for one activity, he can use a surplus existing in another activity. The budget is a guide [a plan]. It is not a binding contract that says, 'Thou will not spend more than $45 a month on utilities!' as we too often see with governmental budgets.

The 'spend-it-or-lose-it' game is not limited to the government sector, however. In a recent IMA [Institute of Management Accountants] survey, members reported four reasons to play this game: (1) 33% said next year's budget will be cut, (2) 30% said they received no recognition or reward for beating their budgets, (3) 20% said they would look bad to their boss, and (4) 17% said their boss encouraged them to spend it all."

Budgeting in the Uncertain Business World

NANCY

"While I have a better understanding of how budgets work in the governmental and nonprofit sectors, it seems manufacturing and merchandising firms need more complex budgeting systems. We start with a strategic plan. From our goals, we develop a target profit. We then create cost and profit equations and conduct CVP analyses until we feel comfortable with the plan.

"CVP analysis is important because many costs vary *in total* with sales. As sales volume changes, total variable costs like materials, labor, shipping, and commissions, change. We need to consider our relevant range because the relationship between sales volume and *unit* variable costs can change outside the range *[variable costs per unit do not change within the relevant range]*. *Total fixed costs do not change within the relevant range*, but they can change for sales volumes outside of it. We also assume step costs are either variable or fixed based on whether their total costs change within the relevant range.

"We need to prepare a cash budget because cash inflows are not known with certainty, and we don't receive all the cash when the sale is made. To make matters worse, cash payments for materials, labor, and overhead do not occur at the same time cash from sales is received, and sometimes do not occur when the resources are used. *Understanding the timing of our cashflows is critical to our short-run success [solvency]*. And if we don't survive the short run, we don't need to worry about the long run!"

The cash-to-cash operating cycle

$% JULIE

"In the merchandising, manufacturing, and for-profit service sectors, a cash-to-cash operating cycle exists because sales cause many activities and their costs. This cycle represents when cash is received and paid due to selling a product or providing a service. Knowing this cycle and our sales forecast, we can prepare our annual cash budget. [Exhibit 4-5 shows this cycle as a timeline. It is a value chain of the cash-related activities created by a sale.]

The Cash-to-Cash Operating Cycle for Multree's Standard Homes

Cashflows	Month 1	Month 2	Month 3	Month 4	Month 5
Cash-ins:	Make sale and collect a 40% down payment.			Deliver house and collect 50% of sales price.	Collect the last 10% of the sales price.
Cash-outs:	• Buy all of the direct materials, pay 1/2 this month. • Pay for 1/3 of the direct labor and variable overhead. • Pay monthly fixed overhead. • Pay sales commission.	• Pay for 1/2 of direct materials. • Pay for 1/3 of the direct labor and variable overhead. • Pay monthly fixed overhead.	• Pay for 1/3 of the direct labor and variable overhead. • Pay monthly fixed overhead.	• Pay monthly fixed overhead. • Pay shipping cost.	• Pay monthly fixed overhead.

Exhibit 4-5

"Just to give you a quick overview, it takes three months to make a house. We sign a sales order in Month 1, receive a 40% down payment, buy all the materials—paying half this month and half next month, and pay the sales commission. For each of the three months needed to build a house, we pay for the labor and variable overhead. So we pay ⅓ of a house's total labor and variable overhead each month. The fixed overhead is paid every month. When we finish the house in Month 4, it is shipped to the customer. We pay the shipping cost and collect ½ of the sales price upon delivery. A month later [Month 5] we collect the last 10% of the sales price.

"Obviously, cash budgeting becomes more valuable when products become more complex and the environment becomes more uncertain. I've listed some factors affecting the importance of cash budgeting [see Exhibit 4-6].

"To show you the details, let's look at each activity in order:

- Making the sale and projecting the cash receipts [Exhibits 4-7, 8, and 9].
- Scheduling production for a manufacturer, or merchandise purchases for distributors and retailers [Exhibits 4-10 and 11].
- Purchasing direct materials [Exhibits 4-12 and 13].
- Building the house [budgeting for the labor and overhead costs, Exhibit 4-14].
- Paying for other operating expenses [Exhibit 4-15].
- Putting it all together into a cash budget [Exhibit 4-16].

Throughout the rest of this meeting, let's look at each schedule in order."

Translating sales into cash

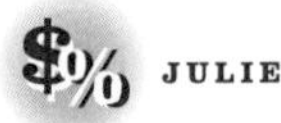

"Our proforma income statement is the starting point for cash budgeting. The first step creates a monthly sales forecast from the income statement's annual sales

The Value of Cash Budgeting

Factors increasing the value of cash budgeting	Factors decreasing the value of cash budgeting
↑ Scarce or expensive resources: money, materials, labor, etc.	↓ Abundance of resources: lots of money in the bank, many available workers, etc.
↑ Long manufacturing or delivery times.	↓ Short cash-to-cash operating cycle.
↑ High operating uncertainty: unreliable suppliers, unskilled or unmotivated workers, poorly maintained machinery, etc.	↓ Highly reliable operating environment.
↑ Complexity and variety: many different types of products or services, customers, or activities.	↓ Little product or activity variety.

Exhibit 4-6

KEY OBJECTIVE 3

Prepare a schedule for cash collections from sales.

volume. Every organization has a different sales pattern, resulting in different sales volumes from month to month. Hotels have more rooms occupied in the summer months. Airlines also have more passengers in the summer and during the holidays. Banks make most of their real estate loans in the summer, but most of their consumer loans in the winter. Brian's budget shows financial aid coming in twice a year. Many governmental operations only receive cash once at the beginning of the year. Many manufacturing and merchandising firms have seasonal patterns. Our sales forecast is very seasonal—most people do not buy houses in the winter, thus we do not build them during the winter. Most of our standard homes are sold to dealers. These sales begin in January, so the dealers have homes in stock when their customers are ready to buy starting in the spring. Custom homes, though, are usually sold to individuals during the summer. Bill developed a monthly sales forecast based on our proforma income statement. The sales forecast is simply our sales volume for each month. [This is the top section in Exhibit 4-7.]

"Units sold are converted into dollars [revenues] in the Sales revenues section. For example, in June we project selling 10 standard homes and 2 custom homes. Each standard home's sales price is $50,000. June sales revenues from standard homes are $500,000 [10 homes × $50,000 each]. Similarly, the revenues from custom home sales in June are $200,000 [2 homes × $100,000 each].

"The Cash collections section calculates when the cash will be collected from the revenues we project each month. Referring back to the cash collection timeline [Exhibit 4-5], we collect 40% in the month of sale, 50% three months later, and the last 10% four months after the sale. This is called a **credit collection pattern**. We can use our credit collection pattern to determine when the cash will be collected from January sales [see Exhibit 4-8 on p. 110].

A **credit collection pattern** *shows the percentage of a month's credit sales to be collected in each subsequent month.*

"We project 5 standard homes sold in January at $50,000 each [total revenues = $250,000]. In the month these houses are sold [January] we will collect 40% of the revenues [40% × $250,000 = $100,000]. When we complete the house and deliver it [three months later in April] we'll receive the balance of the revenues, less 10%. In other words, we'll collect 50% of January revenues in April [50% × $250,000 = $125,000]. We don't ask for the last 10% until a month after the customer has received the house. This is protection to our customers in case some quality problems result which we do not fix. The last 10% of revenues for houses sold

Multree Homes Monthly Sales and Cash Collections Schedule

Sales forecast:	Jan	Feb	Mar	Apr	May	Jun	Jul	Aug	Sep	Oct	Nov	Dec	Totals
Standard homes	5	10	20	20	25	10	5	5	0	0	0	0	100
Custom homes	0	0	2	2	4	2	0	0	0	0	0	0	10
Sales revenues:													
Standard homes ($50,000 each)	$250,000	$500,000	$1,000,000	$1,000,000	$1,250,000	$500,000	$250,000	$250,000	$0	$0	$0	$0	$5,000,000
Custom homes ($100,000 each)	0	0	200,000	200,000	400,000	200,000	0	0	0	0	0	0	1,000,000
Total sales revenues	**$250,000**	**$500,000**	**$1,200,000**	**$1,200,000**	**$1,650,000**	**$700,000**	**$250,000**	**$250,000**	**$0**	**$0**	**$0**	**$0**	**$6,000,000**
Cash collections:													
40% in the month of sale	$100,000	$200,000	$480,000	$480,000	$660,000	$280,000	$100,000	$100,000	$0	$0	$0	$0	$2,400,000
50% three months later				125,000	250,000	600,000	600,000	825,000	350,000	125,000	125,000	0	3,000,000
10% four months later					25,000	50,000	120,000	120,000	165,000	70,000	25,000	25,000	600,000
Total cash deposits from sales	$100,000	$200,000	$480,000	$605,000	$935,000	$930,000	$820,000	$1,045,000	$515,000	$195,000	$150,000	$25,000	$6,000,000

Exhibit 4-7

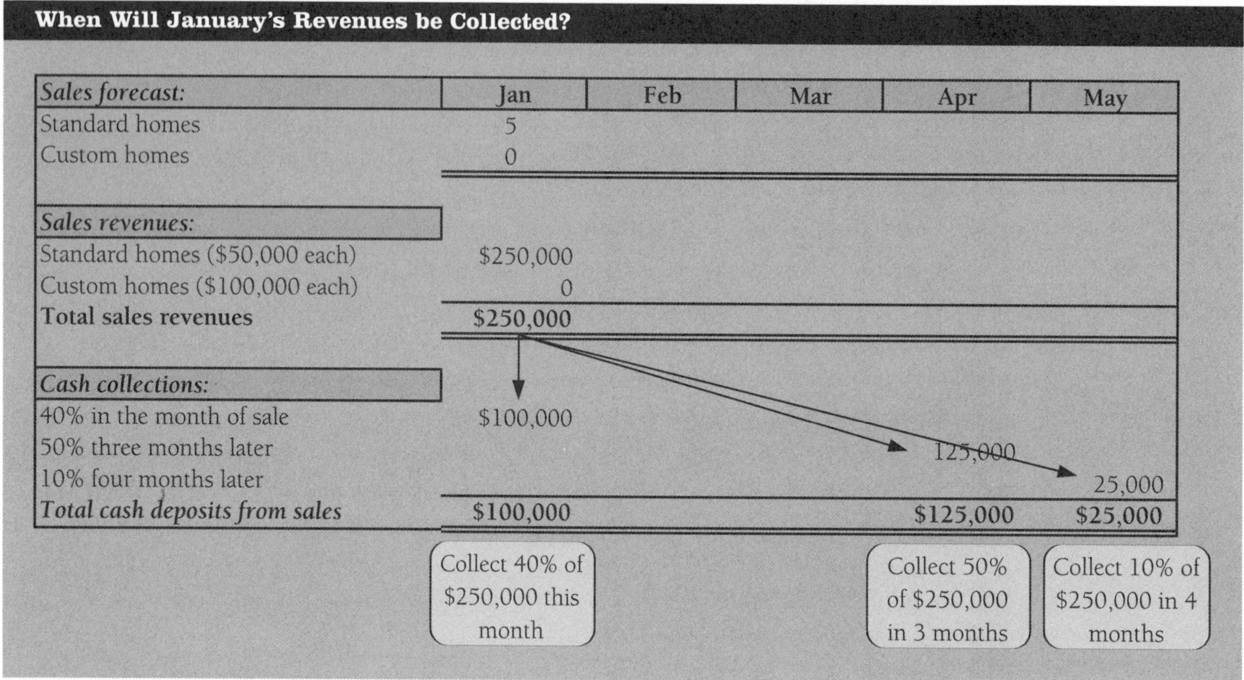

When Will January's Revenues be Collected?

Sales forecast:	Jan	Feb	Mar	Apr	May
Standard homes	5				
Custom homes	0				
Sales revenues:					
Standard homes ($50,000 each)	$250,000				
Custom homes ($100,000 each)	0				
Total sales revenues	**$250,000**				
Cash collections:					
40% in the month of sale	$100,000				
50% three months later				125,000	
10% four months later					25,000
Total cash deposits from sales	**$100,000**			**$125,000**	**$25,000**

Exhibit 4-8

in January won't be received until May [10% × $250,000 = $25,000]. [Exhibit 4-8 illustrates January collections. Go back to Exhibit 4-7 and repeat this process for each month. When you get to June, we'll collect 40% of June's $700,000 revenues (i.e., $280,000) that month, 50% of June revenues three months later in September (50% × $700,000 = $350,000 in the second line of September), and the last 10% in October (10% × $700,000 = $70,000 in that month's column, the third line).]

"This may be clearer if we change our focus from answering the question, 'When will a month's revenues be collected?' to 'How much will we deposit in any month?' In each month we will deposit 40% of that month's revenues, plus 50% of the revenues from sales made three months earlier, plus 10% of the revenues from sales four months ago. [Exhibit 4-9 illustrates May's cash collections.]

"Many companies offer their own credit plans. For example, furniture retailers may allow you to buy at Christmas and not pay for the furniture until May. Manufacturers offer credit terms to their customers, too [e.g., distributors and retailers]. Common credit terms like '2/15, net 30' mean if the customer pays within 15 days he can take a 2% discount, otherwise the entire bill is due in 30 days. Well, 15 days is about one-half of a month. Assume all customers pay in time to take the discount. Everyone buying products in the first half of the month [the first 15 days] will pay in the second half of the month. Customers buying products in the last half of the month will pay in the first half of the next month [within 15 days of the purchase] and take their 2% discount. The credit collection pattern is 98% of ½ of the month's revenues will be collected in that month, and 98% of ½ of the month's revenues will be collected in the following month.

"Credit collection patterns can get complicated for some retailers who have their own credit cards, like Sears. Consider the following hypothetical sales and credit sales pattern:

How Much Cash Will We Deposit in May?

Credit collection pattern	Month of sale	Sales revenues (a)	Percent collected this month (b)	Cash collected this month (a x b)
40% this month	May	$1,650,000	40%	$660,000
50% from three months ago	February	$500,000	50%	250,000
10% from four months ago	January	$250,000	10%	25,000
Cash collected in May			100%	$935,000

Exhibit 4-9

Type of sale	Percentages		Other terms
Cash	**20%**		
External credit cards (e.g., VISA)	**50%**		**Less 5% fee charged by the credit card company**
Sears credit card:	**30%**		
Collected in month of sale		**20%**	
Collected in following month		**50%**	
Collected two months late		**15%**	**+ 18% interest charged on Sears card**
Collected three months late		**10%**	**+ 18% interest charged on Sears card × 2 months**
Never collected		**5%**	
Totals	**100%**	**100%**	

What will be collected in any month?

1. 20% of that month's sales [cash sales],
2. 50% of that month's sales × 95% [external credit card sales less the 5% fee],
3. 30% of that month's sales × 20% [Sears card sales collected in the same month],
4. 30% of the previous month's sales × 50% [Sears card sales from last month collected this month],
5. 30% of sales from two months ago × 15% × 118% [Sears card sales from two months ago collected this month plus interest], and
6. 30% of sales from three months ago × 10% × 118% × 2 [Sears card sales from three months ago collected this month plus two months' simple interest].

Because the cash deposited into the bank for any month can come from six different sources, this is a calculation best left to a spreadsheet program!

"Considering the complexity, uncertainty, and extra costs created by offering credit, many retailers [especially small businesses] do not provide their own credit cards [unless the interest charged more than covers the extra financing costs; in other words, unless they make a profit on their own credit cards]. When a firm only accepts cash, checks, or external credit cards, its collection pattern looks like:

- Collect all cash sales in the month of sale,

- Collect all sales paid for by customers' checks in that month, less an allowance for bad debts, and
- Collect all credit card sales in the same month, less the fee charged by the credit card company."

KEY OBJECTIVE 4

Develop operating budgets (schedules for purchases, labor, overhead, and operating expenses).

Using budgets to coordinate operations

"Using our sales forecast, we need to coordinate with our operations people so the sales forecast will be achieved. In other words, they have to be able to meet the sales forecast. This means everyone has to work together in preparing budgets for material purchases and use, labor, overhead support, and operating expenses. With these detailed budgets, everyone knows what's expected. So, where do we begin?"

Production and merchandise purchases schedules. "Manufacturers begin by transforming the sales forecast into a **production schedule**. Its purpose is to determine how many products must be made each month in order to achieve the sales forecast. The number of products to be made is called a **production quota**."

"I don't understand why we need a production quota. If we plan on selling 100 products in a month, shouldn't we produce 100 products? Shouldn't the production quota be the same as the sales forecast?"

"Oh no! When I worked for a shoe company, the number of shoes made each month always differed from the number sold. To encourage customers to come into the store and buy shoes, we maintained large retail shelf inventories [finished goods inventories]. If we didn't have any shoes on the shelf, customers wouldn't come in the store! Multree Homes customers are different. They will buy a house and then are willing to wait months to get it. For many other products, like shoes, customers want them now. They are not willing to wait for them to be made."

"Of course this may be changing for many products. With the increase in mail/phone order and Internet sales, growing numbers of consumers are willing to wait for products. Companies fortunate enough to be able to make products within the time period customers are willing to wait, like us, do not need to carry significant finished goods inventories. Look back at Multree's proforma income statement we developed in the last meeting [Exhibit 3-1]. We don't need any finished goods [completed product] inventories. We build to order."

"Yes! A similar phenomenon is called 'just-in-time retailing.' One reason Wal-Mart is able to offer low prices on national brand products is its links with suppliers. Suppliers, such as Wrangler Jeans, are linked via computers to Wal-Mart's POS system [point-of-sale cash registers and sales programs]. Because Wrangler knows when and where a pair of jeans is sold by Wal-Mart, it can be replaced within just a few days, without the need for Wal-Mart to maintain large warehouse inventories. Recognizing its customers are willing to wait for their goods if they can order over the Internet, Wal-Mart now has over 10,000 products on its Web site.

> *A* **production quota** *is the number of products to make in order to satisfy the sales forecast. The operating budget which calculates production quotas for each period (e.g., a month) is called a* **production schedule.**

"If a company can make a product within the time a customer is willing to wait, it can eliminate its inventories through just-in-time [JIT] manufacturing. However, for most merchandisers and manufacturers, finished goods inventories are necessary for three reasons:

- Retail shelf inventory is needed to promote sales.
- Sales forecasts are only estimates. If actual sales exceed budget, we better have the inventory to allow it!

• Production and delivery may be unreliable. Inventories provide protection against unforeseen events, such as receiving delays or machine breakdowns.

As with the shoe company, these companies 'produce for inventory.' For example, assume we plan 100 shoe sales this month. To do this, we need a 10% retail shelf inventory [10 shoes]. But if we have 10 shoes in inventory at the beginning of the month, we need to make only 90 more shoes to achieve our sales forecast."

"Well, it's really a little more complicated than that. If we make only 90 shoes, no shoes will be available for retail shelf inventory at the end of the month. With no inventory, will we be able to sell any shoes next month? Logically then, we need to:

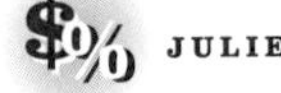

1. Make enough shoes for this month's sales [100 sales forecast less 10 products in beginning inventory], and
2. Make enough shoes to replenish the inventory so we can continue selling shoes next month [for example, to support next month's sales forecast of 200 shoes, we need 20 shoes in this month's ending inventory].

"The formula then becomes:

Production Quota Formula

Production quota = Sales forecast – Beginning inventory + Desired ending inventory

The merchandise purchases schedule shows: (1) the cost of products which have to be bought in order to meet the sales forecast, and (2) when purchases will be paid for.

"Manufacturers prepare a production schedule. Merchandisers [wholesale distributors and retailers] prepare a similar merchandise purchases schedule. Instead of computing how many products to make, merchandisers calculate how much merchandise to buy. Both schedules satisfy the same goal: determining how much will be needed to meet the sales forecast. Manufacturers make products, so they calculate the number of products to make. Merchandisers buy products, so they calculate the dollar value of products to buy. Whether the schedule is prepared in units of product or dollars, the formula is the same.

"The good news is we do not need to learn a new formula for calculating purchases or the production quota. It is just the cost of goods sold calculation used in the income statement for financial accounting. The logic is to solve this formula for purchases. On the income statement, the numbers are dollars. 'Purchases' is the dollars [cost] of merchandise to buy. If we change the numbers from dollars to products, 'purchases' becomes 'production quota' [the number of products to make]. [Exhibit 4-10 demonstrates this using these same simple numbers.]

"Since we want to budget monthly, let me show you how these schedules work with multiple months [Exhibit 4-11 on p. 115]. We need to look at only two months in order to demonstrate the calculations.

"The top half of the exhibit shows the production schedule. The only data we need is the monthly sales forecast and the desired beginning inventory. We save a calculation because this month's ending inventory is also next month's beginning inventory. So once we've calculated January's desired ending inventory, it also becomes February's beginning inventory. [February sales of 200 shoes × 10% = 20 shoes for January's ending inventory, which also is February's beginning inventory. Arrow 'a' shows this in the top half of Exhibit 4-11.] February's ending inventory is March's beginning inventory [March sales of 400 shoes × 10%].

"The totals column is a little tricky. Remember, it is the total of January and February. The time period for the totals column starts on January 1 and ends on

The Merchandise Purchases and Production Schedules

Cost of goods sold section of the income statement	
Beginning inventory	$10
+ Purchases	110
Cost of goods available for sale	$120
Less: ending inventory	(20)
Cost of goods sold	$100

Merchandise Purchases Schedule Merchandisers: solve for purchases (in dollars)	
Cost of goods sold	$100
Less: beginning inventory	(10)
Cost of goods needed for sales	$90
+ Ending inventory	20
Purchases	$110

Production Schedule Manufacturers: solve for production quota (in units)	
Sales forecast	100 products
Less: beginning inventory	(10) products
Products needed for sales	90 products
+ Ending inventory	20 products
Production quota	110 products

Exhibit 4-10

Monthly Production and Merchandise Purchases Schedules

Production schedule

Data section:		January	February	March
Sales forecast (product volume)		100	200	400
Beginning inventory	10%	of this month's sales volume (in units)		

Production Schedule

Production quota	Formulas	January Calculations	January Amounts	February Calculations	February Amounts	Totals
Sales forecast		=	100	=	200	300
Less: beginning inventory	10% of this month's sales	10% x 100 =	(10)	10% x 200 =	(20)	(10)
Products needed for sales			90		180	290
+ Ending inventory	10% of next month's sales	10% x 200 =	20	10% x 400 =	40	40
Production quota			110 units		220 units	330

(Arrows: a — January ending inventory 20 → February beginning inventory (20); b — January beginning inventory (10) → Totals; c — February ending inventory 40 → Totals.)

Merchandise purchases

Data section:	Dec	January	February	March
Sales revenues	$100	$125	$250	$500
Cost of goods sold (COGS) ratio	80%	of revenues		
Beginning inventory	10%	of this month's sales at cost		
Payment schedule	50%	this month, and	50%	next month

Merchandise Purchases Schedule

Merchandise purchases:	Formulas	January Calculations	January Amounts	February Calculations	February Amounts	Totals
Cost of goods sold	Revenues x COGS ratio	$125 x 80% =	$100	$250 x 80% =	$200	$300
Less: beginning inventory	10% of this month's COGS	10% x $100 =	(10)	10% x $200 =	(20)	(10)
Cost of goods needed for sales			$90		$180	$290
+ Ending inventory	10% of next month's COGS	10% x $200 =	20	10% x $400 =	40	40
Purchases			$110		$220	$330
Payment schedule:						
To pay this month	Given percentage x purchases	50% x $110 =	$55	50% x $220 =	$110	
To pay from last month	Given percentage x purchases	50% x $82 =	41	50% x $110 =	55	
Total cash-outs for purchases			$96		$165	$261

(Arrows: a — January ending inventory → February beginning inventory; b — January beginning inventory → Totals; c — February ending inventory → Totals; d — January purchases $110 → February "to pay from last month".)

Exhibit 4-11

February 28. Thus the beginning inventory is the January 1 inventory [arrow 'b'], which we already have calculated. Similarly, the totals column ending inventory is the February ending inventory [arrow 'c']. Also note only two lines add across into the totals column: sales forecast and production quota.

"We need some more information to prepare a merchandise purchases schedule. Sales revenues are the sales prices paid by our customers. *Since we want to know how much to buy, revenues have to be converted into our cost to buy these products [i.e., cost of goods sold].* This 'retail sales dollars-to-cost' conversion calculates cost of goods sold [COGS] using the following formula:

Converting Sales to Cost of Goods Sold (COGS)

Cost of goods sold	=	**Revenues**	×	**COGS ratio**
January COGS	=	**$125**	×	**80%**
	=	**$100**		

An 80% cost of goods sold ratio means, on average, every dollar of sales costs us 80¢ to buy that merchandise. Forecasting $125 in January sales revenues, we will need to buy $100 in merchandise. We want 10% of this merchandise on our retail shelves as beginning inventory. [January beginning inventory = $100 COGS × 10% beginning inventory requirement = $10 *at cost*. Arrows 'a,' 'b,' and 'c' are repeated from the top half of Exhibit 4-11 to illustrate the remaining calculations are the same as in the production schedule.] The only difference is the production schedule is prepared in units of product, but merchandise purchases are calculated in dollars.

"*Calculating merchandise purchases [$110 at cost in January, and $220 in February] answers the question, 'How much should we buy each month?' The cashflow question is, 'When will we have to pay for it?'* So we need two sections for the merchandise purchases schedule. The top section budgets merchandise purchases each month, using the same format as in the production schedule. The bottom section determines when we write the checks. Assume we pay for one-half of our purchases in the month received, and the remainder in the next month. [This is shown using arrow 'd.'] Notice we're paying $41 in January for the last half of December purchases. December purchases equal $82 [$100 in revenues × 80% COGS ratio = $80 COGS, less $8 in beginning inventory @ 10%, plus $10 for ending December inventory, which equals January's beginning inventory]."

NANCY

"Let's see if I can sum up." Everyone chuckled at her pun. "When manufacturers need to prepare a production schedule [or when merchandisers need a purchases schedule]:

- With JIT manufacturing, we can make products while customers wait. We won't need any ending inventory and the production quota equals the sales forecast. Similarly, if merchandisers can obtain and deliver products while their customers wait [JIT purchasing and delivery], they won't need any ending inventory. So, merchandise purchases equal cost of goods sold. Production [or purchases] schedules are not needed in JIT situations.

- If a manufacturer or merchandiser maintains a stable inventory level each month, production quota and sales forecast will be the same [purchases equal cost of goods sold for the merchandiser]. This is what happened at the shoe company. The retail store shelves were always full regardless of next month's sales forecast. Production [or purchases] schedules are not needed in these situations, either, because beginning and ending inventories each month do not change even though sales may change from month to month.

- If companies maintain ending inventories that change every month depending on the next month's sales forecast, production or purchases schedules will be needed.
- Some other situations also require these schedules. For example, sales orders are taken in one month but production is not started until a later month, depending on the particular customer order. Here again, production in a particular month is not for the same products sold in that month."

Direct materials purchases schedule. "Merchandisers purchase finished products. Manufacturers have to make them from materials, labor, and overhead. So manufacturers need to prepare schedules for each of these resources. The amount of resources needed, their costs, and when we pay the bills all are determined by the production quota. At Multree Homes, we start building a house in the month it is ordered. If we sell five homes in January, we'll buy all the direct materials and start building them in January. Our sales forecast equals our production quota.

$% JULIE

"Just like with merchandise purchases, we want to know: 'How much to buy each month?' and 'When to pay for it?' Buying materials is just like a retailer buying merchandise. Thus the direct materials purchases schedule I prepared uses the same logic, format, and formulas as the merchandise purchases schedule. [See Exhibit 4-12.]

"We start with the production quota and compute how much direct materials are needed to achieve it. We budget $15,500 for each standard home and $26,250 for each custom home. Let's walk through the calculations for June:

	Production quota for June	Direct materials budgeted per house	Total budgeted Direct materials cost per month
Standard homes	**10 homes**	**$15,500 per house**	**$155,000**
Custom homes	**2 homes**	**$26,250 per house**	**52,500**
Total direct materials needed for production quota			**$207,500**

[Exhibit 4-13 on p. 119 looks at the relevant numbers for June from the monthly budget in Exhibit 4-12.]

"As we did with the production and merchandise purchases schedules, assume we want a 10% beginning inventory. This allows some materials to be available at the beginning of next month, and as a safeguard [buffer] against supplier delivery delays and bad materials. June's beginning materials inventory should be $20,750 [$207,500 needed for the production quota × 10% beginning inventory requirement]. June's ending materials inventory should be 10% of July's materials needed [$77,500 needed in July × 10% beginning inventory requirement]. The payment schedule is just like the one for merchandise purchases [Exhibit 4-11].

"Each month is calculated in the same way." [Try a few to make sure you understand how the monthly program works in Exhibit 4-12. Some other information you need: on January 1, $10,000 is in beginning materials inventory. For the end of the year, we're going to increase this to a $25,000 December 31 ending

Multree Homes Direct Materials Purchases and Payments Schedule

Production quota	Jan	Feb	Mar	Apr	May	Jun	Jul	Aug	Sep	Oct	Nov	Dec	Totals
Standard homes	5	10	20	20	25	10	5	5	0	0	0	0	100
Custom homes	0	0	2	2	4	2	0	0	0	0	0	0	10
Direct materials needed													
Standard homes ($15,500 each)	$77,500	$155,000	$310,000	$310,000	$387,500	$155,000	$77,500	$77,500	$0	$0	$0	$0	$1,550,000
Custom homes ($26,250 each)	0	0	52,500	52,500	105,000	52,500	0	0	0	0	0	0	262,500
Total DM needed for quota	**$77,500**	**$155,000**	**$362,500**	**$362,500**	**$492,500**	**$207,500**	**$77,500**	**$77,500**	**$0**	**$0**	**$0**	**$0**	**$1,812,500**
Less: beginning DM inventory (10%)	(10,000)	(15,500)	(36,250)	(36,250)	(49,250)	(20,750)	(7,750)	(7,750)	0	0	0	0	(10,000)
Total DM needed for production	$67,500	$139,500	$326,250	$326,250	$443,250	$186,750	$69,750	$69,750	$0	$0	$0	$0	$1,802,500
+ Desired ending DM inventory (10%)	15,500	36,250	36,250	49,250	20,750	7,750	7,750	0	0	0	0	25,000	25,000
Direct materials to purchase	**$83,000**	**$175,750**	**$362,500**	**$375,500**	**$464,000**	**$194,500**	**$77,500**	**$69,750**	**$0**	**$0**	**$0**	**$25,000**	**$1,827,500**
Payment schedule													
Pay 1/2 this month	$41,500	$87,875	$181,250	$187,750	$232,000	$97,250	$38,750	$34,875	$0	$0	$0	$12,500	$913,750
Pay 1/2 from last month	5,000	41,500	87,875	181,250	187,750	232,000	97,250	38,750	34,875	0	0	0	906,250
Cash-out for DM purchases	**$46,500**	**$129,375**	**$269,125**	**$369,000**	**$419,750**	**$329,250**	**$136,000**	**$73,625**	**$34,875**	**$0**	**$0**	**$12,500**	**$1,820,000**

Exhibit 4-12

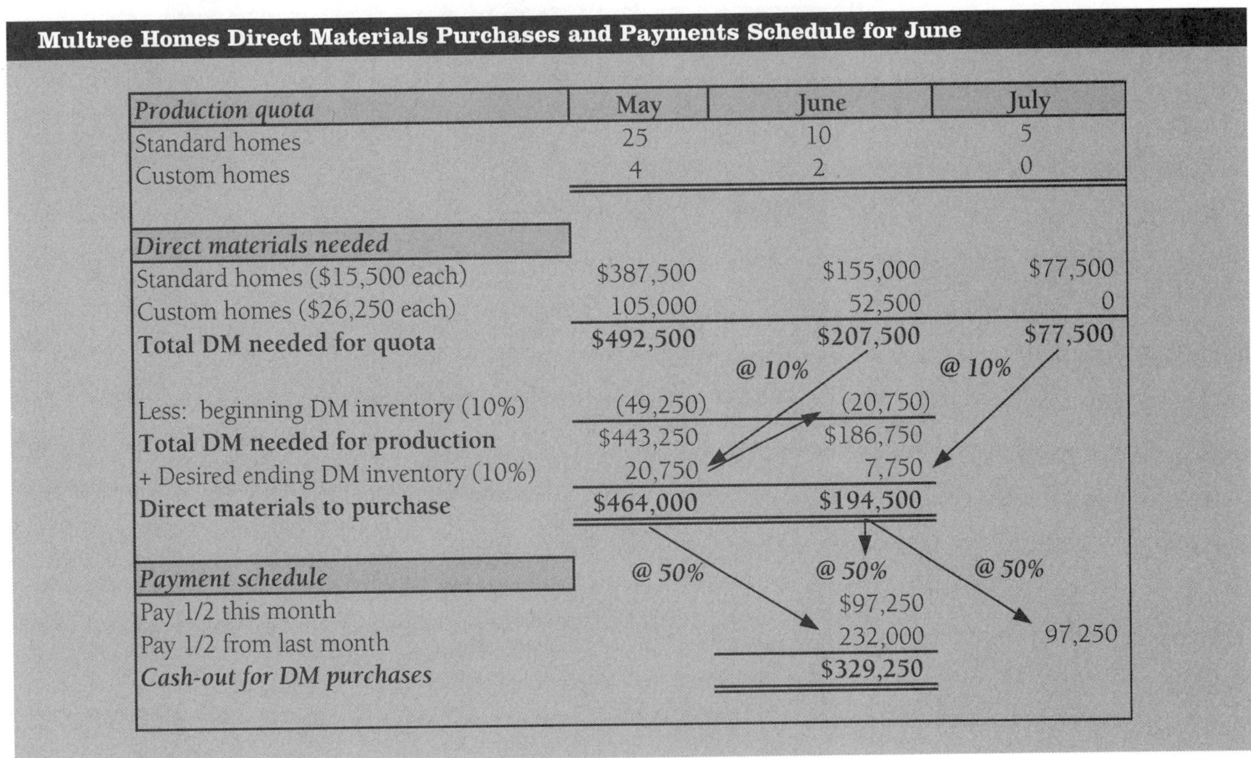

Multree Homes Direct Materials Purchases and Payments Schedule for June

Production quota	May	June	July
Standard homes	25	10	5
Custom homes	4	2	0
Direct materials needed			
Standard homes ($15,500 each)	$387,500	$155,000	$77,500
Custom homes ($26,250 each)	105,000	52,500	0
Total DM needed for quota	**$492,500**	**$207,500**	**$77,500**
		@ 10%	@ 10%
Less: beginning DM inventory (10%)	(49,250)	(20,750)	
Total DM needed for production	$443,250	$186,750	
+ Desired ending DM inventory (10%)	20,750	7,750	
Direct materials to purchase	**$464,000**	**$194,500**	
Payment schedule	@ 50%	@ 50%	@ 50%
Pay 1/2 this month		$97,250	
Pay 1/2 from last month		232,000	97,250
Cash-out for DM purchases		**$329,250**	

Exhibit 4-13

materials inventory. Also remember, these amounts are used as the beginning and ending inventories in the totals column.]

Direct labor and overhead schedule. "Next we'll schedule labor and budget for labor and overhead costs. Start in the same way as we did with direct materials. First, calculate the labor and variable overhead needed for the production quota. For example, labor is budgeted at $10,000 for a standard home, with variable overhead another $2,000. In January we'll start 5 standard homes. Budget $60,000 for January's direct labor and variable overhead [$12,000 labor and overhead × 5 standard homes]. [This is done in the top two sections of Exhibit 4-14.]

"It takes three months to build a house. For simplicity, let's assume we use an equal amount of labor and overhead each month. So, for the five houses started in January, their $60,000 in direct labor [DL] and variable overhead [VOH] will be spent at the rate of $20,000 per month. You can see this payment stream in the 'DL and VOH payments schedule' [$20,000 in January's line 1, $20,000 in February's line 2, and $20,000 in March's line 3].

"The last section adds fixed overhead. Factory supervisors are paid monthly [$16,667 in total each month]. Heat and light is about the same every month, averaging $10,000 a year [$833 per month]. Architectural costs for standard homes involve any changes we want to make in next year's products. We do these design changes in October and pay for them in November. $10,000 is budgeted for standard home architectural changes. Each custom home is somewhat unique, so we budget $10,000 in architectural costs per custom home. These costs are incurred in the month we sign the sale order. We're planning to sell and start four custom homes in May. You'll see $40,000 budgeted for architectural costs in the fixed overhead section.

Multree Homes Direct Labor and Overhead Schedule

Production quota	Jan	Feb	Mar	Apr	May	Jun	Jul	Aug	Sep	Oct	Nov	Dec	Totals
Standard homes	5	10	20	20	25	10	5	5	0	0	0	0	100
Custom homes	0	0	2	2	4	2	0	0	0	0	0	0	10
Direct labor needed													
Standard homes ($10,000 each)	$50,000	$100,000	$200,000	$200,000	$250,000	$100,000	$50,000	$50,000	$0	$0	$0	$0	$1,000,000
Custom homes ($25,000 each)	0	0	50,000	50,000	100,000	50,000	0	0	0	0	0	0	250,000
Total direct labor needed	**$50,000**	**$100,000**	**$250,000**	**$250,000**	**$350,000**	**$150,000**	**$50,000**	**$50,000**	**$0**	**$0**	**$0**	**$0**	**$1,250,000**
Variable overhead needed													
Standard homes ($2,000 each)	$10,000	$20,000	$40,000	$40,000	$50,000	$20,000	$10,000	$10,000	$0	$0	$0	$0	$200,000
Custom homes ($5,750 each)	0	0	11,500	11,500	23,000	11,500	0	0	0	0	0	0	57,500
Total VOH needed	**$10,000**	**$20,000**	**$51,500**	**$51,500**	**$73,000**	**$31,500**	**$10,000**	**$10,000**	**$0**	**$0**	**$0**	**$0**	**$257,500**
DL and VOH payment schedule													
Pay 1/3 this month	$20,000	$40,000	$100,500	$100,500	$141,000	$60,500	$20,000	$20,000	$0	$0	$0	$0	$502,500
Pay 1/3 from last month		20,000	40,000	100,500	100,500	141,000	60,500	20,000	20,000	0	0	0	502,500
Pay 1/3 from two months ago			20,000	40,000	100,500	100,500	141,000	60,500	20,000	20,000	0	0	502,500
Cash-out for DL and VOH	**$20,000**	**$60,000**	**$160,500**	**$241,000**	**$342,000**	**$302,000**	**$221,500**	**$100,500**	**$40,000**	**$20,000**	**$0**	**$0**	**$1,507,500**
Fixed overhead costs													
Supervision	$16,667	$16,667	$16,667	$16,667	$16,667	$16,667	$16,667	$16,667	$16,667	$16,667	$16,667	$16,667	$200,000
Heat & light	833	833	833	833	833	833	833	833	833	833	833	833	10,000
Architectural	0	0	20,000	20,000	40,000	20,000	0	0	0	0	10,000	0	110,000
Cash-out for fixed overhead	**$17,500**	**$17,500**	**$37,500**	**$37,500**	**$57,500**	**$37,500**	**$17,500**	**$17,500**	**$17,500**	**$17,500**	**$27,500**	**$17,500**	**$320,000**

Exhibit 4-14

"Oh, you also must remember a 'trick' in budgeting fixed overhead. Factory building and equipment depreciation usually is part of the fixed overhead budget in proforma income statements. We don't write checks to pay for depreciation, though. It is a noncash cost. Depreciation is just an annual allocation of previously paid costs to buy the plant and equipment. *Because we are not really paying for it now, depreciation is not included in the cash budget.* If we're going to buy equipment or other assets creating depreciation expenses in future periods, we'll budget for those expenditures when they occur [this will be discussed with Exhibit 4-16]."

Operating expenses schedule. "O.K. We've budgeted manufacturing costs [direct materials, direct labor, variable and fixed overhead]. Next, both manufacturers and merchandisers need to prepare a budget for operating expenses. To do this, we need to know which expenses are variable costs and fixed costs based on sales. I've prepared an operating expenses schedule showing this [see Exhibit 4-15].

"Starting with selling expenses, commissions are a variable cost based on the homes sold. Sales personnel earn a $2,500 commission for each standard home sold and $3,000 for each custom home. Commissions are paid in the month of sale. To illustrate for June, commissions are budgeted at $31,000 [($2,500 × 10 standard homes = $25,000) plus ($3,000 × 2 custom homes = $6,000)]. The other selling expense, advertising, is a fixed cost. We start our advertising campaign in December. We do less advertising as the year progresses. As you can see, advertising is budgeted at $10,000 a month during December through February, $8,000 a month for March through May, and $5,500 a month in June and July.

"Some administration expenses are variable costs, and some are fixed. Purchasing is a fixed cost [$200,000 per year for the Purchasing Department, averaging $16,667 per month]. Shipping is a variable cost budgeted at $1,000 per home. In January, 5 homes are started. Three months later they are completed. They are shipped in April. Thus, $5,000 is budgeted in April for shipping. The same pattern exists for the homes started in the other months [e.g., 10 homes started in February are shipped in May, so budget $10,000 in May for shipping]. The other administration costs are basically salaries, and office building and equipment depreciation. They are fixed costs. The total budget is $690,000, of which $86,000 is depreciation. The *cash* administration costs are then $604,000 [averaging $50,333 per month]. Our final expense is income taxes, which are paid quarterly." Julie could hear the subtle boos and hisses from the others. "Well, we have to pay taxes. That and death are the only guarantees in life! So, we better include it in our budget."

Cash budgets and short-term financial planning

KEY OBJECTIVE 5

Create a monthly cash budget.

$% JULIE

"Now, we can develop the cash budget. It's divided into three sections each with its own subtotal [see Exhibit 4-16 on p. 123].

- *Cash from operations* is kind of like a cash-based break-even number for operations. First, we want to know if the cash generated from operations [sales] is sufficient to pay our operating costs [manufacturing costs and expenses]. *Do operations generate a positive cashflow each month?* If not, when are we going to have problems paying our operating costs?
- *Monthly cashflow* is a cash-based break-even number for the month because it includes other cash sources and uses from the non-operational section. Cash comes in and goes out for other events besides building and selling houses. For example, Grandfather Multree invested a lot of surplus cash over the years, generating almost a quarter million dollars in annual investment income! Of course, we also

Multree Homes Operating Expenses Schedule

Sales forecast	Jan	Feb	Mar	Apr	May	Jun	Jul	Aug	Sep	Oct	Nov	Dec	Totals
Standard homes	5	10	20	20	25	10	5	5	0	0	0	0	100
Custom homes	0	0	2	2	4	2	0	0	0	0	0	0	10
Selling expenses													
Sales commissions	$12,500	$25,000	$56,000	$56,000	$74,500	$31,000	$12,500	$12,500	$0	$0	$0	$0	$280,000
Advertising	10,000	10,000	8,000	8,000	8,000	5,500	5,500					10,000	65,000
Total selling expenses	**$22,500**	**$35,000**	**$64,000**	**$64,000**	**$82,500**	**$36,500**	**$18,000**	**$12,500**	**$0**	**$0**	**$0**	**$10,000**	**$345,000**
Administration expenses													
Purchasing	$16,667	$16,667	$16,667	$16,667	$16,667	$16,667	$16,667	$16,667	$16,667	$16,667	$16,667	$16,667	$200,000
Shipping				5,000	10,000	22,000	22,000	29,000	12,000	5,000	5,000	0	110,000
Other cash administration costs	50,333	50,333	50,333	50,333	50,333	50,333	50,333	50,333	50,333	50,333	50,333	50,333	604,000
Income taxes			62,500			62,500			62,500			62,500	250,000
Total administration expenses	**$67,000**	**$67,000**	**$129,500**	**$72,000**	**$77,000**	**$151,500**	**$89,000**	**$96,000**	**$141,500**	**$72,000**	**$72,000**	**$129,500**	**$1,164,000**
Cash-out for operating expenses	$89,500	$102,000	$193,500	$136,000	$159,500	$188,000	$107,000	$108,500	$141,500	$72,000	$72,000	$139,500	$1,509,000

Exhibit 4-15

Multree Homes Monthly Cash Budget

Cash from operations	Jan	Feb	Mar	Apr	May	Jun	Jul	Aug	Sep	Oct	Nov	Dec	Totals
Cash deposits from sales (Exhibit 4-7)	$100,000	$200,000	$480,000	$605,000	$935,000	$930,000	$820,000	$1,045,000	$515,000	$195,000	$150,000	$25,000	$6,000,000
Less: direct materials payments (Exh 4-12)	(46,500)	(129,375)	(269,125)	(369,000)	(419,750)	(329,250)	(136,000)	(73,625)	(34,875)	0	0	(12,500)	(1,820,000)
Less: DL & VOH payments (Exh 4-14)	(20,000)	(60,000)	(160,500)	(241,000)	(342,000)	(302,000)	(221,500)	(100,500)	(40,000)	(20,000)	0	0	(1,507,500)
Less: fixed overhead payments (Exh 4-14)	(17,500)	(17,500)	(37,500)	(37,500)	(57,500)	(37,500)	(17,500)	(17,500)	(17,500)	(17,500)	(27,500)	(17,500)	(320,000)
Less: operating expenses (Exh 4-15)	(89,500)	(102,000)	(193,500)	(136,000)	(159,500)	(188,000)	(107,000)	(108,500)	(141,500)	(72,000)	(72,000)	(139,500)	(1,509,000)
Cash generated from operations	**($73,500)**	**($108,875)**	**($180,625)**	**($178,500)**	**($43,750)**	**$73,250**	**$338,000**	**$744,875**	**$281,125**	**$85,500**	**$50,500**	**($144,500)**	**$843,500**
Non-operational cashflows													
Investment income			$60,000			$60,000			$60,000			$60,000	$240,000
Capital projects expenditures	(10,000)	(10,000)	(10,000)	(10,000)	(10,000)	(10,000)	(10,000)	(10,000)	(10,000)	(10,000)	(100,000)	(100,000)	(300,000)
Dividend payments			(175,000)			(175,000)			(175,000)			(175,000)	(700,000)
Total non-operational cashflows	**($10,000)**	**($10,000)**	**($125,000)**	**($10,000)**	**($10,000)**	**($125,000)**	**($10,000)**	**($10,000)**	**($125,000)**	**($10,000)**	**($100,000)**	**($215,000)**	**($760,000)**
Monthly cash surplus or (deficit)	**($83,500)**	**($118,875)**	**($305,625)**	**($188,500)**	**($53,750)**	**($51,750)**	**$328,000**	**$734,875**	**$156,125**	**$75,500**	**($49,500)**	**($359,500)**	**$83,500**
+ Beginning cash balance	48,939	0	0	0	0	0	0	0	277,375	433,500	509,000	459,500	48,939
Cash balance before financing	**($34,561)**	**($118,875)**	**($305,625)**	**($188,500)**	**($53,750)**	**($51,750)**	**$328,000**	**$734,875**	**$433,500**	**$509,000**	**$459,500**	**$100,000**	**$132,439**
Line-of-credit financing													
Beginning line-of-credit (LOC) balance	$0	$34,561	$153,782	$460,944	$654,054	$714,344	$773,238	$452,970	$0	$0	$0	$0	$0
+ LOC interest expense (1% a month)	0	346	1,538	4,609	6,541	7,143	7,732	4,530	0	0	0	0	32,439
LOC owed before monthly financing	$0	$34,907	$155,319	$465,554	$660,594	$721,488	$780,970	$457,500	$0	$0	$0	$0	$32,439
+ LOC borrowings	34,561	118,875	305,625	188,500	53,750	51,750	0	0	0	0	0	0	753,061
Less: LOC repayments	0	0	0	0	0	0	(328,000)	(457,500)	0	0	0	0	(785,500)
Ending LOC balance	$34,561	$153,782	$460,944	$654,054	$714,344	$773,238	$452,970	$0	$0	$0	$0	$0	$0
Ending cash balance	**$0**	**$0**	**$0**	**$0**	**$0**	**$0**	**$0**	**$277,375**	**$433,500**	**$509,000**	**$459,500**	**$100,000**	**$100,000**

Note: Ending cash balance = Cash balance before financing + LOC borrowings - LOC repayments.

Exhibit 4-16

invest heavily in new equipment every month. *Taking into consideration these non-operational activities, does each month generate enough cash to pay all the bills?*

- *Line-of-credit financing* is the third section. If our bank account is going to be overdrawn in some months, we need to know this now! I've negotiated a line of credit [short-term borrowing from the bank, much like overdraft protection on your personal checking account] to provide any cash needed in those months. While we want to know when we will be overdrawn, our bankers want to know in which months we will have the surplus cash to pay them back!"

Operational and non-operational cashflows. "The lines within the cash from operations section come from the schedules we just prepared. We have three non-operational cash items. The $60,000 investment income is received at the end of each quarter. Except for November and December, we budget $10,000 a month for equipment purchases and upgrades [capital projects expenditures]. In the last two months, no houses are built. This time is used for major manufacturing line changes in the plant due to new product lines and technology. The $100,000 budget in each of these months includes the cost of our workers who are making these changes. The last item in the non-operational cashflows section is the dividend payments from Multree Homes to its owners. That's us. We each want $100,000 a year, paid quarterly." Julie was quick to notice the boos and hisses she heard when discussing income taxes were now replaced with big smiles and congratulatory gestures!

SID

"Hold on. I don't see how we can pay ourselves $175,000 each of the first two quarters [in March and June]. Look at our 'Cash generated from operations' subtotals. Every month from January through May we are spending significantly more than we are bringing in. And this is just for operations! Additionally, we are going to spend another $10,000 on capital projects [equipment purchases] each month. Summing the cash from operations and the non-operational cashflows each month into the subtotal 'Monthly cash surplus/deficit,' we will overdraw our bank account in every month for the first half of the year. Adding up the monthly cash deficits for January through June, we will spend $802,000 more than we deposit! The amount by which we will overdraw our bank account [the monthly cash deficit] ranges from a minimum of $51,750 in June to a $305,625 maximum in March." Julie now noticed the congratulatory gestures were being replaced with something else.

JULIE

Line-of-credit financing. "You're right. We can solve this problem in three ways. We can have a sufficient beginning of the year cash balance. We'll need $802,000 [the sum of the monthly cash deficits through June]. We have only $48,939 in the bank account on January 1, however. Another way is through better cash management. Perhaps we can accelerate some cash inflows or delay some payments. This doesn't look too promising, though. Asking customers for more money sooner may not please them! Delaying payments to suppliers or workers will aggravate them, too! Yes, we can defer our dividends, but that is only $350,000 of the $802,000 needed.

"Alternatively, we can negotiate a **line of credit** with the bank. This is basically overdraft protection on our checking account. Our bankers will do this if we have a good history of cash management and we can show them how much we will need, and when we can pay it back. This is the purpose for the third section of the cash budget.

*A **line of credit** is a short-term loan arrangement with the bank in which money will be placed into our checking account when needed, and repaid when we have a surplus.*

"Let's go over some of the calculations in this section. In January we will spend $83,500 more than we deposit [January's monthly cash deficit]. With only a $48,939 beginning cash balance, we will be overdrawn by $34,561 [January's negative cash balance before financing]. So we will borrow $34,561 against our line of credit [the + LOC borrowings line within this section of the cash budget]. Since we don't have a beginning LOC balance owed to the bank, we will owe it $34,561 at the end of the month. The amount we are borrowing is just enough to keep us from overdrawing our bank account. Our January ending bank account balance is thus projected to be zero. The ending January bank account balance becomes the beginning February cash balance.

"Now look at February. The January ending LOC balance becomes February's beginning LOC balance. Of course, we are going to be charged interest in February for the money we borrowed in January. Our LOC interest rate is 12% per year [1% per month]. One month's interest on the $34,561 borrowed in January is $346 [all amounts are formatted to the whole dollar in this spreadsheet program]. We then will borrow another $118,875 [February's negative cash balance before financing]. At the end of February, we will owe $153,782 on our line of credit [the beginning balance plus interest for the month plus February's borrowing].

"This LOC borrowing pattern will continue through June. Each month we will borrow enough to cover our overdrawn checking account. Finally, in July we project a $328,000 cash surplus [cash balance before financing]. After the bank charges our July interest, the LOC balance will be $780,970. At least we can pay back part of this. The bank will take our entire $328,000 surplus and use it to paydown the LOC. At the end of July we will owe the bank $452,970. The good news is in August we will have enough surplus cash to pay off the LOC and have $277,375 left in the bank. And this allows for our quarterly dividends in March and July!"

"So, maintaining good relationships with our bankers is very important! Because of the seasonal nature of our business and the timing of our cashflows, we need to borrow heavily in the first half of the year, but we make lots of cash in the second half. *If we can show this to our bankers with our cash budget, they will work with us throughout the year.*"

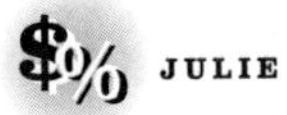

"That's the point! For the entire year, we will generate enough cash to pay all of our bills, invest $300,000 in new equipment [the capital projects expenditures line in the non-operational cashflows section], pay ourselves each $100,000 [dividends], and increase our cash balance from $48,939 [on January 1] to $100,000 by the end of the year. However, we have to break down the budget into months to make sure the timing of our cashflows throughout the year is adequate."

"Wait a minute! Bankers are external users of our accounting information. I only have to give external users our financial accounting system reports [e.g., income statement and balance sheet]. If I give our cash budget to them, should I make it available to other external users? We certainly don't want our competition to get it!"

"You've raised a good ethical question, Jackie. Technically, management accounting information is confidential, and we have a confidentiality standard for ethical conduct. However, I don't think it will be too smart to withhold this information from our bankers. They will demand it as a condition for our line of credit. For example, small businesses applying for federal government-sponsored Small Business Administration [SBA] loans must provide cash budgets for five years. I guess we have to be careful about who we share this information with, and they must protect its confidential nature.

"By sharing this information, our bankers have a suggestion to improve our cash management. The cash budget strives for an ending balance of zero dollars, much like my personal checking account! We should consider maintaining a $10,000 ending balance each month, in case of unforeseen events. Having beginning and ending inventories allow us to buffer [guard] against uncertainty. Maintaining a $10,000 minimum cash balance is just another type of uncertainty buffer for our cash 'inventory.'

"How does maintaining a $10,000 minimum cash balance affect our cash budget? Whenever we borrow on our line of credit, we will borrow enough to result in an ending monthly cash balance of $10,000 instead of $0. So, in January we will borrow $44,561. This will leave $10,000 in our bank account at the end of the month. It will carry over into the February beginning cash balance. Our LOC balance will be $10,000 higher every month until we can pay it off [in August], and we will incur an extra $100 in LOC interest expense each month [1% of the extra $10,000].

"Having a minimum cash balance should be part of our cash management program. I remember this was a big issue back in 1995 when Kirk Kerkorian wanted to purchase Chrysler's outstanding stock and take over the company. One of his main concerns was Chrysler's budgeted $7.5 billion cash reserve. Management believed it was necessary for the automotive industry downturns and cycles. Interestingly, General Motors budgeted a $15 billion cash reserve, Ford $18 billion, and Toyota $26 billion!"

Budgeting's Behavioral Implications

TOMMY

"We also have a lot of other behavioral and ethical issues to consider in our cash budgeting process. I think we should talk about how we are going to do this with our people. We need them to provide the budget information. They also have to be motivated to practice good cash management."

JULIE

"You're right. Let's start by asking, 'What makes the budgeting process successful?'" [Exhibit 4-17 provides some ideas.]

KEY OBJECTIVE 6

Describe how cash budgeting can affect motivation and control.

Participation and motivation

"As you know, I've been holding budget meetings with everyone in the company. It's been a long and involved process, but I feel it's been worth it. Several purposes were accomplished:

- As our management accountant, I need to get all the information [upward communication].
- Everyone else also needs to know a lot of information, so they can plan their operations and coordinate plans with others [downward communication, information sharing, and coordination].
- By sharing information and agreeing on our plans, everyone is committed to the budget [motivation].
- The process is an opportunity to let everyone know we are a team, working together toward common goals [communication, coordination, and using the budget]."

What Makes the Budgeting Process Successful?	
Top management commitment	☑ Budgeting is part of overall good management. ☑ It operationalizes the strategic plan. ☑ It guides day-to-day operational control. ☑ It is the basis for performance evaluation.
Communication to employees about how the strategic plan is going to work	☑ Forces everyone to plan. ☑ Formalizes the planning process. ☑ Provides for financial resource allocations.
Gain employee commitment	☑ Employees participate in determining the budget. ☑ Employees are rewarded for good cash management.
Coordination of value chain processes	☑ Determine how changes in the sales forecast affect purchasing and production processes. ☑ Effect on administrative support processes from changes in production schedules.
Use the budget	☑ Continuously update the budget for changing circumstances. ☑ Budget only for programs that add value.

Exhibit 4-17

"This is called **participative budgeting**. Everyone is significantly involved and makes valued contributions. *Workers tell me they feel like they are part of the company. They feel a responsibility to create value. Quite bluntly, the more involved employees are in making policy, the more motivated and loyal they become, and the more they achieve.* The formal two-way communication process is management's way of saying employees are important. I've talked to too many others in different companies who see themselves as just workers doing a job.

*In **participative budgeting**, everyone jointly works together in preparing the budget. In contrast, with **authoritative budgeting**, management dictates the budget to the organization.*

"Participation is the opposite of **authoritative budgeting** in which top management dictates the budget to the rest of the organization. Imposing the budget is simpler and faster than the participatory approach. Authoritative budgeting works well in small, start-up companies in which management has the best knowledge of operating needs and everyone works closely together.

"It runs the risk of employees not accepting the budget as practical or valid, though. Because employees did not participate in setting the plans and identifying the resources needed to accomplish them, they may not be motivated to achieve the budget. Another problem with imposing a budget on the organization is top management may not understand the process well enough to identify needed resources. We see this too often in the governmental sector, where budgets and resources are provided by people who do not do the work. The people doing the work, denied any participation, may see the budget 'handcuffing' them. Believing their opinions and knowledge are not valued, employees may become frustrated and develop a 'who cares?' attitude.

"In fairness to governmental policymakers, its budgets serve a different purpose than in other sectors of our economy. The primary purpose for governmental budgets is resource allocation: 'While we want to provide all these services, we have only this much money to spend on each one.' Governmental budgets are generally unpopular because their primary purpose is to limit spending. Budgets in nongovernmental organizations are primarily tools for accomplishing the strategic plan. Therefore, in these settings, employee motivation and commitment to the budget is critical for long-run value creation. And participation is often necessary for commitment.

"Of course, participation doesn't always work. Consider countries in which the questioning of authority is not culturally acceptable. In these environments it may be difficult to involve employees, as they may prefer an imposed budget. Participation may not be necessary for commitment and performance. This might explain why participative budgeting is not as widely practiced in Japan as in the United States.

"Even in our economic culture of 'individualism,' participative budgeting is not always needed for proper motivation, though. Employees are loyal to their organizations and committed to budgets for many reasons. When organizational cultures promote loyalty and commitment, authoritarian budgeting may work well."

Performance evaluation

"While participation usually is important in motivating people to live within their budgets, at least in our culture, it may not be sufficient. I see lots of people who participate in setting their budgets, but who spend like crazy!"

"I see that behavior, too. *The other critical component for budget commitment is its use in performance evaluation. People are motivated to do something if it's rewarded.* Rewards can take many forms: money, promotions, better parking places, a corner office with a window, a trophy or plaque everyone can see forever, or maybe just self-satisfaction in a job well done. Regardless of the type of reward we offer with a positive evaluation, good cash management involves a comparison of budgeted cashflows to actual cashflows. This is the last step in the cash management process [Exhibit 4-1]."

"Oh, I understand the link between motivating performance and evaluation. I took too many tests in college. Exams are performance evaluations, and grades are rewards. I never liked them! They were usually too hard and too long. And, all too often, they did not measure the knowledge I learned."

"You've raised two important issues: (1) how difficult should the standards be? and (2) are we measuring the right things? Let's look at each in turn.

"Perhaps the easiest way to make the budget-to-actual cashflow evaluation easier is to 'pad the budget.' This can be done by decreasing budgeted revenues and/or increasing budgeted costs. In accounting, we call this adding **budgetary slack**. *Adding slack to the budget can accomplish three possible goals for the individual being evaluated:*

> **Budgetary slack** *is the reduction in budgeted revenues, or the increase in budgeted costs above reasonable estimates.*

- If management has a history of cutting the budget, adding slack first will result in a reasonable budget after the anticipated cuts.
- Adding slack serves as a protection against unforeseen events [it buffers against uncertainty].
- The easier the budget, the easier to achieve it, and the easier it is to get a good evaluation and rewards."

"How do we avoid the unethical addition of slack? It can't be done by replacing participative budgeting with an imposed budget. I've seen more than one manager who has successfully lobbied for a pet project or a bigger budget in private during lunch or golf with an executive. At least with participative budgeting, such budget

requests may be scrutinized by a lot of people. Accountability is much more effective with public information. Private information allows people to get away with murder!"

JULIE

"I agree. We can avoid the first reason for slack by agreeing not to cut the budget 'across the board.' This is a typical government method in which everyone's budget is cut equally. Borg-Warner top management used to do this until it discovered everyone knew it would happen and padded their budgets accordingly. The justification is that it's fair. Of course, while it may be fair, it may not be right. Granted, some departments may have slack, but other departments may already be operating as efficiently as possible. To cut their budgets means they may not be able to do their jobs. *It's the 'across-the-board' budget cutting that's unethical!*

"How I solved the second reason for slack with my son's college budget was by adding a contingency line. Remember, the last item in his living expenses budget is $62 for emergencies. Often padding is accomplished by inflating specific amounts everywhere. To illustrate this, assume for every material used we will budget more than should be used. By inflating each line item in a budget we're protected against unforeseen events, but the slack is hidden. In contrast, *by adding a contingencies line item and budgeting each resource realistically, if something unexpected happens it will be highlighted.* I believe it's unethical to inflate each item in a budget, and thus hide the slack, as an uncertainty protection method.

"The last reason for slack, making the evaluation easier, is a harder problem to solve. The more important budget achievement is in performance evaluation, the greater the pressure to add slack. How important should it be? In too many organizations, financial performance is the only, or primary, evaluation measure. Shouldn't we equally value customer satisfaction and high-quality products or services? *We really need multiple performance measures tied to all of our strategic plan goals if we want to measure the right things.*"

TOMMY

"Overemphasis on budget goals created a serious ethical issue for Bausch & Lomb in the early 1990s. According to one report of its budget practices, managers appeared to be under a lot of pressure to meet imposed budget goals designed to maintain double-digit growth. Some customers may have been pressured to place large orders at the end of the budget period and offered very favorable credit terms [or threatened with no future sales]. Some orders may have been shipped early so the sales could be recorded in the budget period. Not only did this affect regular orders [wait until the end of the budget period and get special deals], it wreaked havoc on billing, accounts receivable, shipping, and inventory [especially when many orders were returned in the next period].

"Budget-based performance evaluations can create even more difficult ethical dilemmas. One manager at Phillips Petroleum inflated operating results by 33% to avoid a bad evaluation. He was afraid the plant would be shut down because its actual performance was so bad. Is the fear of losing 300 jobs and a whole town sufficient to justify unethical conduct? Is it unethical to solely rely on 'hitting the numbers' in performance evaluation?"

Budgets as security blankets

JULIE

"I remember a Canadian accountant [Ivan Kilpatrick, former vice president at Bombardier, Inc.] saying our ethical responsibility is to guard against 'fantasy forecasts.' Two other ways we can accomplish this are with continuous budgeting and zero-based budgeting."

Continuous budgets.

Good management begins with good planning.
Good planning facilitates day-to-day operational control.
Good operational control makes performance evaluation much easier.

With **continuous budgeting**, *a new month (or whatever time period is used in the budget) is added on to the end of the budget each month so there is always a current 12-month budget.*

"If we lived in an unchanging world, annual budgets might suffice. Our competitive world is always changing, though. Thus we should be continually reviewing and updating our budget. This is called **continuous budgeting**. Companies like Johnson & Johnson and NEC review their budgets monthly, and add another month to it. As a result these firms always have a current 12-month budget.

"The Ritz-Carlton also compares budgeted and actual cashflows monthly. Top management isn't too concerned with differences less than 5%. However, because of the uncertainty in occupancy rates, every month the budget for the next three months is reviewed. The Arizona Public Service Company conducts monthly reviews of its two-year budget.

"By comparing budget to actual each month, a pattern of slack in someone's budget becomes apparent. More importantly, though, *continuous attention to planning moves the organization from a reactive mode to a proactive mode*. Instead of constantly trying to overcome unforeseen problems ['I spend all my time putting out fires!'], we can update next month's budget with plans to avoid anticipated problems."

"I wish we did continuous budgeting when the Boss was still alive! I remember when we introduced the winter skiing chalet custom home for the Lake Tahoe market. Sales convinced the Boss to introduce it in the middle of the production season. We had an avalanche of orders. Although I scheduled a lot of overtime, we never caught up until the end of the year. The salespeople got great Christmas bonuses, but I didn't get anything."

"Well, the Boss said you didn't stay within the annual budget. The Accounting Department had a policy of not allowing changes to the annual budget once it was approved. We didn't want to lose sight of our original plans."

"Yes, and I got screwed! Why can't you bean counters keep the original budget, but also maintain a current budget? The two can be compared to see where unforeseen events forced us to rethink our plans. Such knowledge will help us improve future planning. Then the continuous budget can be compared to actual cashflows, better reflecting our new reality."

"No need to get hostile! The point is well made. *Unless management is willing to recognize when budget changes are necessary, our people will not accept the evaluation system as valid. Then our planning system will collapse.* One of the major reasons many companies go out of business is an unwillingness to review and adjust their budgets when needed. Strict adherence to an unchangeable annual budget is too often heard by subordinates with good ideas in that management phrase, 'You've got a great idea, but it's not within the budget.' I think we can learn from the Japanese. Many Japanese firms prepare six-month budgets primarily to respond to changing circumstances. Their budgets are not used primarily for performance evaluation, and bonuses are not tied to achieving the budget. This fundamental difference with the United States' philosophy of basing rewards on budget performance may explain why Japanese firms have simple budgets, while we have very detailed, time-consuming ones. ITT's budget, for example, occupies 21 feet of shelf space!"

Zero-based and program budgets. "Another way to minimize slack, pet projects, empire-building, and programs that have outlived their usefulness is through **zero-based budgeting**. Each budget year, projects have to be justified in order to be funded. **Program budgeting** requires a multi-year budget with a termination date ['sunset provision'] for each project. These budget techniques attempt to overcome the creeping slack problem found in **incremental budgets**. Incremental budgeting, very popular with governments, does not require program justifications each year. Everyone gets 5% or 10% more [or less] this year depending on the money available. It's like a cost-of-living adjustment [COLA]. Some states do have 'sunset' laws, though, to force program review or discontinuance. As financial pressures increase, companies [e.g., Texas Instruments, Southern California Edison] and governments [e.g., Rochester, New York, the state of Georgia] are switching to zero-based and program budgeting."

> **Incremental budgeting** *increases (decreases) everyone's budget by the same percentage.* **Zero-based budgeting** *requires each project to be justified before it's included in the budget.* **Program budgeting** *does not require annual justification, but does contain a termination date.*

KEY OBJECTIVES SUMMARY

SID

"Well, we've learned a lot about budgeting in this meeting. Doris, can you summarize the important information?"

1. Explain why proforma income statements and CVP analysis have to be translated into a cash budget.

DORIS

"Our proforma income statement shows our budgeted profit for the year. Profit is not cash, however, and we need cash to pay our bills. A cash budget is necessary so we can see the timing of our cash inflows and outflows. We prepare the budget monthly because while the annual cashflow may be sufficient to run our business, in certain months we may have to borrow money from the bank. This becomes obvious when we look at Multree's cash budget [Exhibit 4-16]. While we will have $100,000 in surplus cash by the end of the year, we will have to borrow about $800,000 in the first six months to pay our bills on time. The more the timing of our cashflows differs from when sales are made, the greater the need for a cash budget.

"With a cash budget, we can practice good cash management [Exhibit 4-1]. The budget provides a monthly spending plan, and a basis for performance evaluation [Exhibit 4-2]. Its use in evaluation will motivate our people to take the planning process seriously and to control operations on a day-to-day basis [Exhibit 4-17].

2. Discuss the usefulness of budgets when cash inflows are known.

"Receiving cash is the easy part of good cash management. Granted, organizations whose cash inflows depend upon sales face a great deal of uncertainty. Changing customer preferences, economic conditions, and competition can make sales forecasting quite challenging. However, even when the timing of cash inflows are fairly certain, such as with government and nonprofit entities, the role of budgets in controlling operations still is critical. I learned a few lessons about the benefits from a good cash budgeting process in these environments while going through Brian's college budget. Many of these benefits also apply in the uncertain business world.

- Brian knows the program demands and critical success factors. Day-to-day control knowledge often exists with the people doing the work. Participation in budgeting is critical for a practical budget when the people doing the work have the best knowledge of their needs.

- To succeed, Brian [the people doing the work] needs resources. The budget captures the timing and cost of these resources. Brian's two big resource needs are time and money. These conflict. The less money he has, the more time he must take away from school in order to work. My daughter also goes to college. She is married, has two children, and a full-time job. Her primary resource need is time. But how important can college be, given these other demands on her time? Budgets identify the critical resources needed.

- Julie, Brian's mom, is like top management in an organization. She provides resources to Brian so he can do his job [learn]. The money she provides him buys the time he needs to do the best job he can in school. Budgets demonstrate top management's commitment to provide the needed resources.

- Julie and Brian negotiated his budget and the performance evaluation criteria to monitor his success. Negotiation identified the amount of resources needed.

- Brian is committed to the budget, and is willing to exercise good managerial judgment in achieving it. His rewards depend on it. Not only is the budget the key tool for operational planning, it is also the key tool for management control. Participative budgeting tied to performance evaluation is critical for long-term value creation.

The final lesson learned is for Julie. You better be careful telling this story. A lot of college students may want you to adopt them!

3. Prepare a schedule for cash collections from sales.

"This meeting is really important to me because I have to prepare a budget for our church. I'm its bookkeeper. First, I have to identify the sources of cash inflows. The church receives a monthly allowance from the diocese, parishioner contributions, and gift shop sales. Second, I have to estimate the amounts and timing of these inflows:

- Each year the diocese informs us of our allowance [$1,000 per month received at the beginning of each month].

- Parishioner collections occur only on Sundays and holy days [5 services per day averaging $100 each].

- The gift shop is open on Sundays and holy days. Sales are all on credit and average $50 per day. I send bills at the end of each month to the parishioners for their gift shop purchases. Half pay in the month the bill is received, which is one month after the sale. The other half pay in the following month. Of course, we have no bad debts.

This information appears in the Data section of my cash collections schedule for the first quarter of the year [see Exhibit 4-18]:

Cash Collections Schedule for the Church

Data section		November	December	January	February	March
Diocese allowance				$1,000	$1,000	$1,000
From parishioners	Services per month			30	20	20
	Cash per service			$100	$100	$100
Gift shop sales	Revenues	$250	$250	$300	$200	$200
	Collection pattern:	50%	in the following month			
		50%	in two months			

Cash collections schedule		January	February	March	Totals
Diocese allowance		$1,000	$1,000	$1,000	$3,000
Parishioner collections		3,000	2,000	2,000	7,000
Gift shop sales:	From last month	125	150	100	375
	From two months ago	125	125	150	400
Total cash deposits		**$4,250**	**$3,275**	**$3,250**	**$10,775**

Exhibit 4-18

Calculating parishioner collections is much like calculating sales revenues in a business. Services per month is like sales volume. Average collections per service is like a sales price. Total collections [sales revenues] is simply sales volume multiplied by sales price [e.g., January's collections = 30 services × $100 per service]. In budgeting collections from the gift shop, gift shop sales average $50 per day. January has 5 Sundays and 1 holy day [February and March have 4, November and December have 5]. I need gift shop sales for two months prior to the budget period because of the lag time between sales and collections. To demonstrate, in January the church will collect 50% of December sales [From last month = 50% × $250] and 50% of November sales [From two months ago = 50% × $250].

4. Develop operating budgets (schedules for purchases, labor, overhead, and operating expenses).

"The church is a nonprofit service organization. Because it does not manufacture a product, we don't need a production schedule or direct materials purchases schedule. The gift store needs a merchandise purchases schedule, though. In this schedule, the most important calculation to remember is converting sales revenues into cost of goods sold. We purchase merchandise at cost. Revenues are the sales prices charged to parishioners. We receive merchandise shipments twice a month, so our beginning inventory is 50% of our needs. The church doesn't have a lot of bills, so I pay them monthly. All bills received by the end of the month are paid at the beginning of the next month, just like with my personal bills. Here's the schedule [see Exhibit 4-19].

"Revenues in the Data section come from my cash collections schedule [Key Objective 3]. In the first line of the merchandise purchases schedule, I calculated

Merchandise Purchases Schedule for the Church's Gift Shop

Data section:		December	January	February	March	April
Gift shop	Revenues	$250	$300	$200	$200	$250
	Cost of goods sold	80%	of sales price			
	Beginning inventory	50%	of this month's sales (at cost)			
	Payment schedule	0%	in the month received			
		100%	in the following month			

Merchandise purchases schedule:	January	February	March	April	1st quarter totals
Cost of goods sold (Revenues x COGS%)	$240	$160	$160	$200	$560
Less: beginning inventory (50% of COGS)	(120)	(80)	(80)		(120)
+ Ending inventory (50% of next month)	80	80	100		100
Merchandise purchases	**$200**	**$160**	**$180**		**$540**
Payment schedule:					
To pay this month	$0	$0	$0		
To pay from last month	220	200	160		
Total cash-outs for purchases	**$220**	**$200**	**$160**		**$580**

Exhibit 4-19

cost of goods sold. Merchandise costs us 80% of its sales price. I included April's cost because it's needed to compute March's ending inventory. However, April is not included in the $560 total.

"Beginning inventory is one half of the current month's cost of goods sold. Ending inventory is one half of next month's cost of goods sold. January's ending inventory equals February's beginning inventory, so I didn't need to calculate any ending inventory figures except for March, which is why April's cost of goods sold is included [March ending inventory = $200 April COGS × 50% desired ending inventory]. In the totals column, the beginning inventory is January's beginning inventory, and the ending inventory is from March.

"Because I pay all the bills on the first of the month, cash-outs equal last month's merchandise purchases. Because December's purchases are paid in January, December's revenues appear in the Data section. [If you're confused about any of these calculations, go back and study Exhibits 4-11 and 13.]

"The church doesn't have a direct labor or overhead schedule [it's not a manufacturer], and it has few operating expenses. The real trick with labor and overhead is to figure out when you have to write the checks to pay for these costs. For example, if laborers are paid weekly, ¾ of a month's total wages are paid within the month [the first three weeks] and ¼ is paid in the following month [the last week's wages are paid at the end of the next week which is the first week in the next month]. Also be very careful with both variable and fixed overhead. These resources usually are not paid for at the same time they are used in production, especially the fixed overhead. Many fixed overhead costs may be semiannual [e.g., car insurance] or annual [e.g., property taxes and insurance]. My point is to budget for them when they are paid. Some costs may be the same every month, but some are not [see Exhibit 4-14]. Remember not to include depreciation. We don't write a check for it.

"None of the operating expenses are variable costs based on the number of church services per month. Because the church has so few expenses, and I pay the bills only once a month, a separate schedule isn't needed. For more complex organizations, we need to be aware of when the bills will be paid, and ignore any depreciation included in these expenses. To keep things simple, the operating expenses are included within the cash budget.

5. Create a monthly cash budget.

"Here's the church's cash budget for the first quarter of the year [see Exhibit 4-20]:

The Church's Cash Budget

		January	February	March	Totals
Cash from operations:					
Cash deposits from diocese, collections, gift shop		$4,250	$3,275	$3,250	$10,775
Merchandise purchases for the gift shop		(220)	(200)	(160)	(580)
Operating expenses:	Utilities	(1,000)	(1,000)	(1,000)	(3,000)
	Minister's living expenses	(750)	(750)	(750)	(2,250)
	Insurance	(500)			(500)
	Travel expenses	(200)	(200)	(200)	(600)
	Repairs and replacements reserve	(200)	(200)	(200)	(600)
Cash generated from operations		**$1,380**	**$925**	**$940**	**$3,245**
Non-operational cashflows:					
Bingo proceeds		$200	$200	$250	$650
Charitable contributions (hiring the homeless at the church)		(1,000)	(1,000)	(1,250)	(3,250)
Total non-operational cashflows		**($800)**	**($800)**	**($1,000)**	**($2,600)**
Monthly cash surplus or (deficit)		**$580**	**$125**	**($60)**	**$645**
+ Beginning cash balance		100	0	0	100
Cash balance before financing		$680	$125	($60)	$745
Line-of-credit financing:					
Beginning line-of-credit (LOC) balance		$800	$136	$14	$800
+ LOC interest expense (2% per month)		16	3	0	19
LOC owed before monthly financing		$816	$139	$14	$819
+ LOC borrowings		0	0	60	60
Less: LOC repayments		(680)	(125)	0	(805)
Ending LOC balance		$136	$14	$74	$74
Ending cash balance		**$0**	**$0**	**$0**	**$0**

Note: Ending cash balance = Cash balance before financing + LOC borrowings - LOC repayments.

Exhibit 4-20

In the Cash from operations section, deposits and purchases come from the schedules I just prepared. I then entered each operating expense in this section [no separate schedule was necessary].

"The non-operational items include Friday night bingo games [bringing in $50 each night] and wages we pay the homeless we hire to do janitorial and fix-up work around the church. We pay them in cash each Sunday after church, and budget $250 per week [50 hours per week at $5 per hour].

"We started the year with $100 in our checking account. This is also the beginning cash balance in the totals column.

"On January 1, we owed the bank $800 on our line of credit. The bank will take all $680 we have in the account at the end of January, leaving an ending LOC balance of $136, and an ending bank account balance of $0. These ending balances become the beginning balances in February. In the totals column, the beginning and ending LOC balances come from January and March, respectively.

"At the end of the first quarter, we will have no surplus cash in our bank account, but will owe only $74 on our line of credit. Our minister doesn't like this [nor does the diocese!], so I will do some spreadsheet analysis to solve the problem later [see the Appendix].

6. Describe how cash budgeting can affect motivation and control.

"Budgets can be imposed or developed through participation. They can be annual or continuous. They also can be incremental or zero-based. How do we determine the 'right' budgeting process for our organization? It involves consideration of many complex factors: Who has the information? What's the best way to communicate the organization's goals? How are our people motivated? and How important is financial-budget performance? Ethically speaking, we need to consider the 'human side' of the budgeting process. Here's some budget goals and process comparisons to end my meeting notes [see Exhibit 4-21]:"

Comparing Participative and Authoritative Processes for Certain Budget Goals

Goals	Participative budgeting	Authoritative budgeting
Get needed information:	If best source is employees.	If best source is top management.
Minimize time and effort:	Time and effort increase with more people involved.	Less people involved speeds up the process.
Communicate budget information throughout organization and coordinate operations:	Accomplished by two-way information flows (workers to management, management to workers). Plans understood because workers involved from the beginning of the process.	Downward flow only passes top management information to workers. Because budget is imposed, extra explanation/instruction may be needed for coordination.
Budget commitment:	Through participation and negotiation. Communication fosters better understanding of strategic plan (the "big picture").	Must come from already existing loyalty to organization. Limited understanding of how budget is linked to strategic plan.

Exhibit 4-21

Comparing Participative and Authoritative Processes for Certain Budget Goals		
Goals	**Participative budgeting**	**Authoritative budgeting**
Motivation to do better than the budget:	Participation leads to higher motivation if individual performance is important within the corporate culture.	The budget is not an important motivator if the corporate culture is characterized by workers' pre-existing dedication to the organization.
Driving out slack:	Participation and peer pressure through information sharing. Continuous and zero-based budgets.	Don't allow private lobbying. Continuous and zero-based budgets.

Exhibit 4-21 (continued)

REALITY 101

Budgeting for a Public Utility

Penn Fuel Gas (PFG), Inc. is a Pennsylvania public utility company. Deregulation and the resulting competition in the utilities industry is driving the need for management accountants and modern management accounting techniques. PFG, responding to pressures from its board of directors, bankers, and top management, developed an annual cash budgeting process in 1994. Both budgeted and actual information were desired about:

- Department cashflows,
- Regional lines of business (utility, propane, and merchandise), and
- Types of customers (commercial, industrial, residential).

Amy Snyder, a member of the Valley Forge IMA chapter, was hired as the new budget director. She offers the following three suggestions in developing a cash budget and cash management process.

Learn the business and industry

Public utility industry rules and regulations are very complex. Training courses and the willingness of top management to maintain an "open door" policy are critical success factors. Utility budgeting is difficult because supply and demand depends so much on Mother Nature. For example, the first two years witnessed the most severe and mild winters. The use of average long-run weather trends needs to be supplemented with sensitivity analyses, such as Monte Carlo simulations (see Appendix A). Continuous budgeting is critical because supply and demand can change so frequently.

Another critical success factor in managing the budget process is knowledge of the corporate culture. PFG believes in participative budgeting, and budget-to-actual comparisons are not used as a "hammer" at year-end for the divisions with unfavorable results. Thus, budgetary slack has not been a problem for PFG.

Determine the users' information needs

Management wants two sets of "deliverables" from the management accounting system:

- The annual business plan has two components: a 12-month proforma income statement and a 12-month cash budget. The cash budget is supported by detailed schedules for capital projects and manpower needs.
- The "monthly financial packet" includes income statements and cashflows by region showing (1) current month actual vs. budget and (2) current month actual vs. the same month last year. The monthly information also includes year-to-date actual vs. budget, year-to-date actual compared to last year, and a continuous budget for the remainder of the year. Other required multiyear information is discussed in the next section.

Update the accounting system, or create a new one

Most accounting systems primarily support external financial reporting because it's a legal requirement. Historically, accountants have not been trained to create management information geared toward long-run value creation. This is especially true in the regulated utilities industry. Deregulation and competition are radically changing management's view of how accountants can add value to the firm.

Instituting a new budgeting system is an ideal time to update or develop a new accounting system. At PFG, the new management information orientation is evident in the use of spreadsheet graphics. In addition to the above information, the monthly financial packet includes monthly bar charts for two years showing budgeted vs. actual cashflows and profit. Selected five-year comparative data also is provided for five customer categories. Amy's first suggestion was to use graphical information, instead of table of numbers, as it appeals much better to all levels of users.

Source: West and Snyder, "How to Set Up a Budgeting and Planning System," *Management Accounting*, January 1997. © Institute of Management Accountants.

APPENDIX A

USING SPREADSHEETS TO PLAY GAMES WITH THE BUDGET

"In our last meeting on CVP analysis, I demonstrated how spreadsheet programs can be used to do 'what-if' analysis, 'goal-seeking,' and graphics. [See the Reality 101 section in Chapter 3.] We can play similar games with the cash budget. Let's use Doris's church budget for an example. Both schedules and the cash budget were created within the same spreadsheet program."

What-if?

KEY OBJECTIVE 7

Comment on spreadsheet usefulness in budgeting.

"Doris's minister is not happy with the current budget for the first quarter of the year. The church has no cash in its checking account, and it still owes money to the bank on its line of credit. Let's change some cash management practices for the gift shop and see the effect on the LOC and bank balance:

1. What if all gift shop sales are collected in the next month?
2. What if we raise the gift shop merchandise sales prices so cost of the goods sold drops to 60%?
3. What if we can increase bingo proceeds 20% [to $60 per day]?

Spreadsheet programs have built-in functions to make these changes and see the results. I asked the program just to show the results for the ending LOC balance and the three monthly ending cash balances [see Exhibit 4A-1].

What-if Games with the Church's Gift Shop

Scenario Summary				
	Original	1. Collect sales sooner	2. Raise prices	3. Increase bingo proceeds
Changing Cells:				
Collect_gift_sales	50%	100%	50%	50%
COGS	80%	80%	60%	80%
Bingo_proceeds	$50	$50	$50	$60
Result Cells:				
March_LOC_bal	$74	$99	$0	$0
Jan_cash_bal	$0	$0	$0	$0
Feb_cash_bal	$0	$11	$92	$67
March_cash_bal	$0	$0	$72	$57

Note: Changing cells for each scenario are highlighted.

Exhibit 4A-1

Collecting sales sooner makes things worse [Scenario 1]. Raising sales prices eliminates our LOC balance in January and projects an ending cash balance of $72 [Scenario 2 assumes total revenues will not increase]. Playing bingo longer each day so revenues increase 20% also eliminates the LOC balance, but does not generate as much surplus cash as Scenario 2.

"Raising gift shop prices seems to be the best alternative. Doris's minister, though, was quick to point out I think of 'best' in terms of maximizing profits. The church is not a profit-making organization. Raising gift shop prices creates an ethical problem for the minister, so he prefers Scenario 3."

Goal-seeking

"Spreadsheet programs also have built-in functions for goal-seeking. We already know increasing bingo proceeds will pay off the LOC balance and leave $57 in our bank account [What-if Scenario 3 above]. But suppose we want an ending cash balance of $200? What do the proceeds have to be? All I did was click on the goal-seeking function. The program asked me which cell I wanted to change—I clicked on the ending cash balance—and what I wanted to change it to—I input $200.

Then, it asked me which cell I wanted to change in order to achieve this goal. The program then calculated the bingo proceeds needed. I checked the new ending cash balance, and it was $200! By the way, bingo proceeds will have to increase to $71 per day."

Sensitivity analyses

"Changing some of the data values in the three what-if scenarios we first looked at had a greater effect on the ending cash balance than did changing other values. When changing an estimated amount causes a significant change in the cash balance, we say the cash balance is 'sensitive' to changes in that data. Sensitivity analysis attempts to identify those data estimates having important impacts on cash.

"By changing the Data section values, we can immediately see the impact on our ending cash balance. Often, organizations will develop different budgets portraying the 'best case,' 'worst case,' and 'most likely' scenarios using different values for key variables. Photon Technology International, Inc. has been doing this for years."

Monte Carlo simulations

"Spreadsheet programs also allow us to set up probability distributions for key variables, and run the budget thousands of times [within seconds!] using randomly generated values based on the statistical distributions selected. This is kind of complicated to explain unless you've had a few statistics courses. [For more information see the article on Monte Carlo simulations in the Reading List.]

"All four of these techniques can dramatically improve the budgeting and cash management processes. Who knows what new tricks will be incorporated into spreadsheet programs in the upcoming years! I do know one thing, though. A high-quality management accountant should be very proficient with spreadsheet programs and the games they allow us to play!"

Mainframe and E-budgeting

"Many medium and large companies need more sophisticated budgeting software, however. Spreadsheet programs suffer from many problems:

- As cash budgets become more complex, some vendor programs cannot perform what-if and goal-seeking analyses.
- Spreadsheet programs are not very flexible.
- They are designed for single users.
- Organizations with different departments, using different vendor programs, may not be able to integrate all the spreadsheets when consolidating the budget.
- Not everyone has an adequate knowledge of how to use spreadsheets, especially some of the more sophisticated financial planning tools.

To overcome these problems, some companies use multidimensional or online analytical processing [OLAP] databases to manage the budgeting process. Other organizations use 'e-budgeting' software throughout the firm's Intranet. These more elaborate mainframe programs allow users to interface through custom-designed, user-friendly input screens.

"Regardless of the level of employee and program sophistication, though, we all have to become computer literate if we are going to survive in this highly competitive and computerized economic environment. I'll schedule training sessions for each of you beginning this Saturday morning! Who wants to go first?"

READING LIST*

Baseball and cash management: Ozanian, "The $11 Billion Pastime," *Financial World*, May 10, 1994.

Bausch & Lomb: Maremont, "Blind Ambition: How the pursuit of results got out of hand at Bausch & Lomb," *Business Week*, October 23, 1995.

Borg-Warner and budget cutting: Hanks, Fried, and Huber, "Shifting Gears at Borg-Warner Automotive," *Management Accounting*, February 1994.

Chrysler and cash reserves: Simison, "A Mountain of Cash is Rising in Detroit as Big Three Build Recession Cushion," *The Wall Street Journal*, April 28, 1995, p. A14.

Continuous budgets: Steward, "Why Budgets Are Bad for Business," *Fortune*, June 4, 1990.

E-budgeting: Hornyak, "Budgeting Made Easy," *Management Accounting*, October 1998.

Ethics: Kilpatrick, "It's Time to Face the Music on Budgets," *CMA Magazine*, March 1994.

Grandmother Calendar Company: "A Company Failing From Too Much Success," *The Wall Street Journal*, March 17, 1995, pp. A1, B2.

Human factors in budgeting: Soulier, "A Psychological Model of the Budgetary Process," *The Woman CPA*, January 1980.

Japanese budgeting: Howell and Sakurai, "Management Accounting (and Other) Lessons from the Japanese," *Management Accounting*, December 1992.

Manipulating numbers, cash vs. GAAP: Simon Caulkin article, *The Observer*, March 5, 1995, p. 9.

Monte Carlo simulations: Fordham and Marshall, "Tools for Dealing with Uncertainty," *Management Accounting*, September 1997.

OLAP: Haddleton, "10 Rules for Selecting Budget Management Software," *Management Accounting*, January 1998.

Phillips Petroleum: Silas, "The Moral Dimension of Competitiveness," *Management Accounting*, December 1994.

Sensitivity analysis: Grant, "High-Tech Budgeting," *Management Accounting*, May 1991.

"Spend it or lose it" and governmental cash management: Finch and Mihal, "Spend It or Lose It," *Management Accounting*, March 1989.

Wal-Mart: "Just Get It to the Stores on Time," *Business Week*, March 6, 1995, pp. 66–67; and Shern, "Retailing Revs Up Just in Time for Happy Holidays," *Business UpShot*, Ernst & Young LLP, November 1997.

*Alphabetic by topic, idea, or company referenced.

CHAPTER 5

How Do Things Really Work?

Accumulating Product Costs

KEY OBJECTIVES:

1	*Discuss how work traditionally has been organized and how cost accounting measures work efficiency.*
2	*List the source documents required for direct cost assignment.*
3	*Prepare a predetermined overhead rate and justify its allocation base.*
4	*Explain the need for equivalent units and calculate the average department cost per equivalent unit in a process costing system.*
5	*Describe how WIP is organized in a job costing system and calculate a job's cost.*
6	*[Appendix A] Distinguish between service and line departments, and justify the need for departmental PORs.*

Everyone was ready to start the next meeting. Only Julie was missing. The grandchildren were pretty content with themselves. Now all they had to do was watch the money roll in, or so they believed! If the Boss (Grandfather Multree) was still alive, he'd be proud.

"I think we've really made progress in learning how to run the business, especially with how management accounting information translates our plans into dollars [cashflows]. We prepared our proforma income statement, did our cost-volume-profit [CVP] analysis, and developed a cash budget. Our projected profits will satisfy the provisions of the Boss's will, allowing us to keep the business, and our budget guarantees the cashflow necessary for our operations. Running a business is pretty straightforward! It's just like my smooth-running dune buggy."

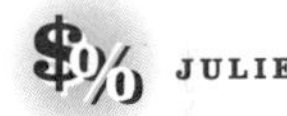

Julie entered the boardroom. "Well, I'm glad you're happy with yourselves! But I want to look under the hood. What I mean is I, too, am happy because all the accounting numbers fit together. However, let's make sure they really happen. Does Multree's operating system support our plans?"

The Next Management Problem: Efficiently Organizing Work

"Yes! We better start worrying about achieving our plans. When I look in our factory, all I see is organized chaos! So far, we only have made our plans. Planning is just the first aspect of good management. Second, we have to control day-to-day operations. Finally, we need to evaluate performance. To accomplish our second and third management functions, we need to understand how things are done. I think we should tour the plant and see how work is organized."

The historic development of scientific management

"First, we need a short history lesson. We began industrialization with 'cottage industries.' Individual trades, such as a blacksmith, were passed down through family generations. It took years to learn a trade because no formal training or educational programs existed.

KEY OBJECTIVE 1

Discuss how work traditionally has been organized and how cost accounting measures work efficiency.

"The first industrial revolution moved us from cottage industries to mass production. Scientific management developed to organize and control this new work environment. Its objective was to maximize operating efficiency through managing time. Trades were divided into small, easily learned tasks. It was just too expensive to have a craftsman do everything within the value chain.

"The goals for scientific management became task specialization and maximizing machinery use. For each task, scientific management identified the one best way to do it. Laborers then learned that one way. Task specialization allowed manufacturers to hire cheap labor instead of expensive craftsmen."

TOMMY

"Maximizing machinery use meant 'run that machine all the time!' That's why the Boss hung those 'Everyone keep busy!' banners throughout the plant. It's still our gospel today."

NANCY

"I don't understand how dividing work into small tasks and running machines all the time accomplishes the objective of maximizing operating efficiency. Can you explain this?"

Justifying scientific management with accounting efficiency measures

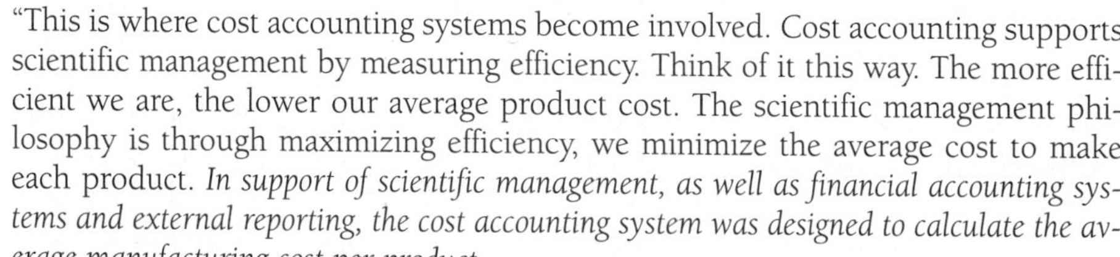

JULIE

"This is where cost accounting systems become involved. Cost accounting supports scientific management by measuring efficiency. Think of it this way. The more efficient we are, the lower our average product cost. The scientific management philosophy is through maximizing efficiency, we minimize the average cost to make each product. *In support of scientific management, as well as financial accounting systems and external reporting, the cost accounting system was designed to calculate the average manufacturing cost per product.*

"Hiring cheap labor minimizes direct labor cost, which scientific management considers a variable production cost. Machines, on the other hand, are very expensive. Machinery creates fixed manufacturing costs. Running machinery all the time minimizes the amount of this fixed cost included in [averaged into] each product. Here's an example. A machine can make 100 products and costs $1,000 a month [ignoring electricity and any other variable operating costs]. This *total* cost does not change if production volume changes [e.g., whether we make 10 or 100 products]. Thus it is a fixed cost. To include the machine's cost in the cost of each product, we have to average ['allocate' in accounting terminology] the $1,000 total cost over the number of products made. If we make 10 products, the *average fixed cost per product* is $100 [$1,000 ÷ 10 products]. If we make 100 products, the average fixed cost *per product* drops to $10.

"Scientific management seeks to minimize variable production costs by hiring cheap labor. It minimizes the average machinery fixed cost *per product* by making as many products as possible. [Exhibit 5-1 illustrates the average cost per product.]

"During the cottage industry era, variable production costs were significant [e.g., the direct labor cost of craftsmen], but fixed costs [e.g., machinery] were not. The first industrial revolution reversed this relationship. Variable costs decreased in importance, while fixed manufacturing costs increased dramatically. With large investments in machinery, maximizing machine use became an extremely important priority. *Remember, scientific management measures efficiency by the average manufacturing cost per product."*

BOB

"This is how work is organized at Multree Homes. We've grouped specialized activities into separate departments so we can operate more efficiently. Each department, like Sawing, Truss Making, Framing, Roofing, and Plumbing, has its own

Calculating the Average Cost per Product

Resource	Cost behavior	If 10 houses are built: Total cost	If 10 houses are built: Average cost per house	If 100 houses are built: Total cost	If 100 houses are built: Average cost per house
Direct labor	Variable: $50 per product	$500	$50*	$5,000	$50*
Machinery	Fixed: $1,000 per month	$1,000	$100**	$1,000	$10**
Sums		$1,500	$150	$6,000	$60

Notes: * Variable costs *per unit* (house) do not change when volume (number of houses) changes within the relevant range.
** Fixed costs *per unit* change inversely with volume (within the relevant range).

Exhibit 5-1

boss and workers specialized in doing that one set of tasks. Each department is responsible for maximizing its output and minimizing its average cost per product."

"So keeping busy usually means we will reduce our unit costs. But how do we coordinate these specialized departments?"

The resulting coordination problem

"Somehow we must balance the production flow. By 'balance,' I mean all the machines and departments are busy all the time. To show you how we do it, here's a little puzzle. I'll buy lunch for the best solution that coordinates production among the departments to minimize machine downtime!"

Scheduling production: An example. "We have three departments and make three products. Each product follows the same processing sequence [Sawing, Framing, then Finishing] but uses different machine times within the departments. Here's the information you'll need about production times in each department for each product."

Sawing department	Framing department	Finishing department
Product A needs 1 week	Product A needs 2 weeks	Product A needs 3 weeks
Product B needs 2 weeks	Product B needs 4 weeks	Product B needs 1 week
Product C needs 3 weeks	Product C needs 1 week	Product C needs 4 weeks

Sid, as the new boss, thought he could devise the fastest production schedule—and when everyone finished, he had [see Exhibit 5-2].

Sid started with product A because he can get it out of Sawing faster than the other products. This minimizes the wait time in the other two departments. Using the same logic, when Sawing finishes product A, it next makes product B, and finally product C. Sid's solution requires 12 weeks. During this time, Sawing is idle 6 weeks, Framing 5 weeks, and Finishing 4 weeks, for a total of 15 idle weeks.

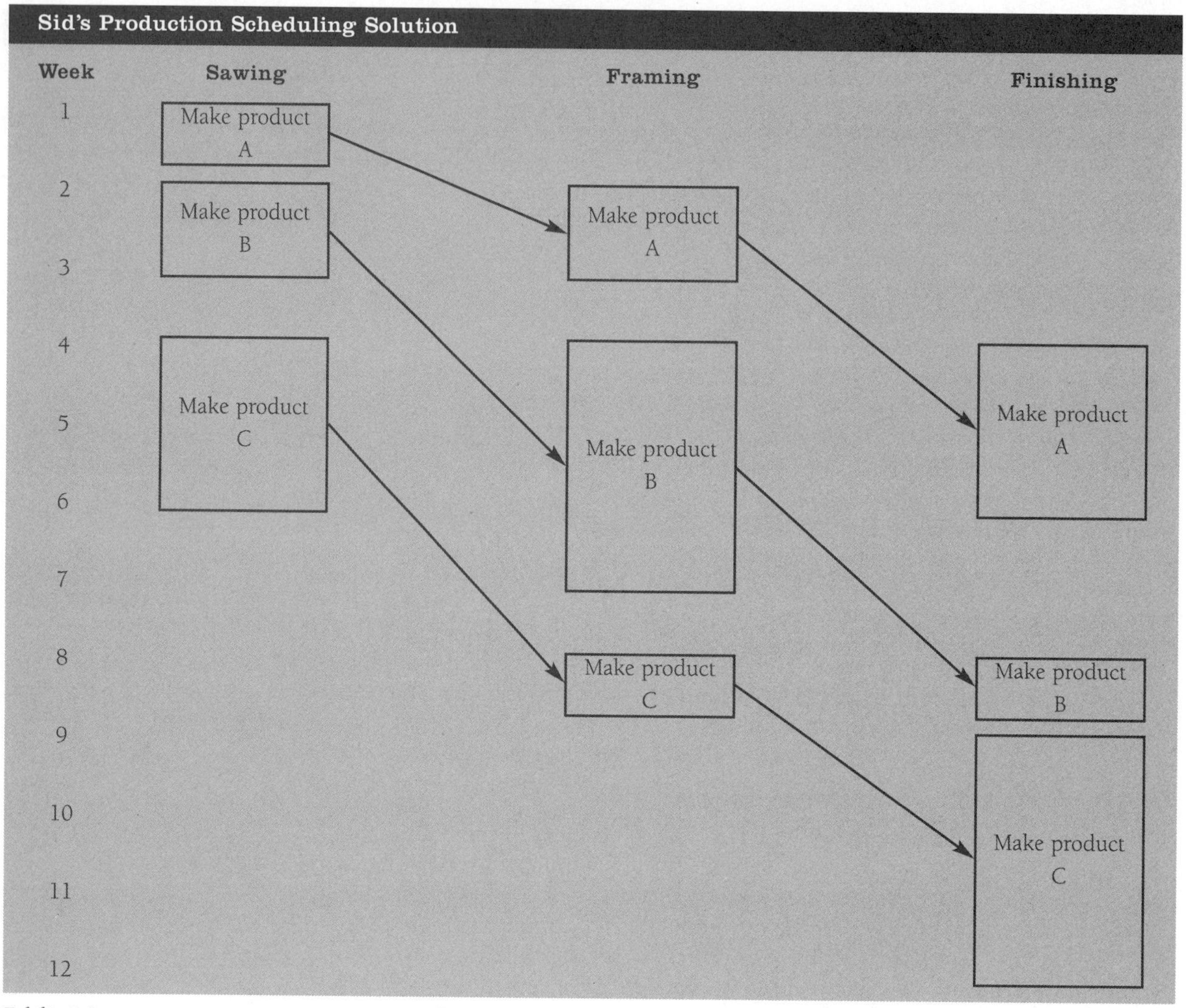

Sid's Production Scheduling Solution

Week | Sawing | Framing | Finishing

1 2 3 4 5 6 7 8 9 10 11 12

Sawing: Make product A; Make product B; Make product C

Framing: Make product A; Make product B; Make product C

Finishing: Make product A; Make product B; Make product C

Exhibit 5-2

BOB

Solving the coordination problem with inventories. "Sid's solution is very interesting. Sawing completes product C at the end of week 6, but Framing cannot start it until week 8. For 1 week, product C sits in inventory. Work-in-process [WIP] inventory is partially completed products waiting to be finished. In Sid's solution, we have some product C in WIP. I like the idea of having WIP. In my solution [Exhibit 5-3] I have some product C WIP at the beginning of week 1 waiting to be worked on by Framing. Similarly, I have some product B WIP at the beginning of week 1 waiting for Finishing to begin working on it. Having WIP allows me to better coordinate production, reduce idle time to three weeks, complete production of all three products in only eight weeks, and make enough product B and C WIP to begin this eight-week cycle again! My logic is to make sure we have enough WIP between departments so everyone can keep busy."

JULIE

"With WIP, each department can operate independently from the others. Now we can accumulate the costs of each department and how much product it makes. We can evaluate the department's performance by calculating the average cost per prod-

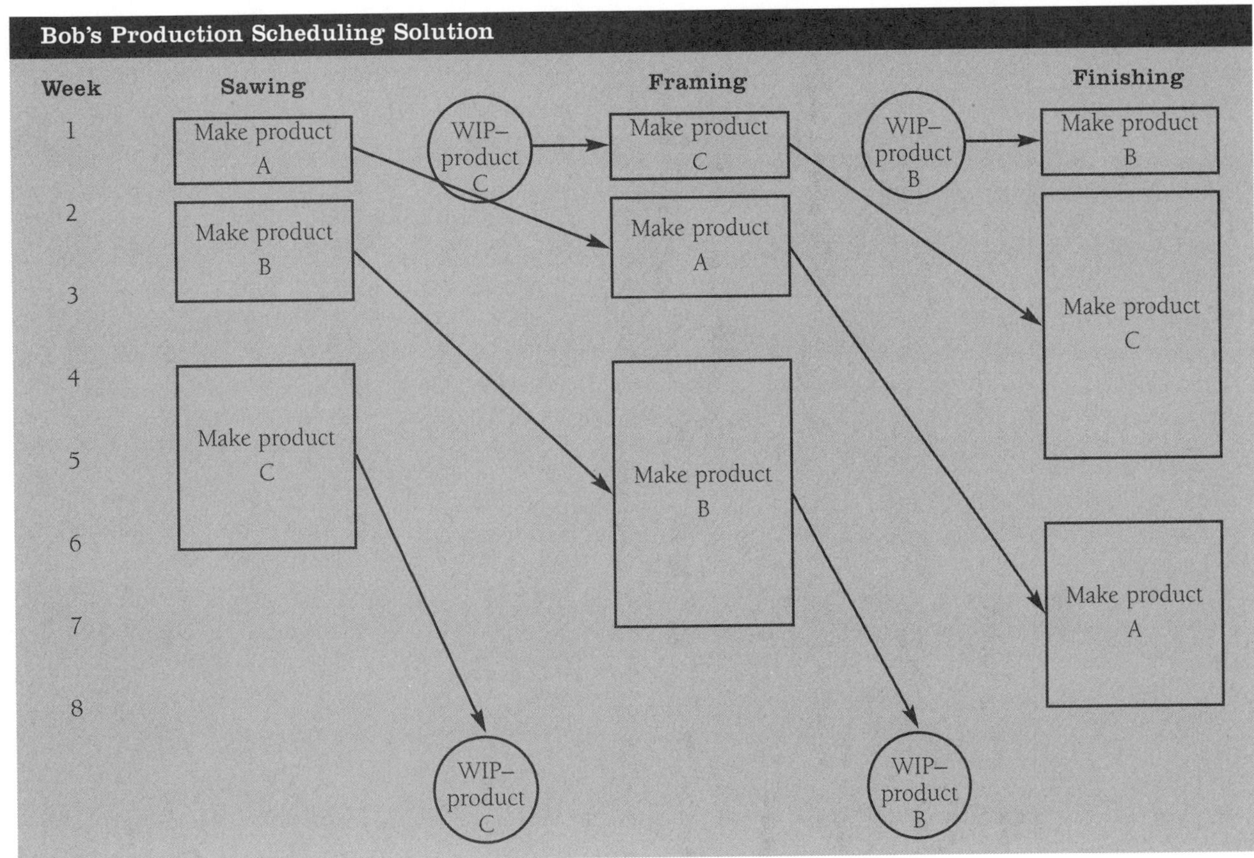

Exhibit 5-3

uct. If everyone is busy all the time, and machinery is being used all the time, the average product cost in every department should be minimized!"

Managing uncertainties with slack. "If everyone is supposed to keep busy, what do you want to do with the two weeks of idle time in Sawing [weeks 7 and 8] and the week 8 idle time in Framing?"

NANCY

BOB

"That's easy! I'll just have them make more WIP. It's a good idea to have some extra WIP in case something goes wrong somewhere. For example, if a machine breaks down in Sawing, having extra WIP between Sawing and Framing allows Framing to keep busy. Having extra resources available in case something goes wrong is called **slack**. Slack resources allow each department to operate relatively independently from the other departments. Each department can keep busy all the time.

> **Slack** *resources are extra people (time), materials, machinery, or other resources available to protect against uncertainties.*

"Extra inventories are just one example of how slack is used to manage these 'uncertainties.' While you may find a better solution to my simple puzzle, think about all the uncertainties if we have another three product lines and five more departments, along with machine breakdowns, material quality and delivery problems, labor shortages, and the like! Of course, we always try to schedule production in the most efficient manner, but we live in a world of uncertainty and things are always changing. In reality, we need many kinds of slack resources." [Exhibit 5-4

The Management Problem: Managing Uncertainties

The uncertainty	Examples	Solutions
1. Unreliable deliveries	1. Missed delivery dates, wrong materials received, wrong amounts received	1. Extra raw materials inventory
2. Unreliable machinery	2. Machine breakdowns, inconsistent output quality	2. Extra machines, extra machine time allowed, extra work-in-process (WIP) inventory
3. Product quality problems	3. Bad raw materials received, bad components made (WIP), bad final products	3. Extra raw materials inventory, extra WIP inventory, extra finished goods inventory
4. Labor problems	4. Poorly educated, poorly motivated	4. Simplify tasks and create specialized departments, allow extra time for each task, hire extra workers
5. Fluctuating product demand	5. Actual orders for standard and custom homes change after they are scheduled to be built and/or construction has started	5. Extra raw materials inventory, extra WIP inventory, extra finished goods inventory

Exhibit 5-4

summarizes some different types of uncertainty and how slack resources are used to manage them.]

"Your use of inventories to maximize efficiency is very interesting because my doctor works on the same principle. A doctor's 'product' is a cured patient. Sick patients waiting to be cured are WIP. The doctor, nurses, staff, and medical equipment are very expensive fixed cost resources. To maximize efficient use of these resources, patients wait in the reception area, each treatment room has a patient waiting, and the doctor and nurses move from one room and patient to another. If we examine other types of services we'll find the same basic idea of how to use expensive resources efficiently."

"Let's see if I understand. To maximize the company's value, we maximize the value of each part separately. That is, *maximizing the efficiency of each department maximizes the overall efficiency of the firm. And if efficiency is maximized, the average cost per product is minimized.*"

"Yes. In each department, workers perform very limited activities instead of complex multi-task activities. Scientific management believes we can get the most out of a person by limiting the difficulty of the tasks we ask her to do. At the department level, each one performs a very limited, specific activity, like welding or framing. To make sure each task is performed as quickly as possible, scientific management uses engineers to determine the 'one best way' to do it. By minimizing the difficulty of a worker's job, we can hire relatively inexpensive labor and quickly train it. By assigning a worker just one task, like operating a drill press, versus requiring that worker to operate more than one machine, scientific management keeps the drill press running all the time. Now that we understand the basic logic of how work is organized, we're ready to take our plant tour."

The plant tour

"All processes [even breathing] convert raw materials into a finished product. Processes use resources [materials, labor, and overhead (e.g., machinery, tools, and buildings)]. Conversion, or production, processes exist in all types of firms. A hospital produces cured patients using medicines and medical supplies, doctors and nurses, and specialized equipment like x-ray machines. A school produces educated students using texts, computers and other equipment, supplies, teachers, and the like. A CPA firm produces tax returns from receipts, using specialized labor [accountants] and equipment [computers and tax software]. At Multree Homes, we manufacture houses.

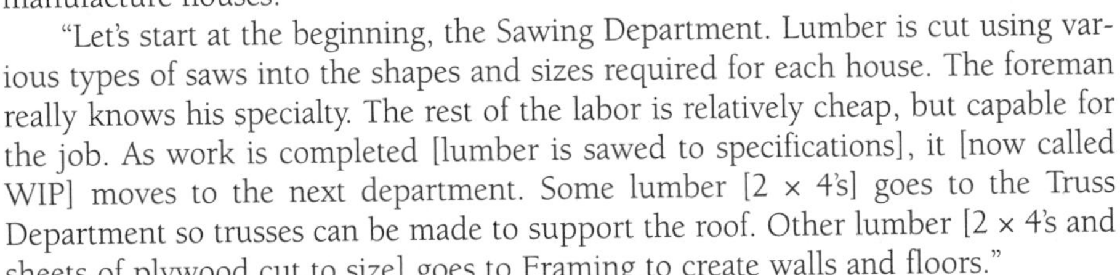

"Let's start at the beginning, the Sawing Department. Lumber is cut using various types of saws into the shapes and sizes required for each house. The foreman really knows his specialty. The rest of the labor is relatively cheap, but capable for the job. As work is completed [lumber is sawed to specifications], it [now called WIP] moves to the next department. Some lumber [2 × 4's] goes to the Truss Department so trusses can be made to support the roof. Other lumber [2 × 4's and sheets of plywood cut to size] goes to Framing to create walls and floors."

Multree's production cycle. "All work goes through the same cycle of activities, whether we're thinking of a bank, law firm, or manufacturer. These activities are *move, wait, set up, run, and move*. They are repeated throughout the production process for each task. [Exhibit 5-5 illustrates this cycle for the Sawing Department.]

Sawing Department Production Cycle

	Production cycle activities				
	Move	**Wait**	**Set up**	**Run**	**Move**
Management activities:	Order lumber from raw materials inventory	Have lumber available when saw is ready	Order sent to Machining Department for saw setup specialist	Schedule workers	Order sawed lumber to be moved to WIP storage area
Operations activities:	Forklift truck moves lumber to Sawing	Lumber stacked next to saw	Specialists set up machines (saws) for the specific work needed	Saw lumber	Forklift truck moves lumber to stock yard

Exhibit 5-5

"To minimize the cost of raw materials, purchase discounts are negotiated for large orders. Because we receive so much at one time, we need to stockpile it somewhere. This is why we have the stock yard [raw materials inventory]. Buying more than we need also provides assurance against uncertainty. Protecting against uncertainty costs money. How much depends on the level of service we get from our lumber suppliers. If the lumber quality is low, we need to stockpile more. If the supplier's deliveries are unreliable [not on time, or not complete], we should keep more lumber in stock to guard against these types of problems. Slack can be expensive, but necessary when resource quality and reliability are low.

"When we're ready to start a house, the lumber is moved to the Sawing Department and stacked next to each saw until needed. Actually, the saws aren't ready yet, but I can't wait to deliver the lumber until the saws are ready because the forklift truck may not be available. This is another example of using slack resources [time and materials] to guard against uncertainties and keep everyone busy. It's better to have the lumber there ahead of schedule than to wait until the last minute and hope nothing goes wrong!

"Before we can begin sawing the lumber, a specialist in setting up machines must adjust the saw settings and the tools it uses. Remember, with scientific management we have different people specializing in individual tasks. The Sawing Department workers are trained only in running the machines. Other workers are trained in setting up and repairing the machines [they work in the Machining Department]. After the lumber is cut, it is moved to WIP [an area in the stock yard] where it waits until the next department needs it. Then the move-wait-set up-run-move cycle starts again for the next task."

Organizing the production process value chain. "Using scientific management, each activity in our value chain's manufacturing process becomes a functional department. The third process in our value chain is manufacturing [see Exhibit 2-5]. It has eleven activities: sawing, framing, rough wiring, rough plumbing, and the like. Each activity is a specialized set of tasks. Scientific management organizes work into specialized functions for greater efficiency, so each activity becomes a separate functional department. Here's how the Boss organized our manufacturing process [see Exhibit 5-6]."

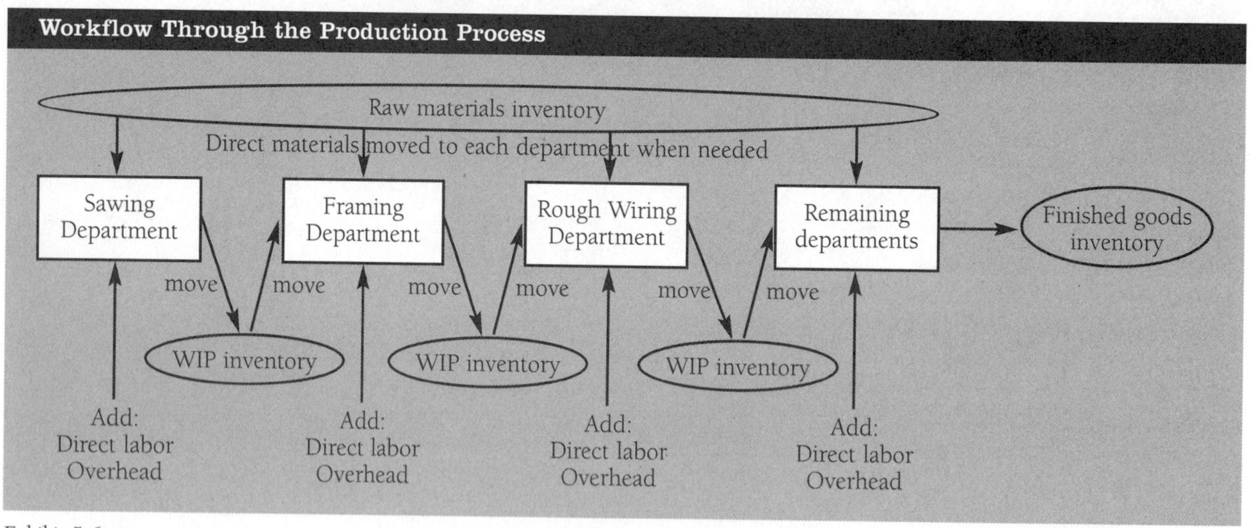

Exhibit 5-6

Why We Inventory Production Costs

"O.K. I understand how and why we organize the activities in our production process. But how does the cost accounting system track the resource and activity costs? How are these production costs assigned to products?"

JACKIE

"*The ultimate objective of a cost accounting system is to determine the cost of our products.* Let's start with product costs. I'll then work backwards through the income statement to see how we track resource and activity costs. What's Multree Homes' primary objective?"

NANCY

"To increase our value by making more money today and in the future. To do this, we must sell houses for more than it costs us to make them."

JACKIE

"Yes! The sum of all the sales prices from the houses we sell is called 'revenues.' The sum of the costs of making all the houses we sold is 'cost of goods sold.' The difference is 'gross profit.' This is the top half of the functional format income statement used for external financial reporting."

Understanding cost of (the) goods (we) sold

JACKIE

"How do we calculate cost of goods sold? First let's think about calculating the number of products sold. Then we will assign costs to those products. Here's the formula in words:

We have 5 products finished and ready to sell at the beginning of the year.
We built 10 products this year.
Therefore, we have 15 products we could sell this year.
We did not sell 2 of these products.
Therefore, we sold 13 products this year.

I've added the accounting terms and costs to the formula, using some simple numbers [see Exhibit 5-7].

The Cost of Goods Sold Calculation

In words:	Accounting terminology	Cost reported on income statement
We have 5 products finished and ready to sell at the beginning of the year.	Beginning finished goods inventory	$45
We built 10 products this year.	+ Cost of goods manufactured	100
We have 15 products we could sell this year.	Cost of goods available for sale	$145
We did not sell 2 of these products.	Less: ending finished goods inventory	(20)
Therefore, we sold 13 products this year.	**Cost of goods sold**	**$125**

Note: Technically we're assuming FIFO.

Exhibit 5-7

"The first cost is beginning finished goods inventory. These products were made last year. Last year we made 10 products, spending $90 in manufacturing costs. This averages $9 a product. Five products were not sold. Since these products were not sold, they became assets on last year's balance sheet. Assets are things we will use in the future to make money. At the end of last year, we planned on selling those five products this year. So they were assets, specifically finished goods inventory. Last year's ending finished goods inventory is this year's beginning inventory. This equals 5 products, costing $9 each, totaling $45 [the beginning finished goods inventory cost in Exhibit 5-7].

"The second cost is the cost of goods manufactured. This year we made 10 products, with total production costs of $100. The average manufacturing cost per product is $10. In total, we can sell 15 products, and the cost of these goods available for sale is $145 [5 products costing $45 in total, plus 10 products costing $100]. If two products are not sold at year-end, this year's ending finished goods inventory is $20. Cost of goods sold is the sum of the 5 products made last year and sold this year [$45] plus the cost of the 8 products made and sold this year [$80]."

"What bothers me about your calculation of a product's cost is only including its manufacturing costs. For each house we sell, we pay our sales people a commission. We have to ship each house to the customer. Each house has a warranty cost budget. Aren't these costs part of the house's cost, too? Is it ethical to ignore them?"

"That's a good point. But remember the historic development of accounting systems we discussed in our first two meetings? Financial accounting systems report on management's stewardship to the investor-owners and creditors. For external reporting, costs are organized on the income statement by function, just as departments are organized by function [sawing, framing, etc.]. The costs of getting a product [merchandise purchases for a merchandiser, cost of goods manufactured for a manufacturer] are reported separately from the costs of getting rid of a product and running the business [selling and administrative expenses].

"The first industrial revolution heralded the age of large factories and mass production. Cost accounting systems were created to track production costs and determine the cost of making products [i.e., cost of goods manufactured]. Once known, cost of the goods sold was calculated and reported on the income statement, and the cost of goods not sold [ending finished goods inventory] was reported on the balance sheet as an asset. Shipping and commissions are not ignored. Rather, they are reported in a different part of the income statement [the expenses section]."

"The ethical issue for accountants occurs when management relies on average product costs in decisions. We need to make them aware that products incur more than just manufacturing costs. The 'product's cost' for financial reporting is determined by GAAP, which defines it to include only manufacturing costs. However, for our needs, we should include manufacturing and nonmanufacturing costs in the 'product's cost.' Management also needs to know which costs are variable and fixed. Thus, for internal reporting, I prepare a contribution margin income statement. For external reporting, Jackie prepares the functionally formatted income statement.

"Not only should we broaden what is included in 'cost,' we also should broaden the meaning of 'product.' With the growth of cost accounting systems in the service sector, the distinction between a 'tangible' product and an 'intangible' service is no longer important. Think of a CPA firm. It provides an income tax service to its customers, but isn't the income tax return a manufactured product? Usually I think of Pizza Hut as being in the food service industry, but doesn't it manufacture pizzas?"

Accumulating manufacturing costs in WIP

"O.K. To satisfy our financial reporting needs, we'll focus on the costs of manufacturing a product. Even for management decisions, we need this information.

Looking back, though [to Exhibit 5-7], can you explain how the cost accounting system recorded the $100 in production costs for the year?"

JACKIE

"Sure. As we spend money in manufacturing, that is, as we use resources in making a house, the resource costs [direct materials, direct labor, and manufacturing overhead] are accumulated in the WIP general ledger account. *WIP includes all the costs of making a product, from start to finish.* I think of WIP as our factory. Resources go in the factory's front door, and finished products leave out the back door. Analogously, the resource costs 'enter the front door' of WIP [costs are debited to WIP]. Until the product is completed, manufacturing costs are accumulated in WIP. These accumulated costs become the cost of the goods manufactured when the product is finished. As the product leaves through the factory's back door, its cost 'leaves WIP through its back door' [i.e., credit WIP].

"Using scientific management, the factory is divided into many functional silos [departments]. *Similarly, the WIP general ledger account can have many subsidiary ledger accounts for the different departments in the factory.* With a separate WIP account for the Sawing Department, for example, we can trace resource costs to it. We can do this for every department [see Exhibit 5-8]."

Cost Flows Through the Production Process

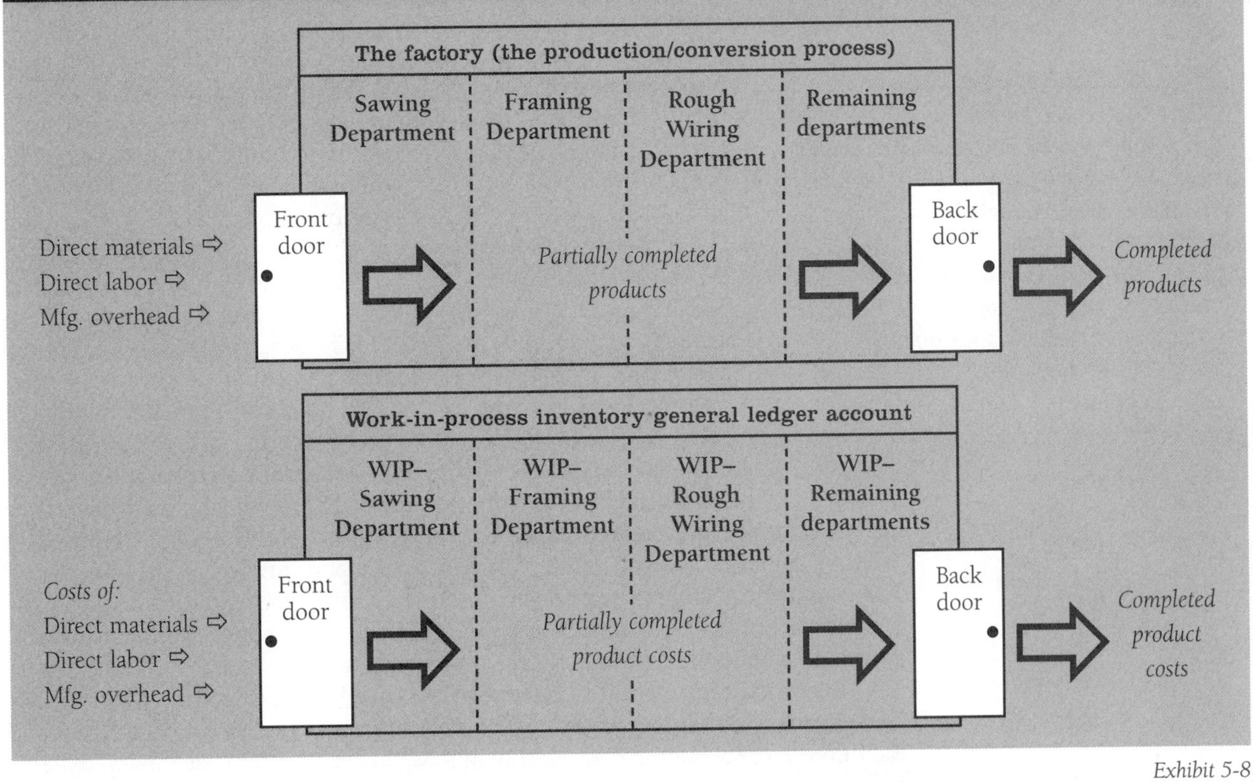

The factory (the production/conversion process)

		Sawing Department	**Framing Department**	**Rough Wiring Department**	**Remaining departments**		
Direct materials ⇨ Direct labor ⇨ Mfg. overhead ⇨	Front door	⇨		*Partially completed products*	⇨	Back door	⇨ *Completed products*

Work-in-process inventory general ledger account

		WIP–Sawing Department	**WIP–Framing Department**	**WIP–Rough Wiring Department**	**WIP–Remaining departments**		
Costs of: Direct materials ⇨ Direct labor ⇨ Mfg. overhead ⇨	Front door	⇨		*Partially completed product costs*	⇨	Back door	⇨ *Completed product costs*

Exhibit 5-8

NANCY

"I get it. As 10 products were being made this year, $100 was spent on direct materials, direct labor, and manufacturing overhead. I see how the cost accounting system, and specifically the WIP general ledger account, mimics the workflow in accumulating the $100. But where did the $100 come from? How much was materials versus labor or overhead? How much was spent in each department? Don't we want to know this information if we are to control operations in each separate department?"

Accounting for direct production costs

"Of course we want to know more specific information. We have two ways for assigning costs, that is, identifying and verifying resource costs, and tracking where they are used. **Cost assignment** is attaching resource costs to something of interest [a 'cost object,' e.g., a specific product, a batch of products, a department, a product line, a geographic sales territory, etc.]. Costs can be assigned through **direct tracing** [e.g., matching specific resources to specific products] or **cost allocation** [e.g., dividing indirect costs among all products made]. Let's look at each cost assignment method in turn."

Costs are **assigned** *to a "cost object" (e.g., a product or department) either by* **direct tracing** *or* **cost allocation**. *Specifically identifying a resource cost to a cost object (direct tracing) is not always possible. Many costs need to be averaged (overhead allocation) in order to be included in a department or product's cost.*

Cost accuracy through physical tracing and source documents. "Before we computerized production scheduling and our cost accounting system, we generated a lot of paperwork to authorize and document resource costs. Let me describe how our manual system worked. Once you understand the paperwork flow, I'll discuss how computerization has replaced much of the paperwork-based controls.

KEY OBJECTIVE 2

List the source documents required for direct cost assignment.

"First, we purchase materials and stockpile them in raw materials inventory. A **purchase order** is the formal source document authorizing a specific purchase of certain resources at a specified price. For example, our purchasing agent works with three lumberyards. After getting the best price, which usually requires a large order, he issues a purchase order specifying all the terms of the purchase. This is a multipart form, with copies going to the stock yard and accounting. When the stock yard receives the lumber, it sends one of the copies, called a **receiving report**, to Accounting [debit raw materials inventory, credit accounts payable]. The receiving report verifies delivery and, with the purchase order, justifies paying the invoice when received from the lumberyard [debit accounts payable, credit cash].

Many source documents are used in cost accounting systems. **Purchase orders** *authorize the purchase and receipt of materials.* **Receiving reports** *document we have the materials and authorize payment.* **Materials requisitions** *track their movement and allow direct tracing of material costs to products (or other cost objects).* **Time cards** *directly trace labor costs to products.*

"When materials are needed for production, a **materials requisition** form is prepared by the department requesting the materials. Upon receipt, I record the materials moved from the stock yard to the factory [e.g., for lumber moved to Sawing, debit WIP—Sawing Department and credit raw materials inventory]. These source documents provide the means to control the acquisition and movement of expensive materials that easily can be traced to products [direct materials], as well as initiate the cost accounting system journal entries.

"To control direct labor costs, we used to have every worker keep a time card. **Time cards** allow us to identify and journalize direct labor to each department and each product. Through source documents, we accurately can trace many material and labor costs. Cost accuracy is not a problem for directly traceable resource usage, that is, direct materials and direct labor."

ERP, EDI, and bar coding. "That's how we used to do it with our manual system. However, production is much more coordinated since we invested in computer systems. And the paperwork has been significantly reduced. Our enterprise resource planning [ERP] system now schedules production and orders materials.

Each product has a bill of materials listing the direct materials needed. The system contains information on when materials should be ordered, their prices, machine times needed and available, manpower requirements, and the like. Thus purchase orders can be automatically created and transmitted directly to suppliers' computer ordering systems via electronic data interchange [EDI] networks. EDI also can schedule shippers for transporting materials and completed homes, and pay them [as well as paying suppliers] with electronic funds transfers from our bank account to theirs. Once received, the ERP system releases materials to production when needed. It also schedules machines and labor to meet delivery dates."

"ERP systems such as ours are not unique. The IMA Cost Management Group's 1998 survey on cost management practices reports over 36% of responding firms have ERP systems in place, and another 19% are planning new systems. ERPs aren't cheap, though. We're averaging about $9,000 per end user in information technology costs. According to a recent Hackett Group study, our costs are about normal [average $9,218; top quartile $11,160; bottom quartile $3,387]."

"As work progresses, laser scanners read bar codes on materials and WIP verifying movement through the plant. Machines and workers have bar codes as well, allowing these resource costs to be traced directly without all the paperwork we used to create. Now we have real-time information on the status and cost of each house.

"Pillowtex, one of the largest pillow manufacturers, has used a similar system since 1990. Not only has it abandoned its manual cost accounting system, production time also has decreased. Virtually all the costs associated with the accounting-related paperwork [costs of the forms, ordering them, storing them, filling out each one, delivering them to everyone who needs a copy, and permanently filing them] have been eliminated!"

"I'll grant you manual systems are becoming obsolete. Hardcopy source documents have been replaced with computer files. But understanding the manual system helps to identify the information needed by the cost accounting system. Only the media has changed, not our information requirements!"

Representing resource usage with T-accounts. "Just to make sure you understand how costs flow through the accounting system, matching the flow of work and resource usage, let me draw you a picture. Accountants aren't always good artists, so bear with me. When drawing people, the best I can do is 'stick people.' I'll do something similar, called T-accounts, for the factory building, departments, and general ledger accounts. I think of a T-account as a building [or department or account]. I won't include the roof, walls, windows, doors, or floors, though. All I'll draw is the 'stick' frame, which looks like a 'T,' hence the name 'T-account' [see Exhibit 5-9].

"Technically, T-accounts are the accountant's picture of a general ledger account. WIP is a general ledger control account. This means it contains many subsets [subsidiary ledger accounts] making up its balance. The subsets of the factory are its departments. Analogously, WIP is made up of subsidiary ledger accounts for each department [e.g., WIP—Sawing Dept.]. So the sum of each department's cost equals the WIP balance.

"Using the T-accounts, we can now answer Nancy's question about how the cost accounting system accumulates the $100 cost of the 10 houses we made. Remember, these numbers aren't realistic. I want to use the smallest numbers I can, so you can concentrate on the ideas without getting bogged down in big numbers. From our source documents [material requisitions and time cards], $10 of resource

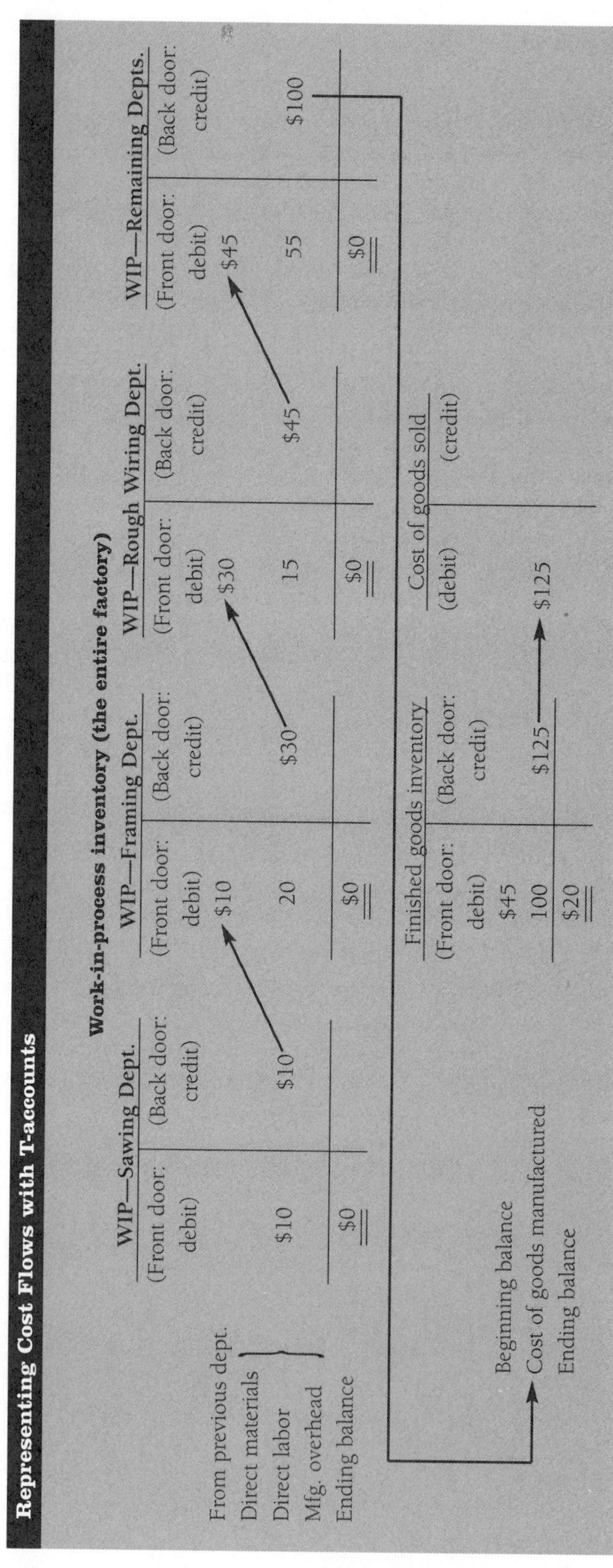

Representing Cost Flows with T-accounts
Work-in-process inventory (the entire factory)
WIP—Sawing Dept.
(Front door: debit)
(Back door: credit)
$10
$10
$0
WIP—Framing Dept.
(Front door: debit)
(Back door: credit)
$10
20
$30
$0
WIP—Rough Wiring Dept.
(Front door: debit)
(Back door: credit)
$30
15
$45
$0
WIP—Remaining Depts.
(Front door: debit)
(Back door: credit)
$45
55
$100
$0
From previous dept.
Direct materials
Direct labor
Mfg. overhead
Ending balance
Finished goods inventory
(Front door: debit)
(Back door: credit)
$45
100
$125
$20
Cost of goods sold
(debit)
(credit)
$125
Beginning balance
Cost of goods manufactured
Ending balance

Exhibit 5-9

costs are incurred in the Sawing Department [debit WIP—Sawing Dept.]. When we finish sawing the lumber, it moves to the next department [debit WIP—Framing Dept., credit WIP—Sawing Dept.]. In addition to the $10 of sawed lumber, another $20 is spent in the Framing Department. When the 10 partially completed houses leave Framing for Rough Wiring, their accumulated cost is $30. We spend $15 in Rough Wiring, so the partially completed houses leaving this department cumulatively cost $45. Each of the remaining departments has its own subsidiary ledger account, and we spend another $55 in these departments finishing the houses. The total cost to build the houses is $100. This is the amount transferred out of the last department when they are completed and leave the factory.

"Completed products leave the factory [credit WIP—the last department] and go to [debit] finished goods inventory until sold. As houses are sold, they leave finished goods inventory [credit their cost from this account and debit cost of goods sold].

"Before leaving T-accounts, let's do an analysis of a general ledger account. A general ledger account has four components: a beginning balance, costs added, costs removed, and an ending balance. Look at the Framing Department again [Exhibit 5-9]. We have no beginning balance. We spend $10 sawing lumber. All the lumber is sawed and moved to Framing, so $10 leaves the Sawing Department account. Because no lumber remains in Sawing, its account balance should be zero.

"Now look at finished goods inventory. Last year's ending balance was $45 [5 houses made last year, costing $9 each, which were not sold last year]. Since we have them ready to sell at the beginning of this year, the beginning finished goods inventory balance is $45 [last year's ending balance becomes this year's beginning balance]. We built 10 houses this year, costing $100 [cost of goods manufactured]. As they are completed, these houses are added to finished goods inventory. The cost of the goods available for sale [15 houses] is $145. We sell 13 houses this year [$125 total cost], leaving an ending balance of 2 houses costing $20 in total. Using a balance equation, we can verify this.

The Balance Equation						
Beginning balance	**+**	**Costs added this period**	**=**	**Costs removed**	**+**	**Ending balance**
$45	**+**	**$100**	**=**	**$125**	**+**	**$20**

The balance equation can be used to verify the ending balance in any T-account [or general ledger account], as well as to calculate any of the four components given the other three values."

Accounting for indirect production costs

"I see how direct materials and direct labor are assigned to each department using source documents, and how we accumulate manufacturing costs in each department with WIP subsidiary ledger accounts. However, I don't understand how overhead [indirect manufacturing costs] gets into the cost of each department. So far, you've only explained direct tracing. How does the overhead allocation process work?"

"Some requisitioned materials, like nails and factory supplies [drill bits, jigsaw blades, etc.], are not worth the effort to directly trace their costs to departments and products. These indirect material costs are charged to overhead. We also cannot directly trace some labor, such as forklift drivers and supervisors, to any particular department. Thus indirect labor is included in overhead.

"Many other resources are indirect costs included in overhead. Factory building costs [heating and lighting, depreciation, property taxes and insurance, building and grounds maintenance, the cafeteria, the first aid station, security, etc.] are not traceable directly to particular departments, so they also are indirect manufacturing costs [another phrase accountants use for overhead].

"If we can see how much of these resources are used in each department, we can trace directly the costs to departments. For example, to make electricity a direct cost, we need separate electric meters for each department. To trace the cost of a machine to a product, we have to measure how much machine time is used on each product. I suppose the plant supervisor can fill out a time card noting how much time he spends in each department. But a lot of his time may not be identifiable with any particular department.

"My point is from a cost-benefit perspective, it just doesn't make sense to try to directly trace many of our production costs. So, *to assign indirect costs to departments or products, we group them together into one account [overhead] and divide up the total [i.e., allocate overhead to departments and products].*"

KEY OBJECTIVE 3

Prepare a predetermined overhead rate and justify its allocation base.

NANCY

JACKIE

The need for predetermined overhead rates. "That makes sense. We accumulate all the indirect manufacturing costs in one general ledger account called overhead. But how does the cost accounting system allocate overhead to departments and products? How frequently should we compute an average overhead cost? Should it be weekly, monthly, quarterly, annually, or for a longer time period?"

"First, let's consider when an average overhead rate should be calculated [your last two questions]. Then we can talk about how we calculate it [your first question]. I've prepared a handout showing the problem with computing the average cost too frequently [see Exhibit 5-10]. In example 1, assume we have only one overhead cost, heating. It is a fixed cost [$1,000 per quarter], but we build a different number of houses each quarter. *Notice how changing production volumes cause the average overhead cost per house to differ from quarter to quarter. Of course, this is only true for fixed costs.* When fixed costs are averaged over output volume [i.e., expressed on a per-unit basis], the fixed cost per house goes down as volume increases. [Review Exhibit 5-1.]

Problems with Calculating an Overhead Rate Too Frequently

Example 1: Output is not constant

Time period	1st quarter	2nd quarter	3rd quarter	4th quarter	Year's total
Overhead cost	$1,000	$1,000	$1,000	$1,000	$4,000
Production volume (houses built)	÷ 10	÷ 40	÷ 25	÷ 5	÷ 80
Average overhead cost per house	$100	$25	$40	$200	$50

Example 2: Overhead cost is not constant

Time period	1st quarter	2nd quarter	3rd quarter	4th quarter	Year's total
Overhead cost	$2,000	$600	$400	$1,000	$4,000
Production volume	÷ 20	÷ 20	÷ 20	÷ 20	÷ 80
Average overhead cost per house	$100	$30	$20	$50	$50

Exhibit 5-10

"If all overhead is a variable cost, quarterly volume changes are not important because the variable cost per house does not change [within the relevant range]. Regardless of the quarterly production volumes, the average overhead cost per home will be the same. Over half of our overhead is a fixed cost, though. So, if we average overhead too frequently, we'll see significant changes in the average cost per house.

"In example 2 [Exhibit 5-10], production volume is the same each quarter, but the heating cost is higher in the winter months. Again, a seasonal factor [changes in volume or cost] causes overhead rate changes."

"I'm sorry, but I do not see a problem. If heating cost is greater in the winter, it should cost more to make a house. I want to know how much more!"

"Why? Which decisions are affected by this information? How does this information help us to manage the company better?"

"Well, if heating cost is higher in the winter, shouldn't we budget for it? Shouldn't we charge more for a product made in the winter if it is more expensive?"

"We did budget for different monthly heating costs in our last meeting when we created our cash budget. But should we raise the sales price on a home just because it was built in the winter, instead of the summer?"

"NO!! Our customers won't allow this! From their point of view, a home made in the summer is identical to one made in the winter. Therefore, both houses should be priced the same."

"I agree. We need to average overhead costs over a longer time period. Because we strategically plan, budget cashflows, and report profits annually, let's calculate an annual average overhead cost. This policy allows two identical products to have the same average overhead cost regardless of when they are made. *We should not let seasonal cost or volume differences affect the product's average cost and sales price.*

"We'll have problems with whatever time period is chosen, though. A year may be too short. If we have the same overhead cost in years 1 and 2, but output is different, the average product cost will be different. This is why Caterpillar uses an average production volume over many years. In contrast, some companies with business cycles shorter than one year recalculate the average each cycle. The time period chosen should make sense for the particular situation. The Boss said it should be annually for us to coincide with our financial accounting cycle."

"But I can't wait until year-end, when we finally know the *actual* overhead cost and output, to get the average overhead rate and incorporate it into a house's sales price. Our sales prices must be high enough to recover all manufacturing costs, including overhead, throughout the year. We need to include overhead in the cost when setting sales prices *at the beginning of the year*. I can't go to a customer who bought a home in March and in December ask him for another $10,000 because I didn't know how much to include for overhead in the original sales price!"

"Remember when we did that housing contract for the Navy? The government made progress payments to us as we built the houses. Each payment covered our construction costs since the last payment, including overhead, and some profit based on the total costs to date. We needed to know how much overhead had been incurred on the houses while we were building them. The idea of an annual *actual* overhead rate won't work for accounting, especially on government contracts!"

"Bill's right. I can't wait until year-end either. I need to control operations on a day-to-day basis. I need to know what my overhead costs should be much more frequently than once a year!"

JULIE

"O.K. *You've identified two problems with overhead allocation:*

- If an average overhead rate is calculated too frequently, seasonal fixed cost and volume changes will affect the average product cost. Our customers won't allow this.
- We cannot wait until year-end in order to know our actual overhead costs and calculate an average rate per house. Our customers won't allow this, and it will inhibit our ability to control operations.

To solve these problems, let's calculate an estimated or **predetermined overhead rate [POR]** to use throughout the year. A POR is the average *estimated* overhead per unit. Here's the formula and rate for this year:

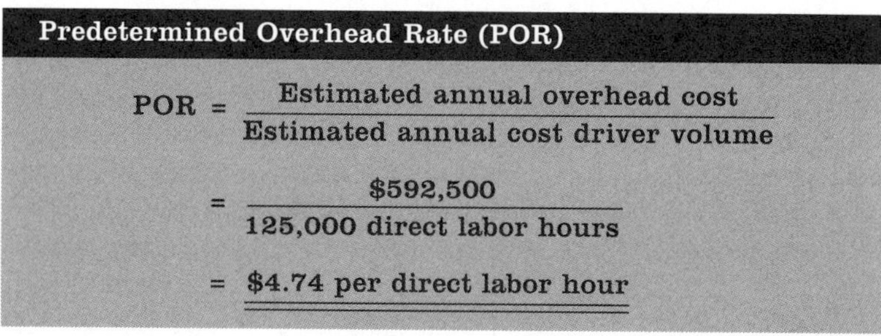

Predetermined Overhead Rate (POR)

$$\text{POR} = \frac{\text{Estimated annual overhead cost}}{\text{Estimated annual cost driver volume}}$$

$$= \frac{\$592{,}500}{125{,}000 \text{ direct labor hours}}$$

$$= \$4.74 \text{ per direct labor hour}$$

Using a POR, we can allocate overhead to products as we are making them, just like we assign direct materials and direct labor to products during production. Simply multiply the POR by the number of direct labor hours worked. If we do a good job in controlling overhead costs throughout the year, the estimated cost should equal the actual cost. If a significant difference results at year-end between the actual cost and the allocated overhead using this estimate, I'll prepare a journal entry to correct the allocation. We have a couple of ways to make this correction, but let's leave the details to the accountants."

NANCY

Choosing an allocation base. "You just used a different formula than in your previous example [Exhibit 5-10]. There you computed an average overhead cost per house. Here you changed the denominator to direct labor hours, and calculated a rate per direct labor hour. Why?"

JULIE

"Good question! *Creating a POR per product [house] makes sense if every product is identical.* However, we make standard homes and custom homes, and each custom home is different. Should every house, standard and custom, have the same overhead cost? Probably not. If different products require different amounts of overhead, they should not be allocated the same overhead cost.

"*So how much overhead should be included in the product's cost when we make different products? It depends on what causes overhead.* The real cause of overhead is called a **cost driver**. The POR denominator should be the estimated overhead cost driver volume. If direct labor causes overhead, the POR should be based on direct labor hours. If two products use the same amount of labor, they should be charged the same amount of overhead. However, since custom homes require more direct labor than standard homes, and labor causes overhead, custom homes should be allocated more overhead, as shown in this illustration:

A **predetermined overhead rate (POR)** *is the estimated amount of overhead cost per unit of its* **cost driver**, *that is, the activity that causes overhead cost. The overhead cost charged (allocated) to a department or product is called* **applied overhead**.

Overhead Allocation Formula						
Formula:	POR	×	Cost driver volume	=	Applied overhead
Standard homes	$4.74/DLhr	×	1,000 DLhrs	=	*$4,740 per house*
Custom homes	$4.74/DLhr	×	2,500 DLhrs	=	*$11,850 per house*

Applied overhead is the overhead cost allocated to a product. For our management needs, consider it a synonym for allocated overhead."

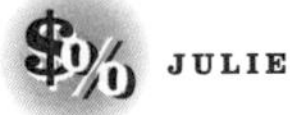

"Since we've invested a lot of money in machinery and computers, much of our overhead is caused by machine usage. Shouldn't we be using machine hours as the overhead cost driver? But some overhead costs are caused by different factors. How do we know which cost driver to use with different types of overhead costs?"

"I've summarized some different overhead costs and potential cost drivers [see Exhibit 5-11]. Be careful, though, these are generalizations for just a sample of overhead costs. Alternative cost drivers can exist in different companies. Each organization needs to look at its individual situation and determine the correct cost driver(s) for the overhead it incurs.

"As more and more overhead becomes fixed costs [e.g., machinery depreciation and building costs] versus variable costs [electricity to run the machines and factory supplies], many organizations choose a driver that measures their capacity. At Multree Homes, our capacity is determined by the amount of labor we have available. We hired enough people to provide 125,000 hours of direct labor time [(1,000 hours per standard home × a production quota of 100 standard homes) + (2,500 hours per custom home × a production quota of 10 custom homes)]. Thus, our POR is calculated using our capacity of 125,000 direct labor hours as our estimated cost driver volume."

"We use many overhead resources, though. Shouldn't we have more than one POR? Should we have different overhead accounts for each cost driver?"

"That depends on the level of detail needed to support our managerial functions of budgeting, controlling operations, and evaluating performance. We use only one POR for allocating all of our overhead. We could have a separate POR for each of our specific overhead costs. But a cost accounting system with multiple overhead accounts and PORs is more expensive than our current one-POR system. Is a more complex system's extra cost justified by better decisions we can make with the more detailed information? We have only one POR, based on direct labor usage, for three reasons:

- Our cost accounting system was designed primarily to support financial reporting. For external reporting, we need only a systematic way to allocate overhead between products sold [cost of goods sold], products unsold [ending finished goods inventory], and products not yet finished [ending WIP]. We do not need multiple PORs to do this.
- Before we automated our production processes, direct labor caused most of our overhead. We didn't have a cafeteria for the workers, or an Information Systems [IS] Department. The Boss did the hiring, and employment law was very simple. So, we didn't need a Human Resources Management Department, either.
- Granted, ethically we always should strive for the most accurate product costs and the best information for good management. But, ethically, we also should compare the cost of more accurate information with its decision-improving

Example Overhead Cost Drivers

Overhead costs	Possible cost drivers	Example POR	Comments	Example costs
Building	Size of departments	$10/Square foot	The size of the departments determines the size of the building and its costs.	Depreciation, repairs and maintenance, insurance, security, grounds
Cafeteria	Meals	$2.00/Meal	The more meals served, the greater the cafeteria costs.	All costs of cafeteria
Human Resources Management	Number of people per department	$12/Worker	The more workers we have, the greater the size and cost of this department.	All costs of HRM department
Information Systems (IS, MIS, CIS department)	1. Report pages	$0.25/Page	1. Some activities only involve creating reports.	1. Printer, paper, delivery, operator time
	2. CPU time	$50/Second	2. Running programs has unique costs.	2. Hardware, software, library, operator time
	3. Consultant time	$250/Hour	3. Designing new programs.	3. Time, office space, computer and software (CAD)
Machinery	Usage	$10/Minute	Machinery will only last so long. Measure life in minutes of use.	Acquisition cost, electricity, repairs and maintenance, insurance
Materials Handling	Volume (in pounds, pallets, cubic feet)	$32/Pallet	Use the factor that causes receiving, storing, moving, etc., costs to be different for each type of material.	Receiving dock and personnel, warehouse costs, forklift and driver, logistics management system
Payroll	Number of paychecks	$44/Check	Every paycheck may cost the same to process.	Department costs, filing and storage, bank account-related costs
Purchasing	Number of purchase orders	$65/PO	Every PO may cost the same to process.	Department costs, forms, distributing POs to all concerned
Setups	Setup time	$25/Setup hour	Individual machine setup costs depend on the hours needed to set up that machine.	Mechanic's time, depreciation of tools and dies needed, supplies

Exhibit 5-11

benefits. Changing our cost driver, or creating multiple ones, increases system complexity and cost. For example, it's expensive to track machine usage per product. But we already collect direct labor hours for payroll. In effect, labor time is free information for allocating overhead. The Boss knew how everything worked. He didn't use much accounting information to run the business, so he never believed the extra accounting system cost was justified.

Here's a simple example of why we use a one-POR allocation system. Consider nails. If a worker counts the nails in each house, nails become a direct material cost. Is it worth it to hire someone to count nails? How accurate will this information be? So we include nails in overhead. Probably the best cost driver is the amount of lumber in a house [measured in board feet]. The more board feet of lumber in a house, the more nails needed. But should we create a separate overhead account for nails with its own cost driver? It's just not that important. Let's include it with the rest of the overhead allocated by direct labor. The more hours worked, the more nails used. It may be the least accurate of these three choices, but it's good enough for our management needs."

BOB

"Wait a minute! Let's not get lost in the accounting arguments. This is the way we do it. I get an annual sales forecast. This determines the capacity we need. I then budget for enough overhead to provide this capacity. I see 'capacity' in terms of the direct labor hours needed for our annual sales, so we use direct labor hours for allocating overhead. This is why the production people think about overhead cost in terms of a direct labor hour."

Process Cost Accounting Systems

NANCY

"I have one more question before we end this meeting. You showed me how work is organized into functional departments by scientific management, and how our cost accounting system mimics this organization by having separate WIP accounts for each department. I see how we assign direct materials and labor costs to departments through directly tracing these resources with source documents. Multiplying the POR by the direct labor hours worked in each department, overhead then is added to the department's cost. How does this get us to the cost of an individual house, though?"

JACKIE

"Actually, once we've resolved the overhead allocation issues, the cost accounting becomes pretty easy. I'll explain how we determine a house's cost in two parts. First I'll describe the cost system for our standard homes [a process costing system]. Then we'll look at custom homes [a job order system]."

Averaging department costs over the products made within it

JACKIE

"We used to make only standard homes. With just one product line, we can cost each home using a **process cost accounting system**. The basic characteristic of this system is organizing WIP by department. We've already discussed this [refer to Exhibits 5-6, 5-8, and 5-9].

A **process cost accounting system** *accounts for production costs by department, and provides an average cost per product for each department. It is used in mass (continuous) production processes.*

"The T-account example [Exhibit 5-9] is a little simplistic, however. Everything started in one department is completed and transferred to the next department. No WIP exists at the end of the month [or year]. But we know WIP between departments is critical for scientific management to work properly. I've prepared a more realistic picture [see Exhibit 5-12]. Rather than using our real costs, though, I've kept the numbers simple so you can focus on the ideas.

"First, look at the Sawing Department's T-account. We spend $1,000 in Sawing this time period [a week, month, year, or whatever we want]. Enough lumber is sawed for 10 standard homes. The average sawed lumber cost per home is $100.

"All the sawed lumber leaves the department and is temporarily stored in the stock yard [as WIP] until requisitioned by Framing. The Framing Department requisitions only 5 houses worth of lumber [$500]. The cumulative total cost to date for the 5 partially completed [framed] houses is $4,000, averaging $800 per house.

"This process continues throughout the remaining departments until homes are completed and transferred out of the factory [and WIP] into finished goods inventory. *To summarize, the fundamental characteristics of a process costing system are:*

- *Each department has its own account* [the general ledger includes a WIP subsidiary ledger account for each department].
- *Costs are accumulated by department.* Source documents trace direct materials and labor to each department. Overhead is allocated to each department using the same plantwide total overhead POR [$4.74 per direct labor hour]. The way we allocate overhead used to be very common. However, many companies now use different methods, based on management's desire for more detailed overhead cost information and more accurate product costs. [Appendix A demonstrates a different method using separate PORs for each department.]
- *A cumulative average cost per product is calculated for each department* and used to cost the output from that department.

The last characteristic warrants clarification. Sawing requisitions, cuts, and bundles lumber by house. Its output is a house's worth of sawed lumber. Thus, the process costing system computes the sawed lumber cost per house. Framing's output is a framed house. So, as with Sawing, an average cost per house is calculated for the Framing Department.

"My point is process costing systems usually calculate the average department cost per unit of whatever that department makes. I didn't illustrate the remaining departments, but let's consider the Truss Department. It makes roof trusses. This is its output. Every house needs a combination of different size trusses. Each size is made in long production runs and stored in WIP until the specific number needed for a house is requisitioned by the Roofing Department. After a long production run of 20-foot trusses, we calculate an average cost per truss. Another average cost per 10-foot truss is computed after completing a production run of this size."

"I understand. With process costing, we calculate the cumulative average cost of whatever each department does. When products leave the last department, this cumulative cost is their manufactured cost [i.e., the cost of the goods manufactured]. Now, I have another question...."

Why not track each house's cost separately?

"It's just too much work! Every standard home is the same, so each one should cost the same. We don't build each house separately, from start to finish, with each house beginning in the first department, moving to the next, and so on, one-by-one, through all departments until finished. Rather, we mass-produce standard homes. *Process costing systems are appropriate for mass-production processes.* Think

Process Cost Accounting Systems

Sawing Department

	WIP—Sawing (Debit)	WIP—Sawing (Credit)
Beginning balance	$0	
Direct materials	300	
Direct labor	200	
Applied overhead	500	
Completed work transferred out		$1,000
Ending balance	$0	

Unit cost calculation			
Resource costs		$1,000	
÷ Work done	÷	10	houses
Average department cost per product		**$100**	**per house**

Framing Department

	WIP—Framing (Debit)	WIP—Framing (Credit)
Beginning balance	$0	
Sawed lumber from WIP	500	
Direct labor	1,000	
Applied overhead	2,500	
Completed work transferred out		$4,000
Ending balance	$0	

Unit cost calculation			
Resource costs		$4,000	
÷ Work done	÷	5	houses
Average department cost per product		**$800**	**per house**

Exhibit 5-12

about a piece of chalk or a writing pen. Does it make sense to try to develop a cost for each pen or piece of chalk individually? No! These are mass-produced commodities, each being identical. At Coca-Cola's Atlanta plant, 2,000 cans of Coke are made per minute. The Janesville, Wisconsin, General Motors plant outputs one car every minute.

"In these mass-production environments, it just isn't worth the effort to try to trace costs to individual products. The easiest way to get an average product cost is to sum all the costs, count the number of products made, and divide the two numbers, resulting in an average cost per product. Examples of mass-produced products include gasoline, milk, paper, pens, concrete, driver's license renewals at the Department of Motor Vehicles, and teeth cleanings by a dental hygienist."

KEY OBJECTIVE 4

Explain the need for equivalent units and calculate the average department cost per equivalent unit in a process costing system.

The need for equivalent units

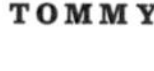

TOMMY

"I think you've oversimplified process costing, Jackie. Look in our factory. It's a mess! It may be organized chaos, but I see WIP lying around everywhere. You've assumed everything is completed in all departments each time period. Isn't it possible to have unfinished work still in a department at the end of the month? Remember, scientific management says, 'Keep busy all the time!' If Sawing finishes cutting the lumber for a house one hour before quitting time, should the workers go home early? No, they keep sawing. So unfinished work should be expected in each department at the end of every day [and at the end of each accounting reporting period]."

JACKIE

"You're right. We should expect beginning and ending WIP *within* each department, as well as stockpiled between departments. When beginning and ending WIP exists within a department, the costing system has to value [place a cost on] the work completed and transferred out, and the uncompleted work remaining in the department [ending WIP]. [Exhibit 5-13 modifies Exhibit 5-12 to illustrate this for the Sawing Department.]

"I prepare monthly financial statements, so assume these costs are for one month. As before [Exhibit 5-12], Sawing used $1,000 in resource costs. The only difference is in the work done. Previously, enough lumber was sawed for 10 houses. Here, 10 houses worth of lumber is completed and transferred out of the department, and another 5 houses worth of lumber is started but only one-half completed by the end of the month.

"Since more work is done for the same cost, the cost of sawed lumber should be lower than $100 per house [the average cost from Exhibit 5-12]. Does this make sense? Because we want to know the cost *per house*, we have to determine how much work was done in terms of *completed houses*. In other words, for the work done, how many products could have been made? This is the logic for calculating **equivalent units**. Equivalent units is the number of products that could have been started, fully processed, and completed with the amount of work done [resources used].

> **Equivalent units** *is a measure of the work done in terms of how many products (units of output from a department) could have been made 'from scratch.'*

"So, how many houses worth of lumber was sawed this month? Lumber for 10 houses was completed and moved out of the department to the stock yard [or it could have been delivered directly to the next department]. Another 5 houses of lumber was one-half complete. Five houses 50% complete is equivalent to 2½ houses fully [100%] complete. Sawing cut enough lumber to make 12½ houses this month: 10 houses completed, plus the equivalent of 2½ houses from the uncompleted work still in the department at the end of the month. *Calculating equivalent*

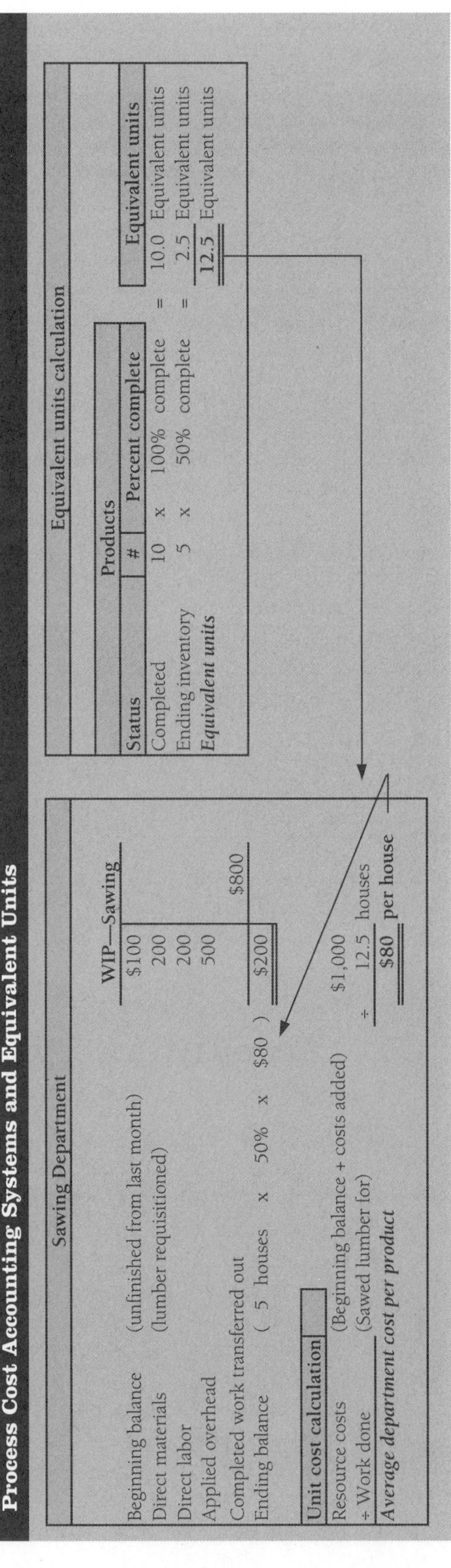
Process Cost Accounting Systems and Equivalent Units
Sawing Department
WIP—Sawing
Beginning balance (unfinished from last month) $100
Direct materials (lumber requisitioned) 200
Direct labor 200
Applied overhead 500
Completed work transferred out $800
Ending balance (5 houses x 50% x $80) $200
Unit cost calculation
Resource costs (Beginning balance + costs added) $1,000
÷ Work done (Sawed lumber for) ÷ 12.5 houses
Average department cost per product $80 per house
Equivalent units calculation
Products
Status # Percent complete Equivalent units
Completed 10 x 100% complete = 10.0 Equivalent units
Ending inventory 5 x 50% complete = 2.5 Equivalent units
Equivalent units 12.5 Equivalent units
Exhibit 5-13

units is just a way to translate partial effort into complete effort. Here's the formula illustrated with the new numbers:

Equivalent Units Formula

	Units	×	Percent complete	=	Equivalent units
From Exhibit 5-13:					
Completed:	**10 houses**	×	**100%**	=	**10 completed houses worth of lumber**
Ending inventory:	**5 houses**	×	**50%**	=	**2.5 completed houses worth of lumber**
Total for the Sawing Department this month				=	**12.5 completed houses worth of lumber**

Once a department's work is translated into equivalent units, the average department cost per unit can be computed. Instead of dividing department cost by output [as done in Exhibit 5-12], simply divide department cost by equivalent units. For Sawing, $1,000 ÷ 12.5 equivalent units = $80 per house. If 10 houses worth of lumber is completed and transferred out, its cost is $80 per house × 10 houses = $800, as shown in the right [credit] side of the Sawing Department's T-account. The Sawing Department's ending WIP cost is $80 per house × 5 houses × 50% complete = $200. [Use the balance equation to check your work.]

"As with allocating overhead and computing PORs, calculating equivalent units can get very complicated. For example, I can determine separate equivalent units for direct materials, labor, and overhead; and using different inventory flow assumptions [e.g., FIFO or weighted average]. Complicated formal reports are often prepared for each department. You don't want to get into all of this unless, of course, you want to be a cost accountant!"

NANCY

Nancy chuckled aloud at this thought, but the others hung their heads, grabbed their hearts, and moaned softly. "Let's leave the details for the accountants then. All we need to understand now is why the equivalent units calculation is required and how it is used in determining the average unit cost of a department's work."

KEY OBJECTIVE 5

Describe how WIP is organized in a job costing system and calculate a job's cost.

Job Order Cost Accounting Systems

BOB

"Well, I've got a custom home to build. Its resource needs are very different from our standard homes. Since it has to be built individually, will it have to be costed individually?"

JACKIE

"Oh yes! For custom homes, we use a **job order cost accounting system**. Job costing is used when products are not all alike. Job costing involves tracing direct costs and applying overhead to each job. A job can be an individual product or a unique batch of products. For example, custom homes are individually made, so each is costed as a separate job. Job costing is appropriate for organizations that make many different kinds of products: printing shops, law firms, CPA firms, and hospitals [where each patient is a job], bridge builders and commercial contractors [where each bridge or shopping mall is a separate job], and when batches of distinct products are made [a wrought iron manufacturer making batches of four-foot-long ornamental fence sections, batches of front screen doors, batches of window guards, and batches of rebar for concrete foundations]."

Job order cost accounting systems *account for production costs by individual product or batch (a 'job'). Each job has a subsidiary ledger account in WIP.*

WIP inventory costs are organized by job

"*The fundamental characteristic of a job shop is the unique difference in products or services.* Since each job is distinct, it uses different amounts and types of resources. Thus, each job has a unique cost. *The fundamental characteristic of job costing is organizing WIP by job instead of department.* Each job has its own WIP subsidiary ledger account.

"Material requisitions and time cards trace resources to jobs rather than to departments. Knowing the direct labor hours worked on a job [or whatever cost driver we use], overhead can be allocated to it. Once a job is finished, its total cost is computed and a formal report prepared. We can calculate job costs with T-accounts, though [see Exhibit 5-14].

WIP Subsidiary Ledger Accounts in Job Costing Systems

		WIP—Job 101		WIP—Job 215		WIP—Job 347	
Direct materials:	Lumber	$8,000		$7,500		$10,500	
	Sheetrock	1,500		900		2,100	
	Cabinets	5,000		3,500			
	Appliances	3,250					
	Other costs	8,500					
Direct labor:	Sawing	1,250		1,000		1,125	
	Framing	1,725		1,400		2,175	
	Wiring	1,475		1,200		1,750	
	Plumbing	1,350		2,500		3,000	
	Other costs	19,200					
Applied overhead @ $4.74/DLhr		11,850		2,891		3,816	
Total job cost			$63,100				
Ending balance		$0		$20,891		$24,466	

Exhibit 5-14

"The job's total cost is removed from WIP when it is finished [credit WIP—Job 101] and goes wherever the job goes [debit finished goods inventory, or cost of goods sold if it is sold and shipped directly to a customer]. The costs of unfinished jobs make up the ending WIP balance. Job 101, an Alpine custom home for the Baldwin family, has been finished and shipped to them. It cost $63,100 [which is credited to WIP—Job 101 and debited to cost of goods sold]. The other two jobs are only partially completed at the end of the month, so their costs remain in WIP because the houses are still in the factory."

"Does this mean we don't need to track costs to departments anymore?"

"Yes, if our only purpose is to generate costs for the financial accounting system. However, if we want management accounting information [e.g., for evaluating and rewarding departments], costs still have to be assigned to departments. While this makes manual job cost systems more difficult, it's not really a problem in computerized systems. Each database record contains data about both the job and the department. By separately sorting on jobs and departments, reports are prepared for job costs and department costs."

“That’s right. When bidding custom homes, I need information on the costs of similar homes built in the past. The detailed information concerning the amount of work required in each department is critical, so I want the job cost reports to identify costs by department. Atlantic Dry Dock uses a similar computerized system. It allows sales personnel to retrieve specific cost information and input it into a spreadsheet program for sensitivity and what-if analyses when preparing custom bids.”

Comparing job and process environments

“With both costing systems, a formal report is prepared for each WIP subsidiary ledger account. In process costing, these accounts are departments, and we get departmental cost reports. WIP subsidiary ledger accounts are created for each job in a job costing system, so we get job cost reports from it.”

“The choice between job and process costing is not as straightforward as it may seem. Each company has unique characteristics requiring different information. Unlike a financial accounting system that is similar for all firms, cost accounting systems differ in many respects as they are custom tailored for each firm. At Multree Homes, we use a hybrid system including both process and job costing. California’s Kunde Estate Winery also uses a combination system. It has a series of wine-making processes, each with an average departmental cost [process costing]. As the different types of wine are processed, each batch is a job with average departmental/process costs allocated to it based on the batch’s time in the process.

“You’d expect Dell Computer to use a process costing system. But Dell does not stockpile computers awaiting customer orders. Each is custom built, containing the unique features a customer wants, so Dell uses a job costing system. Some Hewlett-Packard plants do not account for labor separately, but combine it with overhead. Harley-Davidson does too, but doesn’t keep a WIP subsidiary ledger system by either department or job in its Milwaukee plant. *My point is both cost and management accounting systems are customized to support the unique environments found in organizations.*”

Job costing in nonmanufacturing firms

“Sally Industries creates many of the robotic creatures for movies and entertainment parks. Each is unique with its own budget. Whether a prehistoric monster or a spaceship, each is a separate job. Some job cost reports have over 20 sections, with direct materials, labor, and overhead assigned to each one.

“Maxwell Technologies has designed job order costing software for the Department of Defense. Its program, called JAMIS, has been used on the stealth fighter and by Lockheed, Hughes, Booz Allen & Hamilton, and Vandenberg Air Base.

“*Cost accounting systems are not only for manufacturing firms, though.* All organizations can benefit from job cost information. The word ‘job’ often is not used. Governmental agencies have programs [family counseling, recreational programs, daycare services]. Universities have funded research projects. Services have clients [doctors, repair shops], cases [lawyers, hospitals], or contracts [advertising].

“City governments calculate the average cost of services such as garbage pickup. States calculate the average cost of renewing driver’s licenses or processing unemployment claims [each is a separate department with costs traced to it]. Banks have separate departments for check processing and compute an average cost per check. Similarly, the post office calculates the average cost to process a letter.

Hospitals determine the average cost of services, like x-rays, for insurance and Medicare reimbursements. And part-time students at universities are converted into FTEs [full-time equivalents, an equivalent units calculation!].

"You should realize cost accounting is not restricted to manufacturing. Manufactured products are not different from services. Products and services both use resources, converting them into something a customer wants. Whether in the governmental, service, nonprofit, or manufacturing sector, organizations transform resources into outputs. Cost accounting systems can provide the average cost of these outputs."

KEY OBJECTIVES SUMMARY

SID

"Well, we certainly have learned a lot about how work is organized, and how the cost accounting system can be designed to support our production processes. Doris, can you summarize the key points from today's meeting, please?"

DORIS

1. Discuss how work traditionally has been organized and how cost accounting measures work efficiency.

"Scientific management evolved to support newly emerging mass-production processes. By organizing work into independent departments, each specializing in a particular task, work was simplified. This allowed hiring inexpensive labor that easily could be trained in the one best way to do a task. Industrialization also brought heavy equipment investments. To maximize efficiency, machines were run as much as possible, and everyone kept busy.

"With each department making as much as possible, scheduling and coordinating customer orders became a problem. It was solved by using the extra output [WIP] as buffers between departments. Bad quality or problems in a previous department would not shut down subsequent departments. Extra WIP is one example of using slack resources to manage uncertainties.

"The more products a machine makes, the lower the machine's average fixed cost per unit. Hiring cheap labor also minimizes variable costs. As efficiency increases, the cost per product decreases. Thus, cost accounting systems were designed to calculate the average product cost as a measure of work efficiency [productivity].

2. List the source documents required for direct cost assignment.

"I've got to tell you my story, 'Doris goes to the dentist.' My dentist uses scientific management ideas, which I experienced yesterday. She can't do everything needed for one patient at a time, so the receptionist leads me to a room [the 'move' activity in Exhibit 5-5's production cycle]. There I [WIP] wait for a dental assistant to put on my bib, adjust the chair and lighting, and the like [wait and setup activities]. After a while, the dental hygienist comes in and cleans my teeth [run activity]. I then move to an examining room and repeat the cycle with the dentist.

Finally, I'm moved again to the receptionist to pay the bill and schedule the next appointment. Of course, many other patients are simultaneously experiencing the same cycle [more WIP to keep everyone busy]. Notice all the specialized labor and many production cycles, and WIP!

"The dentist keeps track of special materials she uses for me within my patient record. This is a source document for directly tracing material costs to each patient. When special materials have to be custom ordered, a purchase order [PO] can serve as the source document authorizing the order and tracking it directly to a patient. A copy of the PO goes to the receptionist so he can use it as a receiving report, acknowledging delivery and, with the supplier's invoice, authorizing payment. Her specialists also track their time with each patient on appointment and scheduling sheets. It seems material requisitions and time cards [or their equivalents] are being used to identify direct materials and labor costs to products [patients]. Moreover, the dentist wants to charge patients enough so her overhead costs can be paid. She uses direct labor hours to allocate overhead to each patient visit. Thus, the time cards are the source documents for applying overhead.

3. Prepare a predetermined overhead rate and justify its allocation base.

"The dentist applies overhead using a predetermined overhead rate [POR]. Her overhead consists of many miscellaneous supplies [variable overhead costs], too inexpensive and time-consuming to trace directly to specific patients. She also has significant fixed overhead costs associated with equipment, receptionist and bookkeeper salaries, rent, taxes, licenses, and insurance.

"My dentist figures patients should be charged for overhead according to how much they use. The more time each patient spends with the dentist and/or her specialists, the more overhead resources the patient needs. Direct labor required for each job [patient] drives her overhead costs. Thus direct labor hours is the cost driver for applying overhead [i.e., the denominator for the POR]. Here's her POR calculation [see Exhibit 5-15]:

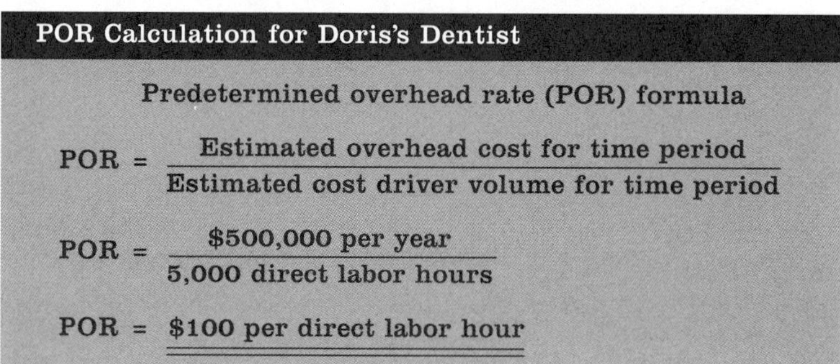
POR Calculation for Doris's Dentist

Predetermined overhead rate (POR) formula

$$\text{POR} = \frac{\text{Estimated overhead cost for time period}}{\text{Estimated cost driver volume for time period}}$$

$$\text{POR} = \frac{\$500{,}000 \text{ per year}}{5{,}000 \text{ direct labor hours}}$$

$$\text{POR} = \$100 \text{ per direct labor hour}$$

Exhibit 5-15

"If my dentist wants more accurate overhead charges to each patient, she can create multiple overhead accounts. For example, the costs of running each type of patient room [cleaning, inspection, treatment, etc.] can be calculated and allocated to patients based on the specialists' hours worked in each room. She can even calculate specialized equipment rates per minute for applying equipment-caused overhead costs. But, she told me, cost accounting just doesn't excite her that much, so one total overhead POR is sufficient.

4. Explain the need for equivalent units and calculate the average department cost per equivalent unit in a process costing system.

"Process costing is used in mass-production processes. Creating thousands or millions of identical products, it doesn't make sense to trace costs to individual products. If each product is the same, it should have the same cost, so costs are traced directly to departments and overhead is applied to each department. Knowing the department's output volume, an average department cost per product can be determined [divide cost by volume]. For example, we have a separate WIP subsidiary ledger account for each department. Dividing the Truss Department's $10,000 cost this month by the 100 trusses made yields a $100 average cost per truss. When Assembly requisitions trusses, the cost is $100 each.

"I have a word processing business which I run part-time in my garage. Direct materials include paper, binders, folders, and envelopes. This month they cost $50. I pay myself $15 per hour [direct labor] and worked 45 hours this month. My $500 per month budgeted overhead consists of computer equipment and garage rent. I plan to work 50 hours per month and allocate overhead using a POR of $10 per hour [$500 ÷ 50 hours]. This month I completed 1 project left over from last month [accumulated cost of $25 last month], started and completed another 9, and started but only half completed 4 other projects. Here's my average cost per project for this month [see Exhibit 5-16].

"To determine the average product cost, I divided my monthly costs by the work I did [$1,200 ÷ 12 equivalent units = $100 per project]. How much work did I do in terms of completed products? I finished 10 projects and half finished another 4 [which is equivalent to completing 2]. I want an average cost per project to charge my customers, so I have to measure my work in terms of projects fully processed from start to finish. Calculating equivalent units is translating the work I did from hours into how many projects could have been fully processed. For the costs incurred and work done this month, it cost $100 [on average] to do a project from start to finish.

"The 10 projects I finished were delivered to customers. $1,000 left WIP with the projects and moved to cost of goods sold. I also have 4 unfinished projects in ending WIP. These have a total cost to date of $200. It costs $100 to do a project from scratch. These 4 projects are half done, so each has incurred one-half [$50] of a completed project's cost.

5. Describe how WIP is organized in a job costing system and calculate a job's cost.

"Many organizations do not mass-produce products or services. Each product or batch may be unique. If so, it probably has a unique cost. Job costing systems organize WIP by job, instead of department, so resource costs can be traced directly [and overhead allocated] to each job.

"I use a process cost system for my word processing projects because I consider each to be the same. Obviously, this isn't always true. When I get special jobs, requiring different resources, I set up an account for each one. Direct materials and labor are traced to each job, and overhead is allocated to it.

"This month I worked on three jobs, as shown [see Exhibit 5-17 on p. 175]. The Jones job from last month was completed. The Chung job was started and completed this month. The Juarez job was started but not completed by month-end.

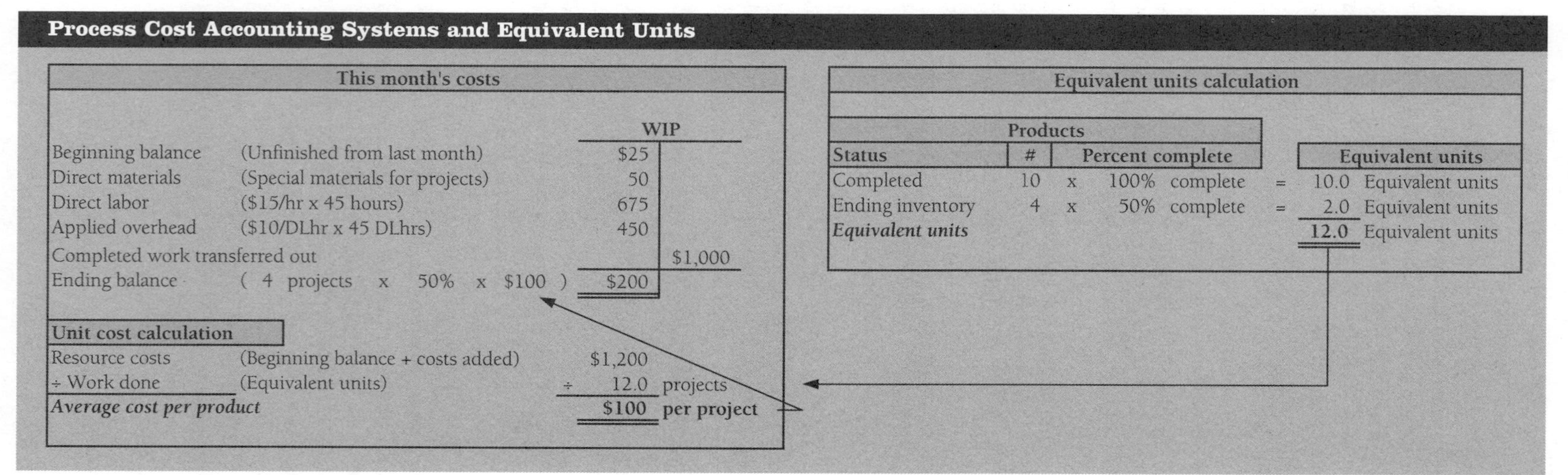

Process Cost Accounting Systems and Equivalent Units

This month's costs

		WIP (debit)	WIP (credit)
Beginning balance	(Unfinished from last month)	$25	
Direct materials	(Special materials for projects)	50	
Direct labor	($15/hr x 45 hours)	675	
Applied overhead	($10/DLhr x 45 DLhrs)	450	
Completed work transferred out			$1,000
Ending balance	(4 projects x 50% x $100)	$200	

Unit cost calculation		
Resource costs	(Beginning balance + costs added)	$1,200
÷ Work done	(Equivalent units)	÷ 12.0 projects
Average cost per product		$100 per project

Equivalent units calculation

Status	#		Percent complete		Equivalent units
Completed	10	x	100% complete	=	10.0 Equivalent units
Ending inventory	4	x	50% complete	=	2.0 Equivalent units
Equivalent units					12.0 Equivalent units

Exhibit 5-16

Doris's Word Processing Job Costs

	WIP—Jones job		WIP—Chung job		WIP—Juarez job	
Beginning balance	$30		$0		$0	
Direct materials	20		10		25	
Direct labor	150		225		75	
Applied overhead	100		150		50	
Completed job cost		$300		$385		
Ending balance	$0		$0		$150	
Hours worked:	10		15		5	

Exhibit 5-17

When jobs are finished, their costs are totaled and transferred from WIP to either finished goods inventory [if stockpiled] or to cost of goods sold [if sold and immediately shipped upon completion]. Because the Juarez job is not done yet, I have an ending balance in WIP. It will become the beginning WIP balance next month."

"Thank you, Doris, for summarizing the important ideas from today's meeting. Now that we understand how work is done and costs accumulated, we can consider how to use this information for operational control and performance evaluation. Let's do this in our next meeting. Good night!"

SID

REALITY 101

Cost Accounting System for GHC's HMO

Group Health Cooperative of Puget Sound (GHC) is the HMO for about one-half million Washington state employees. Typical of most HMOs, its cost system developed for external financial reporting needs. Following a traditional design, cost accounts were created for divisions and departments. Also typical of many accounting systems, whether in healthcare, government, service, or manufacturing, it developed incrementally. As new divisions, departments, and programs have been introduced, stand-alone computer systems were developed. The usual result was experienced by GHC: multiple accounting information systems each serving the specific needs of clinics, hospitals, and administrative departments. Obtaining integrated information was virtually impossible.

GHC management decided to develop a client-server centralized cost system to support its multiple users and locations. These users include senior management, physicians, local managers (at clinics, districts, etc.), contracting specialists, and company analysts. The development process lasted three years. The new system basically is a process costing system with overhead allocated to each 'production' department. Production, or line, departments provide services to patients and are called 'service delivery departments.' The system includes 500 of these departments, which represent about 70% of GHC's total costs.

Additionally, separate overhead accounts and PORs exist for each overhead (staff, support) department. Overhead is allocated from each support department to the other support departments and service delivery departments based on their usage of that service. This is the step method of service department cost allocations (see Appendix A). Overhead represents about 30% of total costs. Overhead accounting involves 26 layers of allocations totaling 180 actual allocations.

Once the overhead from all support departments is allocated to the service delivery departments, the average unit cost of providing each service is calculated. Now, as patients use a particular service, that service delivery department's average unit cost can be charged to the patient. The resulting database stores two million records a month!

The flowchart of the cost accounting system is summarized below:

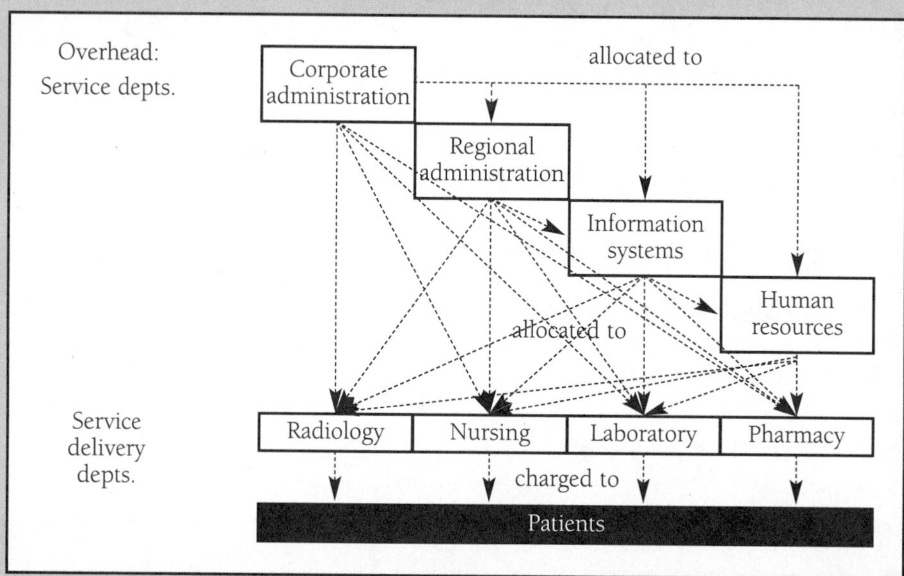

In developing service delivery department rates for charging patients, GHC used the output of each department as the rate base. Some outputs were obvious (x-rays for radiology, prescriptions for the pharmacy, etc.), while others were provided by professional organizations (see 'laboratory' below). Still others were developed by GHC personnel though detailed cost analyses. Samples of the bases include:

Department	Charging basis
Community health services	Number of visits
Dialysis	Treatment hours
Inpatient departments	Inpatient days
Obstetrics	Number of births
Surgery, anesthesia, etc.	Minutes of care
Laboratory	College of anatomical pathology [CAP] units

Complex cost accounting systems, particularly overhead allocation methods, are common and required for Medicare and other types of reimbursements. Both providers of the information and users at GHC consider their new system to be successful, supporting decisions for which relevant information was not previously available.

Source: Lee and Nefcy, "The Anatomy of an Effective HMO Cost Management System," *Management Accounting*, January 1997. © Institute of Management Accountants.

SERVICE DEPARTMENT ALLOCATION METHODS

KEY OBJECTIVE 6

Distinguish between service and line departments, and justify the need for departmental PORs.

NANCY

"In our discussion about overhead allocations, many examples of overhead were mentioned, such as janitorial, equipment repairs and maintenance, first aid, and our factory cafeteria. Lumping all these overhead costs together into one total overhead account, and allocating total overhead with one plantwide POR, really bothers me. Granted, these activities are all indirect production costs when considering individual products [i.e., we cannot see how much of a worker's lunch is consumed when making an individual house; therefore, meal costs cannot be directly traced to products]. However, can't these costs be traced directly to the departments using the services? And since each of these services has a different cost driver, shouldn't they be allocated separately? Our POR allocates all overhead based on the direct labor hours worked in a department [process costing] or on a unique house [job costing]."

What are service departments?

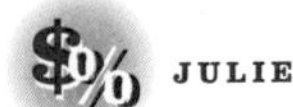
JULIE

"First let's distinguish between production and service departments, and then we'll look at whether these service department costs should be traced directly to production departments. If not, how should we allocate these overhead costs [one total overhead POR, or many PORs]? **Service** [staff, or support] **departments** are not directly involved in making products. **Production departments** [line activities] directly work on the product."

Service departments *provide support to* **production departments**, *which actually make a product.*

Why have service departments?

JULIE

"In other words, when being made, products pass through production departments, but they do not pass through service departments. In building houses, they do not go into the Repairs and Maintenance Department, as they do with Sawing, Framing, or Plumbing. But if the saws break down, without people to repair them, work stops. Service departments are critical for production departments to do their jobs."

NANCY

"Why not have people performing these services right in the production departments? If we could do that, these support costs become part of the department's direct labor."

JULIE

"Well, yes and no. While the people would become direct labor of the department, are they direct labor specifically assignable to products? For example, Sawing is cutting lumber for Job 101. The saw breaks down. Fixing it costs $50. Should this be charged only to the cost of Job 101? Of course not!

"Well then, should we have separate functional departments for each type of support activity? Scientific management says, 'Yes.' Functional 'silos' [independent departments] are an efficient way to organize work. Now that support services are separate departments, how can their costs get into the product's cost and sales price?"

Why allocate service department costs?

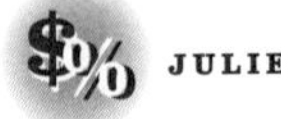
JULIE

"Service department costs are part of the total cost to make houses, even though we cannot measure directly how much of the repair cost on a saw is attributable to each product. Since we cannot trace service department costs [e.g., machine repair costs] directly to individual products, these support costs are included in overhead. They get into the product's cost through applying overhead to production departments and then averaging the production department costs over the products made [calculating a cost per equivalent unit in process costing]. In job costing, the POR applies overhead directly to each job [house].

"Should all the overhead be accumulated in one overhead account and allocated using one POR? Using one plantwide, total overhead POR assumes all overhead is caused by just one cost driver, in our case direct labor hours. Historically, making products or providing services was very labor intensive, and labor caused much of the overhead. Overhead costs were not a significant component of total manufacturing cost, thus any miscosting resulting from one POR was not important.

"Now, with billions of dollars spent on automation, robotics, and computer systems, labor represents only 8%–10% of a product's cost [at least in the electronic, machinery, and automotive industries]. In contrast, overhead is about 25% of total manufacturing cost in these industries [and as high as 66% in the airline industry]. Thus, using direct labor may seriously miscost the overhead charged to each product. It is a systematic method, though, and acceptable for financial reporting. *Using one total overhead POR is what I call the 'financial accounting method' for allocating overhead.*

"Service department costs are included in overhead and allocated to products for three reasons:

- Since they are a cost of making products, production support costs must be included in the product's cost for financial reporting.
- Management control of service departments is enhanced by properly allocating these support costs. We'll talk about this issue in a future meeting [see Chapter 8, Appendix A].
- Separately allocating service department costs may lead to more accurate product costs. This is the issue I want to discuss now."

How should service department costs be allocated?

JULIE

"I call this the 'traditional management accounting method.' Each production and service department will have its own overhead account in WIP. It's easy to see how services have different cost drivers. For example, cafeteria costs are driven by the number of meals served. Janitorial costs are driven by the size of the factory. Similarly, production departments may have unique overhead caused by different drivers. A machining department's overhead may be caused by machine usage, while an assembly department's overhead may be caused by labor usage. Also, as Nancy noted, many overhead costs are traceable directly to production departments [e.g., supplies requisitioned]. So, each department should have its own overhead account and POR. Now we'll make a lot of overhead allocations instead of just one.

"Overhead cost accounting proceeds in three steps:

1. *Directly trace overhead costs to each department.* Supplies requisitioned by the Sawing Department are charged to its overhead account. Costs for preparing meals are charged to the Cafeteria.
2. Now that we know the cost of each service department, *service department costs are allocated to production departments* [and included in the production department's overhead account].

3. Step 2 allocates all service department costs into the production department overhead accounts. Between directly tracing production department overhead to each department and allocating all service department overhead to the production departments [step 2], all overhead is now in production department overhead accounts. *Each production department has its own POR for applying its overhead to the costs of products as they pass through the department.* In total, the production department PORs include all factory overhead and thus allocate all factory overhead to the products.

We have three ways to do step 2. Let's look at the simplest. I'll demonstrate it by using only two service departments and two production departments. [Exhibit 5-A1 illustrates the method.]

"The Cafeteria allocates meal costs to each production department using meals eaten as its cost driver. Repairs and Maintenance allocates its costs to Sawing and Framing based on the hours its people work in each department fixing the equipment. As houses pass through Sawing and then Framing, each applies overhead to the houses using its own POR [Sawing's cost driver is machine hours; Framing's is direct labor hours].

"We'll need a lot of data to demonstrate the product costing error from using one total overhead POR. Work your way very slowly through the following calculations. [Exhibit 5-A2 on p. 181 presents the PORs for each department.]

"The Cafeteria budgets $100 to serve 10 meals. This yields a $10 meal rate [POR]. Since Sawing eats only 1 meal, $10 is allocated from the Cafeteria and included in Sawing's overhead. Framing eats 9 meals, so it is allocated $90. Repairs and Maintenance [R&M] budgets $200 to work 10 hours in the production departments fixing equipment. Using its $20 per hour POR, Sawing is charged $180 [9 hours of R&M work] and Framing is charged $20 for 1 R&M hour. These amounts also are added to the production department overhead accounts. Summing the overhead in each production department's overhead account, a separate POR is developed for each one. [Exhibit 5-A3 on p. 182 uses these PORs to apply overhead to houses as they pass through each production department.]

"Sawing works 90 machine hours on standard homes and 10 machine hours on custom homes [Exhibit 5-A2 data section]. Using its $5 per machine hour POR, $450 of Sawing Department overhead is allocated to standard homes while $50 is allocated to custom homes. Similarly, Framing works 80 direct labor hours on standard homes and 20 hours on custom homes. $400 of Framing Department overhead is allocated to standard homes and $100 to custom homes.

"The total overhead POR calculation is shown, and allocated overhead using multiple PORs is compared to the amounts allocated with a single POR [see the bottom half of Exhibit 5A-3]. Using a single POR, standard homes are undercosted by 6% and custom homes are overcosted by 33%. Think about how serious this problem becomes when we use real costs [big numbers] and many service and production departments!"

NANCY

"Is this miscosting problem with overhead always going to happen when using a single, plantwide overhead rate?"

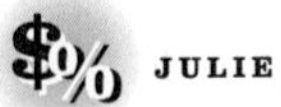

JULIE

"No. *If all products are identical, each should have the same amount of overhead in its cost. Here are the conditions in which multiple PORs yield more accurate overhead allocations and product costs:*

- We make different products.
- They require different amounts and/or types of overhead.
- We have many subsets of overhead, each with a different cost driver.

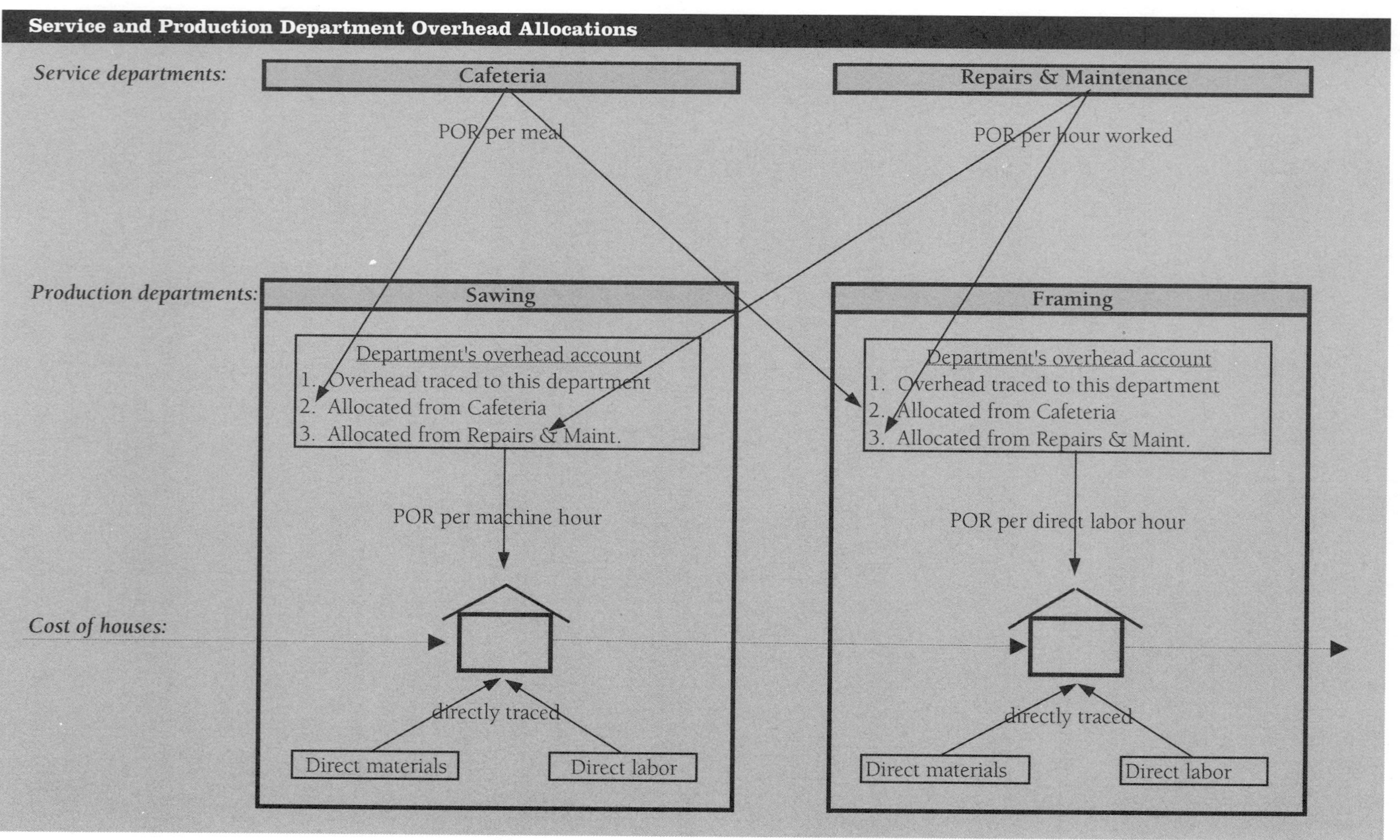

Service and Production Department Overhead Allocations
Service departments:
Cafeteria
Repairs & Maintenance
POR per meal
POR per hour worked
Production departments:
Sawing
Department's overhead account
1. Overhead traced to this department
2. Allocated from Cafeteria
3. Allocated from Repairs & Maint.
POR per machine hour
Framing
Department's overhead account
1. Overhead traced to this department
2. Allocated from Cafeteria
3. Allocated from Repairs & Maint.
POR per direct labor hour
Cost of houses:
directly traced
Direct materials
Direct labor
directly traced
Direct materials
Direct labor

Exhibit 5-A1

Calculating Service and Production PORs

Raw data

				Machine hours worked		DL hours worked	
Department	Overhead cost	Meals eaten	R&M hrs worked	Standard homes	Custom homes	Standard homes	Custom homes
Cafeteria	$100						
Repairs & Maintenance	200						
Sawing	310	1	9	90	10	20	5
Framing	390	9	1	0	0	80	20
Totals	$1,000	10	10				

POR calculations

	Cafeteria		Repairs & Maintenance	
Overhead cost	$100		$200	
÷ Cost driver volume	÷ 10	meals	÷ 10	hours
POR	**$10**	**per meal**	**$20**	**per hour**

							Sawing	Framing
Overhead traced directly to departments							$310	$390
Allocation from Cafeteria	$10 per meal	x	1	meal	=		10	
	$10 per meal	x	9	meals	=			90
Allocation from Repairs & Maintenance	$20 per hour	x	9	hours	=		180	
	$20 per hour	x	1	hour	=			20
Total production department overhead							**$500**	**$500**
÷ Cost driver volume							÷ 100	÷ 100
POR							**$5** per machine hour	**$5** per direct labor hour

Exhibit 5-A2

Comparing Allocated Overhead: Departmental PORs versus Single POR

Using separate PORs for each department (Exhibit 5-A2)

	Allocated Overhead					Standard homes	Custom homes
From Sawing Department	$5 per machine hour	x	90	Machine hours worked	=	$450	
	$5 per machine hour	x	10	Machine hours worked	=		$50
From Framing Department	$5 per direct labor hr	x	80	DL hours worked	=	400	
	$5 per direct labor hr	x	20	DL hours worked	=		100
Total allocated overhead						**$850**	**$150**

Using a plantwide total overhead POR

							Standard homes	Custom homes
Total overhead POR calculation:	$1,000	÷	125	DL hours worked	=	$8 per direct labor hr		
Allocated overhead	$8	x	100	DL hours worked	=		**$800**	
	$8	x	25	DL hours worked	=			**$200**
Over/(under) costed using one POR							($50)	$50
% over/(under) costed							(6%)	33%

Exhibit 5-A3

When these conditions exist, overhead costing can become very complicated—especially when you realize this method is the simplest of the three. It's called the direct method because service department costs are allocated directly to production departments."

"But shouldn't some of the Cafeteria's cost be allocated to Repairs & Maintenance? Don't these people eat in the Cafeteria? Analogously, shouldn't some of the R&M department costs be allocated to the Cafeteria if cafeteria equipment needs to be fixed?"

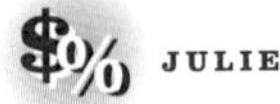

"The Reality 101 section illustrates a more sophisticated method allocating service department costs to other service departments, as well as to production departments. It is called the step method. I also can use an even more complex method called the reciprocal method.

"Do you need to work through the calculations with these other methods? I doubt it. Let's leave it to the accountants. What's important to realize is good management often requires good information. *When the above three conditions exist, better overhead costing results from using multiple PORs.*"

READING LIST*

Atlantic Dry Dock: Barton and Cole, "Atlantic Dry Dock's Unique Estimation System," *Management Accounting*, October 1994.

ERP survey: Krumwiede and Jordan, "Results of 1998 Survey on Cost Management Practices," *Cost Management Update,* December 1998/January 1999, the Institute of Management Accountants.

Harley-Davidson: Foster and Horngren, "JIT: Cost Accounting and Cost Management Issues," *Management Accounting*, June 1987.

Hewlett-Packard: Hunt, Garrett, and Merz, "Direct Labor Cost Not Always Relevant at HP," *Management Accounting*, February 1985.

IT costs (Hackett Group study): "Cost Management Trends," *Cost Management Update,* December 1998/January 1999, the Institute of Management Accountants.

Kunde Estate Winery: Lee and Jacobs, "Kunde Estate Winery: A Case Study in Cost Accounting," *CMA Magazine*, April 1993.

Maxwell Technologies: Williams and Hart, "Maxwell Business Systems' High Flight," *Management Accounting*, November 1996.

Overhead allocation bases: Emore and Ness, "The Slow Pace of Meaningful Change in Cost Systems," *Journal of Cost Management*, Winter 1991.

—— Cohen and Paquette, "Management Accounting Practices: Perceptions of Controllers," *Journal of Cost Management*, Fall 1991.

—— Schwarzbach, "The Impact of Automation on Accounting for Indirect Costs," *Management Accounting*, December 1985.

Overhead proportion of total costs: Banker, Potter, and Schroeder, "An Empirical Study of Manufacturing Overhead Cost Drivers," *Journal of Accounting and Economics*, January 1995.

—— Banker and Johnson, "An Empirical Study of Cost Drivers in the U.S. Airline Industry," *The Accounting Review*, July 1993.

Pillowtex: Klein and Jacques, "'Pillow Talk' for Productivity," *Management Accounting*, February 1991.

Sally Industries: Barton and Cole, "Accounting for Magic," *Management Accounting*, January 1991.

*Alphabetic by topic, idea, or company referenced.

CHAPTER 6

Are We Following the Plan?

The Need for Variance Analysis

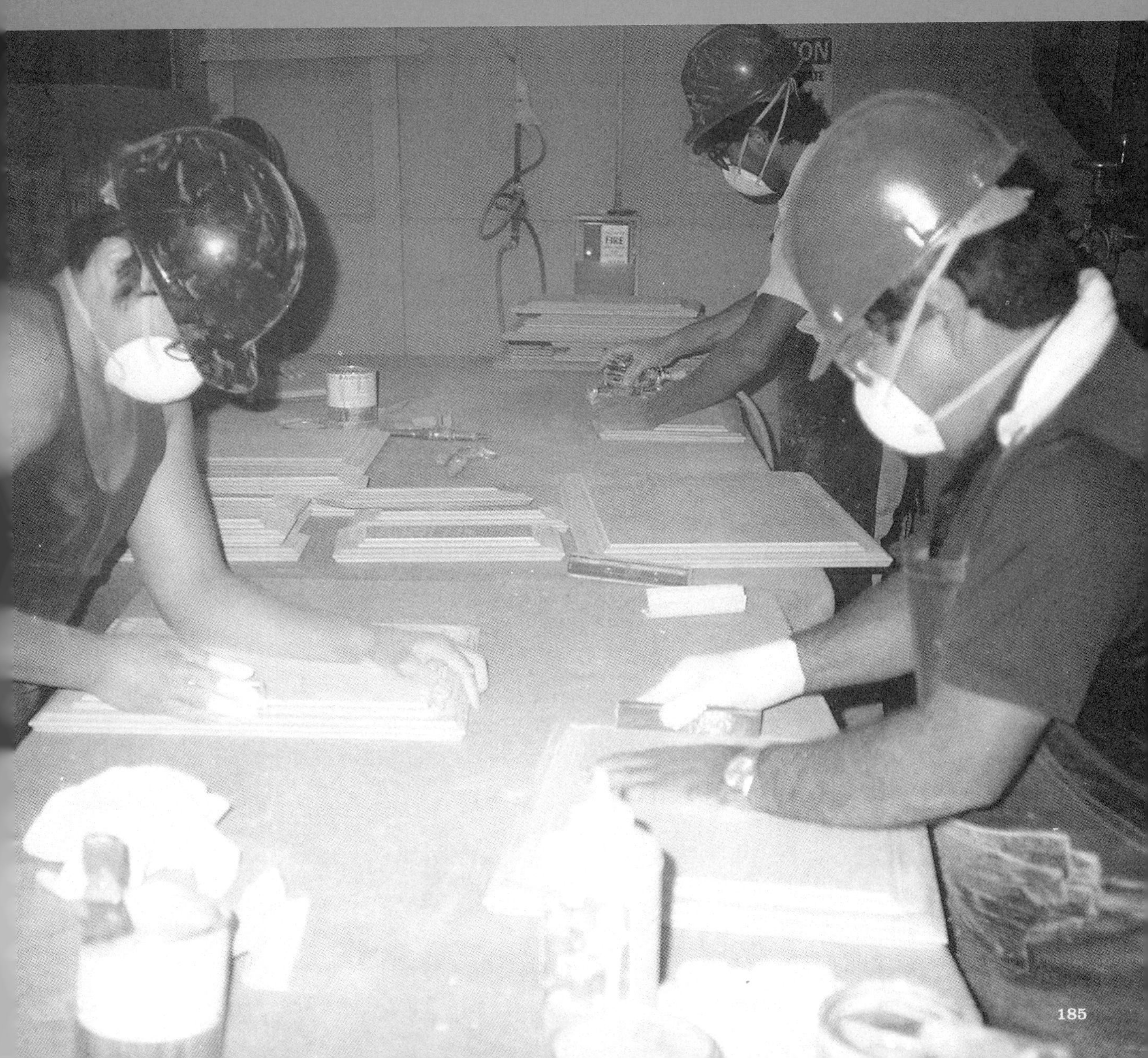

KEY OBJECTIVES:

1	*Explain management by exception and how it is a feedback system.*
2	*Calculate and interpret the sales price and volume variances.*
3	*Define the components of a standard cost card, and list its benefits and limitations.*
4	*Calculate and interpret spending and usage variances.*
5	*Distinguish between boardroom and process control, and explain the usefulness of variance analysis for these strategies.*
6	*Compare ideal and practical standards, and explain why practical standards represent the "one best way."*

The weekly meetings were now pretty relaxed. The grandchildren seemed comfortable with the profit plan and cash budget, and how work is organized to accomplish them. As Doris entered the boardroom, everyone was glad to see her. Or was it the pastries? She turned to Nancy and Tommy.

DORIS

"I see a lot of paperwork spread out in front of you two. But it doesn't look like our CVP [cost-volume-profit] plan or cash budget. It looks like travel brochures. Are you trying to find ways to spend your money?" Everyone laughed as Nancy gathered her new car pamphlets and Tommy put away his Maui leaflets. As he stared out the window at the gray sky, the cold north wind blew through the tree limbs, still ice-covered from the last storm. Snow started to fall yet again. Tommy was very tired of winter! The ominous weather foreboded the meeting.

TOMMY

"Sure! There's no reason to wait. The weather's turning bad again, and Maui looks awfully warm and inviting. By the time I get the credit card bill, we'll have our first big cash bonus!" Julie's head did not rise from her computer reports, but her eyes lifted over her bifocals as she apprehensively gazed out the window and then at Tommy.

KEY OBJECTIVE 1

Explain management by exception and how it is a feedback system.

Reconciling Results with the Plan

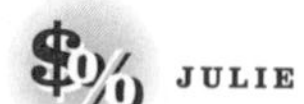

JULIE

"Tell me, how do you know you've actually made that money?" The smiles disappeared from Tommy's and Nancy's faces. As they glanced at each other, they became very quiet. So did the rest of the grandchildren. All knew if Julie was upset, something must be wrong. It started to snow more heavily. The lights flickered. Tommy dropped his donut. As he went to pick it up, his elbow knocked over his coffee.

What's the problem?

JULIE

"Before you start spending the cash, let's make sure we really have it. Just because the CVP 'mathematics' work, we can't assume the originally anticipated results actually have occurred. Periodically, we need to reconcile actual cashflows with our plan. If we're not making the money we expected, we have a problem. Tommy, you seem to have at least one problem!"

"What do you mean?" Tommy looked perplexed as he wiped up the spilled coffee and threw away the donut he retrieved from under the table.

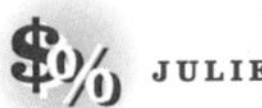

"Well, you want coffee and donuts, but you have none. And I see the donuts now are all gone." As she helped herself to the last one, Tommy frowned.

"I see. A problem is the difference between what I want and what I have. I want a donut, but do not have one. Are you telling us we have a problem with achieving our cash budget and profit goal?"

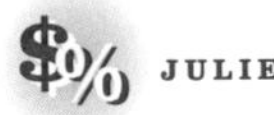

"It appears so. Some things are working right. Some things are going wrong. In accounting, the difference between planned and actual profits or cashflows is called a **variance**. If we are not making our planned profit or cashflow, it can be due to problems with sales [sales variances] and/or problems with cost control [cost variances]."

A **variance** *is the difference between budgeted and actual profits or cashflows.* **Management by exception** *is a management philosophy focusing attention on problems. Variance reports support this philosophy.*

Focusing on problems: Management by exception

"I don't like problems! Let's use today's meeting to identify our problems. I don't care about the areas not having any problems. The Boss had a saying, 'If it ain't broke, don't fix it!' I don't want to waste my time looking at activities going as planned. Let's focus on our problems."

"This is called **management by exception**. The idea is simple. Management does not need control information about activities working well. However, we do need information about activities keeping us from our profit goal. The management accounting system should identify problem areas and provide variance reports about them."

"Hold on a minute. On this morning's news, Chrysler reported last week's sales were 10% higher than sales a year ago. Ford, on the other hand, reported 5% less sales than in the same week last year. In variance reporting, as with financial reporting, shouldn't we be comparing last year to this year?"

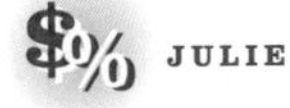

"We can, if this provides useful information to decision makers. Investors use comparisons between last year and this year. They may be defining a variance [problem] as the difference between what we had and what we have. Thus, our external income statement includes a comparison between last year's numbers and this year's. But Tommy knows if we realize our budget, he'll have the money for his Maui trip. As managers, we have some pretty sophisticated plans, from the general strategic plan to the very specific cash budget. To achieve our objectives, we need to accomplish our plans. Reporting on the differences between actual and planned results for *this* year allows us to focus our attention on activities not working as planned, in other words, where we need corrective actions."

"Your argument makes sense to me. If we're trying to improve over last year, we've planned for it within our budget. The budget-to-actual comparisons tell us if we are exercising adequate control, as well as if we are improving over last year. I admit I always have been skeptical of comparisons between last year's actual results and this year's actual results. For example, assume this year's actual results are better than last year's, but we didn't achieve our budget last year and we're going to miss it by even more this year. Just because this year's actual results are better than last year's, are we O.K.? Does the comparison provide the correct message? Are the comparisons of actual results between years meaningful? Who says last year and this year are even comparable?"

"But how can we make sense of the budget-to-actual comparison? For example, we budget a $1,000 profit, but achieve only an $800 profit. The variance is

$200. This doesn't tell me what went wrong, though. It seems we need more detailed analyses. How does variance reporting work?"

Sarah's college dilemma

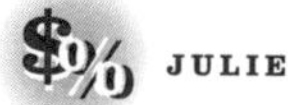
JULIE

"Since you just graduated from college, I'll use my daughter's tuition problem as an example. Sarah is enrolled at the local college, but doesn't have enough money for tuition. To solve her problem [i.e., get back on budget], Sarah wants me to give her $580! When I asked her what went wrong, she provided the following explanation. She didn't provide a comparison with last year [when she also asked for money]. Rather, she explained why she needs $580 this year.

A favorable variance means actual results are better than planned. An unfavorable variance means actual results are worse than planned.

"She planned to work 400 hours last summer at $10 per hour [after tax]. She actually made $8 per hour [after tax], and worked 440 hours. She wanted to earn $4,000. She really earned $3,520 [$8 per hour × 440 hours]. She had a $480 unfavorable 'total earnings' variance. Two things were different from her plan. First, she earned $2 per hour less than budget for each of the 440 actual hours worked. She missed her planned revenues by $880 because of this problem. Call it an unfavorable 'wages earned' variance.

"Her second problem was the difference between budgeted and actual hours. She says this was a problem because she didn't spend her last week of summer with friends at the lake, as she had planned. Instead she had to work. I didn't see a problem, though! Do you? By working another 40 hours, Sarah would have earned an extra $400 according to her budget. She planned to make $10 per hour. If she had, and she also worked 40 more hours, she would have exceeded her budget by $400 [a favorable 'hours worked' variance]. In sum, she lost $880 due to a wage rate problem, but gained an extra $400 by working more hours [a volume problem]. Netting out these two specific earnings or revenue variances, her earnings were $480 less than planned [a net unfavorable variance].

"In addition to her two revenue problems, Sarah had some cost problems. She budgeted $50 per credit for tuition, but the cost actually was $60 per credit. She wanted to enroll for 16 credits, but enrolled for only 15. The increased tuition cost Sarah an extra $150 [$10 more in tuition × 15 credits], an unfavorable 'tuition rate' variance. Of course, she saved $50 according to her budget because of enrolling for 1 less credit [a favorable 'credits' variance]. The total tuition variance was $100 unfavorable [an extra $150 in tuition less $50 of her budgeted costs saved by enrolling for only 15 credits]. [Exhibit 6-1 is Sarah's variance report.]

"Notice Sarah created a management by exception report. She told me only about her problems. She did not include any information about books and supplies, or living expenses. They are within budget. What bothers me about her report is its feedback nature. By 'feedback,' I mean problems are reported *after* they occur. If we had known about the tuition increase *ahead of time*, we could have planned to overcome the problem! Receiving information about problems in time to minimize their effects is called 'feedforward.' It's a shame the college did not tell us about the tuition hike in time to do something about it [e.g., to earn enough money before school began]. Now Sarah has to get a job over the semester break. Communicating 'bad news surprises' after the fact creates all sorts of new difficulties. When problems occur, they must be communicated to those who can fix them. In this way, we can minimize their effects on our plans. Feedback is not a good control philosophy when the information arrives too late to fix the problems."

NANCY

"I don't understand. By getting a new job between semesters, won't Sarah fix her problem? All she has to do is work a couple of weeks."

Sarah's College Dilemma

	Earnings (revenues) variances						
Wages earned:	**(Actual wage rate**	-	**Budgeted wage rate)**	x	**Actual volume**		
	($8 per hour	-	$10 per hour)	x	440 hours	=	($880) U
Hours worked:	**(Actual hours**	-	**Budgeted hours)**	x	**Budgeted rate**		
	(440 hours	-	400 hours)	x	$10 per hour	=	$400 F
Total earnings variance							($480) U

(**Note:** **F** = favorable, **U** = unfavorable, or earned more (F) or less (U) than planned)

	Cost variances						
Tuition rate:	**(Budgeted rate**	-	**Actual rate)**	x	**Actual volume**		
	($50 per credit	-	$60 per credit)	x	15 credits	=	($150) U
Credits:	**(Budgeted credits**	-	**Actual credits)**	x	**Budgeted rate**		
	(16 credits	-	15 credits)	x	$50 per credit	=	$50 F
Total tuition variance							($100) U

(***Note*:** Costs more (U) or less than (F) planned)

Exhibit 6-1

TOMMY

"Did she really 'fix' her problem? When I use the word 'fix,' I mean prevent the problem or correct it in a timely manner that minimizes its impact on her plans. Sarah could have worked a little overtime each week during the summer to make the extra money, if she had known ahead of time about the increased tuition. This would have prevented the problem [or at least minimized it]. Remember, Sarah will need another $580 again in the second semester. She can prevent that problem by working between semesters. She knows about the second semester problem in time to do something about it.

"The college could have communicated the potential tuition hike a lot sooner. College administrators were planning on it well in advance of it happening! Instead, though, they chose to wait until a week before the semester began. By that time, it was too late for Sarah to take any corrective actions. Sarah now has a problem because of the college's failure to communicate exceptional information in time to minimize its impact on the students. If the college administrators were management accountants, and this was an accounting report, would their conduct have been ethical?"

NANCY

"Now I understand. Sarah could not be *proactive*. She did not have timely information. After the fact, she can only *react*. Sarah's management ability is reflected in the variance report. Once she knew conditions had changed, she exercised good judgment, changing her plans to minimize the variance. By working an extra week, Sarah's total variance was limited to $580. It could have been worse. Of course, if she had known about the tuition hike at the beginning of the summer, she wouldn't be asking you for the extra money now. Upon investigation, you now believe the variance was not her fault. So are you going to give Sarah the $580?"

JULIE "Well, let's see. By 'drilling down' into the details, Sarah identified four inputs to her plan which changed: her wage rate, the hours she worked, the tuition rate, and the number of credits she's taking. Some were better than planned [favorable variances], but some were worse than planned [unfavorable variances]. Instead of just saying she needs $580, she used the variances from her plan to present her case. So, I can evaluate her performance based on facts, rather than just on her reputation! I guess I will give her the money."

NANCY "After seeing her variance report, Sarah's explanation makes a lot of sense to me. The report seems useful in evaluating her managerial performance. However, to control operations on a day-to-day basis, we can't wait until the end of a month or year to receive our variance reports. To be proactive, we will need much more timely information. Where do we begin?"

Multree's profit variance report

JULIE "Remember our CVP model? At our third meeting, I presented our proforma income statement for the whole company [Exhibit 3-5], and for our standard homes product line [Exhibit 3-6]. In constructing our profit equation, which is the basis for the contribution margin income statement, we developed some pretty detailed estimates [Exhibit 3-2]. We used these estimates in preparing our profit plan and cash budget. Just as Sarah did, we will look at each of the line items [Exhibit 3-6] and determine whether it is within budget. Some organizations create very sophisticated profit models and go to extremes in measuring variances. Regardless, all use the same basic idea of preparing variance reports by comparing budget to actual results. I have February's **profit variance report** right here [Exhibit 6-2].

A **profit variance report** *reconciles budgeted to actual profit. If budgeted and actual sales volume differ, and variable costs exist, the original budget is converted into a* **flexible budget** *showing expected profit for the actual sales volume.*

"The profit variance report compares planned to actual profit in two steps. First, it begins with the original budget. The per unit column comes from our CVP equation [Exhibit 3-6]. The second column is the total projected profit for 10 standard homes, which is our February sales forecast [Exhibit 4-7]. The fixed costs are from the direct labor and overhead, and operating expenses schedules [Exhibits 4-14 and 4-15]. [In Exhibit 6-2, $1,250 is added to the cash fixed overhead from Exhibit 4-14 for February depreciation, and $7,167 is the month's depreciation added to the cash fixed administration costs from Exhibit 4-15.] February's budgeted profit is $97,083.

"While we planned to sell 10 standard homes, only 9 were sold. Selling one less product reduces our profit by the product's contribution margin per unit [CMU]. If we have no other variances, actual profit is less than budget by $20,000 [a standard home's CMU from Exhibit 3-6]. This is the sales volume variance shown in the third column. Bill will elaborate on this in a minute." Everyone looked at Bill and smiled. He just frowned, though. "The fourth column is a revised, after-the-fact budget for the 9 homes actually sold. It is called a **flexible budget**. If actual sales volume differs from the plan, a flexible budget is needed. *Budgeted* sales revenues, total variable costs, and contribution margin *must be* different when 9 homes are sold than when 10 are sold. It doesn't make sense to compare a budget for 10 homes with actual revenues and costs for 9 homes.

"To illustrate the need for a flexible budget, look at the direct labor line. Originally, $100,000 was budgeted because we planned on selling 10 homes [column 2]. We actually spent $100,000 on direct labor [column 5]. If we calculated a

Multree Homes Profit Variance Report for February

	Standard homes budgeted profit Per unit	Totals @ 10	Sales volume variance (1) home		Flexible budget for 9 homes	Actual profit for 9 homes	Sales price and cost variances	
Revenues	$50,000	$500,000			$450,000	$441,000	($9,000)	U
Less: Variable costs								
Direct materials	$15,500	$155,000			$139,500	$140,000	($500)	U
Direct labor	10,000	100,000			90,000	100,000	(10,000)	U
Variable overhead	2,000	20,000			18,000	18,000	0	
Sales commissions	2,500	25,000			22,500	23,400	(900)	U
Total variable costs	($30,000)	($300,000)			($270,000)	($281,400)	($11,400)	U
Contribution margin	**$20,000**	**$200,000**	**($20,000)**	**U**	**$180,000**	**$159,600**	**($20,400)**	**U**
Less: Fixed costs								
Fixed overhead		$18,750			$18,750	$28,750	($10,000)	U
Advertising		10,000			10,000	15,000	(5,000)	U
Administration		74,167			74,167	77,167	(3,000)	U
Total fixed costs		($102,917)			($102,917)	($120,917)	($18,000)	U
Net income		**$97,083**	**($20,000)**	**U**	**$77,083**	**$38,683**	**($38,400)**	**U**

Note: Favorable (**F**) variances mean actual profit is greater than budgeted profit.
Unfavorable (**U**) variances mean actual profit is less than budgeted profit.

Exhibit 6-2

labor variance by comparing the original budget for 10 homes with the actual costs for only 9 homes, it appears actual cost [$100,000] equals budgeted cost [$100,000], and no variance exists.

"But only 9 homes were made and sold! From column 1, we budget $10,000 for direct labor per house. We should have spent $90,000 if only 9 homes were sold [the flexible budget amount in column 4]. If we spent $100,000 on 9 houses, we overspent by $10,000 [an unfavorable direct labor variance]. By comparing the flexible budget to actual results, both based on the same sales volume, we get a more accurate variance calculation.

"Why do we need flexible budgets? The answer is in understanding cost (and revenue) behaviors. Variable costs, while remaining constant per unit over the relevant range, change *in total* as volume changes. This is also true for revenues. Revenues and variable costs are variable components in our CVP model. *If volume changes, total revenues and variable costs change proportionately.*

"Now that we have a flexible budget for 9 homes, we can compare it to the actual profit for 9 homes [in the fifth column]. The difference between our 9-home budgeted and actual profit is shown on a line-by-line basis in the right column. These variances are due to sales prices and costs."

SID

"Are you telling us February variances were $58,400 unfavorable??" Sid's voice was rising in tempo with his face's color changes. "We originally planned on a $97,083 February profit. We lost $20,000 of it because only 9 homes were sold, so our profit should be $77,083. We lost another $38,400 of that planned profit due to sales price and cost problems. Our actual profit is $58,400 below our original budget!! WE'RE OUT OF CONTROL!!

"So tell me, what went wrong? Let's start with the biggest variances. For each area of responsibility, I want to 'drill down' through these numbers to the details. Why is actual profit less than half of our plan? I see sales variances totaling $29,000, so Bill, let's start with you."

KEY OBJECTIVE 2

Calculate and interpret the sales price and volume variances.

Sales Variances

"Sarah's problems with earning enough money are similar to ours. She identified two specific variances from her summer work. First, her hourly wage is just like a sales price for us. Sarah wanted to make $10 per hour, and we wanted to sell standard homes at $50,000 each. Her second problem concerns the hours worked, which is equivalent to our sales volume. Sarah wanted to work 400 hours. We wanted to sell 10 standard homes. *Sales variances tell us how differences from budgeted sales price and volume affect contribution margin.*"

Sales price variance

"Let's start with the **sales price variance**. It tells us how much of the variance between budgeted and actual contribution margin is due to sales prices not equaling the plan. [The top calculation in Exhibit 6-3 shows this specific variance.]

Multree Homes February Sales Variances

Sales price variance							
Formula:	(Actual sales price	-	Budgeted sales price)	x	Actual volume		
February variance	($49,000 per home	-	$50,000 per home)	x	9 homes	=	($9,000) U
Sales volume variance							
Formula:	(Actual volume	-	Budgeted volume)	x	Budgeted CMU		
February variance	(9 homes	-	10 homes)	x	$20,000 per home	=	($20,000) U
Total sales variance							($29,000) U

Note: F = favorable, U = unfavorable, or earned more (F) or less (U) than planned.

Exhibit 6-3

"Actual sales price is $49,000. This is $1,000 less than budget. In total, for the 9 homes sold, actual revenues and contribution margin are $9,000 below budget. This is an unfavorable variance, which is why a 'U' appears after it. Think of it this way: What's the change in CMU if sales price decreases $1,000? When price goes down $1,000, CMU goes down $1,000. In total, contribution margin and profit go down $1,000 multiplied by volume [9 homes actually sold].

"Variance formulas are very simple. Is actual sales price greater than [favorable] or less than [unfavorable] budgeted sales price? Total contribution margin and profit go down $1,000 if we sell 1 house at $49,000. But we sold 9 homes at this lower price. So, $9,000 of the difference between budgeted and actual profit is due to sales prices below plan. *Actual profit is $9,000 less than planned profit because of a sales pricing problem.*"

Sales volume variance

"Next, consider the effect of a sales volume change on our budget. Each home is worth $20,000 to us. This is its incremental profit, or CMU. Thinking about this from a CVP perspective, what happens to contribution margin if volume decreases by one product? We lose one product's CMU. Sell one more house, make another $20,000. Sell one less house, lose $20,000 of our planned profit.

"The **sales volume variance** measures the difference between budgeted and actual profit due to sales volume not equaling plan. In February, actual sales volume is one home less than budget. Thus, actual profit is $20,000 below budget, an unfavorable variance [the second calculation in Exhibit 6-3].

"In total, February's actual contribution margin and profit are $29,000 less than budget due to problems with sales prices and sales volume. The $29,000 unfavorable total sales variance can be seen in the answers to two CVP 'what-if' questions [see Exhibit 6-4]."

> *The difference between budgeted and actual profit because of unplanned sales prices is the* **sales price variance**. *The* **sales volume variance** *measures the difference in budgeted and actual profit due to an unplanned sales volume.*

Reconciling Sales Variances with CVP What-if Analysis

What-if?	Effect on budgeted contribution margin	
Actual sales price is less than budgeted sales price by $1,000?	Contribution margin decreases by $1,000 per house × 9 homes actually sold =	($9,000)
Actual volume is less than budgeted volume by 1 home?	Contribution margin decreases by $20,000 per house × 1 home =	(20,000)
	Change from budgeted contribution margin (unfavorable variance)	**($29,000)**

Exhibit 6-4

"I'm confused! I've been following along and doing the calculations using my logic. I'm comfortable with the sales price variance. It's just actual sales price less budgeted sales price. The effect on total profit depends on how many homes are sold. So, I multiply the sales price difference by the actual volume sold.

"But when I do the sales volume variance, I don't get your answer. I understand it measures the difference between actual and budgeted sales volume. You multiplied this difference by the *budgeted CMU*. I multiplied it by the *actual sales price*. Here's what I did:

(Actual sales volume	–	Budgeted sales volume)	×	*Actual sales price*	=	Sales volume variance
(9 homes	–	10 homes)	×	*$49,000*	=	($49,000) U

What's *wrong* with my logic?"

JULIE

"Two things. First, by using sales price, you calculated the difference in *revenues* because of a change in volume. Granted, selling one less house reduces revenues, but doesn't it also reduce total variable costs? Selling one less house means losing its sales price. Since we're not going to sell it, though, we won't incur its variable costs. We lose the sales price, but save the variable costs. In other words, by not selling a house, we lose only its CMU [sales price less variable costs per unit]. Your logic identified the effect on sales revenues, but you forgot to consider the effect on *total* variable costs. *This is why thinking about a product in terms of its CMU is so important! A house is not a house, it's really $20,000 in incremental profit.* My point is if variable costs exist, changes in volume will cause changes in both sales revenues and total variable costs. This is why we use CMU and not sales price in the variance logic and formula.

"Your second logical problem is using *actual* instead of *budgeted* sales price, or actual CMU instead of budgeted CMU. The actual sales price and CMU are $1,000 less than budget. We already measured the profit effect from this sales price difference in the sales price variance. By using actual price [or actual CMU] in the volume variance formula, we confuse the price and volume problems. Both problems are commingled in your calculation. Each variance should tell us the *unique* effect on planned profit from a change in price or volume. We don't want the price variance problem to be included in our measurement of the sales volume problem, which will happen if *actual* price or CMU is used in the volume formula."

NANCY

"O.K. I have another question. Actual variable costs total $11,400 more than the flexible budget [Exhibit 6-2]. Shouldn't we next do separate cost variance calculations for these variable costs? And what about the fixed costs?"

JULIE

"Yes. This is the next step in variance analysis. Before looking at these formulas, though, I have to discuss our standard cost card. To drill down to the details, we need some detailed budget information found on it."

KEY OBJECTIVE 3

Define the components of a standard cost card, and list its benefits and limitations.

The Standard Cost Card

JULIE

"A **standard cost card** itemizes the resources used in making a product, and shows their budgeted costs *per product*. Here are summaries of our standard cost cards [see Exhibit 6-5]. The ones used on the shop floor are much more detailed. For example, each direct material has a separate line [lumber, appliances, carpeting, etc.]. Similarly, each department has a line budget for its labor.

"Starting in the right column, each resource has a **standard cost**: its budgeted cost for making one product. A standard cost is a *budget per unit of product*. We budget $15,500 in direct materials and $10,000 in direct labor for each standard home.

A **standard cost card** *presents the budgeted production cost for one product. Each resource has a* **standard cost** *(budgeted cost per product) composed of a* **standard price** *(budgeted purchase price) and* **standard quantity** *(the amount of the resource budgeted for each product).*

"As we all know from economics, price multiplied by quantity equals cost. So, a standard cost is composed of a standard price and standard quantity. **Standard price** is the budgeted price for one unit of a resource [input]. Direct labor is budgeted at $10 per hour. We purchase labor by the hour. We buy carpeting by the roll, wiring by the spool, and paint in 50-gallon drums. Each resource has a budgeted acquisition cost, or standard price, usually calculated as the budgeted net delivered purchase price.

"The amount of each resource we plan on using *to make one product* is called its **standard quantity**. For example, we budget 1,000 direct labor hours for a

Standard Costs

Multree Homes Standard Homes Product Line Standard Cost Card						
Resources	**Standard prices**		**Standard quantities**		**Standard costs**	
Direct materials					$15,500	/house
Direct labor	$10.00	/hour	1,000	DLhrs/house	10,000	/house
Variable overhead	$2.06	/DLhr	1,000	DLhrs/house	2,060	/house
Fixed overhead	$2.68	/DLhr	1,000	DLhrs/house	2,680	/house
Standard absorptive manufacturing cost					**$30,240**	/house
Budgeted annual standard homes manufacturing costs =			**$268,000**	per year +	**$27,560**	/house

Multree Homes Custom Homes Product Line Standard Cost Card						
Resources	**Standard prices**		**Standard quantities**		**Standard costs**	
Direct materials					$26,250	/house
Direct labor	$10.00	/hour	2,500	DLhrs/house	25,000	/house
Variable overhead	$2.06	/DLhr	2,500	DLhrs/house	5,150	/house
Fixed overhead	$2.68	/DLhr	2,500	DLhrs/house	6,700	/house
Standard absorptive manufacturing cost					**$63,100**	/house
Budgeted annual custom homes manufacturing costs =			**$67,000**	per year +	**$56,400**	/house

Notes on the cost equation calculations:

Budgeted fixed overhead allocated to standard homes = $2.68/DLhr x 1,000 DLhrs per house x 100 homes production quota. = $268,000

Budgeted fixed overhead allocated to custom homes = $2.68/DLhr x 2,500 DLhrs per house x 10 homes production quota. = $67,000

Standard variable cost for standard homes line = ($15,500 + $10,000 + $2,060) per home = $27,560

Standard variable cost for custom homes line = ($26,250 + $25,000 + $5,150) per home = $56,400

Exhibit 6-5

standard home and 2,500 hours for a custom home. These are each product's standard labor quantities [or standard labor hours].

"Remember from our last meeting how we allocate overhead to each product? We use a predetermined overhead rate [POR] with direct labor hours as the cost driver. For financial accounting, we need only one total overhead POR. However, for budgeting and profit planning, variable and fixed overhead must be separated. Thus, each has its own standard cost. I've heard over 80% of publicly traded manufacturing companies separate variable and fixed overhead. Our total overhead POR is $4.74/DLhr [total annual budgeted overhead of $592,500 divided by 125,000 budgeted direct labor hours. It's broken down into a variable overhead POR and a fixed overhead POR [see Exhibit 6-6].

Predetermined Overhead Rates

Budgeted variable overhead:		
Indirect materials	$115,000	
Indirect labor	80,000	
Power	62,500	
Total budgeted VOH	$257,500	
Variable overhead POR calculation:		
Total budgeted VOH / Budgeted direct labor hours	$257,500 / 125,000	
Variable overhead POR	**$2.06**	**per DLhr**
Budgeted fixed overhead:		
Supervision	$200,000	
Heat & light	10,000	
Depreciation	15,000	
Architectural costs	110,000	
Total budgeted FOH	$335,000	
Fixed overhead POR calculation:		
Total budgeted FOH / Budgeted direct labor hours	$335,000 / 125,000	
Fixed overhead POR	**$2.68**	**per DLhr**

Exhibit 6-6

"A standard price is the budgeted price for a resource. Variable overhead is budgeted at $2.06 per direct labor hour. The variable overhead standard price is its POR [and the fixed overhead POR is its standard price]. It's like we 'purchase' overhead by the labor hour. Thus, the standard quantities for variable and fixed overhead are direct labor hours. Direct labor time is the overhead cost driver because we believe direct labor causes overhead. Every time we work one more direct labor hour, we should spend $2.06 on variable overhead.

"We talked about using different cost drivers for overhead allocation in our last meeting. Suppose machine usage causes overhead, and the PORs are based on machine hours [e.g., $5.00/Mhr]. The overhead standard quantities become the budgeted machine hours for one product. In preparing the standard cost card line budgets for overhead, the first thing I do is look at the POR. If its cost driver [the denominator] is labor hours, this must be the overhead standard quantity. Alternatively, if the POR is based on something else, like pounds of material used, this becomes the overhead standard quantity. *My point is the POR will tell us the standard quantity to use.*"

Absorption costing

NANCY

"The fixed overhead can't be right! Fixed overhead is not a variable cost. The fixed cost per house [the standard fixed overhead cost] is not a stable number. It changes with volume. The more houses we plan to build, the lower our fixed overhead standard cost. Why is fixed overhead included in the standard cost card? Why does it appear to be a variable cost?"

JULIE

"You must remember the historic development of cost accounting systems. They were created to track production costs. In the United States, for financial and tax accounting, and for governmental contract accounting, a product's manufacturing cost must include a fixed overhead allocation. This is called **absorption costing**. To support external reporting, the cost accounting system, as well as the standard cost card, contain only manufacturing costs [including fixed overhead]. This is why the sum of the resource standard costs is called the 'standard absorptive manufacturing cost.' It's interesting to note not all countries require product costs to be limited to manufacturing costs, including fixed overhead. For example, Canadian manufacturers often use 'variable costing' [sometimes (mis)labeled as 'direct costing'], which includes only variable manufacturing costs in the 'product cost.'"

Absorption costing *includes an allocation of fixed overhead in the product's manufacturing cost. It is required for tax and financial reporting.*

Standard cost card benefits

JULIE

"Developing standard costs and calculating variances is common in the manufacturing sector and increasing in popularity [something like 87%]. About 60% prepare monthly variance reports, 13% weekly, and 22% daily [this is by far the fastest growing percentage]. Standards are also common in the nonmanufacturing sectors [one survey reports two-thirds of manufacturing, high-tech, and service firms use standards and variances]. For example, McDonald's has standards for every aspect of its business, from the number of pickles on a hamburger to the time customers wait in line. On the eastern coast of the United States, Dutch Pantry restaurants receive many types of food prepared at one centrally located plant. Over 150 food items are prepared based on exacting standards.

"UPS also uses detailed standards. In delivering parcels, drivers should walk at three feet per second. They should knock on the door because this saves time over ringing a doorbell. State agencies have standards for the number of claims processed and checks mailed per day. Golf has a standard called 'par' for every hole.

"Hospitals have standards for many lab tests, and use standard costs to bill patients for services and supplies. The federal government uses standard costs for Medicare reimbursements, as do many HMOs and health insurance plans.

"So, a standard cost card provides many benefits to firms in all economic sectors:

- Standard costs provide detailed information for the CVP profit equation and the cash budget.
- Standard prices and quantities support management by exception by allowing detailed variance analysis as we 'drill down' through the profit variance reports.
- A lot of people in many different departments are involved in setting standards. This process facilitates communication, coordination, and participative budgeting. Through standards, people know what is expected of them and what to expect in the future.
- The standard absorptive manufacturing cost provides useful information for setting sales prices and obtaining payments under government cost-plus contracts. The prices and payments received must be sufficient to pay for variable costs, cover a fair share of fixed costs, and provide a reasonable profit.
- By using standards and variances in performance evaluation, they can motivate people to obtain our profit goal.
- Many firms use standard costs in their cost accounting systems for journal entries and inventory valuation. Thus, the standard cost card is invaluable in reconciling financial accounting income to budget."

The need for a budgeted cost equation

$% JULIE

"Of course, the standard absorptive manufacturing cost cannot be used to budget total manufacturing costs. If we want to build another standard home, should we budget $30,240 for manufacturing costs [its standard absorptive manufacturing cost in Exhibit 6-5]? No! As long as we are within our relevant range, total fixed costs will not change if one more house is built. We should budget only for the additional variable costs [$27,560].

"Conversely, if we aren't going to build any homes this month, won't the total fixed overhead still exist? For profit planning and cash budgeting we need to know the variable costs per product and the fixed costs in total. In other words, we need a budgeted cost equation. Some call this a flexible budget equation.

"To provide this information, the budgeted cost equation is included beneath the standard cost card [Exhibit 6-5]. For standard homes, budget $268,000 per year in fixed overhead, plus $27,560 per house [the sum of the standard variable costs]. For any volume within the relevant range, I can tell you how much to budget for production costs.

"However, including only manufacturing costs creates a second limitation with the standard cost card. We also need the equations for selling and administrative costs. Only by combining all cost equations can we construct the CVP profit equation. Please remember, though, the equations are valid only over their relevant ranges.

"A third limitation may exist depending upon how overhead is allocated. We have a traditional cost system allocating all overhead with a direct labor-based POR. We argued about its validity in our last meeting. In most organizations, multiple products are sold [or different services provided], and many different subsets of overhead exist, each with a unique cost. We can more accurately plan and control overhead with multiple PORs, each being a separate line on the standard cost card [as discussed in the Chapter 5 appendix]. For example, about ten years ago Caterpillar set up three overall overhead accounts. These were subdivided into specific subsidiary accounts, each having its own flexible budget equation. I'll talk more about this in a future meeting [Chapter 9]."

Cost Variances

KEY OBJECTIVE 4

Calculate and interpret spending and usage variances.

JULIE

"Now we're ready to look at Multree's cost variances. [Exhibit 6-2 reports summary variances for each cost.] Each cost variance is simply the difference between the flexible budget and actual cost. For example, the direct labor cost variance is $10,000 unfavorable. Using the standard cost card information, we can drill down from summary variances to their two specific variances [spending and usage]. Sarah's logic shows us how."

Spending variances

"First, Sarah calculated a tuition rate variance. **Spending variances** measure the difference between standard and actual price for a resource. I've calculated some of our February spending variances [see Exhibit 6-7]."

Spending variances *measure the difference between expected and actual costs due to unplanned resource price changes.*

Variable cost spending variances. "Variable cost spending variances all use the same formula:

Variable Cost Spending Variance Formula

Spending variance	=	**(Standard price**	−	**Actual price)** ×	**Actual quantity purchased**
For Sarah's tuition (Exhibit 6-1):					
($150) U	=	**($50 per credit**	−	**$60 per credit)** ×	**15 actual credits taken**

Let's look at just one of our purchase orders. Roof panels are 4 foot by 10 foot plywood sheets nailed to the roof trusses forming the roof. Tar paper and shingles are then nailed to the roof panels for waterproofing. This purchase order was for 250 sheets at $23 each. The standard price is $21, so we have a $2 per sheet unfavorable spending variance *for every sheet purchased.* Our actual profit and cashflow are $500 less than budget due to this unplanned price increase.

"When calculating direct labor and variable overhead spending variances, the actual quantity purchased is the actual quantity used. To illustrate, look at the Sawing Department direct labor rate variance for the second week in February [Exhibit 6-7]. That was the week the roof panels were sawed. The actual wage rate was $2 less than budget for each of the 200 hours worked. The result was a $400 increase in actual profits compared to plan.

"The variable overhead spending variance is calculated monthly for the whole factory. Our variable overhead POR is $2.06 per direct labor hour. Actual February variable overhead cost is $18,000, which averages $1.80 for each of the 10,000 hours actually worked. [Actual price × Actual quantity = Actual cost, or Actual price = Actual cost ÷ Actual quantity. $18,000 ÷ 10,000 actual DLhrs worked = $1.80/DLhr.]

Multree Homes Spending Variances

Variable costs formula:	(Standard price	-	Actual price)	x	Actual quantity purchased		
Roof panels (Direct materials)	($21.00 per sheet	-	$23.00 per sheet)	x	250 sheets	=	($500) U
Sawing Dept. labor (Direct labor)	($10.00 per hour	-	$8.00 per hour)	x	200 hours	=	$400 F
Variable overhead	($2.06 per DLhr	-	$1.80 per DLhr)	x	10,000 DLhrs	=	$2,600 F
Sales commissions	($2,500 per home	-	$2,600 per home)	x	9 homes	=	($900) U
Fixed costs formula:	Budgeted fixed cost	-	Actual fixed cost				
Fixed overhead	$18,750	-	$28,750			=	($10,000) U
Advertising	$10,000	-	$15,000			=	($5,000) U
Administration	$74,167	-	$77,167			=	($3,000) U

Note: Favorable (**F**) variances mean actual profit is greater than budgeted profit.
Unfavorable (**U**) variances mean actual profit is less than budgeted profit.

Exhibit 6-7

"I've shown reports for just three variable manufacturing cost variances. We really have a whole lot of them. We can have nonmanufacturing cost variances, too. The sales commission variance [Exhibit 6-7] illustrates this. We budget $2,500 per home for sales commissions. The actual commissions for the 9 homes sold in February were $2,600 each, creating a $100 per home unfavorable spending variance. For the 9 homes sold, actual profit is $900 less than budget. *The important point to remember is spending variances tell us how much actual profits change from budgeted profits due to unplanned pricing events.* While you can memorize a formula, to understand what these variances are telling management, focus on the difference between standard and actual price."

Fixed cost spending variances. "*All fixed cost spending variances use the same formula: budgeted cost less actual cost.* Because total fixed costs do not change with different volumes, the original and flexible budget amounts are the same [as long as they are still within the relevant range]. Thus, flexible budget adjustments affect only contribution margin [revenues and variable costs]. Going back to the profit variance report [Exhibit 6-2] and the sales volume variance, we can see this. Given a $20,000 budgeted CMU, our original budgeted contribution margin is $200,000 based on selling 10 homes. Because we sold only 9, though, contribution margin should be less than the original budget. Should total fixed costs also be lower because only 9 homes were sold? No, not as long as we are still within the relevant range.

"Thus, no flexible budget adjustment is needed. Fixed costs as originally budgeted can be compared directly with actual fixed cost [as seen in the bottom half of Exhibit 6-7]. Each of our three fixed costs was over budget [unfavorable spending variances]. This overspending resulted in actual profit being $18,000 less than plan."

Usage variances

"One reason for a variance is spending more or less than budgeted in acquiring resources. Another reason is using more or less of that resource than budgeted. **Usage, or efficiency, variances** measure this. Instead of focusing on the price of resources, let's turn our attention to *how productively we use them.* Productivity and efficiency tell us about the relationship between inputs and outputs. The more output we get from the same amount of inputs, the more productive we are. The less inputs used in creating our products, the greater our efficiency."

> **Usage, or efficiency, variances** *report the difference between budgeted and actual profit due to using more or less of a resource than planned.*

Variable cost usage variances. "Total variable cost increases as volume increases. Why? Not because the price changes. Variable costs *per unit* are constant over the relevant range. Total variable cost goes up because more resources are needed when more products are made. If Sarah enrolls for another credit, total tuition goes up because the number of credits increases. The tuition rate does not change. *A usage variance measures the profit change from budget due to using more or less of a resource.*

"Well, then, if resource usage changes with volume, how much should be used? We need to know this 'flexible budget' amount so it can be compared with the actual quantity used. I've prepared some usage variance calculations [Exhibit 6-8]. Look at the usage variance for roof panels.

"During the second week in February when Sawing was cutting roof panels, 103 sheets were used. Was this more or less than should have been used? The standard quantity of roof panels is 12 per house. Since 9 homes were built, 108 panels

Multree Homes Usage Variances

Variable costs formula:	(Std. qty. allowed	-	Actual quantity used)	x	Standard price		
Roof panels (Direct materials)	(108 sheets	-	103 sheets)	x	$21 per sheet	=	$105 F
Sawing Dept. labor (Direct labor)	(180 hours	-	200 hours)	x	$10 per hour	=	($200) U
Variable overhead	(9,000 DLhrs	-	10,000 DLhrs)	x	$2.06 per DLhr	=	($2,060) U

Note: Favorable (F) variances mean actual profit is greater than budgeted profit.
Unfavorable (U) variances mean actual profit is less than budgeted profit.

Exhibit 6-8

should have been needed [12 panels per house × 9 houses]. This is the flexible budget amount, or **standard quantity allowed**. Here are some examples:

Standard Quantity Allowed				
Standard quantity	×	Actual output	=	Standard quantity allowed
12 roof panels per house	×	9 houses	=	108 panels
20 hours sawing panels per house	×	9 houses	=	180 sawing hours
1,000 direct labor hours per house	×	9 houses	=	9,000 direct labor hours

Standard quantity allowed *is the total amount of a resource that should be used for the actual number of products made.*

The usage variances [Exhibit 6-8] show the calculations for the same February activities we looked at with spending variances [Exhibit 6-7]. Let's start with direct materials. We budget $21 per sheet for roof paneling, one of our direct materials. 108 sheets should have been used for the 9 houses built, but 103 sheets were actually used. Being more efficient than plan, the 5 sheets not used [at a budgeted price of $21 each] saved us $105 compared to budget. Actual profit is $105 greater than planned profit, a favorable direct material usage variance.

"Turning our attention to direct labor, 180 hours should have been worked in sawing the roof panels, although 200 hours were actually worked. Working 20 hours more than allowed results in actual profit being less than the budget by $200, an unfavorable direct labor usage variance in the Sawing Department.

"Now think about variable overhead. Throughout the plant, we should have worked 9,000 direct labor hours in making 9 standard homes. An unfavorable labor efficiency variance results from working 10,000 hours. According to our POR, labor causes overhead. *If more hours are worked than planned, more variable overhead must have been used than was planned to be used.* In other words, for every direct labor hour worked, $2.06 should be spent on variable overhead. If 1,000 hours more than budget were worked, $2,060 more variable overhead was used [an unfavorable usage variance]."

TOMMY

"Well, the variable overhead usage variance is based on a couple of assumptions. First, we assume labor causes overhead. Then, we assume if more hours are worked, more overhead is used. It's possible we can work more hours and not use proportionately more glue, nails, sheetrock tape, lubricants, saw blades, electricity to run the machines, and the like. *The variable overhead usage variance really measures the cost driver quantity used.*"

JULIE

"By using more [or less] of the items making up variable overhead, its total cost increases [or decreases]. In our direct materials and labor efficiency variances, the portion of actual cost caused by the quantity used is isolated, becoming the focus of our attention in those variances [i.e., focus on the difference between standard quantity allowed and actual quantity used]. With variable overhead, we do not measure the quantities of each item [e.g., lubricants and saw blades]. We cannot trace them to specific products. This is why indirect resources are included in overhead. If we could trace usage directly to products, these items become direct materials. *Because variable overhead represents indirect product costs [resources used], its spending variance has two components: a price variance [e.g., lubricants cost more per gallon] and a usage variance [e.g., less gallons were used than planned].* I'll come back to this idea when we discuss investigating the variable overhead spending variance a little later. Right now, go back to the usage variance examples [Exhibit 6-8] and focus on the standard quantity allowed. It is measured as direct material and labor quantities for our direct variable costs [sheets of roof paneling, hours of labor]. It is not measured as pounds of nails or feet of wire as in the variable overhead usage variance. Instead, all the indirect costs are bundled together into one total variable overhead POR per direct labor hour, as if we really 'purchased' variable overhead by the direct labor hour."

Fixed cost usage variances. "Overhead management and accounting create all sorts of problems! I have to spend some extra time making sure I understand direct versus indirect manufacturing costs, manufacturing versus nonmanufacturing costs, and how the accounting differences affect budgeting and product costing. Here's another one of those overhead issues you should explain. A variable cost efficiency variance results when we use more or less of a resource, like lumber or labor. Can we use more or less of a fixed cost resource, like fixed overhead, resulting in a fixed overhead usage variance? What exactly is fixed overhead?"

"More outstanding questions! Overhead costs we budget with cost drivers not related to production volume, like the weather, are considered fixed overhead because they are not influenced by fluctuations in production volume. Another way to think about this is to realize fixed overhead is the cost of certain resources we need just to be able to make the first house. For example, we need a factory building which creates a fixed overhead cost [rent or depreciation]. The building needs to be heated, lighted, insured, and maintained. We have to pay property taxes on it. Fixed overhead is the cost of having productive capacity available to use in making products or providing services. Can we use more or less of this capacity [e.g., the factory]?"

"Of course we can! We're not working at maximum capacity now. The capacity we use depends on the amount of business we have. Since this capacity is very expensive, we should calculate a fixed overhead, or capacity, usage variance! But how can we measure the 'cost' of capacity?"

"A number of ways exist, depending on the type of control information we want. Generally speaking, we want to know how efficiently we use the entire plant. Accounting theoreticians are currently working on measuring capacity usage. As an example of one issue, should unused [surplus] capacity be measured from a cost perspective? By this I mean should we 'cost' excess capacity by allocating overall plant costs [e.g., rent or depreciation, utilities, taxes, and insurance]? Or should we 'cost' surplus capacity using the CMU of products that could be made with it? Capacity is not just a manufacturing issue, though. We also should measure sales capacity and administrative capacity. The issues are complex and best left for a more advanced discussion of cost accounting."

"O.K. I think we should summarize profit variance analysis. We begin with a profit variance report which highlights summary variances by line item in the income statement [Exhibit 6-2]. To further analyze the summary variances, we then drill down to specific variances. Simple formulas calculate the difference between planned and actual profit for each line item. We calculated the sales variances for Multree [Exhibit 6-3]. The same formula for a spending variance [Exhibit 6-7] and for a usage variance [Exhibit 6-8] can be used with each variable cost. Usually with fixed costs, only spending variances are calculated. Here's my summary of profit variance analysis [see Exhibit 6-9]."

Reporting and Investigating Variances

"I understand the math. But have you answered my original questions? Why do we have a $29,000 unfavorable sales variance? I realize $9,000 is due to sales price

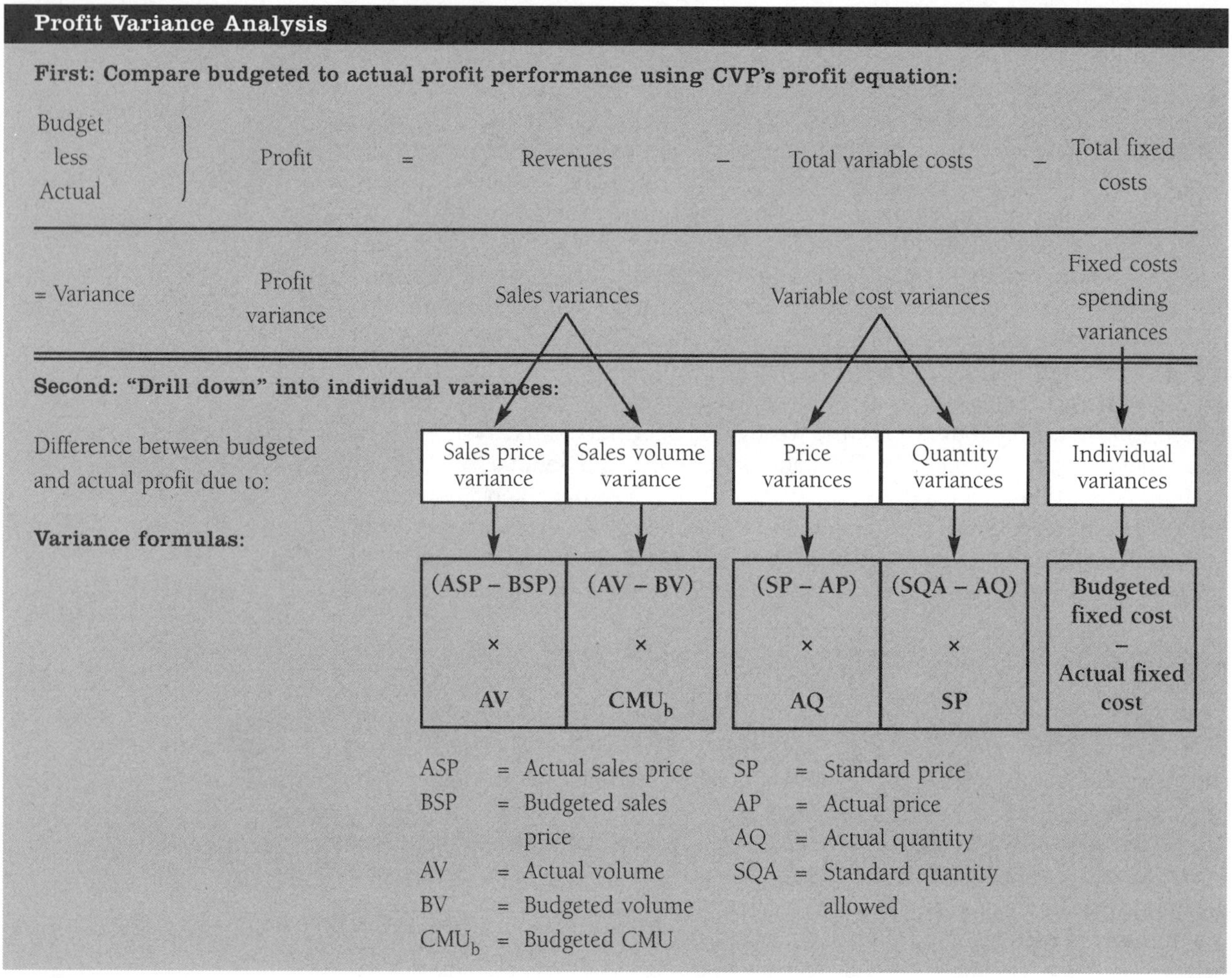

Profit Variance Analysis

First: Compare budgeted to actual profit performance using CVP's profit equation:

Budget less Actual	Profit	=	Revenues	−	Total variable costs	−	Total fixed costs
= Variance	Profit variance		Sales variances		Variable cost variances		Fixed costs spending variances

Second: "Drill down" into individual variances:

	Sales price variance	Sales volume variance	Price variances	Quantity variances	Individual variances
Difference between budgeted and actual profit due to:	Sales price variance	Sales volume variance	Price variances	Quantity variances	Individual variances
Variance formulas:	(ASP − BSP) × AV	(AV − BV) × CMU_b	(SP − AP) × AQ	(SQA − AQ) × SP	**Budgeted fixed cost − Actual fixed cost**

ASP = Actual sales price
BSP = Budgeted sales price
AV = Actual volume
BV = Budgeted volume
CMU_b = Budgeted CMU

SP = Standard price
AP = Actual price
AQ = Actual quantity
SQA = Standard quantity allowed

Exhibit 6-9

problems, and another $20,000 due to sales volume problems. What caused these problems? I also don't know why we have $29,400 in unfavorable cost variances! As with sales variances, the cost variances can be decomposed into spending and usage problems. But *why* did we have all these variances? Your accounting report does not tell me this!"

What is control?

JACKIE

"The reports are not supposed to provide information on variance causes! Remember scientific management. Value chain processes are broken down into small groups of tasks, each organized into a separate department often called a 'functional silo.' Accordingly, as a separate department, Accounting's responsibility ends with 'running the numbers.' I create the report. It's management's responsibility to run the business. It's your responsibility to investigate and solve problems!"

TOMMY

"Don't you have an ethical responsibility to report problem causes within variance reports? Isn't this critical control information?"

JACKIE

"Well, it may be. And I do have a role to play in identifying variance causes. To understand the accountant's traditional role in investigation, we should consider what 'control' means for upper management and for shop floor [lower-level] managers. Top management asks two questions:

- Has the target profit been achieved?
- Are the departments under control?

Remember, historically accounting information was designed for upper management. Scientific management tells us they want aggregate, summary numbers. The profit variance report does this. And it itemizes variances by responsibility area [sales, production, administration].

KEY OBJECTIVE 5

Distinguish between boardroom and process control, and explain the usefulness of variance analysis for these strategies.

"This is what I call 'boardroom control.' Top management 'controls' the company by reviewing summary accounting reports. Moving down the management hierarchy, lower-level managers are motivated to minimize their variances because they know top management will hold them accountable for variances occurring in their departments. Thus, lower management is motivated to control day-to-day operations. Controlling day-to-day operations is what I call 'process control.'

"Top management cannot get involved in all the details of running the business on a daily basis. The bigger the company, the more this is true. They 'manage by the numbers' relying on monthly or weekly summary variance reports to tell them if the company is under control and target profits are being achieved."

Where to begin investigating variances?

JACKIE

"Because so many specific variances can be calculated, variance reports have to direct top management's attention to the most significant variances. I do not want to bury you in too many details. Where do we begin? Many firms employ one or a combination of the following strategies:

- Start with the largest variances, as measured in dollars.
- Only investigate variances falling outside some acceptable limits.
- Use management judgment in deciding which variances should be investigated."

"The first strategy makes sense to me. The largest variances have the greatest effect on our profits. I'm interested in dollars, and I want variances reported as total dollar amounts because every dollar of a variance is one less dollar of profit for me!"

TOMMY

"I like the second strategy better! Suppose we have two variances—one is \$1,000 and the other \$100. The first variance is only 1% of the standard cost [e.g., the flexible budget for labor is \$100,000] but the second is 100% of standard. Expressing variances as percentages of standard cost helps us judge their significance. Regardless of the total dollars involved, a 100% variance means it's more likely the system is out of control. Using some kind of limit [percentage of standard, or standard deviation from it] is just like how my furnace controls temperature. It will not turn on until the temperature deviates two degrees from what I set it to be. While a temperature within this range is not exactly what I want, it is acceptable."

"The Boss preferred the third strategy. He did not rely upon accounting numbers to run the business. He pretty much knew what was going on. He knew the significant problems causing large variances. He did review my variance reports, though. Any variances surprising him were investigated. That's where I came in. The Boss circled the ones he wanted more information about. I then had to go down to the plant and ask why they happened."

"And that's why accountants too often are characterized as the 'cop on the block.' Workers only saw you when they were in trouble! No wonder accountants traditionally have not been well liked by operations personnel!"

NANCY

"We now have the information technology to develop more sophisticated and detailed variance reports [e.g., bar coding and scanning, touch screens, data warehousing, etc.]. For example, I saw a company develop an on-line, real-time system that reported cost variances to the departments when they actually happened. Because department workers were alerted to variances as they occurred, corrective actions could be taken to minimize the problem's impact on planned profits and to prevent the problem from recurring. Then, workers input the source and cause of variances so the variance reports could answer whether departments were again 'under control.' The variance reports provided more accurate performance evaluation information for boardroom control, while also motivating shop floor process control. Why don't we do this?"

JACKIE

"It's just a cost-benefit decision. The Boss only wanted to look at exceptional variances. Therefore, we only investigated exceptional variances. He just didn't see the need to investigate every variance, whether real-time or after the fact. When he wanted more information about a variance, he asked me to get it. In this way, the Boss practiced scientific management and management by exception. He believed it was a more efficient investigation strategy than developing the sophisticated management accounting system you described."

NANCY

"Of course, the Boss was thinking like upper management. Upper management and lower management have different information needs, at least according to scientific management. If we're interested in process control, though, drilling down into spending and usage variances still will not be sufficient!

"Also consider this. Not only has Multree Homes changed over the years, so has its upper management. We don't know the business as well as the Boss did. It's bigger and more complex. We need accounting information to help us run the business. Maybe we should consider investing in a better management accounting system!"

JULIE

"If we are going to keep our traditional variance reporting system, though, another way to focus top management on the important variances is not to report variances about insignificant activities. Trane Company, for example, designed the Pueblo, Colorado, plant's standard cost system to not report most direct material variances since about ¾ of its parts only represent 3% of production costs. Labor variances are no longer reported because labor represents less than 5% of total production costs. On the other hand, Sally Industries—a Jacksonville, Florida, firm making robots for amusement and theme parks—reports all labor variances on a job-by-job basis because it is one of the highest costs incurred. Both companies, following the KISS principle [keep it simple, stupid] identify the important activities and limit variance reports to them.

"In determining which variances to investigate, though, about half of major manufacturers use dollar or percentage limits. The other half rely on judgment. Only 1% use statistically set limits. The Ritz-Carlton hotel chain uses percentages, and allows each hotel a 5% profit variance each month. Variances within this limit are not considered significant and thus are not worthy of upper management investigation. Or so traditional management accounting theory goes."

NANCY

"O.K. Let's see if I understand control and the role of variance reports. Top management wants after-the-fact information about whether target profit has been achieved and departments are under control. Variances tell us about the differences between planned and actual profits. However, we have to conduct special investigations to discover their causes and determine if operations are in control. This is boardroom control.

"Process control concerns day-to-day operations management. Variances can support operational control if the information system captures variance causes and sources. Variances can provide feedforward information to the shop floor, as well as feedback information to top management. We have to decide if the more sophisticated information system is worth the investment."

Understanding variance causes: Drilling down into the "black box"

"Theory be damned! Let's get real. How can we assume departments are under control unless we drill down to the specific variance causes? Look at variable overhead in our profit variance report [Exhibit 6-2]. Having no variance, variable overhead costs must be under control. But when we look at its spending and usage variances [Exhibits 6-7 and 6-8], each is more than 10% off standard. The total variances may be too aggregated to give us the control information we need. The two variable overhead variances canceled out each other! How do we really know if departments are under control without more detailed information? How can we use variances in performance evaluation, thus motivating shop floor process control, without knowing their causes? I want to know why actual contribution margin and profit is $29,000 less than plan due to sales problems. You accountants still have not answered this question!!"

Doris felt the tension building. She emptied the coffee pot and made fresh decaffeinated as her attempt at process control. ("No more caffeine for him!" she thought to herself. Or is this boardroom control?) She then retrieved her best pastries from the back of the refrigerator. Bill grabbed the first one, wiped his brow, and began timidly.

"We can think of many possible explanations for sales price and volume problems. *Often, we suspect many separate problems make up a summary monthly variance.* Fortunately, only one problem explains both sales variances. It's competition. Our competitors are underpricing us in the standard home line. We've dropped the price but continue to lose sales. I do have some good news, though. Custom home sales are better than budget. We just sold two, when none were planned!"

"Competition, huh? The Boss drove out all the local competition years ago. Where are these competitors coming from?"

"Well, some are selling standard home kits. Others are willing to ship manufactured homes from distances not practical 20 years ago. I even saw a company selling over the Internet! Competition is coming from everywhere. We used to be able to differentiate our product based on geographic location. However, our geographic region is no longer 'sacred territory.' Competition is fast becoming global. You can see this in the other sales-related variances.

"Competition is the underlying cause for the sales commission spending variance [Exhibit 6-7]. To encourage our sales people to work harder, I'm offering a $100 bonus for each standard home sold. This increases the commission to $2,600 per home. The $5,000 unfavorable advertising variance is from new advertising media [developing a Web site] to promote standard home sales.

"Competition also is the culprit for the $3,000 unfavorable administrative cost variance. These are extra Purchasing Department costs incurred in trying to find new suppliers offering lower material prices."

"I know why our fixed overhead budget variance is $10,000 unfavorable! Again, it's competition. This is extra architectural cost for standard home design changes in an attempt to better differentiate our product and maintain sales. I don't have any idea, though, why we have material and labor variances for the roof panels and Sawing Department, or what's going on with variable overhead. I guess Jackie will have to go down to the shop floor and ask those people."

"I did! Let's start with the roof panel $2 per sheet unfavorable price variance [Exhibit 6-7]. Lumber prices are very volatile. Ten-foot sheet prices increased $2. The purchasing agent didn't anticipate it in preparing the budget. Our standard homes are 26 feet long. Thus, the Sawing Department cuts every third 10-foot sheet to only 6 feet in length. The 4-foot length left over is usually scrapped. Knowing about the price increase, Sawing Department personnel saved the scraps to minimize the number of sheets needed. Cutting one of the 4-foot scraps in half, and combining each half with two other 4-foot scraps, equals saving one 10-foot sheet. This is why we have a favorable roof panel usage variance [Exhibit 6-8]. Of course, it required more work by the sawing people. Hence the $200 unfavorable labor usage variance. Some temporary people were hired to help. We did not have to pay them normal fringe benefits, so their labor rate was only $8 per hour [versus our $10 standard rate], resulting in the $400 favorable labor rate variance [Exhibit 6-7].

"To understand the variable overhead spending variance, we should drill down to the specific items comprising it. [This is done in Exhibit 6-10.]

Specific Variable Overhead Spending Variances

Variable overhead resources	Variable overhead POR (per DLhr)	Flexible budget for 10,000 DLhrs actually worked	Actual variable overhead cost for 10,000 DLhrs	Variable overhead spending variances
Indirect materials	$0.92	$9,200	$9,000	$200 F
Indirect labor	0.64	6,400	4,000	2,400 F
Power	0.50	5,000	5,000	0
Total VOH	**$2.06**	**$20,600**	**$18,000**	**$2,600** F

Exhibit 6-10

Line management knows they are accountable for their variances. Working 10,000 direct labor hours resulted in unfavorable labor usage and variable overhead usage variances. Knowing this, they cut back on machine maintenance and training. Less factory supplies were used because of less maintenance activities, resulting in a favorable indirect materials spending variance. A lot of February's indirect labor is for maintenance and training. To save money, these activities were not done, resulting in a favorable indirect labor spending variance. By cutting back on maintenance and training, they were able to offset the unfavorable variable overhead usage variance."

"We should reconsider how our people view overhead cost control. Maybe we should be more like Starbucks coffee shops. While most employees are part-time, the company spends over $1,000 training each one. This involves 25 hours of training from formal courses in 'Coffee Knowledge 101' to friendly customer service methods. To Starbucks, overhead cost control is not minimizing this month's cost. Rather, it's investing in training and in employee health and morale to increase long-term value.

"Knowing the causes of the spending variance, favorable variances do not necessarily mean 'good news.' If we use less material or labor than their standard quantities, have we lowered the product's quality and hurt our long-term value? The favorable spending variance results from not doing maintenance and training. How will this affect long-term value? If a favorable fixed cost spending variance occurs in research and development because a highly promising, but very expensive, R&D project was delayed, is this 'good news'? *A favorable variance means actual profit is greater than budget. This, however, is a short-run idea* as profit is a short-run measure [e.g., for a month or year]. When we consider long-run value, both favorable and unfavorable variances may be good or bad news."

"The fixed overhead budget variance should be itemized just like variable overhead spending [in Exhibit 6-10]. I don't have an itemized report, though, because we already know what happened [the extra spending on architectural changes caused the entire $10,000 unfavorable variance]."

Sid's frustration was beginning to show as he sat through the detailed explanations. He realized his interest was not in the details. Finally, he felt compelled to interrupt.

"Enough! All I want to know is whether the departments are under control. Obviously, they are not! Or, at least, they *were* not. My question now is have these problems been identified and solved?"

"The variance reports are not designed to tell us this, either. Traditionally, in part due to the influence of scientific management, accounting's role in management has been limited to 'bean counting.' We do not solve problems; we are 'number crunchers.'"

"We better rethink accounting's role in management control. No longer can you afford to hide in the back room, only coming out to play 'cop on the block' investigating why variances happened after the fact. The new role for management accountants will be in problem solving. I expect you to become part of our top management team! You shouldn't be investigating variances up to a month after they happened. Your reports should provide variance causes and whether the underlying problems have been fixed. Only with this type of more detailed information can we turn our attention to the problems *still* existing!"

"We've uncovered a lot of problems with these variance reports. Obviously, they are not telling us everything we want to know. However, they provide a lot of useful control information. Here's my summary [Exhibits 6-11a and b].

"Traditional variance analysis and after-the-fact 'boardroom' control treat the organization as a 'black box.' If we have no variances, we have no problems serious enough to warrant investigation. The only way to turn the black box into a 'glass box' is by drilling down to specific variances and then identifying their real sources and causes. Over ten years ago, Caterpillar management discovered that three separate accounting systems were necessary to satisfy its information needs: one for product costing, one for operational control, and one for performance evaluation."

The One Best Way: A Well-Engineered Process

"You know, it doesn't make any difference how sophisticated our accounting system is if the standards are bad. We saw this with Sarah's college dilemma. She failed to anticipate the tuition increase. Her standard price [budgeted tuition rate] was not correct, and this caused the tuition rate variance [Exhibit 6-1]. Is it possible some of our variances result from bad standards and not from control problems?"

Contributions of Variances to Control	
For boardroom control	**For process control**
1. Measures whether target profit has been achieved.	1. Directs top management to who to ask first.
2. Identifies where profit problems occurred.	2. Motivates line management to control operations by avoiding variances that are used in performance evaluation.
3. Itemizes variances in terms of spending and usage.	3. Focuses line management and workers on profit and how it is affected by their day-to-day control activities.
4. Prioritizes problems in terms of profit.	

Exhibit 6-11a

Problems with Traditional Variances

The problem:	Explanation:	Example:
1. Total variances are too aggregated when investigating if departments are under control.	Specific spending and usage variances can offset each other, resulting in total variances not appearing significant.	The VOH spending and usage variances canceled out each other in Exhibit 6-2.
2. Variance reports are timely for boardroom control, but not for process control.	Monthly variances are not timely enough for managing day-to-day activities.	Sawing workers thought they were doing a good thing by using roof panel scraps. But this will increase home costs when the roofs are assembled. The extra seams may also reduce quality.
3. Favorable variances are not necessarily good news. Unfavorable variances are not necessarily bad news.	Favorable and unfavorable only indicate a variance's effect on budgeted profit.	The VOH spending variance is favorable, but it resulted from not doing maintenance and training. Conversely, an unfavorable variance may be good news if it results from performing activities preventing more costly problems later.
4. A monthly variance often is the total of many different problems.	Variances do not tell us about their causes and whether the problems causing them have been corrected.	The most significant problem in Framing, a machine breakdown, has been fixed. Top management should not have to investigate this after receiving the monthly variance report.
5. One problem can cause many variances across different departments. This inhibits correct performance evaluation.	If variance reports do not identify sources and causes, and link together the variances caused by a single factor, the wrong people may be rewarded or punished.	Even though the roofers did their best to produce high-quality roofs with the materials they had available, all the unfavorable variances resulting from using the roof panel scraps sent from the Sawing Department resulted in the roofers being punished (no bonuses).

Exhibit 6-11b

SID

Sid began to settle down. Maybe Doris's decaf coffee and special pastries were working. "The Boss believed in a well-engineered process. If operations are designed efficiently, standard quantities represent the 'one best way' to do things. Achieving our standards, then, is the correct way to behave. Achieving standards means we will hit our target profit. While this is a short-run perspective, accomplishing our annual profit goal will lead us to our long-term value creation objective. I believe a well-understood and designed process allows 'management by the numbers.' In other words, we can use accounting numbers as the primary basis for judgment and action. If our standards communicate the 'one best way' to do activities, we only need to focus on exceptions [variances]. This is how scientific management and management by exception are related. But if our standards are bad, they may not represent the one best way. Are our standards O.K., Bob?"

Ideal versus practical standard quantities

KEY OBJECTIVE 6

Compare ideal and practical standards, and explain why practical standards represent the "one best way."

"I think so! This is the way the Boss always did things. We've engineered our standard quantities using time and motion studies pioneered by Frederick Taylor back in 1882 as a key component of scientific management. Of course, today we use computer modeling programs [CAD/CAM] to provide a precise understanding of each task and movement. Our industrial engineer has studied the product and resource characteristics, labor requirements, and WIP [work-in-process] movements. These are incorporated into our standard quantities. Here are two resource standards, one for 2 × 4 lumber, and one for sawing 2 × 4's [see Exhibit 6-12].

Standard Quantities for 2 × 4 Lumber Sawing

2 × 4 lumber standard quantity			
8-foot long 2 × 4 lumber		100	pieces
Allowance for scrap	10%	10	pieces
Allowance for rejects	5%	5	pieces
Standard quantity		115	8-foot long 2 × 4s

Sawing labor		
Ideal sawing time	10	hours per house
Stacking sawed 2 × 4s	20	
Idle time during saw setup	4	
Inspecting materials	5	
Allowance for rework	5	
Break time	1	
Cleanup time	2	
Miscellaneous activities	3	
Standard labor time	50	hours per house

Exhibit 6-12

"An **ideal standard quantity** is the minimum amount of a resource needed given our current operating conditions [plant layout, equipment quality, etc.]. We ideally need 100 eight-foot long 2 × 4's for framing each home. Ideally, only 10 labor hours are required in Sawing to cut them to the correct size."

"Why do we have to cut them? Can't we just purchase the framing lumber in the correct length? This would eliminate all the sawing labor!"

"No we can't. The ideal standard is not practical. A **practical standard quantity** allows for uncertainties. For example, walls are seven feet high. But we cannot buy 7' lengths because the saw mill has a ¼ inch tolerance. The actual length can be ¼ inch too short or long. We need exactly 7' lengths, so we buy 8' lengths and cut them to size. We also have to buy 10% more than needed because some

Ideal standard quantities *do not allow for any waste or loss in the use of our resources.* **Practical standard quantities** *include realistic expectations for problems like poor quality materials, equipment breakdowns, and labor downtime.*

lumber has knots in it or is warped. We scrap the bad lumber. Finally, our saw is not perfect. Sometimes lumber is not cut to exactly 7' because the saw gets out of alignment or the blade becomes dull. Allowing for all these uncertainties, our practical standard quantity is 115 pieces of 2 × 4 framing lumber.

"Our engineer also has considered all the uncertainties in the labor time needed to saw the framing lumber. Sawed lumber has to be stacked, laborers sit around a total of 4 hours while the saws are set up, 5 hours are used in inspecting incoming lumber [and scrapping the bad 10%], and on average 5 hours of reworking [re-sawing or sanding edges to size] are needed due to an imperfect sawing process [Exhibit 6-12]. We also allow for break time [required by law], time to clean up, and time for other activities."

TOMMY

"Yes! Those other activities are important! Three hours are needed to look for tools, gloves, pallets, ask for help, talk with each other, and the like. Most importantly, it includes time to go to the bathroom. If we don't budget time for this activity, they will go to the bathroom anyway, and maybe more often than is really necessary!" Everyone laughed.

NANCY

"So, our practical labor standard time becomes 50 hours per house in Sawing? No wonder we're having competition problems!"

TOMMY

"The Japanese believe in ideal standards and work to achieve them. They do this to support their total quality management [TQM] and just-in-time [JIT] strategies. Some companies use 'stretch goals' targeted to be accomplished in some intermediate time period. Boeing set stretch goals in 1992 to be achieved by 1996 for its 777 aircraft line. For Toshiba's new VCR line, the stretch goals are to produce it with half the parts and in half the time of its older VCRs. Mead Corporation expects 3% annual productivity improvements."

$% JULIE

"Well, we're not the Japanese! Mead lost more than 300 [of 900] managers within three years of implementing its stretch goals. General Electric management rejected them as well, because lower management did not believe they were attainable. Most of our managerial motivation research concludes people are best motivated with tight but achievable standards. I'm told another major wood products company has a 20% waste factor in its standards. We have only 15% with our framing lumber.

"You may not like it, but we do have to be practical. If not, our standards will always underestimate the amount of resources we will really need. Using ideal standards in our CVP model and cash budget will overestimate our profit and underestimate cash outflows. Even Frederick Taylor factored in these uncertainties in developing practical standards workers were expected to accomplish. This is why Bethlehem Steel and other major industrial revolution manufacturers hired his firm."

SID

"As I see it, we're not being very efficient!" Sid again started to lose his control reviewing the numbers in Exhibit 6-12. Doris, now becoming the 'control engineer' for these meetings, was quick with a fresh pastry and more decaf coffee. "I think we should investigate this idea of stretch goals, and move more toward ideal standard quantities. Julie, get in touch with the IMA and see what its publication service and library have on stretch goals and productivity improvement. I'll schedule a future meeting on this topic [Chapter 11]."

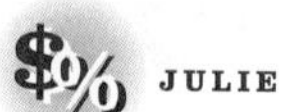
JULIE

"You better schedule more than one [Chapters 12 and 13, too!]."

The costs and benefits of poor quality

BOB

"I know we are wasting 15% of our framing lumber and most of the sawing labor hours. But it's just too expensive to eliminate all of the uncertainties. It's cheaper to allow for scrap and rejects than to reengineer our processes and get perfect quality from our suppliers. And we can get some great prices from the saw mill if we are willing to accept some warped or knot-filled lumber. This is just good old-fashioned business practice. It's a cost-benefit decision.

"I remember when the Boss used to walk the plant. One day he watched a $200 graphite saw blade being replaced. Lots of people were standing around. The Boss went bananas! The workers thought they could avoid the scrap by replacing the dull blade before the engineers said it was necessary. They didn't realize it's cheaper to scrap lumber and use the blade longer! The Boss didn't mind pushing a little more bad production during the day because blade changing was very expensive and time-consuming, and should be done only when people are not normally working. In his mind, the benefits from eliminating the extra waste were less than the costs from the lost working time.

"So, both standard quantities and prices are based on what's practical. Standard prices include the most economical shipping methods and discounts we should receive for large orders containing some bad lumber. Our standard prices and quantities result from a well-understood process designed in the one best way. The budgeted slack resources [allowances for waste], as we discussed in our cash budgeting meeting, recognize the uncertainties we face. Much like Best Baking Company's standards, ours are engineered costs validated by years of experience."

Using standards to communicate what's expected

NANCY

"All right. I'm convinced. When we communicate with workers through the budgeting process, or when we hire new people, standards provide them with the information to do their jobs in the most efficient manner."

TOMMY

"We should be careful, though. Just because we 'scientifically' measure activities, this doesn't mean we are measuring the correct activities. Standards, by representing how work should be done, communicate what's expected. We have to know when conditions have changed and adjust our standards so they remain accurate enough for good management."

JULIE

"That's already part of our standard costing system. When variances occur, we investigate the significant ones. Variances are caused by inefficiencies or changes in our environment. If bad standards cause a variance, they need to be updated. But I agree with your idea, Tommy. Standards cannot be based solely on past performance, under the assumption nothing has changed. Standards have to be forward looking. Levi Strauss of Canada changes its standards whenever variance investigation identifies they're out of date. Making and selling jeans in over 60 countries, Levi's standards are used worldwide. They must be current and correct. Citizen Watch Company updates its standards every three months. A 1% variance triggers investigations which require a review of its processes. Tightly controlling production through variance investigation is becoming more common in Japan, too."

TOMMY

"As our competition tightens their standards, we should consider driving out the long-accepted waste in ours. I don't like not doing a high-quality job. I teach my kids to always do their best. But this isn't our best!"

BOB

"I appreciate your position, but your kids are the last kind of people we want to hire! We don't want workers tinkering with work methods. Remember the Boss saying, 'If it ain't broke, don't fix it!'? Using good scientific management methods, engineers designed our processes by dividing them into small, easily learned tasks. This allows hiring cheap labor and not investing a lot of money in training. We can hire and lay off people as needed. Labor then is a variable cost. They are not supposed to think. They're supposed to do what they are told. If they're not bored, the jobs are designed wrong!"

TOMMY

"So, you're arguing we are doing a quality job. We're living to our standards, and they define what quality is. Our problem is not designing quality into our standard quantities, at least from our competition's and customers' perspective. We don't inspect work until the houses are completed. Quality control is a separate department at the end of the manufacturing process. And the guys in rework are working more than the guys in production! I still believe we should rethink what quality is and drive out waste from our standard quantities. Think about the airline industry. Do you want maintenance personnel using practical standards that allow for a certain acceptable amount of quality problems?

"With our practically engineered standards, workers are not motivated to improve processes. Acceptable poor quality [waste] may no longer be possible in our globally competitive market, though. Empowering our people to suggest improvements, training them in high-quality methods, and rewarding them for driving out waste may be the only ethical strategy to follow in today's world—at least if long-run value creation is our true objective!"

SID

"Well, I see we still have a lot to talk about with how work should be done. Our discussion of quality problems and how they are continued through our standards will have to wait until a future meeting [Chapter 11]. Doris, can you summarize what we have covered today, please? And please bring me that last pastry!"

KEY OBJECTIVES SUMMARY

DORIS

"We covered six important ideas in today's meeting:

1. Explain management by exception and how it is a feedback system.

"Management by exception focuses on problems. A problem is the difference between planned and actual results. In accounting, a problem is called a variance. Planned results are communicated through our proforma income statement. To identify problems, the proforma income statement is compared to actual revenues and costs. When planned and actual sales volume are different, a flexible budget is prepared for the actual sales volume. The flexible budget adjusts revenues, total variable costs, and contribution margin from the original plan to the budgeted amounts for the actual sales volume. A profit variance report compares the original budget to the flexible budget, and then the flexible budget to actual profit, identifying sales price and volume variances and cost variances.

"The profit variance report is used primarily to evaluate a company's performance. Thus it is a feedback report. Top management wants to know if the profit plan was achieved. Investigating variances, top management discovers if departments are under control. Profit variances result from operational problems. If department managers did a good job in identifying and solving problems, their variances were minimized [kept within acceptable limits], resulting in favorable performance evaluations. If variances have not been corrected, top management intervention may be needed.

"Notice the feedback nature of this control strategy. Top management negotiates budgets and standards with subordinates. It maintains a 'hands-off' policy by not intervening on a day-by-day basis to minimize variances. This is lower management's responsibility [according to scientific management]. Rather than preventing or minimizing problems, top management only becomes involved after the fact. Because variance reporting was originally designed for top management, it does not capture information on the sources and causes of the problems creating the variances, nor does it report if the problems have been identified and corrected. Thus, variance reports are not suitable for day-to-day process [shop floor versus boardroom] control.

2. Calculate and interpret the sales price and volume variances.

"I was playing golf with my dentist the other day. We had many variances! In addition to our golf variances, she told me about some of her business variances last month. I think she did this because she wanted me to pay for the game. Here's her budget information [see Exhibit 6-13]:

Selected Information from Doris's Dentist's Budget

Revenue information		
Insurance patients:	8 per day x 23 Days/month =	184 Patients/month
Anticipated insurance reimbursement:		$100 /patient
Budgeted contribution margin per patient (CMU):		$50

Resources	Standard Costs		
	Standard Prices	Standard Quantities	Standard Costs
Direct materials: X-ray film	$1.00 /slide	8 Slides/patient	$8.00 /patient
Direct labor: Dental hygienist	$10.00 /hour	0.5 Hours/patient	$5.00 /patient
Variable overhead	$20.00 /DLhr	1.0 DLhr/patient	$20.00 /patient
Fixed overhead	$30,000 /month		

Exhibit 6-13

"Most of her business is routine preventive dental care for patients enrolled in our local HMO [health maintenance organization]. My dentist plans on seeing 184 HMO patients a month. The HMO used to pay her $100 per patient [this is her budgeted charge]. Budgeting $50 per patient in variable costs, her budgeted CMU is $50.

"Last month, she saw 200 preventive care patients, but the HMO changed its reimbursement amount to $90. According to the health plan, patients receive two free preventive care visits a year. Thus my dentist cannot bill them for the $10 reduction in her HMO reimbursement. Because sales price and volume differed from budget, my dentist's actual contribution margin was $1,200 less than plan due to these two variances [see Exhibit 6-14].

Dentist's Sales Variances

Sales price variance					
Formula:	(Actual sales price	- Budgeted sales price)	x	Actual volume	
February variance	($90 per patient	- $100 per patient)	x	200 patients	= ($2,000) U
Sales volume variance					
Formula:	(Actual volume	- Budgeted volume)	x	Budgeted CMU	
February variance	(200 patients	- 184 patients)	x	$50 per patient	= $800 F
Total sales variance					($1,200) U

Note: Earned more (F) or less (U) than planned.

Exhibit 6-14

Of the total $1,200 unfavorable sales variance, $2,000 [unfavorable] was due to the $10 reduction in her HMO reimbursement [sales price]. This was partially offset by seeing more patients than planned [the $800 favorable sales volume variance from each of the 16 additional patients who should provide $50 in incremental profit (i.e., budgeted CMU)].

3. Define the components of a standard cost card, and list its benefits and limitations.

"Of course, she incurred some variable and fixed cost variances, further reducing actual profits as compared to her budget. Before 'running the numbers,' though, some ideas about standard costs should be clarified. Standard cost is a resource's budgeted cost in making one product. Every resource has a standard cost, which is composed of a standard price and standard quantity. The standard price is the budgeted net delivered purchase price for a resource. For example, my dentist buys X-ray film by the slide. Her dental hygienist is paid by the hour. Variable overhead is allocated using direct labor hours. You can see these standard prices in the budgeted information presented with the previous learning objective summary. That summary also lists the standard quantities; the amounts of each resource budgeted for a product [or service]. While we have only some of the dentist's resource information, resource standard costs are usually summarized in a standard cost card [Exhibit 6-5]. The sum of all of the resources' standard costs is called the standard absorptive manufacturing cost of a product or service. This is an absorptive cost whenever fixed overhead is included in each product's budgeted and actual cost.

"Standard cost cards provide many benefits, including detailed budget information for CVP and variance calculations, serving as a vehicle for communication and coordination in the budgeting process, budget information for price-setting, motivating people to achieve the profit plan, and more efficient cost accounting.

"Standard cost cards also have some limitations. First, the standard absorptive manufacturing cost cannot be used to budget total manufacturing costs. A cost equation is needed for that purpose. Second, standard cost cards usually contain only manufacturing cost information. Other budgeted costs must be obtained elsewhere.

4. Calculate and interpret spending and usage variances.

"Comparing actual profits to flexible budget profits, summary variances can be calculated for each line item in the income statement. These summary variances can be itemized into spending and usage variances. Spending variances compare budgeted and actual resource prices. Usage variances compare how much of a resource should have been used [standard quantity allowed] with the actual quantity used.

"Spending variances exist for variable and fixed costs. All variable cost spending variances use the same formula. Fixed cost spending variances use a formula based on total fixed costs. Here's my dentist's variances [see Exhibit 6-15]:

Dentist's Spending Variances

Variable costs formula:	(Standard price	-	Actual price)	x	Actual quantity purchased		
X-ray film (DM price variance)	($1.00 per slide	-	$0.90 per slide)	x	2,000 slides	=	$200 F
Dental hygienist (DL rate variance)	($10.00 per hour	-	$10.50 per hour)	x	110 hours	=	($55) U
Variable overhead spending variance	($20.00 per DLhr	-	$19.00 per DLhr)	x	210 DLhrs	=	$210 F
Fixed costs formula:	Budgeted fixed cost	-	Actual fixed cost				
Fixed overhead budget variance	$30,000	-	$32,000			=	($2,000) U

Note: Costs more (**U**) or less than (**F**) planned

Exhibit 6-15

Because a spending variance concerns resource prices, actual price is subtracted from standard price. When standard price is greater than actual price, a favorable variance results. Actual profit is greater than planned profit by this price difference *for each resource purchased*. In other words, the extra total profit is the price difference multiplied by the resource quantity purchased. For X-ray film, the actual price per slide is 10¢ less than standard for each of the 2,000 slides purchased at this favorable price. Buying a large quantity resulted in a lower price.

"The dental hygienist worked ten overtime hours. Being paid time-and-a-half, his average wage for the month was slightly higher than standard. The 50¢ per hour unbudgeted spending results in a $55 unfavorable variance.

"To calculate the variable overhead spending variance, actual cost [$3,990] is divided by actual direct labor hours [210 hours (110 hygienist hours + 100 dentist hours)] to create a rate [$19] which can be compared to the variable overhead POR [$20/DLhr]. Spending $1 per hour less than budget for each of the 210 hours worked results in a $210 favorable variable overhead spending variance. It can be due to spending less on the indirect resources purchased or using less resources than planned.

"Fixed cost spending variances simply compare the total budgeted fixed cost with the total actual fixed cost. My dentist expected to spend $30,000 while actually spending $32,000. The extra $2,000 [an unfavorable fixed overhead spending, or budget, variance] is due to an increase in her liability insurance premium.

"Now, look at her usage variances [see Exhibit 6-16]:

Doris's Dentist's Usage Variances

Variable costs formula:	(Std. quantity allowed	-	Actual quantity used)	x	Standard price	
X-ray film (DM usage variance)	(1,600 slides	-	1,500 slides)	x	$1 per slide	= $100 F
Dental hygienist (DL efficiency variance)	(100 hours	-	110 hours)	x	$10 per hour	= ($100) U
Variable overhead efficiency variance	(200 DLhrs	-	210 DLhrs)	x	$20.00 per DLhr	= ($200) U

Note: Costs more (U) or less than (F) planned

Exhibit 6-16

Each of her 200 patients should have 8 X-ray slides taken, so 1,600 slides should have been used [the standard quantity allowed]. Only 1,500 slides were taken, though. While this results in a favorable usage variance [100 slides not used at a $1.00 budgeted price], is it good news? Yes, if the slides were not needed. No, if they should have been taken, but were not. While actual profit is greater than budget, was patient service quality maintained?

"My dentist budgets ½ hour per patient for the hygienist. The hygienist saw 200 patients last month, so the standard hours allowed are 100. The hygienist is very personable, and talked with patients 10 hours too much. Budgeting $10 per hour, this reduced actual profit $100 below plan. Now, if this made the patients more comfortable [who likes to have his teeth cleaned?] and keeps the patients returning every six months, maybe the unfavorable variance is good news!

"We assume if more labor hours are worked, more variable overhead [supplies] should be used. Labor causes overhead. It's the variable overhead cost driver. Working an extra 10 hours, with a $20 per hour budgeted variable overhead rate [POR], she should have $200 less profit than planned from using more supplies during the extra hours worked. Since the extra 10 hours resulted from talking to patients, instead of cleaning teeth, I don't believe the variance! The variable overhead usage variance really measures whether more of the cost driver was needed than planned [i.e., direct labor hours]. It does not measure whether more variable overhead items were used. Variable overhead usage is mixed up with spending in the variable overhead spending variance.

"Notice, we do not have any fixed cost usage variances. While some could be created, my dentist is only interested in fixed cost spending. To her, capacity usage is not an important management control problem.

5. Distinguish between boardroom and process control, and explain the usefulness of variance analysis for these strategies.

"Boardroom control is the after-the-fact analysis of profit variances to answer two top management questions: were target profits achieved, and are the departments under control? It is a feedback system. Variances inform top management about the differences between target and actual profit. Summary variances are computed for each income statement line item. Each summary variance can be broken down into a spending and usage component. However, using good scientific management practices, an after-the-fact investigation must be conducted to determine the underlying variance causes. Variances do not tell us why they happened or whether they have been corrected. Variances at best identify who to ask first in seeking their causes.

"While we can create more sophisticated information systems capturing variance sources and causes, our top management believes the cost is greater than the benefit from this better information. So variances answer the first control question, but only point us in the right direction for seeking after-the-fact information about whether departments are under control. If we want to drill down to the causes, turning the black box into a glass box and becoming more proactive instead of reactive, we'll need a more detailed and expensive cost accounting system.

"Process control concerns real-time shop floor [operational] management. Line management is motivated to control day-to-day operations because process problems create profit variances, and variances are used in performance evaluation. Avoiding variances is the key to rewards. Through their use in performance evaluation, variances motivate shop floor control. However, they do not provide all the information needed for correct evaluation because variance sources and causes are not identified. They only show us where the variances occurred. Profit variances were created primarily for top management [boardroom] control. While the use of variances in evaluation influences process control, variance usefulness for day-to-day control is limited.

6. Compare ideal and practical standards, and explain why practical standards represent the "one best way."

"Ideal standards do not include any allowances for uncertainties. They represent what could be done if nothing goes wrong. Practical standards allow for quality problems in materials and machinery, and in our people. Practical standards provide realistic budgets and profit projections.

"Engineers have analyzed our processes and designed the best way to make houses. The amount of materials needed and the time required, allowing for all of our uncertainties, are the basis for the standard quantities. Thus, practical standard quantities represent the one best way to do work, even though they allow for an acceptable amount of waste. From a cost-benefit perspective, we've assumed it's just too expensive to eliminate all the problems and remain profitable.

"Our workers accept standards as the one best way. Actually, it's a love-hate relationship. They love the freedom standards provide. As long as workers stay within the standards, Jackie will not come down and bother them. This is how I drive my car. I admit I speed. But I try not to go more than 5 miles per hour over the limit. As long as I stay within this limit, I won't get a speeding ticket. Jackie's like the cop on the block. If I have a variance [speeding too much], I'll get a ticket! This is when I hate the system!

"I also see practical standards as the one best way. I tell my grandchildren to stay in the backyard. As long as they do, I won't investigate what they are actually doing. I realize they may still get into trouble in the backyard; I only hope I don't find out about it! My kids love the freedom, but hate the punishment if something bad happens. Me, too!"

"Thank you, Doris. You did a good job. Since I've had so much fun in this meeting, I think I'll make an appointment with my dentist! Good night all."

REALITY 101

"The Santa Clause" Movie Variances

Nine of the eleven highest grossing movies used special effects to make the impossible possible. While the special effects industry has exploded in quality through the use of computer-aided design (CAD), direct labor represents 65% to 70% of direct costs. Over 30 independent visual effects companies compete with special effects divisions of the major film studios for this business. Accurate budgeting and cost control are critical to receiving the contract and delivering the effects in a profitable manner. Standard costs and variance reports are critical management control system components, as demonstrated in Buena Vista Visual Effects' contract for "The Santa Clause" movie.

Visual effects shots can range from $5,000 to $50,000 each. High profile movies can budget between $5 and $10 million just on special effects, representing about 20% of the total movie's budget. Buena Vista, based on prior movies, has developed a series of standard costs for certain effects. These are used to create budgets and bid proposals for new movie projects. For example, the budget for "The Santa Clause" is shown in Exhibit 6-17.

To support process control, the management accounting staff developed a job cost variance reporting system that can be accessed on-line and in real-time. By including a column for updated estimated costs to complete, the online reports provide an early warning system (a feedforward control mechanism). The variance report approximately half-way through the project looked like Exhibit 6-18 on page 222.

Source: Scalice, "Lights! Cameras!...Accountants?" *Management Accounting*, June 1996. © Institute of Management Accountants. (Amounts used are for illustration only.)

Budget for "The Santa Clause"

Resources	Standard price	Standard quantity	Standard cost
Effects shots (9 scenes)			
Effects editor	$1,200/week	15 weeks	$18,000
Digital scanning operator	$1,000/week	20 weeks	20,000
Film recording operator	$1,000/week	20 weeks	20,000
Composite artist	$1,200/week	44 weeks	52,800
Raw film stock	$0.65/foot	25,000 feet	16,250
Film processing	$0.72/foot	30,000 feet	21,600
Total effects shots			**$148,650**
Creative/production staff			
Effects supervisor	$2,000/week	26 weeks	$52,000
Effects producer	$1,600/week	26 weeks	41,600
Screening room	$95/hour	130 hours	12,350
Total production staff			**$105,950**
Reindeer and sleigh			
Computer animator	$1,200/week	30 weeks	$36,000
Graphics artist	$1,000/week	25 weeks	25,000
Miniature/model maker	$900/week	36 weeks	32,400
Total reindeer and sleigh			**$93,400**
Summary			
Total direct costs			**$348,000**
Production overhead	@ 65% of direct costs		226,200
Total production costs			**$574,200**
Profit mark-up			86,130
Contract price			**$660,330**

Exhibit 6-A1

Job SC: The Santa Clause Movie					
	Cost Variance Report				
Resources	**Cost to date**	**Cost to complete**	**Total costs**	**Budget**	**Variances**
Effects shots (9 scenes)					
Effects editor	$9,500	$8,500	$18,000	$18,000	
Digital scanning operator	11,000	10,000	21,000	20,000	($1,000)
Film recording operator	8,500	11,500	20,000	20,000	
Composite artist	27,000	27,000	54,000	52,800	(1,200)
Raw film stock	9,000	10,000	19,000	16,250	(2,750)
Film processing	10,000	11,650	21,650	21,600	(50)
Total effects shots	**$75,000**	**$78,650**	**$153,650**	**$148,650**	**($5,000)**
Creative/production staff					
Effects supervisor	$20,000	$30,000	$50,000	$52,000	$2,000
Effects producer	20,000	21,600	41,600	41,600	
Screening room	5,350	6,000	11,350	12,350	1,000
Total production staff	**$45,350**	**$57,600**	**$102,950**	**$105,950**	**$3,000**
Reindeer and sleigh					
Computer animator	$20,000	$18,000	$38,000	$36,000	($2,000)
Graphics artist	22,000	5,000	27,000	25,000	(2,000)
Miniature/model maker	33,000	0	33,000	32,400	(600)
Total reindeer and sleigh	**$75,000**	**$23,000**	**$98,000**	**$93,400**	**($4,600)**
Total direct costs	**$195,350**	**$159,250**	**$354,600**	**$348,000**	**($6,600)**

Exhibit 6-A2

READING LIST*

Absorption costing: McNair and Vangermeersch, *Management Accounting Guideline 42: Measuring the Cost of Capacity*, Society of Management Accountants of Canada and the Institute of Management Accountants.

Best Baking Company: Mager, "Valuing Production Using Engineered Costs," *Management Accounting*, March 1993.

Boeing and stretch goals: See stretch goals.

Caterpillar: Jones, "Product Costing at Caterpillar," *Management Accounting*, February 1991.

Citizen Watch Company: Cooper, *When Lean Enterprises Collide: Competing through Confrontation*, Harvard Business School Press, 1995.

Dutch Pantry: Boll, "How Dutch Pantry Accounts for Standard Costs," *Management Accounting*, December 1984.

Ethics and standard setting: Raiborn and Payne, "TQM: Just What the Ethicist Ordered," *Journal of Business Ethics*, 1995.

General Electric and stretch goals: See stretch goals.

Levi Strauss (Canada): "America's Most Admired Corporations," *Fortune*, March 6, 1995.

Mead Corporation and stretch goals: See stretch goals.

Overhead, separating VOH and FOH: Cress and Pettijohn, "A Survey of Budget-Related Planning and Control Policies and Procedures," *Journal of Accounting Education*, Fall 1985.

Problems with traditional variances: Johnson, "Performance Measurement for Competitive Excellence"; Kaplan, "Limitations of Cost Accounting in Advanced Manufacturing Environments," *Measures for Manufacturing Excellence* (Kaplan, ed.), Harvard Business School Press, 1990.

Sally Industries: Barton and Cole, "Accounting for Magic," *Management Accounting*, January 1991.

Starbucks: Rothman, "Into the Black," *Inc.*, January 1993.

——-: Teitelbaum, "Companies to Watch," *Fortune*, August 24, 1992.

Stretch goals: Merchant, "How Challenging Should Profit Budget Targets Be?" *Management Accounting*, November 1990.

——-: Sherman, "Stretch Goals: The Dark Side of Asking for Miracles," *Fortune*, November 13, 1995.

——-: Tully, "Why To Go For Stretch Targets," *Fortune*, November 14, 1994.

Surveys of standard costing use: Cohen and Paquette, "Management Accounting Practices: Perceptions of Controllers," *Journal of Cost Management*, Fall 1991.

——-: Gaumnitz and Kollaritsch, "Manufacturing Cost Variances: Current Practice and Trends," *Journal of Cost Management*, Spring 1991.

Toshiba and stretch goals: See stretch goals.

Trane Company: Clements and Spoede, "Trane's Soup Accounting: It's a System of Utter Practicality," *Management Accounting*, June 1992.

Variance reports include sources and causes: Thomas and Mackey, "Activity-Based Cost Variances for Just-in-Times," *Management Accounting*, April 1994.

*Alphabetic by topic, idea, or company referenced.

CHAPTER 7

But, What If We Do . . .?

Incremental CVP Analysis for Unplanned Events

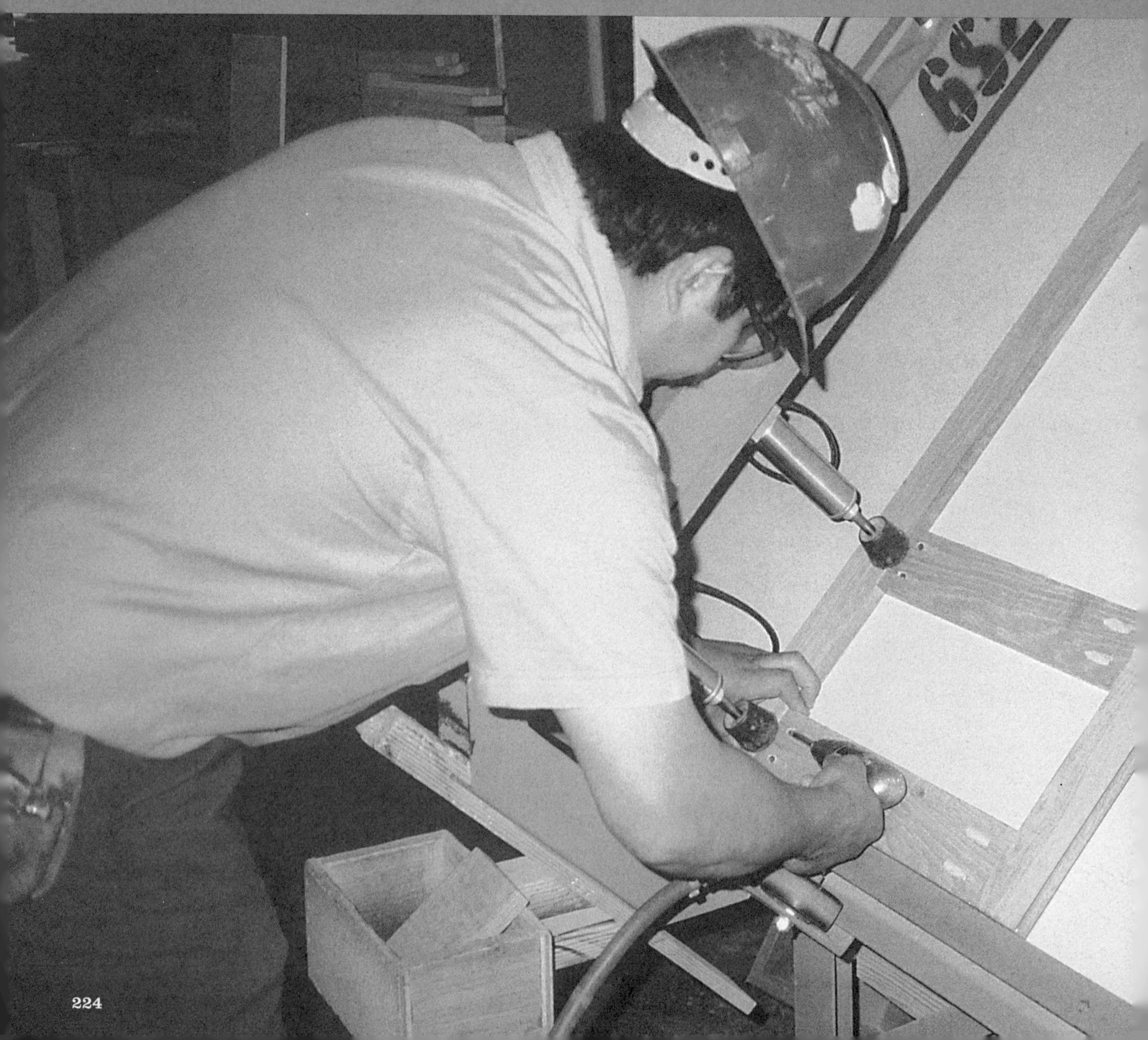

KEY OBJECTIVES:

1	*Explain the need for a markup policy with budgeted sales.*
2	*Use incremental CVP analysis to determine special sales prices.*
3	*Determine whether an intermediate product should be sold or processed further.*
4	*Calculate the relevant cashflows from transferring intermediate products.*
5	*Compute the relevant cashflows for a make-or-buy decision.*

Slowly the grandchildren were forgetting the heated arguments during the last meeting. Things were just beginning to settle down. The "control freaks" [as Nancy thought of them] had been creating new variances daily. Strewn all over the conference table, variance reports captured and consumed their interest. Sales and production mix variances, industry volume and market share variances, competition sales prices, and who knows what other variances, each had a separate report. Nancy knew a library was being created when carpenters began building a bookshelf for all the management accounting texts and trade magazines neatly stacked in the corners of the boardroom. Finally, when they tried to create variances for donut variety and quality, Nancy had to interject.

"Enough is enough! You're becoming more obsessed with measuring and not enough with doing! Sure, the variances have uncovered things we didn't plan on, but what problems have they identified? Variances should indicate opportunities for improvement. They should signal where we need to make some new decisions. Variance analysis involves more than comparing planned to actual resource usage. Of course, we should be concerned with efficiency [productivity], which is what cost variances measure. But shouldn't we also devise reliable methods for short-run change management?

"We must consider how effectively we work. Efficiency, or productivity, deals with how well we do something. By 'well,' I mean the amount of output obtained for the inputs used. Effectiveness, on the other hand, concerns getting the job done right. As you learned Friday night, I'm a very efficient dart player. It doesn't take me five minutes to get ready to throw the first dart. I don't make long elaborate arm gestures, or dance around the tables when I hit the bull's-eye. My dart throwing also is very reliable. I usually cluster the darts quite closely. I'm not very effective, though, as I rarely hit the dart board!"

"Nancy has a point!" As the undercurrent of chuckling continued, its focus changed from Nancy's poor dartsmanship to Julie's poor attempt at a pun. "Maybe we don't need detailed variances for boardroom control. For management by exception, we want only enough information to determine any new actions [decisions] now needed. We should use these 'dollar-and-cents' measures to prioritize our problems. Attack the biggest variances first. Suggest short-run changes or corrections."

"What do you mean by 'short-run' decisions? How do they differ from long-run decisions? Why is it important to recognize a difference between them?"

JULIE

"Well, think about our mission statement and strategic plan. These are long-run decisions developing objectives and goals, strategies to accomplish them, and ways to measure our success. Once we develop our annual plan, and as we manage day-to-day activities, we make short-run decisions keeping us 'on track' or exploiting new opportunities. To achieve or improve on the annual plan, new short-run unplanned actions may be needed. Thus, the time frame differentiates short- and long-run decisions. Because we develop a profit plan annually, as do most firms, short-run decisions affecting plan achievement usually span less than a year. Long-range decisions affect a year or more."

BOB

"The second difference between short- and long-run decisions involves the types of constraints we face. In the short run, we're constrained by the annual plan and resource availability. My job is to get the most from our current resources. Long-run decisions, on the other hand, usually relate to capacity issues, like expanding production or developing new products. Financing 'capital budgeting' decisions, like plant expansion, is part of our annual strategic plan, and we have a line item for it in our cash budget. The most important strategic constraint is financing these decisions. Once we've decided on the amount of resources to make available, short-run operating decisions are constrained by that resource capacity."

Short-term decisions usually are influenced by existing physical resource *constraints. Long-range strategic decisions usually are influenced by existing* financial *constraints.*

JULIE

"From an accounting perspective, here's why it is important to distinguish between short- and long-run decisions. Because the constraints are different, the types of analysis and relevant accounting information change as we move from long-run strategic to short-run operational decision making. *In this meeting, we'll consider management accounting information for unplanned short-run operating decisions.* We'll discuss capital budgeting decisions in a later meeting [Chapter 14]."

BILL

"O.K. Looking at our variance report from last week's meeting, the biggest problems are in sales. I'm trying to create some short-run fixes. One idea is to go back to the Canadian government and see if they need any more prefabricated stations for the Royal Canadian Mounted Police."

SID

"Oh yeah. I remember the 'mountie huts' as we called them." This brought about general laughter from those who were around when the Boss first introduced the idea. "It was a deal the Boss made on his last fishing trip for Northern Pike at Great Slave Lake in the Canadian Northwest Territories. They only wanted 20 [huts, not fish], and we could build them during our slow season when lots of surplus capacity existed. The Boss was confident about our ability to build them better and cheaper than the competition. However, Bill's predecessor, the marketing vice president who was fired shortly afterward, rejected the opportunity based on her profit projection [see Exhibit 7-1]."

Which Products Should We Be Selling?

JACKIE

"I worked with the marketing vice president on that bid. We used our cost accounting system's numbers, based on absorption costing primarily designed for external financial reporting. The predetermined overhead rates [PORs] were a little different from this year's. For variable overhead, the POR was $3.00 per direct labor hour. For fixed overhead, it was $5.00/DLhr. After allocating the $2,000 design costs over the 20 huts, estimated manufacturing costs averaged $12,100 per hut."

NANCY

"Where did the percentages come from for marketing costs, administrative costs, and profit?"

Bid Sheet for Mountie Huts

Costs:						Per job	Per hut
Direct design and architectural (not included in budgeted overhead)	$25	per hour x	80	hours =		$2,000	$100
Direct materials							8,400
Direct labor	$10	per hour x	200	hours =			2,000
Variable overhead	$3	per hour x	200	hours =			600
Fixed overhead	$5	per hour x	200	hours =			1,000
Total manufacturing costs							$12,100
Allocated marketing costs	10%	of manufacturing costs =					1,210
Allocated administrative costs	28%	of manufacturing costs =					3,388
Total costs							**$16,698**
Profit	20%	of total costs =					3,340
Projected bid price per mountie hut							$20,038
Actual bid price per mountie hut							$20,000

Exhibit 7-1

Budgeted sales and markups to hit our target profit

KEY OBJECTIVE 1

Explain the need for a markup policy with budgeted sales.

"The numbers came from the financial accounting income statement. Let's take a look at our current proforma to see how those percentages are calculated [the left side of Exhibit 3-4]. Annual marketing expenses are $345,000 [$280,000 sales commissions + $65,000 advertising]. Dividing this into the $3,655,000 total manufacturing costs yields a 9.439% marketing-to-manufacturing cost ratio. I rounded it to 10%. Similarly, the $1 million of administrative costs is 27.35978% of manufacturing costs. I rounded this to 28%. Finally, the $1 million profit divided by $5 million in total costs is 20%. These ratios are the same as those used in the mountie hut analysis.

"Let me interpret these numbers for you. On average for all products we plan to make and sell, marketing costs equal 10% of manufacturing costs. Administrative costs average 28% of manufacturing costs. So, whenever we prepare a bid for a job, we first estimate the manufacturing costs. Then, we mark up manufacturing costs 10% for marketing expenses, and add another 28% for the job's fair share of the administrative costs. Last, we mark up the job's estimated total cost another 20% for the average profit we want. Does this make sense?"

"I think so. *Here's the logic of markups.* The sum of the sales prices from all products [revenues] must be high enough to cover all costs and return a desired profit. So, determining the sales price involves three steps. First, we develop a reasonable estimate of the job's manufacturing cost. We next add an allocation for the job's 'fair share' of other costs [marketing and administrative expenses]. Finally, we add an average profit amount we want from each job."

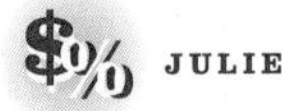

"O.K. You're logic is correct. However, there is a more important issue: *when should we use a markup policy in pricing our products?* A **markup** is the amount added to cost for setting a sales price. Marking up cost to arrive at a sales price is called a **cost-plus pricing strategy**."

A **cost-plus pricing strategy** *begins with a product's or service's cost and then adds an amount to cost (a* **markup***) in determining its sales price. Markups include any costs not part of the base cost, and a normal profit.*

Cost-plus pricing strategies. *"The first problem is defining the product's or service's 'cost.'* Usually, manufacturing firms start with production cost [i.e., standard absorptive manufacturing cost] and add a markup to it. The markup must be sufficient to return a fair share for the other costs and for profit. Merchandisers, following the same strategy, often base their markups on the merchandise's purchase cost. Service providers usually begin with an estimate of materials [if any] and labor costs, and then mark up that cost in setting a price.

"A related second problem involves understanding what the markup must include. In each of these three situations, the base 'cost' to be marked up did not include all the costs of the firm. In other words, markups usually include some costs as well as some profit. The manufacturer's markup must include all expenses [nonmanufacturing costs] and a desired profit. The merchandiser's markup includes all of the company's remaining costs plus an adequate profit amount. The service provider's markup, if based on direct labor, includes all the other costs in addition to the profit it wants.

"So, 'cost' can be measured in many different ways. Each time cost is defined differently, the markup changes. Here's an example of how this can cause problems. Profit sharing on international telephone calls has been a serious concern for the Federal Communications Commission. International rates are shared with foreign telephone companies, who measure their costs much differently than American companies. Foreign accounting techniques, such as increasing costs for inflation, have resulted in about 75% of every international revenue dollar going to foreign companies.

"How does this work? Assume, for example, American and foreign telephone companies agree to a 100% markup on cost in determining their rates, and these rates are used to allocate [divide up or share] the international telephone revenues. Because foreign companies report a higher cost, their markups and rates are higher than U.S. firms. Thus, they get a greater share of the international phone revenues.

"The mountie hut bid used three markups. Two were based on manufacturing cost [the 10% markup for marketing expenses, and the 28% markup for administrative expenses] and one was based on total cost [the 20% markup for profit]. The bid could have used only one markup, though. A 65.6% markup on manufacturing cost results in the same sales price [from Exhibit 7-1: $12,100 × 165.6% = $20,038]. Using just one markup based on manufacturing cost means the markup must include all nonmanufacturing costs plus profit. In the mountie hut bid, separate markups were used to better convey what each included."

BILL

"Often, a markup policy is considered to be a long-run strategic decision because the markup is determined from our annual proforma income statement, and it applies to all homes sold throughout the year. The pharmaceutical industry, though, considers cost-plus pricing as a multiyear strategic decision. As new drugs are developed and patented, a firm is protected from competition during the patent's life. So, over the new drug's life, its sales price must recover research and development costs, the production and operating costs incurred each year, and return a sufficient profit. Consider how important this is when it may cost $300 million in research and development to develop a single drug, only 1 in 1,000 projects lead to a breakthrough treatment, and only 30% of marketed drugs recover their investments!"

JULIE

"So, the third problem in using a cost-plus pricing strategy is determining which products it should be used with. In pricing normal products, that is, sales comprising the planned revenues in our proforma income statement, a standard cost-plus strategy

should be used. Regardless of the base cost used [e.g., manufacturing cost, purchase cost, direct labor cost], the markup must cover the remaining costs and provide a normal profit.

"Here's another way to think about it. Each product's sales price must generate a CMU [contribution margin per unit]. But, how much? Enough so the sum of the CMUs [i.e., the total contribution margin from all products sold] pay the total fixed costs, with enough left over to achieve our profit goal. But, this is true only for the products included in our original $6 million sales budget."

"Does this mean cost-plus pricing strategies should be used only with mass-produced products? It seems jobs like the mountie huts are special circumstances. Do special jobs not included in our proforma sales projection incur the normal marketing and administrative costs? Should these costs be allocated to special jobs using our normal markups [the 10% and 28% markups used in Exhibit 7-1]?"

"Cost-plus pricing strategies apply equally to mass production [process systems] and job shops [specialty products]. In job shops, though, the bidding and markup procedures may be more complicated, due to each job's uniqueness. FMI Forms, for example, uses multiple PORs for its different printing machines when bidding jobs. Atlantic Dry Dock has a sophisticated cost variance system to provide information for its bids on ship repairs and conversions [large variances are frequent in this business]. Because these jobs are part of their annual budgeted sales, each job's sales price must be high enough to cover a fair share of all costs and the desired profit.

"Cost-plus pricing also is needed in the governmental sector. Subcontractors have detailed rules for allocating indirect costs and profits to government work. The U.S. government has developed Federal Acquisitions Regulations and Cost Accounting Standards Board pronouncements specifying how to classify and allocate overhead and operating expenses to government contracts. Once this 'full, absorptive cost' is determined, government subcontractors are allowed a normal markup for their profit.

"So, when do we use a pricing strategy that includes indirect cost allocations and normal profit recovery? We use normal markups on all products included in our annual sales forecast. It does not make any difference whether the products are mass produced, custom jobs, government work, or services."

"The Boss never intended the mountie huts to be part of normal sales, though! It was a special job to avoid laying off workers by using surplus capacity, and to generate some extra profit. *The marketing VP, however, followed a very strict policy of using the normal markup with all products* [standard homes, custom homes, and special order jobs]. Thus, the huts had to provide enough revenues to cover a fair share of indirect costs [overhead, marketing, and administrative costs] and part of the planned profit. Saying this a different way, the mountie huts had to provide a normal CMU.

"Why was the job rejected? To provide a normal CMU, the huts had to be priced at $20,000. The mounties already had another bid for $16,000 per hut. The marketing vice president decided not to pursue the order because we wouldn't make a normal profit by matching the competitor's bid, and we'd report a loss at any price below $16,698!" [This is the total average cost per hut in Exhibit 7-1.]

"Are you suggesting in some situations, like the mountie huts, it may not be appropriate to use absorption costing and normal markups?"

Market-based pricing strategies. *"In two situations we may not be able to obtain a normal markup.* First, when the market, and not our cost, determines sales prices. And second, with special orders not originally included in our annual budget, such as the mountie hut job.

"When competition is keen, normal markups may not be possible. Consider the Orlando hotel market. While normal occupancy rates are under 80%, Harris Rosen's properties [about 6% of the 85,000-plus hotel rooms] average over 95%. Rosen attributes much of his $100 million net worth to pricing strategies. He discounts normal room rates daily to achieve a goal of 100% occupancy. Normal industry practice shuns this, preferring empty rooms in order to maintain normal markups.

"Abandoning normal markup policies also is commonplace in the airline industry. In the computer chip industry, Intel often cuts prices in response to growing competition. Rupert Murdoch's newspaper price war in Great Britain is another example. By cutting the *Times* price to 35¢, he forced similar price cuts by the *Daily Telegraph* and the *Independent*." Tommy chuckled to himself as he remembered how the price war led to millions of dollars of losses by each newspaper.

"Cost-plus pricing has been the backbone of regulated industry price-setting. However, as industries become deregulated, market factors drive lower prices. Southwest Airlines in the United States and EuroBelgian Airways in Europe have become quite profitable using no-frills, low pricing strategies to gain market share from more established airlines. Now, many competitors match Southwest's advertised 'special' rates.

"Even when competition is not intense, a normal markup policy may not be desirable. For example, when entering a new market, normal markups may be abandoned to gain initial market share. Penetration, or predatory, pricing strategies using very low initial prices can keep out future competition. Texas Instruments did this to combat future competition in the handheld calculator market back in the 1970s. A major reason Japanese firms gained control of the FAX machine market was pricing 40% below U.S. manufacturers. Hewlett-Packard used the same strategy with computer printers to combat the Japanese. DuPont's initial below-normal markup pricing for nylon led to its use in automobile tires [a new market]."

Special sales and price-setting

NANCY

"O.K. I understand when market forces may cause us to abandon a cost-plus pricing strategy on normal business. But the mountie huts job was not part of the annual sales forecast. It was a special order. Why did the Boss think we could get that order given our strict adherence to a normal markup policy for all business?"

JULIE

"He did not think a normal markup policy should be used with special orders. Our regular pricing policy is based on full absorptive cost plus a normal profit. *With special sales not envisioned in the annual profit plan,* we can use a different pricing strategy called **incremental pricing**. With incremental pricing, *we consider only those costs unique to the special order. The logic is simple: any sales price greater than the order's incremental costs will yield extra profit.* So, in pricing special jobs not considered as part of our normal business, we need to identify the order's relevant costs."

An **incremental pricing policy** *determines the minimum, or break-even, price just covering the product's or service's incremental cost.*

"What do you mean by 'relevant costs'?"

NANCY

JULIE

Identifying relevant cashflows. "Every decision affects the future. No decision can change the past, however. Nothing we can do will change what has already happened. The past cannot be altered. Let me illustrate. Doris just gave me the receipt for our donuts. She spent $20. [We like our donuts!] Some are going to be left over. She can't undo the purchase and get her money back. But she can sell the extra donuts. This is a future action. Having four extra donuts, should she price them at $5 each, in order to recover the $20 cost? Of course not! No one will pay $5 for an old donut. If so, send them in. First, I'll fire them. Then, I'll make them our customers!

"The office staff may pay 50¢ for a donut. What happens if she sells the four donuts for 50¢ each?"

 NANCY

"That's easy! Doris will collect $2 and the donuts will have a net cost of $18."

JULIE

"But, is the $18 relevant to her decision? She already spent the $20. It's gone. This is called a **sunk cost** because the money has been spent. Doris has two alternatives: don't sell the four donuts, or sell the four donuts. Will she incur any new costs in selling them? No. Nor will she incur any new cost in not selling them. This decision has no relevant costs. How about revenues? If she does not sell the donuts, no new revenues will result. That's simple. If she sells them for 50¢ each, Doris will have $2 in new revenues. *What will be different in the future if the donuts are sold?* Doris will be $2 richer. The $2 future cashflow is the only relevant cashflow for this decision! The $20 already spent is irrelevant. Doris must choose between having $2 or not having $2.

A **sunk cost** *has already been incurred. The money has been spent. It's irrelevant to any decision we are now considering.*

"Here's a more realistic situation. We have a house left over from an old product line, and Bill hasn't been able to find a normal customer for it. It cost $25,000 when originally built last year. If we spend $10,000 for some alterations, we can sell it to a contractor for $12,000 or to a distributor for $15,000. What should we do?

"The distributor sale creates $5,000 in incremental cashflows: $15,000 less the $10,000 in alteration costs. Selling to the contractor generates incremental cashflows of $2,000. We spend $10,000 in the future and collect $12,000 in the future. So, we'll be $3,000 richer if we sell to the distributor. In deciding between alternatives, *we can calculate the incremental cashflows for each alternative and then compare them for our decision.* As a profit maximizer, the alternative generating the most future cash is the one I'll choose!

"As an accountant, I like seeing an analysis showing all of the incremental costs and revenues because I know all of the relevant items have been considered. But, we have a simpler approach. Didn't you just compare the two sales prices? That's the most efficient analysis. You simply looked at the one difference between the two alternative incremental cashflows, which is the sales prices. Notice the $10,000 to be spent fixing up the house is irrelevant to the decision of who to sell the house to. Granted, it is an incremental cashflow. But, it's the same for each alternative. Thus, it cannot affect the *difference* between the alternatives. A decision is a choice between two or more alternatives. Not all future cashflows are relevant for the decision! **Relevant cashflows** for making a decision [i.e., choosing between alternatives] must occur in the future and be different between the alternatives. Why? We only have the resources to do one or the other, but not both. Let's summarize these ideas using the old home sale [see Exhibit 7-2].

In making a decision (choosing between alternatives), only the relevant cashflows should be considered. **Relevant cashflows** *are the differences between the incremental cashflows of each alternative.*

"Using net income to choose between the two alternatives, we will reject both as any sales price less than $35,000 yields a loss [$25,000 original cost + $10,000 fixing up costs]. Rejecting either one is a bad decision, though. The problem from basing the decision on net income is it includes irrelevant costs, which can confuse the issue. This should be a simple decision. Selling to the distributor increases cash

Incremental and Relevant Cashflows in Decision Making

Cashflows	Alternatives			Cashflow classifications		
	Contractor	Distributor	Difference	Incremental?	Relevant?	Why?
Sales price	$12,000	$15,000	$3,000	yes	yes	The sales prices occur in the future and are unique to the alternatives, thus they are incremental cashflows. Because they are different, the net change in revenue ($3,000) is relevant for the decision.
Fixing-up costs	$10,000	$10,000	$0	yes	no	Because this cost will happen in the future, it is an incremental cost for each alternative. It is not relevant in choosing between the alternatives, though, because it is not different (it's the same for both alternatives).
Original cost	$25,000	$25,000	$0	no	no	Sunk costs have already happened. Incremental cashflows are the future cashflows caused by selecting a specific alternative. Sunk costs cannot affect the difference between the alternatives' future cashflows.
Net income (sales price - fixing-up costs - original cost)	($23,000)	($20,000)	$3,000	no	no	Net income should not influence the decision because it includes a sunk cost and a future, incremental cost which is not different for the two alternatives. The $3,000 difference is relevant, but it is the differential cashflow from the sales price difference. Focus on the relevant item: the sales price difference.

Exhibit 7-2

$5,000. Selling to the contractor increases cash $2,000. These are the incremental cashflows of each alternative. We're $3,000 richer selling to the distributor. The net cashflow between the alternatives is the only relevant number!

"This also is true with Doris's donuts. Selling the leftover donuts for 50¢ each results in an $18 net cost. But, by not selling them, Doris gives up an extra $2 in real cash. *In special short-run sales decisions, consider only the incremental cashflows in computing a minimally acceptable price. To maximize our profit when choosing between alternatives, base the decision on the difference in incremental cashflows [i.e., the relevant, net cashflows].*"

KEY OBJECTIVE 2

Use incremental CVP analysis to determine special sales prices.

Using surplus capacity. "Now, let's use cost-volume-profit analysis [CVP] to identify the relevant cashflows for the mountie hut job, and price it using an incremental pricing strategy. First, which numbers are relevant? It depends on the alternatives we're considering. Here, our two alternatives are take the mountie hut job or don't take it. The second alternative [reject the order] maintains the status quo, in other words, Alternative 2 is, 'Don't do anything different.' Alternative 2 does not change our cashflows. The difference between Alternatives 1 and 2, then, is the job's incremental cashflows. Thus, all of the mountie huts incremental cashflows are relevant to this decision. Here's my analysis [see Exhibit 7-3].

Incremental Cashflow Analysis for Mountie Huts

			Relevant cashflows	
Costs:			Fixed costs for job	Variable costs per hut
Design and architectural	$25 per hour x	80 hours =	$2,000	
Direct materials				$8,400
Direct labor	$10 per hour x	200 hours =		2,000
Variable overhead	$3 per hour x	200 hours =		600
Fixed overhead	$5 per hour x	200 hours =	n/a	
Total manufacturing costs			$2,000	$11,000
Shipping & setup costs			18,000	
Allocated marketing costs	10% of manufacturing costs =		n/a	n/a
Allocated administrative costs	28% of manufacturing costs =		n/a	n/a
Total costs			**$20,000**	**$11,000**
Allocate fixed costs to each hut			÷ 20 huts	
Average fixed cost per hut			$1,000	1,000
Average total cost per hut				**$12,000**

Exhibit 7-3

"Let's start with the manufacturing costs. Design and architectural costs are unique, direct fixed costs of this job. Materials, labor, and variable overhead are variable costs. *Variable costs usually are incremental costs relevant to a future cashflow analysis.*

"The fixed manufacturing overhead, though, has an 'n/a' [not applicable, or not relevant] in the fixed costs column. *Usually, allocated fixed costs are not relevant for two reasons.* Much of the fixed overhead represents sunk costs. For example, factory depreciation included in fixed overhead is the accounting write-off of a cost actually paid in the past [i.e., expensing part of the original asset cost when purchased]. So, depreciation is not a future cash cost. [It was not included in the cash budget, either.] Second, ask if the total fixed overhead will change by accepting this order. We had surplus capacity available for building the mountie huts. Surplus capacity situations usually mean we are still within our relevant range. If so, total fixed costs will not change by accepting a special order. Mountie huts create no new fixed overhead cost, so it is not relevant.

"The marketing and administrative costs also are allocated. These are mixed costs [part variable and part fixed], so we should specifically identify if any of these costs are needed on this job. No new variable costs are necessary. As with fixed overhead, the fixed marketing and administrative costs will not change in the future, as long as we are still within the relevant range. Thus, they are not relevant.

"However, we should always ask if any new unique fixed costs will occur because of the order. This job requires $18,000 in shipping and setup costs. Because it is a future cashflow unique to this order, it is relevant. We actually have two relevant fixed costs: shipping and setup, and design and architectural. Because the order is for exactly 20 huts, and the customer wants a bid price per hut, the two relevant fixed costs are averaged [allocated] over the 20 huts, yielding a $12,000 average incremental cost per hut. The minimum sales price we could have accepted was $12,000. This is the mountie hut break-even sales price."

NANCY

"Wait a minute! We could have won the order. If we matched the competition's $16,000 price, we would have made an extra $4,000 cash per hut! That's more than the profit originally desired [$3,340 in Exhibit 7-1]. No wonder the last marketing vice president was fired! Now, how does CVP analysis help us price this special order?"

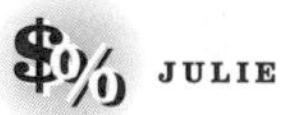
JULIE

"We have incremental variable costs and incremental fixed costs. Let's use CVP analysis to find the minimum sales price [the break-even sales price]. This [see Exhibit 7-4] will verify our previous calculations.

"CVP analysis involves five numbers: sales price, variable cost per unit, total fixed costs, volume, and profit. To break even, profit is zero. Since we know the incremental variable cost per hut, the incremental fixed cost, and volume, all we do is solve the profit equation for the break-even sales price. The minimum sales price must include $11,000 per hut for the incremental variable costs, plus $1,000 per hut for the fixed costs [$20,000 ÷ 20 huts].

"We also can see this graphically [see Exhibit 7-4]. At the break-even volume [20 huts], contribution margin equals fixed costs. If no products are made and sold, we have no revenues or variable costs, thus contribution margin is zero. We now have two points [X-Y coordinates] for drawing the contribution margin line [($0, 0 huts) and ($20,000, 20 huts)]. The slope of the contribution margin line is the contribution margin per hut [CMU]. CMU is $1,000. If variable costs are $11,000, break-even sales price must be $12,000 [sales price – variable cost = CMU]. Any sales price greater than $12,000 will produce an incremental cash profit.

"We also can use CVP analysis to solve for a special order volume. Suppose the Royal Canadian Mounted Police reject our bid and counter with an $11,500 sales price. Since this is below our break-even price, we probably should reject the order. However, we could make a counteroffer for more huts at $11,500 per hut. How

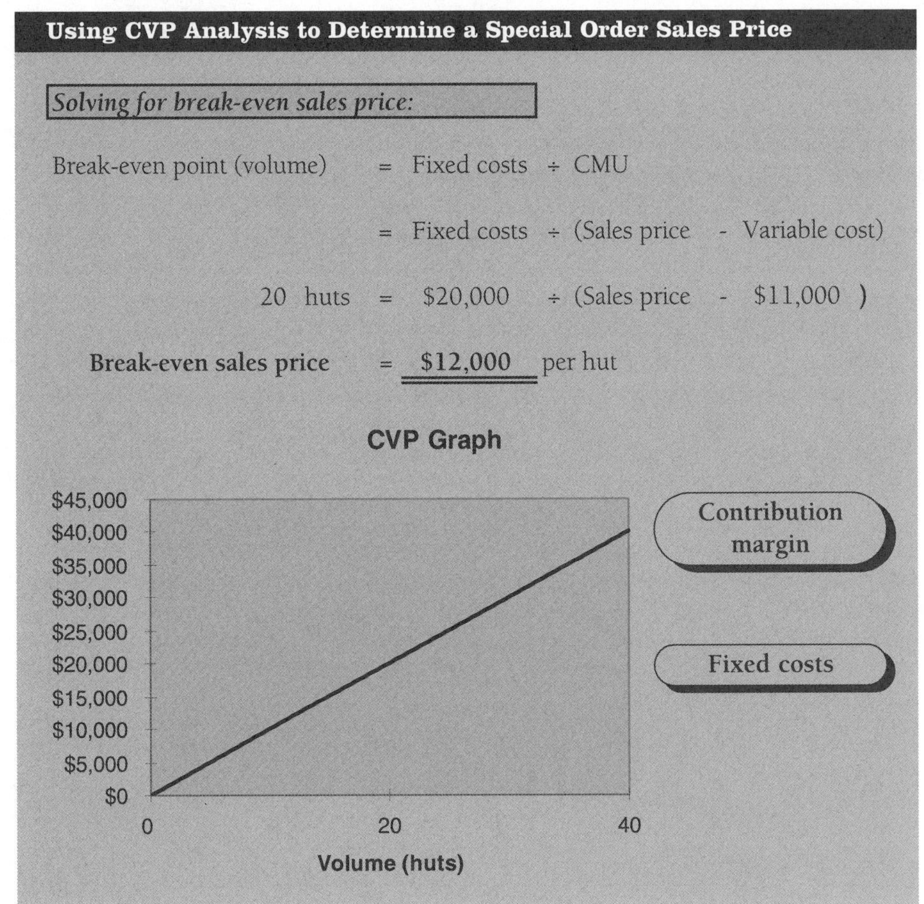

Exhibit 7-4

many huts must be ordered at $11,500 each so we can break even? [Exhibit 7-5 demonstrates this analysis.]

"Originally [Exhibit 7-4], the huts' minimum price was $12,000. With variable costs of $11,000 each, CMU was $1,000. Now [Exhibit 7-5], the huts' CMU is $500. Sales price decreases $500, so CMU decreases $500. How many $500 bills are needed to pay for the $20,000 in incremental fixed costs? To break even, 40 huts must be ordered if the sales price is $11,500 each [$20,000 fixed costs ÷ $500 CMU = 40 huts].

"Graphically, decreasing CMU by $500 reduces the slope of the contribution margin line, shifting it to the right [rotating clockwise from the origin]. The new line shows contribution margin is less than fixed costs for sales below 40 units; that is, we lose money. For sales above 40 huts, though, contribution margin exceeds fixed costs, resulting in a profit."

"Well, what if we want a $10,000 profit on a 40-hut order? Using incremental CVP analysis, an extra $10,000 profit ÷ 40 huts = an extra $250 CMU. Each hut has to generate another $250 in CMU. Now the bid price becomes $11,750. Right?" Nancy knew she could solve the profit equation again, but that's too much work: ($20,000 fixed cost + $10,000 profit) ÷ 40 huts = $750 CMU. Needing a $750 CMU with $11,000 variable costs, sales price has to be $11,750."

"Right! With special orders not affecting our normal business, incremental CVP analysis leads us to the profit-maximizing decision. It allows us to calculate the

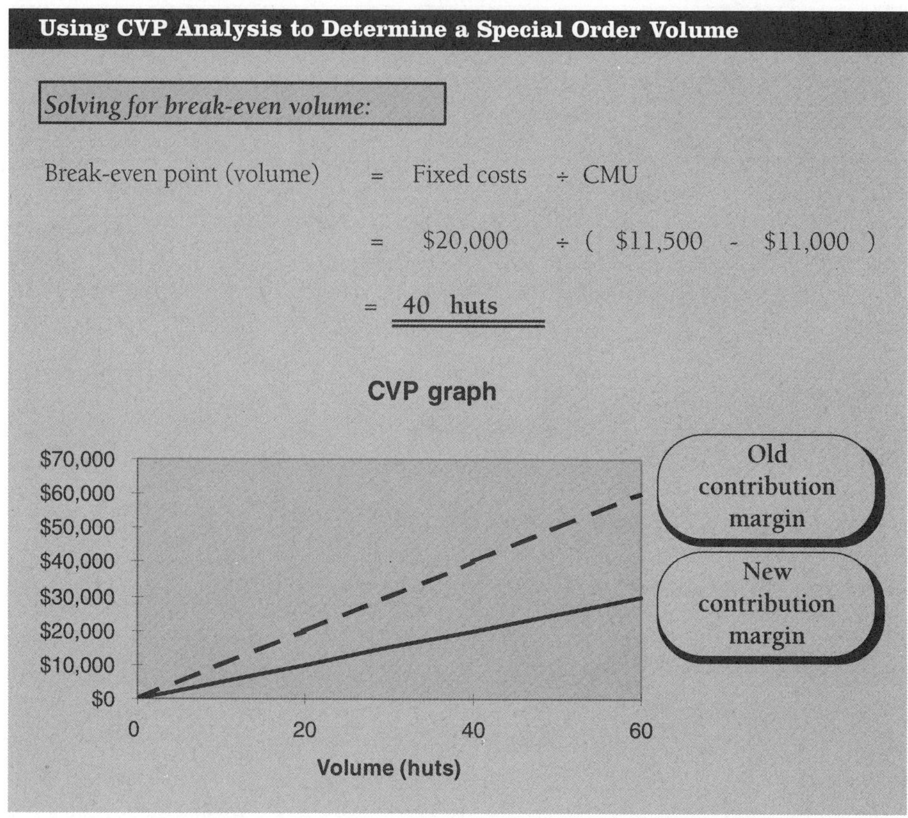

Exhibit 7-5

minimum [break-even] sales price for our incremental pricing policy. Any price above it yields extra cash profit. However, *we should use incremental pricing only with special orders not affecting normal budgeted sales*. Our regular products must be sufficiently marked up so their sales prices provide enough for the company's other costs and our planned profit."

Trading off normal sales for special orders

JULIE

"Now, consider one last pricing situation. What happens if we do not have the surplus capacity for a special order?"

Opportunity cost considerations. "In this situation, some normal sales must be given up if we want to accept the special order. Normal sales generate a planned CMU. For standard homes, our budgeted CMU is $20,000. What if we have to give up making and selling two standard homes so we can accept the mountie hut job? We have to give up two $20,000 CMUs. In other words, we give up the opportunity to have $40,000 from the two standard homes [used to cover fixed costs and create profit]. Because this is a unique future cashflow associated with the job, it's relevant to our decision. If we sell the mountie huts at a break-even price, and we have to give up $40,000 in normal profit to do this, we're $40,000 worse off. This is the **opportunity cost** of accepting that job. An opportunity cost is the net cashflow given up when choosing an alternative. Only less profitable [suboptimal] alternatives have an opportunity cost."

An **opportunity cost** *is the net cashflow given up by not choosing the most profitable alternative.*

"I want to make sure I understand this opportunity cost idea. Our two alternatives are (A) accept the job and give up selling two standard homes, and (R) reject the special order and sell the two homes. Here are some price-setting scenarios for (A):

1. Price the job to break even. A's incremental cashflows = $0. R's incremental cashflows = $40,000. Profit-maximizing decision: choose R. If we choose A, we give up the opportunity to have another $40,000. Thus, A has a $40,000 opportunity cost.

2. Price the job to provide a $10,000 cashflow [hut sales price = $12,500]. We still should choose R because it creates $30,000 more cash. This is the net cashflow between the two alternatives. If we choose A, we give up having another $30,000. The less profitable alternative, A, has a $30,000 opportunity cost.

3. Price the job to provide a $40,000 incremental cashflow. If the order is for 20 huts, the sales price = $14,000 [($20,000 incremental fixed costs + $40,000 profit) ÷ CMU = 20 huts. CMU = $3,000. Thus, sales price = $11,000 variable costs + $3,000 CMU = $14,000]. Now both alternatives provide the same incremental cashflow, and neither has an opportunity cost. So we are indifferent between the alternatives and our decision must be based on some other criterion than profit maximization. What other criteria are relevant? Can we talk about this next?"

"O.K. But, before we do, try this new scenario. We have three alternatives: A's incremental cashflow is $10, B's is $8, and C's is $3. Which alternative should we choose, and what are the opportunity costs of choosing the other two less profitable alternatives?"

"Obviously we should choose A because it provides $2 more than B and $7 more than C. B's opportunity cost is $2 [the net cashflow given up if B is chosen]. Here's my logic. I should choose A if I'm a profit maximizer. If I instead choose B, I've given up the opportunity to have another $2. B has a $2 opportunity cost. Similarly, C's opportunity cost is $7. I should choose A, but I instead choose C, giving up the opportunity to have another $7. How can I justify choosing a less profitable alternative, though? What reasons provide a greater marginal utility for me than the extra $7 I could have had?"

Considering externalities. "Consider Doris's donuts again. Being a profit maximizer, she should sell the 4 leftover donuts. She can get $2 for them. But is $2 worth her effort? Maybe not! She may very willingly give up the extra $2 in order to take home the leftovers and offer them to her husband if he will do the dishes! In other words, getting the dishes washed is worth more than $2 to Doris.

"Returning to the contractor-distributor decision [Exhibit 7-2], selling to the contractor has a $3,000 opportunity cost. However, we may choose this alternative because we believe it will lead to future sales at normal prices. Conversely, selling to the distributor may cause other distributors to ask for special prices. Thinking about the mountie hut job, we might accept a price below $12,000 if we believe this will lead to a new market and future profitable sales.

"All decisions probably have **externalities**. These are hard-to-quantify outcomes affecting our ability to maintain long-term value. Externalities may lead us to choose a lower-profit alternative. In other words, they may be more important than the opportunity cost of that alternative. Externalities may provide more long-run

In decision making, ***externalities*** *should be identified. These are hard-to-quantify effects from choosing an alternative.*

value than the current net cashflow given up. For example, Ben and Jerry's can make the same quality ice cream at a lower cost if it changes its commitment to the environment. But to them environmental concerns are more important than the extra profit. Mitsubishi discontinued sales to Circuit City, its biggest customer at the time, to focus on small retailers offering more personalized customer service."

BILL

"Oh, I can think of some externalities affecting pricing decisions. How about off-season versus peak-season hotel rates? Most of a hotel's costs are fixed. Variable costs, like room cleaning, are minimal. With low variable costs, prices can be significantly reduced during off-seasons and they will still have a healthy contribution margin!

"To encourage highly profitable sales, normal markups may be temporarily abandoned on complementary products. Loss leaders often encourage people to shop at a particular grocery store. Offering special package meal rates at fast-food restaurants increases total sales and contribution margin. Professional baseball teams offer discounted tickets to special groups, with the expectation of higher concession and souvenir sales. Once an alternative's externalities are identified, we should try to quantify their cashflow effects. In this way, externalities can be included in the incremental cashflow and CVP analyses.

"While many decisions may appear to be short-term, they may have strategic, long-run externalities. When Sears approached Whirlpool for special prices, it made sense to abandon the normal markup policy. Starting with special sales to Sears, Whirlpool has turned Sears into its major customer, selling 40% of its appliances as Kenmore products. Although Whirlpool has a high-quality reputation, Sears' quality reputation may be even stronger. As the public discovered Kenmore appliances were made by Whirlpool, Whirlpool's quality image also increased.

"Of course, General Motors had a different experience. Automobile manufacturers often make special fleet sales to car rental companies like Hertz, Avis, and Enterprise. GM finally reduced fleet sales 50% because reselling the rental cars hurt its long-run normal sales.

"San Diego County decided on a multiple markup strategy for trash dumping. The county built a $134 million recycling plant, but cities within the county are not required to dump there. Finding cheaper sites in other counties, the cities' response caused the county to develop a four-rate system: from a low of $58 per ton if the city signed a 20-year dumping contract, to $235 per ton with no long-term commitment.

"Another externality involves legal constraints. U.S. price discrimination laws prohibit charging different prices for the same product to competing customers in the same market, unless the price difference can be justified by unique manufacturing, selling, or distribution costs. Foreign countries also prohibit certain pricing strategies. To counteract foreign predatory pricing, antidumping laws force foreign suppliers to charge a fair price when in competition with domestic firms."

NANCY

"Let's see if I have the big picture. I've summarized the two pricing strategies [Exhibit 7-6]."

BILL

"While your summary highlights important differences, these pricing strategies really complement each other. Both cost and market considerations are relevant in many price-setting decisions. Traditionally, cost-plus pricing has been the initial analysis. Market, competitive, and legal externalities then are considered, which can lead to price adjustments. However, if product or service revenues cannot cover all costs and provide an acceptable profit in the long run, a firm should question what it considers to be its core competency in the industry-wide value chain. My point is cost must be a primary concern in all price-setting decisions. Thus, I

Pricing Strategies Comparison

Logic	When to use it	Accounting information needed	Some externalities to consider
Cost-plus pricing Marks up "cost" in setting a satisfactory price. The markup should provide a sales price and total revenues high enough to cover all costs and a normal profit.	1. On normal sales included in the annual budget. 2. When required by the customer (e.g., government work).	1. The cost base (e.g., standard absorptive manufacturing cost, purchase cost, incremental direct cost). 2. Other costs which must be included in the markup. 3. Profit which must be covered by the markup.	1. Short-run market and competitive pressures. 2. Need to maintain price stability during short-run market fluctuations (e.g., seasons). 3. Layoff costs, rehiring and training costs, employee morale from rejecting new business. 4. Long-run need to recover all costs and generate a satisfactory profit. 5. Long-run effects on market share. 6. Government regulations guide how the cost base is measured, how costs are allocated, and how markups are computed.
Incremental pricing Determines the minimum (break-even) price. Any price above this creates a positive cashflow.	1. On special orders that do not affect normal, budgeted sales. 2. When short-run market and competitive externalities do not allow a normal markup. 3. Penetration pricing strategy for new market development.	1. Incremental variable and fixed costs for each alternative (e.g., special order). 2. Incremental CVP analysis.	1. Effect on short-run normal sales which should cover all budgeted costs and the planned profit. 2. Product quality from maintaining a stable, experienced work force (vs. hiring and laying off in #3 above). 3. Impact on competitors from taking away some of their business. 4. Antidiscrimination pricing laws. 5. Effect on long-run sales (e.g., normal customers discover special deals, and also want lower prices). 6. Need to develop new markets.

Exhibit 7-6

wasn't surprised when a manufacturing survey reported about 70% of firms used full cost with markup [cost-plus] pricing, 18% used market pricing, and 12% used incremental pricing. And about half of the firms using cost-based pricing used markups based on manufacturing costs."

Selling Intermediate Products

"Looking over my notes on the mountie hut job, one of the reasons they were interested in us was our high-quality windows. As you know, we make our own windows. I've always thought this is one of our core competencies."

"Windows are one of the special features our marketing people emphasize to prospective customers. If we're so good at it, maybe we should consider selling windows!"

KEY OBJECTIVE 3

Determine whether an intermediate product should be sold or processed further.

Sell now or process further

"You're talking about a 'sell-or-process-further' decision. This is a decision about what to do with **intermediate products**. These are products which can be sold as is, or processed further into another product. For example, windows are an intermediate product if we can sell them now or use them to build houses. If we make a strategic decision not to sell windows, they are just components of our final product [a house], and are part of work in process [WIP]."

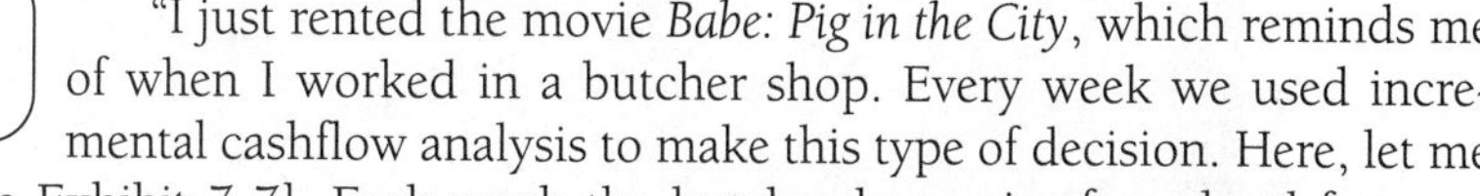

Intermediate products *can be sold as is, or processed further into a final product.*

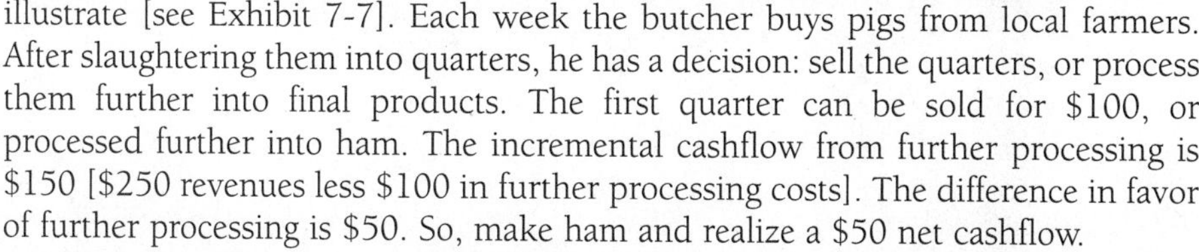

"I just rented the movie *Babe: Pig in the City*, which reminds me of when I worked in a butcher shop. Every week we used incremental cashflow analysis to make this type of decision. Here, let me illustrate [see Exhibit 7-7]. Each week the butcher buys pigs from local farmers. After slaughtering them into quarters, he has a decision: sell the quarters, or process them further into final products. The first quarter can be sold for $100, or processed further into ham. The incremental cashflow from further processing is $150 [$250 revenues less $100 in further processing costs]. The difference in favor of further processing is $50. So, make ham and realize a $50 net cashflow.

"The second quarter can be sold for $75 or processed into pork chops, which yields the same incremental cashflow. So, the butcher is indifferent between selling the quarter or making pork chops. Here's where an externality is important. I'd let the workers decide. Around Christmas, they may want to work more, so make pork chops. In the summer, they may want to play softball [work less], so sell the quarter.

"The third quarter can be sold for $50, or processed into sausage yielding a $40 incremental cashflow. Processing further has an opportunity cost of $10. With the fourth quarter, the butcher loses money making pickled pigs feet [the incremental cashflow is a negative $10]. Even if the fourth quarter cannot be sold, pickled pigs feet should not be made. Besides, I hated dusting the jars each Monday morning."

"Your analysis seems incomplete to me. Shouldn't you include the cost of buying and slaughtering the pig? Don't these costs have to be included for a true measure of profit?"

JULIE

"If we want to know the net income from a pig, you are correct. But all the costs incurred in obtaining the four quarters are irrelevant to the decision about what to do with the already existing quarters, which is selling the quarters or processing any of them further. The butcher already has the four quarters. They could have been given to him free, or he could have paid $1 million for them. So what? The

Sell-or-Process-Further Decision

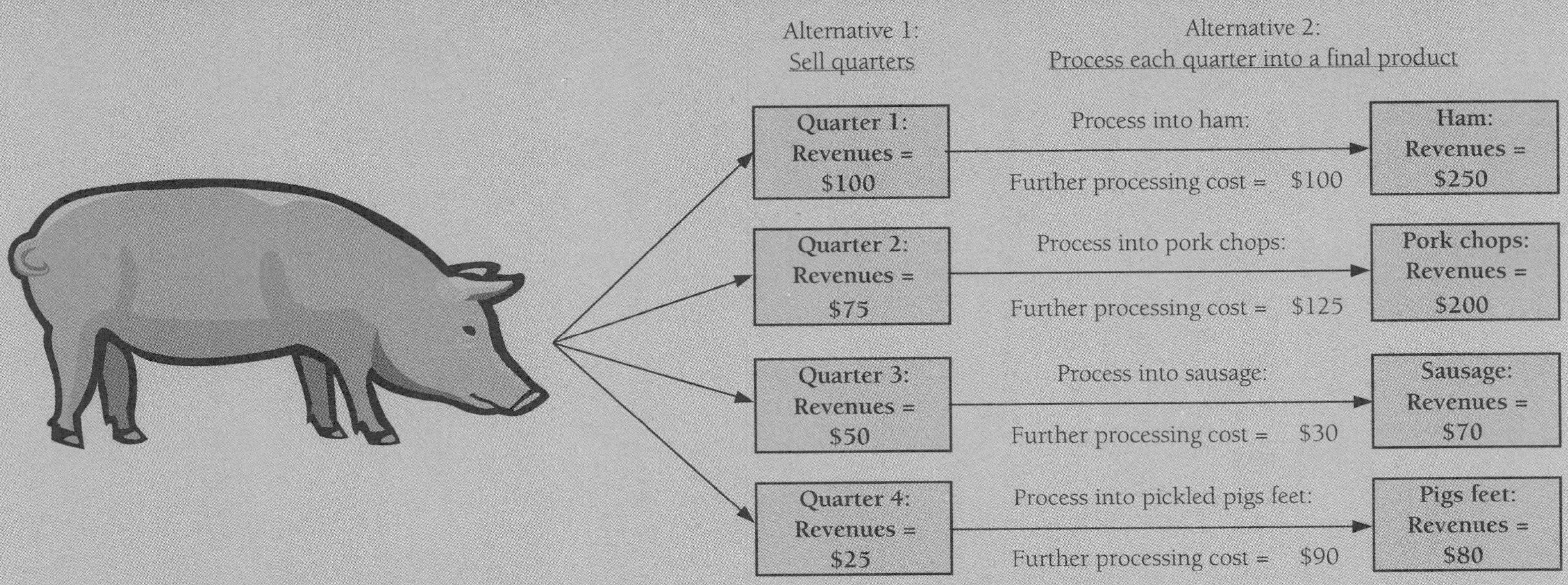

Alternative 1: Sell quarters	Alternative 2: Process each quarter into a final product		
Quarter 1: Revenues = $100	Process into ham:	Further processing cost = $100	**Ham: Revenues = $250**
Quarter 2: Revenues = $75	Process into pork chops:	Further processing cost = $125	**Pork chops: Revenues = $200**
Quarter 3: Revenues = $50	Process into sausage:	Further processing cost = $30	**Sausage: Revenues = $70**
Quarter 4: Revenues = $25	Process into pickled pigs feet:	Further processing cost = $90	**Pigs feet: Revenues = $80**

Incremental cashflows:	Alternative 1	Alternative 2: Process further						
Intermediate products	**Sell now**	**Final product revenues**	-	**Further processing costs**	=	**Further processing net cashflow**	**Difference between 1 and 2 (net cashflow if processed further)**	**Decision**
Quarter 1:	$100	$250	-	$100	=	$150	**$50**	Process further
Quarter 2:	75	200	-	125	=	75	**0**	?
Quarter 3:	50	70	-	30	=	40	**(10)**	Sell
Quarter 4:	25	80	-	90	=	(10)	**(35)**	Sell

Exhibit 7-7

costs of creating four quarters are sunk. That cash is gone. Remember, decisions are forward looking. Given that the butcher already has four pig quarters, what should he do with them now? To identify the relevant cashflows, we first must identify the alternatives *currently being considered.*"

KEY OBJECTIVE 4

Calculate the relevant cashflows from transferring intermediate products.

Transfer pricing

NANCY

"Now, getting back to the windows, I think we should sell them. Clearly, this is a high-quality product we can differentiate from our competition. But who should make the decision to sell windows or send them to Assembly for our houses [i.e., process further]? How will we know which decision is best?"

TOMMY

"I think the window-making department should make the decision. They are the most knowledgeable people about window production and market conditions."

SID

"Well, you're suggesting we let them run the window-making department just like it was a separate company. This means we are changing their responsibilities. Right now, as a manufacturing department, their responsibilities are to make high-quality windows, within budget, and on time for Assembly. Their new responsibilities will be to make as much money as possible. Of course if we do this, Assembly must be able to buy windows from whomever offers the best price [assuming equal quality and on-time delivery]."

JULIE

"If we give the window department the decision-making power to determine who to sell to, we have just made it a real **profit center**. The decision to sell to an external customer [real customers not related to the company] or an internal customer [another department, division, or company within the same overall firm] is called a **transfer** decision. The price charged by our new window company to Assembly is called a **transfer price**. *The transfer [internal sale] decision has two parts:*

> *If part of a firm is given the power to determine who to sell its products (or services) to, it is a* **profit center**. *When a profit center sells to another part of the company, the sale is called a* **transfer**, *and the internal sale price is a* **transfer price**.

- Should they transfer instead of buying from and selling to other companies?
- If they decide to transfer, what amount should be used as the transfer price?

To answer these questions:

- *They should transfer whenever it creates a positive net cashflow for the overall firm.*
- *The correct transfer price depends on how we evaluate and reward the managers.*"

TOMMY

"Oh, I've got something to say about how our people should be evaluated and rewarded, and how this affects their motivation to maximize our profit!"

SID

"I'm sure you do! But I don't want to consider how to motivate our people to make the right decisions. Today's meeting is about identifying the relevant information they need. Let's save your ideas for our next meeting, and focus on determining when transfers should happen."

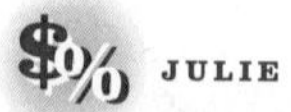
JULIE

Calculating the transfer's relevant cashflow. "We know they should transfer whenever it increases overall Multree profit. First, let's identify the alternatives and the relevant data [Exhibit 7-8]. Then [in Exhibit 7-9], I'll create a worksheet for presenting the information and calculating the transfer's relevant cashflows.

"In situation 1 [Exhibit 7-8], our new window company has sufficient surplus capacity to supply Assembly while maintaining its current normal sales to regular customers. Remember, it's now a profit center. So, Assembly is just like any other

Relevant Information for the Transfer Decision

	Situation 1		Situation 2
Situation 1:	Window company has sufficient surplus capacity to make the windows desired by Assembly, while continuing to sell to all outside customers.	*Situation 2:*	Window company is selling all of the windows it can make to outside customers at its normal sales price.
Alternatives:	1. Transfer windows to Assembly, or 2. Do not make any more windows.	*Alternatives:*	1. Transfer windows to Assembly, or 2. Sell windows to outside customers.
Relevant cashflows:		***Relevant cashflows:***	
For buyer: (Assembly)	Purchase cost from outside supplier = $85.	For buyer: (Assembly)	Purchase cost from outside supplier = $85.
For seller: (Windows)	Incremental window-making cost if transferred = $50.	For seller: (Windows)	Normal outside sales price = $100. Normal costs saved if transferring (vs. selling outside) = $10.

Exhibit 7-8

The Transfer Pricing Decision for Profit Center Managers

Range of mutually acceptable transfer prices to both managers:	*Situation 1:* Seller has excess capacity, so transferring does not affect outside sales	*Situation 2:* Seller has no excess capacity, so transferring reduces outside sales
Ceiling price (set by buyer: Assembly)	*Outside purchase cost* $85	*Outside purchase cost* $85
Floor price (set by the seller: Windows)	*Incremental window cost if transferring* $50	*Normal outside sales price less normal costs saved* $90*
Relevant cashflow (to the overall firm: Multree)	*Ceiling - Floor* $35	*Ceiling - Floor* ($5)
	Transfer increases Multree's cashflows	Transfer decreases Multree's cashflows

*Multree's premium windows sell for more than those sold by other suppliers.

Exhibit 7-9

customer. Assembly can place an order with the window company whenever it wants, or it can buy windows from another window maker. Upon receiving an order from Assembly, the window compay can (1) transfer windows to Assembly or (2) refuse to transfer. Its break-even price is the minimum price covering the average incremental costs of the transferred window [$50]. Any price above this creates extra cash for the window company. As with any seller, the higher the price, the better! So, the $50 average incremental window cost is a floor transfer price [as shown in the middle column of Exhibit 7-9].

"Assembly is the buyer of windows. It can buy similar windows from an unrelated company for $85. So, it will not pay more for the same windows from our window company. This is the maximum price Assembly is willing to pay. Of course, any price lower than $85 will save Assembly money. As with any buyer, the lower the window's cost, the better! Thus, the $85 outside purchase cost is the ceiling transfer price [as shown in the middle column of Exhibit 7-9].

"How do we feel as the parent company? We can make windows for $50 or buy them for $85. Making windows and transferring them to Assembly saves us $35. This is the net cashflow from transferring. It is simply the ceiling [maximum] price Assembly [the buyer] is willing to pay, less the floor [minimum] price the window company [the seller] must charge [as shown in the middle column of Exhibit 7-9].

"Now, consider situation 2 [the right columns in Exhibits 7-8 and 7-9]. Instead of having sufficient capacity for the order, assume the window company is currently selling every window it can make to outside customers for $100. In other words, it is producing at maximum capacity for external sales. The window company's floor price changes from situation 1 because its alternatives change [as seen in the right column of Exhibit 7-8]. To transfer a window, it has to give up selling the window to a regular, outside customer for $100. Not to lose any money, the window company has to sell that same window to Assembly for the same price as the outside customer is willing to pay, unless, of course, some costs will be saved by transferring. For a regular customer, windows have to be crated, costing $10. The windows do not have to be crated if transferred to Assembly. The $10 saved can be passed on to Assembly through a reduced sales price. In other words, the window company is indifferent between selling to an outside customer for $100, or transferring to Assembly at $90 [assuming no externalities].

"However, the buyer [Assembly] still will not pay more than $85 [the same as in situation 1]. So, in situation 2, the transfer's net cashflow is a negative $5 per window. Windows should not be transferred because transferring has a $5 opportunity cost. In other words, Assembly should buy windows from an outside source, and the window company should continue to sell all the windows it can make to outside customers until outside prices rise above $90. Until then, and as long as the window company is operating at full capacity, no transfers should happen.

"*In both situations, Multree's net cashflow from transferring is the ceiling price minus the floor price.* To determine when transfers should occur in either situation, only four accounting numbers are relevant: the outside purchase cost to the buyer [Assembly], the seller's average incremental cost to transfer, its normal [outside] sales price for the intermediate product, and any normal costs saved by transferring instead of selling to outside customers.

"Since we are allowing the managers to make the transfer decision, we might ask them to set the transfer price. If so, they can agree to any price between the floor and ceiling. Whenever the ceiling is greater than the floor, a range of mutually acceptable transfer prices exists. In situation 1, they can agree to any price between $50 and $85.

"In situation 2, though, no range exists as the floor is greater than the ceiling. This has two implications. First, the parent company [Multree] does not want a transfer. This will result in a $5 negative net cashflow [bottom row, right column of Exhibit 7-9]. Second, the managers will not be able to agree on a transfer price because no mutually acceptable range exists [the ceiling price is less than the floor price]. So, the motivation of the managers not to transfer is congruent with the company's desire and no transfer will result.

"In situations when they should agree to transfer, whether they need to agree on a transfer price, and their motivation to negotiate it, depends on how we evaluate and reward them. I have something to say about that, too, but as Sid wishes with Tommy's comments, I'll wait until the next meeting."

"Let's see if I understand how to decide to transfer. The two columns [of Exhibit 7-9] identify the four relevant cashflows when the seller has sufficient surplus capacity, and when the seller has to give up outside sales in order to transfer. The difference between the maximum price the buyer is willing to pay [the ceiling] and the minimum price the seller will accept [the floor] determines whether the transfer should happen. This difference is the net cashflow to the parent firm. When transfers should happen, a range of mutually acceptable transfer prices exists, bounded by the ceiling and floor."

Transfer pricing for services and multinationals. "Transfer pricing is widely used in many different organizational settings. A survey of Fortune 500 manufacturers reported 92% use transfer prices. Some companies are creating profit centers out of corporate services. PacTel's [Pacific-Telesis Group] legal department has to compete with other law firms for the rest of the company's legal business. Weyerhauser has turned all of its corporate services into profit centers. It claims these managers now provide better service to the operating divisions, and search for external business. Of course, the operating divisions can obtain these services from outside sources if they are not happy with the quality of in-house service. Teijin Seiki, in Japan, motivates higher quality and lower costs by setting the transfer price at the ceiling whenever the net cashflow is negative. Instead of allowing external purchases, which maximizes short-run overall profit, Teijin Seiki expects the selling division to find ways to improve so the transfer becomes profitable [i.e., the floor price becomes lower than the ceiling].

"The real fun with transfer pricing won't begin until we become a multinational enterprise [MNE], though. A 1995 Ernst & Young survey reported transfer pricing was the most important management issue with MNEs. During his 1992 campaign, President Clinton claimed the U.S. was losing over $11 billion in taxes due to MNE transfer pricing strategies. Setting transfer prices, whether transfers are required or not, affects foreign and domestic taxable profits, income taxes, and tariffs. Usually multinationals require transfers and set transfer prices to minimize taxes and tariffs, avoid foreign currency fluctuations, and move cash out of risky political environments. For example, Wind River Systems, a silicon valley software manufacturer, has a transfer pricing system company management credits with much of its financial success. Its average global tax rates are less than 35%, compared to 50% for other multinationals."

TOMMY

"O.K. Maybe we should consider moving our corporate headquarters to a low tax location, like Ireland, Puerto Rico, or the Cayman Islands! I can live in any of those countries!!"

JULIE

"I can too! But we better watch out for the Internal Revenue Service. It settled with Toyota for almost $1 billion in alleged back taxes due to setting artificially high transfer prices to U.S. subsidiaries. Of course, we could work with the IRS and get approval for our international transfer prices in advance, but that process costs at least $500,000 and the transfer prices are good for only three years! Many countries are issuing transfer pricing regulations [e.g., Canada, Europe, Japan, and South Korea]. At least multinationals are creating many new jobs for tax accountants and lawyers! Now, if you really want to move to another country, try Japan. While the IRS is attempting to collect over $12 billion from other countries due to their transfer pricing strategies, many Japanese firms are hiring IRS officials to fight the IRS!"

Production Decisions

BOB

"Before we move to another country, I have some production problems with windows we should discuss. We may wish to consider buying windows, either in the short run until we solve the problems, or permanently [long-run outsourcing]. I'm afraid we may not have a core competency in window making, as we believed when analyzing the transfer decision."

KEY OBJECTIVE 5

Compute the relevant cashflows for a make-or-buy decision.

Short-term make-or-buy decisions

BOB

"Our main problem is with installing windows. They don't always fit within the window frames when assembly workers install them. Thus, we have a lot of rework in Assembly. In the short run, I think we should consider buying windows, at least until these problems are solved. Since I hope this is only a short-run special decision, an incremental cashflow analysis seems appropriate. What are the alternatives? And, what are their incremental cashflows?"

JACKIE

"Looking at the window's standard cost card, its production cost is $70. But Purchasing tells me windows can be bought for $85 each. Our decision is to make windows or buy them. Comparing these two costs, the decision is simple. Continue making the windows."

NANCY

"For this decision, is it correct to use the window's standard cost? Doesn't it include an allocation of the entire plant's fixed overhead? Is fixed overhead relevant? Is the allocated variable overhead relevant? The entire plant's variable overhead is allocated with one plantwide POR. I suspect most of the variable and fixed overhead does not apply to window making. Thus, I don't expect a lot of the variable and fixed overhead will change in the future if we buy windows instead of making them!

"I see where the $85 purchase cost came from. We used it in our transfer pricing decision [Exhibit 7-9]. We also used $50 for the incremental cost of making a window for our homes. Shouldn't this be the incremental window production cost for our make-or-buy decision?"

JULIE

"Normally, I'd agree with you, Nancy. *From Multree's perspective, the transfer decision is a simple make-or-buy analysis when the seller has surplus capacity* [situation 1 in the middle column of Exhibit 7-9. In situation 2 (the right column) *when the seller has no surplus capacity, transferring is a sell-or-process-further decision.*]. But I did a special study of the window costs, and I think we should use $90. Here are the window-making costs relevant to this make-or-buy decision [see Exhibit 7-10].

"The standard cost card uses our cost accounting system PORs, which are not relevant costs for this decision. The PORs are for all the variable and fixed overhead of the entire factory. These are plantwide averages for all variable and fixed overhead, and all direct labor hours worked. As we discussed in the cost accounting

Window Make-or-Buy Decision

Budgeted incremental cost for transfer pricing decision			
Resource	**Standard price**	**Standard quantity**	**Standard cost**
Direct materials			$35.00 /window
Direct labor	$10.00 /hour	1 hour/window	10.00 /window
Variable overhead	$5.00 /hour	1 hour/window	5.00 /window
Fixed overhead			n/a
Incremental cost per window			**$50.00 /window**

Special cost analysis for make-or-buy decision			
Resource	**Expected price**	**Expected quantity**	**Expected cost**
Direct materials			$35.00 /window
Direct labor	$10.00 /hour	1 hour/window	10.00 /window
Variable overhead	$5.00 /hour	1 hour/window	5.00 /window
Rework	$10.00 /hour	4.0 hours/window	40.00 /window
Incremental cost per window			**$90.00 /window**
Less: window's purchase cost			(85.00) /window
Net cashflow if buying window			***$5.00 /window***

Exhibit 7-10

meeting [Chapter 5, Appendix A], for a decision only affecting one particular department, we probably should compute a separate POR for that department. When calculating the incremental cost for the transfer decision, we discovered window-making variable overhead is $5 per direct labor hour. A lot more variable overhead items are used in making a window than are used on average per direct labor hour for making an entire house.

"The fixed overhead allocated to windows in the standard cost card also is not relevant to this short-run decision. We don't expect fixed overhead to change if we buy windows once in a while, instead of making them. So, I adjusted the overhead costs for the transfer decision [see the top panel in Exhibit 7-10].

"When preparing the incremental cost analysis for the make-or-buy decision [bottom panel in Exhibit 7-10], I also used the overhead costs from the transfer decision, as well as the rework cost Bob mentioned. I know the $40 rework cost seems high, but think about what's involved. An assembly worker spends extra time trying to square the window [fit it into the frame in the wall], finally gives up in frustration, goes over to window making and gets a specialist, and then assists the specialist in fixing the problem. Including the time other assembly workers must wait, and the time of the specialist, this averages 4 hours per window!

"The bottom panel provides the incremental cashflow analysis for a short-term make-or-buy decision. We can save $5 per window by buying windows, assuming we have no short-run externalities [e.g., different quality, inability of supplier to deliver windows on time]."

"Wow! We should be buying windows. Possibly, this should be a permanent, strategic decision."

Strategic outsourcing

"Now, you're talking about outsourcing. Outsourcing is a long-run decision to buy instead of make a component. Sometimes support services are outsourced, like payroll, legal, data processing, and the like. Medical clinics often outsource lab work [e.g., blood analyses] and x-rays. When governmental services are outsourced to the private sector, this is called privatization. Outsourcing first class mail has been estimated to reduce postage 25%. However, remember from our discussion at the beginning of this meeting, long-run decisions often involve changing our capacity [the resources we make available]. This changes the cost analysis, as well as introduces many externalities."

Outsourcing (originally discussed in Chapter 1) is a long-run strategic decision to stop making a component (or providing a service), and instead obtain it from an outside source.

Externalities and outsourcing. "One consideration I want to discuss is the $40 rework costs in Assembly. Julie only discovered this hidden cost because she actually talked to the assembly workers. This is one reason why I don't like practical standard quantities. Knowing this problem will happen, we budgeted the 4 hours in Assembly's standard labor time. In other words, this problem is buried in its standard quantity. Thus, rework does not show up as a labor usage variance. If we did not include estimated rework in the standard quantities, it would create usage variances."

"Well, even if we take rework out of the standard quantities so it appears in a cost variance whenever rework is needed, I still would not have discovered it unless I talked to the assembly workers. The labor usage variance is charged to Assembly, where it occurs. It is not charged to the window-making department where it is caused."

"Wait a minute, Julie. You're assuming the rework is caused by problems in making the windows, and it will go away [we'll save $40] if windows are purchased instead of manufactured. What if the problem is really caused in Framing? Then this rework cost will still occur if windows are purchased."

"Well, in that case, the rework cost is not relevant to our make-or-buy decision! The incremental window-making cost drops to $50 [see Exhibit 7-10, $90 'make' cost – $40 rework]. So, we should not buy windows for $85. I guess our traditional cost variance system isn't as useful as it should be! Are there any other externalities we should consider?"

BOB

"Oh, a few:

- Quality: Will the supplier provide high-quality windows on a continuing basis? How important is high-quality windows to our customers [more generally, how important is product quality]?
- Service: Can we work with the supplier on design changes as we change floor plans in upcoming years? Can the supplier be as responsive to customer preference changes as we can by continuing to make windows? Will we receive complete orders on time?
- Cost: Is the $85 a 'low-ball,' one-time special price just to get our business? Can we sign a long-term supply contract providing price and delivery stability? Will future supplier prices increase or decrease? How financially sound is the supplier?
- Labor: How will outsourcing affect employee morale? Will we lose some really good people, or can they be retrained and used in different departments? What are the relevant labor-related costs with outsourcing? For example, we should consider severance pay, unemployment compensation, retraining, health insurance, pension, and other fringe benefits costs savings.

- Management knowledge: Does our window-making knowledge help us in other areas when redesigning houses? Will this knowledge be lost if we stop making windows?

Strategic outsourcing is very popular. For example, all of the components for Dell, Zeos, and Gateway computers are made by other suppliers. Toyota outsources 75% of its parts, while at General Motors it's 53%."

"Well, it's pretty clear we must consider many strategic issues before we decide to outsource any activities. When activities are outsourced, we can't watch them as closely. So, we must be very careful not to outsource components or services critical to customer satisfaction and high quality. Gillette, for example, attributes much of its success to not outsourcing, and maintaining tight internal quality controls. Gillette supplies one-third of the 20-billion-per-year razor blade market. Since 1990, U.S. sales have increased 54%, and 71% worldwide. AC International began business as a virtual company [outsourcing everything in its value chain], but ended up internalizing all production activities due to customer complaints. Now it's the world's second largest bicycle water bottle manufacturer."

Incremental cashflow and CVP analysis for outsourcing. "Often, outsourcing decisions affect production capacity. If we permanently outsource window making, fixed overhead may change. Equipment may be sold and salaried managers laid off. And, that part of the factory might be used for something else. We do not expect these events will happen in a short-run make-or-buy decision. But in the long-run decision, they become relevant cashflows. I've redone the short-run analysis to reflect the long-run relevant costs for an outsourcing decision [see Exhibit 7-11].

Long-Run Cashflow Analysis for Outsourcing Windows

			Relevant cashflows	
			Fixed costs per year	Variable costs per window
Incremental costs to make:				
Direct materials				$35
Direct labor	$10 per hour x	1 hour =		10
Variable overhead	$5 per hour x	1 hour =		5
Variable manufacturing costs				$50
Net cost to buy windows:				
Purchase cost				$85
Fixed overhead saved			$20,000	
Net annual cashflow from using capacity for duct making			25,000	
Outsourcing cost ($85/window less $45,000 in fixed cost savings)			($45,000)	$85
Allocate fixed costs over annual window volume			÷ 1,000	
Average fixed cost saved per window			($45)	(45)
Average net outsourcing cost per window				$40
Net saved per window if outsourced				$10

Exhibit 7-11

"After further investigation, Bob and I believe the rework costs are due to problems in framing the houses. So, it won't make any difference if we make or buy windows. The rework cost will still exist unless we fix the problem in Framing. It now is irrelevant to the make-or-buy decision because it is not a difference between the alternatives. In the short run, we make windows for $50 or buy them for $85. This is the same analysis we used in the transfer pricing analysis [Exhibit 7-9].

"The long-run outsourcing decision, though, creates a change in fixed overhead. We can save $20,000 per year if we stop making windows. Now, what do we do with the space previously used to make windows? We believe this capacity can be used to make the air ducts for the house's heating and cooling system. Currently, we are buying prefabricated air ducts. Making ducts will save us $25,000 a year. So, if we outsource windows, a total of $45,000 per year will be saved. This savings reduces the $85 purchase cost if outsourced. In the long run, our average annual home production quota should require 1,000 windows. Allocating the $45,000 annual savings over the 1,000 windows reduces the net average purchase cost to $40 per window [as seen in the bottom part of the *Net cost to buy windows* section of Exhibit 7-11]."

NANCY

"I think I understand. If we permanently outsource windows, they'll cost us $85 each. However, we'll save $45,000 a year, which averages $45 a window. So, our net cost to buy windows is $40. We project a $50 cost to make them, so we're saving $10 a window if we buy them. It seems this [Exhibit 7-11] is the same incremental cashflow analysis [with a known volume] you used for the mountie huts [Exhibit 7-3]. It even looks like the same spreadsheet program!

"Of course, the $85 purchase price may not be stable for a whole year, or for many years. Assuming we need exactly 1,000 windows every year, what is the maximum purchase price we can accept before outsourcing becomes the less profitable alternative [i.e., before it begins to incur an opportunity cost]?"

JULIE

"We show a $10 per window average net cashflow for outsourcing [Exhibit 7-11]. The purchase price has to increase $10 for this to disappear. So, outsourcing is the more profitable alternative as long as the purchase price does not exceed $95 and we use 1,000 windows per year. At a $95 cost, we're indifferent between making or outsourcing windows [assuming no externalities]. By the way, we can use incremental CVP analysis to verify this [see Exhibit 7-12].

CVP Analysis for Maximum Outsourcing Cost

Solving for maximum purchase price:

Break-even point (volume)	=	Δ Fixed costs	÷ CMU
	=	Δ Fixed costs	÷ (Purchase price - Variable cost)
1,000 windows	=	$45,000	÷ (Purchase price - $50)
Maximum purchase price	=	**$95**	**per window**

Exhibit 7-12

"Since this is an incremental analysis, I used the delta sign [Δ] to mean 'change in.' Fixed costs go down $45,000 per year from outsourcing. Outsourcing 1,000 windows, this averages $45 per window. The difference between the variable production costs and the purchase price cannot exceed this limit. In other words, if our incremental production cost is $50, we should not pay more than $95 to buy a window. Again, this is exactly the same logic and analysis used with the mountie huts in determining their break-even sales price [Exhibit 7-4]."

NANCY

"O.K. I get the idea. Once we understand the relationships between variable and fixed costs, volume, and profit, CVP analysis becomes a very powerful tool for decision making. We must be careful, though, to make sure the numbers are valid [i.e., we are still within the relevant range]. Here's my last question for the day." That thought brought big smiles to everyone's faces! "Let's assume we can get a long-term price of $85, but the number of windows needed each year changes [which only makes sense because our sales forecast changes every year]. What window volume will change our decision? In other words, when will making windows become the cheaper alternative? And, don't tell me this is again just the same analysis you've already done for the mountie huts!!"

JULIE

"I'm sorry, but it is. We've already done this analysis [Exhibit 7-5]. At an $11,500 sales price, the mountie huts generate a $500 CMU. The minimum order volume must be 40 huts to break even. At less than 40, we lose money. An order greater than 40 provides extra contribution margin and profit. Now, let's use the same logic with outsourcing the windows [see Exhibit 7-13].

CVP Analysis for Maximum Outsourcing Volume

Solving for break-even volume:

Break-even point (volume)	=	Δ Fixed costs	÷ CMU
	=	$45,000	÷ ($85 - $50)
	=	**1,286 windows**	

Exhibit 7-13

"Outsourcing saves $45,000 a year. This is offset by the extra $35 per window purchasing cost [compared to making]. How many '$35 bills' will we have to spend before the $45,000 savings is used up? As long as we don't need more than 1,286 windows a year, the $45,000 savings will be greater than the total extra cost of buying the windows. If we buy more than 1,286 windows in a year, we'll spend more than $45,000 in purchasing costs. The 1,286 window annual volume is the indifference volume for outsourcing."

NANCY

"O.K. I give up! You've convinced me! CVP analysis is the accountant's gift to management! Once we realize which costs are variable versus fixed, and incremental versus sunk, we can identify the alternatives and calculate each one's incremental cashflows. In comparing them, the alternative with the positive net cashflow should be chosen unless externalities are more important. Even though less profitable alternatives have an opportunity cost, externalities may cause us to choose them. Incremental CVP analysis allows us to play 'what-if' games and do sensitivity analysis. Did I get it right? Doris, how does this compare with your meeting notes?"

KEY OBJECTIVES SUMMARY

"Well, your summary is much more succinct and it sure does sound good! Five important ideas were discussed today:

1. Explain the need for a markup policy with budgeted sales.

"Not all homes are priced exactly the same. So, our sales force needs some guidance in negotiating prices. On average, for all sales included in the annual plan, each home's estimated manufacturing cost must be marked up 65% [from Exhibit 3-4: ($345,000 selling expenses + $1,000,000 administrative expenses + $1,000,000 net income) ÷ $3,655,000 manufacturing costs = 65% (rounded up)]. This provides a sales price high enough to cover a fair share of Multree's expenses and profit. A markup [usually expressed as a percentage of cost] is the amount added to a base cost in setting the sales price. The base cost differs from firm to firm, and industry to industry. In the manufacturing sector, base cost is usually standard absorptive manufacturing cost. Thus, the markup must be high enough to pay for a fair share of the company's expenses and target profit. Determining the sales price by adding a markup to cost is called cost-plus pricing.

"Why do we need a 65% markup on manufacturing cost? To cover all of our budgeted costs and provide our desired profit. Of course, this applies only to the sales included in our annual plan. We do not need to achieve this markup on special sales which are not part of the original $6 million projected revenues.

"And, while a 65% markup is our pricing goal, Bill knows current market conditions may not always allow it. If this markup becomes an 'ironclad' rule, we may lose business and not achieve our target profit. Market-based pricing may have to drive the decision-making process in the short run. Hopefully, any unfavorable sales price variances can be overcome with increased sales volume [favorable variances] so we still can achieve our profit plan.

"I'm the troop leader for my granddaughter's Girl Scout Troop. Our annual cookie sale provides our funds. Everybody loves Girl Scout cookies! Here's our annual cost equation: $300 per year in annual operating costs + $2 purchase cost per box. We plan to sell 100 boxes this year. To cover all costs, our markup on purchase cost must be 150%. Total purchase cost for 100 boxes is $200. Other costs and profit equal $300 [our profit goal is zero]. $300 ÷ $200 = 150% markup on purchase cost. This is a $3 markup per box [$2 purchase cost × 150%]. So, cookies must be priced at $5 per box [$2 purchase cost + $3 markup].

2. Use incremental CVP analysis to determine special sales prices.

"With special orders, we can use incremental pricing. Any price greater than the order's incremental cost provides extra cash. In addition to good cookies at $2 per box, we can buy broken cookies for $1 a box. Each order incurs $20 in processing and paperwork costs [an incremental fixed cost]. We think we can sell 20 boxes. Using incremental CVP analysis, the minimum break-even sales price for 20 boxes is $2. Here's my calculation [based on Exhibit 7-4]. [See Exhibit 7-14.]

"The girls did a market survey discovering we can sell broken cookies for $1.50 per box. Since this is below the $2.00 break-even price, we won't sell them unless

CVP Analysis for Broken Cookies

Solving for break-even sales price:

Break-even point (volume)	=	Fixed costs	÷	CMU
	=	Fixed costs	÷	(Sales price - Variable cost)
20 boxes	=	$20	÷	(Sales price - $1.00)
Break-even sales price	=	**$2** per box		

Exhibit 7-14

we think we can sell more than 40 boxes. This is the break-even volume based on a $1.50 sales price. I used the incremental CVP calculation [Exhibit 7-5] to solve for volume. [See Exhibit 7-15.]

Broken Cookies Break-Even Volume

Break-even point (volume)	=	Fixed costs	÷	CMU
	=	$20	÷	($1.50 - $1.00)
	=	**40 boxes**		

Exhibit 7-15

3. Determine whether an intermediate product should be sold or processed further.

"Many firms have final and intermediate products. Intermediate products can be sold as is, or processed further into a final product. In deciding whether to sell an intermediate product now or process it further, consider only the incremental cash-flows of the two alternatives.

"My Girl Scouts bought the broken cookies. We can sell the broken cookies door-to-door for $1.50 a box. Alternatively, we can open each box, crush the cookies, and make ice cream. I know a number of parents with new ice cream makers [never-been-used Christmas gifts!]. So, all we have to do is buy the ingredients and containers [about $3.00 per half-gallon]. Budgeting for normal scrap [cookies eaten during the process] and allowing for ice cream loss during 'quality-control testing' [Girl Scouts eating the ice cream], I figure each box of broken cookies will yield one-half gallon of ice cream. Now, how much should we price a half-gallon? Yesterday I paid $5.29 at the grocery store [a 'special' price] for one-half gallon of Dreyer's 'Girl Scout Thin Mint Cookie' ice cream.

"If we sell broken cookies, our incremental cashflow is $1.50 per box. To be indifferent between selling now or processing further into ice cream, a half-gallon must be priced at $4.50. $4.50 minus $3.00 in further processing costs provides a $1.50 incremental cashflow, which equals the incremental cashflow from selling the cookies. It seems to me we should be able to sell ice cream for more than $4.50, especially considering we deliver! I'll have the Girl Scouts do another marketing survey. If we can sell the ice cream for more, let's do it. Otherwise, let's sell the broken cookies to normal customers.

"We have a couple of externalities to consider, though. Dreyer's has a quality reputation, which commands a premium sales price. Will our ice cream be as high quality? If we decide to sell the broken cookies to our regular customers, will this reduce the number of normal cookies sold at regular prices? Also, the Girl Scouts are afraid the ice cream will melt while they are delivering it. So, they decided to buy 50 boxes of broken cookies and sell them after the regular orders have been delivered.

4. Calculate the relevant cashflows from transferring intermediate products.

"My husband and I were going over our household budget last week. We've decided we are a charitable nonprofit organization. Among our many subsidiaries are the Boy Scouts and Girl Scouts [my husband is a troop leader, too]. We are the 'parent' company because we donate any money needed to cover their costs [i.e., money needed but not raised through events like selling cookies]. The Boy Scout and Girl Scout troops are real profit centers. They decide who to buy from and sell to.

"The Boy Scouts need cookies to include in their gift packages given to people in need. They're willing to buy boxes of broken Girl Scout cookies and use the good cookies in their gift packages. [They'll eat the broken ones!] Another Girl Scout troop has offered to sell broken cookies to them for $1.75 a box.

"Our Girl Scouts have two choices. First, when they order boxes, they simply can order more hoping the Boy Scouts will buy them. [This is the surplus capacity situation shown in the middle column of Exhibit 7-9.] The incremental cost of ordering extra boxes is $1.00 per box. The incremental cost if the Boy Scouts have to buy from another Girl Scout troop is $1.75. The net cashflow in favor of my troop supplying the Boy Scouts [transferring] is 75¢ a box. If they transfer for any price between $1.00 and $1.75, both will make some extra money, and so will I [75¢ per box]! This is shown in the middle column of my cookies transfer pricing worksheet [Exhibit 7-16].

"The second choice is ordering exactly 50 boxes, which is what the Girl Scouts think they can sell to regular customers. Now, the Girl Scouts' alternatives are sell the boxes to regular customers for $1.50, or sell them to the Boy Scouts. Unless we can save some incremental costs by selling to the Boy Scouts [versus selling to normal customers], we need the same $1.50 price obtainable from regular customers. This is shown in the right column of my worksheet. Whenever the Boy Scouts need broken cookies, I'm 25¢ per box better off if the Girl Scouts sell them to the Boy Scouts, rather than selling them to outside customers.

"As the parent company, I see the first scenario as a short-run make-or-buy decision. I, through the Girl Scouts, get boxes of broken cookies for $1.00, or I, through the Boy Scouts, buy them for $1.75. Transferring [selling from a profit center to another part of the company] saves the parent company, me, 75¢. I see the second scenario as a sell-or-process-further decision. I, through the Girl Scouts, can sell boxes now for $1.50, or process them further into gift baskets. Selling now has a $1.50 incremental cashflow. By processing further [transferring], I give up the $1.50, but save $1.75 because the Boy Scouts will not have to buy from another Girl Scout troop. The net cashflow in favor of transferring is 25¢.

5. Compute the relevant cashflows for a make-or-buy decision.

"Some of my Girl Scouts suggested we bake cookies instead of buying broken cookies for our ice cream. As with any short-run decision, we should compare the in-

The Cookies Transfer Pricing Decision

Range of mutually acceptable transfer prices:	Transferred product or service comes from seller's surplus capacity	Transferred product or service is taken from the normal retail sales of the seller
Ceiling price (set by buyer: Boy Scouts)	*Outside purchase cost* $1.75	*Outside purchase cost* $1.75
Floor price (set by the seller: Girl Scouts)	*Incremental cost* $1.00	*Normal sales price - Incremental costs saved* $1.50
Relevant cashflow (to the overall firm: Doris)	*Ceiling - Floor* <u>$0.75</u>	*Ceiling - Floor* <u>$0.25</u>

Exhibit 7-16

cremental cashflows of each alternative. Then we should consider externalities. Buying broken cookies costs $20 per order plus $1.00 per box. Our ice cream market survey indicates we need 10 boxes. So, the 'buy' alternative's incremental cost is $30. Baking the same number of cookies costs $18 [$1.80 per box]. Baking cookies creates a $12 net cashflow.

"When will buying be cheaper than baking? It costs $1.80 per box to bake cookies. If we need only 10 boxes, buying will never be cheaper unless the $20 fixed ordering cost decreases! For 10 boxes, the average purchase cost is $3 [($20 order cost + {$1 per box × 10 boxes} = $30) ÷ 10 boxes = $3 average cost per box]. Until baking cost exceeds $3 per box, buying cookies doesn't make sense. Using incremental CVP analysis [Exhibit 7-12], we can verify this. [See Exhibit 7-17.]

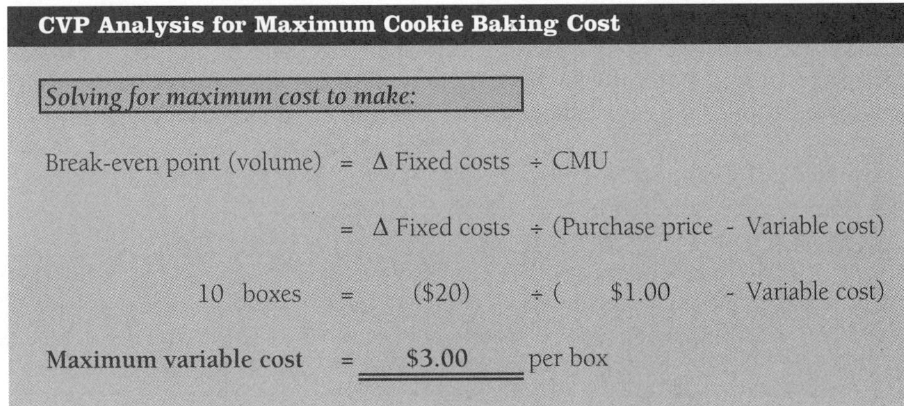
CVP Analysis for Maximum Cookie Baking Cost

Solving for maximum cost to make:

Break-even point (volume)	=	Δ Fixed costs	÷ CMU
	=	Δ Fixed costs	÷ (Purchase price - Variable cost)
10 boxes	=	($20)	÷ ($1.00 - Variable cost)
Maximum variable cost	=	**$3.00**	per box

Exhibit 7-17

Baking saves the $20 ordering cost. But baking incrementally costs 80¢ per box more than buying [$1.80 versus $1.00]. So, we're trading off a higher variable cost for a fixed cost saving. For only 10 boxes, variable baking costs are $8 more than buying. This is less than the $20 fixed cost saved by baking, so baking is the less expensive alternative. When will the higher variable cost equal the fixed cost saving? When it costs $3 to bake the cookies. As long as we need only 10 boxes, and the baking cost is less than $3 per box, we should bake instead of buy.

"Well, we know buying boxes of broken cookies is more expensive than baking cookies when only 10 boxes are needed. How many boxes are needed for buying to be the cheaper alternative? 25 boxes is our indifference volume [see Exhibit 7-18].

CVP Analysis for Indifference Cookie Volume

Solving for break-even volume:

Break-even point (volume)	=	Δ Fixed costs	÷ CMU		
	=	($20)	÷ ($1.00	-	$1.80)
	=	25 boxes			

Exhibit 7-18

"If we need less than 25 boxes, baking is the cheaper alternative. Sometimes, using the CVP equation in its factored form [break-even point = (fixed costs + profit) ÷ CMU] confuses me, though. Remembering the equation is simple algebra . . ." Everyone began to boo Doris at this point. The day had been long enough! ". . . I just solved for the volume that equates the two alternative's costs:"

Outsource cost equation = Baking cost equation
$20 + ($1 × Volume) = $1.80 × Volume
Volume = 25 boxes

At this point, everyone began to smile. They knew Doris had finished summarizing how incremental CVP analysis can support decision making for unplanned events. Sid, sensing this, interrupted Doris.

SID

"Thank you Doris. I don't know about the rest of you, but I'd sure like some Girl Scout cookies! Doris, do you have any extra boxes of broken cookies? I'll gladly pay more than $1.50 each for all of them so we can end this meeting!"

REALITY 101

Public Utility Deregulation and Transfer Pricing

Historically, the utility industry has had little use for transfer pricing. Regulatory agency rules determined how costs were allocated to a utility company's segments when setting rates for the generation and sale of resources, and for the cost of transmitting electricity, gas, or water from the utility company to the customer (e.g., a city).

In 1996, the Federal Energy Regulatory Commission began deregulation. Utility companies must now separate three lines of business: generation (e.g., creating electricity, gas, water), transmission (e.g., electric and gas lines), and marketing. Each division is a profit center. Generation decides whether electricity should be sold to other utilities or municipalities. Transmission can sell the use of its lines to Generation or to other suppliers. Marketing can buy resources from and sell to any interested customer. For example, Denver's electricity may be generated in Tacoma, Washington, and travel through lines owned by a utility in Utah. One goal of the new deregulation requirements is to prevent a utility from denying its customers access to other utility sources by claiming no transmission capacity is available, or by charging exorbitant rates for use of its transmission system.

Deregulation allows divisions of the same utility to buy and sell between themselves (transfer), as well as buy and sell to other utilities and end users. Implementing a transfer pricing system at Sierra Pacific Power (SPP) in Reno, Nevada, has resulted in numerous benefits and problems.

Traditionally, in the regulated environment, each SPP division budgeted its own costs. When Transmission delivered electricity, gas, or water to end customers, the actual cost of generating the resources was moved out of the Generation Department and into the Transmission Department. This is a typical process costing system.

Now, the departments are separate profit centers (divisions) and negotiate the cost of their services as part of the annual budgeting process. The new "budgeted cost" is actually a transfer price. By transferring a budgeted cost, instead of actual cost, the supplying division is better motivated to control costs. As part of the new cost control consciousness, comprehensive reviews of all internal functions are being conducted, looking for ways to improve operations and reduce costs.

Deregulation also has created some transfer pricing problems. Before electricity is sold from Generation to Transmission, Transmission conducts an internal capacity study to determine its transmission needs and capacity. Outside suppliers wanting to sell electricity to transmission or use its lines also need the capacity study. Because Transmission must decide who to buy resources from, it first has to decide who it will sell these capacity studies to. To solve this problem, Transmission prepared a transfer pricing worksheet (see Exhibit 7-19).

Due to deregulation, the Transmission Division has a new marketable service: capacity studies. Of course, deregulation allows independent consultants to perform these studies. Independent consultants in the Reno area charge $120 per hour for the study. To be competitive, SPP's Transmission Division prices this service at $100 per hour for external customers. Budgeted study cost for an outside customer is $70 per hour, and for an internal customer (e.g., Generation), $60 per hour.

Regardless of the amount of external study business Generation has, it should always do studies for Generation, even if this means giving up some external business. Generation and Transmission can negotiate a mutually acceptable price within the $60–$120 per hour range if Transmission has the surplus capacity to do it without giving up any external studies. If Transmission has to give up an external study job, the transfer price range narrows to $90–$120 per hour.

Source: Interviews with Carolyn Bonari and Richard Minetto of Sierra Pacific Power.

Transmission Capacity Study for Transfer Pricing

Range of mutually acceptable transfer prices:	Transmission Division has the surplus capacity to do a study for Generation	Transmission must give up doing a study for an outside supplier in order to do a study for Generation
Ceiling price (set by Generation)	External cost for a study **$120 per hour**	External cost for a study **$120 per hour**
Floor price (set by Transmission)	Internal study incremental cost **$60 per hour**	Normal external supplier study price, less costs saved doing an internal study **$90 per hour**
Relevant cashflow to SPP	Ceiling - Floor **$60 per hour**	Ceiling - Floor **$30 per hour**

Exhibit 7-A1

READING LIST*

AC International: Kirk, "It's About Control," *Inc.*, August 1994.

Atlantic Dry Dock: Barton and Cole, "Atlantic Dry Dock's Unique Cost Estimation System," *Management Accounting*, October 1994.

British newspaper price wars: Reuters, "A Price War Grows Hotter," *New York Times*, August 3, 1994.

EuroBelgian Airways: "Now Lifting Off in Europe: No-Frills Flying," *Business Week*, November 28, 1994.

Dell and Zeos and outsourcing: Tully, "You'll Never Guess Who Really Makes . . .," *Fortune*, October 3, 1994.

FCC and international calls: "Accounting Changes on International Calls Proposed by the FCC," *The Wall Street Journal*, July 13, 1990, p. A2.

FMI Forms: Rodgers, Comstock, and Pritz, "Customize Your Costing System," *Management Accounting*, May 1993.

General Motors: Taylor, "GM's $11,000,000,000 Turnaround," *Fortune*, October 17, 1994. Outsourcing: see Toyota.

Gillette: Koselka, "It's My Favorite Statistic," *Forbes*, September 12, 1994.

Hewlett-Packard: Yoder, "How HP Used Tactics of the Japanese to Beat Them at Their Game," *The Wall Street Journal*, December 8, 1994, p. A1.

Internal Revenue Service and transfer price-setting (APAs): Borkowski, "Section 482, Revenue Procedure 91-22, and the Realities of Multinational Transfer Pricing," *International Tax Journal*, Spring 1992.

Japan hiring IRS agents: Abramson, "Ex-Tax Collectors Help Foreign Firms Fight U.S. Efforts to Get More Funds," *The Wall Street Journal*, October 18, 1993, p. A16.

Mail and outsourcing: Schine, Dunham, and Farrell, "America's New Watchword: If It Moves, Privatize It," *Business Week*, December 12, 1994.

Mitsubishi: Berss, "We Will Not be a National Chain," *Forbes*, March 27, 1995.

Pacific-Telesis: Stevens, "Lawyers and Clients," *The Wall Street Journal*, July 24, 1995, p. B8.

Pricing in the pharmaceutical industry: Holmes, "Research RX: Is Health Care Reform a Bitter Pill for the Pharmaceutical Industry?" *Management Accounting*, November 1993.

Pricing practices survey: Shim and Sudit, "How Manufacturers Price Products," *Management Accounting*, February 1995.

Rosen's hotel pricing: McDowell, "His Goal: No Rooms at the Inns," *New York Times*, November 23, 1995, pp. C1, C8.

San Diego County: Bailey, "California Cities Face Heftier Trash Fees," *The Wall Street Journal*, July 27, 1994, p. A2.

Teijin Sieki: Kawada and Johnson, "Strategic Management Accounting—Why and How," *Management Accounting*, August 1993.

Toyota: "The Corporate Shell Game," *Newsweek*, April 15, 1991. Outsourcing: Taylor, "The Auto Industry Meets the New Economy," *Fortune*, September 5, 1994.

Transfer pricing and relevant cashflows: Thomas, "A Contingency Theory for Organizational Transfer Pricing: Opportunity Cost and Market-Based Factors," *Journal of Accounting and Financial Studies*, Spring 1998.

Transfer pricing survey: Tang, "Transfer Pricing in the 1990s," *Management Accounting*, February 1992.

Weyerhauser: Johnson and Loewe, "How Weyerhauser Manages Corporate Overhead," *Management Accounting*, August 1987.

Wind River Systems: Fraser, "Controlling Global Taxes," *Inc.*, August 1993.

*Alphabetic by topic, idea, or company referenced.

CHAPTER 8

Will Our People Do This?

Motivation and Control Through Accounting Information

KEY OBJECTIVES:

1	*Describe the motivational relationship between planning, control, and evaluation.*
2	*Discuss the evolution from clan control to accounting control and accounting's control hierarchy.*
3	*Explain three motivational problems with using accounting information in performance evaluation.*
4	*Prepare a segmented income statement and explain its usefulness in evaluating segments and managers.*
5	*Compute ROI and residual income, and explain their motivational implications.*
6	*Summarize five ethical concerns with management's use of accounting control measures.*
7	*[Appendix A] Demonstrate how service department and common cost allocations can support cost control.*

Nancy felt the Boss's grandchildren had learned a lot about running the business in the past few months, but things still were not going as planned. Variances abounded. Bill was complaining about the lack of standard home sales. Bob was worried about unfavorable cost variances from scheduling disruptions for custom home sales. Their last board meeting was spent entirely on new ideas to solve Multree's problems. Nancy needed a walk through the tree-covered hills. She was having fun with her job but still felt nervous, just like when she used to toboggan down these hills as a child. That, too, was fun. But, like Multree Homes, things weren't quite under control. Back then it added excitement. Now, though, as she looked down the hill, all she could do was shiver.

If things are going to improve, Multree's people have to make it happen. Management cannot make an organization work. It can plan, attempt to control, and evaluate. But employees have to be motivated to follow through. *Responsibility and authority come from the top of the organization, but power comes from the people supporting management.* Employees make the day-to-day operating decisions.

All of the sudden, Bruno the Dog went racing by chasing a Frisbee. She watched as Bruno joyfully responded to each of Tommy's commands. She smiled as she enjoyed their antics. Then a frown crossed her face as she wondered why Tommy didn't have any motivation and control problems with his dog. Her dogs never came when she called, unless it was time to eat at the dinner table with her! They were motivated just enough to do the minimum in life: bark at the delivery truck, lift a leg when necessary, eat [as often as possible], and sleep on the furniture the rest of the time!

Nancy was even more impressed with Bruno the Dog's behavior when Tommy wasn't around, like staying in the yard even when the gate was open. Unlike her dogs, Bruno made good decisions without Tommy's supervision. That's real control!

NANCY

"Tommy, I've always wondered what your secret is with Bruno the Dog. Why does he do what you want, instead of only what he wants? Why is he so happy to see you, when my dogs just bury their heads under the furniture pillows?"

TOMMY

"I have no secrets! It's just good old common sense. First I plan. Start with a good pedigree. Bruno is a purebred border collie. Then control. Make sure the dog knows what you want. Train and educate. Make sure you communicate in a simple, direct, and consistent manner. Finally, evaluate. Praise and reward in a way that motivates the behavior you want.

"You're really thinking about our problems at Multree, though, aren't you? You're worried our people aren't motivated to implement our strategy and plans, and improve our value. Tell you what. Since I grew up with our workers, I'll prepare something on motivation and control from their perspective for today's meeting."

KEY OBJECTIVE 1

Describe the motivational relationship between planning, control, and evaluation.

The Motivational Cycle: Budgeting, Control, and Evaluation

SID

As the meeting began, the strain and apprehension from the last two meetings still was strong in the room. The wall paneling seemed darker than usual. "If we really understand a process [it's a glass box], everyone knows the one best way to do things. The problem is this isn't always possible. With black box processes, we have to rely on our people's judgment because we don't know what's going on inside the box. So we have to trust them to make decisions in the best interests of the company—that is, exercise good judgment. During the past week, I visited each of our departments. Our people were not very happy to see me. Often, like our children and pets, they thought they were in trouble. I guess that's the nature of management by exception. Workers only see management when something is wrong. They avoided me whenever possible. Those who did talk to me didn't share much information. One thing is obvious. Some of our problems are caused by employee relationships." Everyone noticed the foreboding tone in his voice. This was not going to be a fun meeting!

How to get employees to do what we want

TOMMY

"I know we have some behavioral problems. *Motivation is what we really mean when using the word 'control.'* Here's what I do with my dog, how it may relate to our people, and its relationship to the three basic management decisions [see Exhibit 8-1].

Training My Dog Is Like Motivating Our People and Running Our Business

Training my dog	Motivating our people	Running our business
1. Buy known traits so less training is required.	1. Hire trained professionals.	1. ***Plan for the future:*** Strategies, proformas, cash budgets.
		Daily monitoring and control:
2. Teach commands.	2. Educate employees.	2. Employee training programs, participatory budgeting.
3. Communicate what is expected.	3. Communicate with employees about what is needed, problems, performance, and ways to improve.	3. Monitor activities, communicate about and fix problems.
4. Reward to motivate (love, cookies).	4. Provide feedback on employee performance, and appropriately reward them.	4. ***Evaluate past performance:*** Measure performance and reward people in ways that will motivate the behavior we want.

Exhibit 8-1

The concept is simple:

I'll give you what you want, if you give me what I want.

However, implementing this is difficult! *We have two problems: motivation and measurement.* Has your boss ever asked you what you want—in other words, what motivates you? Usually, rewards mean money. Sometimes sufficient monetary rewards are not possible, though. Here's where our managerial creativity becomes important. We should ask our people what motivates them and then find a way to make those rewards possible.

"The second problem is how to measure performance. We can directly observe it, but this is not practical in many large, complex organizations. So we usually rely on some type of measurement system, like the accounting system. While it produces 'hard numbers' people can rely on, traditionally the numbers focus only on outputs and costs. In other words, we treat the process as a black box."

"I see! In measuring performance, the problem is ignoring how things are done. It's like the old saying, 'The proof is in the pudding' or, 'If customers buy it, it must be good.' Just because we see an output, for example a sale, we can't assume the right things have been done." She smilingly stared at Bob's pack of cigarettes.

"I hoped to learn more about these problems by taking a psychology course last summer. But it wasn't offered because department budgets are based on student enrollments, and summer courses don't count. So, by offering summer courses, students won't take the same course during the regular semesters, and the department's funds then go down. While students may be better off by offering summer courses [improving customers' value], the department is punished. *Lesson 1: Incentives motivate behavior.* Just like training dogs.

"Not offering the course was O.K., though, because it would have been taught by Professor Easy. He tells great stories and students love him. It's an easy 'A' and students reciprocate by giving him an 'A' on student evaluations. Since it's the only output measure used to evaluate teaching quality, he gets good raises every year. Is he motivated to improve the course? He could require computer projects, but if the technology doesn't work right, his student evaluations might go down. Since the technology is not within his control, and student evaluations are the only measure used to evaluate his performance, he's not willing to take that risk. *Lesson 2: Performance measures also motivate behavior.*

"I wonder if the college is really measuring teaching quality. Of course, how do you measure it? Maybe it should be a black box! *Too often, we choose one easy, inexpensive output measure and hope it is good enough.* Evaluating teaching by relying solely on student evaluations may be cost-benefit justified. It's just too costly to effectively evaluate the process. The costs from identifying the critical success factors for high-quality teaching, and then measuring the process [getting inside the black box], are greater than the benefits from a better evaluation of teaching performance."

"Nancy identified four dimensions to a good 'control' system [as shown in Exhibit 8-2].

"We discussed goal congruence in our first meeting. To motivate others to do what we want, we have to offer them acceptable rewards. To earn rewards, performance measures are needed. The measures should be limited to activities people control. If we don't give a person the authority and power to do something, how can we hold her responsible for it when evaluating her performance? *Motivation can break down because of inadequate rewards, measuring the right things in the wrong way, or measuring the wrong things.*

The Motivational Cycle

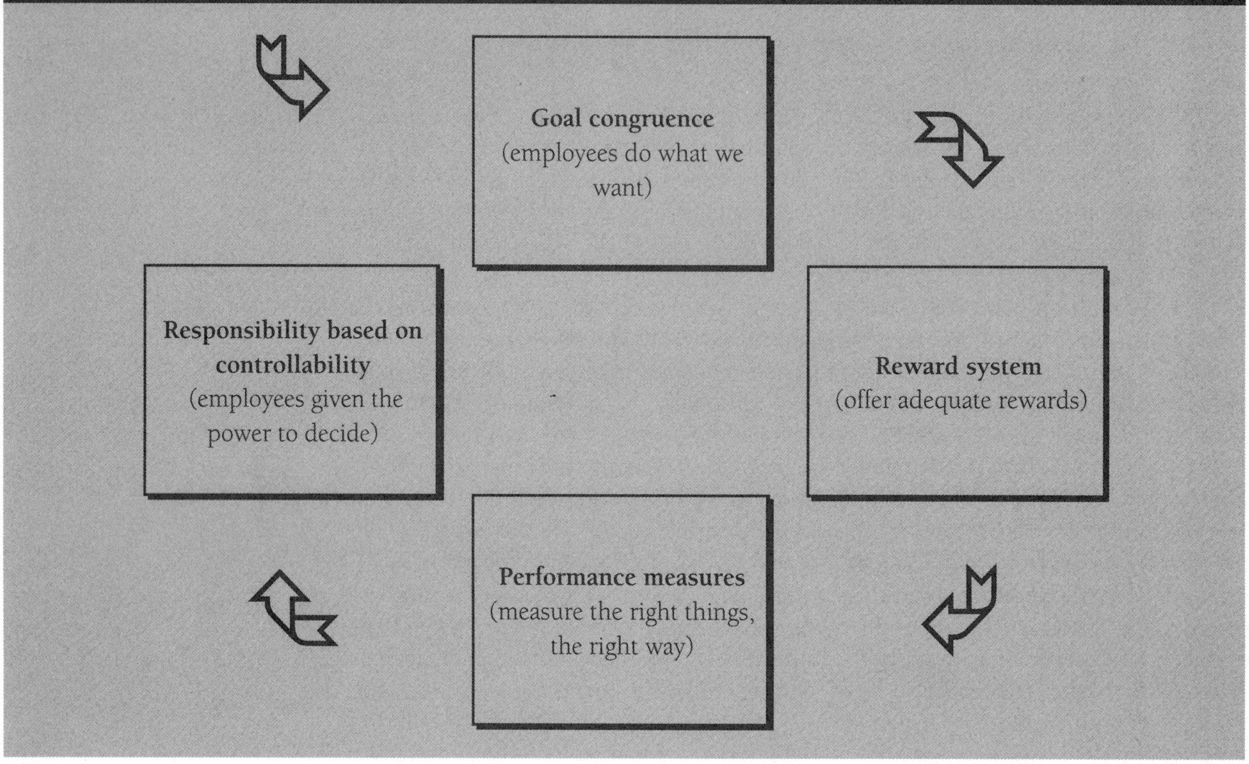

Goal congruence
(employees do what we want)

Reward system
(offer adequate rewards)

Performance measures
(measure the right things, the right way)

Responsibility based on controllability
(employees given the power to decide)

Exhibit 8-2

"The budgeting process identifies who is responsible for Multree's activities. The person budgeting something should be the person responsible for it. During the planning process, performance measures reflecting our goals should be developed jointly with the people responsible for planning and implementing each goal. The measures should guide day-to-day monitoring and control, as well as evaluation. If people know how they are doing in real-time, periodic performance evaluations should not provide any negative surprises [bad news]. Our people then will see a consistent pattern with what is expected on a daily basis and their evaluations."

TOMMY

"On the other hand, by looking only at the output of a process [i.e., not looking inside the black box] we may motivate people to manipulate it in undesirable ways. Professor Easy may throw out a bad exam score because he is overly concerned with student evaluations.

"Relying solely on one or two output measures may encourage behaviors that decrease long-run value. Thus, our measurement system may create a big ethical problem for us as well as our employees!"

"I guess we better ask ourselves, 'What do we really want our people to do?'"

SID

We want them to exercise good judgment

TOMMY

"Well, if I may generalize, they should use good judgment. They should make goal-congruent decisions without direct supervision. Goal congruence is when employees do things that are in the best interests of the company, or a dog does what its master wants. The opposite of goal congruence is dysfunctional behavior, making decisions that benefit an individual but hurt the company's value. If we properly motivate our people, decisions improving their own well-being also improve the firm's value."

"So, *good judgment is goal-congruent decision making!* And good decisions come from

- People who are properly motivated,
- Who exercise good judgment, and
- Who have good information.

The management accounting system must provide relevant information for their decision-making needs, as well as evaluation information about what they have done and how they have done it. Now, how do we know they are exercising good judgment?"

Organizational Control Systems: Finding the Right Mix of Strategies

KEY OBJECTIVE 2

Discuss the evolution from clan control to accounting control and accounting's control hierarchy.

"Remember the old adage, 'If you want it done right, do it yourself'? However, as our responsibilities grow, this becomes less practical. With small organizations, the owner can observe processes directly. The Boss used direct observation as a substitute for doing everything himself. He didn't need to rely on hard, verifiable accounting performance measures. Instead, he used soft information. Salary raises were based on his belief about how well each person was increasing firm value."

Clan control

"As organizations grow, direct observation becomes more difficult. What did the Boss do when direct observation wasn't possible any more?" Everyone turned to the Boss's portrait hanging ominously above the head of the boardroom table. They could hear him emphatically say, "Hire family!"

"Clan control involves hiring people who share our values. Many personal characteristics promote it: family, religion, professionalism, culture, common goals [partners], and ethics. We expect shared values in professional service firms [law firms, doctors, etc.], some government entities [schools, city councils], and non-profit groups [Peace Corps, Red Cross]. People in these organizations usually are internally motivated. *When goal congruence comes from within the people, the need for formal accounting control measures is not as important.*"

"This is exactly what I expect from all of our people!! Just as I expect it from my children. I don't have problems with my oldest daughter. I tell her not to be home too late, and she's always home around 8:00. 'Too late' means the same thing to both of us. She knows it's important to me. Sharing my goals and values, I don't need to monitor her performance. I think Julie feels the same way about her son. She doesn't monitor his college budget."

"Clan control was the Boss's primary motivational system. He knew the people and processes. Multreeville was built around the company. Everyone had a common goal. So the Boss did not need to rely on accounting numbers when evaluating performance. The budget was used only for communicating goals and making plans, not as a basis for evaluation by reporting variances.

"This type of 'family' is not restricted to small firms, however. ABB [Asea Brown Boveri], a multinational leader in environmental control systems, robotics, and super-fast trains, requires all managers to learn English as part of its clan control strategy."

Market control

TOMMY

"While common values are one way to assure goal congruence, the marketplace is another. Instead of being motivated internally, competition provides an external motivation. If a competitor can provide our product or service more cheaply than we can, our future is in jeopardy! Thus, many firms are dropping products and services provided more cheaply or better by others. Outsourcing is a primary control in business and government. Governments are outsourcing [privatizing] many services like garbage collection, fire protection, and community programs, as budget pressures force them to reconsider government's role in society. The efficiency of market control also is seen in the movement from regulated services to deregulated competition.

"In your case, Sid, you won't have to monitor when your daughter comes home if a market control exists. For example, the city can have an 8:00 p.m. curfew. If your daughter isn't home on time, she'll be fined!"

Bureaucratic controls

TOMMY

"Of course, market controls do not always exist. As firms grow, clan controls may prove ineffective. So, organizations create bureaucratic controls."

Centralization: rules and regulations. "One way to control a process is with specific rules. Scientific management supports this type of control by dividing processes into smaller activities. Engineers analyze activities and devise rules for the best way to perform them. Then people are trained to follow the rules. McDonald's is a good example. We don't want workers making decisions about how big the hamburger is or how many pickles are on it. To make sure hamburgers are identical, regardless of whether they're made in San Jose or London, supervisors closely monitor the process."

SID

"Yes! I have to impose a rule with my younger daughter. Not coming home 'too late' means something completely different to her! So I replaced soft control information ['Don't be home too late'] with the hard rule, 'I'll pick you up at 8:00 p.m.!'"

TOMMY

"Rupert Murdoch exemplifies centralization, involving himself in decisions across many of his diverse companies. He believes top management cannot truly understand a business unless it becomes involved in day-to-day decisions. It is not unusual to find him writing an editorial for his newspapers, or negotiating a deal to exchange guns for special event tickets through one of his television stations. Similarly, Southwest Airlines' CEO approves all purchases over $1,000."

Decentralization: substituting good judgment for rules. "For many reasons, organizations, especially multinationals, decentralize decision making. Divisional managers are expected to make goal-congruent decisions without top management 'staring over their shoulders.' Decentralization involves replacing specific rules with good judgment whenever flexibility is needed because of local conditions. Johnson & Johnson and Wal-Mart are examples of very successful decentralized companies.

"Many firms centralize some decisions and decentralize others. In multinationals transferring goods or services between international subsidiaries, top management often dictates transfer prices. About 70% of decentralized firms transferring domestically also preset transfer prices. Some believe the mix of decentralization and centralization depends upon the subsidiary's nation. Countries with a more authoritarian society may be better served with a centralized organization [e.g., France, Germany, Italy, and eastern Europe].

"Often the mix is determined by which decisions top management wants to control directly. A common example is investment decisions. Divisions are decentralized for operating decisions but have to obtain approval for capital projects. Many highly decentralized companies now centralize their information systems, such as at Dial."

SID

"Now you're talking about my son! I rely more on his judgment than I do with my younger daughter. All he needs is a rule like, 'Be home by 8:00 p.m.' I see! Until clan control is established, I use rules to control my kids. As their good judgment develops, they have more freedom. I have less need for direct observation and can rely on output controls [don't be home too late, or be home by 8:00 p.m.]. Some day, all I'll have to do is go to bed without worrying, knowing when I arise the kids will be home, the car will be in the garage, and no police will be at the door! This is how I want this business run!"

Accounting control systems

JULIE

"The further we move from do-it-yourself and clan control, the less we may be able to rely on soft information [feelings and beliefs] in evaluating performance. Since organizations need to measure performance as the basis for rewards, direct observation is replaced with formal measures. Management also wants hard information so people cannot argue about its accuracy. So they use accounting numbers."

NANCY

"Oh, this is interesting! You're saying *management accounting information now serves two roles*:

- *Supporting* good judgment and decisions by providing relevant and accurate information, and
- *Motivating* good judgment and decisions because it is used to evaluate performance."

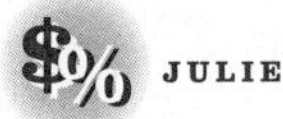

JULIE

How much accounting control do we need? "The question we must answer is, 'How much accounting control is needed?' Many organizations have accounting systems only for external financial reporting. GAAP-based numbers, while hard, may not be relevant for evaluating how well our people are creating value. All control systems probably are imperfect, though. So a mix of controls is needed, which differs in each organization. Even within the same organization, the types of controls change over time."

NANCY

"Yes! I experienced that throughout college. My first undergraduate courses had many formal controls, like homework and daily quizzes. As I progressed, my grades depended more on one or two exams. Smaller class sizes also allowed for better direct observation by the professor. I hear many masters courses don't even have exams! Professors may believe the longer students are in college, the greater their motivation to learn, and the more good judgment they display. The need for detailed, hard control numbers declines and soft evaluation data [e.g., student participation] provide a less expensive, effective control system.

"I guess the characteristics of the people in any organization determine the best mix of controls. When processes are observable and/or good judgment prevails, accounting numbers may not need to be the primary control system." [Exhibit 8-3 summarizes these ideas.]

How Much Accounting Control Do We Need?

Control system	"The contract"	Source of motivation	Role of accounting information in control
Clan control	Be home before it is "too late"	Shared values	Secondary (informal, infrequent direct observation is primary source of control)
Market control	Be home before curfew	External (the police)	Secondary (primary source is external—police ticket)
Bureaucratic rules (centralized)	I'll pick you up at 8:00	Compliance with parental authority	Shared (frequent direct observation, or accounting system when direct observation not practical)
Bureaucratic rules (decentralized)	Be home by 8:00	Good judgment	Primary (accounting system measures the outputs from the black box)

Exhibit 8-3

The accounting control hierarchy. "Accounting control emphasizes the effect on profit and cashflows from the actions people take. Even in a nonprofit firm, the profit/cashflow goal is one of its primary responsibilities [e.g., stay within budget, generate more funds so we can do more]. Usually, we identify three levels of increasing profit responsibility. [See Exhibit 8-4.]

Responsibility Centers Used in Accounting Control Systems

Cost center:	Its budget covers only the costs incurred in it. Cost center activities create costs, such as in a production department, warranty service center, accounting department, or computer information center. Cost variances traditionally have been the primary accounting control measures.
Profit center:	Its budget includes revenues and costs. Profit centers normally are product lines or sales territories, but can be as small as an individual salesperson. A profit center's activities create revenues and incur costs. Sales and cost variances traditionally have been the primary accounting control measures.
Investment center:	Its budget involves investment and profit activities. Investment center activities involve asset purchases that are used to generate profits. Examples include companies or divisions within a corporation. Primary accounting evaluation measures include sales and cost variances, and traditionally have expressed profit in relation to the investment (e.g., return on investment, residual income, and economic value added).

Exhibit 8-4

"Establishing profit-based responsibility centers is very common. About 95% of organizations with formal budgets prepare responsibility center performance reports. Their importance was obvious to Honda Motor Company's new president. One of Nobuhiki Kawamoto's first decisions established product line profit centers. His goal was to separate the less profitable automobile business from the more profitable motorcycle and power equipment lines."

Accounting control measures responsibility in terms of the profit or cash resulting from activities. **Cost centers** *are measured by cost variances.* **Profit center** *reports include cost and sales variances.* **Investment center** *reports compare budgeted and actual profit in terms of the investment made.*

 NANCY

"So far, we've discussed general behavioral issues with motivating our people. *Obviously, how they are evaluated affects their motivation to exercise good judgment.* You've described three levels of profit responsibility. Can we get more specific and look at how accounting control at each level motivates them? Will our accounting control system do what we want it to do?"

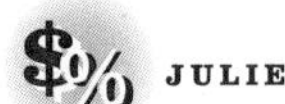 JULIE

"Only if we do it right! We must guard against measuring the wrong things or measuring the right things in the wrong way. Let's start with cost centers."

Standard Setting, Variances, and Cost Center Evaluation

KEY OBJECTIVE 3

Explain three motivational problems with using accounting information in performance evaluation.

 JULIE

"Three behavioral problems may result from a poorly designed accounting control system. We can see many examples by looking at how we evaluate cost centers. Remember, though, these problems also affect profit and investment centers."

Participation and legitimacy

"First, motivation can break down if our people do not trust the accounting system. Trust should result if they believe it is legitimate. Participation does not guarantee legitimacy, but without it, expecting people will embrace the system is naïve.

"A primary accounting control for cost centers is cost variance reports. *Our people can participate in two ways:*

- Through participating in setting budgets [standard prices and quantities], and
- Through identifying why budget-to-actual differences [cost variances] happened.

In our sixth meeting, we discussed two types of standard quantities: ideal and practical. Ideal standard quantities do not include allowances for wasted materials, labor downtime, machine breakdowns, or quality problems. Practical standards include these allowances. Ideal standards usually are not attainable, but practical standards are.

"Using ideal standards, when a machine breaks down a variance results. If the workers cannot control machine maintenance, should they be held responsible for this variance? Workers may become demoralized when they are constantly held accountable for events they cannot control. This motivational problem is avoided with practical standards. Practical standards include an allowance for machine breakdowns, so no variance results."

 TOMMY

"Generals Patton and Montgomery used practical standards to motivate goal congruence in World War II. Both began with spiritless armies. But, through a series of achievable goals, their armies turned into successes." Nancy giggled as she remembered the movie *Stripes* and John Candy as a "lean, mean, fighting machine."

"Allowing workers to participate in setting standards helps to assure these allowances are adequate. It's a check on the engineer's beliefs by the people doing the work. Thus, practical standards are more likely to be accepted as legitimate.

"If practical standard quantities are just a continuation of those used in previous years, though, we're building an organizational culture that accepts [legitimizes] waste. Remember, scientific management already has evaluated the cost and benefits of allowing waste. So, workers may not have any incentive to improve.

"More generally, if management allows this year's budget to be based on last year's [incremental budgeting], will workers improve? Spending less than budget can mean next year's budget will be reduced! Thus we see the all too common 'spend it or lose it' strategy prevalent in the governmental sector. Amazingly, budgeting policies may be encouraging negative behavior!

"Participation also may introduce slack into standard quantities. Slack is adding even more allowances for loss. For example, instead of budgeting 1 hour for downtime, workers may want 1½ hours. The motivation for slack can be good or bad. It's bad if the real reason is to make getting rewards easier. If people are motivated to do as little as possible, slack allows this 'satisficing' behavior. On the good side, slack hedges against uncertainty."

NANCY

"I did this in college! How many three credit courses turn out to be six credits worth of work? By enrolling for less courses, I was budgeting slack into my schedule. Of course, it meant I was on the '10-year plan' for an undergraduate degree!"

JULIE

"Slack may be necessary because many uncertainties exist. Systems problems abound [machine breakdowns, material shortages, WIP quality problems], people are not properly trained, or they are asked to do something different than planned. Multinationals have unique uncertainties due to the political, cultural, and economic differences . . ."

NANCY

"Let's see if I understand. *Participation supports legitimacy*. Usually it results in good practical standard quantities to use in cost variances. Because people believe practical standards can be attained, they are better motivated to achieve the company's budget goals. However, budget games, like trying to get too much slack, may result if people are motivated to do less rather than more."

Who's responsible?

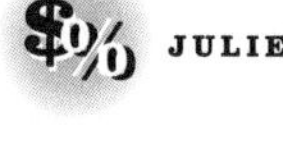

JULIE

"Not participating in setting standards was our first motivational problem with using accounting information in performance evaluation. The second problem is assigning responsibility for the variances. Historically, accountants believed variances occurring in a department are its responsibility. Scientific management supports this because it designs departments to be independent functional silos."

TOMMY

"Here's how cost variance reports are too often used in performance evaluation. Because the financial accounting system 'books' are closed each month to produce an income statement, monthly variance reports also are prepared. Each department manager receives her variances. If the reasons for the variances are not known, top management sends down the accountant. If a manager can't provide the reasons, she has to interrupt workers and ask them who remembers what happened last month. If a variance was caused in a preceding department, the accountant has to go there and verify it. Of course, that manager will have to investigate this 'bad news' surprise. Too often, the managers appeal responsibility for unfavorable variances back and forth, resulting in bad feelings toward each other. Top management becomes unhappy because of all the infighting. Workers don't want to communicate and cooperate, and ultimately, the motivation for teamwork [being part of the family] breaks down. Our workers don't understand why we allow this to happen."

"And this is why operating personnel think of accountants as the 'cop on the block.' They see me only when something is wrong and they're going to be held responsible for it! I really hate that part of my job."

"Now wait a minute. Let's not get defensive about cost variances. It's the accounting system's role to report where variances occurred. Then management acts, calling for an investigation if needed. This is management by exception. It's just another example of how scientific management isolates different activities [accounting is a functional silo separate from management]. How can we investigate a variance until after we discover it happened? And until we investigate, how do we know who's responsible? You people just need to understand if you don't create any variances, we won't have any of these investigation problems!"

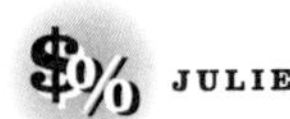

"STOP! Maybe we shouldn't rely on a monthly financial accounting system to run our business. *We can have a real-time information system for variance analysis.* When a problem occurs, the workers [not top management] are in the best position to identify why it is happening. If the problem is caused by something that happened in another department, those workers should be involved in fixing it. Many Japanese firms use visual control systems to fix problems, called 'andon.' The Saturn plant has an andon cord any worker can pull when a problem is discovered. Pulling the cord stops the entire production line, and people run to the problem in order to fix it and get production going again.

"Thus, the responsibility for the variance can be determined and agreed upon in real-time as the problem happens. This information can be input into the accounting system noting it has been fixed. This increases investigation efficiency. It also increases the effectiveness of the accounting system in performance evaluation by providing the relevant information we need. Ditch Witch, a world leader in trenching equipment, and CCSSCo, a Los Angeles sandwich company, did this. Ditch Witch did it to solve quality problems. CCSSCo's motivation was to improve processes through an operational audit."

"I don't understand. If Framing Department workers spend too much time framing a house, the unfavorable labor usage variance is their responsibility."

"Very few production systems have truly independent processes, whether making houses, providing medical treatments, preparing tax returns, or running a city government. What if the unfavorable Framing labor variance happened because lumber was warped, or cut to the wrong length? Are you going to penalize Framing personnel in their performance evaluations? Think back to our variance reporting meeting [Chapter 6]. Roof panel prices increased $2, causing an unfavorable direct material spending variance, which was charged to Purchasing. Two variances resulted in the Sawing Department because of this, and numerous variances happened the next month in Assembly. One variance can cause many other variances 'down the line,' both in that month and succeeding months! *Just because a variance occurs in one department does not mean it was caused by that department. Without knowing why variances resulted, we ethically cannot use them in performance evaluation.*"

What gets measured gets done

"Also look at our February variance report [Exhibit 6-2]. It shows no variable overhead variance. But when we drilled down into the 'black box' we discovered a $2,060 unfavorable usage variance [Exhibit 6-8]. Knowing about this variance, and being motivated not to have unfavorable variances, the manager canceled machine maintenance and employee training to create an offsetting favorable spending variance [see Exhibit 6-7]. Are we correctly using our accounting system? Are we promoting decisions leading to long-run value? It seems we're telling our people, 'Hey, only one factor is important in your evaluations, don't have any unfavorable variances.' Is this ethical?"

JULIE

"Well, maybe not. *An overemphasis on one measure will focus people on it.* Maximizing short-run profit [avoiding cost variances] at the expense of long-run value is not good judgment. This is the third motivational problem with using accounting information in performance evaluation."

"I thought good judgment is goal-congruent decision making. Our evaluation system is simple: If you want bonuses, raises, or promotions, don't have any unfavorable variances. By doing whatever it takes to avoid variances, our people are doing what we want . . . Oh! The problem is not with the accounting system, it's with us! *We're communicating the wrong information about what we want!* We don't want them inappropriately creating a favorable variance that hurts long-term value. I guess we're measuring the right things, but in the wrong way!"

"Our production manager canceling machine maintenance and employee training is not an uncommon reaction. In 1994, a USAir maintenance manager placed an airplane in use even though its warning system didn't work, just to save money." USAir was losing $2 million per day at the time. Five major crashes occurred between 1989 and 1994. Hopefully, the accounting system and how it was used did not contribute to any of these disasters!

"If I may summarize,

- Our people should participate in setting standards and determining their performance measures [feedforward information].
- The measures should be tied to our strategic plan and budget.
- The measures should be achievable.
- We should provide frequent feedback [hourly, daily, weekly, or whenever appropriate].
- By using the same measures in evaluation, performance reports will not contain any negative surprises."

Segmented Income Statements and Profit Center Evaluation

JULIE

"Now, lets look at profit centers. To evaluate them, our income statement is divided into profit center 'segments.' For example, I'll segment Multree's income statement into two profit centers, one for each product line. Another common way to segment is by sales territories. Often, income statements are first segmented by product line, and then each line is further segmented into territories. Territories then can be segmented again into sales offices. Each sales office also can be segmented into individual salespeople. In other words, we can keep dividing the income statement into smaller and smaller segments. These **segmented income statements** are used to evaluate profit centers and their managers." [Exhibit 8-5 is Multree's proforma income statement segmented into product lines.]

A **segmented income statement** *includes "mini-income statements" for each profit center.*

Segment profitability and common cost allocations: controllability versus GAAP

JACKIE

"This is our financial accounting system income statement using absorption costing. Cost of goods sold is based on the standard absorptive manufacturing cost

Multree Homes Proforma Income Statement

	STANDARD HOMES			CUSTOM HOMES			COMPANY TOTALS	
	Per unit	%	Totals @ 100	Per unit	%	Totals @ 10	%	Totals
Revenues	$50,000	100%	$5,000,000	$100,000	100%	$1,000,000	100%	$6,000,000
Less: cost of goods sold	(30,240)	(60%)	(3,024,000)	(63,100)	(63%)	(631,000)	(61%)	(3,655,000)
Gross profit	**$19,760**	**40%**	**$1,976,000**	**$36,900**	**37%**	**$369,000**	**39%**	**$2,345,000**
Less: expenses								
Advertising	542	1%	54,167	1,083	1%	10,833	1%	65,000
Sales commissions	2,333	5%	233,333	4,667	5%	46,667	5%	280,000
Administration	8,333	17%	833,333	16,667	17%	166,667	17%	1,000,000
Totals	(11,208)	(22%)	(1,120,833)	(22,417)	(22%)	(224,167)	(22%)	(1,345,000)
Net income	$8,552	17%	$855,167	$14,483	14%	$144,833	17%	$1,000,000

Notes: Cost of goods sold is the standard absorptive manufacturing cost for each product. All expenses are allocated using relative sales revenues. All numbers are formatted to whole amounts. Per unit expenses are averages.

Exhibit 8-5

[from Exhibit 6-5]. Expenses are allocated to each profit center based on the product line's relative sales. Since standard homes provide 5/6 of total revenues [$5 million of $6 million], this segment is allocated 5/6 of each expense. The custom homes line is allocated 1/6 of the expenses because it provides 1/6 of total revenues. This is called an 'ability to bear' allocation method. Its logic is the more revenues a segment creates, the greater its ability to bear the company's expenses, and larger segments probably use more of these activities so they should be charged more than smaller segments."

TOMMY

"Our managers really don't like this way of allocating expenses because they don't have any control over the administration costs. They also don't like the way their net income changes if the *other* product line's sales change! Let me show you. What happens to custom homes net income if standard homes sales drop to $4 million? Custom homes will now provide 20% of total revenues [$1 million ÷ $5 million], so custom homes will be allocated 20% of each expense, instead of the 17% [1/6] it is now allocated [in Exhibit 8-5]. The custom homes manager, by doing absolutely nothing different, is charged more costs and her net income goes down."

NANCY

"Let's see if I understand. Using this income statement to evaluate our product line managers, the custom homes manager will be punished for something she did not do! While this violates our controllability rule in performance evaluation, it does satisfy GAAP. We know product lines cause these common costs. We just don't know how to allocate them in a better way, like based on cause and effect."

JACKIE

"You're right. While holding the segment managers responsible for them may not be correct, good reasons exist for allocating overall company costs. Think about administration expenses. These include activities like payroll and computer information systems [often called 'corporate overhead' or 'common costs']. The company provides these services to profit centers because it's cheaper than having the profit centers doing them [or cheaper than outsourcing]. Without a centralized accounting department, for example, each profit center would have to maintain its own accounting department. Because segments use these services, they should be charged for them. Fireman's Fund uses allocations to set insurance premiums. Since each type of insurance uses corporate overhead, its premium [sales price] should recover its total costs, which should include a corporate overhead allocation. Also, by allocating corporate services, segment managers may be motivated to pressure better cost control of these services. The better services control their costs, the lower their allocation will be to the profit centers.

"Common cost allocations also are required for rate setting in regulated industries. Hospitals have specific allocation rules for Medicare and insurance reimbursements. Similarly, governmental contractors must follow detailed federal allocation rules for government cost-plus contract billings. Of course, we have to be careful in following all the different rules. Stanford University was embarrassed to discover it had charged federal research contracts for a yacht and the president's home furniture, among other things!

"Multinationals also have interesting allocation problems. To illustrate, if a certain percentage of a product's cost [62.5% for cars] comes from NAFTA member countries, the product gets special tariff treatment. With parts made all over the world, how much of a car's cost really comes from member countries? NAFTA includes common cost allocations in the product's cost. Thus, many parts originating in member countries get allocated common costs through international transfer prices. Increasing the cost of parts from member countries makes it easier to receive special tariff treatment."

“I agree with you! Services provided to profit centers somehow should be charged to them. As with allocating manufacturing overhead to products, these charges should be based on a cause-effect relationship. In other words, we need to identify the real cost drivers for these services. It may not be correct to allocate service costs with relative sales ratios [the 5/6 and 1/6 for standard and custom homes]. Ethically, activities in one profit center should not change costs allocated to other profit centers. Sadly, though, about 60% of segmented firms do not allocate common costs with cost drivers representing how the segments use those corporate services.

JULIE

“A 1998 IMA survey reported some interesting statistics. 60% of the surveyed firms charge operating segments for corporate services [40% charge for specific services based on the amount used and 60% use a standard charge]. Of those allocating specific services, 20% used a transfer price including some profit. And here's some interesting statistics on companies allocating corporate services based on sales.”

% of firms allocating common costs based on sales	Allocation amounts as a percentage of sales
10%	> 10%
25%	5% to 10%
50%	1% to 5%
15%	< 1%

Evaluation and motivation: does GAAP motivate long-run value?

TOMMY

“We have another motivational problem with segments ‘absorbing’ all costs. We just addressed problems with corporate overhead allocations to profit centers. Now let's look at fixed manufacturing overhead allocations to products. Because fixed overhead is included in the product's cost, it is part of cost of goods sold. The amount of fixed overhead in cost of goods sold affects the segment's gross profit and net income. To understand how allocating fixed overhead affects motivation, I'll start with a question. Why is the average product cost lower when production volume is higher?”

NANCY

“Because we use absorption costing and most of our overhead costs are fixed. But why is this relevant to motivating profit center managers?”

JULIE

Absorption costing, motivation, and ethics. “How does absorption costing affect motivation? Look here [Exhibit 8-6]. This information comes from our standard cost card [Exhibit 6-5]. Since we're planning on making 100 standard homes, the average fixed overhead cost per house is $2,680 [$268,000 ÷ 100 houses in the ‘100 homes’ column]. Absorption costing includes this in the product's cost.

“We have the capacity to make 150 homes, though. Maximizing output, the average fixed overhead drops to $1,787 [$268,000 ÷ 150 houses in the ‘150 homes’ column]. The more homes we make, the lower the average fixed cost per home.

“If we make and sell 100 homes, all $268,000 of the fixed overhead appears on the income statement [as shown in the bottom half of Exhibit 8-6, ‘100 homes built’ column]. What happens if we make 150 homes, but sell only 100? Since we allocate fixed overhead to each house, and 50 are not sold, 50 houses worth of fixed overhead do not appear on the income statement. These 50 unsold houses are ending finished goods inventory [an asset on the balance sheet]. These 50 homes move

Absorption Costing's Effect on Financial Statements and Performance Evaluation—Multree's Standard Homes Product Line

Manufacturing resources	Budgeted costs		Average absorptive manufacturing cost @ production volumes of:			
			100 homes		150 homes	
Variable production costs	$27,560	per house	$27,560	per house	$27,560	per house
Fixed manufacturing overhead	$268,000	per year	2,680	per house	1,787	per house
Standard absorptive manufacturing cost			$30,240	per house	$29,347	per house

Where is the fixed overhead cost if sales =		*100 homes?*			100 homes built	150 homes built
Fixed overhead on income statement in cost of goods sold:						
$2,680	per house x	100	homes	=	$268,000	
$1,787	per house x	100	homes	=		$178,667
Fixed overhead on balance sheet in finished goods inventory:						
$2,680	per house x	0	homes	=	0	
$1,787	per house x	50	homes	=		89,333
Total fixed overhead					$268,000	$268,000

Note: Average fixed overhead per house is formatted to whole numbers.

Exhibit 8-6

$89,333 of fixed overhead from the income statement to the balance sheet. On the income statement, cost of goods sold is $89,333 lower. Thus, profits are that much higher.

"To avoid this problem, we can use 'variable costing' [sometimes called 'direct costing']. All $268,000 of fixed overhead is deducted in calculating net income, regardless of the number of houses made. Fixed overhead is not included in the predetermined overhead rate, or the product's cost. Basically, the contribution margin income statement does this by including fixed overhead with the other fixed costs [Exhibit 8-7 highlights this].

"Look at the 'Make 100, Sell 100' columns of each income statement. When sales and production volumes are equal, the two income statements show the same profit because all fixed overhead appears in both. When sales and production volumes differ, absorption costing allocates fixed overhead between the income statement [sold products] and the balance sheet [unsold products]. We just saw $89,333 of fixed overhead moving to the balance sheet [in Exhibit 8-6]. The income statements [in Exhibit 8-7] verify absorptive costing-based profit goes up $89,333 because of this. Look at the 'Make 150, Sell 100' columns."

NANCY

"Do we want production volume changes to change net income, *even though sales don't change*? This is what absorption costing does. *We shouldn't be maximizing output if we can't sell it, just to manipulate our performance measures [segment income]*."

JULIE

"Champion International, a major U.S. paper manufacturer, suffered from this problem. A paper-making machine costs hundreds of millions of dollars. Basing performance evaluations on absorptive cost motivated managers to run these machines all the time. However, sales are seasonal and paper prices radically change during different seasons. Even if sales prices were not high enough to create a profit, paper still would be made and stockpiled in order to minimize the average cost. Finally, Champion had to abandon absorption costing. Interestingly, Canada and the United Kingdom allow variable costing for external reporting. Northern Telecom, the Canadian telecommunications equipment manufacturer, developed a contribution margin format with a bottom line adjustment also reporting absorption-based profit."

TOMMY

"We also should consider how absorption costing affects our customers' perception of us. Sometimes, firms can blindly allocate too many activities in too much detail, resulting in some crazy prices not supported by the marketplace. For example, I don't like our hospital because it allocates costs and charges a profit on materials used. I just received my hospital bill for a minor outpatient treatment. The hospital charged me $7.00 for an aspirin! Well, I know the cost accountant and got him to do some research. The aspirin's purchase cost was only 0.6¢. However, it was ordered by a doctor [allocate 50¢], inventoried by a pharmacist [allocate 60¢], and served by a nurse in a paper cup [11¢]. Then add 20¢ for record keeping and $2.08 for bad debts, malpractice insurance, and other overhead. The aspirin's full absorptive cost became $3.50. The hospital wants a 100% profit [markup] on cost, so another $3.50 was added, bringing my charge to $7.00!"

NANCY

"This really bothers me, too! My dune buggy just had a tuneup. The auto mechanic charged me $2.50 for the same spark plugs I can buy at Kmart for $1.00. Granted, all of her costs must be recovered in sales prices before any profit is made. But as a customer, I really hate burying these costs in the 'cost of a spark plug.' At least list the overhead charge and profit separately. I can understand and accept that! How ethical is it to allocate overhead *and profit* into the cost of parts and materials if it radically miscosts the materials and hurts customer relations? When I think about our competition and our position on the industry's value chain, is it

Comparing Income Statement Formats

Financial accounting uses a functional, absorption costing income statement

	Make 100 Sell 100	Make 150 Sell 100
Revenues	$5,000,000	$5,000,000
Less: cost of goods sold		
Variable manufacturing costs	2,756,000	2,756,000
Fixed overhead	268,000	178,667
Total COGS	(3,024,000)	(2,934,667)
Gross profit	$1,976,000	$2,065,333

Management accounting uses a contribution margin income statement*

	Make 100 Sell 100	Make 150 Sell 100
Revenues	$5,000,000	$5,000,000
Less: variable manufacturing costs	(2,756,000)	(2,756,000)
Contribution margin	2,244,000	2,244,000
Less: fixed overhead	(268,000)	(268,000)
Gross profit	$1,976,000	$1,976,000

Difference in profit *$89,333*

**Note:* Only the manufacturing costs are included to focus on the different accounting for fixed overhead.

Exhibit 8-7

possible our cost allocation methods actually hurt our ability to create long-run value and differentiate ourselves from our competition?"

KEY OBJECTIVE 4

Prepare a segmented income statement and explain its usefulness in evaluating segments and managers.

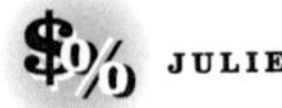

Segmenting the contribution margin-based income statement. "Cost allocations make it difficult to determine a segment's real profit. By affecting the segment's reported profit, allocations also affect the manager's motivation to improve firm value. Reported income can be manipulated by simply changing inventory levels. Maybe we shouldn't make these allocations! We use the contribution margin income statement for planning and control because it supports cost-volume-profit [CVP] analysis. We also can use it to report profit center income and evaluate segment managers in the absence of allocated fixed overhead and operating expenses [see Exhibit 8-8].

"Tommy complained about allocating fixed overhead and administration costs to each segment because they are not controllable by the segment managers. If these costs cannot be traced directly to the segments, we won't allocate them. When we segment the income statement, the common fixed costs will be reported only in the 'Company Totals' column. They include two of the fixed overhead costs [depreciation, heat and light] and the administration costs. The other two fixed overhead costs [architectural and supervision] can be traced directly to each product line, though. They will be classified as 'direct' fixed costs of the segments. Each product line also has its own advertising budget. This, too, is a direct fixed cost.

"Calculating the contribution margin for each segment and then subtracting its direct fixed costs results in a mini-income statement. The segment's profit, called the **segment margin**, reports the profit directly contributed to the overall firm. Since we are segmenting by product line, I labeled the segment margins as 'product line margins.' For budgeting and performance evaluation, segment margins provide a better measure of the profit each segment generates than do the net incomes reported for each segment in the financial accounting method [Exhibit 8-5 format]. Standard homes contribute $1,840,000 [and custom homes $185,000], which is used first to pay the $1,025,000 in common company costs. The remainder is Multree profit."

The profit contributed directly by a segment is called its **segment margin**. *The sum of all segment margins is used to pay for the company's common costs, with anything left over being profit.*

"Hold on a minute. How will our managers react if segment margins are used to evaluate their performance? Can we hold them accountable for all their direct costs? For example, the standard homes product line manager doesn't have the power to control his own salary! If he did, I wonder how large it would be!"

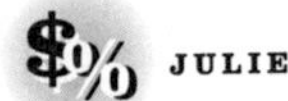

"You're right, Tommy. However, he does control his advertising budget and architectural costs. We also assume all variable costs [and, thus, his segment's contribution margin] are under his control. All we have to do is modify the income statement format a little to convey this information [see Exhibit 8-9 on p. 281].

"By separating a segment's controllable and uncontrollable direct fixed costs, a new subtotal is reported. The **controllable segment margin** is the segment's profit resulting from the manager's decisions [the activities she controls]. When evaluating the manager's performance, use profit variances only from the line items through controllable segment margin. Here are the salient points for preparing this income statement:

Controllable segment margin *reports the profit resulting from activities under the segment manager's control.*

- First, fixed costs are separated into those traceable directly to each segment versus those common to all segments.
- Second, within each segment, separate controllable from uncontrollable direct fixed costs.

Multree Homes Proforma Income Statement

	STANDARD HOMES			CUSTOM HOMES			COMPANY TOTALS	
	Per unit	%	Totals @ 100	Per unit	%	Totals @ 10	%	Totals
Revenues	$50,000	100%	$5,000,000	$100,000	100%	$1,000,000	100%	$6,000,000
Less: variable costs								
Direct materials	15,500	31%	1,550,000	26,250	26%	262,500	30%	1,812,500
Direct labor	10,000	20%	1,000,000	25,000	25%	250,000	21%	1,250,000
Indirect materials	1,000	2%	100,000	1,500	2%	15,000	2%	115,000
Indirect labor	500	1%	50,000	3,000	3%	30,000	1%	80,000
Power	500	1%	50,000	1,250	1%	12,500	1%	62,500
Sales commissions	2,500	5%	250,000	3,000	3%	30,000	5%	280,000
Totals	(30,000)	(60%)	(3,000,000)	(60,000)	(60%)	(600,000)	(60%)	(3,600,000)
Contribution margin	$20,000	40%	$2,000,000	$40,000	40%	$400,000	40%	$2,400,000
Less: direct fixed costs								
Advertising			50,000			15,000		65,000
Architectural costs			10,000			100,000		110,000
Supervision			100,000			100,000		200,000
Totals			(160,000)			(215,000)		(375,000)
Product line margin			$1,840,000			$185,000		$2,025,000
Less: common fixed costs								
Depreciation								15,000
Heat & light								10,000
Administration								1,000,000
Total								(1,025,000)
Net income								$1,000,000

Exhibit 8-8

Multree Homes Proforma Income Statement

	STANDARD HOMES			CUSTOM HOMES			COMPANY TOTALS	
	Per unit	%	Totals @ 100	Per unit	%	Totals @ 10	%	Totals
Revenues	$50,000	100%	$5,000,000	$100,000	100%	$1,000,000	100%	$6,000,000
Less: variable costs								
Direct materials	15,500	31%	1,550,000	26,250	26%	262,500	30%	1,812,500
Direct labor	10,000	20%	1,000,000	25,000	25%	250,000	21%	1,250,000
Indirect materials	1,000	2%	100,000	1,500	2%	15,000	2%	115,000
Indirect labor	500	1%	50,000	3,000	3%	30,000	1%	80,000
Power	500	1%	50,000	1,250	1%	12,500	1%	62,500
Sales commissions	2,500	5%	250,000	3,000	3%	30,000	5%	280,000
Totals	(30,000)	(60%)	(3,000,000)	(60,000)	(60%)	(600,000)	(60%)	(3,600,000)
Contribution margin	**$20,000**	**40%**	**$2,000,000**	**$40,000**	**40%**	**$400,000**	**40%**	**$2,400,000**
Less: controllable direct fixed costs								
Advertising			50,000			15,000		65,000
Architectural costs			10,000			100,000		110,000
Totals			(60,000)			(115,000)		(175,000)
Controllable segment margin			**$1,940,000**			**$285,000**		**$2,225,000**
Less: uncontrollable direct fixed costs								
Supervision			100,000			100,000		200,000
Totals			(100,000)			(100,000)		(200,000)
Segment margin			**$1,840,000**			**$185,000**		**$2,025,000**
Less: common fixed costs								
Depreciation								15,000
Heat & light								10,000
Administration								1,000,000
Totals								(1,025,000)
Net income								**$1,000,000**

Exhibit 8-9

- Third, to calculate controllable segment margin for each segment, subtract the controllable direct fixed costs from contribution margin.
- Finally, subtract the uncontrollable direct fixed costs from the controllable segment margin to compute the segment margin.

What do we use these segment subtotals for?

- *Use segment margin to measure a segment's direct profitability.*
- *Use profit variances through controllable segment margin to evaluate the segment manager's performance."*

Dropping a segment

SID

"While the segmented contribution margin income statement supports evaluation, it still does not provide all the information needed for all decisions. For example, should we stop making custom homes? Can't we use this capacity more profitably?"

BILL

"Not in our case! Remember, the Boss started the custom homes line because it is very profitable and generates more standard home sales. Many potential customers are drawn by our custom home brochures, but end up buying standard homes."

NANCY

"I agree. Look at the custom homes segment margin. If we drop this line, our company profits will go down $185,000."

JULIE

"Well, maybe. *While segment margin tells us the profit generated by a segment, it does not tell us exactly which costs will be eliminated by dropping a product line. Adding or dropping a segment may involve other relevant costs and externalities not reflected in the income statement.* For example, we spend $100,000 a year on custom home supervision. Will we fire these people if custom homes are dropped, or will we keep them and move them to different jobs? My point is not all of a segment's direct costs are relevant to a different decision situation [e.g., dropping a segment versus measuring its profitability]. Segment margins may not reflect long-run value.

Segmented contribution margin income statements support evaluation, but they do not always present all the relevant information needed for other types of decisions, such as a strategic add-drop decision.

"Also consider the common fixed costs. I don't expect depreciation or heat and light will change if we drop custom homes. The equipment and factory building are shared by both segments. We won't dispose of any equipment or reduce the size of the factory building, so these costs will not change [and, therefore, are not relevant costs between the two alternatives of keep the line or drop it]. Administrative costs will change if we drop the line, though. About 75% of Purchasing's activities involve custom homes. I expect declines in other corporate services, too, like accounting."

BILL

"How about other relevant revenues and costs not obvious from just looking at the segment margin? For example, what effect will dropping custom homes have on standard homes sales? In the gaming industry, casinos lose money on drinks and food [free drinks to gamblers and very inexpensive buffets]. Should these lines be dropped? Of course not! They bring in gambling business. Another consideration is how we can use the extra capacity resulting from dropping a segment. Could we use it to sell windows, for example?

"Can we identify any relevant externalities? Do we need to maintain a product line for image recognition, or because of competition? Will dropping a line hurt the community? Will adding or dropping a line adversely affect the environment?"

JULIE

"Our income statement is not designed to report all the relevant items for what is normally called an 'add-drop' decision. This is a special strategic decision requiring a special accounting analysis. However, some income statements report the profit effect from dropping a line. Amtrak and the Canadian passenger-rail system routinely report the costs saved by abandoning routes so their governments can consider this in rate-setting and route-abandoning decisions. Usually, though, we have to modify the income statement to report this information."

Transfer pricing and the motivation to transfer

"I'm still bothered because the contribution margin income statement appears to treat segments as independent operations. In our last meeting, we considered turning the Windows Department into a profit center and selling windows to other builders. If Assembly wants windows, it can buy them from the Window Department. However, will the managers want to transfer? When two segments buy and sell between themselves, both segments' profits are affected. The transfer price is a cost to the buyer and sales price to the seller. Since the transfer price will affect the reported profit and evaluation of each manager, it will also affect their motivation to transfer. Is it possible the transfer price may motivate them not to transfer when they should?"

"Well, they shouldn't have a choice! Windows should be supplied to Assembly and Multree homes should be made first, before any windows are sold to others!"

"So, we can use a rule-based control system, but Windows will not be a profit center because the manager cannot make the transfer decision."

"Then why do multinationals require transfers between international subsidiaries? And why are the transfer prices set by corporate headquarters?"

"Multinationals use transfer pricing for special reasons: minimizing income taxes and tariffs, moving money out of foreign subsidiaries, and the like. Requiring transfers and/or presetting the transfer price replaces decentralized decision making with centralized rules. Since the decisions to transfer and to set the price are no longer controllable by the managers, we should not include any of the transfer's profit in their controllable segment margins. If we don't distinguish the uncontrollable transfer profit from profit on external [normal, controllable] sales, the evaluation system's legitimacy is compromised, which may adversely affect the managers' motivation to exercise good judgment. So we should segment international subsidiaries into internal sales [transfers] and external sales [to companies not part of the overall organization]. Then transfers and external sales can be evaluated using the control system we've established for each one."

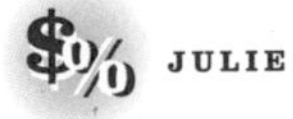

"Bell Communications Research [Bellcore] set up corporate service departments as profit centers, and these departments determined their transfer prices. Other profit centers then decided if they wanted to use ['buy'] these services, such as word processing, secretarial support, graphics, and publishing. Because the transfer prices were so high, though, departments did the work themselves or outsourced it. A lot of money was wasted because the corporate services were not being used. So in some situations we see a justification for requiring transfers and presetting the transfer price."

"Only when the managers are free to decide both (a) whether to transfer and (b) the transfer price, can we hold them responsible for these decisions and the resulting profits appearing in their segment margins."

"Fortunately, we already provide them with the relevant information for both decisions. Look at the transfer pricing worksheet from our last meeting. [Exhibit 7-9 is reproduced here as Exhibit 8-10. Exhibit 7-8 provides the background information.]

"Windows and Assembly know they should transfer whenever the ceiling price is greater than the floor price. Multree benefits by $35 per window if Windows has

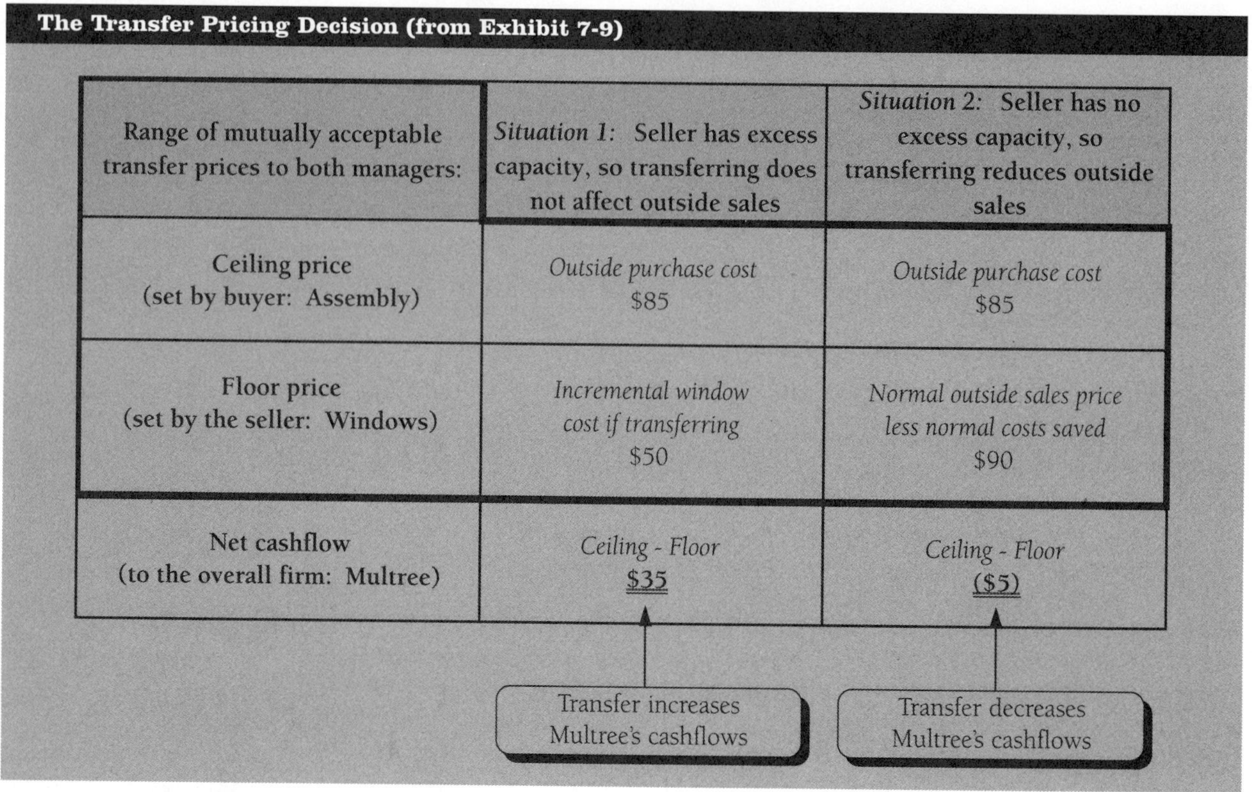

The Transfer Pricing Decision (from Exhibit 7-9)

Range of mutually acceptable transfer prices to both managers:	*Situation 1:* Seller has excess capacity, so transferring does not affect outside sales	*Situation 2:* Seller has no excess capacity, so transferring reduces outside sales
Ceiling price (set by buyer: Assembly)	*Outside purchase cost* $85	*Outside purchase cost* $85
Floor price (set by the seller: Windows)	*Incremental window cost if transferring* $50	*Normal outside sales price less normal costs saved* $90
Net cashflow (to the overall firm: Multree)	*Ceiling - Floor* $35	*Ceiling - Floor* ($5)

Exhibit 8-10

surplus capacity and transfers. If Windows does not have any surplus capacity, no transfer should happen [transferring will cost Multree $5 per window]. In this situation, they should transfer only when Windows has surplus capacity.

"The transfer price determines how much of the $35 extra cashflow appears in each segment margin. For example, if the transfer price is $85 [the ceiling], all of the $35 appears in Windows' segment margin as extra profit. It sells a window to Assembly for $85. Since it costs $50, Windows' profit is $35. Assembly sees none of the transfer's extra cashflow in its segment margin. Whether it buys from someone else for $85, or from Windows for $85, Assembly's cost of a window is the same.

"What if the transfer price is $50? All of the $35 appears as Assembly's profit. Instead of paying $85, it gets a window for $50. Saving $35, Assembly's profit goes up $35. Windows sells at its break-even price [sales price = $50, cost = $50]. *My point is the transfer price is a profit-sharing rule between the two segments.*

"While either the floor or ceiling could be accepted by both managers, realistically they won't agree to either one. If the price is set at the ceiling, all the profit is in Windows. That manager will get rewarded. The Assembly manager has no extra profit and gets no extra reward. Therefore, the Assembly manager [the buyer] will not accept the ceiling price. [Why should I make a decision creating extra profit for Multree when someone else will get all the recognition and reward, and I get nothing?]

"What if the transfer price is the floor? All of the profits are in Assembly, and that manager gets rewarded. Since none of the profit created by their joint decision to transfer appears in Windows' segment, that manager [the seller] will not accept the floor price.

"However, they can agree to any price between the ceiling and floor. This is why I call it the 'range of mutually acceptable transfer prices.' Once they know to transfer, all they have to do is agree on how to share the profit they have created."

"Are you telling me the two managers may decide not to transfer even though they know they should, simply because they may not be able to agree on how to share the profit [i.e., what the transfer price should be]?"

"Yes, accounting theorists argue this is a potential 'cost' of decentralization. If we let them make decisions, we have to accept the possibility of some bad decisions!"

"I hire people to exercise good judgment. Not transferring when they should is wrong. If I hear about it, they're fired!"

"Well, maybe we can avoid that by presetting the transfer price at the midpoint. That seems fair. Each participated equally in the decision and each gets one-half of the profit. Transfer pricing seems simple!"

"If we do that, are transfer profits reported in each segment controllable by its manager? How do we evaluate and reward them? Transfer pricing is complex and poses many ethical issues for the management accountant."

"I disagree with you, Julie, and I agree with Nancy. Transfer pricing is simple. Given the relevant information, managers know if they should transfer. They also know the range of mutually acceptable prices when negotiating the transfer price. I don't reward people for coming to work on time and just doing their job! Profit center managers shouldn't be rewarded for making such a simple and expected decision!"

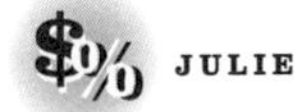

"O.K., Sid. But realize you've changed how we reward them. Profit center managers *were* rewarded based on how much profit each segment generates, which included profits from transfers. Now you don't want to include part of that profit [from transferring] in figuring their rewards. *Deciding when to transfer is relatively simple, but the correct transfer price depends on how we reward them.* So the accounting system supports how you *now* want to evaluate and reward them, I'll segment each profit center into internal [transfers] and external sales. We can continue to evaluate them on their profit from regular sales, without it being mixed up with transfer profits."

"I can think of many different ways to reward managers for increasing Multree's profit by transferring. Each may require a different transfer price in order to correctly motivate and evaluate the managers."

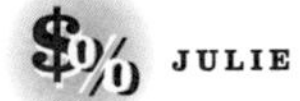

"I can, too. Based on our discussion so far, *I suggest the following transfer prices*:

- *If we require a subsidiary to transfer* everything it makes to another segment, it's a cost center. So, *transfer at standard cost*. We want the supplying manager to control quality, delivery, and cost. We expect the final product [a house] to cover all fixed costs, including the Windows Department fixed costs.

- If the subsidiary is required to transfer, but *it can use its surplus capacity to sell to other builders, deduct the standard cost of transferred windows from the cost of the windows sold to other builders*. Windows' segment margin will report the profit from outside sales. Because transfers are required, we expect the home's sales price to cover all fixed costs. Transferring at standard cost accomplishes this goal.

- *If the subsidiary is a real profit center, segment transfers from outside sales. The correct transfer price depends on how we reward the managers* for transferring when they should. We can preset the transfer price if we have a rule for how they should share the reward. For example, if they will be equally rewarded, set the transfer price at the midpoint of the range of mutually acceptable transfer prices. With no reward for transferring, set it at the ceiling. If we want them to determine how much reward each receives, they will have to negotiate a transfer price.

"I know you want to see more details on how the transfer prices support good judgment and create valid variances for performance evaluation in each of these situations. Because this will take some time, I suggest we save this discussion for a different meeting [i.e., an intermediate management accounting course] and turn our attention to investment centers for the rest of this meeting."

Evaluating Investment Centers

KEY OBJECTIVE 5

Compute ROI and residual income, and explain their motivational implications.

JULIE

"In addition to profit-making decisions, investment center managers make asset investment decisions. Even nonprofits and governments have profit and investment centers, like the sports program at our university, or its Foundation [fund-raising segment]. The Canadian postal service [Canada Post] purchased Purolator Canada Limited [a courier service] and operates it as an investment center. To evaluate investment centers, let's measure segment margin in terms of our investment in the segment."

Return on investment

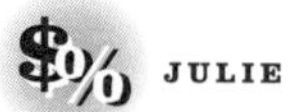
JULIE

"Investing in a segment is like putting money in a savings account. The interest rate is the profit you earn on that investment. This is called **return on investment [ROI]**. Simply, it's profit divided by investment. However, for performance evaluation, we break down ROI into two ratios: **profit margin** and **asset turnover**. DuPont developed ROI as a way to evaluate its many investment centers in the early 20th century. It also was embraced by General Motors a few years later when DuPont's CFO was hired by Alfred Sloan after he took over GM. Actually, the DuPont method is far more complicated than these two ratios. It's an integrated evaluation system for drilling down from ROI through profit margin and asset turnover to specific profit variances and budgets. I'll show you this 'pyramid of accounting control measures' later [in Exhibit 8-14]. Right now, let's focus on Multree's ROI [Exhibit 8-11].

Return on investment (ROI) *is the profit earned on money invested, expressed as a ratio of profit to the investment amount. ROI is the mathematical product of two ratios:* **profit margin** *(profit as a percentage of sales), and* **asset turnover** *(how many sales dollars result from a $1 investment).*

"Starting with the standard homes asset turnover ratio, a dollar investment generates two dollars in sales [the $1 investment 'turns over' 2 times into $2 of sales]. The profit margin tells us each sales dollar creates 37¢ in profit. Therefore, each dollar invested provides 74¢ in profit, so standard homes has a 74% ROI. For custom homes, a $1 investment turns over into $1 of sales, which generates 19¢ in profit, for a 19% ROI. In total, a $1 investment in Multree Homes increases sales 1½ times, with each sales dollar creating 17¢ in profit. So, each $1 invested in our company earns 1½ × 17¢, or 25¢ [Exhibit 8-11 percentages are formatted to one decimal place: ⅙ of 1.5 = 25%]."

Residual income

NANCY

"I see a problem with ROI. Two customers enter an automobile dealership. Customer A says, 'I have a 20% ROI and want to buy the Mercedes!' Customer B says, 'Oh, I only have a 10% ROI, so I suppose I have to take the Geo.' When the sales manager investigates further, customer A's 20% ROI is on a $10,000 investment. Customer B's 10% ROI is on a $500,000 investment. Guess who gets the Mercedes and who gets the Geo!"

Return on Investment (ROI)

ROI = $\frac{\text{Profit}}{\text{Investment}}$	=	$\frac{\text{Segment margin}}{\text{Segment sales}}$	x	$\frac{\text{Segment sales}}{\text{Segment assets}}$

Standard homes:		Profit margin		Asset turnover
ROI = $\frac{\$1{,}840{,}000}{\$2{,}500{,}000}$	=	$\frac{\$1{,}840{,}000}{\$5{,}000{,}000}$	x	$\frac{\$5{,}000{,}000}{\$2{,}500{,}000}$
ROI = 73.6%	=	*36.8%*	*x*	*2.0 times*

Custom homes:		Profit margin		Asset turnover
ROI = $\frac{\$185{,}000}{\$1{,}000{,}000}$	=	$\frac{\$185{,}000}{\$1{,}000{,}000}$	x	$\frac{\$1{,}000{,}000}{\$1{,}000{,}000}$
ROI = 18.5%	=	*18.5%*	*x*	*1.0 times*

Multree Homes:		Profit margin		Asset turnover
ROI = $\frac{\$1{,}000{,}000}{\$4{,}000{,}000}$	=	$\frac{\$1{,}000{,}000}{\$6{,}000{,}000}$	x	$\frac{\$6{,}000{,}000}{\$4{,}000{,}000}$
ROI = 25.0%	=	*16.7%*	*x*	*1.5 times*

Exhibit 8-11

$% JULIE

"That's an interesting story! Sometimes it makes sense to express profit in percentage terms, but sometimes comparing dollars makes sense. Wanting to compare profits to our investment *in dollars*, we can calculate the investment's **residual income**. This is the profit remaining after subtracting the cost of funding an investment. For example, we have the opportunity to invest $100 and earn 10%. However, we have to borrow the $100 at 11% interest. We'll lose money on this investment! The investment's profit is $10, but the interest is $11. The residual income is a negative $1 [our net loss after paying interest on the loan is $1]. General Electric was one of the first major corporations to use residual income. [Exhibit 8-12 demonstrates the calculation for Multree Homes.]

Residual income *is the remaining profit after deducting the cost of the capital invested.*

"Money [funding investments] is not free. When we consider how profitable an investment is, shouldn't we consider the cost of getting the money? Many ways to measure this 'cost of capital' [COC] exist. We can discuss this in a finance meeting [i.e., a finance course]. Here [Exhibit 8-12] I used our company's 20% average cost

Residual Income

Residual income	=	Investment	x (	ROI	-	COC)
Standard homes:						
$1,340,000	=	$2,500,000	x (	73.6%	-	20%)
Custom homes:						
($15,000)	=	$1,000,000	x (	18.5%	-	20%)
Multree Homes:						
$200,000	=	$4,000,000	x (	25%	-	20%)

Note: ROI is the investment's return and COC is the company's cost of capital.

Exhibit 8-12

of capital. *As long as the investment's ROI is greater than its cost of capital, it will generate a positive residual income.* Making and selling standard homes requires a $2.5 million investment. After deducting the cost to get this money, the segment has a $1,340,000 surplus, or residual, income. Overall, Multree Homes' ROI is 5% greater than the cost of funding our assets. In dollars, the 5% surplus ROI equals $200,000 in residual income.

"Using residual income to evaluate segments, should we drop custom homes? Before we do, consider all relevant revenues and costs, and externalities! We sell more standard homes because we have custom homes. If we drop custom homes, we'll hurt standard home sales, overall company ROI, and residual income."

Comparing ROI and residual income

JULIE

"We usually think the best way to compare different things is by finding something they have in common. ROI often is thought to be good for comparing different size investments. To illustrate, we can compare our two product lines based on ROI. The standard homes ROI is 74%, while the custom homes ROI is 19%."

NANCY

"Sure, for the same size investment, I'd rather have 20% instead of 10%. But, for different size investment centers, I'd rather have a 10% return on $1 million than a 20% return on $100,000! So when should we use ROI and when should we use residual income?"

JULIE

"ROI is one of the most common evaluation measures used by stockholders, who can replace top management if they are not happy with the company [i.e., its stock price and dividends]. So, my primary motivation is to 'go forth and maximize ROI'! Also, it's easily understood [a savings account interest rate], and it's free [we don't have to do anything extra and costly to the accounting system in order to get this ratio].

"So why use residual income? It provides a 'hurdle rate,' or a minimum acceptable rate of return. Any investment center with an ROI below this minimum is costing the company money. I always want to maximize ROI, but if segments do not provide a positive residual income, they need to improve or we should consider dropping them. Going back to your example, if the cost of obtaining investment funds is 15%, that $1 million investment center with a 10% ROI isn't as good as the $100,000 investment center with a 20% ROI!"

"So these measures complement each other. ROI provides a way to compare segments by computing relative profits [percentages of their assets]. Residual income expands this comparison to include dollars of profit after adjusting for the investment's cost. *We need to consider both their relative and absolute profits in evaluation.*"

Will ROI and residual income motivate good investment [planning] decisions? "I see how ROI and residual income are used in evaluating performance, but will they motivate good investment [planning] decisions? Investments are multi-year decisions, but ROI and residual income are one-year measures. My concern is how a single-year evaluation measure affects long-run planning decisions. Look at this analysis [Exhibit 8-13].

Annual ROI and Residual Income for a Multi-Year Investment

Data section

Benefits: Machine reduces cash costs $30,000 per year for 5 years.
Costs: Machine costs $100,000.
Depreciation expense is $20,000 per year for 5 years.
Cost of capital (COC) = 14%.

Solution section

Year	ΔProfit	÷	Investment	=	ROI	-	COC	=	Surplus ROI	Residual income
1	$10,000	÷	$100,000	=	10.0%	-	14%	=	(4.0%)	($4,000)
2	10,000	÷	80,000	=	12.5%	-	14%	=	(1.5%)	(1,200)
3	10,000	÷	60,000	=	16.7%	-	14%	=	2.7%	1,600
4	10,000	÷	40,000	=	25.0%	-	14%	=	11.0%	4,400
5	10,000	÷	20,000	=	50.0%	-	14%	=	36.0%	7,200

Notes: ΔProfit = $30,000 saved less $20,000 in new depreciation.
Investment amonts are the beginning-of-year net book values.

Exhibit 8-13

"We should buy this machine. Its average ROI over five years is 15%. Total residual income is $8,000. Over the five years, it will generate $150,000 in cash [for a $100,000 initial cost]. However, if I'm evaluated with ROI or residual income, I won't invest in it! For the first two years, ROI is less than the minimum 14%, and thus residual income is negative. Using either measure, I'm going to be punished for two years in my performance evaluation!"

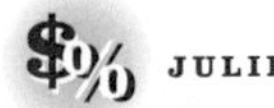

"I have to agree with you! *How we measure profit and investment in evaluating performance influences investment decisions.* You used financial accounting numbers in both the numerator and denominator. Here's another example of *motivating bad decisions because we use the wrong accounting information.* We should be focusing on cashflows and future value in planning decisions. But our evaluations use single-year accrual-based financial accounting numbers. *What gets measured gets done!*"

TOMMY

"I can't ethically support evaluating investment centers solely with ROI or residual income! To motivate correct planning decisions, we should evaluate performance by comparing budgeted and actual cashflows each year. In performance evaluation, we should ask, 'Did this investment provide the extra $30,000 cash this year as projected?'"

JULIE

Will ROI and residual income motivate good control decisions? "Overemphasizing profit in evaluating performance also affects day-to-day operational control decisions. For example, to improve this year's profit, let's cancel research and development, advertising, employee training, and machine maintenance. These expenses on the income statement reduce this year's profit, ROI, and residual income.

"How badly will this damage our long-term value? Is this the type of behavior we want to motivate? Instead of managing activities to improve long-run value, managers may be motivated to make decisions that best influence short-term profits reported on the financial statements. Don't underestimate how strong this motivation can be! We're talking about top management, who is very close to the stockholders. Stockholders only have access to financial accounting information. If the financial accounting numbers don't 'sing the song' stockholders want to hear, they're out of a job! Further exasperating the problem, top executives often are rewarded with a company's stock, increasing their motivation to base investment decisions primarily on the financial statement effect."

SID

"Some companies believe requiring stock ownership motivates a long-run value perspective. At Campbell's Soup, top management must own stock valued between one-half and three times their annual salaries. Eastman-Kodak, Gerber Foods, Hershey Foods, Union Carbide, and Xerox have similar programs. But if this motivates actions that improve stock prices at the expense of long-term value, how can we overcome this problem?"

The need for economic value added (EVA)

JULIE

"AT&T replaced stock rewards with stock options. But it's not clear how this changes top management's potential motivation to base decisions on financial accounting income effects. Instead of changing rewards, consider changing how we measure profit and investment. **Economic value added [EVA]** is a set of adjustments to residual income that is believed to better measure the value from decisions affecting segment profit and investments."

> **Economic value added (EVA)** *modifies residual income by adjusting profits and investments from the accounting system values to measures better reflecting shareholder value.*

SID

"Look, if the ship's compass is wrong, let's not use it! The accruals and allocations in our accounting system may be leading us off-course. Tell me more about EVA!"

JULIE

"First, the accounting system is not completely wrong. It's just not as accurate as you think it is. Rarely are any measures perfect. In part, good judgment means knowing when measures are good enough and when they need to be changed. EVA adjustments are complicated. Changes like this to our accounting system are expensive. But many firms believe the benefits far exceed the costs."

SID

"O.K. What types of adjustments should we consider? How do we know if we should use EVA instead of ROI or residual income?"

JULIE

"About 200 different types of adjustments have been proposed. In measuring income, amounts we should consider changing include how much should be in revenues [e.g., for long-term contracts of sale, and projected sales from current finished goods inventory], how inventory costs are calculated [LIFO, FIFO, etc.], and which expenses not to include in income [R&D, personnel training costs, depreciation, goodwill amortization, etc.].

"In valuing the segment's investment, consider changing asset values to better reflect market values, eliminating deferred income tax and LIFO reserves and goodwill, and revaluing intangibles, just to name a few. Interestingly, the cost of capital is adjusted to an opportunity cost measure, the return from similar competitive investments.

"But before changing the accounting numbers, we should see if the changes yield significantly different values, how much managers can influence the new values, whether people understand them, and how hard it is to get the information."

"One characteristic management has always valued in performance evaluation numbers is hardness; we can verify the numbers. This is a fundamental tenet of financial accounting. EVA numbers can be very soft. It seems understanding and agreeing with EVA measures are more important than how the measures are calculated."

"That may not be too difficult. Remember, EVA is just an extension of the performance evaluation measures we've been using. Let me show you how the measures are linked together as we drill down through the management hierarchy [see Exhibit 8-14].

"Many organizations use EVA, like AT&T, Briggs & Stratton, Eli Lilly, Georgia-Pacific, Olin, and Tenneco. Coca-Cola began using EVA in the 1980s. EVA justified dropping its pasta and wine lines and refocusing on Coke's core competencies. Quaker Oats adopted it in 1992, and used it to justify abandoning its trade loading policies. Trade loading [multi-month food ordering] was responsible for up to $100 billion in grocery wholesale inventories, adding $20 billion to American grocery bills. The U.S. Postal Service adopted EVA in 1995, and [for the first time in 6 years] reported a budget surplus. On-time deliveries and customer satisfaction also increased.

"Probably the most important reason for EVA's motivational success is the rewards tied to it. To illustrate, John Blystone left GE to become CEO of SPX [a multi-billion dollar auto equipment company in Muskegon, Michigan]. Through EVA, he's able to lure managers from other firms. In 1996, his key managers earned up to 200% of base pay in EVA bonuses. EVA proponents argue the extra measurement cost is justified by the motivational benefits from better matching individual performance to the firm's long-term value goals. So achieving these goals justifies the huge bonuses and stock options paid to top executives.

"If we're still worried about the EVA numbers, or just don't think their benefit exceeds their cost, we do have another performance evaluation tool which also reflects long-run value creation. It's called a balanced scorecard."

Does Our Accounting System Support Good Judgment?

SID

"Let's save that for a future meeting [Chapter 14]. Before changing how we evaluate performance, let's make sure we're using accounting measures correctly."

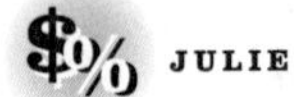

"I see five problems with using accounting information in evaluating performance:

- Segments may not be comparable.

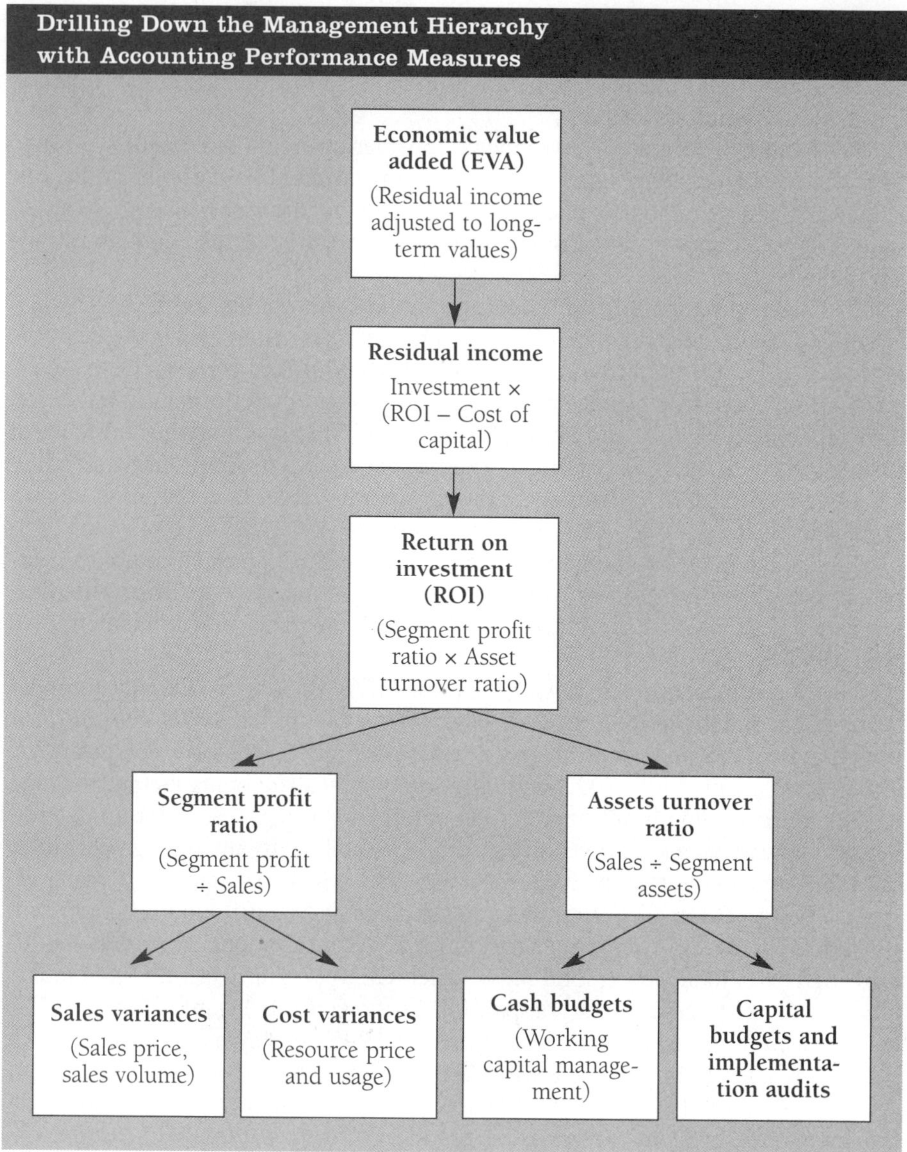

Exhibit 8-14

- Segment managers may be placed in conflict with each other.
- Comparing last year and this year may not correctly evaluate performance.
- Managers may be motivated to maximize accounting's reported profit instead of long-run value.
- We may need nonfinancial process measures in addition to the output measures accounting systems usually report.

KEY OBJECTIVE 6

Summarize five ethical concerns with management's use of accounting control measures.

Deadly parallel evaluations

"All too often, accounting information is used to compare segments and managers by basing rewards on who has the most segment margin. This is called a 'deadly parallel' evaluation strategy. It creates two problems. *First, the segments may not be comparable, and perhaps they shouldn't be.* Some ['cash cows'] are well established with mature product lines. Others ['rising stars'] are very new with promising product lines just being developed but with relatively poor profit performance to date. How can we compare them? The older segment's assets are fully depreciated, its depreciation expense is low [thus higher income in the numerator of its ROI], and its asset values are very low [small denominator]. Its ROI is quite high. The new segment has a large depreciation expense and asset base because its assets are new. Thus its ROI is quite low. Will their ROI's provide a valid comparison? Which has the greater potential to create long-run value?

JULIE

"Comparing segments located in different countries also can be difficult for multinationals, due to differences in tariffs, tax laws, foreign currency exchange rates, and imposed transfer prices. My point is in comparing segments, we have some serious measurement problems. To make segments comparable, will we have to change how income and assets are measured from segment to segment? Once we realize the changes needed to make segment ROIs comparable, the EVA adjustments may not introduce such a significant extra cost!

"The second problem is putting managers in competition with each other. We're all supposed to be part of the same team, working for the overall organization's goals. Does this happen with transfers? With a deadly parallel evaluation strategy, the segment manager with the most profit gets the biggest reward. Since transfer prices determine how much of the transfer's extra cashflow appears in each segment margin, managers fight [negotiate] over the transfer price. When they can't agree on a transfer price, they may not transfer when they should. If managers are not in competition with each other for raises and bonuses based on their segment margins [including transfer profits], they won't care about the transfer price, and they will transfer when they should. My point is comparisons need to be made very carefully."

Comparing last year to this year

JACKIE

"We don't do these types of segment comparisons in financial accounting! Income statements usually include both this year's results and last year's. I judge performance by comparing this year to last year, not by comparing budgeted to actual performance."

JULIE

"You're right, of course. However, financial accounting's goals are not the same as management accounting's. Financial accounting information is used by people outside the company. An investor's value is increased if the stock price goes up. So he compares last year to this year to try to forecast the future prices. The problem is it doesn't tell us whether we have achieved our goals. While profits may have increased from last year, both year's profits may be horrible!

"Another reason why comparing last year's actual performance to this year's may lead to an incorrect evaluation is last year may not be comparable to this year. To see the fallacy in a 'this year to last year' comparison, mortgage interest rates were very low two years ago. All home builders sold a lot of houses. Interest rates went up dramatically last year. Everyone sold less homes, and reported significantly less profits. We foresaw this in our strategic plan and offered mortgage loans at a lower rate. As a result, we sold more homes than budgeted, and made more profit than planned. Even though the economy killed the home building industry, and our profits were much lower than two years ago, we still had an outstanding year! Year-to-year comparisons cannot reveal this. *Only by comparing this year's budget to actual performance can we know if we accomplished our goals!"*

Behaviors financial accounting can motivate

JULIE

"Many organizations traditionally measure performance on a single short-run dimension, profit. However, an overemphasis on short-run financial accounting profit may not motivate our people to focus on the critical success factors leading to long-run value.

"Why use financial accounting numbers in performance evaluations? It's easy, cheap, the numbers are hard, and most importantly, top management must satisfy stockholders. Since external owners [stockholders, bond holders, and bankers] only get financial accounting reports, management is motivated to 'control' these numbers. I just can't argue with that motivation! Because their job security depends on the financial statements, top management also will hold everyone else accountable for how their activities affect financial accounting income.

"*Since the financial accounting numbers always are going to be important, we must guard against decisions made primarily to influence these numbers at the expense of long-run value.* Cost center managers may cancel research and development, machine maintenance, or employee training to avoid unfavorable variances. Purchasing agents may buy unjustifiably large orders to get discounts, or buy lower quality materials resulting in favorable price variances. Profit center managers may maximize output to minimize the average product cost. They also may manipulate sales to create favorable variances and extra profits."

TOMMY

"Don't underestimate how strong this motivation is! In December of 1993, to bolster annual segment profit, a Bausch & Lomb division manager pressured its distributors into buying up to two-year supplies of contact lenses at prices well above normal. Not having any choice, all but two complied [the two were dropped in January]. While this created favorable 1993 sales variances, a new manager took over in mid-1994 after the lack of 1994 sales led to a 37% profit decline, a stock price decline from $50 to $32 per share, and a class action lawsuit by the stockholders.

"I know some believe 'financial income managing' is part of their jobs. As long as it's allowable to choose different accounting methods [revenue recognition, depreciation, inventory, etc.], these managers believe their conduct is ethical. I want to know how we can avoid decisions made to enhance short-run earnings at the expense of long-run value!"

Process versus output measures

JULIE

"Part of the problem is cultural. Stockholders are important to American businesses. This isn't as true in Japan. The other part of the problem is our 'black box' mentality. Accounting numbers tell us about outputs, or the results of processes. *We need to look inside the black box, turning it into a 'glass box.'* Effective motivation begins with measuring the processes creating financial results, rather than just measuring the results. Traditional accounting information just doesn't tell us the whole story. Relevant evaluation information is missing. With cost centers, practical standard quantities [and the resulting cost variances] bury quality and inefficiency problems. Segment profits may not correctly measure controllable costs and revenues due to allocations of common costs. ROIs probably need adjustments before segments can be compared.

"*We need to supplement financial measures with nonfinancial process measures better reflecting current and future cashflows.* Both in 1994 and 1995, Rubbermaid was voted 'America's most admired company' because of its commitment to product quality and customer service. MBNA America believes maintaining credit card customers is its most important value-creating activity. Thus, it measures daily customer representative performance on 14 critical success factors [like answering the phone by the second ring and processing requests within one hour]. IBM measures 7 factors including customer satisfaction and employee morale. McDonald's uses the 'QSC' criteria: product quality, customer service, and store cleanliness.

"These companies believe nonfinancial measures better predict future cashflows than do traditional accounting numbers because the nonfinancial measures show value changes before the accounting numbers will. In summary, we must remember:

> **What gets measured gets done, but**
> **if we measure the wrong things, even though very accurately,**
> **the wrong things will be done.**
> **And, if we reward what's measured,**
> **the wrong things may be done very well!**

KEY OBJECTIVES SUMMARY

"Let me summarize the six major ideas discussed in today's meeting:

1. Describe the motivational relationship between planning, control, and evaluation.

"People have two sources of motivation, internal and external. We hope they are internally motivated to improve the organization [clan control]. By offering acceptable rewards, we also hope to externally motivate goal congruence [bureaucratic and accounting controls]. So, organizations design control systems by recognizing the following linkages:

- *Control* means people are motivated to do what we want them to do.
- *Motivation* requires knowledge about what they want, and a reward system to give it to them.
- The *reward system* requires an evaluation system based upon performance measures.
- *Performance measurement* requires assigning responsibilities [usually through the budgeting process].
- *Responsibility* requires controllability over the factors measured.
- *Controllability* requires participation in developing measures, and the ability to influence the activities needed to do one's job.

2. Discuss the evolution from clan control to accounting control and accounting's control hierarchy.

"Detailed accounting controls may not be necessary when people already are motivated to act in the firm's best interest [clan control]. In these environments, accounting information is used primarily for decision making, rather than for motivation. As organizations grow and complexity increases, personally monitoring processes becomes less likely. So bureaucratic rules are created, and decisions are made at the top [centralization]. When management believes some decisions can be made better by people doing the work, and the people use good judgment, they're allowed to make decisions [decentralization].

"The more removed top management is from day-to-day operations, the greater the need for accounting information to evaluate performance. Relying only on accounting controls creates evaluation and ethical problems, though. Ethical problems include not providing complete, objective, and relevant information. Without high-quality information, evaluations may not be correct and/or considered legitimate by the people being evaluated. If this happens, goal congruence may break down. Focusing only on output measures creates the opportunity for people to manipulate the process in undesirable ways [maximizing output to minimize average cost, sacrificing long-run value for short-run profit].

"Accounting measures exist on three managerial levels. Cost centers conduct activities that incur costs, so they are evaluated with cost variances. Profit centers are responsible for revenues and costs, and are evaluated with sales and cost variances. Investment centers are responsible for profits and investments, so their performance is measured using profit based on the investment required to maintain them.

"Process controls are costly. They are evolving to include both financial [profit, cashflow] and nonfinancial [quality, customer satisfaction] measures. The incremental benefits from better control and evaluation should be weighed against the incremental costs of a more detailed management accounting system. Control and evaluation include a portfolio of clan, market, bureaucratic, and accounting systems. Managers need to be aware of the factors determining, and changing, the best combination of control systems, as well as the potential problems with using accounting controls.

3. Explain three motivational problems with using accounting information in performance evaluation.

"If our people do not believe the system legitimately measures their performance, goal congruence may break down. So, involve everyone in the planning process. This assures they understand our strategic plan, critical success factors, and who is responsible for each process. They also should participate in creating the standards used to evaluate them. Involving them in the planning process increases the likelihood they will accept the performance evaluation system as legitimate.

"Our second problem concerns who is responsible for variances. Remember, variances are output measures. To correctly assign responsibility, we have to know why the variance happened. We need to get inside the black box. Its real cause may not be within the department where the variance occurred. Without knowing a variance's source and cause, how can we correctly evaluate performance? Traditionally, and partly due to scientific management, accountants believed their responsibility ends with identifying where a variance happened. Then it's management's responsibility to identify sources and causes. If we wish, the accounting system can capture this information and include it in the cost variance reports. This should increase the efficiency of the overall control system and the effectiveness of the accounting system. Perceived as a more legitimate system, our people should be better motivated to achieve Multree's goals.

"'What gets measured gets done' is our third problem. When rewards are important and only short-run profit-based output measures are used, we may be promoting dysfunctional behaviors.

4. Prepare a segmented income statement and explain its usefulness in evaluating segments and managers.

"I use one room of my home to run a business. I sell diet aid products [weight loss pills, vitamins, health bars, etc.] and plastic storage containers [like Tupperware®]. Here's the data on each:

Profit items	Diet aids	Plastic containers
Sales price	$10	$20
Sales volume	100 units	100 units
Merchandise cost per unit	$8	$14
Phone calls and travel	$50	$100
Business licenses and forms	$200	$100

The phone calls and travel are my decisions, and don't depend on the amount of business I do. I need a separate business license for each product line, and special forms for ordering merchandise. I also incur $50 in room-related costs [utilities, insurance, taxes]. My segmented income statement looks like this [see Exhibit 8-15].

Doris's Profit Analysis for Her In-Home Businesses

	Diet Aids			Plastic Containers			Totals	
	Per unit	%	Totals @ 100	Per unit	%	Totals @ 100	%	$
Revenues	$10	100%	$1,000	$20	100%	$2,000	100%	$3,000
Less: variable costs	(8)	(80%)	(800)	(14)	(70%)	(1,400)	(73%)	(2,200)
Contribution margin	$2	20%	$200	$6	30%	$600	27%	$800
Less: controllable direct fixed costs			(50)			(100)		(150)
Controllable segment margin			**$150**			**$500**		$650
Less: uncontrollable direct fixed costs			(200)			(100)		(300)
Segment margin			**($50)**			**$400**		$350
Less: common fixed costs								(50)
Net income								**$300**

Exhibit 8-15

My only variable costs are merchandise purchases. Phone calls and travel are controllable direct fixed costs of each product line. I have no control over the direct fixed costs for licenses and forms. Since both product lines share the one room, room costs are common to the segments.

"To prepare a segmented income statement, first separate fixed costs into direct and common. Direct fixed costs are deducted from each segment's contribution margin to compute its profit [segment margin]. Next, within each segment, direct fixed costs are classified as controllable or uncontrollable, with the subtotal 'Controllable segment margin' added.

"Use controllable segment margins to evaluate managers. It looks like I'm doing a good job managing what I control with both product lines. Segment margins evaluate the profit center [versus its manager]. I'm not making any money on diet aids. I should consider dropping it unless I can increase sales or reduce controllable direct fixed costs. The common fixed costs aren't relevant to this decision because they will not change if I stop selling diet aids. However, I always need to identify any relevant externalities [e.g., some diet aid customers buy plastic containers].

5. Compute ROI and residual income, and explain their motivational implications.

"I've invested assets in my business, such as office furniture, a computer, fax machine, copier, file cabinets, and a telephone answering machine. Is my $10,000 investment justified? Here's my ROI [Exhibit 8-16]. It's for both segments combined because I cannot trace any assets directly to either one.

Doris's Return on Investment (ROI)

$$\text{ROI} = \frac{\text{Profit}}{\text{Investment}} = \frac{\text{Segment margin}}{\text{Segment sales}} \times \frac{\text{Segment sales}}{\text{Segment assets}}$$

ROI		Profit margin		Asset turnover
ROI = $300 / $10,000	=	$300 / $3,000	x	$3,000 / $10,000
ROI = 3%	=	10%	x	0.3 times

Exhibit 8-16

"I'm happy with a 10% profit margin, but my 0.3 times asset turnover ratio is not acceptable. To increase my 3% ROI, I need to increase sales. This may require more advertising. But more advertising will increase expenses, reduce profit, and reduce ROI until new sales are realized. The problem with ROI [and residual income] is it's a short-run measure. I have to be careful to avoid decisions increasing ROI today at the expense of future value.

"If I borrowed the $10,000, I should consider its cost in computing the return I'm earning on it. I didn't have to borrow the money, but I could have invested it elsewhere. How does investing in this business compare to depositing the money in my 5% savings account? Residual income will tell me this [see Exhibit 8-17].

"I'm using an opportunity cost [the interest I can receive on a competing investment in my savings account] for the cost of my invested capital. The negative $200 residual income is the profit I'm giving up by keeping the business. If it wasn't for the externalities [free diet aids and storage containers, meeting new people, etc.], I'd drop the business! As it is, though, these intangible benefits are more important than the extra $200 I could have.

Doris's Residual Income

Residual income	=	Investment	x (	ROI	-	COC)
($200)	=	$10,000	x (	3%	-	5%)

Note: ROI is the investment's return and COC is the company's cost of capital.

Exhibit 8-17

6. Summarize five ethical concerns with management's use of accounting control measures.

"Julie identified the following problems:

- Segments may not be comparable.
- Segment managers may be placed in conflict with each other.
- Comparing last year and this year may not correctly evaluate performance.
- Managers may be motivated to maximize accounting's reported profit instead of long-run value.
- We may need nonfinancial process measures in addition to the output measures accounting systems usually report.

A common way to evaluate and reward people is by comparing their performance. Whoever does the best job gets the best reward. If investment centers are very different, though, their ROIs and residual incomes may not be comparable. The accounting numbers do not support the evaluation strategy, and may need to be modified.

"What happens when they have to make cooperative decisions like transferring? Should managers be placed in competition with each other for rewards? This is what deadly parallel evaluations do. To evaluate its unique profit contribution to the organization when transfers take place, each profit center should be segmented into internal and external sales. To properly motivate correct transfer decisions, the transfer price we use will depend on our reward system.

"Comparing this year with last year creates another comparability problem. Each year may be very different. If we want to know whether our strategic and profit plans have been achieved, we need to compare this year's budget to actual results, rather than last year to this year.

"Even if we don't evaluate performance by comparing segments or years, managers still may be motivated to do things increasing short-run financial accounting income at the expense of long-run value. As long as financial accounting numbers are used to evaluate top management, this motivation will exist. We can use other performance measures like EVA and process controls. But can we convince stockholders also to use these new measures?"

"We have a lot of unresolved problems. To better understand their financial effects, segment profitability, and to better motivate good judgment, we may have to change what our accounting system measures. Before we do, however, I want a report from Marketing, Production [including purchasing], and Accounting about your problems. In our remaining meetings, we'll look at how we can fix them, and the management accounting information needed to plan, control, and evaluate any new strategies we adopt. We'll start with our cost accounting system. It seems our product costing system may be masking some of our more serious problems. Good night!"

SID

Movie Making and Magical Accounting: Where Did All the Profits Go?

Tying key personnel rewards to organizational performance has become a significant trend in many industries, both profit-making and nonprofit. The growing use of stock option plans and EVA attest to this. But, as early as 1950, Jimmy Stewart negotiated a movie profit-based contract with Universal Studios. In the ensuing 50 years, though, no other industry has been subject to more publicized lawsuits, actor disdain, and distrust of industry accountants due to these profit-sharing contracts. At the heart of the controversy is how profit is calculated.

Batman, Coming to America, Forest Gump, Rain Man, and *Who Framed Roger Rabbit?* are among the top 40 most successful films in box office sales, but none have reported a profit! For example, *Coming to America* grossed over $350 million, but reported an $18 million loss. Less than 5% of all movies have shown a profit for actor profit sharing. The reason is in how a movie's profit (segment margin) is adjusted to residual income through a series of common cost allocations and imputed interest charges. The income statement for *Police Academy 4* illustrates how this is done.

Police Academy 4 **Income Statement Highlights**	
U.S. theater and television revenues	$15.3 million
Foreign theater and television	23.5
Pay television	8.8
Video sales	5.0
Total revenues	**$52.6 million**
Less: cost of goods sold (direct production costs)	–15.1
Gross profit	$37.5
Less: direct distribution costs	–17.6
Segment margin	**$19.9 million**
Less: studio charges	
Production overhead (15% of direct production costs)	2.3
Advertising overhead (10% of direct advertising costs)	1.0
Distribution overhead (34.5% of gross revenues)	18.2
Imputed interest (cost of capital charge specially computed)	4.6
Total studio allocations and charges	–$26.1
Residual income	**–$6.2 million**

Revenues are not as straightforward as you may expect. Theater sales are about only 45% of gross box office receipts. When multiple films are sold (as double features, or to television networks) the price must be allocated between films. Video sales usually are made to a subsidiary at a transfer price which is 20% of the subsidiary's price to retailers. So, 80% of the video's revenues are not reported in the film's segment margin.

Direct production costs include charges for equipment, props, and costume rentals. The "costs" are transfer prices from other studio profit centers. The transfer prices may be based on the cost of replacing what's rented, even if it's returned in the same condition.

The real fun begins with the allocations, though. In Art Buchwald's lawsuit over *Coming to America* profit sharing, the court threw out the production overhead. Using direct production costs as the overhead cost driver appears reasonable until it was discovered many costs (e.g., actor salaries) are not related to how overhead resources are really used. The advertising overhead also was ignored as its cost driver does not represent how this overhead is incurred. Similarly, it's very difficult to believe distribution overhead is caused by gross sales and is really in the 25%–50% industry range. For example, the $18.2 million distribution "fee" charged to *Coming to America* was more than Paramount's worldwide distribution network actual cost for the entire year! (In fairness to Paramount Studios, the case was appealed and subsequently settled out of court).

The cost of capital charge ("imputed interest") for the residual income calculation also raises some interesting accounting questions. Interest charges (usually 125% of commercial prime rate) begin when costs are accrued (e.g., allocations), not when actually paid. Revenues received are not used to reduce net costs until the end of the accounting period. Thus, interest is charged on money not yet spent, and interest earned on revenues is ignored. Worse yet, prepaid nonrefundable revenues are not credited to the film until after it is released. Even though bills are paid from revenues, these costs are still included in the "investment" used to calculate the interest charge.

Perhaps the movie industry accountants should make a musical since they're so good at making the books sing the song studio managements want to hear! (Or at least a magician's TV special, in that a $20 million profit on *Police Academy 4* can be turned into a $6.2 million loss.)

Source: Bengel and Ikawa, "Where's the Profit?" *Management Accounting*, January 1997. © Institute of Management Accountants.

APPENDIX A

SERVICE DEPARTMENT ALLOCATIONS AND COST VARIANCES

Overhead allocation bases, motivation, and ethics

"In our cost accounting meeting [Chapter 5], we considered cost accuracy and accounting system cost in deciding how to allocate overhead. However, from today's meeting it appears we also should consider some behavioral and ethical issues. Our primary means of evaluation is through cost control efforts. The overhead allocated to departments affects their total costs, evaluations, and rewards. Thus, our people really care about how overhead is allocated, and it affects their decisions!

"Consider what Hitachi and Tektronix did. Both are heavily automated with direct labor being only a small percentage of manufacturing costs. Upper management wanted to continue replacing labor with equipment. Direct labor was chosen for their overhead allocation base so managers would be motivated to continue automating processes. Why? Because their PORs were incredibly high [very large overhead in the numerator, very low direct labor in the denominator]. This gave the appearance of labor being very expensive. Every time one hour is worked, a large overhead cost is charged to it. While this distorted labor and overhead costs, top management believed motivating behavior with an accounting control system was more important and could be accomplished best through a high overhead cost allocation [because it affected performance evaluations and rewards].

"The direct labor-based overhead allocation should have motivated plant managers to continue automating processes, congruent with management strategy. Every time they saved an hour of labor, they avoided a huge overhead allocation, reduced their costs, and created large favorable variances. But because continuing automation further increased overhead costs and reduced labor costs, the POR actually increased! Even though plant managers were automating processes, they could be allocated more overhead, adversely affecting their rewards. So bad decisions were being made because the labor cost was so overstated. Confoundingly, by focusing on direct labor reduction, which was only 3%–7% of manufacturing costs, managers were not attending to the activities driving the vast majority of their costs. Ultimately, Tektronix had to replace its one-POR allocation system with a multiple POR system.

"On the other hand, Peterson Ranch, a fruit and nut producer in central California, had more success with its overhead allocations. It allocated equipment costs to its farms based on the size of the equipment. Management's goal was to motivate smaller, more efficient equipment purchases. Ranch managers responded appropriately.

"So we see successful and unsuccessful examples of using overhead allocations to motivate behavior. Regardless, is choosing an allocation base primarily to motivate behavior ethical, especially if it does not represent the true cause-effect relationship driving overhead cost? Is purposely distorting product costs ethical?"

$% JULIE

"Personally, I think these were bad decisions from an ethical point of view because *better ways exist to motivate people*. Automation may be an appropriate goal for maintaining our competitiveness and increasing the firm's value. However, if this is one of our goals, motivating people to look for process improvements through automation should be part of our strategic plan. And everyone should participate in the strategic planning process. Further, our cash budget, specifically the capital budget portion for equipment purchases, should include money for these improvements. We'll know if they're making these investments. By involving everyone in the planning and budgeting process, they know to continue automating. We do not need to distort product costs through inaccurate overhead allocations just to motivate them.

"This is only my opinion, though. Involving everyone in the planning process provides feedforward control and positive reinforcement. I believe this motivates people better than the threat of punishment [negative reinforcement] through feedback information [unfavorable variances]. Apparently, many managers and accountants believe cost allocations should be used to motivate employees. The Hitachi and Tektronix examples are not unique. In spite of all the arguments to the contrary, direct labor still appears to be the predominant choice for allocating overhead. Although the statistics are about ten years old, 62%–94% of surveyed companies use direct labor as their overhead cost driver."

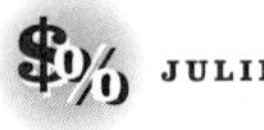

"When control issues dominate the need for accounting information, accuracy may be a secondary goal. Remember how stewardship requires hard data over soft, more relevant, data for external performance reporting?"

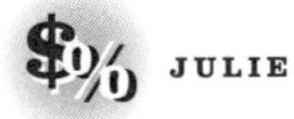

"Oh, I understand what you're saying. Stockholders are willing to sacrifice relevance for reliable information. But as managers, are we as willing to sacrifice accuracy and relevance for motivational needs, especially if better ways exist to motivate goal congruence? Accounting information is used for decision making (planning, monitoring, and evaluating). Because one of management's decisions concerns how to evaluate performance, accounting influences behaviors. Both uses of accounting information are equally important. We should not sacrifice one goal for another. Considering both uses, should we allocate overhead if it is not controllable by the people and segments receiving the allocations? If we decide to allocate, how should we do it?"

We have the same problems with allocating manufacturing overhead and corporate overhead

JULIE

"The word 'overhead' has two meanings in practice. Production overhead is indirect manufacturing costs not traceable directly to products. Corporate overhead is the cost of overall firm services. As we discussed before [in the Appendix to Chapter 5] manufacturing overhead often is incurred in service departments. Service department costs can be allocated to production departments. And production departments can have their own PORs.

"Service department overhead allocations affect total production department cost and cost variances. Similarly, allocating corporate overhead to segments [profit centers] affects their costs, segment margin, and profit variances [see Exhibit 8-5].

"Because allocating common costs can adversely affect motivation in two ways, traditional management accounting has concluded:

- Allocating fixed overhead to products may motivate managers to maximize output [which minimizes the average product cost]. So, do not allocate fixed production overhead to products [i.e., use variable costing and the contribution margin income statement].
- Allocating corporate costs to profit centers does not accurately measure segment profit, and these costs are not controllable by segment managers. Therefore, do not allocate common costs to segments [Exhibits 8-8 and 8-9].

However, not allocating service costs to the departments using them also may create behavioral problems. Not allocating these costs means the services are free to their users. St. John's Hospital provided free meals to all employees. The cafeteria incurred massive unfavorable cost variances, though, because employees took more than they could eat, sampling various entrees and throwing away what they didn't like. After the hospital began charging departments, the reduction in waste was so great the cafeteria began to show favorable variances."

"To slightly misquote a Shakespearean play, 'To allocate, or not to allocate. That is the ethical question!' Of course, if we allocate in the wrong way, we may see the same behavior as if we do not allocate. Our custom homes manager told me she didn't care whether corporate costs are not allocated to her profit center [Exhibit 8-9], or allocated using relative revenues [Exhibit 8-5]. The allocations are not based on the amount of the services she uses. Since she's going to be charged whether or not she uses the services, she might as well use as much as possible!

"How can we allocate manufacturing overhead to production departments [the users of the overhead services], and allocate common corporate costs to segments [the users of those services], in a way that motivates cost control and supports proper performance evaluation?"

Solving the allocation problem by recognizing who controls prices and usage

$% JULIE

"All activities [and their revenues and costs] are controllable. Our problem is identifying who controls what. Here's the logic of my proposed allocation method:

- *Service providers are responsible for controlling their costs.* For example, the cafeteria manager is responsible for controlling the costs of providing food.
- *Service users are responsible for controlling their usage of the services.* This means production departments should be charged for manufacturing overhead based on the amount used. Profit centers also should be charged for corporate services based on the amount used.

Interestingly, the method I'm going to demonstrate has been proposed for universities. Academic departments [those providing courses to students, like History and Mathematics] should be treated as profit centers. Their controllable segment margins include allocations of common university services [e.g., admissions and records costs, university accounting and computing services, and financial aids].

"So you can better understand the problems with allocating common costs incorrectly, let's look at two situations. Both are based on the cafeteria example we've looked at before [in Chapter 5, Appendix A]."

Situation 1: "The cafeteria provides meals to two departments, Sawing and Framing [see Exhibit 5A-2]. Its budget is $100 for providing 10 meals [1 to Sawing and 9 to Framing]. The cafeteria's POR is $10 per meal. Sawing budgets $10 for meal costs and Framing budgets an allocation of $90. The cafeteria's actual cost is $110. Allocating actual cost, the meal rate becomes $11 for the 10 meals eaten. Sawing is charged $11 for its one meal, and Framing is charged $99 for its nine meals. Both users end up with unfavorable variances due to the cafeteria overspending on meals. *By allocating actual costs, the cafeteria manager is able to shift responsibility for his cost control failures to the users.* The users are punished with unfavorable variances for activities they do not control. *Allocating actual costs provides no incentive for the cafeteria to control its costs!*"

Situation 2: "The cafeteria's $100 budget includes $20 for variable meal costs [$2 per meal] and $80 for fixed costs, averaging $10 per meal based on a budget of 10 meals. Framing eats 8 meals [1 less than budget] and Sawing eats no meals. Actual cafeteria costs are $96 [right on budget: $2/meal × 8 meals = $16, plus $80 in fixed costs]. Framing originally budgeted $90 for 9 meals, but is allocated all $96. Framing incurs a $6 unfavorable cost variance because Sawing ate a different number of meals than it budgeted. In other words, Framing ate less meals and is charged more because of another segment's actions.

"Here's the moral of my story: *Allocating actual costs, or allocating fixed costs using a rate [a POR], violates the controllability axiom for goal congruence [see Exhibit 8-2].*"

Situation 3: "Here's how we solve the problem:

- Variable cafeteria costs are caused by resource costs [standard prices for carrots and Jell-O] and the meals actually eaten [actually quantity used]. So, *allocate variable service costs to users by charging them the standard meal price multiplied by the meals actually eaten.*

- Fixed costs are caused by the size of the cafeteria. So, *allocate budgeted fixed costs to each user based on the relative size of the users.* Capacity [size] causes fixed costs.

Here's how this allocation system works. Actual variable cafeteria costs are $36 for 12 meals [Sawing eats 4 meals and Framing 8]. Actual variable meal cost averages $3 per meal. The cafeteria manager budgeted $2 per meal, though. Framing and Sawing should be charged only $2 per meal because the cafeteria manager said this is all it should cost. Only $24 should have been spent on variable food costs [$2 per meal × 12 meals actually eaten]. The $12 unfavorable spending variance [$1 per meal] is the responsibility of the cafeteria manager, so don't allocate it to the users. Only charge them the $2 standard price. This is the meal price they budgeted [contracted for] in their department's overhead.

KEY OBJECTIVE 7

Demonstrate how service department and common cost allocations can support cost control.

"Now, Sawing only budgeted to eat 1 meal, but actually ate 4 meals. Charging it $2 per meal for 4 meals, Sawing has a $6 unfavorable usage variance ['meals eaten' cost variance]. This is simply the usage cost variance formula [from our Chapter 5 meeting]: $2/meal × (1 meal – 4 meals). Framing eats 8 meals, but budgeted 9. So, it has a favorable meals eaten variance: $2/meal × (9 – 8 meals). Let me summarize how and why variable service costs are allocated:

- *Variable service costs are charged to users at the standard rate multiplied by the actual meals eaten.*
- *The food spending variance remains in the cafeteria account because it's the responsibility of the service provider.*
- *The usage variances are in the users' accounts because they are responsible for the number of meals they eat.*

Now, let's look at fixed costs. The cafeteria budgeted $80. Why? Because of how big it is. The bigger its size, the greater its fixed costs. How big is it? We built the cafeteria big enough to serve 20 meals. Why 20 and not 40? Because Sawing can eat a maximum of 6 meals, and Framing 14. That's how big the user departments are. Because Sawing can eat 6 of 20 meals if its running at maximum capacity, it's responsible for 30% of the cafeteria's size [6 ÷ 20 meals]. So Sawing is responsible for 30% of the cafeteria's budgeted fixed costs, and that is the amount it should be allocated [30% × $80 = $24]. Running at full capacity, Framing could eat 14 of the 20 meals. It's responsible for 70% of the cafeteria's size and, therefore, 70% of its budgeted fixed cost. Allocate Framing 70% of $80, or $56.

"Each user 'contracts' for services at a mixed cost: Sawing = $2 per meal + $24 per year, and Framing = $2 per meal + $56 per year.

"If the cafeteria's actual fixed costs are $75 instead of the $80 budgeted, users are still allocated the budgeted amounts. Thus, *any cafeteria fixed cost spending variance remains in its account.* It's the responsibility of the cafeteria manager. Obviously, if we use real numbers and allocated all services to all users, the calculations get pretty complex. But that's why we have cost accountants and spreadsheet programs! So, we're not going to do any of these calculations.

"You need to understand the basic idea. Variable service costs are allocated to users at the budgeted rate × actual amount of services used. Fixed service costs are allocated using budgeted fixed costs × the relative size of each user. This leaves the spending variances in the service provider accounts, and the usage variances in the users' accounts. This allocation method promotes correct evaluation because it's based on who controls which aspects of the service's total costs."

READING LIST*

$7 aspirin: McFadden, "The Legacy of the $7 Aspirin," *Management Accounting*, April 1990.

ABB: Taylor, "The Logic of Global Business: An Interview with ABB's Percy Barnevik," *Harvard Business Review*, March–April 1991.

Bellcore: Kovac and Troy, "Getting Transfer Price Right: What Bellcore Did," *Harvard Business Review*, September–October 1989.

Campbell's Soup: Berman and Alger, "Reclaiming the Patrimony," *Forbes*, March 14, 1994.

CCSSCo: Strefeler and Thomas, "Operational Auditing Using Socio-Technical Systems Analysis," *Internal Auditor*, April 1994.

Champion International: Constantinides and Shank, "Matching Accounting to Strategy: One Mill's Experience," *Management Accounting*, September 1994.

Corporate services allocations reasons: Fremgen and Liao, *The Allocation of Corporate Indirect Costs* (Institute of Management Accountants), 1987.

Dial: Robinson, "Decentralize and Outsource: Dial's Approach to MIS Improvement," *Management Accounting*, September 1991.

Ditch Witch: Thomas and Mackey, "Activity-Based Cost Variances for Just-in-Times," *Management Accounting*, April 1994.

Ethics and income manipulation: Bruns and Merchant, "The Dangerous Morality of Managing Earnings," *Management Accounting*, August 1990.

EVA: Stewart, *The Quest for Value* (HarperCollins Publishers, Inc.), 1991.

——- Tully, "The Real Key to Creating Wealth," *Fortune*, September 20, 1993.

——- *Fortune*, December 11, 1995, also has many firm-related EVA articles.

Fireman's Fund: Crane and Meyer, "Focusing on the True Costs in a Service Organization," *Management Accounting*, February 1994.

Hitachi: Hiromoto, "Another Hidden Edge—Japanese Management Accounting," *Harvard Business Review*, July–August 1988.

Honda Motor Co.: Miller, et al., *Business Week*, September, 13, 1993.

IBM: Kirkpatrick, "Breaking Up IBM," *Fortune*, July 27, 1992.

IMA survey on corporate allocations: King, "Determining What's Fair in the World of Corporate Charges," *Cost Management Update*, October 1998.

Manipulating income with absorption costing: Koehler, "Triple-Threat Strategy," *Management Accounting*, October 1991.

NAFTA: Agami, "Accounting for NAFTA," *Management Accounting*, May 1994.

Northern Telecom: Sharman, "Time to Re-examine the P&L," *CMA Magazine*, September 1991.

Peterson Ranch: Keller and Krause, "'World Class' Down on the Farm," *Management Accounting*, May 1990.

Practical standards: Merchant, "How Challenging Should Profit Budget Targets Be?" *Management Accounting*, November 1990.

Quaker Oats: Sellers, "The Dumbest Marketing Ploy," *Fortune*, October 5, 1992.

Rubbermaid: Jacob, "Corporate Reputations," *Fortune*, March 6, 1995.

Rupert Murdoch: Cox, "How Do You Tame a Global Company? Murdoch Does It Alone," *The Wall Street Journal*, February 14, 1994, pp. A1, A6.

SPX: Martin, "Another GE Veteran Rides to the Rescue," *Fortune*, December 29, 1997.

St. John's Hospital: (modified from) Hoshower and Crum, "Controlling Service Center Costs," *Management Accounting*, November 1987.

Stanford University: Shao, "The Cracks in Stanford's Ivory Tower," *Business Week*, March 11, 1991.

Tektronix: Jonez and Wright, "Material Burdening," *Management Accounting*, August 1987.

Transfer pricing and reward systems: Thomas, "A Contingency Theory for Transfer Pricing: Market-based and Reward System-based Factors," *Journal of Accounting and Finance Research*, Winter 1998.

Universities and common cost allocations: Leenhouts, "Contribution Analysis: One Way to Optimize Resources," *KPMG Management Issues For Colleges and Universities*, February 1998.

USAir: Frantz and Blumenthal, "USAir Safety Lapses Alleged," *New Orleans Times-Picayune*, November 13, 1994, p. A6.

*Alphabetic by topic, idea, or company referenced.

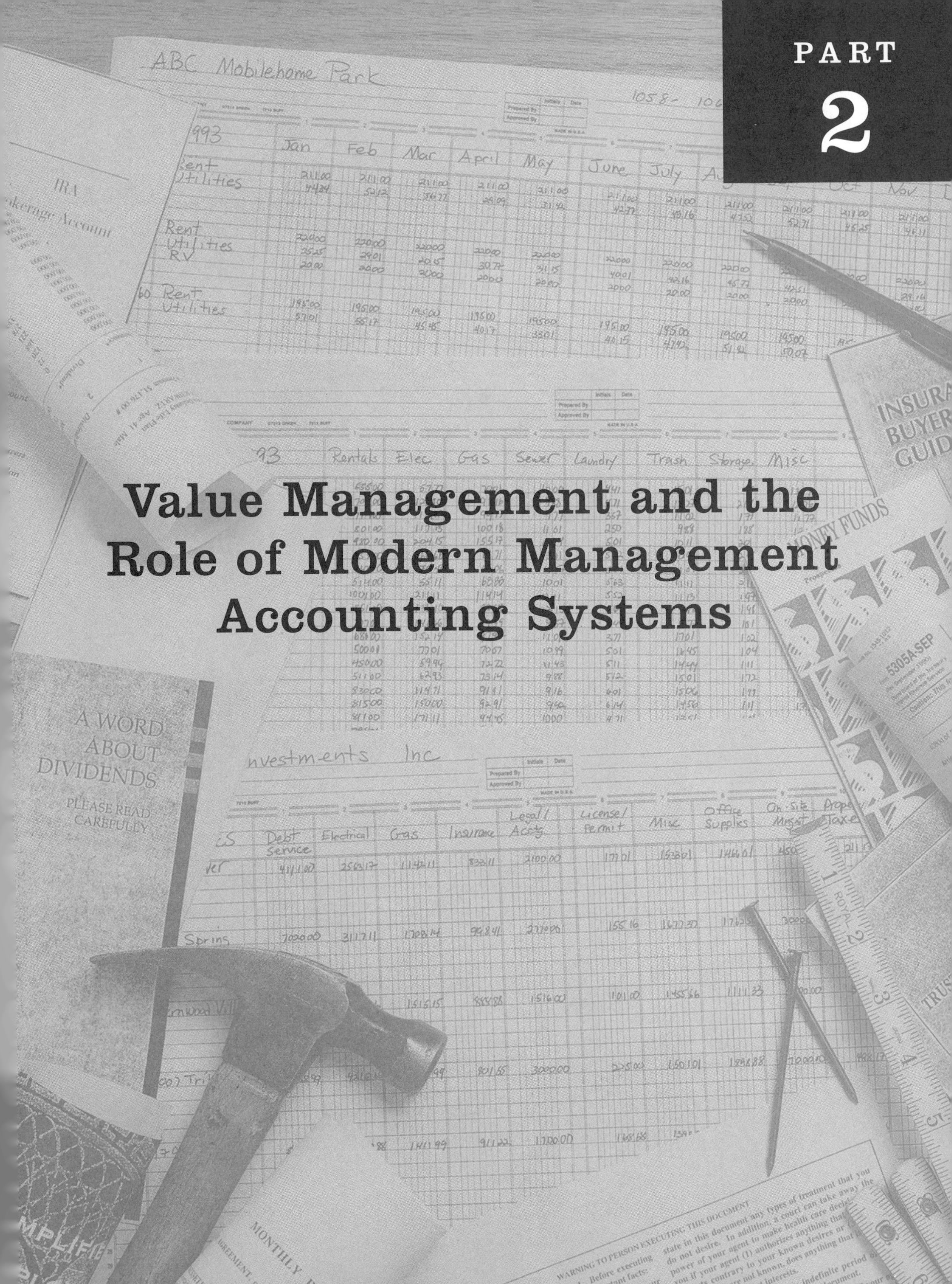

PART 2

Value Management and the Role of Modern Management Accounting Systems

CHAPTER 9

What Did it Really Cost Us?

Activity-Based Costing

KEY OBJECTIVES:

1	*Identify situations that create a need for new cost systems.*
2	*Explain the three production characteristics justifying ABC.*
3	*Describe how ABC uses resources and activities to calculate product costs.*
4	*Compare the allocation of batch costs in a traditional cost system and an ABC system.*
5	*Discuss how different cost allocations can affect income statements and profits.*
6	*(Appendix A) Summarize the differences between ABC's Bill of Activities and a traditional standard cost card.*

KEY OBJECTIVE 1

Identify situations that create a need for new cost systems.

The Crisis

After reviewing Multree's financial statements for the last three months, Sid and Jackie were more than worried. They identified four problems causing lower profits and keeping them from Multree's profit goal:

- *The sales mix is changing from plan.* Sales of the more expensive custom homes are increasing while standard home sales are declining. Profits should be going up, but instead they are going down.
- *Sales keeps scheduling special custom home orders.* They can't explain why competitors are pricing their standard homes so much lower than ours. Nor can they explain why our custom homes are priced so much lower than the competition.
- *Production costs are significantly over budget.* Workers too often stand idle while setup crews work overtime. Work-in-process inventories lay everywhere as production schedules change to accommodate custom home orders.
- *Purchasing can't order the materials for the custom homes fast enough.* These people are also working overtime, and purchasing costs are out of control.

Achieving their target profit for the year didn't look too likely. Thus, Sid decided today's meeting should address the crisis Multree Homes is facing. Each person had reviewed the financial reports. As Sid walks in, many are arguing, and pointing fingers at the others. Waving his hands over his head, Sid quiets everyone down and begins . . .

SID

"The company's in a turmoil! New competitors have entered our markets. They are competing vigorously for our well-established standard homes product line, offering price concessions, quality, and service options new to our market. The company is under siege and all our decisions seem to be wrong! Our competitors must be dumping their standard homes at prices that are not cost justified. We thought they would be doomed, but instead they seem to be prospering. We are the ones who are suffering!"

JACKIE

"Based on our accounting information, though, we are making the right decisions. Although we have many standard homes in inventory which aren't selling, demand for custom homes is increasing. They are twice as profitable as standard homes [having a $40,000 contribution margin per unit (CMU) compared to the standard homes' $20,000 CMU]. Our cashflow should be doubling!"

"This doesn't make any sense to me. Standard home sales always create most of our profits, but we can't sell them at our normal prices. You say the custom homes are even more profitable, and we are selling more of them. Cashflows should be increasing, but profits are falling. Are we getting the right information? It seems like our problems are mostly with sales and our competition. Bill, what do you think?"

Markups and marketing problems

"We have a mixed strategy selling both low-volume specialty products [custom homes] and high-volume commodity products [standard homes]. We set prices by marking up cost to achieve our profit goal. Unfortunately, our commodity line [standard homes] suffers from tough price competition. When we discussed pricing strategies [Chapter 7], we decided on the following average markup for all homes:

Average sales price for all homes [Exhibit 3-4]	**$ 54,545**	
Less: Average manufacturing cost (COGS)	**(33,227)**	
Average profit	**$ 21,318**	
Average markup ($21,318 ÷ $33,227)		**65% (rounded up)**

"As I see it, three factors cause our sales problems:

- Customers can get standard homes cheaper from our competition.
- Competitors are charging much more for custom homes. This makes it easier for our salespeople to sell custom homes as compared to standard homes.
- Our salespeople earn an average of $500 more in commissions on custom homes.

"Our markup percentage is similar to the industry average. *If our standard home sales prices are too high, could our costs be too high? Similarly, if our custom home prices are too low, could these costs be understated?*"

"I've compared our income statements with industry averages and our total costs seem reasonable based on the revenues we make. So do our profit margins. If we have a costing problem, it must be in determining the cost of specific product lines."

Production problems

"This seems reasonable to me! According to our cost variance reports, we are looking less and less efficient. Our standard costs show we should be much more efficient in high-volume production [standard homes] than with specialty products [custom homes]. I've prepared some comparisons between product lines [see Exhibit 9-1].

"For each of these activities, standard home costs are less than custom home costs. But, the sales staff can't sell our high-volume products. Scheduling keeps pushing the low-volume, more expensive custom homes. Every time we start another custom home, an expensive setup is needed. Production foremen can't stay within their budgets making only custom homes! This sales mix change creates three problems for production:

Comparisons Between Product Lines		
Production activities	**Standard homes**	**Custom homes**
Construction (direct labor hours):	1,000 hours per house at $10 per hour	2,500 hours per house at $10 per hour
Setups:	1 setup at $1,500 for each batch of 5 houses	1 setup per house at $2,000 each
Materials handling:	1 setup at $1,000 for each batch of 5 houses	$1,000 per house
Architectural costs:	$10,000 per year for the entire product line	$10,000 per house

Exhibit 9-1

- Workers spend less time actually making products and more time waiting on setup crews.
- Setup crews work overtime, but still can't keep up.
- Production overhead costs are over budget due to increasing setups and overtime."

"Wait a minute! You mean to tell us we're not as efficient with custom homes, but that's where we make more money? And we're more efficient when making standard homes, but that's where we are losing money? This really doesn't make sense!"

Purchasing problems

"I agree! Look at purchasing costs. We have the new automated materials ordering system for standard homes. We order materials in batches for each five houses, so we build them five at a time. However, purchasing agents are working a lot of overtime due to the increase in demand for custom homes. To minimize their costs, the Boss required three bids for each major direct material. Thus, we are using more and more suppliers."

Bob was particularly sensitive because of a roof tile problem last spring. The lowest bid came from a high-quality Taiwanese producer. The truck carrying the parts from its factory literally missed the boat, though, and sat dockside for six weeks. From a cost and quality point of view, it was an excellent purchase. However, more expensive substitute parts had to be ordered on a rush basis, creating chaos in production. Because the home was delivered late, a lot of customer goodwill was lost. And some of the tiles were still sitting in inventory.

"Yes! This also is costing us more money on the shop floor. My friends tell me since purchasing started shopping around, we can't get the same technical support from our regular suppliers. They used to help us with product design and manufacturing problems. But that was when we ordered a lot more from them. Since they are getting less business from us now, our major suppliers just aren't as cooperative. When called for help, they put us on a waiting list. We can't expect they will give us the same quality of technical support we used to enjoy because our orders are too small."

Symptoms of accounting system failure

"Factory people think our problems are in sales. We're using the same quality machines and people as our competition. Our cost overruns are due to the custom homes. We should either raise the price substantially, or stop making them!"

JACKIE

"No! Custom homes are our most profitable line. We can't drop them. I agree with you, though. We need to raise the price. We can't lower the price on our standard homes because if we lower our markup, we won't achieve our target profit. Maybe we should drop the standard homes line!"

Both Bill and Bob choked on their donuts. They know sooner or later custom home sales will drop if prices keep going up. If standard home prices don't drop, they won't sell, either. They think accounting is nuts. Together they prepared a list of symptoms signaling the need for a new accounting system [Exhibit 9-2].

Symptoms of Accounting System Problems

Where observed	The symptoms	The conflict
Sales	1. Competitors' sales prices on standard products (our high-volume products) appear unrealistically low.	Compared with industry averages, accounting reports show our sales prices are based on average markups yielding a normal profit.
Sales	2. Customers still buy our specialty products even as we keep raising prices. But competitors do not want to be in our specialty products market even though it appears very profitable.	Accounting reports show abnormally high profits for specialty products, which should increase competition but doesn't.
Production	3. Production management wants to drop the specialty line because it's too expensive and expand high-volume product lines because these products can be made more efficiently.	Accounting reports show specialty products are more profitable than commodity products.
Production	4. The costs of some activities are out of control, such as purchasing, setups, and materials handling.	Even though specialty products appear more profitable, the unfavorable overhead cost variances support Production's belief that they are more costly than commodity products (standard homes).
Accounting	5. Sales and Production are suspicious of accounting reports that show high-volume (commodity) products are less profitable than low-volume (specialty) products.	Sales and Production are in conflict due to conflicting accounting reports.

Exhibit 9-2

You Need a New Cost System When . . .

KEY OBJECTIVE 2

Explain the three production characteristics justifying ABC.

NANCY

"I may not be a true businessperson yet, but if we drop custom homes as Production suggests, and if we drop standard homes as Accounting suggests, won't we be out of business? Another thing seems pretty clear, too. That rigid cost-plus pricing formula is changing our sales mix for the worse. Whenever Sales quotes a custom home price, Accounting provides the direct costs [i.e., direct materials and labor], allocates production overhead using a $4.74 per direct labor hour predetermined overhead rate [POR], and then adds the 65% markup on manufacturing costs to cover allocated operating expenses and achieve our profit goal.

"The $50,000 standard home sales price also is based on its total manufacturing costs [direct and allocated] plus the required 65% markup. By 'required,' I mean our markup cannot be changed unless we are willing to give up our profit goal. It seems our sales prices are driven by our costs. In other words, costs determine sales price. But, if I understand what Bill is saying, our competition [the marketplace] really determines the maximum price we can charge for both our standard and custom homes. We can't sell standard homes at our normal price. Worse yet, we can't make custom homes fast enough, which is killing Purchasing and Production! If Jackie is correct, the problem is not with our total costs. It must be with how our accounting system charges those costs to our two product lines. *Can our accounting reports be misleading us about the real costs of each product line?*"

Quiet fell over the room.

JULIE

"Well, you know it's possible. When the weather changes, I change my clothes. Maybe operating conditions have changed due to our change in sales mix. Perhaps our cost-volume-profit analysis is no longer valid and we should change it. It is based on two critical assumptions:

- Costs can be classified as variable or fixed.
- These classifications are valid over some relevant range of volume."

Overhead is the real culprit

JULIE

"Direct materials and direct labor are variable costs we trace directly to each product line. Some of the variable and fixed overhead costs, though, are really step costs. We graphed these in our earlier meeting [Exhibit 3-3]. Further complicating our product costing efforts, overhead costs are different within each of our product lines. But, that's not how we allocate overhead into each product's cost. Here's how it's done in our cost accounting system:

In many traditional cost accounting systems, direct labor is used to allocate overhead. If this doesn't represent a true cause-effect relationship, products may be miscosted.

- First, we assume all overhead costs, including step costs, are either variable or fixed.
- Next, we group all variable overhead costs together, and all fixed overhead costs together.
- Then, predetermined overhead rates [PORs] are calculated for the variable and fixed overhead. Our variable overhead POR is $2.06 per direct labor hour. Our fixed overhead POR is $2.68 per direct labor hour.
- Finally, every home, standard and custom, is charged exactly the same amount per direct labor hour worked. The total amount of overhead cost allocated to both standard and custom homes is $4.74 multiplied by the direct labor hours worked on them."

BOB

"But, that's not how most of our overhead costs really behave! Costs like purchasing and setups do not vary with the labor hours worked directly on building each house. They do change, though, as we change our product mix, so they are not fixed costs either. *If we use direct labor to allocate all overhead, and labor does not cause much of the overhead, we're not accurately matching the overhead really used to the products.* For example, a custom home should not be charged the same overhead as a standard home if different overhead items are used. We need to divide the overhead into its various components. I've graphed how the overhead costs I talked about earlier [Exhibit 9-1] really behave [see Exhibit 9-3].

"Our cost accounting system allocates indirect labor costs for setups and materials handling as variable overhead. They are variable costs for custom homes, but they're step costs for standard homes. Standard home setups are $1,500 for each

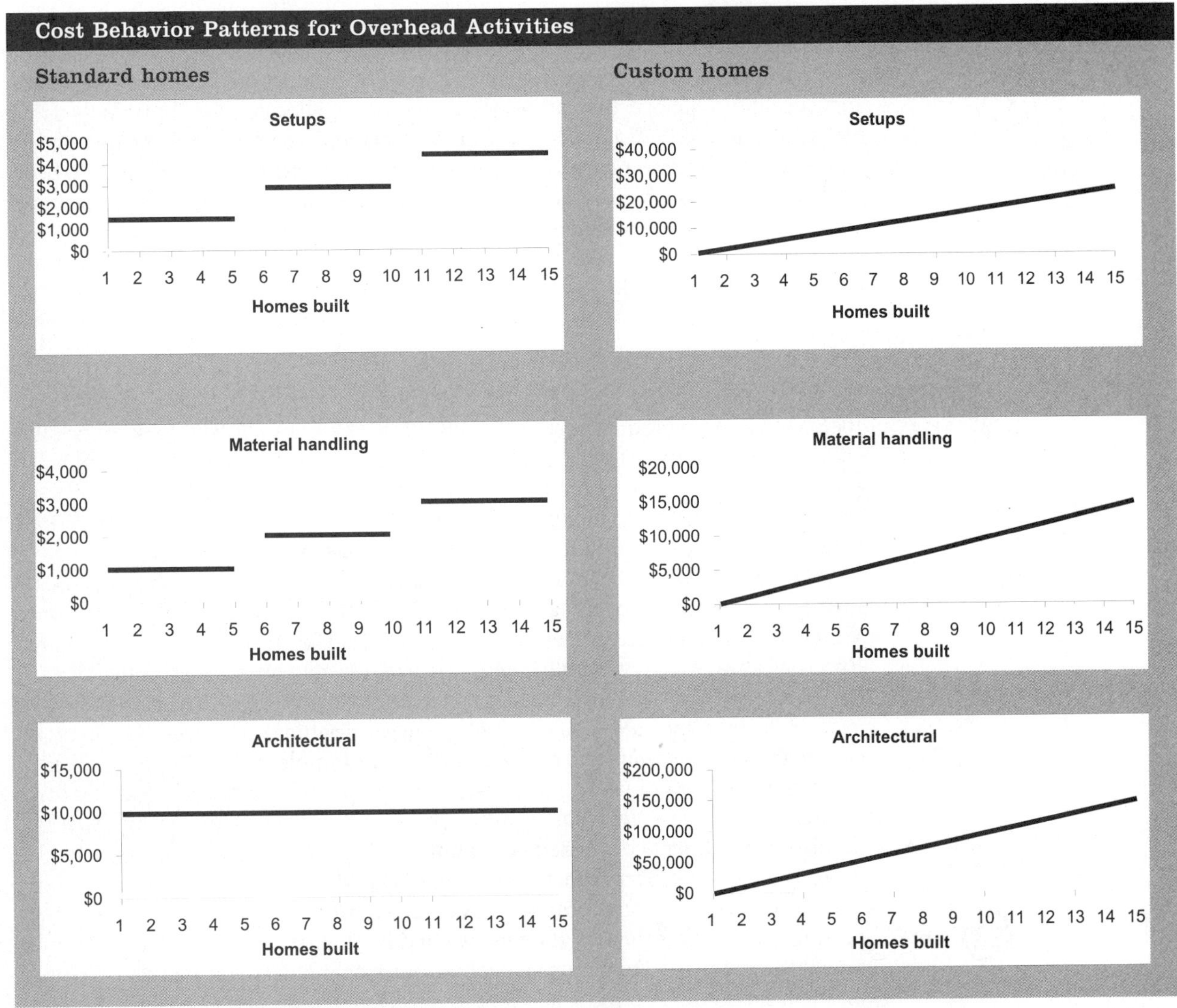

Exhibit 9-3

batch of five houses [see Exhibit 9-1]. Their materials handling costs are another $1,000 per batch. Architectural costs are allocated as part of fixed overhead. This is a fixed cost for standard homes, but each custom home requires its own architectural work. Therefore, this cost is really a directly traceable variable cost for custom homes!

"Each subset of overhead caused by a different type of activity is called a **cost pool**. We have many different overhead cost pools. *Each overhead cost pool should be charged to products based on its cause-effect relationship.* Assume purchasing costs are caused by the number of purchase orders issued. The number of purchase orders for standard and custom homes then can be used to allocate Purchasing Department costs. Most of the purchasing costs should be charged to custom homes because they require most of our purchase orders! In other words, each

> *Subsets of overhead having their own unique causes (cost drivers) are called* **cost pools**.

overhead cost pool should have its own allocation method [its own POR]. The accounting system should account for each cost pool separately."

"Well, that's just your perspective as head of production. From Jackie's financial accounting perspective, all overhead should be allocated to all products using the same rate [POR]. Tommy, as our human relations specialist, probably supports Bob because allocating each cost pool separately should result in better overhead cost variances, which are used in performance evaluations. From Sid's, Julie's, and my perspective, we want an allocation method congruent with how we budgeted for these activities and costs in the strategic plan and cash budget. From a marketing perspective, what do you think, Bill?"

Operating expenses: another culprit

"In setting sales prices, as long as I'm stuck using a markup based on cost, let's get the most accurate product cost we can. But I think we also should look at the allocations of nonmanufacturing costs like advertising, sales commissions, and shipping. These can be traced directly to product lines, but that's not how we allocate them in our accounting reports. It seems we have the potential for some serious miscosting of our two product lines with these costs as well!"

"While everything you say is true, financial reporting requires systematic methods for allocating overhead and nonmanufacturing costs to our product lines. We always have allocated manufacturing overhead by using direct labor hours. Expenses always have been allocated based on the relative sales revenues of each line. But, I see your point. *If the cost accounting system is going to be used to help us manage the business, rather than just for financial reporting, these types of allocations don't make sense when different cost pools exist.* For example, at Weyerhaeuser [one of our major suppliers of wood products], accounts payable costs are caused by three different cost drivers: the time required to service each of its operating divisions, number of documents processed, and number of invoices received for payment. So, its Accounts Payable Department costs were divided into three separate cost pools."

"Jackie's right. Cost allocations always have been done to satisfy financial reporting needs. That's the way the Boss wanted it. Financial accounting reports must satisfy the needs of external users such as our stockholders and bankers. The real problem is twofold and more subtle, though. Grandfather had an instinct for costs and pricing. He didn't rely on only the accounting data for pricing decisions. Most of what he did was based on his knowledge of the business. We just don't have his experience. *When we rely on the cost numbers for pricing, we become vulnerable to costing errors.* Thus, we are unable to plan strategically. This is a new competitive world. One not faced by the Boss. *If we try to run the company only 'by the numbers,' we may not be able to achieve our strategic plan and create long-term value.*

"Management's interpretation and understanding of the accounting numbers influences its decisions. Misinterpretations can lead to poor decisions. When I look back at our accounting systems problems [Exhibit 9-2], I wonder if the real problem is conflicting information or opinions and judgments. The issue we're concerned with is managing by the numbers versus using good management judgment!"

Different products can use different resources

"Let me try to clarify what's going on. Management accounting systems exist only because they are useful. The cost of changing the current system must be justified by improved decisions or risks avoided. The first key point is to realize the existing system was justified under old operating conditions. What has changed? Most importantly, we now have more than one product line made in the same factory. Only in the past few years have we built both standard and custom homes.

"Consider the resources needed to make these different products. If all products use the same amounts of the same resources, they will have the same cost. For example, in a factory making only one mass-produced product, like ball-point pens, each pen costs the same. The important question is, 'When won't products have the same per-unit cost?'" [Exhibit 9-4 summarizes the situations in which products should have different costs.]

When Will Products Have Different Costs?
When multiple product lines exist and Different products use different resources and activities and/or Different products use different amounts of the same resource or activity.

Exhibit 9-4

"I see what's happening. Complexity drives costs. The more complex our methods and products, the greater our costs. It's like when I was in school. One semester I had 3 courses. The next semester I had the same number of credits, but 6 courses. Six courses made keeping track of everything much harder. Like the number of classes I took, the more products we make, the harder it is to accurately track costs to each one."

Consumption ratio tests

"I see the need for a better way to assign costs to products and measure product profitability. When I see conflicts between marketing and production caused by the product cost and profitability numbers coming from our accounting system, I know we might have a costing problem. But installing a new cost system will be expensive. Before we invest a lot of money in it, do we have any simple 'tests' available to help us verify a miscosting problem?"

"Yes. In production, we look at consumption ratios. I had lunch with Jackie and our setup foreman the other day. Jackie tells me the cost accounting system allocates four times as much overhead to standard homes as to custom homes. However, our setup foreman tells me the actual setup time ratio is more like 3:2. These ratios don't agree! If the setup foreman is correct, and he should know, the cost accounting system is allocating too much setup cost to standard homes and not enough to custom homes."

"Well, if this is true, I better verify it. Let me run some numbers [Exhibit 9-5].

"My analysis confirms Bob's suspicions. First, let's look at production quotas. *If a standard and custom home use the same types and amounts of overhead*, ten times as much total overhead should be charged to standard homes as is charged to custom homes [production quotas are 100 standard homes to 10 custom homes, or a 10:1 ratio]. To make this happen, *the cost accounting system should use a volume-based cost driver*, such as a production quota, to allocate overhead.

"Since the direct labor hours are different for each product line [1,000 hours for standard homes versus 2,500 hours for custom homes], we use direct labor hours to allocate overhead. In this way, each home, whether standard or custom, gets charged the same amount of overhead per hour worked on it. Because direct

A Consumption Ratio Test for Setups

How does the cost accounting system allocate setup costs?
(Overhead is allocated using direct labor hours)

	Standard homes		**Custom homes**
Standard direct labor hours per home	1,000		2,500 DLhrs/house
× Production quota	× 100		× 10 Houses
Total direct labor hours per product line	100,000		25,000 DL hours
Direct labor consumption ratio		**4 to 1**	

Actual consumption ratio

	Standard homes		**Custom homes**
Budgeted setups	20		10 Per product line
× Setup hours (time to setup)	× 150		× 200 Hours per setup
Total setup hours per product line	3,000		2,000 Setup hours
Setup hours consumption ratio		**3 to 2**	

Exhibit 9-5

labor is a variable cost, total direct labor cost depends on production volume. So, if we allocate overhead using direct labor hours, we're still using a volume-based cost driver. Because we work four times as many hours on standard homes as compared to custom homes, the cost accounting system allocates four times as much total overhead to standard homes." [Exhibit 9-5 shows how this 4:1 direct labor consumption ratio is calculated.]

"But what *if some overhead costs do not vary directly with production volume* [e.g., step costs like setups]? Then *using a volume-based cost driver may incorrectly allocate overhead to products, distorting their costs*. Setups [a step cost per Exhibits 9-1 and 9-3] are a good example of an overhead activity whose cost is caused by a non-volume-based cost driver. In other words, setup costs are not variable costs based on production volume or direct labor hours. To correctly cost each product line, the line should be charged setup costs based on the number of setups required. The number of setups is the cost driver causing setup costs. And the product lines 'consume' setups in a different ratio than they use direct labor hours [i.e., a 3:2 ratio versus the 4:1 direct labor hours ratio as shown in Exhibit 9-5]. When we see a difference between the volume-based consumption ratio used to allocate overhead and a specific overhead activity's consumption ratio, we may need a different allocation method, like activity-based costing."

NANCY

"O.K. Let's see if I understand what's happened. Say our setup costs are $5. The cost accounting system charges $4 to standard homes and $1 to custom homes because we're using a volume-based cost driver [direct labor hours]. But we should be charging $3 to standard homes and $2 to custom homes."

JULIE

"Correct! I think we should do some more detailed analyses of our overhead activities. First, I'll explain what activity-based costing is and how it works. Then, I'll show you how our traditional costing system miscosts our two product lines."

KEY OBJECTIVE 3

Describe how ABC uses resources and activities to calculate product costs.

Activity-Based Costing Systems

"Many companies in our situation have changed how they cost products. They are using **activity-based costing [ABC]**. ABC figures the cost of each **activity** [the work we do]. Then, products are charged for the activities they use, like setups.

JULIE

ABC differs from traditional product costing systems in two fundamental ways:

- **Allocating overhead into product costs is much more detailed.**
- **Nonmanufacturing costs often are included in the product's cost.**

"Because ABC is so different, many companies have two accounting systems. They continue to allocate overhead in a more traditional, simple, and less costly way for financial reporting. This often is called the 'peanut butter approach' because it satisfies GAAP through spreading overhead equally to all products. These companies then have a separate ABC-based management accounting system to support decision making. Often, ABC is done with computer software, separate from the financial accounting system. I can get a current list of available software by calling the Institute of Management Accountants using its 800 number if you wish."

ABC systems *trace resources directly to activities, and then activities to products and services.* **Resources** *are assets needed to perform activities.* **Activities** *represent the work done in providing a service or making a product.*

Resources

"ABC is a two-step method. First, resource costs are traced to activities. Second, activity costs are charged to the products. **Resources** are the assets we use in doing work [activities]. I've grouped our resources into four categories [see Exhibit 9-6].

JULIE

Resource Categories	
1. *People:*	Direct labor, indirect labor, supervisors, purchasing agents, sales personnel, management, administrative staff, Computer Information Systems personnel, the accounting group, etc.
2. *Materials:*	Direct materials, indirect materials, purchasing forms, invoices, office supplies, etc.
3. *Direct technology:*	Tools and equipment used by people in performing activities. Their use can be traced directly to the activity.
4. *Facilities:*	Buildings and grounds, heat and light, property taxes and insurance, etc.

Exhibit 9-6

"People do work, or in the ABC jargon, they perform activities. Thus, all labor costs are directly traceable to activities. We also can trace many material costs directly to activities. Similarly, people use tools and equipment when doing specific activities, so we can trace these costs to activities.

"Facilities pose a problem, though. Often we cannot see how much of the building is used in issuing a purchase order [a specific activity] or in paying our bills. Facility costs still need to be allocated. I could measure the square footage of each department, allocate building costs to departments using their square footage, and then somehow allocate the department charge to activities done within it. This seems too costly, though. Maybe we can do this in the future if we believe it will help our product pricing decisions. I've decided on a simpler approach. Each house, custom and standard, gets allocated an equal amount of these costs. . . ."

Activities

"Wait a minute. Before we can trace resource costs to activities, don't we have to know what everyone does? How can we get a list of activities each person or group does? Is it as simple as just asking everyone to make a list of what they do?"

JULIE

"Well, it often is a lot more complicated. But, as a first step, this is a good idea. Let's keep it simple and somewhat general. We don't want people listing all the specific tasks they go through in doing something [e.g., punching a phone number into a fax machine]. I was just thinking about the Weyerhaeuser Payroll Department services and activities. When I had lunch with the controller last month, he listed some of these:

Payroll services	Activities
• Preparing normal paychecks	• Verify accuracy of employee timecards
• Preparing special paychecks	• Input payroll data into computer system
• Updating employee records	• Update master records files on the computer
• Issuing payroll reports	• Process changes in employee deductions, etc.
• Preparing special labor studies	• Review edit reports
• Labor distribution reporting	• Journalize payroll
• Processing deferred compensation and stock options	• Process changes, corrections, etc.
• Payroll tax reporting	• Print paychecks
	• Distribute paychecks
	• Prepare bank transfers
	• Respond to employee inquiries

"Unless we are doing a detailed analysis of a department's activities, for example, to redesign how the work is done, we should keep this as simple as possible [the KISS principle]. Start with the major activities. Once we have a list of the major activities a person does, we then can ask how much time it takes and what tools and equipment are used."

"Of course, making a list of all the resources used in each activity a person does can be a time-consuming, detailed, and costly process! Is it really worth it? Most of my friends who work in the factory and office won't want to take the time to do this right. They just won't see the benefit."

"You're right, Tommy. In most ABC projects, a pilot study is done first. Often simple surveys of the workers provide rough information about major activities performed, time used, resources needed, and the like. While this isn't very accurate, it provides us with a starting point. Fireman's Fund did this to approximate how much time its people spent on activities like soliciting business, screening policy applications, and processing the paperwork. After we make some rough ABC analyses, certain areas will appear to warrant a more detailed study. As specific analyses get more detailed, we have many software programs available to help us. Doing the calculations is not the difficult part of the process.

"What's really hard is motivating individuals to do the background work necessary for ABC. But, to improve specific activities and our entire operation, we ultimately will have to do this. If people are given the time, training, management support, and rewards for improving their work, hopefully we can get their acceptance. Also, if we keep losing money, motivation may be simple. As one Campbell Soup plant controller bemoaned, 'We've got to improve what we're doing or we'll go out of business!' Everyone hated ABC, but they knew they had to do it right because their jobs depended on it!"

"I agree with everything you just said, but we need to use our real reasons for improving operations. We have to keep away from 'finger-pointing.' Our workers cannot feel they are being blamed for problems we discover. Nor can they feel their jobs are being threatened. If they think they'll be punished by the ABC results, the study may be sabotaged. We have to identify and communicate the positive impact of their efforts to everyone involved. We also have to do this in a way everybody trusts!

"The results from an ABC study have to be consistent with what our people know and do. Their trust in ABC is essential. I'm sure we can earn that trust, however, if it appears ABC is not just another accounting study. The accounting staff spends very little time on the shop floor. We usually see them only when they're bearing bad news like cost variance reports! They're thought of as 'bean counters' and the 'cops on the block.' Building trust will require the accounting people working with the factory people. Developing this trust over time will happen only if everyone is an equal member of the team."

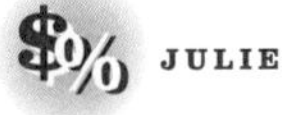

"Well, hopefully . . . At the very least, though, it will allow some agreement on priorities. Again, let's just keep the analysis as simple as possible in our first attempt to use ABC. Let's also keep our goal simple: a more accurate product cost for standard and custom homes. I've prepared a sample of the activities we do [see Exhibit 9-7]. This is just a partial list to illustrate the idea."

Example Activities at Multree Homes

Departments:	Activities:
Sales:	1. Advertising 2. Answering customer inquiries 3. Taking sales orders 4. Coordinating sales with production 5. Customer follow-up after completion
Production:	1. Schedule production 2. Order materials 3. Set up equipment 4. Rough framing, roofing, install windows, carpeting, etc.
Warehousing and Shipping:	1. Receive materials 2. Inspect materials 3. Store materials 4. Deliver materials to production 5. Prepare completed houses for shipping 6. Load trucks 7. Deliver to retailers or customers
Accounting:	1. Pay bills 2. Prepare payroll 3. Run cost accounting system and create reports 4. Run financial accounting system and create reports 5. Collect revenues from customers
Computer Information Systems:	1. Run order entry system 2. Prepare production schedules 3. Process manufacturing data into costing system 4. Run accounts receivable and payable systems 5. Issue reports from general ledger system 6. Prepare sales reports and forecast information

Exhibit 9-7

Cost drivers and activity levels

What causes a cost is called a cost driver. Labor is a resource. The wage rate is the price of a unit (hour) of labor. Its cost driver is the hours worked on an activity. So, the resource cost charged to this activity is the wage rate times the hours worked. Once all resource costs are traced to an activity, like setting up machines, then the setup cost can be charged to each product based on the number of setups it requires. The number of setups is this activity's cost driver.

"For product costing, we need to charge activity costs to products. This is done with cost drivers. In many preliminary ABC studies, *a cost driver often is the output of an activity*. For example, purchasing costs may be caused by the number of purchase orders issued. To keep it simple, we can divide Purchasing Department costs by the number of purchase orders and charge each house for the number of purchase orders it requires using this cost per purchase order. The number of purchase orders becomes the cost driver for the purchasing activity. Both resources and activities have cost drivers. Here's an example using some very simple numbers [see Exhibit 9-8]."

"Well, Julie, this works pretty well as long as each purchase order takes about the same amount of time to prepare. I've seen this simple assumption used in many ABC studies. I've been rethinking this, though, and it isn't true for us. Standard home purchase orders are created by our new ordering system. Custom home purchase orders are manually prepared. Even though our proforma income statement shows a sales forecast of 100 standard homes and only 10 custom homes, I'll bet custom home purchasing requires almost 80% of the Purchasing Department's time!"

"You're probably right, Bob. It's important not to be too simple! The output of an activity may not be its cost driver. *A cost driver is what really causes a cost.* We'll need to work closely with our purchasing agents to correctly identify the real cost driver. This is another example of why teamwork is so critical."

"To help us better identify cost drivers and assign costs to products, activities often are organized into four levels." [These are presented in Exhibit 9-9 on p. 326.]

"You know, I don't think the numbers have to be perfect to identify miscosting problems. They need to be good enough so they're not misleading. The accounting system will be good enough when it helps us better understand the physical activities people do and how they are related. Organizing our activities into these levels should help."

"You are right. The issue is, 'What does it cost us to do things that increase value?' But, I'm still a little nervous with all this behavioral talk. Why didn't the Boss need this information?"

"Look, you have to remember the Boss knew the business really well. He knew which activities caused costs. The economic conditions were radically different then, too. We operated in prosperous times with little competition. The Boss just didn't need formal information from the accounting system to run the business. He also knew the accounting numbers were primarily to keep the IRS and bankers happy. We want to use the numbers in running the business, though."

"I'm sorry, but I still don't understand why we shouldn't try to develop the most accurate costs possible. How can we justify compromising the accuracy of our accounting system?"

"Look at it this way, Nancy. You are driving your car down the highway. If you know your car and are a good driver, you can estimate your speed without a speedometer. But, if you don't have a good understanding, you need the speedometer."

"Yes! That is what professional race car drivers do. They are excellent drivers who know their cars really well. What if a driver is somewhere in between having no understanding and having total understanding, though?"

"Then it is just a matter of accuracy. You probably can be satisfied with a little inaccuracy in the speedometer. Say, 10% or so."

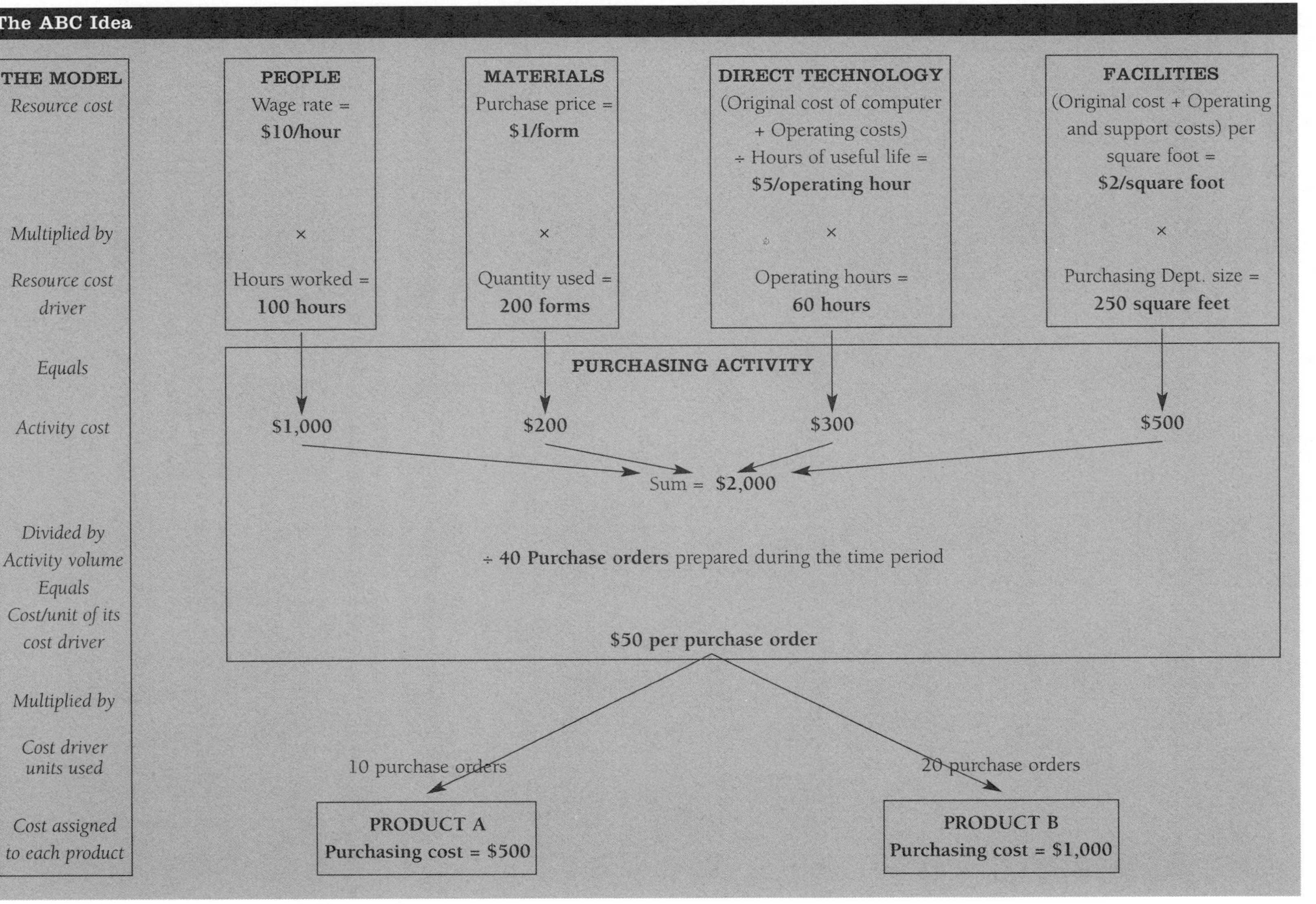

The ABC Idea
THE MODEL
Resource cost
Multiplied by
Resource cost driver
Equals
Activity cost
Divided by Activity volume
Equals Cost/unit of its cost driver
Multiplied by
Cost driver units used
Cost assigned to each product
PEOPLE
Wage rate =
$10/hour
×
Hours worked =
100 hours
MATERIALS
Purchase price =
$1/form
×
Quantity used =
200 forms
DIRECT TECHNOLOGY
(Original cost of computer + Operating costs)
÷ Hours of useful life =
$5/operating hour
×
Operating hours =
60 hours
FACILITIES
(Original cost + Operating and support costs) per square foot =
$2/square foot
×
Purchasing Dept. size =
250 square feet
PURCHASING ACTIVITY
$1,000
$200
$300
$500
Sum = $2,000
÷ 40 Purchase orders prepared during the time period
$50 per purchase order
10 purchase orders
20 purchase orders
PRODUCT A
Purchasing cost = $500
PRODUCT B
Purchasing cost = $1,000

Exhibit 9-8

Activity Levels in ABC Systems	
Product (unit)-level activities	These activities are needed every time an individual product is made. They are traced directly to each product.
Batch-level activities	These activities are needed every time a batch of products is made. They are traced directly to batches and then allocated equally to each product in the batch.
Product line-level activities	These activities are unique to individual product lines. Product line costs are allocated equally to each product in the product line at Multree. In other companies, specific activities might be allocated separately based on their unique cost drivers (different cause-effect relationships).
Facilities-level activities	These activities are associated with a facility, such as the factory or administration building. At Multree, they are allocated to all products equally. As with product-line activities, these might be allocated separately based on their unique cost drivers (different cause-effect relationships).

Exhibit 9-9

JACKIE

"Hold your horses, Slim. If I'm 10% over the speed limit and I'm caught, the ticket is pretty expensive! Oh, but I see the moral in your story. Under certain conditions, it makes sense to buy a better speedometer. I guess our accounting system choices are like the speedometer. The system is more or less valuable depending on our needs and our knowledge of the business."

They stopped the meeting for lunch, and to think about these ideas. After lunch, the meeting began again. The room was filled with apprehension.

NANCY

"O.K. I think I understand. With traditional cost allocations, all overhead is allocated in the same way to every product using one overhead rate [often based on direct labor hours]. And I remember that nonmanufacturing costs, even though they can be traced directly to specific products or product lines, commonly are allocated using relative sales revenues." [See Exhibit 8-5.]

BILL

"That is my understanding, too. Our financial reports charge nonmanufacturing costs, like sales expense, to the time period reported [a monthly or annual income statement]. These costs are not assigned to individual products, as we do with direct manufacturing costs like direct materials and labor. To be consistent for our auditors, we use revenues as the basis for allocating expenses to product lines. For example, last year custom home sales accounted for 20% of our revenues. So that product line was allocated 20% of all expenses, even though my sales force spent 80% of its time with custom home buyers!"

JULIE

"That's correct, Bill. No wonder we have miscosting problems! The good news is ABC can include both manufacturing and nonmanufacturing costs. All resource costs are traced to activities, and activities are charged to the products using them. This, in turn, should provide more accurate product costs. I've drawn a picture comparing our traditional costing to ABC [see Exhibit 9-10].

"ABC has four activity categories. These aren't perfect, but they will improve our measures enough to avoid some of our worst mistakes. Let's relate the four ac-

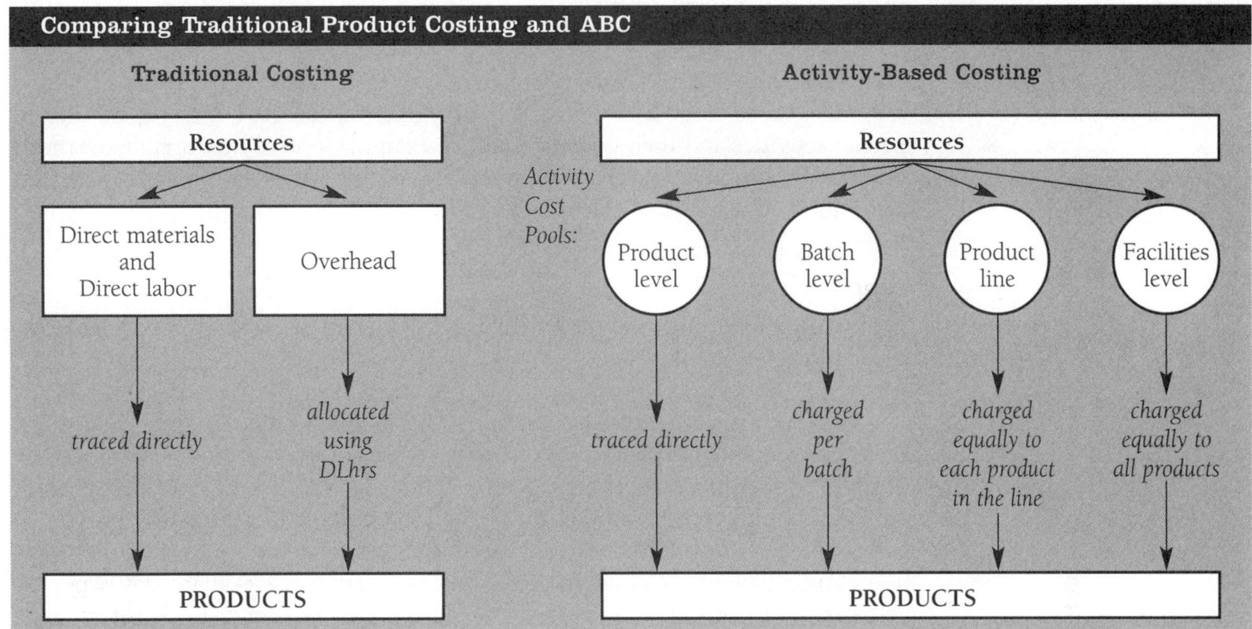

Exhibit 9-10

tivity levels to their narrative descriptions [Exhibit 9-9] and the earlier cost behavior graphs [Exhibit 9-3].

Activities usually are organized into four levels: **product** *or service unit,* **batch** *(a group of products),* **product line**, *and* **facilities**. *When costing a product, unit-level activities are variable costs. Batch-level activities are step costs. Product line and facilities-level activities are fixed costs.*

- **Product [or unit]-level activities** happen each time we make another product. These are direct variable costs. For our custom homes [see Exhibit 9-3] these include setup, material handling, and architectural costs. All are unique to each custom home made.
- **Batch-level activities** are step costs. For standard homes, setups and material handling are batch-level costs [see Exhibit 9-3]. Every time we make another batch of five standard homes, we incur another level of these costs.
- **Product line-level** costs are direct fixed costs of a product line. Standard home architectural costs are an example [see Exhibit 9-3]. We budget $10,000 per year for architectural changes to this product line [see Exhibit 9-1].
- **Facilities-level** costs include common costs for the entire company. They cannot be traced directly to any product line. When costing products and services, these are fixed costs."

SID

"But even with ABC, we still have the responsibility to know the business well enough so we can identify situations where the accounting system is causing problems. Hopefully though, we will have fewer situations to watch out for with ABC. The accounting system can't do it all for us, but it can make good management easier! Knowledge about the company can be in the people and/or the information system. This 'information mix' depends on the particular people, the situation, and the accounting system's sophistication. As our business becomes more complex, we should consider the need for a more detailed, costly accounting system."

NANCY

"So the idea is to make activities more visible by turning the overhead cost 'black box' into a glass box. But, before we install an ABC system, how serious are these miscosting problems?"

KEY OBJECTIVE 4

Compare the allocation of batch costs in a traditional cost system and an ABC system.

How Did We Miscost Our Products?

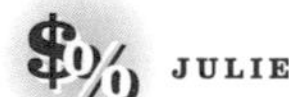

JULIE

"To calculate the costing errors, compare how we assign costs to products with how we budget those costs. By looking at the budget, we can get a pretty good idea of specific activities and their cost drivers. For example, one of the variable overhead components, indirect labor, is composed of two activities [setups and materials handling]. Let's look at setup costs."

A setup costs example

JULIE

"First, we'll look at how the traditional costing system charges setup costs to standard and custom homes."

Traditional setup cost allocation. "In Exhibit 9-11, the top calculation shows our variable overhead POR. Variable overhead includes indirect labor. One component of indirect labor is setup costs. Of the $257,500 total variable overhead, $50,000 is budgeted for setup costs. The middle calculation shows the portion of the variable overhead POR representing setup costs. The bottom calculation shows the setup cost allocations to both product lines. Every house is charged 40¢ per direct labor hour for setups. Because a standard home needs only 1,000 direct labor hours to complete, a $400 setup cost is charged to it. Custom homes require 2,500 direct labor hours, so they are allocated $1,000 each for setups."

Allocating Setup Costs as Part of the Variable Overhead POR

$$\text{Variable overhead POR} = \frac{\text{Budgeted variable overhead}}{\text{Budgeted direct labor hours}} = \frac{\$257{,}500}{125{,}000\text{ DLhrs}} = \$2.06/\text{DLhr}$$

$$\text{Setup costs portion of the variable overhead POR} = \frac{\text{Budgeted setup costs}}{\text{Budgeted direct labor hours}} = \frac{\$50{,}000}{125{,}000\text{ DLhrs}} = \$0.40/\text{DLhr}$$

	Standard homes	Custom homes
Variable overhead POR for setups	$ 0.40 /DLhr	$ 0.40 /DLhr
× Standard direct labor hours per house	× 1,000 DLhrs	× 2,500 DLhrs
Setup costs allocated to each house	**$ 400 per house**	**$ 1,000 per house**

Exhibit 9-11

ABC setup cost allocation. "Let me show you how we budgeted for setup costs, and how we can allocate them using ABC. Because custom homes are unique, each setup takes more time than for standard homes. We also make standard homes in batches of five. Each custom home is made individually, so it needs its own setup. Each batch of standard homes costs less to set up than a custom home because of these two differences. In the top calculation of Exhibit 9-12, we budget $1,500 to set up a batch of five standard homes, and $2,000 for each custom home.

"Because we have a sales forecast of 100 standard homes, we plan 20 setups and a $30,000 budget. Planning to sell 10 custom homes, each with its own setup, $20,000 is budgeted for this product line. The middle calculation shows our $50,000 total budget for setups [the same $50,000 shown in the middle calculation of Exhibit 9-11]: $30,000 for standard homes and $20,000 for custom homes.

ABC Setup Cost Allocation

	Standard Homes	Custom Homes
Standard labor rate	$ 10.00 /hour	$ 10.00 /hour
× Standard labor hours per setup	× 150 hours	× 200 hours
Standard setup cost	**$ 1,500 /setup**	**$ 2,000 /setup**
× Originally budgeted setups	× 20 setups	× 10 setups
Budgeted setup costs	$30,000	$20,000
÷ Product line volume	÷ 100 houses	÷ 10 houses
ABC cost per house	**$ 300 /house**	**$ 2,000 /house**

Exhibit 9-12

According to our ABC analysis, a standard home should be allocated $300 for setup costs [the bottom calculation in Exhibit 9-12]. Our traditional cost allocation [$400 in Exhibit 9-11] overcosts standard homes by $100. ABC also shows custom homes should be charged $2,000 for setup costs. The traditional cost allocation [$1,000 in Exhibit 9-11] undercosts each custom home by $1,000!

"Why? Direct labor hours do not cause setup costs. Hewlett-Packard already knows this. At its Boise Surface Mount Center, labor accounts for only 2% of its costs. Hewlett-Packard changed its labor-based allocations to 10 cost pools. It then discovered over 75% of its 57 products were miscosted, with one-fifth miscosted by 20% to 100%.

"We make two product lines [see Exhibit 9-1]. They each need the same activity [setups] and resource [setup time], but the setup times are different. This is an example of different products using different amounts of the same resource [the last characteristic in Exhibit 9-4]. *By directly tracing this resource to an activity and then directly tracing the activity to each product line, we develop a more accurate product cost.*"

A purchasing cost example

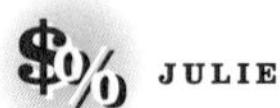
JULIE

"Here's another example. We currently budget purchasing costs as part of our general and administrative expenses. Purchasing costs represent $200,000 of the $1 million budget for these expenses."

JACKIE

Traditional purchasing costs allocation. "In our financial statements, all expenses are allocated to the two product lines using their relative sales revenues. This results in a standard home being allocated $1,667 for purchasing costs. A custom home is allocated $3,333 of the purchasing costs [see the top half of Exhibit 9-13]."

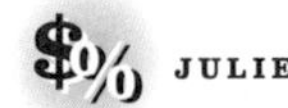
JULIE

ABC purchasing costs allocation. "As with setups, purchase orders are a batch cost for standard homes. However, with all the different suppliers we use for our custom homes, we issue twice as many purchase orders for one custom home as we do for a batch of five standard homes. Each custom home purchase order also takes three times as long to process as compared to standard homes. On this basis, I figured 25% of the total Purchasing Department time and cost should be charged to standard homes and 75% to custom homes. We can't use the number of purchase orders as our cost driver [as in Exhibit 9-8] because the activities and costs per purchase order are different for standard homes versus custom homes. Here's

Purchasing Costs Allocations					
Traditional allocations:		Standard homes		Custom homes	Totals
Originally budgeted revenues		$5,000,000		$1,000,000	$6,000,000
Relative revenue ratios		5/6		1/6	
Traditional cost allocation	@ 5/6 =	$166,667	@ 1/6 =	$ 33,333	$200,000
÷ Product line volume		÷ 100 homes		÷ 10 homes	
Allocated cost per house		**$ 1,667 /house**		**$ 3,333 /house**	
ABC allocations:		**Standard homes**		**Custom homes**	**Totals**
ABC purchasing cost allocation	@ 25% =	$ 50,000	@ 75% =	$150,000	$200,000
÷ Batches per product line		÷ 20 batches		÷ 10 batches	
ABC cost per batch		**$ 2,500 /batch**		**$ 15,000 /batch**	
÷ Houses per batch		÷ 5 houses/batch		÷ 1 house/batch	
ABC cost per house		**$ 500 /house**		**$ 15,000 /house**	

Exhibit 9-13

how I came up with the relative times. Assume it takes one hour to create the purchase orders for a batch of five standard homes:

Time for a batch of 5 standard homes	**1 hour**
Number of batches planned	**× 20 batches**
Total time needed for standard homes	**20 hours**
Each custom home purchase order takes 3 times as long as a standard home purchase order	**3 hours per home**
Need twice as many purchase orders	**× 2**
Purchasing time needed for one home	**6 hours per home**
Custom homes sales forecast	**× 10 custom homes**
Total time needed for custom homes	**60 hours**

"So, standard homes need 25% [20 hours ÷ (20 + 60 hours)] of Purchasing's time. Custom homes need 75%." [The bottom half of Exhibit 9-13 shows how these time ratios are used to cost both product lines.]

NANCY

"We've really miscosted our product lines with purchasing costs! Using our traditional costing system, a standard home's cost is overcosted by $1,167 [$1,667 – $500]. Custom homes are undercosted by $11,667 [$3,333 – $15,000]."

BILL

"We put together many other examples of the miscosting problems with our traditional system. [The complete analysis is in Appendix A, Exhibit 9A-5.] When we go back and look at all the different activities, our traditional cost allocations overcost standard homes by $1,876. If we abandon the cost-plus pricing strategy and markup we have been locked into, we can lower the sales price and again compete successfully in this market. Also, look at custom homes. Traditional allocations undercost them by $18,756 each, so we are underpricing them. No wonder we're losing money as our sales mix changes to more custom homes!"

NANCY

"Let's see if I understand what's happened. *While traditional cost allocation methods may be acceptable for financial [external] reporting, they can cause serious product costing [and pricing] errors when organizations:*

1. *Make different products or provide different services, and*

2. *Different products or services use different activities and resources, or*

3. *They use the same activities and resources, but in different amounts.*

If so, we better not group all the overhead together and then allocate it using just one assumed cause-effect relationship [e.g., direct labor hours]. Nor should we assume all expenses are correctly charged to product lines by allocating their costs based on product line relative sales revenues. This may be O.K. for financial reporting, but it sure isn't good enough for management decisions, such as product pricing!"

Miscosting services

"The miscosting caused by traditional allocations is not limited just to manufacturers like us. It happens in merchandising, service, and governmental organizations, too. When I broke my leg skiing last winter, the hospital bill was outrageous! My insurance paid only 80% after a healthy [pun intended] deductible. After some investigation, I discovered nursing care can vary from 5% to 70% of the time a patient is in the hospital. It depends on the illness or injury's severity, called acuity level. While I didn't require much nursing care, I was charged the same room rate as anyone else in that ward. The room rate included a charge for 24-hour nursing availability. Because of my complaints to the insurance company, the hospital conducted an ABC study of nursing care. Now, as each patient is admitted, they are rated on a 5-point acuity scale. Patients are charged a fixed hourly rate multiplied by the average hours their acuity level requires. Actually, ABC is becoming quite popular in healthcare management, especially in measuring the costs of specific treatments."

"I'm really worried about Uncle Tom and Aunt Harriet. They're on Medicare now. Costs increase every year, as do their deductibles. Medicare should require ABC! I just read a report stating Medicare requires hospital operating costs to be allocated based on patient-days. The amount reimbursed is based on the number of days a Medicare patient is in the hospital. Patient costs have at least two cost drivers, though: costs of admission and per-day treatment costs. Admission costs are substantial, but most people do not stay a long time. The elderly, though, stay much longer. By averaging admission costs over patient-days for both non-Medicare and Medicare patients, the per-day average is inflated for the longer-staying Medicare patients. The report's authors estimated Medicare is overbilled between $66 million and $2 billion per year!"

"Many service firms are moving to ABC to overcome problems from competitors, regulators, and governmental downsizing and outsourcing. For example, the U.S. Postal Service began accepting credit cards based on its ABC study. AT&T's breakup and deregulation lead to an ABC study of its business billing center. Union Pacific Railroad now uses ABC to figure freight charges. Their charges are based on four activities: the cost of loading and unloading [cost driver is tons of freight per shipment], moving freight [cost driver is gross ton miles], the cost of the train [cost driver is freight car miles], and switching freight trains [cost driver is yard-train switching minutes]."

"Hughes Aircraft had to dump its 50-year-old accounting system because its labor-based allocations no longer represented the true cost drivers. The federal government's Defense Department demanded better cost estimates. Not only did Hughes' ABC pilot studies provide more accurate cost estimates, they also streamlined the government reporting process!"

Why Don't We Know What Went Wrong?

NANCY

"Now that I understand the cause of our costing and pricing problems, how do our cost allocations affect the projected profits from decisions such as changing our sales mix? Isn't this the 'bottom line' concern we all have?"

JULIE

"This is not a simple question to answer, Nancy. We normally prepare two different types of income statements, contribution margin-based for internal decision making, and functional format for financial reporting. With ABC, we can prepare a third kind of income statement based on activity levels."

KEY OBJECTIVE 5

Discuss how different cost allocations can affect income statements and profits.

Contribution margin-based income statements

"First, remember we use contribution margin income statements and cost-volume-profit analysis to support our decisions. This system assumes all costs are either variable or fixed, including batch costs. In our profit planning, we projected contribution margins per house of $20,000 for standard homes and $40,000 for custom homes. With our original sales mix of 100 standard and 10 custom homes, we projected a total contribution margin of $2.4 million [see Exhibit 3-4]. This covered our $1.4 million in fixed costs, and provided our $1 million profit goal. Changing the sales mix to 80 standard and 20 custom homes should not have changed our total contribution margin, fixed costs or profits. So, we originally didn't think this was a bad idea. Bill and I prepared an analysis [see Exhibit 9-14]."

NANCY

"So you're saying our variable and fixed costs assumptions originally led us to believe the sales mix change would not change our profits. However, an ABC analysis shows this new mix will actually increase our costs, and lower our profits by $230,000!"

Functional form income statements

JACKIE

"We make some different assumptions and cost allocations with functional income statements for financial reporting. When using the financial accounting system for forecasting and inputting the new sales mix into this system, it shows higher costs and lower profits of $26,200."

NANCY

"Wait a minute! Our contribution margin analysis said profits wouldn't change. The ABC analysis shows profits going down by $230,000 if we change our sales mix. Our financial accounting system says only $26,200. Which is correct? Why do the income statements show different profits?"

JULIE

"Actually, both the contribution margin and functional format statements are wrong! Remember, Nancy, the contribution margin analysis says if total contribution margin doesn't change, profits will not change [at least within the relevant range]. But, when we rebudgeted activities, profits decreased $230,000. Our assumptions about variable and fixed costs were wrong.

"With our financial accounting system, the $26,200 lower profit is caused by cost of goods sold [our product costs], which is calculated using absorption costing. While we are projecting to sell 10 fewer houses in total with this new sales mix, our production costs appear to increase $26,200!" [Exhibit 9-15 on p. 334 shows this change.]

"My point is simple. If we don't rebudget our costs based on the activities causing them, both income statements will project the wrong profits. Both are based on some bad assumptions about our cost behaviors:

- Both assume indirect labor is a variable cost. Really, it's made up of two batch costs: setups and materials handling.

Contribution Margin-Based Profit Projection

STANDARD HOMES			CUSTOM HOMES			COMPANY TOTALS
CMU	Volume	Contribution margin	CMU	Volume	Contribution margin	Contribution margin
$20,000	100	$2,000,000	$40,000	10	$400,000	$2,400,000
$20,000	80	$1,600,000	$40,000	20	$800,000	$2,400,000

Bad assumptions:

Activities:	Explanation:	Effect on total costs if we had correctly budgeted these activities:	
Indirect materials: setups and materials handling	Treated as variable costs, but really batch costs. (If our standard home volume is not a multiple of 5, our batch size, we would have projected the wrong cost.)		$ 0
Architectural	Treated as a fixed cost, but really a product-level variable cost for custom homes.	10 extra custom homes × $10,000 =	$100,000
Administration: shipping	All administrative costs treated as fixed costs, but this is really a product-level variable cost.	New total volume is 10 less than original volume × $1,000 per house =	$ (10,000)
Administration: purchasing	All administrative costs treated as fixed costs, but this is really a batch cost.	The extra work due to increased custom homes requires a budget increase* =	$140,000
INCREASE IN TOTAL COSTS:			$230,000

* Change in purchasing costs:	Costs	Cost change
Original budget	$200,000	
Allocation to standard homes @ 25%	$ 50,000	
Save 20% (80 instead of 100 homes)	× (20%)	$ (10,000)
Allocation to custom homes @ 75%	$150,000	
Double the sales volume	× 100%	+$150,000
Net purchasing costs change		+$140,000

Exhibit 9-14

Financial Accounting Profit Projection						
Standard homes volume change		=	(20)	homes		
Sales price	$ 50,000					
Less: COGS	(30,240)					
Gross profit	$ 19,760	×	(20)	homes	=	$(395,200)
Custom homes volume change		=	10	homes		
Sales price	$100,000					
Less: COGS	(63,100)					
Gross profit	$ 36,900	×	10	homes	=	369,000
Net change in gross profit						$ (26,200)

Bad assumptions:

1. The POR stays the same. For each direct labor hour worked on a house, we charge $4.74 for total overhead. With the change in sales mix, our total direct labor hours increase. The more hours worked, the more overhead allocated to the products, whether or not total overhead really increased. We really don't know how much our overhead should change unless we rebudget the activity costs creating it. As we just saw with the previous analysis, we need to rebudget indirect labor and architectural costs.
2. The total general and administrative expenses stay the same. We should rebudget the shipping and purchasing activities, though, because they will change with this sales mix and volume change.

Exhibit 9-15

- Both assume architectural costs are fixed. This is true for standard homes, but not for custom homes. Because each custom home needs special architectural work, it is a variable product-level activity for custom homes.
- Both assume administrative costs are fixed. However, this includes purchasing [a batch-level activity] and shipping [a product-level variable cost]."

ABC income statements

"Rebudgeting our setup, architectural, shipping, and purchasing costs, I've created two ABC-based income statements, segmented by product line. [Exhibit 9-16 shows the projected profits with the original sales mix and volume. The projected profits with the new sales mix is presented in Exhibit 9-17.]

"Later we will take a look at a detailed analysis of the ABC costs used in these income statements [Exhibit 9A-2]. Custom homes are individually made, so they do not have any batch-level costs. Product line costs are averaged [allocated] over the sales volume within each line. In Exhibit 9-17, the number of houses in each line changes, so the amount allocated to each house is different from our original projection [Exhibit 9-16]. Facilities costs are averaged over all houses, standard and custom. The new sales mix is ten less houses in total than the original volume, so the amount charged to each house changes. When we express a fixed cost as a per-product amount, whether product line level or facilities level, it will change when volume changes.

"This brings up a really good observation, though. *All three costing techniques make some cost allocation assumptions. Thus, we have no right or wrong methods.* The

ABC-Based Income Statement (Using original sales projection)

	STANDARD HOMES			CUSTOM HOMES			COMPANY TOTALS	
	Per unit	%	Totals @ 100	Per unit	%	Totals @ 10	%	Totals
Revenues	$50,000	100%	$5,000,000	$100,000	100%	$1,000,000	100%	$6,000,000
Less: Costs								
Product (unit) level	30,500	61%	3,050,000	86,000	86%	860,000	65%	3,910,000
Batch level	1,000	2%	100,000	0	0%	0	2%	100,000
Product line level	1,600	3%	160,000	11,500	12%	115,000	5%	275,000
Facilities level	6,473	13%	647,273	6,773	7%	67,727	12%	715,000
Total costs	($39,573)	(79%)	($3,957,273)	($104,273)	(104%)	($1,042,727)	(83%)	($5,000,000)
Net income	**$10,427**	**21%**	**$1,042,727**	**($4,273)**	**(4%)**	**($42,727)**	**17%**	**$1,000,000**

Exhibit 9-16

ABC-Based Income Statement (Using revised sales projection)

	STANDARD HOMES			CUSTOM HOMES			COMPANY TOTALS	
	Per unit	%	Totals @ 80	Per unit	%	Totals @ 20	%	Totals
Revenues	$50,000	100%	$4,000,000	$100,000	100%	$2,000,000	100%	$6,000,000
Less: Costs								
Product (unit) level	30,500	61%	2,440,000	86,000	86%	1,720,000	69%	4,160,000
Batch level	1,000	2%	80,000	0	0%	0	1%	80,000
Product line level	2,000	4%	160,000	5,750	6%	115,000	5%	275,000
Facilities level	7,088	14%	567,000	7,400	7%	148,000	12%	715,000
Total costs	($40,588)	(81%)	($3,247,000)	($99,150)	(99%)	($1,983,000)	(87%)	($5,230,000)
Net income	**$9,413**	**19%**	**$753,000**	**$850**	**1%**	**$17,000**	**13%**	**$770,000**

Exhibit 9-17

best method depends on the situation. When we experience the conditions listed in Exhibit 9-4, though, ABC usually will produce more accurate product costs.

"We must remember all cost behavior assumptions are just that—*assumptions*. At best, they provide rough approximations for budgeting. This is the lesson the Boss wanted us to learn. It also explains why he treated budgeting as an approximation process. When he was alive, he made very simplistic assumptions. He didn't have sophisticated technologies and people to identify true cost behaviors. It would have been too costly to do this.

"Now, with greater competition, we need better accounting information, and we have more educated people and sophisticated computer systems. We can make better approximations based on a better understanding of the resources needed for various activities and which products use each activity."

BOB

"ABC is how we've always budgeted, though! We just never created an accounting system based on how we do things. I'm beginning to understand why traditional systems haven't been very useful in running our business. They were designed for other purposes, like external reporting. Maybe we should investigate how Elgin Sweeper combined ABC and the contribution margin format into its income statement. I hear Bradford Soap Works integrated ABC into its general ledger system."

SID

"For most of the time the Boss ran things, we were much smaller. He really understood how the business worked and what our competition was doing. With small businesses, most of the information needed to run them is informal and 'in the head' of the owner. As businesses grow and become more complex, the owners become more removed from day-to-day operations. Informal information from hands-on experience needs to be replaced with more formal information. While we don't have all the information we need, ABC is a good start. It gives us a better understanding of product costs when different products use different activities and resources. It also helps us see the resource costs of each activity.

"So, let's do ABC. It tells us something new:

- What activities really cost.
- Which activities are used in various products."

BILL

"Just having better cost information doesn't solve our crisis, though. I also need information about our customers, industry, suppliers, and competition. In other words, I need to know more about our environment. I'll go along with ABC, but what should we do next?"

The costs and benefits of ABC

JULIE

"We need a more detailed and accurate product costing system, such as activity-based costing, to support many types of decisions."

Strategic uses for ABC.

- "*Adding or dropping product lines.* If we can't increase our custom home prices, we may want to consider dropping them. All 2,500 products reported on the income statement of Scovill Manufacturing's Schrader Bellows Division appeared profitable until it changed to ABC and discovered only 550 were.
- *Product pricing.* Now that we know standard homes are less costly than we thought, we can meet our competition's sales prices. Through our product differentiation efforts, custom home prices can be raised.

- *Outsourcing a component [make-or-buy]*. We can investigate cost reduction strategies with suppliers and customers across our industry-wide value chain. I suggest we talk about this in our next meeting. Stratus Computers successfully did this in its make-or-buy decisions for many of its components.
- *Product redesign*. By reengineering our products, we may be able to reduce total product line costs over its life cycle. This, too, is a good topic for our next meeting.
- *Process redesign*. Similarly, we can redesign our processes to improve quality and reduce costs. Product and process redesign should be the topics of subsequent meetings.
- *Customer profitability analysis*. Bill believes some customers are more expensive to support than others. We can use ABC to analyze the activities customers demand and their costs. For example, Farrall, Inc., discovered less than 10% of its customers created 230% of its profits! Obviously, the company was losing money on many of its customers."

NANCY

ABC system costs. "These are important decisions we're now considering. It seems we should upgrade our costing system before we do anything else! Why haven't we done this yet?"

SID

"Remember, Nancy, management accounting systems usually are somewhat inaccurate! Relevance is their most important attribute. Creating the information needed for all potential decisions is rarely justified. It costs too much. But information costs are changing with the development of relational databases and computer software. Regardless, we must know the limitations of our accounting system. Traditional systems such as ours usually average indirect costs [overhead and expenses] over all products. We usually don't create new, more detailed cost pools for better direct tracing of these costs to the products. The tradeoff is between more cost accounts for greater product cost accuracy and the additional cost of doing this. Every dollar spent on an upgraded accounting system reduces our profits by a dollar! We can justify additional accounting costs only through improved decisions."

JULIE

"And not all ABC efforts are successful, as Hewlett-Packard found out at its Colorado Springs Division. It's very easy to create too many cost pools and drivers, and not have the top management and administrative support necessary. However, 89% of firms implementing ABC believe it's worth the effort, even though it often took more time and cost more than expected, at least according to a recent survey I read."

NANCY

"O.K. I see your point. We really should upgrade our costing system, though. Better cost information should improve our pricing decisions. Improved decisions should increase the value of our company. This is the ultimate objective, isn't it? Of course, even with the perfect management accounting system, we will have to change how we think about the business. The accounting system cannot improve Multree's value. While traditional methods may still work in many situations, too many managers are discovering the real key to long-run success is through changing their perspective about how things should be done. We must begin to think strategically and break out of the scientific management-driven 'silo thinking' we've become accustomed to."

KEY OBJECTIVES SUMMARY

DORIS

"Before we leave, let's make sure I have good meeting notes. We have covered five topics in this meeting.

1. Identify situations that create a need for new cost systems.

"Exhibit 9-2 summarized these situations. As I see it, we can see symptoms of costing system problems in three departments:

- *Sales:* Our competition is pricing commodity products lower than us, but we are pricing specialty products lower than them.
- *Accounting:* Specialty products seem to be more profitable than commodity products.
- *Production:* Managers want to drop specialty products because they are too costly, and focus on the more efficiently produced commodity products. This is opposite from what Accounting is suggesting.

"The important point is to recognize the cause of these problems. The accounting system averages indirect costs so products look like they cost the same. They don't. If we were running a motel, cleaning costs would not be the same for a room with a retired couple and a room with college students staying there for spring break! When products or services are different and indirect costs are large, cost differences will be hidden. In service industries, almost all costs are indirect [expenses]. Even in sales we see this phenomenon. Some customers demand little attention while others demand a lot. Right now, few accounting systems really tell us this.

2. Explain the three production characteristics justifying ABC.

"Exhibit 9-4 summarized these. Traditional cost allocations can miscost products when:

- We make more than one product line.
- Different products use different resources and activities.
- Different products use different amounts of the same resources and activities.

I remember from our product costing [Chapter 5] meeting that if we can trace all resource costs directly to specific products, everyone can agree on the 'one, true product cost.' The more indirect costs allocated to products, though, the less accurate our product cost becomes. We don't have a problem, and don't need ABC, if all products use exactly the same activities and resources. We could simply divide the total costs by the number of products. But when we have different products using resources and activities in various ways, we need ABC to trace as many costs as possible directly to our products.

"Consumption ratio comparisons can provide us with a quick test to see if we may be miscosting our products. My sister, Enid, can use these with her catering business. She contracts with the federal government to supply sandwich platters to a federally subsidized elderly care facility. Enid provides two types of platters: regular sandwiches and dietetic sandwiches. Making platters involves four activities: move and wait, setup, run [make sandwiches], and inspect. Here are the consumption ratios:

Sandwich Platters Consumption Ratios

	Batch size	Move & wait	Setup	Run	Inspect
Regular platters	10	1 hour	½ hour	10 hours	0 hours
Dietetic platters	1	½ hour	1 hour	1 hour	0.1 hours
Consumption ratios	10:1	2:1	1:2	10:1	0:0.1

"Obviously, these products consume different amounts of her overhead activities. However, Enid uses the same $4 overhead rate per direct labor hour for each product, so regular platters are allocated 10 times the overhead dietetic platters are. Each requires one direct labor hour, but 10 regular platters are made in a batch, while dietetic platters are made one at a time. Differing from this 10:1 volume-based allocation ratio, regular platters consume twice the move and wait resources as dietetic platters. We see the opposite relationship for setups. And, regular platters use no inspections, versus one six-minute inspection for each dietetic platter. These two products use different activities, as well as using the same activities but in different amounts. So, I expect they are miscosted because Enid is charging them the same $4 rate for overhead. To see how serious a problem this is, we need to calculate the ABC costs.

3. Describe how ABC uses resources and activities to calculate product costs.

"ABC is a two-stage process. First, resources are traced to activities. Activity costs then are charged to the products using them. How activities are charged to products depends on the type [level] of activity. Four activity levels normally are used in ABC systems:

- *Product [unit] level:* These are direct variable costs of specific products. Examples include direct materials, direct labor, sales commissions, and in our case, shipping.
- *Batch level:* These are step costs traditionally assumed to be either variable or fixed. We trace batch-level activities directly to product lines and then allocate them to the products made in that batch. Setups, materials handling, and purchasing are good examples.
- *Product line level:* These usually are direct fixed costs of a product line. They should be traced directly to each line and then allocated to only those products. Advertising, architectural costs, and product line supervision are good examples.
- *Facilities level:* These are indirect fixed costs of having facilities available. We still have to allocate these costs like we do in any cost system. Examples include heating, building depreciation, insurance, and property taxes.

4. Compare the allocation of batch costs in a traditional cost system and an ABC system.

"In traditional systems, batch costs are treated as either variable or fixed costs. Because they are not traceable directly to specific products, they are considered part of overhead. Traditional systems allocate overhead to products using some volume-based approach, such as direct labor hours or machine hours. The problem is many of these activities may not be caused by the number of hours worked [a measure related to production volume].

"ABC breaks down these costs into those caused by individual products [product-level costs traced directly to products] and those which are not. Costs not caused by production volume [such as batch, product level, and facilities costs] are allocated in different ways based on their cost drivers. The idea is simple; the better we trace our activity costs, the more accurate our product costs will be.

"Here's the standard cost cards for Enid's two sandwich platters [see Exhibit 9-18].

Sandwich Platter Standard Costs

	Regular platter					Dietetic platter				
Direct materials					$13.78					$18.78
Direct labor	$12.22	x	1.0 hour	=	$12.22	$12.22	x	1.0 hour	=	$12.22
Overhead:	$4.00	x	1.0 hour	=	$4.00	$4.00	x	1.0 hour	=	$4.00
Standard cost					**$30.00**					**$35.00**
+ Markup @	80%				$24.00					$28.00
Sales price					**$54.00**					**$63.00**

Exhibit 9-18

"The federal government allows her $12.22 per hour for wages and benefits. It also allows an 80% markup for administrative and shipping costs and a reasonable profit. Allocating $4 of overhead to each product, regular platters cost $30 and dietetic platters cost $35. Currently, she bills the government $54 per regular platter and $63.00 for each dietetic platter.

"Now, let's look at the ABC costs [see Exhibit 9-19].

"Allocating each batch-level overhead activity separately, regular platters cost $27.83, but dietetic platters cost $50.55. Using a single volume-based overhead rate overcosted regular platters $2.17 and undercosted dietetic platters $15.55!

5. Discuss how different cost allocations can affect income statements and profits.

"Each of the three types of costing systems we have considered is based on cost behavior assumptions. Traditional systems assume all overhead can be allocated to products using a volume-based rate [a POR often based on direct labor hours]. A contribution margin approach assumes all costs are either variable or fixed. ABC identifies variable, step [batch], and fixed costs.

"When we use the allocation techniques from these methods to budget costs, budgeting errors often result. With traditional systems, be careful with fixed overhead. Even though we allocate it with a rate as if it were a variable cost, it is not.

Sandwich Platter Activity-Based Costs

	Regular platter					Dietetic platter				
Direct materials	$13.78	x	10	platters	= $137.80	$18.78	x	1	platter	= $18.78
Direct labor	$12.22	x	10	platters	= 122.20	$12.22	x	1	platter	= 12.22
Overhead:										
Move & wait	$12.22	x	1.0	hours	= 12.22	$12.22	x	0.5	hours	= 6.11
Setups	$12.22	x	0.5	hours	= 6.11	$12.22	x	1.0	hours	= 12.22
Quality inspection	$1.22	x	0	inspections	= 0.00	$1.22	x	1	inspections	= 1.22
Total cost per batch					$278.33					$50.55
Average cost per sandwich platter					**$27.83**					**$50.55**
+ Markup @	80%				22.27					40.44
Sales price					**$50.10**					**$90.99**

Exhibit 9-19

Also be aware of how nonmanufacturing costs behave. They are not always fixed, indirect costs. When budgeting, we cannot assume all costs are either variable or fixed, as is done in the contribution margin approach. Some are step costs and should be identified with their true cost drivers. This method often assumes administrative costs are indirect, fixed costs. This may not always be true, either.

"Even with ABC we should be careful. Some may think because product line and facilities costs are allocated to each product [for product pricing and profitability analysis purposes], these are variable costs. As we saw when our product mix changed, these allocations to each product can change, too!

"Here's what happened to Enid. The federal government just changed the maximum reimbursement rates. It won't pay more than $52 for a regular platter, but it will go as high as $92 for dietetic platters. Since Enid cannot bill more than $63 using her current cost system, she can't capitalize on the new higher rates for dietetic platters. Nor is she willing to lower her billing rate for regular platters. She can't afford to give up her normal profit. So, she's considering not providing the platters to the elderly facility.

"After looking at the ABC costs, though, she can make a normal profit on both types of platters and still be within the new government limits. For Enid, ABC provides a better picture of each product's real profitability, and allows her to keep the elderly care facility business."

Lumpy Lettuce: A Pervasive Management Control Problem

CCSSCo makes prepackaged sandwiches for vending machines. Ham and cheese sandwich production travels through five departments: Ham Preparation, Cheese Preparation, Lettuce Preparation, Assembly, and Packaging. Each department's performance evaluation is based on traditional cost variance reporting. This has caused serious problems in hitting daily production quotas, labor and materials usage, and in producing high-quality sandwiches.

Consider Lettuce Preparation. Each sandwich should contain two green leaves of lettuce. Workers are rewarded for avoiding lettuce and labor usage variances. They often generate favorable variances by not processing lettuce as they should. Lettuce cores, yellow leaves, and lumps are often found in the Tupperware® containers by Assembly workers. To fix the problem, assembly workers have to take the time to discard bad lettuce and search for good lettuce. This results in unfavorable lettuce and labor usage variances in that department. These workers quickly learned doing the right thing would be punished! So, they started putting lumpy lettuce in the sandwiches. When the sandwiches got to Packaging, these workers could not easily cut and insert them into the cardboard containers. Many were rejected and many others had to be reworked. Often less-than-appealing sandwiches ended up in the vending machines.

To solve this problem, CCSSCo conducted an ABC study of the entire process. Here, ABC was not used to better allocate overhead or cost products. Instead, it was used to improve the production process. After identifying activities performed in the departments, workers determined what could go wrong with each activity. These problems then were mapped in a matrix and linked together to identify cause-effect chains. For example, lumpy lettuce causes too much (or too little) to be used in Assembly. This, in turn, makes it difficult to level the sandwiches, cut them diagonally, and/or insert them in the cardboard packages. The point is one variance can be transported "down the line," wreaking havoc in subsequent activities. From the matrix, 51 critical problems were identified.

CCSSCo realized cost variances are simply the costs of problems occurring within activities. A general ledger coding system was created to calculate the cost variances resulting from these critical problems. Each activity was numbered along with its major problems. As each problem occurred, the resulting cost variance was coded by the workers to identify the problem, its source, and its cause. Instead of calculating cost variances in terms of direct labor usage or direct material usage, they now were based on activities. The new accounting system reported cost variances in terms of problems, that is, the costs to identify and fix them. An example report for one shift is shown in Exhibit 9-A1.

In order for an activity-based cost variance reporting system to work, the workers coded these problems as they occurred. The first number in the code identifies what problem happened. The second number is its cause. To avoid false cause coding, the workers responsible for the cause had to agree to it. In this system, employees had to work together in identifying and correcting problems. The long-run benefit was everyone became motivated to prevent problems occurring down the line from the work they did.

Source: M. F. Thomas, *An Application of Socio-Technical Systems Analysis to Accounting Variance Control Theory*, 1985.

Example Cost Variance Report

Variance	Problem	Cause	Labor cost	Bread usage	Lettuce usage	Total cost
21.10	Mustard spreading machine jammed	Soggy bread	$20.00	$2.50		$22.50
38.12	Sandwiches needing to be remade in Packaging	Lumpy lettuce	$25.00	$4.00	$8.00	$37.00
Shift cost variances			$45.00	$6.50	$8.00	$59.50

General ledger codes:
10: Soggy bread
12: Lumpy lettuce
21: Mustard spreading machine jammed
38: Sandwiches needing to be remade in Packaging

Exhibit 9-A1

APPENDIX A

ABC ANALYSIS AND BILLS OF ACTIVITIES

KEY OBJECTIVE 6

Summarize the differences between ABC's Bill of Activities and a traditional standard cost card.

JULIE

"Once we determine the costs of our activities, these can be organized by level within a Bill of Activities. Each product line has its own Bill of Activities [see Exhibit 9A-2 on pp. 344 and 345]. We also have included some notes about resource costs and cost drivers.

"In our traditional cost system, each product line has its own standard cost card. Traditional systems do not trace resource costs to activities. Instead, resources are charged to products through direct tracing [direct materials and labor] or through allocating variable and fixed overhead with predetermined overhead rates [PORs]." [The standard cost cards for each product line are shown in Exhibit 9-A3 on p. 346. They were originally presented in Exhibit 6-5. The PORs were first presented in Exhibit 6-6. They are reproduced in Exhibit 9A-4 on p. 347.]

"Let's compare ABC's Bill of Activities with traditional costing's standard cost card:

- Only two overhead allocations are made in traditional costing. All variable overhead is allocated with one 'all-inclusive' POR. All of the fixed overhead is allocated using its own POR. In ABC, each variable overhead item is separately costed to products. Indirect materials and power are traced directly to products as

ABC Analysis and Bills of Activities

Multree Homes
Standard Homes Product Line
Standard Bill of Activities

Activities	Standard prices		Standard quantities		Standard costs		Resource and cost driver notes:
Product (unit)-level activities:							Traced directly to each house.
Direct materials					$15,500	/house	
Direct labor	$10.00	/hour	1,000	DLhrs/house	10,000	/house	
Indirect materials					1,000	/house	
Power (per machine hour)	$1.00	/Mhr	500	Mhrs/house	500	/house	Power is for the tools and equipment used by workers.
Sales commission	5%	of sales price			2,500	/house	
Shipping					1,000	/house	Each house is shipped separately.
Total product-level costs					*$30,500*	*/house*	
Batch-level activities:							100 houses are planned for in 20 batches of 5 houses each.
Materials handling	$1,000	/batch	0.20	batches/house	200	/house	Workers are paid $10/hr, 100 hours needed per batch of 5 houses.
Setups	$1,500	/batch	0.20	batches/house	300	/house	Workers are paid $10/hr, 150 hours needed per batch of 5 houses.
Purchasing	$2,500	/batch	0.20	batches/house	500	/house	25% of Purchasing Dept. costs are for these 20 batches.
Total batch-level costs	*$5,000*	*/batch*			*$1,000*	*/house*	
Product line-level activities:	**Budgeted fixed costs**		**Budgeted volume**				
Supervision	$100,000	/year	100	houses/year	1,000	/house	Direct cost of the product line. Allocate equally to each house.
Advertising	$50,000	/year	100	houses/year	500	/house	Direct cost of the product line. Allocate equally to each house.
Architectural	$10,000	/year	100	houses/year	100	/house	Direct cost of the product line. Allocate equally to each house.
Total product line-level costs	*$160,000*	*/year*			*$1,600*	*/house*	
Facilities-level activities:							
Heat and light	$8,000	/year	100	houses/year	80	/house	80% of total manufacturing time is for this product line.
Depreciation	$12,000	/year	100	houses/year	120	/house	80% of total manufacturing time is for this product line.
Remaining administration	$690,000	/year	110	houses/year	6,273	/house	Purchasing and Shipping separately accounted for. Remaining administration costs are allocated equally to all houses.
Total facilities-level costs					*$6,473*	*/house*	
Standard activity-based cost					$39,573	/house	

Exhibit 9-A2

ABC Analysis and Bills of Activities

Multree Homes
Custom Homes Product Line
Standard Bill of Activities

Activities	Standard prices	Standard quantities	Standard costs	
Product (unit)-level activities:				
Direct materials			$26,250 /house	Traced directly to each house.
Direct labor	$10.00 /hour	2,500 DLhrs/house	25,000 /house	
Indirect materials			1,500 /house	
Power	$1.00 /Mhr	1,250 MLhrs/house	1,250 /house	Power is for the tools and equipment used by workers.
Sales commission	3% of sales price		3,000 /house	
Shipping			1,000 /house	Each house is shipped separately.
Architectural			10,000 /house	Each house is uniquely designed.
				Because each custom home is made to order, batch-level costs are really product-level costs:
Batch-level activities:				
Materials handling	$1,000 /batch	1 batch/house	1,000 /house	Workers are paid $10/hr, 100 hours needed per setup.
Setups	$2,000 /batch	1 batch/house	2,000 /house	Workers are paid $10/hr, 200 hours needed per setup.
Purchasing	$15,000 /batch	1 batch/house	15,000 /house	75% of Purchasing Dept. costs are for these 10 houses.
Total product-level costs			*$86,000 /house*	
Product line-level activities:	**Budgeted fixed costs**	**Budgeted volume**		
Supervision	$100,000 /year	10 houses/year	10,000 /house	Direct cost of the product line. Allocate equally to each house.
Advertising	$15,000 /year	10 houses/year	1,500 /house	Direct cost of the product line. Allocate equally to each house.
Total product line-level costs	*$115,000 /year*		*$11,500 /house*	
Facilities-level activities:				
Heat and light	$2,000 /year	10 houses/year	200 /house	20% of total manufacturing time is for this product line.
Depreciation	$3,000 /year	10 houses/year	300 /house	20% of total manufacturing time is for this product line.
Remaining administration	$690,000 /year	110 houses/year	6,273 /house	Purchasing and Shipping separately accounted for. Remaining administration costs are allocated equally to all houses.
Total facilities-level costs			*$6,773 /house*	
Standard activity-based cost			**$104,273 /house**	

Exhibit 9-A2 (continued)

Multree Homes Standard Homes Product Line Standard Cost Card							
Resources	Standard prices		Standard quantities		Standard costs	
Direct materials					$15,500	/house
Direct labor	$10.00	/hour	1,000	DLhrs/house	10,000	/house
Variable overhead	$2.06	/DLhr	1,000	DLhrs/house	2,060	/house
Fixed overhead	$2.68	/DLhr	1,000	DLhrs/house	2,680	/house
Standard absorptive manufacturing cost					$30,240	/house
Budgeted annual standard homes manufacturing costs =			$268,000	per year +	$27,560	/house

Multree Homes Custom Homes Product Line Standard Cost Card						
Resources	Standard prices		Standard quantities		Standard costs	
Direct materials					$26,250	/house
Direct labor	$10.00	/hour	2,500	DLhrs/house	25,000	/house
Variable overhead	$2.06	/DLhr	2,500	DLhrs/house	5,150	/house
Fixed overhead	$2.68	/DLhr	2,500	DLhrs/house	6,700	/house
Standard absorptive manufacturing cost					$63,100	/house
Budgeted annual custom homes manufacturing costs =			$67,000	per year +	$56,400	/house

Exhibit 9-A3

product-level costs. Indirect labor is broken down into its two batch-level activities: setups and materials handling. Similarly, each of the four fixed overhead activities is separately allocated with ABC. Factory supervision and architectural costs are product-line direct costs. Depreciation and heat and light are facilities-level costs. Thus, ABC has many more overhead allocations than does a traditional costing system.

- When costing products, ABC includes all costs while traditional cost systems [designed primarily for GAAP and financial reporting] only include production costs.

- When we make multiple product lines and they use different resources and activities, or the same ones but in different amounts, we should expect different product costs. The product costs should reflect the different resources and activities consumed by each product line.

Predetermined Overhead Rates

Variable overhead:	
Indirect materials	$115,000
Indirect labor	80,000
Power	62,500

Variable overhead POR calculation:

Total variable overhead / Budgeted direct labor hours	$257,500 / 125,000	
Variable overhead POR	**$2.06**	**per DLhr**

Fixed overhead:	
Supervision	$200,000
Heat and light	10,000
Depreciation	15,000
Architectural costs	110,000

Fixed overhead POR calculation:

Total fixed overhead / Budgeted direct labor hours	$335,000 / 125,000	
Fixed overhead POR	**$2.68**	**per DLhr**

Exhibit 9-A4

The product cost differences between our traditional costing system and ABC are detailed here [Exhibit 9A-5]."

Comparison of Traditional Cost Allocations and ABC

Activities/Resources	Traditional allocation method	Standard Homes			Custom Homes		
		Traditional cost allocation	ABC cost allocation	Over/(under) costing with traditional method	Traditional cost allocation	ABC cost allocation	Over/(under) costing with traditional method
Manufacturing costs:	Based on POR:						
Indirect materials	$0.92 /DLhr	$920	$1,000	($80)	$2,300	$1,500	$800
Indirect labor: materials handling	$0.24 /DLhr	240	200	40	600	1,000	(400)
Indirect labor: setups	$0.40 /DLhr	400	300	100	1,000	2,000	(1,000)
Power	$0.50 /DLhr	500	500	0	1,250	1,250	0
Total variable overhead	*$2.06 /DLhr*	*$2,060*	*$2,000*	*$60*	*$5,150*	*$5,750*	*($600)*
Architectural costs	$0.88 /DLhr	880	100	780	2,200	10,000	(7,800)
Supervision	$1.60 /DLhr	1,600	1,000	600	4,000	10,000	(6,000)
Depreciation	$0.12 /DLhr	120	120	0	300	300	0
Heat and light	$0.08 /DLhr	80	80	0	200	200	0
Total fixed overhead	*$2.68 /DLhr*	*$2,680*	*$1,300*	*$1,380*	*$6,700*	*$20,500*	*($13,800)*
Total overhead costs	**$4.74 /DLhr**	**$4,740**	**$3,300**	**$1,440**	**$11,850**	**$26,250**	**($14,400)**
	Based on relative revenues:						
Expenses:							
Sales commissions	Standard homes	2,333	2,500	(167)	4,667	3,000	1,667
Advertising	@ 5/6 of	542	500	42	1,083	1,500	(417)
Purchasing	total revenues.	1,667	500	1,167	3,333	15,000	(11,667)
Shipping	Custom homes	917	1,000	(83)	1,833	1,000	833
Remaining administrative costs	@ 1/6 of	5,750	6,273	(523)	11,500	6,273	5,227
	total revenues.						
Total expenses		**$11,208**	**$10,773**	**$436**	**$22,417**	**$26,773**	**($4,356)**
Total allocated costs		**$15,948**	**$14,073**	**$1,876**	**$34,267**	**$53,023**	**($18,756)**
Direct materials	Direct tracing	15,500	15,500	0	26,250	26,250	0
Direct labor	Direct tracing	10,000	10,000	0	25,000	25,000	0
Average cost per product		**$41,448**	**$39,573**	**$1,876**	**$85,517**	**$104,273**	**($18,756)**

Exhibit 9-A5

ABC overview: Cokins, Stratton, and Helbing, *An ABC Manager's Primer*, Institute of Management Accountants and CAM-I (Irwin Professional Publishing), 1993.

——: White, *The 60 Minute ABC Book Activity-Based Costing For Operations Management*, CAM-I (Consortium for Advanced Manufacturing-International, Bedford TX), 1997.

ABC implementation survey: Krumwiede, "ABC: Why It's Tried And How It Succeeds," *Management Accounting*, April 1998.

AT&T: Hobdy, et al., "Activity-Based Management at AT&T," *Management Accounting*, April 1994.

Bradford Soap Works: Gammell and McNair, "Jumping the Growth Threshold Through Activity-Based Cost Management," *Management Accounting*, September 1994.

Elgin Sweeper: Callan, Tredup, and Wissinger, "Elgin Sweeper Company's Journey Toward Cost Management," *Management Accounting*, July 1991.

Farrall, Inc.: Cooper, et al., *Implementing Activity-Based Cost Management: Moving From Analysis to Action*, Institute of Management Accountants (Montvale, NJ), 1992.

Fireman's Fund: Crane and Meyer, "Focusing on True Costs in a Service Organization," *Management Accounting*, February 1993.

Healthcare management and ABC: Baker, *Activity-Based Costing and Activity-Based Management for Health Care*, Aspen Publishers (Gaithersburg, MD), 1998.

Hewlett-Packard: Merz and Hardy, "ABC Puts Accountants on Design Team at HP," *Management Accounting*, September 1993.

Hewlett-Packard's Colorado Springs Division failure: Landry, Wood, and Lindquist, "Can ABC Bring Mixed Results?" *Management Accounting*, March 1997.

Hughes Aircraft: Haedicke and Feil, "Hughes Aircraft Sets the Standard for ABC," *Management Accounting*, February 1991.

Medicare: Hwang and Kirby, "Distorted Medicare Reimbursements: The Effect of Cost Accounting Choices," *Journal of Management Accounting Research*, Fall 1994.

Post Office: Carter, Sedaghat, and Williams, "How ABC Changed the Post Office," *Management Accounting*, February 1998.

Scovill Manufacturing: Cooper, "Schrader Bellows Cases," Harvard Business School cases 186-272, 1986.

Stratus Computers: Boisonneault, "Activity-Based Costing for Make/Buy Decisions at Stratus Computer," *Target*, March/April 1992.

Union Pacific: Rotch, "Activity-Based Costing in Service Industries," *Journal of Cost Management*, Summer 1990.

Weyerhaeuser payroll cost drivers: Pederson, "Weyerhaeuser: Streamlining Payroll," *Management Accounting*, October 1991.

*Alphabetic by topic, idea, or company referenced.

CHAPTER 10

Should We Start All Over?

Strategic Cost Management

KEY OBJECTIVES:

1	*Discuss how industry-wide value chains and accounting information aid firms in identifying their core competencies.*
2	*Demonstrate the use of strategic partnering and activity-based management performance measures in managing suppliers.*
3	*Create activity-based management measures for customer satisfaction and explain the role of ABC in managing customer relations.*
4	*Illustrate product line management with target costing, simultaneous engineering and quality function deployment, and life cycle costing.*

Just as the turn of the 20th century heralded the scientific method, allowing dramatic advances in productivity, the turn of the 21st century has ushered in a similar revolution, setting the stage for a new form of management activity. This new skill is *continuous improvement in a dynamic environment*. To be successful, companies will have to:

- Change the goods and services they provide and the way they produce them (Chapter 10), and
- Develop methods focusing on quality, service, and cost (Chapters 11–13).

In this globally competitive environment evolving from the new communications and logistics age, *the only truly sustainable competitive advantage companies have is to learn faster than their competition*. Realizing future meetings must have this common theme, Julie scheduled each one to introduce procedures and describe ways companies can use accounting information to support learning and continuous improvement activities.

Strategic Value Chain Management: What Business Are We In?

KEY OBJECTIVE 1

Discuss how industry-wide value chains and accounting information aid firms in identifying their core competencies.

"Remember the problems we discussed in our last meeting? I've been thinking about them from a 'big picture' point of view. Specifically, I'm looking at our industry's value chain and where we are on it [see Exhibit 2-3]. I'm beginning to wonder if we're really focusing on the right things.

"It seems we have two different management problems: generating long-term and short-term value. *Long-term value is created by our line of business and our strategies within this line of business. Short-term value is created by how well we operate [efficiency] within our plan*. Everything we've done so far seems to be part of short-term value creation."

"Are you saying accounting numbers like contribution margin, net income, standard costs and cost variances, and even activity-based costing [ABC] are just short-run profit measures? In other words, have we been executing the Boss's long-run plan without checking to see if it still works today?"

Sid's cigar almost dropped out of the corner of his mouth as his expression changed. "Even worse, I really don't think we know exactly what was the Boss's long-term plan. We might need to change it."

JULIE

"You're right! We need some **strategic cost management** for Multree Homes. This uses accounting information to help determine what we should be doing within our industry, and how we can manage value chain processes. Where do you want to start, Bill?"

> **Strategic cost management** *evaluates industry-wide value chain processes to identify how and where a firm can create a sustainable competitive advantage and long-term value.*

Develop the industry's value chain "from cradle to grave"

BILL

"Well, I started to think about this when Jackie and I took a strategic management class. We developed an industry-wide value chain for the pizza business. Value chains help us view our company strategically. Look at the value chain our team created [see Exhibit 10-1].

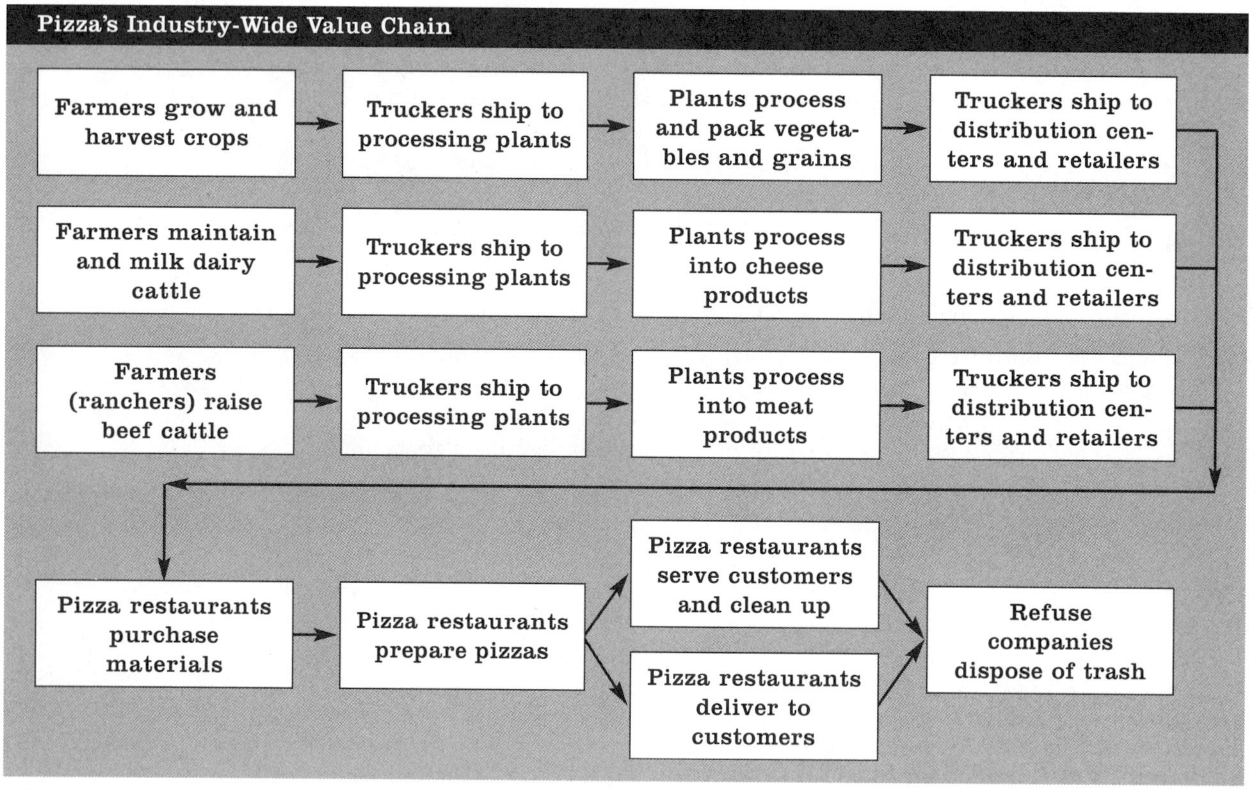

Pizza's Industry-Wide Value Chain

Farmers grow and harvest crops → Truckers ship to processing plants → Plants process and pack vegetables and grains → Truckers ship to distribution centers and retailers

Farmers maintain and milk dairy cattle → Truckers ship to processing plants → Plants process into cheese products → Truckers ship to distribution centers and retailers

Farmers (ranchers) raise beef cattle → Truckers ship to processing plants → Plants process into meat products → Truckers ship to distribution centers and retailers

Pizza restaurants purchase materials → Pizza restaurants prepare pizzas → Pizza restaurants serve customers and clean up / Pizza restaurants deliver to customers → Refuse companies dispose of trash

Exhibit 10-1

"We set up the value chain to show products or services provided by different businesses within the industry. Businesses are described by the various services they perform: farming, shipping, processing, preparing and serving pizzas, and garbage disposal. In our project, we have two branches within the pizza restaurant business. The top box represents traditional eat-in restaurants. The bottom box illustrates how some pizza businesses differentiate themselves by adding delivery service."

Identifying opportunities with return on investment (ROI). "We then prepared a financial analysis of the companies on the chain. We added return on investment [ROI] calculations to each business group. For example, we found farms with ROIs ranging from 3% to 8%, and disposal companies with ROIs of 15% to 30% [see Exhibit 10-2]."

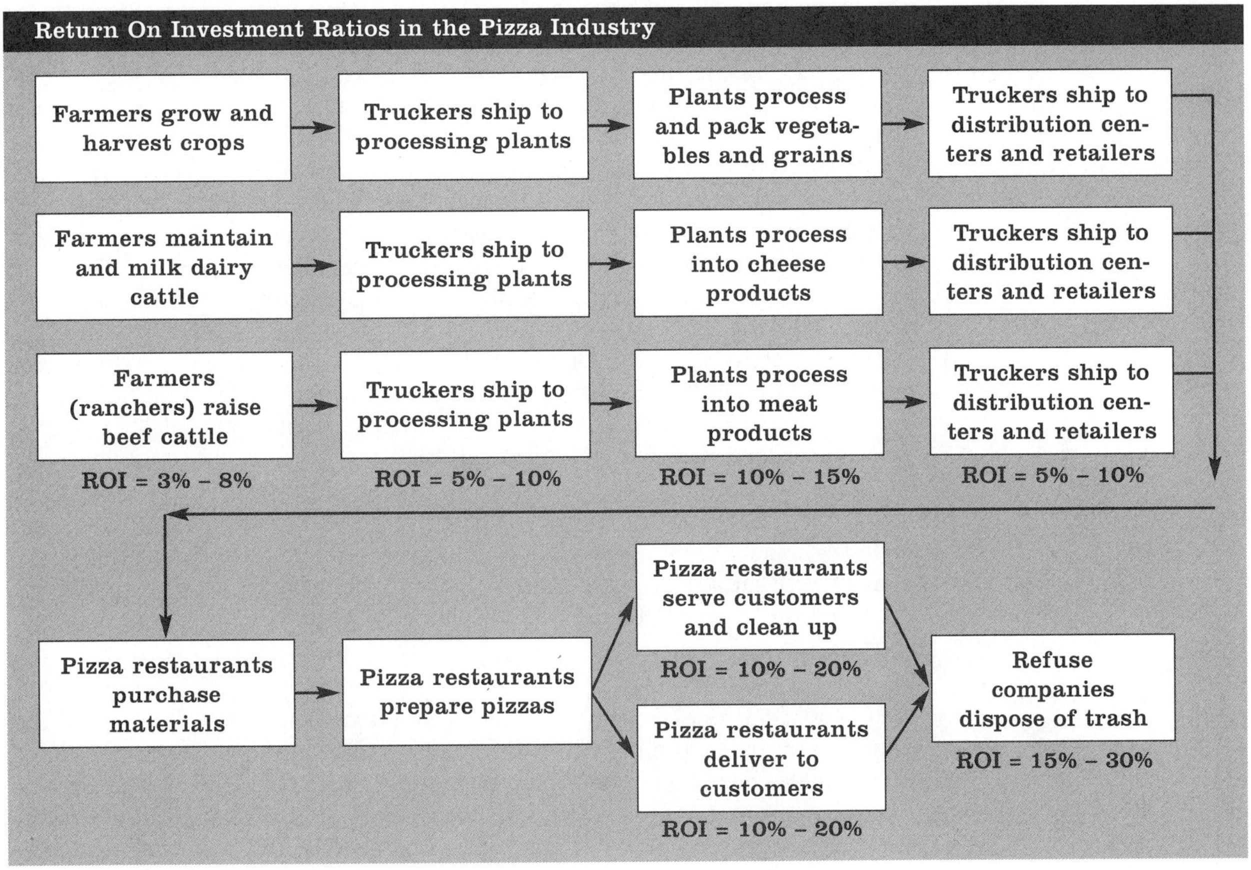

Return On Investment Ratios in the Pizza Industry

Farmers grow and harvest crops →	Truckers ship to processing plants →	Plants process and pack vegetables and grains →	Truckers ship to distribution centers and retailers
Farmers maintain and milk dairy cattle →	Truckers ship to processing plants →	Plants process into cheese products →	Truckers ship to distribution centers and retailers
Farmers (ranchers) raise beef cattle →	Truckers ship to processing plants →	Plants process into meat products →	Truckers ship to distribution centers and retailers
ROI = 3% – 8%	ROI = 5% – 10%	ROI = 10% – 15%	ROI = 5% – 10%

Pizza restaurants purchase materials → Pizza restaurants prepare pizzas → Pizza restaurants serve customers and clean up (ROI = 10% – 20%) / Pizza restaurants deliver to customers (ROI = 10% – 20%) → Refuse companies dispose of trash (ROI = 15% – 30%)

Exhibit 10-2

"Sometimes companies can increase value and profits by combining unique sets of activities along the value chain. For example, both Iowa Beef Processors and Tropicana perform shipping activities. Tropicana reduces the cost of shipping orange juice by locating its plants near major markets. Instead of making orange juice at the Florida groves, it ships frozen orange concentrate, and then mixes it with water at the plant. This significantly reduces shipping costs. Iowa Beef accomplishes the same result with the opposite strategy. Its plants are near cattle ranches because shipping processed meat is much cheaper than shipping cattle." Nancy thought to herself how good Iowa Beef's idea was, especially after driving behind some cattle trucks last summer on her vacation!

"Through an analysis of its industry's value chain, Federal Express identified a competitive niche in the delivery process. Customers are willing to pay a premium for expedited deliveries directly to specific recipients. The increased customer value was so great, United Parcel Service [UPS] successfully entered this market. In response, the U.S. Postal Service now provides this service. To counter the Post Office's entry into special delivery, some believe by allowing Federal Express and UPS to deliver first class mail, postage cost could decrease 25%.

"Using the idea of moving up and down the value chain to improve profits, we thought our restaurant also should do garbage disposal as a way to differentiate itself. We discovered one disposal company with a 30% ROI, so this seemed like a good idea. For pizza deliveries, we'd return to the customers' homes to take away the empty boxes. It was pretty exciting for awhile as adding disposal should have improved our profits. However, we become less confident when we presented our idea to the class, as they discovered some flaws with our strategy. While the customers liked the idea, several students mentioned they just wouldn't pay the extra amount necessary to make it profitable."

"I see you learned when profit analysis is important." The grandchildren all chuckled. "*The objective of value chain analysis is to identify lucrative activities reducing industry costs [i.e., costs to the ultimate consumer] and increasing our profits.* Let other companies provide less profitable goods and services. However, we can't look only at ROI. You wanted to take just one of the disposal company's activities. ROI is the return for all the activities the disposal company does. You needed a detailed study of just this activity: the cost of picking up and disposing the boxes and the extra revenue you might be able to get for it. *ROI is a rough guide for looking at industry goods and services; it is not a precise measure for the potential profitability of specific processes within a service* [such as disposal]."

"Yes, we learned a valuable lesson. To use the value chain, we needed to find representative companies spanning one or more of these processes. Unfortunately we made a slight error. The only companies we could find for the disposal activity were garbage disposal firms. They do a lot more than just pick up garbage. That was the only process we were thinking of adding to the pizza restaurant, though."

ABC and CVP analysis to evaluate opportunities. "So we sharpened our pencils, went back to our analysis, and noticed something we previously ignored on the value chain. Some companies span food preparation, delivery, cleanup, and disposal. For example, caterers make money even though they do all those low-value activities like delivery, cleanup, and disposal. Why? Because caterers prepare only large orders.

"You see, preparation and sale of the pizza itself is a very profitable activity, as Papa Murphy's, a chain of pizza preparation stores, discovered. Customers pick up the pizzas and then cook them at home. However, we need large orders to make money if we are going to cook and deliver pizzas, clean up, and then dispose of the garbage. So, by moving down the value chain and linking together delivery and cleanup, we have differentiated ourselves and captured the large pizza order market." [Exhibit 10-3 shows the cost-volume-profit (CVP) analysis for the pizza operation.]

"We considered the costs of each activity involved in providing this special service. From an ABC perspective, each 'batch' of pizzas [each large order] incurs special [incremental] costs that do not depend on the size of the batch [the number of pizzas ordered]. These costs include delivery, return for cleanup, cleanup, and disposal. We estimated these costs at $80 per order. With each pizza bringing in $10, its contribution margin per unit, we need a minimum order of 8 pizzas to break even. We set a $20 minimum profit goal, so customers must order 10 pizzas for free delivery, cleanup, and disposal."

"Our marketing analysis also showed competitors add a surcharge for large pizza delivery orders. By not adding an extra charge, and by offering these special services, we were able to capture all the large pizza order business from our com-

Cost-Volume-Profit Analysis for Pizza Delivery, Cleanup, and Disposal

	Per pizza	%	Totals for 10 pizzas
Sales revenues	$15	100%	$150
Less: variable costs	(5)	(33%)	(50)
Contribution margin	$10	67%	$100
Less: batch costs			
Delivery			25
Return			25
Cleanup			10
Disposal			20
Total batch costs			($80)
Net income			$20
Break-even point:	*8 pizzas*		

Exhibit 10-3

petitors. We also discovered because this is a university town, we have quite a substantial large order business after Saturday football games!"

"I see some key lessons to learn about industry value chains:

- *When choosing where we want to be on our industry's value chain, we have to be careful to find truly representative companies for the financial comparisons.*
- *ROI is an aggregate measure of value useful in evaluating industry-level goods and services.*
- *When we attempt to differentiate ourselves by adding new services, detailed CVP and ABC analyses are necessary."*

Define our company by where it spans the value chain

"But, how can we apply these ideas to our company? Specifically, why are we where we are on our industry's value chain?"

What are our core competencies? "Each industry segment can generate a different ROI in providing its goods and services. To sustain value within an industry segment, we must maintain a superior ROI compared to our competition. If we have a core competency in a particular segment, it will result in that higher ROI. We define where we are by our core competencies. **Core competencies** are the activities unique to our business, in other words, our competitive advantages. Consider Disney Enterprises. Disneyland and Disney World have some of the longest lines I've ever stood in! But, they move people quickly. One of Disney's core competencies is moving people. This is why the City of Oakland, California, hired them to analyze its transportation system. One of McDonald's core competencies is moving new products in and out of its product mix to meet ever-changing customer demands in the fast food industry. Value often comes from the unique combination of our value chain processes. So, we need to closely monitor core competencies to maintain our competitive advantage.

Core competencies *are those processes and activities a firm does best. They result in products or services yielding long-run value to the firm.*

"Remember when we were discussing how to create value in our second meeting? Exhibit 10-4 relates our services within the industry [Exhibit 2-3] to our value chain processes [Exhibit 2-5]. Our core competencies are in the last three industry goods and services: building houses, selling them, and providing customer and warranty service.

Where We Are on the Industry-Wide Value Chain

Industry goods and services (Exhibit 2-3)	Multree Homes value chain (Exhibit 2-5)
Sell houses	1. Customer order-taking
	1.1. Sales
	1.2. Credit check (Finance)
	1.3. Accounts receivable
Build houses	2. Materials acquisition (inbound logistics)
	2.1. Scheduling
	2.2. Purchasing
	2.3. Receiving, inspecting, RMI storage
	2.4. Delivery to factory
Build houses	3. Manufacturing
	3.1. Lumber sawing
	3.2. Wall assembly (framing)
	3.3. Rough wiring
	3.4. Rough plumbing
	3.5. Wall finishing (including insulation, windows, and door hanging)
	3.6. Roof construction
	3.7. Finish carpentry
	3.8. Top-off plumbing
	3.9. Finish electric
	3.10. Carpeting
	3.11. Inspection
Build houses	4. Shipping (outbound logistics)
	4.1. Packing
	4.2. Shipping
	4.3. Set up at retail dealer, customer lot
Sell houses	5. Close sales
	5.1. Customer walk-through and inspection
	5.2. Bill customer (customer's bank)
	5.3. Collect and deposit cash
Customer (warranty) service	6. After-sale customer services
	6.1 Provide warranty work
	6.2 Survey customer satisfaction
	6.3 New product and service advertising

Exhibit 10-4

"We could be a general contractor building subdivisions of tract homes. But, think of the core competencies we need to develop. We have to be really good 'crystal ball gazers' so we can forecast where housing demands will be far enough ahead of time to buy the land cheaply. We must have the legal expertise to get through all the governmental bureaucracies for environmental impact studies, zoning permits, and subdivision plans. Finally, we have to be supervision experts over all the subcontractors who actually build the houses [the electricians, plumbers, carpenters, roofers, etc.].

"Our primary core competency is eliminating a lot of the coordination and overhead general contractors have. This is the main reason our homes can be produced more efficiently [faster and at a lower cost]. Often, a home buyer has to wait six to nine months when buying in a new subdivision. We can deliver the same home more quickly."

BILL

"Financing and interest represent a huge cost to the contractor's customers, and a major savings to ours. Subdivision builders must obtain multimillion dollar construction loans for long time periods. The bank is paid back over a long time period, as each house is completed and sold. This adds a substantial amount of interest to the ultimate cost of their subdivision homes."

TOMMY

"Coordinating the subcontractors is usually the builder's greatest headache! Every time it rains, the building lots previously graded and staked must be redone. The concrete foundation workers wait on the earth-moving equipment and engineers. The framers wait on the foundations. The electricians and plumbers wait on the carpenters. And the list goes on and on."

JULIE

"Identifying core competencies is receiving more attention by management accountants. I just read a new monograph by the Society of Management Accountants of Canada. It lists the core competencies of many well-known companies. [A summary of these competencies is presented in Exhibit 10-5.] We also need to continually evaluate them within our strategic plan as part of our environmental analysis. Timex failed to do this. At one time, it had about half of world sales due to its core competency in low-cost precision manufacturing. Timex failed to see the development of digital technology, though, which made its manufacturing process obsolete until it could catch up with its competition."

Core Competencies in Well-Known Companies

Company	Core competencies	Products or services
AT&T	Technological leadership through Bell Labs	Telecommunications products
Honda	Small engine production	Motorcycles, snowmobiles, lawnmowers, snow blowers, chain saws
IBM	Research and development, experienced sales force	Mainframe computers and software
Microsoft and Apple	Imagination	New ways to use information technology
Procter & Gamble	Research and development, marketing and distribution	Ivory soap, Tide laundry detergent, Folgers coffee, Crisco, Pampers
Xerox	Information processing	Developed icons, pull-down menus, mouse

Source: Adapted from The Society of Management Accountants of Canada, *Value Chain Analysis for Assessing Competitive Advantage*, Management Accounting Guideline 41, © The Society of Management Accountants of Canada, 1996.

Exhibit 10-5

NANCY

Validating our core competencies with accounting information. "So far, everything you've said makes sense. But, how do we know if these are our core competencies? What accounting analyses help us identify them?"

JULIE

"Well, let's compare our standard home costs to what it costs a general contractor to build the same homes. Most of the manufacturing activities [process 3 in Exhibit 10-4] are outsourced by general contractors. Subcontractors specialize in each activity. For example, separate companies exist for carpentry, plumbing, electric, heating and air conditioning, carpeting, roofing, painting, and the like. Using ABC information, we can compare our financial performance to theirs. [Exhibit 10-6 illustrates the ABC-based income statement comparisons. Percentages formatted to whole numbers.]

ABC-Based Income Statement Comparisons

	MULTREE'S STANDARD HOMES			GENERAL CONTRACTOR		
	Per unit	%	Totals @ 100	Per unit	%	Totals @ 50
Revenues	$50,000	100%	$5,000,000	$80,000	100%	$4,000,000
Less: costs						
Product level	$30,500	61%	3,050,000	61,000	76%	3,050,000
Batch level	1,000	2%	100,000	0	0%	0
Product line level	1,600	3%	160,000	5,000	6%	250,000
Facilities level	6,473	13%	647,273	4,000	5%	200,000
Total costs	($39,573)	(79%)	($3,957,273)	($70,000)	(88%)	($3,500,000)
Net income	**$10,427**	**21%**	**$1,042,727**	**$10,000**	**13%**	**$500,000**

Exhibit 10-6

"While general contractors make about the same profit per house as we do, they have to sell it for 60% more than we charge. Further, they can build only half the houses we do in a year. Their product [unit]-level costs are much higher because of outsourcing direct labor and materials. We build our houses in batches of five. They don't have batch-level costs because each house is built separately. Their product line-level costs are much higher due to architectural and financing costs. They don't have a factory like ours, though, so their facilities-level costs are less."

BOB

Outsourcing non-core competencies. "Once we establish our core competencies, we can consider outsourcing non-core competency activities other firms do better than us. This is common in all economic sectors. Many hospitals outsource supplies purchasing and logistics to Baxter International. Seton Medical Center in Daly City, California, estimates this saves it about $300,000 a year. BFI contracts disposal services from many cities. Toyota outsources about 75% of its parts production. United Parcel Service [UPS] outsources its customer service centers. *Combining our core competencies with the outsourced non-core competencies makes us more efficient and competitive than if we did it all ourselves.*"

NANCY

"We're seeing this trend in colleges throughout the country. Over time, they have evolved into mini-cities, providing housing, food, clothing, recreation, health care, and transportation to their 'citizens.' Of course, this is costly. Between 1980 and 1995, inflation rose 85%, family income 93%, and college tuition 256%, with no end in sight! Competition for students is becoming intense, with college bidding wars for top-quality students. What are a university's core competencies? Its faculty. Some schools differentiate themselves on their research expertise. Others on their teaching. While some differentiate themselves as high-quality 'party' schools, or with their athletic programs, these may not be sustainable advantages.

"To survive, universities will have to identify their core competencies and outsource other activities that can be provided at a lower cost. We're already seeing this as many outsource activities like food services [to Marriott] and bookstores [to Barnes and Noble]."

TOMMY

"By the mid-1990s, around 80% of the Fortune 500 companies were spending about $9 billion outsourcing support activities. A Pitney Bowes survey reports 17% of its respondents outsource more than 20% of their total operations, and 38% outsourced at least 11%. Computer services are often prime candidates because the costs are so high for remaining current with the ever-changing technology [hardware as well as software]. J. P. Morgan, Chevron, Sun Microsystems, Eastman Kodak, and Unilever are all following this strategic trend."

JACKIE

"Many companies also outsource accounting services. Payroll was one of the first applications. I remember a time when all companies thought they had to do their own payroll. It was just too sensitive and dangerous to let out of their control. A few years ago, we considered letting Payroll Processors, Inc. handle paycheck preparation and the related reporting requirements for payroll taxes and fringe benefits. While we decided not to do it then, now I wish we had! As soon as I get the opportunity, I'm going to do an ABC analysis of our payroll costs. As many businesses and local governments have discovered, a specialty firm may be able to do it for less."

NANCY

"Now I understand. *In determining where we belong on our industry value chain, we use ABC profit comparisons to confirm the core competencies we identified with aggregate accounting measures such as ROI. Then we should consider outsourcing our noncore competency activities.*"

Managing Value Chain Relationships with Suppliers

KEY OBJECTIVE 2

Demonstrate the use of strategic partnering and activity-based management performance measures in managing suppliers.

SID

"As firms outsource and downsize operations, it becomes even more important to consider how our suppliers and customers affect core competency activities. In other words, we need to manage our strategic relationships throughout the industry value chain. The way we traditionally dealt with suppliers was through competitive bidding to obtain the lowest price. We then evaluated and rewarded purchasing agents based on direct materials purchase price variances. On the surface, this made a lot of sense."

TOMMY

"Well, yes and no! Remember our meeting on value creation [Chapter 2]? We thought our purchasing process was well managed. We got multiple bids and bought large quantities for special discounts. But this resulted in large stockpiles of materials, like lumber. We stored it outside in the stockyard. We had to buy a new forklift truck and hire a driver just to move it around. We bought a lot of tarps to cover it, protecting the lumber from rain and snow. We built a chain-link fence for security, and bought two German Shepherds. But, they got a little too friendly. Ultimately, we offered bonuses to over half our workforce if they would adopt a pet dog! Finally, we built that large warehouse. Of course, the extra maintenance, insurance, property taxes, and the like cost us over $10,000 every year. Was purchasing in large lots really saving us money?

"And, remember our meetings on cost variance analysis [Chapter 6], and motivation and control [Chapter 8]? With our traditional accounting system, cost variances influence the way managers act because variances are used as the primary performance evaluation measures. For example, purchasing price variances measure how well the purchasing agent is meeting budgeted costs for materials and components. If she buys in larger lots than originally planned, or buys lower quality materials than planned, a favorable materials purchase price variance results and she is rewarded. Her best strategy is to constantly shop the marketplace for special deals. Using the traditional scientific management strategy, she is responsible only for meeting production needs as cheaply as possible. She doesn't even have to talk to the production manager as long as the materials are available when needed. And if we've got lots of materials on hand, she doesn't have to be picky about quality. The manufacturing people throw away materials they can't work with. She is not responsible for inferior quality or stacks of excess raw materials causing extra storage costs and waste throughout the process. The result?

Cost minimization often is at the expense of quality and waste in other activities

When we change to a value chain approach, we have to consider the impact of each activity on another. Our focus shifts to coordination and management of the value chain processes as a whole, not solely individual activities viewed in isolation from each other [a traditional scientific management result]. The purchasing manager needs to consider the activities of our entire value chain. Cost management is no longer a matter of getting the best bids on a day-to-day basis. Instead, supplier activities and their resulting costs are managed with negotiated long-term contracts and ongoing relationships. We should use our purchasing manager to coordinate vendors and our activities. At Saturn, suppliers have offices within its automobile plant!"

Strategic partnering and ABC

BOB

"This way of managing supplier relationships along the industry's value chain is called **strategic partnering**. Its objective is to reduce the number of activities performed by eliminating redundant activities, and increase the commitment of suppliers to us, as well as provide cost savings for both of us.

Strategic partnering *builds long-run relationships with a few suppliers to eliminate activities not adding value, increase vendor quality, and reduce costs across the value chain.*

"For example, Procter & Gamble installed order-entry computers in Wal-Mart stores, significantly reducing these activity costs by eliminating duplicate activities performed by the two companies. Dell Computers contracts with Roadway Services to track all of its inbound and outbound shipments. Shipping and logistics now are tracked by just one company rather than two. Through strategically partnering with certain travel agencies, hotels, and rental car companies, Price Waterhouse discovered it could save about $10 million a year on travel costs."

BILL

"A KPMG study reports strategic partnering is a competitive necessity in retailing, with 96% of retailers sharing information with their suppliers and customers. In managing their inventories, 71% involve suppliers, and 78% involve customers. One conclusion in Ernst & Young's 'Connected Manufacturing Enterprise' project is that value chain relationships will be more important 'assets' in creating value than owned assets [e.g., property, plant, equipment, and inventories] by 2008."

NANCY

"O.K., show me how strategic partnering can work for us."

BOB

An ABC analysis of value chain processes. "We just completed a value chain analysis with one of our roof panel suppliers. We buy ¾-inch plywood sheets in large lots from different suppliers [whoever offers the lowest price]. They come in 10-foot lengths [4 feet wide]. Our standard home's roof is 26 feet long. To cover each side of the roof, we need four 10-foot sheets and two sheets cut to 6 feet. So, in total, we need 12 sheets per house. We throw away the odd 4-foot pieces. To make the roof, we nail 12 boards and seal 5 seams. This is the way we, and every other builder, have been making roofs for as long as I can remember.

"Looking at the value chain from creating roof panels in our supplier's plant through the completion of the roofs in our plant, our goal was to determine which activities actually drive these costs, and if we can reduce the number of activities in the chain. We discovered plywood is made by a continuous process. As it comes out of the process, our suppliers cut it into 10-foot sheets, the industry standard length, for packaging. All their packaging, storage facilities, and trucks are set up to handle 10-foot sheets.

"Well, we wondered why they couldn't make 13-foot sheets for us. Our main supplier wouldn't consider this, but one of our secondary suppliers started to work with us on the idea. Working together, we were able to eliminate many activities. Now, we send our truck to their plant, pay for two machine setups [to cut 13-foot sheets for us and then return to 10-foot sheets], and loading. The supplier gets his same markup, along with a long-term contract as our sole supplier. While we incur the extra pick up and delivery cost, all of our other costs are reduced." [You can see the value chain activities and ABC analyses in Exhibits 10-7a and b. Exhibit 10-7a shows the original value chain activities and costs. Exhibit 10-7b (p. 365) shows the revised activities and costs.] "With strategic partnering, we were able to reduce these costs by 37% [$149.70]. One of our supplier's activity costs increased, but two decreased and three were eliminated. On our side of the value chain, we incur one new activity (pickup and delivery) but four activity costs are reduced and two eliminated."

SID

"I'm sold on this approach! We need to do this for all our major suppliers and really take advantage of these opportunities. One other point before we go on. Think about our savings in purchasing if we stop obtaining multiple bids and we work with the same group of companies all the time!"

BOB

Technical support and other advantages. "Our partnering with this supplier provides another advantage. Because of the way we design roof trusses, we are less interested in the roof sheet's strength and more interested in its waterproofing capability. If its waterproofing can be improved, we may be able to eliminate one layer of felt. The improved waterproofing will cost more, but the reduced stress tolerance will lower our supplier's production costs. Because we've guaranteed a long-term contract, our supplier is motivated to invest in the necessary research and development. Our supplier sees an additional benefit from a new and unique product line to sell to other builders as well! They're just delighted! The risk of a new product development has dropped considerably.

"Of course, we're not the first company to think of strategic partnering. Ford uses it quite successfully, too. One of its suppliers, Progressive Tool and Industries Company, designed a mechanical bat wing for use in installing its components within Ford's Louisville plant. Lear Seating no longer just provides seats to Ford. It now provides complete interior assemblies, including doors and instrument panels. Ford credits its strategic partnering efforts for reducing cost by over $700 per car."

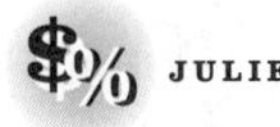

JULIE

"Strategic partnering with suppliers also creates cost savings in purchasing and accounts payable. We can install an EDI [electronic data interchange] system for ordering, shipping, and paying invoices. Wal-Mart and Kmart require suppliers to use their EDI systems. Stride-Rite's EDI system with its customers reduces delivery time

Activity-Based Costing and Redesigning the Value Chain—Original Costs

	Standard prices		Standard quantities		Standard costs	
Supplier activities:						
Rolling the plywood	$1.00	per foot	120	feet per house (a)	$120.00	per house
Setup for cutting into 10' sheets	$100.00	per batch of 1,000 sheets	0.012	batches per house (b)	1.20	per house
Packaging	$5.00	per batch of 10 sheets	1.2	packages per house	6.00	per house
Storage	$2.00	per package (10 sheets)	1.2	packages per house	2.40	per house
Loading trucks	$0.50	per package	1.2	packages per house	0.60	per house
Delivery	$250.00	per truckload (8 packages)	0.15	loads per house	37.50	per house
Total costs					**$167.70**	per house
Markup @ 50%					83.85	per house
Material cost to Multree					**$251.55**	per house
Our activities:						
Receiving and unpackaging	$75.00	per truckload	0.15	loads per house	$11.25	per house
Move 1/3 of sheets to sawing	$45.00	per truckload	0.15	loads per house	6.75	per house
Cut 6' lengths and return to storage	$125.00	per truckload	0.15	loads per house	18.75	per house
Move sheets to assembly	$50.00	per move (c)	0.2	moves per house	10.00	per house
Nail to roof trusses	$7.50	per sheet	12	sheets per house	90.00	per house
Seal seams	$4.00	per seam	5	seams per house	20.00	per house
Multree's cost of roof paneling					**$156.75**	
Total cost of roof paneling					**$408.30**	per house

Notes:

(a): Need 12 sheets per house.

(b): Need 12 sheets of the 1,000.

(c): 1 move for each batch of 5 standard homes.

Exhibit 10-7a

Activity-Based Costing and Redesigning the Value Chain—Revised Costs for New Activities

	Standard prices		Standard quantities		Standard costs	
Supplier activities:						
Rolling the plywood	$1.00	per foot	104	feet per house (a)	$104.00	per house
Setup for cutting into 13' sheets	$200.00	per batch of 1 truckload	0.04	loads per house (b)	8.00	per house
Packaging					0.00	per house
Storage					0.00	per house
Loading trucks	$10.00	per truckload	0.04	loads per house	0.40	per house
Delivery					0.00	per house
Total costs					$112.40	per house
Markup @ 50%					56.20	per house
Material cost to Multree					**$168.60**	per house
Our activities:						
Pickup and delivery	$100.00	per truckload	0.04	loads per house	$4.00	per house
Receiving and unpackaging	$50.00	per truckload	0.04	loads per house	2.00	per house
Move 1/3 of sheets to sawing					0.00	per house
Cut 6' lengths and return to storage					0.00	per house
Move sheets to assembly	$40.00	per move (c)	0.2	moves per house	8.00	per house
Nail to roof trusses	$7.50	per sheet	8	sheets per house	60.00	per house
Seal seams	$4.00	per seam	4	seams per house	16.00	per house
Multree's cost of roof paneling					**$90.00**	
Total cost of roof paneling					**$258.60**	per house
COST SAVINGS FROM REDESIGN					***$149.70***	per house
					37%	

Notes:

(a): Need 8 sheets per house.

(b): Each truckload contains 200 sheets. We get charged for 2 setups.

(c): 1 move for each batch of 5 standard homes.

Exhibit 10-7b

to 1½ days. So, strategic partnering is not just for supply relationships. For example, the IMA [Institute of Management Accountants] included a 'Financial Software Supplement' with its August 1998 *Management Accounting* issue reporting on dozens of strategic partnerships with software vendors."

NANCY

"Strategic partnering can eliminate many activities not adding value to our products, as well as provide incentives and ideas for new products. Strategic partnering also allows us to work with companies whose core competencies are different than ours, so the combined relationship can be world class! We don't have to perform activities we previously thought we needed, but just didn't do very well."

ABM vendor performance measures

JULIE

"In traditional systems, quality is assured by excess inventory stocks to guard against poor quality materials or not having them when needed. Strategic partnering eliminates the need for large inventories. When we change our management philosophy, we need new performance measures supporting these new management objectives. *Our new objectives are high-quality materials, delivered on time, at an acceptable cost.* These new measures are part of **activity-based management [ABM]**. ABM focuses on our processes and activities to:

- Identify activities adding value to the user of that process,
- Eliminate activities not adding value, and
- Create performance measures equally emphasizing quality, service, and cost.

Let me illustrate some of these measures for managing supplier relationships."

> *Axioms from Chapter 1:* What gets measured gets done; suitable control motivates good judgment and good judgment requires good information. **Activity-based management (ABM)** *is a strategy to maximize value by focusing on the quality, service, and cost of processes and activities.*

Vendor performance index (VPI). "The **vendor performance index [VPI]** measures how expensive a supplier is when it creates extra work for us. Let's call the extra work 'nonvalue-added activities.' The VPI formula is:

Vendor Performance Index (VPI)

$$\text{VPI} = \frac{\text{Materials purchase cost} + \text{Nonvalue-added costs}}{\text{Materials purchase cost}}$$

Examples of nonvalue-added activity costs for one of our suppliers are shown in Exhibit 10-8.

"I calculate VPI monthly for each supplier. The optimal value for VPI is 1. This results when materials purchase cost plus $0 in nonvalue-added costs is divided by materials purchase costs. In other words, a VPI of 1 is ideal because the supplier creates no extra work for us. With a 1.2 VPI, this company is causing us an extra 20¢ in nonvalue-added costs for every dollar of materials we purchase from it. We've got some work to do in getting better performance from this supplier! VPI can be lowered with strategic partnering. For example, AlliedSignal was able to reduce its supplier nonvalue-added activity costs by $50 million in 1994 alone."

> *Many ABM vendor performance measures exist. The* **vendor performance index (VPI)** *relates the cost of extra work created by a supplier to the amount we purchased.* **On-time delivery** *and* **complete order filling ratios** *relate the number of on-time and complete orders to total deliveries received. Many ABM measures are graphically displayed using spreadsheet programs.*

On-time delivery and complete order filling. "Two other measures of supplier quality I calculate are the **on-time delivery ratio** and the **complete order**

Vendor Performance Index

Nonvalue-added activities	Labor hours	Labor cost at $10/hr
Inspection	10	$100
Processing paperwork	2	20
Returning bad materials	3	30
Waiting for late deliveries	5	50
Totals	20	$200
Materials purchase cost	$1,000	

$$VPI = \frac{\text{Materials purchase cost} + \text{Nonvalue-added costs}}{\text{Materials purchase cost}}$$

$$VPI = \frac{\$1{,}000 + \$200}{\$1{,}000}$$

$$\mathbf{VPI = 1.2}$$

Exhibit 10-8

filling ratio. The first is the percentage of deliveries we receive on time. We consider a delivery 'on time' if we receive it the day it is supposed to arrive. The second ratio is the percentage of orders received that include everything we ordered. I also create a graph within my spreadsheet program showing the number of late [or early] deliveries, and the days late [or early] for each supplier [see Exhibit 10-9].

"Adams Supplies is either early or late half the time, but not by more than a couple of days. Only 80% of their deliveries are complete, though. Murry Electric is anywhere from 2 days early to 3 days late 40% of the time, but their deliveries are always complete. Woods Lumber has the best on-time delivery ratio, arriving when they are supposed to 67% of the time. However, when they miss a date, it's often by 2 to 5 days! Also, they are horrible in delivering everything we order [a 41% complete order filling ratio]."

"Our purchasing people typically select suppliers based on the lowest bid. Why? Because they're evaluated with only one measure, the direct materials purchase price variance. Remember, what gets measured gets done. Too often, quality and delivery performance suffer, hindering our ability to create value for our customers. Strategic cost management and ABM measures can help us overcome these problems in two ways. First, we're using a customer's view of 'cost.' Materials and parts costs include more than just the net delivered purchase price, which is what our standard prices are based upon. Secondly, we're measuring cost from a 'cause-effect' perspective, linking all purchasing value chain costs to individual suppliers. 'What's measured gets done' works well when we measure the right things in the right way!

On-Time Delivery and Complete Order Filling

Suppliers	Total deliveries	Deliveries on time	On-time delivery ratio	Complete orders received	Complete order filling ratio
Adams Supplies	20	10	50%	16	80%
Murry Electric	10	6	60%	10	100%
Woods Lumber	27	18	67%	11	41%

Late Deliveries by Suppliers

# of Late Deliveries
0 1 2 3 4
(5) (4) (3) (2) (1) 0 1 2
Days (Late)/Early
Adams Supplies
Murry Electric
Woods Lumber
Woods Lumber
Murry Electric
Adams Supplies

Exhibit 10-9

"I've talked to a lot of our workers about your graphs, Julie. They all like them because graphs are easier to understand than most of the accounting reports they receive. Most ABM measures can be displayed graphically, making the information more user-friendly. I know some of our workers and managers have requested microcomputers in their departments so they can create spreadsheet graphics about their activities. We should put enough money in our budget for these!"

"I think I'm beginning to get your idea, Julie. *When we devise performance evaluation measures, whether for our employees or suppliers, we cannot look just at cost variances. We also need to create ABM measures for the critical performance factors of quality and delivery.*"

"By combining vendor ABM measures with strategic partnerships, we're adding value to our customers. We should consider what Levi-Strauss does. It reduced material costs by negotiating long-term supplier contracts. Contracts are automatically renewed each year as long as suppliers maintain measures such as on-time delivery and complete order filling within an acceptable range."

KEY OBJECTIVE 3

Create activity-based management measures for customer satisfaction and explain the role of ABC in managing customer relations.

Managing Value Chain Relationships with Customers

"We also need to manage the other end of our value chain, our relationships with customers. Based on Julie's and Bob's discussion of vendor management, I see two ways we can do this. First, we should be able to create ABM measures just as we did for our suppliers. Second, we can use ABC with customer-related activities."

ABM customer performance measures

NANCY

"That makes a lot of sense, Bill. I've been thinking about our vendor performance measures. Aren't we suppliers to our customers?"

"Well, yes, I suppose so. Where do you want to go with this idea, Nancy?"

Using vendor performance measures on ourselves. "If we want to evaluate the quality of our suppliers, we measure our satisfaction with them by using ABM measures such as the:

- Vendor performance index [VPI],
- On-time deliveries ratio, and
- Complete order filling ratio.

Well, from our customers' perspective, we are their suppliers. Should they calculate these measures about our performance as their supplier? If so, shouldn't we measure our performance to our customers using this same type of accounting information?"

"I see your point, Nancy. That's a really good idea! Julie, let's start calculating these performance measures on ourselves. If we wait for our customers to report our performance to us, we will be reacting to that information. I don't want to operate in a reactive mode. This is not a characteristic of high-quality performance, customer satisfaction, or a world-class organization. I want to operate in a proactive mode. Bill, as vice president of marketing, I want you to take charge of gathering this information. Julie, work with Bill in developing a spreadsheet program to report it on a timely basis."

BILL

Customer satisfaction measures. "I know another ABM measure we can use to measure customer satisfaction. It's called a **snake chart**. To create it, I've surveyed our customers and identified which product or service attributes they think are important, and how well we perform on each attribute. We can load this data into the management accounting system and present it graphically. Here's the snake chart I developed [see Exhibit 10-10].

> A **snake chart** *graphically displays product or service attributes customers think are important along with how well the provider performs on each attribute.*

"Let's see what our customers have to say about each of the six attributes they think are important. The least important is having different types of homes [Variety in types of homes]. You'll notice we do this very well, but it is not that important to our customers. We're about average on our ability to customize homes, but we can do better. It's not our highest priority, though, because it is not critically important to our customers. On-time delivery is the most important attribute. We know this, and we do it excellently. It's one of our highest priorities. Customers also think complete order filling is important, and we do a very good job here. Construction/installation support is not highly valued by our customers, but it is somewhat important to them. We need to do better here. Notice how important warranty service is, and how poorly we do it! This should be a very high priority in our strategic plan."

"This can't be right! We differentiate our products on their high quality. It's part of our vision statement and strategic plan."

"Yes, but the Boss's idea of high quality was responding to service calls within 24 hours. For the 20 calls a day we average, we've been able to respond within 24

Customer Satisfaction Snake Chart

Attributes:	Customer ratings: Importance	Customer ratings: Performance
Variety in types of homes	2	8
Ability to customize floor plans	7	6
On-time delivery	10	10
Complete order filling	8	9
Construction/installation support	5	2
Warranty service	9	4

Ranking scales: Importance	Ranking scales: Performance
1 = Least important	1 = Very bad performance
10 = Most important	10 = Outstanding performance

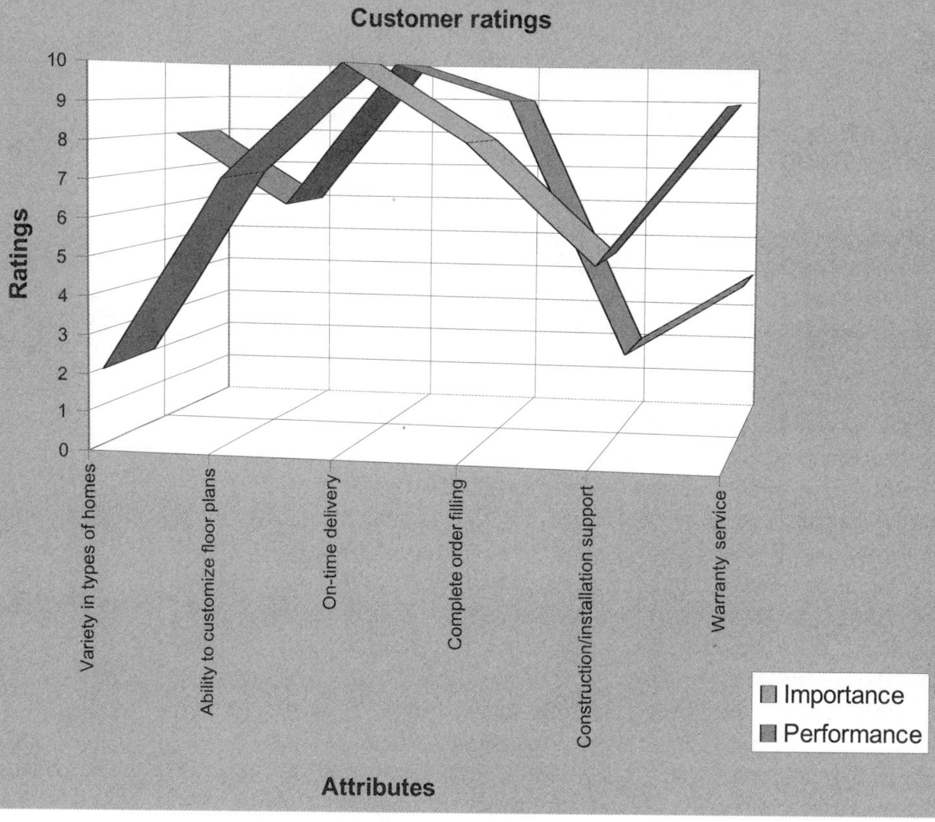

Customer ratings

Ratings: 0 1 2 3 4 5 6 7 8 9 10

Variety in types of homes
Ability to customize floor plans
On-time delivery
Complete order filling
Construction/installation support
Warranty service

Importance
Performance

Attributes

Exhibit 10-10

hours 95% of the time. Our customers, though, only consider the 20 calls per day, which should not happen!"

"When Bill and I were studying how the Boss did things, we discovered something else. He was a big proponent of scientific management. High quality was viewed on a department-by-department basis [another example of scientific management's silo thinking]. Production did a good job if 90% of everything worked right. Quality Control did a good job if it caught another 5% of quality problems. Then, the Warranty Service Department was responsible for fixing the last 5% of quality problems in the field when customers discovered them. With each department, people did a 'good enough job,' and then 'threw the product over the wall' to the next department.

"We need to stop thinking about the provision of goods and services in terms of independent departments, each performing separate activities. Instead, *we must look at value from the customer's perspective in terms of processes which create value, rather than in terms of our departments*. This is what value chain analysis and strategic cost management means. This explains the rating of 4 for warranty service on the snake chart. It's not good enough to respond within 24 hours 95%, or even 100%, of the time. From our customers' perspective, warranty calls should not occur!"

"We have to understand what drives value from the customer's perspective. Levi-Strauss knows this. Custom-fitting jeans are highly valued. So, for an extra $10 at some stores, customer measurements can be taken and sent to Levi's Tennessee plant where jeans are made specifically for that customer."

Customer management with ABC

"You know, I had a very interesting meeting with another lumber company last week. Woods Lumber hasn't been doing a very good job as our main lumber supplier [see Exhibit 10-9], and now it wants to raise prices again. Merrywood Lumber and Supply's marketing manager and management accountant just completed an ABC analysis of delivery costs for different types of customers—individual home builders, subdivision contractors, and manufacturers like us. Their goal was simple: to get our business. I was really surprised because they never were that interested in us as a customer. We sat down and worked together for a day, sharing a lot of information. After they showed me their ABC analysis [Exhibit 10-11], I understood why they were now interested in getting our business.

"Remember our meeting about motivation and control [Chapter 8]? We used to allocate selling and administrative expenses based on each product line's sales revenues. Julie showed us how this distorted the product lines' profitability, though. She recommended we start using a contribution margin income statement without allocating the common costs to each line. Then, in our meeting last week [Chapter 9], she showed us how we could get an even better picture of each line's profits by using ABC.

"Well, Merrywood Lumber and Supply used to do the same type of revenue-based allocations. Its original analysis appears at the bottom [of Exhibit 10-11]. When segmenting its income statement by type of customer, individual home builders appeared to be the most profitable [13%]. Customers like us didn't seem to be profitable [only 3%]."

"In its ABC study, cost driver volumes were tracked for each of the three customers [e.g., for activity 1, 14,000 items loaded for individual home orders]. Next total activity costs were measured [e.g., $85,000 for loading trucks]. Average ABC costs then were developed by dividing total activity costs into total activity cost driver volume [e.g., $85,000 loading costs ÷ 34,000 items = $2.50 per item]. Using the ABC cost driver rates and customer cost driver volumes, activity costs were allocated to each customer group. For example, individual home customers account for $35,000 of the $85,000 total loading costs in activity 1 [$2.50 per item × 14,000 items = $35,000]. After looking at the three activities in its value chain's delivery process, Merrywood now charges customers using average activity costs!

"Merrywood's ABC analysis reveals a 27% loss for individual home builders because of all the time drivers sit around waiting for the owner to show, and then for a forklift to unload the trucks. Worse yet, individual sites are scattered all over the place, so a lot more miles are driven getting to them. Merrywood also discovered most orders are for only one of each item, with many different items in a single order. This added complexity further drives up costs.

Activity Analysis of Customer Delivery Costs

Delivery process activities	Cost drivers		Individual homes	Subdivisions	Manufacturers	Totals	Average ABC costs
1. Load trucks	Number of items	*Total items:*	14,000	18,000	2,000	34,000	
		Actual costs:	$35,000	$45,000	$5,000	$85,000	$2.50 per item
2. Delivery	Miles driven	*Total miles:*	1,000	900	100	2,000	
		Actual costs:	$5,000	$4,500	$500	$10,000	$5.00 per mile
3. On-site time	Hours at the job site	*Total hours:*	150	60	40	250	
		Actual costs:	$3,000	$1,200	$800	$5,000	$20.00 per hour
Total delivery costs by type of customer			**$43,000**	**$50,700**	**$6,300**	**$100,000**	

New profit analysis	Individual homes	Subdivisions	Manufacturers	Totals
Sales revenues	$75,000	$400,000	$125,000	$600,000
Less: Cost of goods sold	(52,500)	(300,000)	(100,000)	(452,500)
Less: allocation of delivery costs (based on activity costs)	(43,000)	(50,700)	(6,300)	(100,000)
Profit by type of customer	($20,500)	$49,300	$18,700	$47,500
Profit ratio	(27%)	12%	15%	8%

Original profit analysis	Individual homes	Subdivisions	Manufacturers	Totals
Sales revenues	$75,000	$400,000	$125,000	$600,000
Less: Cost of goods sold	(52,500)	(300,000)	(100,000)	(452,500)
Less: allocation of delivery costs (based on revenues)	(12,500)	(66,667)	(20,833)	(100,000)
Profit by type of customer	$10,000	$33,333	$4,167	$47,500
Profit ratio	13%	8%	3%	8%

Exhibit 10-11

"The ABC analysis shows manufacturers are really its most profitable customers [15%]. This makes sense because drivers don't have to go as far to get to us, they don't have to wait a long time for unloading, and we order single items in large quantities. Needless to say, I was able to negotiate much better prices than we get from Woods Lumber. The customer-based ABC analysis is saving us hundreds of dollars per home! Most importantly, because Merrywood's profits are increasing, it's willing to strategically partner with us. We're working on an EDI system for ordering and payments which will reduce purchasing and accounts payable costs. And by sharing our production schedule with Merrywood, it's able to provide more frequent deliveries, reducing our need to store large materials inventories."

NANCY

"Wow! Should we do an ABC analysis of our customers? Is it possible different types of customers require different activities from us?"

JULIE

"Perhaps, Nancy, but I doubt it. Our customers are all basically the same in terms of the activities they want from us. ABC is often time-consuming and costly. Let's make sure the benefits from getting the information are greater than its costs. Last meeting [Chapter 9] we discovered our standard and custom home lines required different activities. They also used different amounts of the same activities. These activity cost drivers were not related to direct labor hours worked on the houses. So, when we allocated overhead to each house using direct labor hours, we miscosted standard and custom homes."

BILL

"Retailing profits really took a beating during the 1990s. The survivors were the ones who knew customer activity costs. Many gather this information in data warehouses, which are used by 96% of retailers with sales over $1 billion, according to an Ernst & Young survey. Many also have turned to selling over the Internet. E-commerce and EDI can significantly reduce inventory, ordering, shipping, and billing costs. For example, Wal-Mart now offers thousands of products through its Web site. What do these trends tell us? *If customers place different demands on us, identifying the costs of customer-based activities justifies ABC.* This just isn't our situation, though."

Customer-based ABC in the service sector

JULIE

"Managing customers with ABC information is important in the service sector because service providers often deal with many types of customers. Consider a bank. A business customer who comes in every day to make deposits is more costly than a nonbusiness customer whose paycheck is directly deposited from work. Business customers also bring a variety of deposit items with them, such as coins, various denominations of dollar bills, checks, and credit card charges. So, when I worked for the bank, ABC customer analyses made sense. Only half of the top 10 most profitable banks during the mid-1980s are still around. First Tennessee National's ABC studies shed some light on this phenomenon. 30% of its certificates of deposit generated 88% of its CD profits. Another 30% resulted in a 7% average loss. For example, 3-month $500 CDs incurred greater processing costs than revenues. It also analyzed 3-year loans. $50,000 loans were profitable only over the first 19 months. $20,000 and $3,000 loans were never profitable."

NANCY

"I see. *The idea is to charge customers for the services they use.* Those not using certain services should not be charged for them. Clearly, ABC is needed to identify activities causing different customer costs."

TOMMY

"That's all true. Some customers make extensive use of automated teller machines. Every time I use my ATM card I am charged two dollars, and I'm charged another dollar by my bank when it processes the transaction! I also get charged for each check I write. I don't think I like ABC!!

"I also remember working at the hospital. Some patients [customers] require treatment in Intensive Care, Maternity, Surgery, or the Outpatient ward. Obviously, the services they receive and the activities performed [e.g., nursing care, feeding, and occupancy costs] are very different. With the increasing costs of healthcare management, insurance companies and HMOs are developing standard protocols which doctors and hospitals must use. Now everyone will receive the same tests and treatment for a specific illness because that's all the doctor will be paid for by the insurance company or HMO. The reimbursement received is based on the equivalent of a standard cost card and bill of activities!"

NANCY

"It's like that at college, too. Different customers [students] use different activities, and they get charged for them. I paid a special fee for the health center, a parking permit, and the computer lab. As Merrywood Lumber is doing with its customers, like us, the service sector uses ABC to identify activity costs and customer profitability."

KEY OBJECTIVE 4

Illustrate product line management with target costing, simultaneous engineering and quality function deployment, and life cycle costing.

Product Line Strategic Cost Management

BILL

"So far, we've talked about managing *processes* up and down the industry's value chain. We also should consider managing the *products* themselves. Looking at individual processes is O.K., but this only improves costs by maybe 20% or 30%. *Most of the costs are locked in by the time we finish designing a product. How we design a house determines the vast majority of costs.* That's why it's so expensive to change things.

"Last year, our marketing team wanted to add that big picture window on the second floor of our winter chalet home. They were sure it would increase sales by 20%. We couldn't do it, though, because of all the problems the redesign created. One wall needed to be moved, increasing the stress load on the roof. Engineering didn't think it would withstand a really heavy snowfall. We also had to change the plumbing design if the wall was moved. The changes went on and on. Our sales problems with that product line all began with the original architectural plans. It was designed and 'thrown over the wall' to manufacturing. They built it and then passed it along to sales and service. The warranty problems encountered in the field were incredible! How can we avoid these problems in the future?"

SID

"Well, Bill, I really don't know. This is the way new products always have been handled. Each department is responsible for its own activities and processes within our value chain. That's what scientific management is all about. In the old days, we had little competition and lots of demand. 'Get the product out the door' was our motto. Each department had its responsibilities and we all worked as fast as we could. Whatever it cost us to make a house was not critical because we could add our markup, sell it, and make a profit."

BILL

"Yes, but that's not how it is anymore. *Our competitors have the same equipment and technology. They can do anything we can. Any advantages we have are temporary.* We can't afford to have very many product lines fail. We must carefully cost our new products in light of what customers will pay for them. Remember, value is in the eyes of the customer. To avoid disasters, first we'd better find out what customers will pay. Then, we can determine how much to spend on making our houses."

JULIE

"I have a suggestion. Let's consider three value chain processes in managing a product line throughout its entire life:

- In the research and development stage, determine the total costs we can spend on a product given our sales projection and desired profit. This is called target costing. Since we commit the vast majority of our costs through our design choices, let's make sure the product can be manufactured, sold, and serviced profitably.

- When designing the product, involve everyone—including the customer. This is called simultaneous engineering and quality function deployment. Since we're locked into most of our costs before we make the first product, let's make sure we give customers what they want. Let's do it right the first time, starting with how we design the product.
- Budget and track total product costs over the product's entire life. This is called life cycle costing. Since we have a target cost, let's make sure we don't exceed it."

Target costing

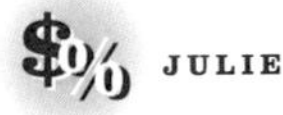

"With regulated services, and in markets with little competition, such as a pharmaceutical company's patent on a new drug, prices often are based on cost plus a markup. For example, government regulatory agencies allow publicly owned utilities a sufficient markup providing a fair ROI to investors. Governmental contracting also is based on cost-plus pricing. Firms won't work for the government unless they can earn a fair profit."

"Of course! That's how the Boss always did it at Multree Homes, too. It makes sense to me. We have to make an adequate profit. So, each product's sales price should be determined by adding a reasonable markup to its cost."

"Well, the traditional American strategy of costs driving prices worked well when competition was not so intense. But, in highly competitive markets, customers and competition really set the allowable sales price. **Target costing** starts with estimating total sales revenues for the product's entire life. Second, a desired total profit is determined. The difference is the target cost: the total we can spend on the product throughout its life.

Target costing *is a market-based approach to determine the total allowable lifetime cost of a product by subtracting a profit goal from estimated lifetime revenues.*

"Consider how H. J. Heinz used this idea. While cat food prices were falling, Heinz raised its price for 9-Lives cat food. After losing significant market share, it started to address the problem from the customer's perspective. First, management determined the price its market was willing to pay. Then, working backwards, it determined the maximum costs it could spend on cat food. Through target costing, strategic partnering, and modernization, it is again a major player in the cat food market.

"Target costing was pioneered at Toyota, and the Japanese have been using it for some time. A 1995 survey reported its use by industry: 100% in transportation, 88% in electrical, 83% in machinery manufacturing, and 75% in equipment manufacturing. Target costing is especially important with products having fairly short lives, like our winter chalet design. In many industries, product lives are becoming much shorter. Consider 3M. 'Post-It' notes are a relatively new product, but now a main profit source. During the 1990s, 3M's strategy was to generate 70% of sales five years in the future from products not yet existing! The Japanese have a motto for this, 'The faster we abandon current products, the more profitable we will be!' Daihatsu, Chrysler, Ford, General Motors, Mercedes-Benz, Nissan, and Toyota all use this technique in deciding whether to introduce new automobiles. In the electronics industry, Compaq, Panasonic, Sharp, and Toshiba rely on target costing.

"Using target costing with our winter chalet home, I estimate we will be able to sell this design for two years before changing customer desires will force us to abandon it. Given current competition, I think we can sell it for $75,000 and sell 10 over its 2-year life. This may not seem like a lot, but in two years we can spin off another related product. We can continue this strategy for quite a long time, staying ahead of our competition by changing our product line frequently. In the long run, this will be very profitable!"

SID

"O.K., but I want a 20% return on cost from these homes during their 2-year life. What do the numbers look like, Julie?"

JULIE

"Total revenues have to equal 120% of costs. The formula looks like this:

Target Costing Formula

Target cost	=	**Total lifetime revenues**	–	**Desired lifetime profits**
	=	**\$75,000 × 10 homes**	–	**20% of target cost**
	=	**\$625,000**		

Can we do this? We can't take our normal one-year research and development time. Nor can we spend another six months drawing architectural plans. We need to find a way to speed up the time to market."

Simultaneous engineering and quality function deployment (QFD)

BOB

"Our next step, then, is to design the house right, the first time, from the customer's perspective. **Simultaneous engineering** involves everyone in the design process, including customers. Bill's job is to make sure customer desires are known, and we find a way to incorporate them into the original design. For example, let's get that picture window in the second floor."

TOMMY

"It won't be easy, though. When I was working for Boeing, our simultaneous engineering goal was to reduce manufacturing time from over a year to six months. We used to design planes with three independent design teams. Only after they finished the initial designs did the teams get together and consult the manufacturing people. Often parts couldn't be manufactured or were too expensive. Millions of hours a year were lost in revisions! Boeing changed its design strategy to simultaneous engineering with the 777. Through strategic partnering and computer-aided design [CAD programs], rework costs and delivery times were cut in half."

> **Simultaneous engineering** *includes people from all the value chain processes in the initial design of a product or service.*
> **Quality function deployment (QFD)** *assures the product's characteristics (functions) are what the customers want.*

BILL

"**Quality function deployment [QFD]** starts the simultaneous engineering process with the functions customers want in a product or service. Borland used QFD to introduce its Quattro Pro® spreadsheet program. It included spreadsheet templates for many uses, tutorials, and extensive help explanations. It also was designed to minimize the huge technical support costs incurred by the industry leader. Quattro Pro® was introduced in 1993 for \$49 [compared to \$495 for its competitor's program]. Following the same logic, but not with the same success, Microsoft's Windows 95® operating system took over a year longer to market than expected in the hope of providing a workable 'plug and play' feature. The goal was to eliminate customer problems when upgrading hardware.

"The chalet home's QFD study shows it needs to be fairly narrow, but tall. Land is expensive near ski resorts and lots are small. Big trees are everywhere and tall homes provide a better view and more living space. Big picture windows are necessary, as are decks. Well-sloped roofs help keep off the snow. Of course, the house better include superior insulation and a wood-burning stove!"

JULIE

"This is where I add value." Julie shouldn't have paused at this point, but she did. Everyone started laughing as they thought she had just volunteered to carry in the firewood! "No, no! QFD requires good ABC information so we can plan the costs of adding these product attributes. Let me illustrate by showing the QFD analysis for adding that picture window [see Exhibit 10-12]."

ABC Quality Function Deployment (QFD) Analysis

Picture window activities	Original ABC analysis	Revised ABC analysis
Purchase glass	$500	$600
Purchase framing materials	50	50
Cut frame lumber	100	100
Package glass for shipping	25	25
Special installation labor	75	100
Extra sealing materials	0	25
Warranty work	250	0
Budgeted cost	$1,000	$900
Target costing allowance	$900	$900
Drift	($100)	none

Note: The chalet home is a purchased kit (package) assembled at the site.

Exhibit 10-12

BOB

"When the target cost is not currently attainable a 'drift' exists. This is the difference between the target cost and the original ABC cost [$100 in Exhibit 10-12]. The management problem is to eliminate the drift. With these windows, we've always had a leakage problem causing the high warranty cost. To eliminate the drift, we went back to the glass manufacturer. Our glass supplier was eager for the business and worked with us in designing a better quality window pane. We agreed to spend more in installation and sealing, and for the extra cost to make the glass. Our supplier agreed to provide any resulting warranty work. The right column [in Exhibit 10-12] shows how we eliminated the $100 drift. Now, Bill has his picture window!

"QFD is more than just assuring our ultimate customer desires, though. It's also designing for manufacturability. By this I mean designing products so manufacturing costs are minimized, as well as logistics and service costs. I've seen a lot of engineering studies showing for every dollar spent in simultaneous engineering and QFD, $8 to $10 is saved in 'downstream' costs [e.g., production, shipping, and warranty work]. Why? Once products are designed, it's very difficult to change them. About 80% of the product's total cost over its entire life is locked in during its design.

"One way to design for manufacturability is to use current parts in new products. This cuts down on the costs associated with designing, making, and using new parts. Caterpillar requires all new products to contain at least 80% current parts. Another way is to reduce product complexity. ABC shows us how complexity drives cost. The Japanese have done this for a long time. For example, by reducing VCR parts 50%, sales prices dropped by about $1,000 over ten years. Hewlett-Packard used common parts in designing its inkjet printers. QFD convinced H-P engineers to abandon their 'super-duper' design for the simpler product customers wanted. IBM was able to cut its microcomputer costs in half in just two years by using less floppy drives and motherboards."

$% JULIE

"Our management accounting system can provide information on our simultaneous engineering and QFD success. For example, here's some of the measures Carrier, the world leader in air conditioning and heating, uses:

- Percentage of standard components used in new products,
- Percentage of purchased parts from certified vendors,
- Percentage of suppliers on EDI,
- Complexity cost ratio [complexity-created costs divided by production costs], and
- Total number of components required.

Other measures reported in a recent survey appearing in *Management Accounting* include:

- Time to market,
- Number of design changes,
- Degree of innovation [design awards, customer surveys], and
- Customer evaluations [like a snake chart]."

Life cycle costing

$% JULIE

"One last step before we're done. To finish our product line strategic management, we have to budget our life cycle costs, make sure we are within the target cost, and devise accounting reports to track the cumulative costs over all of the product's five life cycle stages:

- Design,
- Market introduction,
- Sales growth,
- Maturity, and
- Market decline.

Life cycle costing provides the big picture budget for all value chain processes within each stage of a product or service's life cycle. The target cost for our chalet home line is $625,000. We need to budget costs for each life cycle stage within this target. [Exhibit 10-13 illustrates the budgeted costs.]

Life cycle costing *projects whether target costs for a new product or service can be obtained by budgeting value chain process costs across all stages of a product's life cycle.*

"Once we have target costs for each process, we should do a process-by-process ABC analysis to make sure we can hit the targets. ITT Automotive has developed 'cost tracking sheets' for this purpose, which I may be able to adapt to our chalet homes. Finally, we can accumulate target costs by life cycle stage, compare them to projected revenues, and calculate target profits by stage [see Exhibit 10-14 on p. 380].

"Bill then can map life cycle stage profit projections to time periods over the chalet home's 2-year life. As we incur process costs throughout the chalet home's

Target Costing for Value Chain Processes

Value chain processes	Life cycle stages					Totals
	Design	Introduction	Growth	Maturity	Decline	
Research and development	70%	10%	5%	5%	10%	100%
	$109,375	$15,625	$7,813	$7,813	$15,625	$156,250
Marketing	10%	40%	20%	10%	20%	100%
	$12,500	$50,000	$25,000	$12,500	$25,000	$125,000
Sales and production*	0%	10%	20%	60%	10%	100%
	$0	$31,250	$62,500	$187,500	$31,250	$312,500
Customer service	0%	5%	15%	50%	30%	100%
	$0	$1,563	$4,688	$15,625	$9,375	$31,250
Totals	**$121,875**	**$98,438**	**$100,000**	**$223,438**	**$81,250**	**$625,000**

*Note: This includes value chain processes 1–5 from Exhibit 10-4: order-taking, purchasing, manufacturing, delivery, and closing.

Exhibit 10-13

Target Costing for Life Cycle Analysis

Life cycle stages	For each stage			Cumulative		
	Revenues	Costs	Profits	Revenues	Costs	Profits
Design	$0	$121,875	($121,875)	$0	$121,875	($121,875)
Introduction	75,000	98,438	(23,438)	75,000	220,313	(145,313)
Growth	150,000	100,000	50,000	225,000	320,313	(95,313)
Maturity	450,000	223,438	226,563	675,000	543,750	131,250
Decline	75,000	81,250	(6,250)	$750,000	$625,000	$125,000
Totals	$750,000	$625,000	$125,000			

Life Cycle Revenues, Costs, and Profits

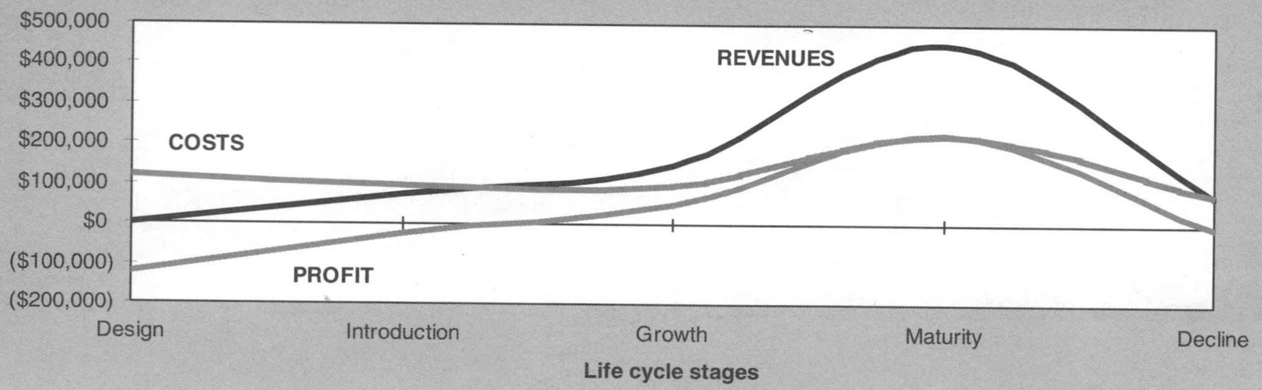

Exhibit 10-14

life cycle, I'll prepare revenue, cost, and profit variance reports to make sure we are still on target." Julie smiled as she realized her pun. Even accountants can be humorous (a little)!

SID

"It seems we're well on our way to developing an effective strategy for managing our industry-wide value chain, linkages with our suppliers and customers, and for managing new product development. Strategic cost management can provide many ABM measures and ABC analyses to support our efforts. Before we adjourn, Doris, can you summarize today's meeting?"

KEY OBJECTIVES SUMMARY

DORIS

"Here is what I remember about today's meeting. Four key ideas were stressed.

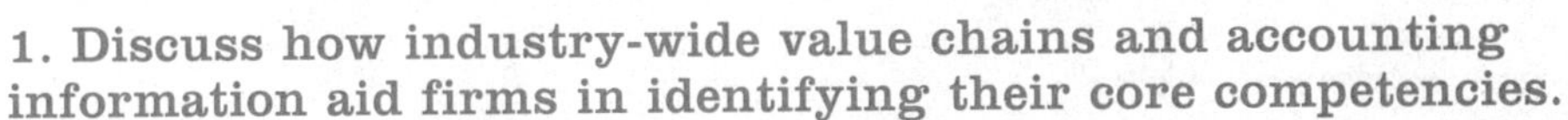

1. Discuss how industry-wide value chains and accounting information aid firms in identifying their core competencies.

"Financial accounting systems are designed for external reporting based on GAAP. These systems are primarily oriented toward short-term value measurement: measuring the income created during a time period, usually a year; and the historical cost of assets, liabilities, and firm equity. Strategic cost management is concerned with creating long-run value. While we can use some information from traditional accounting systems, ABC information combined with CVP analysis is needed for strategic management.

"We should begin by developing value chains of the activities 'from cradle to grave' defining the industry. Using these industry-wide value chains, we can identify the activities our company does. Accounting measures, such as ROI, assess whether our activities represent competitive core competencies. Using ABC and CVP analysis, we then can evaluate the profitability of our core competencies and pursue changes improving our long-run value.

"Applying this to my grocery store example [Chapter 2, Key Objective 2 summary], I'm thinking about having groceries delivered to my home. I always seem to work late and have a hard time getting to the store. I reproduced my value chain and the ABC-CVP analysis [see Exhibit 10-15].

"Assuming I work during the time I would otherwise go to the store, I can earn another $25 [the three unit-level activity costs]. The batch costs increase $7 due to not being able to use coupons and the delivery charge. It looks like I'd be better off having my groceries delivered. Instead of going shopping, I'll just outsource this non-core competency!" Everyone laughed as they knew how much Doris hated grocery shopping after work. "Using value chains, we can redesign our organization to capture the most profitable set of industry-wide activities given our capabilities.

2. Demonstrate the use of strategic partnering and activity-based management performance measures in managing suppliers.

"A value chain approach suggests the benefits from focusing on the overall system are significant. Value chain economies justify long-term relationships with a few

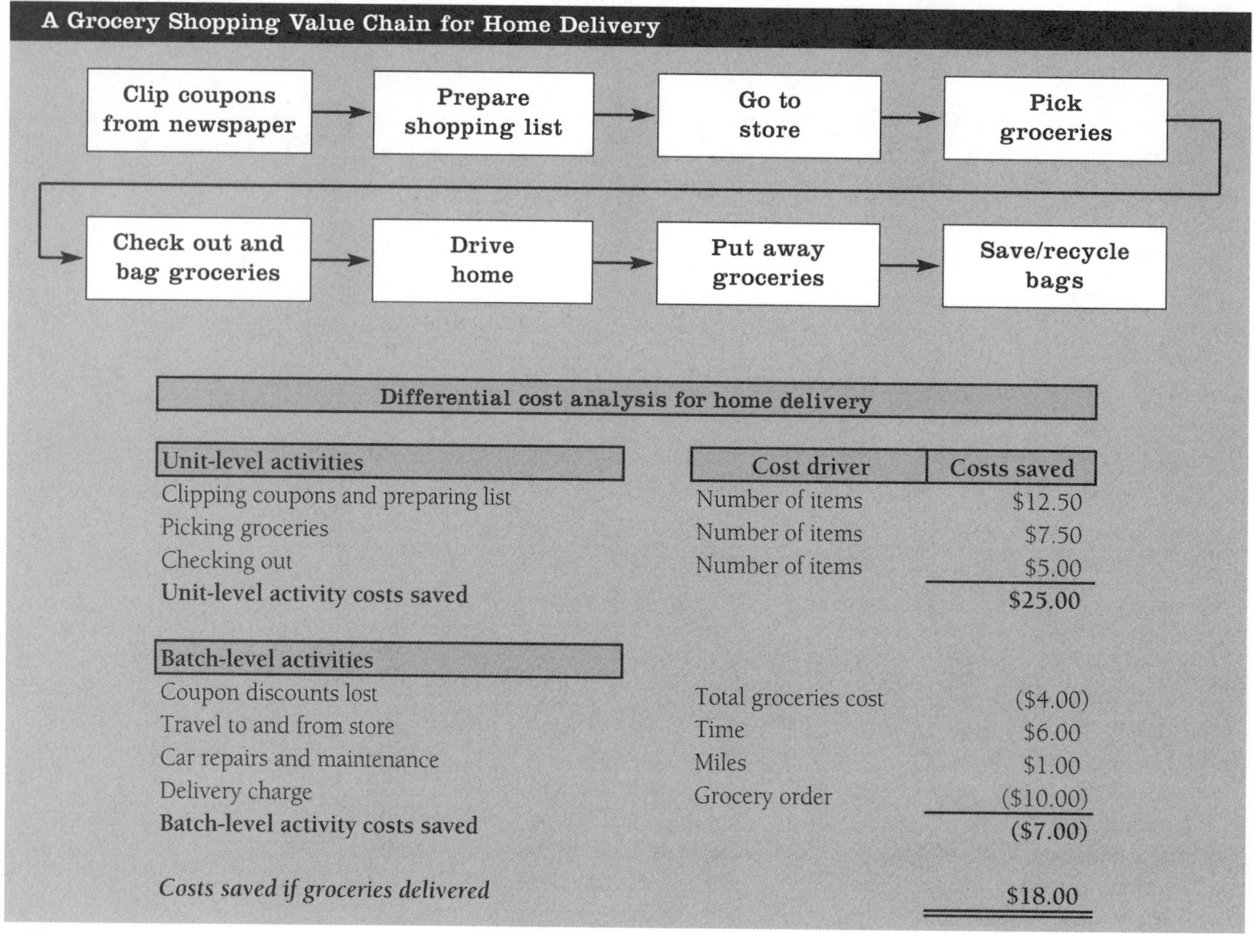

Differential cost analysis for home delivery	Cost driver	Costs saved
Unit-level activities		
Clipping coupons and preparing list	Number of items	$12.50
Picking groceries	Number of items	$7.50
Checking out	Number of items	$5.00
Unit-level activity costs saved		**$25.00**
Batch-level activities		
Coupon discounts lost	Total groceries cost	($4.00)
Travel to and from store	Time	$6.00
Car repairs and maintenance	Miles	$1.00
Delivery charge	Grocery order	($10.00)
Batch-level activity costs saved		**($7.00)**
Costs saved if groceries delivered		**$18.00**

Exhibit 10-15

suppliers, rather than seeking competitive market bids from many different companies.

"Too often, we sacrifice quality and service for cost minimization. When the Boss was alive, cost variance reports were the only performance evaluation measures used. With strategic partnering, though, the accounting system can focus on ABM financial and nonfinancial performance measures to help coordinate and improve these value chain relationships. For example, three nonfinancial measures appropriate for supplier management include a vendor performance index [VPI], on-time delivery, and complete order filling.

"Thinking about grocery deliveries reminds me of the problems I'm having with home newspaper deliveries. I think I'll calculate these measures for that supplier relationship. [See Exhibits 10-16 and 10-17.]

"These were the costs incurred last month. Let me explain some of the non-value-added activities I included in VPI. I have *USA Today*, *The Wall Street Journal*, and the local newspaper delivered each morning. I then bring these papers to the office for your use. I'll wait one-half hour for late deliveries, and this happens twice each week. When deliveries are incomplete I go to the local coffee shop [Starbucks] and buy them. The time lost driving to Starbucks is the differential time compared to driving directly from home to work. Once a week, at least one paper will be missing. Of course, I buy a cup of coffee whenever I'm there.

Home Newspaper Delivery Analysis: Vendor Performance Index

Nonvalue-added activities	Cost driver	Volume Hours	Volume Other	Cost
Waiting for late deliveries	time	4.0		$40
Driving to Starbucks and work	time	2.0		20
Driving to Starbucks and work	miles		50	5
Buying replacement newspapers	papers		4	3
Buying coffee	taste		4	12
Standing in line	time	2.0		20
Total nonvalue-added costs				**$100**
Monthly bill for newspapers				$200

$$\text{VPI} = \frac{\text{Newspaper cost} + \text{Nonvalue-added costs}}{\text{Newspaper cost}}$$

$$\text{VPI} = \frac{\$200 + \$100}{\$100}$$

$$\text{VPI} = 3.00$$

Exhibit 10-16

Newspaper On-Time Delivery and Complete Order Filling

Suppliers	Total deliveries	Deliveries on time	On-time delivery ratio	Complete orders received	Complete order filling ratio
Multreeville News Publishers	22	14	64%	18	82%

Exhibit 10-17

"These ABM measures show the cost and frequencies for three critical success factors concerning home newspaper deliveries. After considering the cost and quality of this service, I think you should be reading these papers over the Internet!

3. Create activity-based management measures for customer satisfaction and explain the role of ABC in managing customer relations.

"Value chains allow us to define our goods or services in unique ways, maximizing their value to our customers. Not only do we have to manage supply-side value chain relationships, we also have to satisfy our customers. From our customers' point of view, we are a supplier to them. Therefore, we need measures reflecting customer value. In addition to the vendor performance measures shown earlier, we can do snake charting. I think I provide a valuable service to Multree Homes. I hope you agree! To find out, I've prepared a short questionnaire for each of you. I'll use Julie's spreadsheet program to graphically display the results. Please take a minute to complete the form now. [See Exhibit 10-18.]

Satisfaction Snake Chart for Doris's Performance

Attributes:	Owners' ratings	
	Importance	Performance
Arrives to work on time	4	8
Has coffee and donuts prepared before owners arrive	10	10
Error-free typing	3	8
Telephone answered promptly	8	9
Pleasant attitude	8	8
Never parks in owners' spaces	10	8

Ranking scales	
Importance	Performance
1 = Least important	1 = Very bad performance
10 = Most important	10 = Outsanding performance

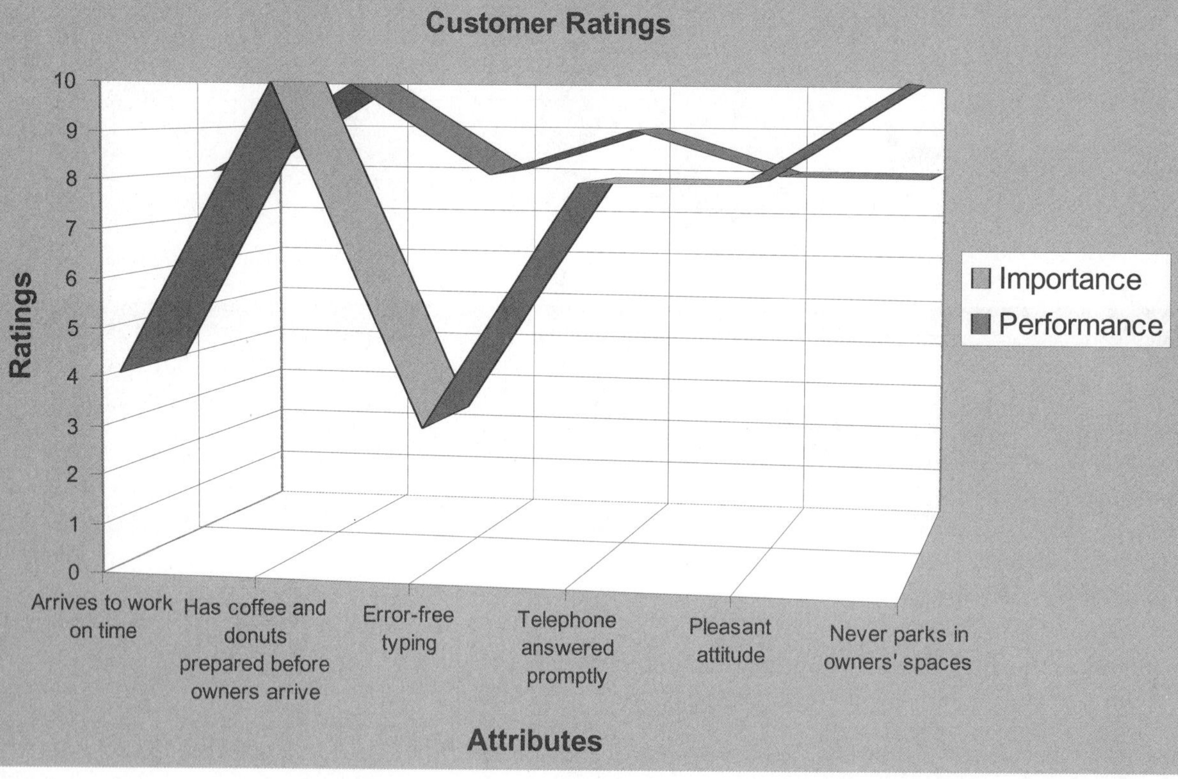

Customer Ratings

Ratings
10
9
8
7
6
5
4
3
2
1
0

Importance
Performance

Arrives to work on time
Has coffee and donuts prepared before owners arrive
Error-free typing
Telephone answered promptly
Pleasant attitude
Never parks in owners' spaces

Attributes

Exhibit 10-18

"Ah . . . I see you do highly value my services. Bringing coffee and donuts, and promptly answering the phone are important to you. So is my pleasant demeanor. I seem to be doing a very good job on these critical success factors. Only arriving to work on time and error-free typing are not considered very important. But, I do a good job on these satisfaction factors, too. I'll work on not parking in your spaces. Overall, my evaluation looks pretty good. May I please have a raise, then?!?

4. Illustrate product line management with target costing, simultaneous engineering and quality function deployment, and life cycle costing.

"The last topic we discussed concerns managing product lines throughout their life cycles. Simultaneous engineering and QFD, combined with target costing and life cycle costing for all the activities in a product's life cycle, reduce the chances of failure. New product introduction should begin with target costing. Target cost is the total cost we can spend on a product for all value chain processes throughout its life cycle. The market sets revenues and we set target profit. Whatever is left over becomes our target cost. Once the target cost is determined, we need simultaneous engineering and QFD to ensure:

- The product is designed to satisfy customer desires, and
- It can be built, marketed, delivered, and serviced within our total target cost.

Finally, we should break the target cost into value chain processes and life cycle stages. You want a super-duper secretary who can perform word processing, spreadsheet, and database tasks. Let's try these analyses on my service. It's a little bit different, kind of like a nonprofit analysis, because we do not have a market to dictate revenues. In the governmental sector, though, target revenues are what the agency expects to receive in the government's budget, and the target profit is zero. This means nonprofit and governmental services set target costs equal to amounts funding sources provide.

"Let's assume you are not willing to spend more than $5,000 for better resources and improved skills, you want a 20% ROI [$1,000], and 'revenues' are the hours and wages saved through my increased productivity. This means my labor savings have to be at least $6,000 if I'm a 'super-duper' secretary.

"I've identified this service's quality attributes, the value chain processes, and four life cycle stages lasting until I retire in three years. I've presented my analysis here [see Exhibit 10-19].

Quality Function Deployment (QFD)

For Super-Duper Secretary

Quality attributes for this service	Target costs
High-quality computer system	$3,000
High-quality software programs	500
Expertise in WordPerfect®	400
Expertise in Quattro Pro® spreadsheet	400
Expertise in dBase® database program	400
Budgeted cost	$4,700
Target costing allowance	$5,000
Drift	none

Exhibit 10-19

"I see five quality attributes for my QFD analysis: high-quality hardware and software, and expertise in three types of programs. My budgeted costs are within your target cost. It appears this can be done for the $5,000 limit you have set.

"My target costing budget covers four value chain processes and four life cycle stages. The value chain processes include buying the stuff, training, maintaining everything, and managing all the frustration. I have $3,000 for hardware and software in my QFD budget. This covers buying and maintaining everything. I have another $2,000 in the QFD budget for obtaining expertise. My value chain processes break this amount into training [$1,000] and frustration management [$1,000]. In thinking about this service's life cycle, I eliminated the decline stage because I don't see productivity decreasing once I've 'matured' in my computer expertise. I'll also retire in three years. I've created a chart showing my target costing budget [see Exhibit 10-20].

Target Costing for Value Chain Processes

Value chain processes	Life cycle stages				Totals
	Research	Learn	Growth	Maturity	
Determine what I need and buy it	70%	10%	10%	10%	100%
	$1,750	$250	$250	$250	$2,500
Training programs to learn the programs	0%	60%	20%	20%	100%
	$0	$600	$200	$200	$1,000
Maintaining hardware and software	0%	0%	40%	60%	100%
	$0	$0	$200	$300	$500
Manage all the frustration	10%	40%	30%	20%	100%
	$100	$400	$300	$200	$1,000
Totals	**$1,850**	**$1,250**	**$950**	**$950**	**$5,000**

Exhibit 10-20

"Finally, I've projected my labor savings, which won't begin until I reach my growth stage. In other words, I don't expect any increased productivity while researching what to get and learning how to use it. I've presented my life cycle revenue, cost, and profit graph [see Exhibit 10-21].

"Two observations should be noted. First, the budgeted cost is within your target cost. Second, you may realize $2,000 more in total savings than target. I think this justifies my training sessions in Hawaii. If you agree to cover the extra costs, I'll adjust the budgets and start packing my bags. Meeting adjourned?"

SID "Wait a minute, Doris. You've done a wonderful job for us. I think you deserve that raise. But, your life cycle analysis shows we won't see any extra savings until you reach the maturity stage of this life cycle. Let's schedule Hawaii for then! Now we can go home."

Target Costing and Life Cycle Analysis

Life cycle stages	For each stage			Cumulative		
	Labor savings	Costs	Savings	Benefits	Costs	Savings
Research hardware and software needs	$0	$1,850	($1,850)	$0	$1,850	($1,850)
Learn software programs	0	1,250	(1,250)	0	3,100	(3,100)
"Growth" (experiential learning)	1,600	950	650	1,600	4,050	(2,450)
Maturity (normal increased productivity)	6,400	950	5,450	$8,000	$5,000	$3,000
Totals	$8,000	$5,000	$3,000			

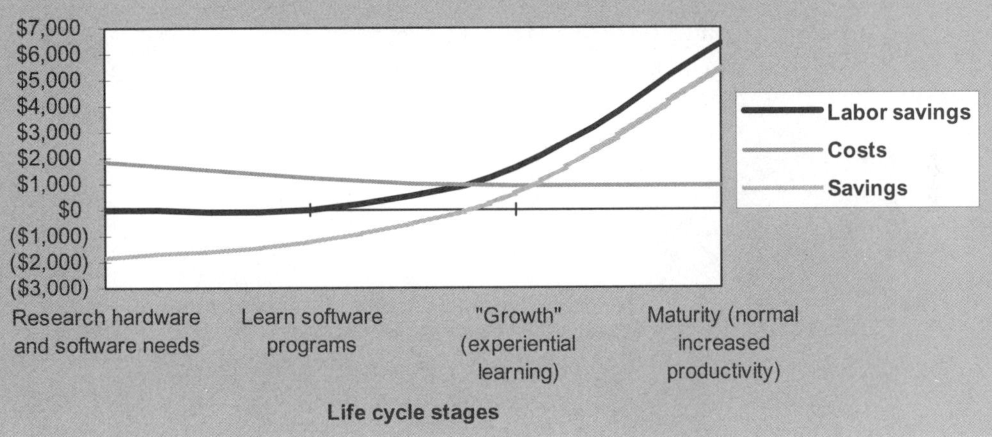

Exhibit 10-21

REALITY 101

Outsourcing and Virtual Companies in the Service Sector

Virtual companies perform only their core competencies. All other value chain processes are outsourced. A virtual company's objective is to maximize the value added by each strategic partnership, while minimizing the investment in permanent staff, assets, and working capital. **Super Bakery, Inc.**, founded in 1983 by Franco Harris (former fullback for the Pittsburgh Steelers professional football team), exemplifies how a manufacturer can become a virtual service company. It supplies donuts and related baked goods to institutions such as schools.

Through outsourcing, strategic partnering, and a customer-based ABC system, Super Bakery sales growth has averaged 20%–30% each year from 1986–1994, when it reached $8.5 million, with only a staff of 9 full-time people. Its profits are twice the industry average.

The institutional food market was mature, with little growth, when Super Bakery entered the market. To be successful, it had to develop a unique product for specialized customers (an example of product differentiation and life cycle management to increase value). The company pioneered "low-calorie, vitamin-enriched donuts that taste delicious and meet USDA standards" targeted to school systems nationwide. To do this, the donuts are vacuum sealed and refrigerated.

To manage supplier and customer value chain processes, it works with school systems to obtain government subsidized commodities (flour, sugar, etc.). It also works with its distributors to reduce inventory carrying costs through a just-in-time manufacturing and delivery system. Super Bakery does not make the donuts, though. Franco Harris hired a master baker to create the recipes and assure quality control. The actual manufacturing is done at three subcontracted plants in New York, Indiana, and California. The company has no investment in plant, equipment, or factory personnel and support services. These are examples of strategic partnering and value chain strategic cost management.

In deciding which activities to outsource, it researched the services most important to customers (a snake chart idea). The services customers most valued became Super Bakery's core competencies. The order management process had the biggest influence on customer satisfaction. Its activities are shown below.

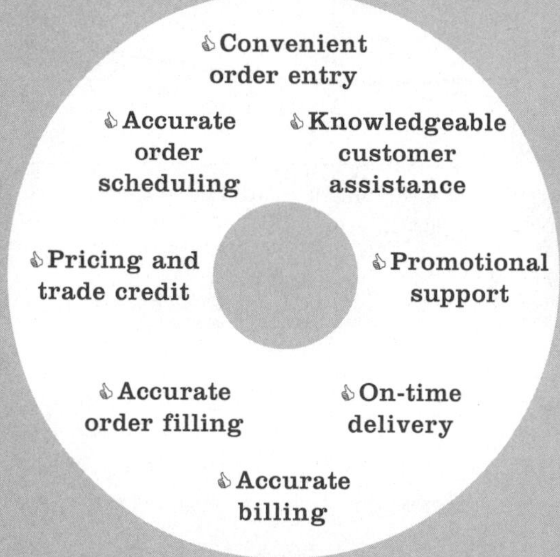

When segmenting a business, for example, to measure customer profitability, traditional accounting systems allocate sales and administrative expenses using revenue percentages (see Original profit analysis in Exhibit 10-11). This assumes each customer's order costs the same. In many businesses, though, customer service costs vary dramatically. Profitable accounts often end up subsidizing unprofitable ones, with management none the wiser. For Super Bakery, freight costs varied with location, order size, and shipping distance. Thus, it needed a customer-based ABC system. By developing a relational database system, costs are known by customer, product, order, broker, territory, manufacturer, and freight company. It also provides costs by customer for overdue receivables. For delinquent customers, interest charges are built into the prices.

An advantage of outsourcing is the company does not have to manage those processes, it only needs to measure outcomes. Managing processes is the responsibility of the subcontractor. Super Bakery developed the following nonfinancial ABM system to measure subcontractor performance:

Value chain service activities	ABM measures
• Order entry speed	• Customer complaints
• Order accuracy	• Correct orders
• Order fill rate	• Complete order filling
• On-time delivery	• Hours early or late
• Accuracy of shipments	• Correct shipments
• Damaged shipments	• Damaged orders returned
• Order filling time	• Days from order receipt to delivery
• Incorrect billings	• Pricing errors, customer complaints

Source: Tim Davis and Bruce Darling, "ABC in a Virtual Corporation," *Management Accounting*, October 1996. © Institute of Management Accountants.

READING LIST*

ABM: McNair, "Implementing Activity-Based Management: Avoiding the Pitfalls," *Statements on Management Accounting 4CC*, Institute of Management Accountants and Arthur Andersen LLP (Montvale, NJ), 1998.

Baxter International: "Why Some Customers Are More Equal than Others," *Fortune*, September 19, 1994.

Boeing 777: Templin and Cole, "Manufacturers Use Suppliers to Help Them Develop New Products," *The Wall Street Journal*, December 19, 1994.

Carrier: Swenson, "Managing Costs Through Complexity Reduction at Carrier Corporation," *Management Accounting*, April 1998.

College outsourcing: Maddox, "Beyond the Company Town: The Future of Outsourcing," and Salluzzo, "Colleges and Universities Must Focus on Their Value Relative to Their Costs," *Management Issues for Colleges and Universities*, KPMG, March and April, 1997.

Data warehousing and E-commerce: "Data Warehouse Is The Latest Competitive Tool," and "Electronic Commerce Revolutionizes Supply Chain," *Business UpShot*, Ernst & Young LLP, November 1997.

Dell Computers and Roadway: see "Value chain management" citation.

Disney and the City of Oakland: see "Value chain management" citation.

EDI at Wal-Mart and Kmart: Borthick and Roth, "EDI for Re-engineering Business Processes," *Management Accounting*, October 1993.

Ernst & Young strategic partnering study: "Special Report: Manufacturing in the 21st Century," *Business UpShot*, Ernst & Young LLP, September 1998.

Federal Express, UPS, and the Post Office competition: Schine, Bunham, and Farrell, "America's New Watchword: If It Moves, Privatize It," *Business Week*, December 12, 1994.

First Tennessee National: Sweeney and Mays, "ABM Lifts Bank's Bottom Line," *Management Accounting*, March 1997.

Ford: "Warning to Automotive Suppliers: It's the Right Way or the Highway," *Executive UpShot*, Ernst & Young LLP, December 1996.

Hewlett-Packard: "How H-P Used Tactics of the Japanese to Beat Them at Their Game," *The Wall Street Journal*, September 8, 1994.

Iowa Beef and Tropicana: see "Value chain management" citation.

ITT Automotive: Schmelze, Geier, and Buttross, "Target Costing at ITT Automotive," *Management Accounting*, December 1996.

KPMG strategic partnering study: Williams, "Keep Customers in the Supply Chain," *Management Accounting*, February 1998.

Levi's: "Custom-Made, Direct From the Plant," *Business Week/21st Century Capitalism*, 1994.

Pitney Bowes outsourcing survey: Williams, "Outsourcing," *Management Accounting*, December 1997.

Price Waterhouse: Schwab, "Price Waterhouse's Experience," *Management Accounting*, August 1990.

Procter & Gamble and Wal-Mart: see "Value chain management" citation.

Quattro Pro: Fisher, "Using 'Usability' to Sell Spreadsheets to the Masses," *The New York Times*, February 6, 1994.

Simultaneous engineering and QFD ABM measures: Hertenstein and Platt, "Why Product Development Teams Need Management Accountants," *Management Accounting*, April 1998.

Timex: see "Value chain management" citation.

Toyota outsourcing: Taylor, "The Auto Industry Meets the New Economy," *Fortune*, September 5, 1994.

UPS outsourcing: see "Value chain management" citation.

Value chain management: San Miguel, "Value Chain Analysis for Assessing Competitive Advantage," *Management Accounting Guideline 41*, The Society of Management Accountants of Canada, Institute of Management Accountants, and Consortium for Advanced Manufacturing-International (CAM-I) (Hamilton, Ontario), 1996.

Vendor management 5-step program: Casher and Metzger, "Leverage Your Vendor Relationships and Enhance Your Bottom Line," *Management Accounting*, March 1998.

*Alphabetic by topic, idea, or company referenced.

CHAPTER 11

How Do We Begin the Improvement Process?

Total Quality Management and Continuous Improvement

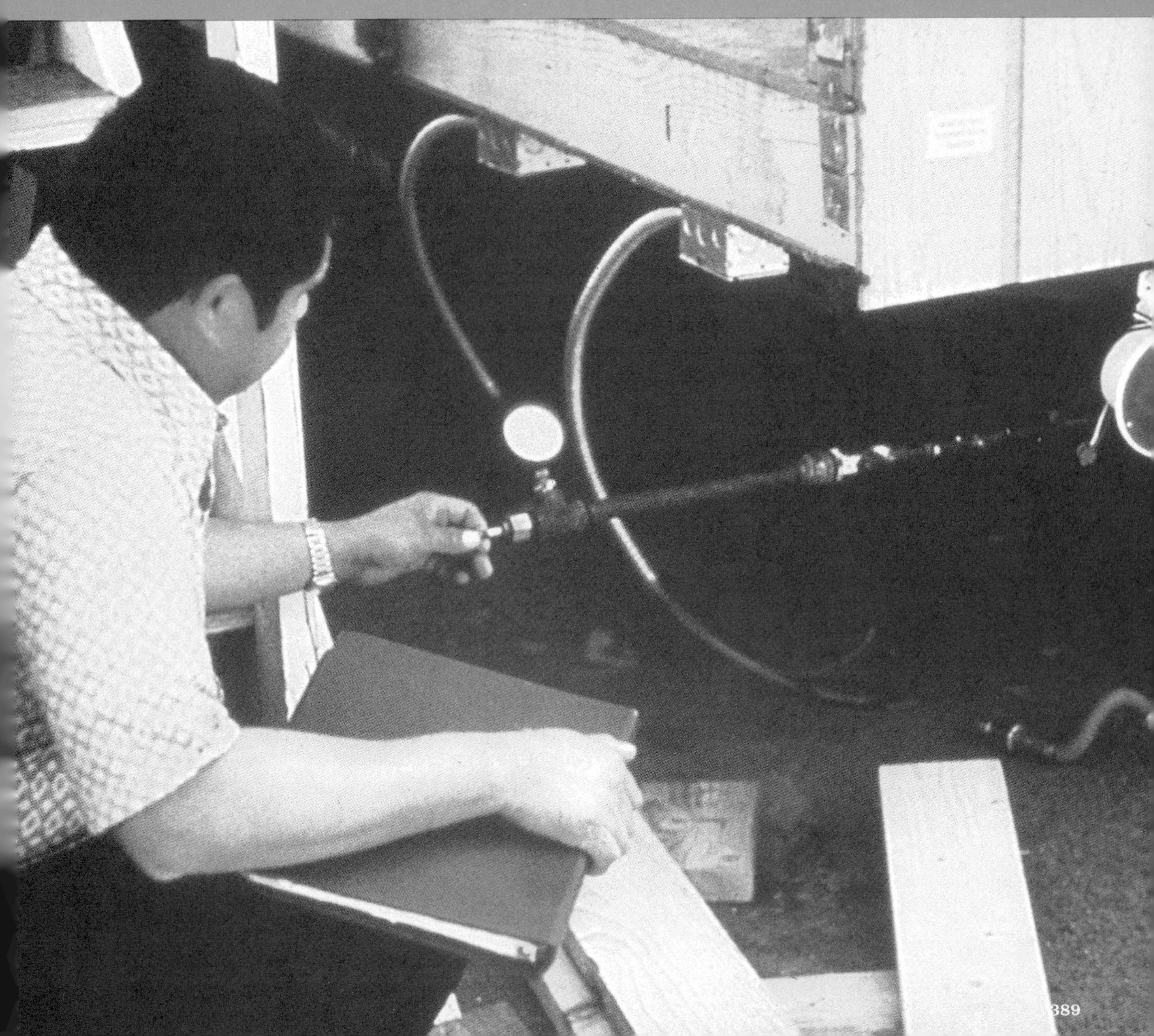

KEY OBJECTIVES:

1	*Discuss total quality management's three critical success factors of quality, service, and cost.*
2	*Define the four quality costs and create a costs of quality report.*
3	*Explain how to identify value-added and nonvalue-added activities, and how continuous improvement with kaizen costing supports TQM.*
4	*Calculate the inefficiency and cost created by nonvalue-added activities.*
5	*Prepare a fishbone diagram and Pareto chart, and discuss the need for 2nd generation ABC in eliminating quality problems.*
6	*Identify ways to motivate a TQM mentality.*

Doris found the conference room a lot quieter than normal. Everyone was very subdued. Their faith in the Boss was shaken. Could the Boss have made a strategic mistake? Maybe, though, his management practices were appropriate for the world he lived in. However, the world has changed radically. Is there a better way to manage the company now? Can they actually do better than the Boss?

"You know, I'm still thinking about our last meeting on strategic cost management. We viewed our company from its position within the industry-wide value chain. Working with both our suppliers and customers are critical to our success, so we focused on strategic partnering with our suppliers and on customer satisfaction measures.

"Simultaneous engineering and target costing really opened my eyes, though. Customer-focused design teams increase our chances of success with new products. Using these ideas, I'm confident we can develop plans maximizing our long-term value."

What Is the TQM Mentality?

"As I see it, our next problem is how we can improve *internal* management. How can we perform our internal operations more effectively and efficiently on a day-to-day basis? We have to get better at understanding and improving our internal value chain processes or our competition will kill us!"

Quality of conformance: executing the plan

"I agree. Quality function deployment [QFD] and simultaneous engineering are concerned with what I call the 'quality of design,' that is, designing products and services from the customers' perspective. *Now, we have to make sure each product is built, priced, delivered, and serviced according to their expectations.* I call this 'quality of conformance.' Developing target costs isn't good enough if we don't have operational techniques to manage the 'drift' [making sure actual life cycle costs equal target costs]. The best way to do this is by eliminating all wasteful activities. *In other words, let's do only those things adding value to our customers, and let's do them in the most efficient way possible. This is the TQM mentality."*

"I've always thought our product quality was under control. Historically, Americans have defined acceptable quality as allowing for a certain number of quality problems and defects. They know no one is perfect. We budget a lot of money for quality testing and reworking products so we stay within acceptable reject rates. We also spend a lot on warranty work fixing problems our customers discover. We're very customer-oriented. This is the way the Boss always did things."

SID

"However, the world has changed, and we need to change too! The Japanese don't have acceptable reject rates. Their philosophy is zero defects. *Today, the only truly sustainable competitive advantage is to learn faster than our competition.* We have to learn how to continuously improve our products and services. This is what **total quality management [TQM]** is all about! It's really a philosophy of customer satisfaction through:

TOMMY

- Better product quality,
- A commitment to customer service, and
- Minimizing total cost.

Total quality management (TQM) *is a strategic and operational commitment to increasing value through improving product (service) quality and customer service, while decreasing cost.*

Many American companies have lost significant market share to foreign competition in our new global economy. Consumers no longer just shop for the best price. They 'surf the net' for products and services satisfying their interrelated needs of quality, service, and cost. Part of the reason for our lost market share is the historical belief that higher quality and service must cause higher costs. Xerox discovered just the opposite, though. Through purchasing better materials, scrap costs decline. So do inspection and storage costs. With higher quality, we should see manufacturing, rework, and warranty costs also go down. Xerox reported savings of over $200 million during a four-year period in the early 1990s just from their quality improvement programs!

"Motorola is another good example. In 1994, it reported a $2.4 billion operating income. Its management attributed $2 billion to quality improvements. They also believed quality programs improving customer satisfaction helped increase revenues by 380%, profits by 800%, and stock prices 600% over an eight-year period. 'World-class' firms believe high quality actually leads to higher profits due to more sales volume and lower total costs across each product's value chain, as well as over its life cycle."

"We're also seeing this customer focus on higher quality and service used to increase value through product differentiation. Federal Express attempted to differentiate itself by introducing personal computer software allowing customers to place orders and track deliveries. In response, UPS formed a partnership with Prodigy for a similar service. Now both are investing in new airline delivery services. The effects from decreasing overall costs through better quality and service have resulted in some pretty big price reductions to large-volume customers. We'll see even more price reductions as other ways to differentiate themselves with quality and service disappear.

BILL

"National quality awards are contributing to this new emphasis on quality. For example, Japan awards the Deming Prize. Mexico bestows the Premio Nacional de Calidad. The United States has the Malcolm Baldrige Quality Award. Past winners include Cadillac, Federal Express, Motorola, Ritz-Carlton, and Texas Instruments. When Armstrong won the Baldrige Award, its stock price rose about 4%."

"We also have an international quality certification program called ISO 9000. In adding value to our products, this quality certification is another important product differentiation tool. Through its ISO 9000 program, DuPont reduced

BOB

defect rates for a computer part over 70%. Many well-known firms [e.g., DuPont, Eastman Kodak, General Electric, IBM, and Motorola], along with the U.S. Department of Defense and NATO, require their suppliers to be ISO certified. The last I heard, the number of American firms obtaining ISO certification was over 2,000.

"In the European Union [formerly the European Economic Community], ISO certification is required. In the United Kingdom alone over 17,000 firms are certified."

JULIE

"ISO certification is impacting management accounting, too. The quest for certification begins with strategic planning, proceeds through the evaluation of current quality, documentation of quality initiatives and their results, and to the development of monitoring and control systems. We'll have even more new work to do because in 1995 the first ISO environmental management standards were issued. I've prepared a list of how management accounting information can support TQM [see Exhibit 11-1]."

Management Accounting's Role in TQM

- ☑ Influence change by measuring the costs of current quality activities.
- ☑ Determine the activities adding value to our products (or services) and those not adding value.
- ☑ Provide relevant cost information for proposed changes.
- ☑ Monitor and report the financial impact of quality programs.

Exhibit 11-1

Linking value to operational conformance

SID

"O.K. I'm convinced! Tell me, how can we use TQM to improve our processes? How can we ensure operations support our long-term plan for creating value? Where do we begin?"

BILL

"That's easy! Start with our customers. They determine our value. We need to account for the activities our customers consider important. They tell us to focus our attention on *three critical success factors:*

- Quality,
- Service, and
- Cost.

KEY OBJECTIVE 1

Discuss total quality management's three critical success factors of quality, service, and cost.

Quality means our product does what it is supposed to do. When customers purchase our product, they expect a set of characteristics. For example, do we build a Geo to last for 50,000 miles, or a Mercedes to last for 200,000 miles? Each car has a different set of characteristics consumers expect. I went back and looked at our snake chart [see Exhibit 10-10]. Our customers identified two quality characteristics: variety in our standard homes line, and the ability to custom design a home.

"If quality is whether the product does what it is suppose to do, *service is whether the organization does what it's supposed to do [again, from the customers' perspective]*. From our snake chart, customers also identified four services: on-time delivery, complete order filling, customer support, and warranty service."

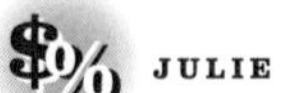

JULIE

"Cost is not just the manufactured cost of our homes. While 'product cost' includes only the manufacturing costs in our financial statements [i.e., cost of goods sold], *our customers include all costs they incur throughout their entire value chain.* [Refer back to Exhibit 10-4.] These costs include planning custom homes or choosing from the different standard home floor plans, credit checking, shipping, setup, closing the sale, and warranty work. The best way to minimize the total cost to our customers is by doing all these activities right the first time.

"We look at each critical success factor separately. Some companies, such as Federal Express, combine them into an overall score. Federal Express measures 12 service attributes which are weighted and combined based on customer complaints. This score is reported weekly."

A customer-focused strategy

"Without measures capturing all the aspects of value, we can make serious mistakes. Too often, firms focus only on cost-cutting to the detriment of value-creating quality. Jackie thought we could save money by switching back to 'normal' coffee and giving up our gourmet coffees. Doris reminded her of why we first changed to gourmet coffee years ago. As a cost-cutting strategy, some big coffee producers, like General Foods and Procter & Gamble, switched to lower-quality coffee beans and large batch runs which reduced freshness. They were competing on cost at a time when many consumers were actually willing to pay more for higher-quality gourmet coffees. Their mistake was not measuring the value customers placed on taste. Today, of course, both have complete gourmet coffee product lines, such as the coffee we're drinking right now!

"Even when nonfinancial measures exist, such as the importance of taste to coffee lovers, these measures can be misused. It's possible to measure the wrong things. Don't forget, what gets measured gets done, whether it's right or wrong [i.e., supports our strategic plan]. Remember when Domino's Pizza used to guarantee delivery within 30 minutes? Management didn't realize the unintended actions of its young drivers to achieve this goal. Some were more concerned with on-time delivery than with safety. In 1993, a traffic accident caused by one of its drivers resulted in a $99 million judgment against Domino's and the end of that policy.

"My point is simple. *First, we need multiple measures of quality, service, and cost.* Being too simple and relying on only one performance measure creates the potential for not achieving all of our quality goals. The second point I want to make is *no one TQM factor should dominate the others.* Fast delivery for Domino's Pizza certainly adds value to the customer, but taken too far, this goal created problems! Too much emphasis on any one accounting measure is often counterproductive. That's why managers need many measures to fully capture all the aspects of value creation."

"Even the Internal Revenue Service is jumping on the 'quality–customer satisfaction' bandwagon! It conducts an annual 'Customer Satisfaction Survey.' The surveys have focused its attention on improving customer service, and have resulted in the IRS's Tax System Modernization and Compliance 2000 programs."

Justifying Change with Costs of Quality (COQ) Reports

"I have doubts about whether TQM will work for us. I'm willing to give it a try, though. But what we're talking about is changing our corporate culture, the way the Boss did things. That can be difficult. As you all know, the Boss earned a lot of credibility around here with our workers. Will they believe quality changes really are an improvement? To win them over, we first need proof that quality problems really do exist!"

BOB

"While I agree, I just don't think quality costs are a problem. Scrap, rework, and rejects never exceed 10% of our production costs. We've been operating with scrap, rework, and rejects for years. They're a fact of life! A long time ago our engineers designed the one best way to do things using good scientific management principles. At that time, and still today, we believed the costs of eliminating all quality problems was greater than the benefit (i.e., the extra value created for our customers). So, we designed acceptable allowances for scrap, rework, and spoilage into our standard quantities. All my direct materials standard quantities have a 5% scrap factor built into them. For new products, I budget 10% scrap rates. Also, my standard labor hours include rework time. This is the way we always have set our standards. It's what the Boss wanted. After all, allowing for these costs in our standards is only practical."

JULIE

KEY OBJECTIVE 2

Define the four quality costs and create a costs of quality report.

"Our workers are motivated to achieve practical standards because they are fair and obtainable. However, many TQM-oriented firms are using ideal standards, including some of our competitors. Eventually they will undercost us, underprice us, and drive us out of business! This is why target costing is so important. We have to continually improve to survive. Each year, our practical standards should be approaching our ideal standards, and should average the target cost. Our target costs cannot include allowances for bad quality because:

- Our customers do not value bad quality and will not pay for it.
- Our competition won't allow for it. They will work on improving quality and service while lowering costs.

When Motorola and Texas Instruments started TQM, they used costs of quality [COQ] reports to justify quality improvements. COQ reports showed how serious their quality problems were, and where they were. Throughout the 1990s, it appears *the major use for COQ reporting has been to motivate a cultural change to TQM.* So, until our people embrace TQM, we will need COQ reports to accomplish three objectives:

- Report the money spent on quality management [to prove quality problems exist and motivate people to think about their seriousness].
- Identify quality control activities consuming the most resources [to improve activities having the greatest impact on profit].
- Track the improvements in quality over time [to justify the changes we've made and sustain the motivation for continuing quality control]."

COQ categories

JULIE

"Let's begin by asking, 'What are the costs of quality?' Are they just scrap, rework, and rejects? The president of Eastman Kodak has the best definition I've seen: **costs of quality [COQ]** represent all the costs that would disappear if we had perfect materials and did everything right the first time. Therefore, COQ includes all the costs of conforming to design specifications, as well as the costs of failing to conform. When companies first started to report COQ back in the 1980s, many discovered COQ was 20% to 30% of their revenues! I worked for a bank in 1980. I remember the banking industry spent $435 million to rework faulty magnetic ink codes on checks. That was about one-half of all check processing costs!

Costs of quality (COQ) *include all costs of preventing, correcting, and detecting quality problems, as well as the opportunity costs of not correcting problems before they reach our customers.*

The costs of doing it right (conformance). "COQ includes four activity costs organized into two categories. The first category is **conformance costs**. Conformance activities either prevent or detect quality problems. **Prevention costs** are what we spend to keep quality problems from happening. Costs of designing products and processes to avoid defects and training people to do things right the first time are good examples. **Appraisal costs** result when materials, subassemblies, and/or products are tested to assure conformance to design specifications."

Conformance costs *are incurred to make sure our products (services) perform as expected. They include costs to prevent quality problems* (**prevention costs**)*, and to test product quality* (**appraisal costs**).

The costs of doing it wrong (nonconformance). "When we discover bad parts, subassemblies, and/or products, we have two options: rework them or reject them. Scrapping parts or subassemblies, rework, and defective products create **internal failure costs**. These costs result when defects are discovered before the product reaches the customer. Bad products reaching our customers create **external failure costs**. These come from fixing customer-discovered problems, and lost future sales from unhappy customers. Whether products fail internally or externally, the costs to correct them [or not correct them!] represent **nonconformance costs**." [Exhibit 11-2 provides examples of the four quality costs.]

Nonconformance costs *result from product failures.* **Internal failure costs** *are the costs of fixing or rejecting bad products before customers receive them. The costs resulting from customers discovering quality problems are called* **external failure costs**.

"The Boss always believed a certain level of nonconformance is tolerable because it's just too expensive to eliminate all defects. Thus, we currently assume a 5% defect rate will give us the minimum total quality costs. This is just good economics. We need to find the optimal mix of conformance and nonconformance costs that minimizes total quality costs."

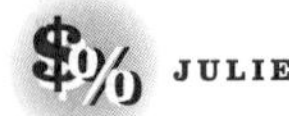

"Here's where we have a debate! The Boss's belief is not the TQM view. TQM is a never-ending quest toward zero defects. Our ultimate objective should be to eliminate bad products. We must keep them from reaching our customers! Our first quality control priority, then, should be to prevent problems from occurring. Our second priority should be to detect and correct problems before customers buy our products. We should invest in conformance activities until nonconformance is eliminated. Once nonconformance disappears, conformance costs will begin to decline.

"So the TQM view believes cost minimization is not the correct objective if it sacrifices product quality and customer service! Together, quality, service, and cost lead to long-run value from our customers' perspective. If we can differentiate ourselves from our competition on quality and service, cost is less important for creating long-run value. Only when our competition provides equal quality products and service do we have to compete on cost. Think back to our meeting on creating value [Chapter 2]."

"Oh, I get it. This is just the old adage, 'an ounce of prevention is worth a pound of cure!' I'll buy that. But you still haven't shown us how COQ reports can justify investing a lot of money on conformance in order to achieve our long-run TQM objective."

"Two types of reports will justify the money spent on TQM:

- Short-run annual reports comparing budgeted to actual quality costs [to make sure we achieve our annual TQM goals].
- Year-to-year reports showing whether our budgeted quality costs are approaching our target costs [zero nonconformance and minimum conformance costs].

Costs of Quality

☺ **Prevention costs examples:**
- New equipment to improve quality and prevent problems
- Training in new methods to improve quality and prevent problems
- Rewards to motivate high quality
- ISO certification
- Technical support to suppliers
- Preventive maintenance

😐 **Appraisal costs examples:**
- Inspection of materials
- Process inspection within each activity
- Final inspection of finished products
- Test equipment

☹ **Internal failure costs examples:**
- Scrapping bad materials
- Reworking subassemblies
- Reworking finished products
- Rejecting defective products
- Retesting reworked components or finished products

☹ **External failure costs examples:**
- Warranty work
- Product replacements
- Recalls
- Product liability insurance, legal fees, etc.
- Handling customer complaints
- Lost sales and customers

Exhibit 11-2

With these, we will know if we're on track toward our zero defects TQM objective."

Short-term reports for operational quality management

JULIE "Let's begin with short-term annual COQ reports. These show quality costs by category and compare actual costs to our annual COQ budget. Consider our total COQ now [Exhibit 11-3]."

JACKIE "Wow, this report looks pretty good! We saved 10% of our budget! It sure seems Sid and Bob are correct. Our quality costs are under control."

JULIE "I really don't agree. Look at our budget. We budgeted $900,000 for COQ, mostly in nonconformance costs [61% of the total budgeted COQ]. Also look at our actual costs. We spent 50% less than budget on conformance costs. This probably explains why we have all the unfavorable variances in nonconformance costs. While we expected about 60% of our quality costs to be in nonconformance, they actually were about 80%. The budget presents a horrible picture of our quality, and actual costs are even worse! Actual external failure costs alone were more than half of our total COQ."

BOB "You're right, Julie. We reduced the prevention and appraisal costs by 50% to recover some of our other losses. I guess we can't just cut costs without thinking about which costs we're cutting! When we reduce conformance costs, we hurt our

Annual COQ Report: Total Quality Costs for Multree Homes						
	Budget		Actual		Variance	
	$	%	$	%	$	%
Prevention costs:						
New equipment	$120,000		$70,000		$50,000	
Training	20,000		5,000		15,000	
Rewards	40,000		10,000		30,000	
Technical support to suppliers	10,000		0		10,000	
Preventive maintenance	60,000		40,000		20,000	
Totals	**$250,000**	28%	**$125,000**	15%	**$125,000**	50%
Appraisal costs:						
Inspection of materials	15,000		12,000		3,000	
Process inspection	20,000		11,000		9,000	
Final inspection	35,000		27,000		8,000	
Test equipment	30,000		0		30,000	
Totals	**$100,000**	11%	**$50,000**	6%	**$50,000**	50%
Conformance costs	*$350,000*	*39%*	*$175,000*	*22%*	*$175,000*	*50%*
Internal failure costs:						
Scrapping bad materials	25,000		26,000		(1,000)	
Reworking subassemblies	75,000		82,000		(7,000)	
Reworking finished products	85,000		89,000		(4,000)	
Retesting	15,000		20,000		(5,000)	
Totals	**$200,000**	22%	**$217,000**	27%	**($17,000)**	(9%)
External failure costs:						
Warranty work	65,000		75,000		(10,000)	
Product liability insurance	10,000		10,000		0	
Handling customer complaints	25,000		33,000		(8,000)	
Lost sales and customers	250,000		300,000		(50,000)	
Totals	**$350,000**	39%	**$418,000**	52%	**($68,000)**	(19%)
Nonconformance costs	*$550,000*	*61%*	*$635,000*	*78%*	*($85,000)*	*(15%)*
Total COQ	$900,000	100%	$810,000	100%	$90,000	10%

Note: Positive variances mean actual cost is less than budgeted cost.

Exhibit 11-3

value. Favorable variances are not always good news! If we had spent what we should have on prevention and appraisal activities, nonconformance would have decreased."

"I think a major reason for increasing nonconformance is the lack of quality control motivation in our workers. Budget cuts in prevention activities, cutbacks in labor time allowed for process and final inspections, and not buying the new test

TOMMY

equipment all sent a clear message to our workers: quality control is not important! Is this the message we really want to send them? Is this what caused such high estimates for the 'Lost sales and customers' [in external failure costs]?"

JULIE

Opportunity costs in COQ reports. "More than likely. You should know, though, all the other costs represent cash expenditures. The lost sales and customers is an opportunity cost. We never really measured this cost before. Bill estimated the lost home sales due to poor quality. I then multiplied that volume by the contribution margin per house [CMU]."

JACKIE

"I don't know if I like this. In financial accounting reports, we do not include opportunity costs. I don't think our bank would approve! Estimating the external failure cost, which could be the most important cost of all, introduces 'soft data' into our reports. If the data is not 'hard' [verifiable, auditable], can we really rely on it? What's more important to me is whether anybody will believe it!"

TOMMY

"You've identified a really important ethical issue. Is it 'right' to use only hard data, and 'wrong' to include 'soft,' estimated data? Remember, management accounting does not have the same goals as financial accounting. The management accounting system's objective is to provide useful, relevant information helping everyone improve decisions and increase value. This system does not have to follow GAAP rules. Good decisions need relevant information, whether based on hard or soft data. Of course, management accountants have an ethical obligation to disclose any measurement issues, such as estimates and special calculations."

JULIE

The importance of lost sales. "You also identified another important issue, believability. How did Bill and I develop this opportunity cost? Can it be measured? Westinghouse believes its total external failure costs are 3 to 4 times the external failure costs it can measure with 'hard data.' A quality research firm president believes 20% of customers with complaints will be lost. In the automobile industry, some believe one satisfied customer tells 8 other potential customers, but one dissatisfied customer tells 22 other people."

BILL

"Back in the early 1990s, Samsung's Chairman, Lee Kun Hee, believed his firm was in crisis not because of the hard numbers [of Samsung's 36,000 employees, 1/6 were needed to repair 20,000 defective products per year], but rather because he believed its competitiveness would erode due to quality problems as South Korea began opening its markets to foreign products.

"All organizations can really save quality costs by listening to customer complaints. Hampton Inns refunded over $1 million to dissatisfied customers in 1993 under its guaranteed refund policy. One major complaint was not having irons and ironing boards in the rooms. An annual investment of about $500,000 was required to change this, but Hampton Inns believed solving this problem generated an additional $11 million in annual revenues. Customer delight is what TQM is all about. Ritz-Carlton reports more than 90% of its customers return. In our industry, one of the leading home builders estimates 60% of its sales come from referrals."

Trend reports on the effects of long-run quality changes

JULIE

"With our company, COQ looks pretty bad. Our objective should be to eliminate nonconformance, and ultimately reduce prevention and appraisal costs. In simultaneous engineering, QFD, and target costing, we should plan to achieve this objective. We should create annual [or more frequent] TQM budgets. Over the long run, budgeted COQ should look like this. [See the Exhibit 11-4 graph.]

"Time period 1 is where we are now, spending $900,000 on COQ with most of it in nonconformance costs. In the next five periods, let's eliminate nonconformance

Long-Run COQ Budget

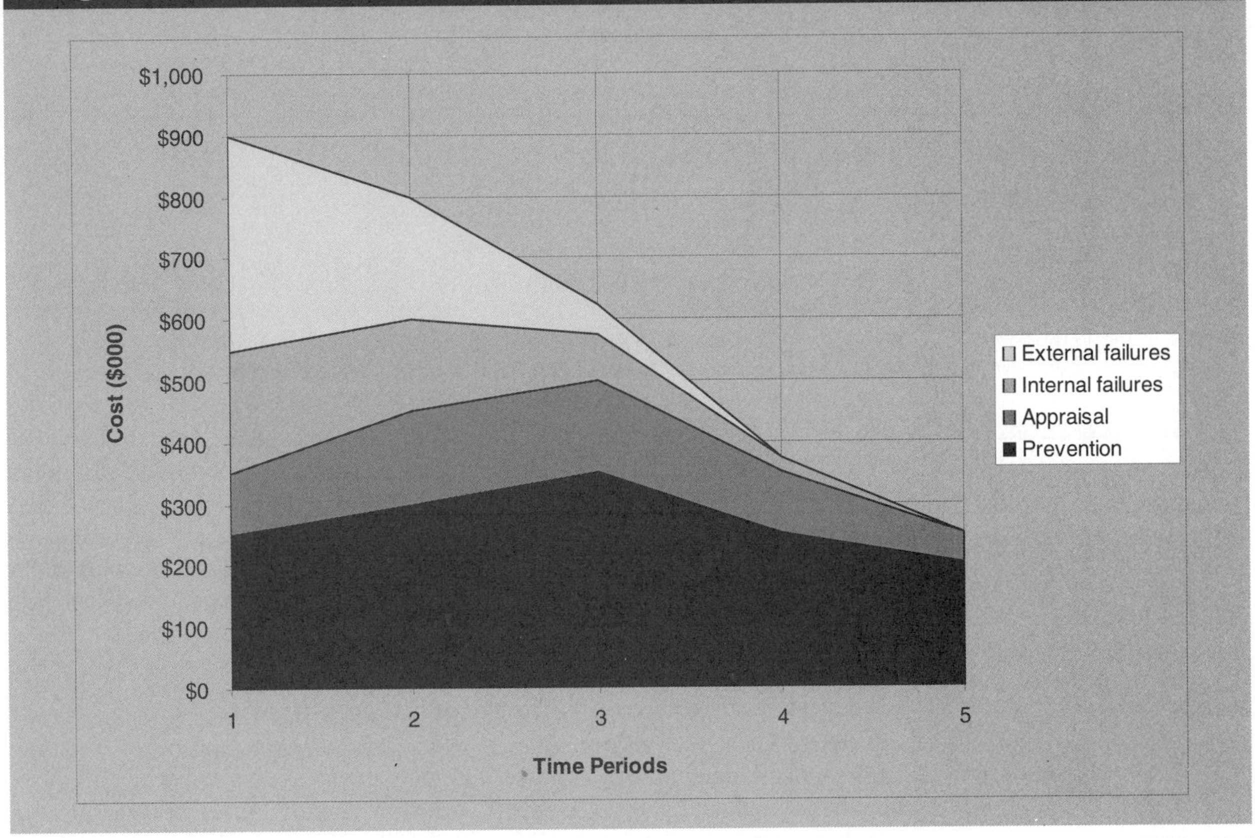

Cost ($000)

$1,000
$900
$800
$700
$600
$500
$400
$300
$200
$100
$0

1 2 3 4 5

Time Periods

External failures
Internal failures
Appraisal
Prevention

Exhibit 11-4

costs [external failures first] and minimize appraisal. If we do the right things right the first time, we should be able to reduce total COQ to under $300,000. Each time period, I'll take the budgeted costs [from Exhibit 11-4] and compare them to the period's actual costs using the COQ [Exhibit 11-3] report format."

KEY OBJECTIVE 3

Explain how to identify value-added and nonvalue-added activities, and how continuous improvement with kaizen costing supports TQM.

Getting Started: Process Value Analysis (PVA)

SID

"Well, you've demonstrated the need for quality improvements and provided us with a way to budget and monitor them. But this is not going to be easy! COQ reports should convince everyone we need to change our culture and focus on TQM. How are we going to get everyone working together, though? How do we begin implementing TQM?"

BOB

"You're right. This is not a simple process. Many methods are available, and they go by different names [process mapping, operational auditing, socio-technical systems analysis, etc.]. One of the more popular names currently being used is **process value analysis [PVA]**. Regardless of the name, all have the same goal: to develop a map of how we work. The focus is on identifying problems affecting quality, service, and cost. I've summarized the major PVA steps in this list [Exhibit 11-5.]

Process Value Analysis (PVA)

1. Define the major processes and link them together within an internal value chain.
2. List the sequential activities required to accomplish each process.
3. For each activity, identify specific steps (actions) that must be done.
4. Determine who benefits from completing each activity (i.e., an activity's internal customer).
5. Ask the internal customer what value is created by that activity, and label activities as value-added versus nonvalue-added.
6. Create activity cost tables to prioritize nonvalue-added activities for elimination based on the costs saved.
7. Analyze value-added activities for ways to improve quality and efficiency.

Exhibit 11-5

Process value analysis (PVA) *is a method to identify value-added and non-value-added activities and their costs. Its objective is to identify opportunities for quality, service, and cost improvements.*

"The first step is creating our internal value chain. It shows the major processes and activities within each process. We did this in our last meeting [see Exhibit 10-4]. To determine the specific steps or actions required for each activity and the resources needed, we need to involve the people who do the work. They know their jobs better than anyone else. The problem I'm having is how to get them involved."

We have both external and internal customers

TOMMY

"Of course! As a result of our reliance on scientific management, people too often work in isolation from others on the value chain. Departments [formal organizational boundaries] separate different types of work. To illustrate, sawing is done in a separate department from framing. TQM defines quality from the customer's perspective. The framers are *internal customers* of the Sawing Department. However, these two groups seldom communicate because they are physically separated. They're at different ends of the factory! To make matters worse, we cut lumber for a batch of five standard homes, move it to WIP inventory [back to the stock yard] where it sits until requisitioned by the framers sometime later [which could be weeks]. Not only are our workers physically separated, their work is separated by time!"

JULIE

"Tommy's right. In our last meeting about strategic cost management, we discovered organizations must work with those surrounding them on the industry value chain. Many accounting measures can be developed to assess our value from an external customer's perspective. I've listed some here [see Exhibit 11-6].

"Since strategic cost management is concerned primarily with external relationships, good strategic cost management should result in external TQM.

"Similarly, within our internal value chain, people must work together. Look again at our internal value chain [Exhibit 10-4]. It shows six processes with activities within each process. Each activity consumes resources in doing its work. The resources are processed [transformed] into outputs. The output of an activity becomes a resource used in the next activity. As a simple illustration, the output from Activity 4.1, Packing, becomes the input for Activity 4.2, Shipping. *Each activity exists to serve the next activity, so the next activity is the 'internal customer' of the previous one.* From the Shipping Department's perspective, activity-based management [ABM] measures should be developed for the quality of goods and services received by previous departments, such as Packing. I've listed a few examples for the Shipping Department as an internal customer [Exhibit 11-7]."

Measuring Value to External Consumers: Some Examples	
Critical success factors	**Management accounting system measures**
Quality	↳ Number of warranty claims
	↳ Average number of warranty claims per home
	↳ Ratio of customer testimonials to homes sold
Service	↳ Time to approval for sales contracts
	↳ Time to approval for loan agreements
	↳ Warranty work time to completion
Cost	↳ Sales price variance using competition's prices
	↳ Warranty cost as a percentage of profit per house
	↳ Costs of quality reports

Exhibit 11-6

Measuring Value to Internal Consumers: Packing Measures Created by its Customer, Shipping	
Critical success factors	**Management accounting system measures**
Quality	↳ Amount of damage during shipment due to poor packaging materials
	↳ Extra time required in shipping because of poorly packaged components
Service	↳ Time waiting to load houses and packaged components
	↳ Time waiting for packaging materials
	↳ Percentage of boxes not adequately labeled
Cost	↳ Cost of rework or replacement for damage caused during shipment
	↳ Extra cost from time trying to find building site (due to poor directions, maps, etc.)

Exhibit 11-7

We have both value-added and nonvalue-added activities

"O.K. We're going to focus on internal customers, and do the right things from their perspectives. But what are the right things?"

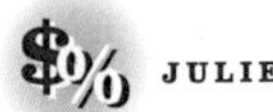

"Some, but not all, of our activities affect the customer's perception of value. For example, if we don't nail the walls together, or paint the house, its value decreases. Activities changing our product's value to the customer are called **value-added activities**. On the other hand, customers are not willing to pay for wasteful activities. These are called **nonvalue-added activities**. The product's [or service's] value is not increased because of these activities. Here are some examples [Exhibit 11-8].

Value-added activities *increase the worth (sales price, value) of products and services to customers.* **Nonvalue-added activities** *do not create an extra benefit for customers.*

"Processing activities take inputs [resources, WIP] and convert them into outputs [WIP, finished products] valued by the next internal customer. Thus value is added to WIP until it becomes a finished product. Nonvalue-adding activities do not change the product [or WIP]. Moving, storing, waiting, and a lot of the inspection activities add nothing to our product. By redesigning how we do value-adding activities and by increasing quality, nonvalue-adding activities can be eliminated without adversely affecting our customers [i.e., the final product's value]."

Examples of Value-Added and Nonvalue-Added Activities

Value-added activities	Nonvalue-added activities
Sawing lumber	Moving materials, WIP, and finished goods back and forth from production areas to storerooms
Framing the house	Storing materials, WIP, and finished goods in warehouses, storerooms, or stock yards
Installing windows and doors	Waiting for materials, WIP, or finished goods to be moved, or to arrive from storage
Plumbing and wiring the house	Inspecting materials, WIP, or finished goods (most, but not all, inspection activities)
Laying the carpet	Reworking bad WIP or products
Nailing shingles on the roof	Disposing of scrap materials and/or rejected products

Exhibit 11-8

ABM goals. "With these differences in mind, we basically have two ABM goals:

- *Eliminate nonvalue-added activities.*
- *Perform value-added activities as efficiently and effectively as possible.*

Some people confuse ABC [activity-based costing] and ABM. They are not the same things. ABC is concerned with costing activities. ABM deals with identifying activities, classifying them in terms of the value they add to customers, and improving them. ABM measures 'put the teeth' into quality improvement programs by providing performance measures and accountability. A recent IMA Statement on Management Accounting [4CC] reports the number of firms it knows are using ABM has grown from 3,000 in 1994 to over 15,000 by 1997. I wonder how many now have ABM strategies!"

NANCY

"It seems ABM and ABC have to go together. I wonder if ABM should precede ABC? What's the role for the management accountant in ABM-ABC systems?"

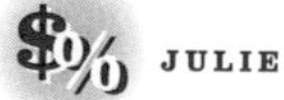

JULIE

"Some accounting researchers believe ABC and ABM should co-exist. They've even developed another acronym to add to the 'alphabet soup' of management accounting acronyms. It's called ABCM [activity-based cost management]. Many aspects of ABC and ABM can exist independently, though. For example, we can develop activity-based costs just to be used in product costing without an improvement program. We also can develop ABM measures without ABC, like a vendor performance index, or complete order filling and on-time delivery ratios. Personally, I think the value added by ABC is increased when it is a component of an ABM strategy. The management accountant has an important role to play here. I should participate, if not lead in:

- Creating and maintaining an ABM data warehouse,
- Creating and maintaining the ABC database,
- Developing desktop decision support systems [often using spreadsheet graphics],
- Developing ABM performance measures and reports to compare planned and actual results, and
- Educating our people in the types of information they can have to help them do their jobs better.

But let's not get ahead of ourselves. Once we've identified our value chain processes and activities, and determined each activity's internal customers, we need to have these customers classify activities as value-adding or nonvalue-adding [see steps 1–5 in Exhibit 11-5]. Now let's consider how we can label activities."

Work the value chain backwards to identify which activities add value. "Perhaps the hardest part of PVA is agreeing on which activities are value-adding or nonvalue-adding. You can't ask the person doing the work. Obviously, she'll say everything she does adds value! *We must ask those who use the output from an activity, in other words, the internal customers.* One of our vinyl window components suppliers, Dayton Technologies, suggests we ask the customer if he is willing to pay for each particular activity! The point is well made [Tommy paused as everyone began chuckling because he didn't realize his "quality" pun]; to classify activities we should work backwards through the value chain.

"For strategic cost management, we began at the end of the value chain with our external customers. We created a snake chart for the critical success factors involving quality, service, and cost. Similarly, we start at the end of our internal value chain and ask those in the last process which activities performed in the preceding process really add value for them. If an internal customer doesn't see the value in a preceding activity, the people doing that work have to justify it. Otherwise, it gets classified as a nonvalue-adding activity."

Making PVA work

"O.K. Scientific management created many efficiencies in the production-oriented world of the early to mid-1900s, although it isolated people in departments. In the customer-oriented world of the 21st century, however, we have to recognize and manage the supplier-customer relationships, both externally and internally. How are we going to bring our people together to do PVA when they have been isolated for so long?"

Using storyboards to bring people together. "One method is storyboarding. Storyboards are process maps created by the people doing the work. Begin storyboarding by having each person list his activities on cards. Then pin the cards to a big board. A string can be used to link the cards together, showing the flow of work throughout the system. I had a lot of fun doing this when I worked for General Electric. After we finished our storyboard, it was amazing to hear all the comments like, 'This isn't right!' and 'This doesn't make sense!' This helped us classify activities as value-added and nonvalue-added. Once we finished, the activities were retyped on red and green cards—red for nonvalue-added activities and green for value-added activities.

"You know, workers often have good ideas for process improvements but no way of communicating them. Storyboarding allows internal customers to interact with those providing goods and services to them. At General Electric, we redesigned the work flow, reduced WIP by $4 million, and cut in half the total lead time. This is an example of how storyboards facilitate employee empowerment."

"So what you're saying is for TQM and PVA to work, we have to change two management philosophies:

- *As members of top management, we must be committed to TQM and let everyone know it.*
- *However, we cannot do PVA. As managers, we can provide only training and support. The people doing the work have to do the analysis and make the changes [employee empowerment]."*

JULIE

The dangers of "managing by the numbers." "Too bad. This isn't how management has usually approached its problems, especially when in financial and competitive crises. Too often, organizations are managed by the numbers. This strategy relies upon hard data [usually restricted to easy-to-obtain data], and ordinarily focuses only on reducing costs. On the surface this makes sense because if costs go down, profits go up. But it's a short-term mentality."

TOMMY

"Here's an example our people always have hated. We need to reduce costs by 10%, so cut everyone's budget by this percentage. Across-the-board budget cuts achieve the goal and appear fair because everyone seems to be equally affected. Are they ethical, though? Cutting the budget means less resources are acquired for both value-added and nonvalue-added activities."

BILL

"Decreasing the resources needed for value-added activities is bad. We learned this lesson in our conformance costs budget-cutting [see Exhibit 11-3]. Sooner or later the customer suffers as quality and service decrease, while total value chain costs increase. The customer ill-will results in increased nonconformance costs, lost market share, and a further loss of profits."

JULIE

"Managing by the numbers is not an attempt to understand why costs exist. What many traditional managers and accountants fail to realize is:

> ***Costs cannot be managed***
> **because costs are only an outcome from work that is done.**
> **To maximize value,**
> ***activities have to be managed.***
> **Well-managed activities result in higher quality, better customer service, and lower costs.**

Logically, this should begin by classifying activities as value- or nonvalue-added. If we do not start here, we run the risk of wasting our time trying to do the wrong things more efficiently. *My point is if an activity is unnecessary, what's gained by increasing its efficiency?* Nonvalue-adding activities must be eliminated entirely. What we have to do first is find the core problem making these activities necessary and attack it.

"This changes our approach to improving processes. Consider quality inspection. The traditional management approach is to find better ways to do inspections. The TQM approach is to eliminate the cause for quality testing. Some inspection always may be valued by our customers [e.g., final inspection, like turning on the lights, furnace, and stove, flushing the toilets, making sure windows open and doors lock, etc.]. If it is a value-added activity, how can we minimize its cost? By having our suppliers guarantee their components work right the first time and making sure each of us does the right things right the first time, many inspection activities can be avoided. Also, if everything is done right the first time, no rework is needed!

"Consider the effects for Tennant Company when it adopted the TQM philosophy. Tennant makes industrial cleaning machinery. Before management decided to build it right the first time, rework activities required about 10,000 square feet of the shop floor. TQM does not come easily or quickly. It took eight years for Tennant to realize a reduction from 33,000 rework hours to 4,800. Rework space dropped to 2,000 square feet. Defect rates dropped 50%, and shipping within 24 hours increased from 47% to 75%."

TOMMY

"At least we are not part of the regulated service, governmental, or nonprofit sectors! Everyone, at one time or another, has complained about poor quality service and lack of customer concern from many of these organizations. The lack of adequate service in the nonprofit and governmental organizations often can be related to 'managing by the numbers' and across-the-board budget cuts [as well as across-the-board increases]. If these organizations emphasized quality, reported COQ, and tied COQ to employee rewards, perhaps they wouldn't have the bad reputation they often receive!"

SID

Continuous improvement programs and kaizen costing. "All right! We won't do across-the-board budget cutting, and we will bring our people together empowering them to do PVA, recommend changes, and implement improvements. But we just can't destroy everything we do now. We need a strategy to guide our change efforts and an accounting system to support them."

TOMMY

"We need to systematically change, one small step at a time, to prove we are improving. If our first few changes are successful, more people will support TQM. However, since we're going to change the accepted ways of doing things, we better be able to show results quickly."

JULIE

"Rather than completely redesigning our value chain, which is a large undertaking, let's take those 'small steps' in improving our processes. **Continuous improvement** programs represent a TQM strategy of making minor improvements on a continuing basis. Procter & Gamble effectively used this strategy with its grocery distributors and retailers, increasing its profits by $50 million. One of the improvements was a new EDI [electronic data interchange] network for computer ordering, processing, shipping, and simultaneous payments. Prior to EDI, about 31% of its orders required some manual correction activities. After EDI, this was reduced to about 6%.

> **Continuous improvement** *programs are part of a TQM strategy focusing on gradual improvements over time.* **Kaizen costing** *supports continuous improvements through frequent revisions to (lowering of) standard costs as improvements are made.*

"Kaizen is the Japanese word for continuous improvement. **Kaizen costing** systems use standard costs to support these programs. The main difference from traditional standard cost systems is how frequently standards are revised. Continuous improvements continually reduce standard costs. Thus standard costs need to be adjusted each time an improvement is made."

TOMMY

"Now wait a minute, Julie. Are you suggesting we recreate our standards every week or month? As it is, they're always wrong. Nobody believes in them or the resulting cost variances. It's bad enough we have to go through that horrible process once a year! I doubt our people are willing to do it more frequently."

JULIE

"Traditional management practices often use financial accounting information for performance evaluation. Top management is evaluated on accounting numbers like net income and return on investment [ROI]. Once a year, it creates a budget to achieve the net income and ROI goals. Too often, budgets and standards are imposed on the workers without their significant involvement. Sadly, the only performance evaluation measures are variances. *If what gets measured gets done, and only variances are used to evaluate and reward performance, our people will be motivated to minimize cost [avoid variances], often at the expense of quality and service.* This is just another example of managing by the numbers.

"The easiest way to increase profit is by reducing the average product cost. The more products made, the less the fixed costs per unit. So we maximize production regardless of whether it can be sold. If it ends up in inventory, who cares? Inventory is a current asset on the balance sheet, so it is good. By the way, workers can save time and increase output by skipping their inspection and testing activities, which results in more favorable cost variances.

"Consider how kaizen costing is used at Shionogi Pharmaceutical. Workers set the standards, which they revise after each batch is completed. Continuous improvement programs work only when employees are empowered to improve activities and are rewarded for their successes. Kaizen costing, then, also requires employee empowerment. Our workers are smart. They understand this. Their involvement in simultaneous engineering and target costing is continued into setting and frequently revising standards.

"To answer your concern about how frequently we should revise standards, it depends. Levi Strauss (Canada) management is willing to revise standards whenever a variance investigation notes they are no longer current. Citizen Watch management budgets a 3% reduction in materials costs annually, but revises standard labor times quarterly.

"Kaizen costing also has been used with target costing and product life cycle management. No one expects the life cycle average target cost will be achieved from the beginning. It takes time to learn and improve. The target cost is simply the average standard cost we must achieve over its life cycle. [Exhibit 11-9 relates target costs and kaizen standard costs.]

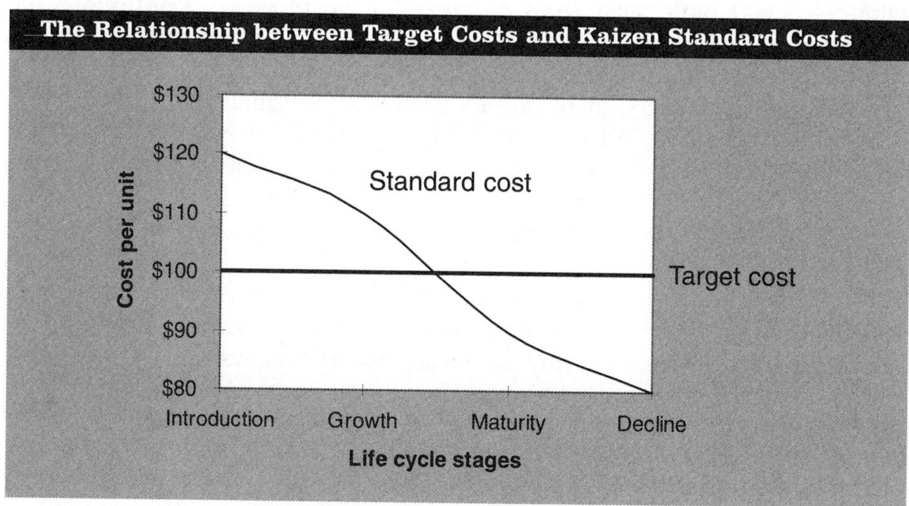

Exhibit 11-9

"Hewlett-Packard combined target and kaizen costing in developing and marketing its Inkjet printers. It wanted Inkjets to replace dot matrix printers, a market dominated by Epson. Employees set target and kaizen costs to beat Epson. They even went so far as to wear 'Beat Epson' football jerseys! The first Inkjet was priced around $1,000. After seven years of continuing improvements, with the resulting price and cost reductions, a basic Inkjet sold for around $250, effectively ending the life cycle of dot matrix printers."

TOMMY

"Employee empowerment is a central theme in TQM. PVA, continuous improvement, and kaizen costing will not work without it. I'm still worried, though. As our standards keep going down, people may be even more motivated to increase output and inventories, and ignore quality, in order to create favorable cost variances."

JULIE

"You're right. Kaizen costing alone will not support TQM. Remember, TQM includes three critical success factors: quality, service, and cost. We need TQM measures of quality [Exhibits 11-3 and 11-4], ABM measures of service [Exhibits 11-6 and 11-7], and kaizen cost measures for our continuous improvement strategy to succeed."

"It seems to me we've developed some good control measures. As long as we also use them to reward people, they should be motivated to do the right things right the first time. Continuous improvement programs require two more types of management accounting information, though. Since we're only going to make small improvements on a continual basis, which nonvalue-added activities should we eliminate first? For the value-added activities, which quality problems should we attack first?"

Measuring the Impact of Nonvalue-Added Activities

KEY OBJECTIVE 4

Calculate the inefficiency and cost created by nonvalue-added activities.

"As an engineer, I'd like to use the storyboards to create a table listing the steps within each activity. The table should identify whether they are value-added or not. Here's an example for wall framing [Exhibit 11-10]."

PVA for Framing Walls

Process 3: Manufacturing

Activity 3.2: Wall assembly (framing)

Steps in Activity 3.2	Classification
1. Requisition lumber (2 × 4 studs) from WIP.	Nonvalue-added
2. Process material requisition form (check for materials availability, schedule forklift and driver).	Nonvalue-added
3. Forklift driver picks lumber from stock yard.	Nonvalue-added
4. Forklift driver delivers lumber to Assembly.	Nonvalue-added
5. When delivered, stack according to when and where 2 × 4's will be used.	Nonvalue-added
6. Set up jigs to hold walls in place.	Nonvalue-added
7. Lay down 12' 2 × 4's for bottom of walls in the jigs.	Value-added
8. Measure and mark every 18" along the 2 × 4 for the location of the wall studs.	Value-added
9. Get nails and brackets from raw materials inventory.	Nonvalue-added
10. Pick up each 8' 2 × 4 wall stud and set it on the mark.	Value-added
11. Nail the stud in place using 90° angle brackets.	Value-added

Exhibit 11-10

"Your table really surprises me! How can we be doing so many nonvalue-added activities? We must be wasting a tremendous amount of resources. No wonder we're in trouble! O.K., Julie, you're our CMA. How can we measure the effects of all these nonvalue-added activities?"

Lead time efficiency (LTE) ratio to measure wasted time

"Just for the framing activity, over half of the steps do not add value to our homes. First, let's measure the time currently needed for this activity [lead time or cycle time] and compare it to the optimal time if all nonvalue-added steps are eliminated. Working with the framers, Bob, Tommy, and I timed each step. Nonvalue-adding activities account for 12 hours of the total time it takes to frame the walls. Value-added time is only 4 hours. [Total time involves four people working four hours each.] The **lead time efficiency [LTE] ratio** measures the inefficiencies caused by nonvalue-added activities [as shown in Exhibit 11-11].

Lead Time Efficiency (LTE) Ratio

Process 3: Manufacturing
Activity 3.2: Wall assembly (framing)

$$\text{LTE Ratio} = \frac{\text{Value-added time}}{\text{Value-added} + \text{Nonvalue-added time}} = \frac{4 \text{ hours}}{4 + 12 \text{ hours}} = 25\%$$

Exhibit 11-11

Lead, or cycle, time is the total time it takes to do something (an activity, process, or group of value chain processes). The **lead time efficiency (LTE) ratio** *compares value-adding time to lead time.*

In framing, 75% of our time is 'wasted,' doing things that add no value from our customers' perspective. The ideal situation has no nonvalue-added time, so our LTE ratio goal is 100%. While framing's 25% LTE ratio doesn't look very good, it is much better than many traditional batch manufacturers who have LTE ratios of 10% or less!

"Long lead times increase inventory costs, too. Consider how long it takes to receive lumber. If supplier lead time is twice as long as production lead time, we will need enough lumber for two batches [10 standard homes at 5 homes per batch]. To make matters even worse, suppose total lead time is five times greater than the time customers are willing to wait. We'll need five standard homes completed and available for sale before Bill gets our first customer. The raw materials and finished goods inventories costs could be eliminated if we can reverse these relationships. For example, if total lead time is less than the time a customer is willing to wait for a home, we can build to order without the need for any inventories [just-in-time manufacturing and delivery]!"

BILL

"Dell Computer does this. It builds each computer to customer specifications, and maintains no finished goods inventory. Each computer is a separate job in Dell's job order cost accounting system. To satisfy its customers, Dell had to reduce total lead time from ordering components through shipment to the customer to five or six days."

Activity cost tables provide relevant costs

JULIE

"Referring back to the 7 PVA steps [Exhibit 11-5], step 6 involves calculating activity costs. Once the people performing an activity list the resources they need, my job is to work with purchasing, human resource management, and others to identify standard resource prices. Multiplying standard resource prices by the standard resource quantities needed for an activity, I can develop standard resource costs. Summing these standard costs, I know the activity's cost. This is a lot like creating a standard cost card for a product, as we did in our standard costing [Chapter 6] meeting. [Exhibit 11-12 presents the summary activity costs for framing.]

"A continuous improvement strategy involves making small continual changes over time. Since we are not going to eliminate all nonvalue-added activities simultaneously, we need to prioritize them. In other words, which should we eliminate first? The activity cost tables provide information on the processing time and costs for each activity. We'll start with those activities having the greatest effect on our profits. According to the framing cost table [Exhibit 11-12], we can save $284 per house by eliminating its nonvalue-added activities. Do any other activities offer a greater savings?"

Activity Cost Table

Process 3: Manufacturing

Activity 3.2: Wall assembly (framing)

Steps in Activity 3.2	Classification	Time (hours)	Cost
1. Requisition lumber (2 × 4 studs) from WIP.	Nonvalue-added	0.5	$20
2. Process material requisition form (check for materials availability, schedule forklift and driver).	Nonvalue-added	1.0	45
3. Forklift driver picks lumber from stock yard.	Nonvalue-added	3.5	90
4. Forklift driver delivers lumber to Assembly.	Nonvalue-added	1.5	50
5. When delivered, stack according to when and where 2 × 4's will be used.	Nonvalue-added	3.0	30
6. Set up jigs to hold walls in place.	Nonvalue-added	2.0	40
7. Lay down 12' 2 × 4's for bottom of walls in the jigs.	Value-added	0.5	15
8. Measure and mark every 18" along the 2 × 4 for the location of the wall studs.	Value-added	1.0	11
9. Get nails and brackets from raw materials inventory.	Nonvalue-added	0.5	9
10. Pick up each 8' 2 × 4 wall stud and set it on the mark.	Value-added	0.5	5
11. Nail the stud in place using 90° angle brackets.	Value-added	2.0	200
Totals:			
Value-added activities		4 hours	$231
Nonvalue-added activities		12 hours	284
Totals		16 hours	$515

Exhibit 11-12

Relevant costs versus ABC costs. "I must warn you, however, to be very careful using this type of information. I included only the incremental resource costs. Our goal is to measure the impact [cost savings] from eliminating nonvalue-added activities. Thus I considered only the materials and labor costs saved. These are the only costs that really will change if we get rid of the nonvalue-added activities.

"I did not include the allocated warehouse costs for the space used to store the lumber. If we don't use that space for something else, we aren't going to save any money. Similarly, I didn't include the forklift costs because we are not going to get rid of the forklift. We should consider only the relevant costs; the costs really disappearing when nonvalue-added activities are eliminated. This is why I could not use activity costs from the ABC system [Chapter 9]. ABC uses absorptive costs, which include allocations of fixed overhead such as building depreciation, property taxes, and insurance included in the product line and facilities-level costs. Fixed costs do not change in total [within the relevant range]; therefore these won't go away when eliminating nonvalue-added activities. Now if we can eliminate a lot more inventory, enough to sell the warehouse, we really can save the fixed costs associated with it. Sooner or later the cumulative effect of incremental improvements will result in batch [step] cost savings. Ultimately, some fixed costs associated with product line and facilities-level activities also will be relevant in our analysis."

Using cost tables in target costing. "My point is we can develop different types of activity cost tables for different purposes. Here I'm using the cost tables for a specific TQM purpose—the costs saved from doing away with nonvalue-added activities. The Japanese use cost tables to show how different materials and methods change an activity's cost. With this information, they evaluate trade-offs to achieve target costs when designing new products, and in strategic cost management. Maintaining cost tables is a primary role for Japanese management accountants. Thus they must be knowledgeable about emerging technologies, new materials, and changing production methods. Hewlett-Packard's management accountants also maintain activity cost tables for use in product design and modification. Their system, called 'COSTIT,' allows design engineers to conduct 'what-if' analyses at their work stations."

Improving Value-Added Activities

NANCY

"Eliminating nonvalue-added activities obviously reduces our costs, shortens lead times, makes us more responsive to customers' needs [flexibility], and improves customer service. But cost and service are only two of the three critical success factors for long-term value creation. How are we going to attack our quality problems?"

KEY OBJECTIVE 5

Prepare a fishbone diagram and Pareto chart, and discuss the need for 2nd generation ABC in eliminating quality problems.

Costing quality problems within value-added activities

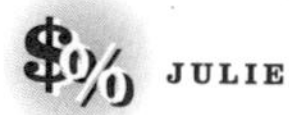
JULIE

"I agree with you! Quality, service, and cost are equally important in TQM. I don't want to imply we should eliminate nonvalue-added activities before attacking quality problems. Increasing efficiency by eliminating nonvalue-added activities is one TQM goal. Another is improving efficiency in value-added activities. The third TQM goal is identifying quality problems, their causes, and their costs. The TQM approach I use begins with fishbone diagrams to identify problem causes. Then 2nd generation ABC costs quality problems, and Pareto charts prioritize them."

TOMMY

Fishbone diagrams to identify problem causes. "Just as we brought all the workers together to do storyboards, let's have them determine why quality problems happen. In ABC, resources are traced to activities. The four types of resources are people, materials, direct technology [tools and equipment], and facilities. Each of these resources, if not perfect, can cause quality problems. One way to discover and organize quality problem causes is with a **fishbone diagram**. This is a cause-effect diagram with the head of the fishbone representing the problem and the spine identifying the problem causes. Each of the ABC resources has its own 'spine line.' Technically, it's called an Ishikawa diagram [named after the person who invented it]. After studying how Xerox used one to identify problems in customer billing, Bob and I got together with the installers and inspectors to create one for our leaking window problem [Exhibit 11-13]."

*A **fishbone diagram** organizes problem causes into the four ABC resource groups (people, materials, direct technology, and facilities) and links them to a quality problem.*

NANCY

"Your fishbone diagram does a good job detecting quality problem causes. But this is just the first step in solving them. I do a lot of fishing with one of the window installers. He says these causes are not independent from each other. To illustrate, sometimes the sealant doesn't stick because it is not laid properly, or the dispenser doesn't work right, or its too hot. By fixing one cause, we may fix a bunch of other causes! We need to know the core reason a problem exists. Creating fishbone diagrams is just the beginning of our quest to discover which problems should be fixed first."

JULIE

2nd generation ABC to cost quality problems. "I agree! As we did with nonvalue-added activities, we need a way to prioritize quality problems. I suggest

Fishbone Diagram for Leaking Windows

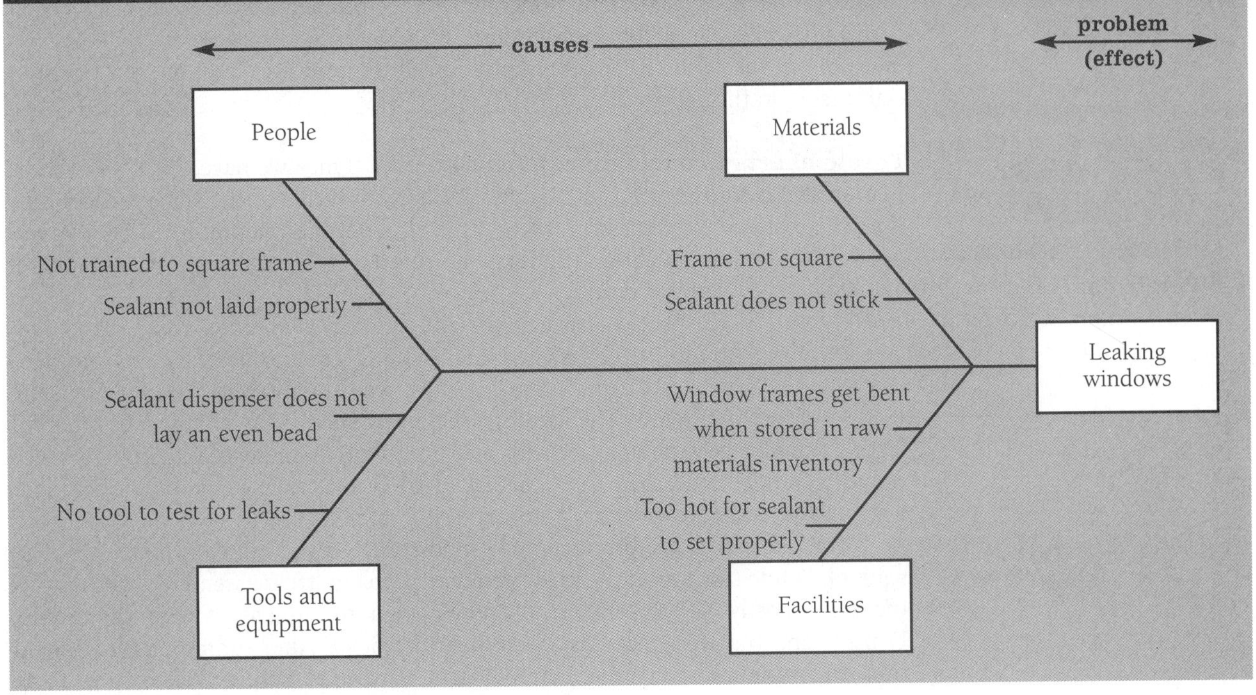

causes

problem (effect)

People

Materials

Not trained to square frame

Sealant not laid properly

Frame not square

Sealant does not stick

Leaking windows

Sealant dispenser does not lay an even bead

Window frames get bent when stored in raw materials inventory

No tool to test for leaks

Too hot for sealant to set properly

Tools and equipment

Facilities

Exhibit 11-13

it should be those costing us the most money. Activity-based costing can help us here. If we have to replace a leaking window, for example, our activity cost tables provide the cost of doing this.

"Rather than replacing the window, perhaps we can fix the leaks. Regardless of whether we replace a window or rework it, correcting this problem results in cost variances. What we need to do is trace our problems and cost variances back to their underlying causes. This is what **2nd generation ABC** does. Think back to how CCSSCo workers identified quality problems, fixed them, and kept track of the resources used in reworking the sandwiches [Chapter 9's Reality 101, Exhibit 9-A1]. A traditional standard cost system reports an unfavorable direct labor usage variance of $45.00, and unfavorable bread and lettuce usage variances of $6.50 and $8.00, respectively. Instead of reporting cost variances for each resource within a department [a scientific management functional silo], their management accounting system reported the cost variances in terms of the quality problems causing them: soggy bread jammed the mustard spreading machine creating a $22.50 variance, and lumpy lettuce caused $37.00 in cost variances."

> **2nd generation ABC** *systems identify cause-effect relationships in quality problems, and report cost variances in terms of problems and their causes.*

NANCY

"Wow! This is the same logic used in the COQ report! Let's report costs in terms of the activities causing them. Traditional cost accounting systems report costs and variances in terms of resources used within departments. These systems track direct materials, direct labor, and overhead, as well as their cost variances [e.g., Sawing Department direct materials usage variance, Framing's direct labor rate variance]. To understand cause-effect linkages, we need to trace resources and their costs to activities.

"The COQ report shows us the 'big picture.' Conformance problems in one department can cause problems and variances in any subsequent department or even in the hands of the customer! Our COQ report [Exhibit 11-3] shows our conformance problems caused many nonconformance problems. *We need the COQ report to identify where our quality problems are. We also need 2nd generation ABC cost variances to cost their causes.* Now we know COQ is significant, and we can prioritize our attack on the causes."

BOB

Pareto charts to communicate problems. "Once we have this type of information, we can prioritize our quality problems in terms of their effects on profits [i.e., the cost variances these problems create]. A vertical bar graph, called a **Pareto chart**, shows the relative importance of quality problem causes in terms of cost.

A **Pareto chart** *is a bar graph of quality problems expressed in terms of each problem's cost and the cumulative costs for all problems.*

"We experimented with this for assembling roof trusses, and found it to be a very useful tool to communicate quality problems between departments. At first we thought we had a lot of quality problems. The fishbone diagram contained over a dozen. After collecting the ABC cost variance data for a month, though, many of the problems were only theoretical and adequately controlled by our workers. Five major problems were identified and their costs graphed [see Exhibit 11-14]."

TOMMY

"The most serious problem was incorrectly sawed lumber [cuts were not square]. While this wasn't the most frequent problem, truss assemblers knew it was the most costly to fix. Historically, they tried to discuss it with the Sawing Department, but were told 'they were just too picky.' After running a 2nd generation ABC system and creating Pareto charts, Sawing personnel had to agree to accept responsibility for the $325 cost variance and take the problem seriously.

"Our traditional cost variance reports never showed us this, or helped us communicate and solve the problem. The $325 variance was buried in the Truss Department's cost variance report as part of its unfavorable direct materials usage, direct labor usage, and variable overhead usage variances. Also, the Boss assumed the truss assemblers were responsible for these variances. Hard feelings continued between truss assemblers and saw operators as one group was blamed for another's problems. With this new TQM-based information, however, everyone is getting along, and the problem was simply solved by increasing the conformance costs budget in Sawing [more money for saw blades prevents this problem]. By getting people in different departments to work together with management and our management accountant, this problem has been eliminated!"

Benchmarking to identify inefficiencies and suggest improvements

SID

"Now we know which quality problems to attack first. Major improvements should result from eliminating quality problems and nonvalue-added activities. Once we accomplish these goals, is our continuous improvement strategy complete? What if our competition also does this? How can we increase the efficiency of our value-adding activities?"

BOB

"Once we are doing things the best we can, let's find out who is better at performing activities similar to ours. If we can study their techniques, we may be able to improve ours. This is called **benchmarking**. We may find benchmarking to be less costly than trying to 'reinvent the wheel' and make all the mistakes another firm has already made and solved!"

Benchmarking *is studying the best practices of other firms to learn how they perform activities similar to ours.*

Pareto Chart for Roof Truss Assembly

Data section:

Problems	Costs	Cumulative percentages
Cuts out of square	$325	33%
Clamps out of square	300	63%
Poor fit	125	75%
Split wood	75	83%
Warped wood	50	88%
Other	125	100%
Total cost variances	$1,000	

Pareto chart:

$1,000 $900 $800 $700 $600 $500 $400 $300 $200 $100 $0

100% 80% 60% 40% 20% 0%

Cuts out of square | Clamps out of square | Poor fit | Split wood | Warped wood | Other

Costs

Cumulative percentages

Exhibit 11-14

"Hold on a minute, Bob. Isn't this just corporate spying? Is this ethical? If so, how do we obtain information about best practices?"

"Well, at one time it might have been thought of as spying. Back at the end of the 1800s, Andrew Carnegie required frequent information about his competitors and used it to underprice them. Robert Camp changed this perception with his 1989 book about Xerox's benchmarking project. After Xerox lost its industry leadership to Japanese firms, IBM, and others, it began this strategy to find out why. Granted, in those days, about 80% of the benchmarking studies were on competitors. Now, however, it's just the opposite situation. About 80% is on firms in other industries. It's not considered spying any more!

"L.L. Bean is considered to have one of the best order-filling processes in mail-order sales. It has allowed firms from all sorts of industries to study its methods. General Mills reduced machine setup times [and lead time] from 8 hours to 10 minutes by studying race car pit crews. With the 767 jet, Boeing set a target cost 25% below its average cost to build a jetliner. To achieve this target, manufacturing lead time had to be reduced from 18 months to 8 months over a four-year period. Boeing benchmarked General Electric's heavy manufacturing to convince its workers this goal could be accomplished. This is really an important point for us. We must demonstrate the need to improve activities. *Most people around here think we're pretty efficient already!*"

JULIE

"I agree! Ultimately, we should benchmark all of our processes, even the services provided to our internal customers. Lucent Technologies did this with its finance operations. Benchmarking 22 finance departments in other companies, Lucent not only increased its efficiency, it also developed an internal customer mentality [all employees are now called 'colleagues']. Applied in the banking industry, and also applicable to all service organizations, multidimensional balanced benchmarking considers four dimensions to service quality: profitability, service quality, marketing effectiveness, and productivity. Just thinking about the ABM measures we've considered in the last two meetings, I can imagine benchmarking lab test accuracy and efficiency in a hospital, claims-processing efficiency for an insurance company, check-processing accuracy at a bank, and response time for police, fire departments, and ambulance services, just to name a few!

"Many firms routinely conduct benchmarking studies, including Alcoa, DuPont, Hewlett-Packard, Johnson & Johnson, Eastman Kodak, and Motorola. Note how many are Malcolm Baldrige Award winners. As a result of this growing practice, professional organizations are creating benchmarking databases. The IMA has the Continuous Improvement Center. Other databases are available through the Consortium for Advanced Manufacturing-International [CAM-I], the Hackett Group, and Price Waterhouse."

KEY OBJECTIVE 6

Identify ways to motivate a TQM mentality.

How Do We Motivate Our People to Practice TQM?

SID

"O.K. I think TQM will be our new philosophy. Our objective is customer delight for both external and internal customers. Our strategies will be process value analysis and continuous improvement. But, as I said before, this will require a change in our organizational culture. This will not happen 'overnight.' Most successful TQM programs require years to implement. Once implemented, we will need an ongoing commitment to maintain this new culture."

JULIE

"I've been tracking the survey statistics. A 1991 international survey reported monthly use of quality information: 70% of Japanese firms, 55% of German and U.S. firms, and 51% of Canadian firms. In a 1992 IMA survey, 51% of firms said they reported COQ and another 31% said they should. By 1996, an IMA survey reported while 82% of firms were involved in TQM projects, only 33% calculated COQ, although another 40% believed it was a good idea. A 1998 survey reported only 9% create COQ reports.

"Why aren't these statistics more supportive of TQM? Two reasons seem to dominate the surveys. Most organizations 'have the religion.' COQ reports were important in grabbing top management's attention and motivating TQM programs. Now that they have the religion, COQ reporting no longer is considered necessary. Specific nonfinancial ABM measures capture more timely and relevant information for individual programs and priorities.

"The second reason is the prevalence of financial accounting systems and the lack of relevant management accounting systems. Financial accounting systems are not designed to identify or report COQ. Here's my speculation. Most organizations have accounting departments because they need to produce financial accounting information [income statements, balance sheets], collect money from customers, and pay the bills. The accountant's role in managing the business traditionally has been quite limited. Many organizations don't even have management accounting positions. Thus we have what has been labeled as a 'cultural gap' between accountants and quality managers."

Why most TQMs fail

"I've heard 70% to 80% of companies trying TQM have not considered their efforts successful. They cite four reasons why.

"First, traditional organizational cultures are often not congruent with TQM. People are organized into functional departments. Separated from each other, they do not interact with internal and external customers. Top executives also are isolated from 'workers.' Managers plan, organize, control, and evaluate. Workers just do the work. This manager-worker dichotomy often results in a 'we-them' mentality.

"To break down these functional silos and organizational barriers, organizations are developing cross-functional teams. For example, the Internal Revenue Service developed these types of teams in creating its 'Cost Management Information System.' The teams used PVA to identify value-added and nonvalue-added activities, and developed ABM ratios, such as LTE, to measure efficiency. Grand Rapids Spring & Stamping went even further with cross-functional teams, developing 'minicompanies.' Each is responsible for developing TQM measures for quality, delivery, cost, safety, and morale. The minicompanies not only empower employees, they force attention on the suppliers and customers for each value chain process.

"Second, traditional reward systems often do not promote people working together. We calculate variances for each department, and these become the most important, or only, performance evaluation measures. Customer delight, high quality, and service are not measured or rewarded, especially internal customer satisfaction. The last survey statistics I've seen date back to 1992, but they support this. For 77% of the surveyed firms, only some employees were evaluated with COQ measures, while for 53% 'none or almost none' of the performance evaluations used COQ.

"Empowering our people through allowing them to benchmark and develop ABM measures supporting TQM may help solve this problem. Caterpillar's Wheel Loaders and Excavators Division did this. Through benchmarking AT&T, IBM, and Texas Instruments, and working with Price Waterhouse, employees developed an integrated combination of financial and nonfinancial performance measures focused on customer responsiveness and flexibility.

"Third, TQM often is a reaction to crisis. Companies are looking for a quick fix to their problems. Problems are identified within departments, attributed to individual departments, and fixed within them without adequate consideration of their internal customers. Changing the 'we-them' mentality into a 'supplier-customer team' mentality is not quick or easy.

"The last reason concerns how TQM has become a formula for success, reduced to a set of procedures offered by management 'gurus.' Many American firms are in crisis from the new global economy, reduction of international trade barriers, and resulting competition. Their quest for solutions has created a renaissance in

management consulting. TQM has become a product, with nearly a thousand versions, each offered by a management expert. TQM consulting has become a billion dollar industry."

Changing the culture to a continuous benchmarking and learning system

NANCY

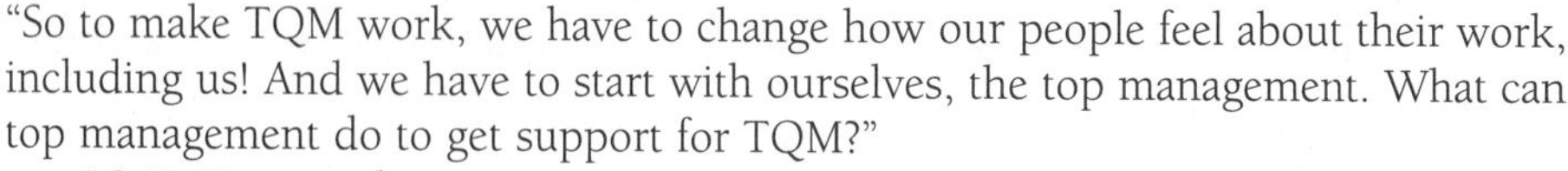

"So to make TQM work, we have to change how our people feel about their work, including us! And we have to start with ourselves, the top management. What can top management do to get support for TQM?"

TOMMY

"O.K. First, we have to practice it ourselves. *Top management must be committed to TQM as a 'way of life.'* Lip service will not suffice. We have to do it in our activities, showing our people we support them by training them, providing the physical and financial resources they need, and rewarding them for continuous improvement. We cannot just dictate 'TQM will be done!' If it is not rewarded, why will they want to do it?

"Second, no more 50% budget cuts in prevention and appraisal costs. *Management must train employees in quality control and give them the power to fix things without getting our approval first [employee empowerment].* This means we are going to redefine what 'work' is. It is no longer just hammering nails into walls, monitoring a machine, answering a phone, or preparing an accounting report, paycheck, vendor payment, or the like. 'Work' must begin with understanding what our internal and external customers want. Then identify problems as they happen, correct them immediately, and prevent them from happening again. Fortunately, many 21st century workers are highly educated, possessing technical degrees beyond high school. Some factory workers have college degrees, including masters' degrees and Ph.D.s. Top management has to make sure employees have the opportunity for continuing professional education so they can continuously learn how to improve.

"We also have to motivate employees to want to learn. *This means we have to reward them for improving their activities.* To begin, they cannot be afraid of losing their jobs. Too often, TQM is a reaction to a crisis. Who wants to improve a process if it means she will lose her job?"

JULIE

"*We will need multiple performance measures.* We cannot just evaluate performance using sales and cost variances, ROI or residual income, or even EVA [economic value added]. Other important measures include getting our work done on a timely basis [service: on-time delivery and complete order filling], and doing it right the first time [quality: number of rejects and complaints, costs of quality]. We should measure the change in standards from year to year [standard costs should be going down if we are continually improving], as well as actual performance against standards within each year. Target costing and kaizen standards are useful here."

TOMMY

"Let's also be careful not to develop too many measures, though. This may only confuse people. Keep it simple. Ask four questions:

- What are the critical success factors for this activity?
- How can we measure performance on each factor [financially and nonfinancially] in a way that is understood and accepted as valid by everyone?
- How will this measure improve performance?
- How will this measure hinder improvement?

Also remember, we cannot look at departments in isolation from other departments. It's too easy to look for quick fixes for a department's problems without considering their impact on others up and down the value chain. Thus, *TQM must start with our value chain, identifying processes and activities, external and internal customers, and what the quality outputs are from each activity.* Focus on activities rather than departments.

"TQM is not just a series of procedures and quality measures. It cannot be reduced to a formula provided by an outside consultant and served on a 'silver platter.' Everyone has to be intimately involved from simultaneous engineering through delivery and service to our external customers. *We'll know we have succeeded when people come to work excited about the prospects of discovering and solving new problems.*" [Exhibit 11-15 summarizes these ideas.]

TQM Problems and Prescriptions

Reasons why TQM initiatives fail:	**Recommendations:**
1. Incongruent organizational culture	⇨ Top management must be committed to TQM
	⇨ Top management cannot dictate that TQM will happen
	⇨ Employees must be empowered to do it
2. Reward system does not support TQM	⇨ Reward employees for TQM activities
	⇨ Use multiple, easy-to-understand measures
3. The search for a quick fix	⇨ TQM must start with value chain processes and activities
	⇨ Change from a department focus to an activity focus
4. TQM becomes a formula rather than a philosophy	⇨ Develop employee excitement for TQM

Exhibit 11-15

KEY OBJECTIVES SUMMARY

DORIS

"Our TQM meeting stressed six major ideas. Here's my summary of each one.

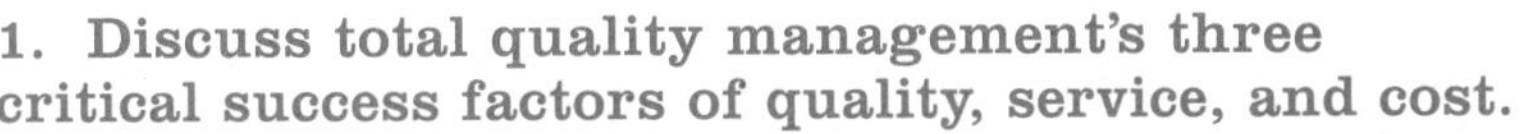

1. Discuss total quality management's three critical success factors of quality, service, and cost.

"Financial accounting is backward-looking, presenting historical data about past revenues and costs. Making decisions based on how they affect financial accounting net income may not create value. We must focus our efforts on the source of long-term value, our customers. TQM's customer focus helps us understand effective and efficient performance. Our TQM goal is to make sure every product is built, priced, delivered, and serviced according to customer expectations. We create value by delighting our customers. This applies to both internal and external customers. So our problem is how to increase value on a day-to-day basis.

"Three critical success factors determine value. Quality is conformance to design. Our products and services should do what they are supposed to, based on our customers' expectations. Similarly, when we service customers, we should be doing what they expect. Within each industry, then, we see firms all along a spectrum from generic, inexpensive products and services to high-quality, expensive ones. Each firm seeks to satisfy a specific market niche having unique expectations.

"Obviously, the level of quality and service affects cost. Cost, from the customers' perspective, includes all the value chain costs. Customers also will include the opportunity costs they associate with any trouble encountered in obtaining the levels of quality and service expected. Not treating our customers right the first time makes us a more costly provider, and will lead to lost customers and sales in the future.

2. Define the four quality costs and create a costs of quality report.

"This report reflects our debate about the costs versus benefits of improving quality. COQ reports motivate change. With them, we can estimate the effect of investments in conformance. We also can analyze the impact of incremental improvements, with less risk and more assurance that we're following a good strategy. This is important because not everyone believes these investments are justified.

"We discussed how to organize quality costs into an overall report. The COQ report categorizes quality costs into prevention, appraisal, internal failures, and external failures. Prevention [not allowing problems to happen] and appraisal [testing] are called conformance costs because these activities assure conformance to design specifications and customer expectations. Nonconformance costs arise from internal and external product failures [we found the bad product, or the customer did]. Here's a COQ report I prepared for typing memorandums. You can see how I classified my quality-related activities into the four COQ categories [see Exhibit 11-16].

"As you can see, I have a pretty good distribution in both budgeted and actual quality costs. Most planned costs are for conformance activities [76%], with prevention costs dominating the budget [60%]. Ideally, no nonconformance costs should be budgeted. I'll work on that. For the actual costs, we came in under budget on the spelling course [$100 favorable variance]. I spent more time proofreading and editing [$100 U], my boss didn't have as many rewrites as expected [$50 F], but it took more time than budgeted to correct the ones he found [$100 U]. Between us, though, we didn't find them all, which explains the unfavorable variances in external failure costs [$150 U].

"It's also important to prepare COQ graphs like the one in Exhibit 11-4. Because existing processes undergo continuous improvements, this information is critical in measuring our long-run TQM success.

3. Explain how to identify value-added and nonvalue-added activities, and how continuous improvement with kaizen costing supports TQM.

"Simply stated, customers are willing to pay for value-adding activities, like installing cabinets and carpeting. If we do not provide these activities, the value of our product decreases. We perform many activities, though, customers do not care about, such as stockpiling inventories, moving stuff around, and reworking bad products. These are nonvalue-adding activities that we should eliminate. Doing the right things [value-added activities] right [quality] the first time [efficiency] is our objective.

"Identifying what the right things are begins with methods like process value analysis [PVA]. First, develop the value chain. Storyboards are helpful for this. For each activity, identify the internal customers and ask them to classify it as value- or nonvalue-adding. Working backwards through the value chain, internal customers justify preceding activities.

Annual COQ Report: Total Quality Costs for Typing Memos

Quality activities:

	Budget	Actual
Spell checking and grammar program	$100	$100
Boss's rewrites	250	200
Word processing program training	500	500
Answering phone calls from recipients about confusing or missing information	50	100
Spelling and grammar courses	1,000	900
Correcting errors discovered by Boss	150	250
Proofreading	300	400
Preparing and mailing replacement letters	150	250

COQ report:

	Budget		Actual		Variance	
	$	%	$	%	$	%
Prevention costs:						
Word processing program training	$500		$500		$0	
Spelling and grammar courses	1,000		900		100	
Totals	**$1,500**	**60%**	**$1,400**	**52%**	**$100**	**7%**
Appraisal costs:						
Spell checking and grammar program	100		100		0	
Proofreading	300		400		(100)	
Totals	**$400**	**16%**	**$500**	**19%**	**($100)**	**(25%)**
Conformance costs	*$1,900*	*76%*	*$1,900*	*70%*	*$0*	*0%*
Internal failure costs:						
Boss's rewrites	250		200		50	
Correcting errors discovered by Boss	150		250		(100)	
Totals	**$400**	**16%**	**$450**	**17%**	**($50)**	**(13%)**
External failure costs:						
Answering phone calls from recipients about confusing or missing information	50		100		(50)	
Preparing and mailing replacement letters	150		250		(100)	
Totals	**$200**	**8%**	**$350**	**13%**	**($150)**	**(75%)**
Nonconformance costs	*$600*	*24%*	*$800*	*30%*	*($200)*	*(33%)*
Total COQ	$2,500	100%	$2,700	100%	($200)	(8%)

Exhibit 11-16

"As we identify problems, we need a strategy to guide our change efforts. Continuous improvement involves making small changes continually over time. The idea is we cannot fix everything right now. Successful small changes encourage more changes [i.e., continual improvements]. Success is measured financially by lower costs. Kaizen costing systems require continuous changes to our standard costs reflecting the improvements made. In this way we capture the cost savings from our TQM programs through declining kaizen standard costs. With new products, our long-range goal is for kaizen standards to average their target costs.

4. Calculate the inefficiency and cost created by nonvalue-added activities.

"But which activities should be improved first? We can prioritize nonvalue-added activities by developing lead time efficiency [LTE] ratios. LTE ratios measure the inefficiency created by nonvalue-added activities. Mathematically, it is value-added time divided by total processing time [lead, or cycle, time]. My grandson is living on campus at our local college. We calculated his homework LTE ratio [Exhibit 11-17].

Lead Time Efficiency (LTE) Ratio for Homework

Activities	Classification	Time (minutes)
Plan the time needed to do it	Nonvalue-added	10
Clean up desk	Nonvalue-added	5
Get food and drink (munchies)	Nonvalue-added	20
Find textbook	Nonvalue-added	15
Locate syllabus and homework assignment	Nonvalue-added	20
Locate chapter and class notes	Nonvalue-added	5
Do homework assignment	Value-added	120
Save it for class	Nonvalue-added	5

$$\text{LTE Ratio} = \frac{\text{Value-added time}}{\text{Value-added} + \text{Nonvalue-added time}}$$

$$= \frac{\text{120 minutes}}{120 + 80}$$

$$= 60\%$$

Exhibit 11-17

"He wastes 40% of his time on activities he shouldn't have to do. If he was neat and orderly, much of the time wasted cleaning up his desk and looking for things could be avoided. By eating the good food regularly served in the dorms three times a day, he wouldn't be spending so much on 'junk food.' He could be working at his part-time job more instead of wasting time. He earns $12 per hour. Using this opportunity cost with the costs of the food he buys [$5], I was able to construct an activity cost table for homework [Exhibit 11-18].

"I help him financially. I'm willing to pay him $12 an hour for doing school work instead of going to his job. However, I don't think I'm willing to pay for his nonvalue-added activities!!

5. Prepare a fishbone diagram and Pareto chart, and discuss the need for 2nd generation ABC in eliminating quality problems.

"He also complains about all the value-added time it takes to do his homework. I wonder how much of his value-added time is due to quality problems. Together we

Activity Cost Table for Homework

Activities	Classification	Time (minutes)	Cost
Plan the time needed to do it	Nonvalue-added	10	$2
Clean up desk	Nonvalue-added	5	1
Get food and drink (munchies)	Nonvalue-added	20	9
Find textbook	Nonvalue-added	15	3
Locate syllabus and homework assignment	Nonvalue-added	20	4
Locate chapter and class notes	Nonvalue-added	5	1
Do homework assignment	Value-added	120	24
Save it for class	Nonvalue-added	5	1
Totals:			
Value-added activities		120	$24
Nonvalue-added activities		80	21
Totals		200	$45

Exhibit 11-18

constructed a fishbone diagram to identify reasons why his homework sometimes does not get turned in [Exhibit 11-19].

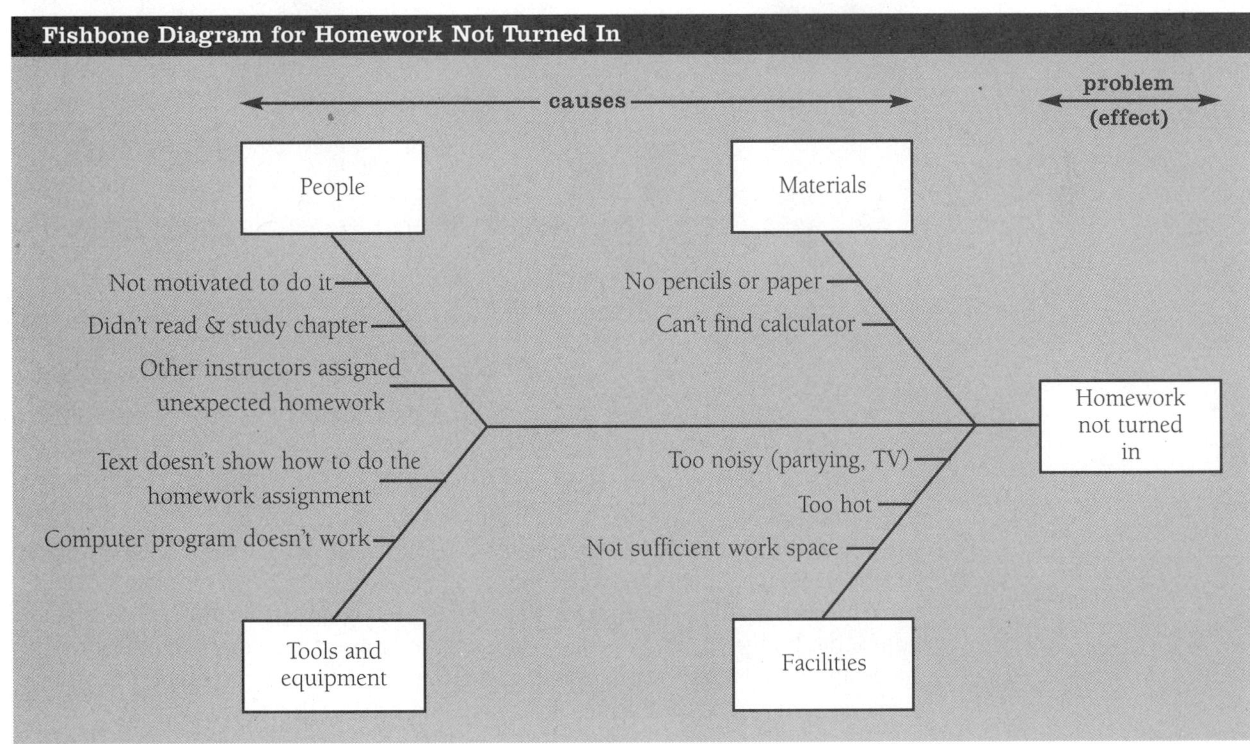

Exhibit 11-19

Once we organized the potential problem causes within the fishbone diagram, we calculated the activity-based cost variances to correct them. Most of these costs were the opportunity costs of his time. Next we prioritized the problems in terms of how much they cost him in a Pareto chart [Exhibit 11-20].

Pareto Chart for Homework Not Turned In

Data section:

Problems	Costs	Cumulative percentages
Didn't study chapter	$18	23%
Unexpected homework	24	53%
Too noisy	12	68%
Bad text	8	78%
Computer problems	4	83%
Other	14	100%
Total cost variances	$80	

Pareto chart:

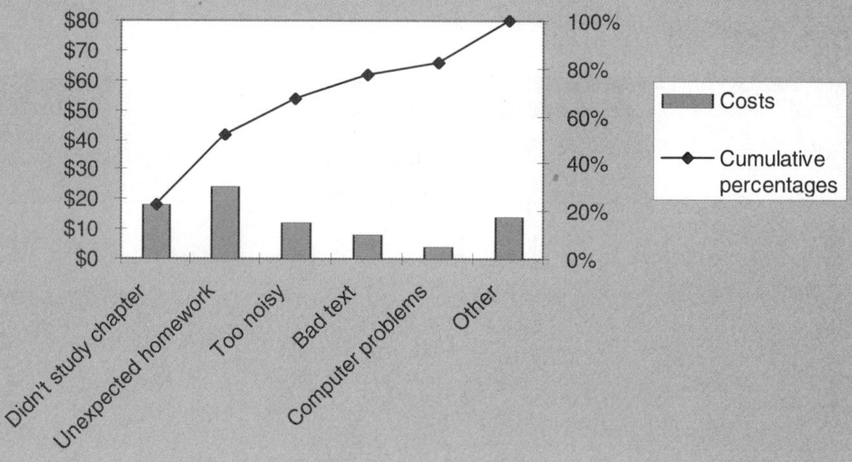

Exhibit 11-20

He may be right. Most of these problems are not under his control. However, I asked him to observe his girlfriend's study habits. This is called benchmarking. Its done to learn how the best perform our activities, so we can improve them. She's a straight 'A' student. Having identified a number of strategies, he can begin to make small improvements over time [continuous improvement programs]. He also can continually adjust his budgeted study times [standard labor hours] as each improvement is made and calculate labor usage variances using the new standards [kaizen costing]. Looking at his grades last semester, I suggested he start this right away!

6. Identify ways to motivate a TQM mentality.

"TQM is not something we can plan to do, then do it, and finally sit back smiling to ourselves when it is done. It really is an attitude people carry with them every day. TQM is not implementing a set of procedures or preparing specific quality cost reports. It's a change in our culture. How do we change our culture?

"First, top management must lead the way. We have to be intimately involved so our workers believe we take TQM seriously, and it is part of our culture. We cannot dictate TQM to others, though. If everyone is to practice TQM daily, they must be empowered to do it. This means we have to train them, allow them to make quality control decisions, set continuous improvement standards, and communicate across departmental borders. We also have to reward them in meaningful ways. All this must begin by recognizing that people are not confined to departments and professional specializations. Rather, they are part of value chain processes and activities."

"Good job, Doris. O.K. We've done enough for one meeting. Let's come back tomorrow excited about the prospect of finding and solving our quality problems!"

REALITY 101

General Marble, a TQM Success Story

General Marble is the largest U.S. manufacturer of bathroom countertops and vanities for do-it-yourself home centers, supplying Home Depot, Payless Cashways, Builders Square, Menards, and others. The president, Hans Wede, just finished a phone conversation with one of his most important customers. Three complaints were made: an inability to make high-quality products, ship correctly, and bill the right amounts. The company was in a financial crisis. Hans felt it was going "down the drain." The eight internal value chain processes, their LTE ratios, and the percentage of orders correctly processed the first time (CPFT) indicated a tremendous amount of nonvalue-added activities (see Exhibit 11-21):

General Marble's Nonvalue-Added Activities

Value chain processes	LTE ratios	CPFT
Order entry	2.4%	53%
Planning	5.9%	22%
Scheduling	9.8%	18%
Manufacturing	0.7%	52%
Warehousing	0.0%	95%
Shipping	1.8%	90%
Billing & accounts receivable	6.3%	73%

Exhibit 11-A1

The international CPA firm of Coopers & Lybrand was hired to oversee General Marble's TQM efforts. Coopers & Lybrand used its "Breakpoint BPR^{SR} Methodology." Six teams were trained in this method. The quality problems they identified included not adhering to schedules, machine unreliability, inventory inaccuracies, damaged shipments, and absenteeism. After developing their TQM vision statement, it was communicated to everyone in the company. All were motivated to improve, from top management to the shop floor, as they recognized the company was in a survival mode. Everyone was trained in TQM.

Their reengineering efforts affected all of the value chain processes. In purchasing, an EDI system was installed with certified vendors. The number of suppliers was cut from 1,200 to 85, eliminating 80% of the small transactions. Deliveries were scheduled as frequently as every two days to reduce unnecessary inventory.

A materials resource planning (computerized scheduling) program was installed for manufacturing with bar code scanning. Orders were now scheduled according to when they were needed for its customers, instead of according to how easy it was to make an order. (The original method allowed each department to schedule orders in a way that maximized machine usage and kept the department workers busy. As orders were not synchronized across departments, this method built up sizable WIP throughout the plant.)

A computerized cost accounting system, ASK MANMAN, and new performance measures were installed by Accounting. The new TQM measures included adherence to schedule, CPFT, on-time shipments, complete order filling, and total processing costs. The results were quite impressive:

- Inventory was reduced from $5.9 million to $3.8 million.
- Order fulfillment increased to 100%.
- Lead time was reduced to five days.
- On-time delivery increased from 40% to 100%.
- Procurement costs were reduced $120,000.

Top management realized that TQM is a never-ending process, though. Thus they have three continuous improvement goals: maintain high quality, 100% fill rates, and 99.8% on-time deliveries.

Source: Bokman, "Anatomy of a Turnaround," *Management Accounting*, December 1996. © The Institute of Management Accountants.

READING LIST*

Managing Quality Improvements, Statement on Management Accounting 4-R, Institute of Management Accountants, 1993.

Implementing Activity-Based Management: Avoiding the Pitfalls, Statement on Management Accounting 4CC, Institute of Management Accountants, 1988.

Automobile industry and lost sales: Carr and Tyson, "Planning Quality Cost Expenditures," *Management Accounting*, October 1992.

Carnegie: Johnson and Kaplan, *Relevance Lost: The Rise and Fall of Management Accounting* (Harvard Business School Press), 1987.

Caterpillar: Hendricks, Defreitas, and Walker, "Changing Performance Measures at Caterpillar," *Management Accounting*, December 1996.

Citizen Watch: see kaizen costing citation.

Boeing's 767 benchmarking: Tully, "Why to Go for Stretch Targets," *Fortune,* November 14, 1994.

COQ related to revenues: Ostrenga, "Return on Investment Through the Cost of Quality," *Journal of Cost Management*, Summer 1991.

COQ use surveys: *International Quality Study* (Ernst & Young and the American Quality Foundation), 1991. "Cost Management—Quality Link," *Cost Management Update* (IMA), September 1992. "Calculating the Cost of Quality," *Cost Management Update* (IMA), June 1996. Sjoblom, "Financial Information and Quality Management—Is There a Role for Accountants?" *Accounting Horizons*, December 1998.

DuPont: Brewer and Mills, "ISO 9000 Standards: An Emerging CPA Service Area," *Journal of Accountancy,* February 1994.

Federal Express and UPS: Greising, "Watch Out for Flying Packages," *Business Week*, January 30, 1995.

General Electric storyboarding: Stewart, "GE Keeps Those Ideas Coming," *Fortune,* August 1991.

Grand Rapids Spring & Stamping: Roehm, Klein, and Castellano, "Blending Quality Theories for Continuous Improvement," *Management Accounting,* February 1995, and "The Next Generation of Employee Empowerment," *Management Accounting,* March 1998.

Hampton Inns: "Why Some Customers are More Loyal than Others," *Fortune,* September 19, 1994.

Internal Revenue Service: MacArthur, "Cost Management at the IRS," *Management Accounting*, November 1996.

ISO certification: Borthick and Roth, "Will Europeans Buy Your Company's Products?" *Management Accounting*, July 1992.

Japanese activity cost tables: Yoshikawa, Innes, and Mitchell, "Japanese Cost Management Practices," *Handbook of Cost Management,* Brinker, ed. (Warren, Gorham & Lamont), 1992. *Implementing Target Costing,* Accounting Guideline 28, Society of Management Accountants of Canada, 1994.

Kaizen costing: Cooper, *When Lean Enterprises Collide* (Harvard Business School Press), 1995. Monden and Lee, "How a Japanese Auto Maker Reduces Costs," *Management Accounting,* August 1993.

Levi Strauss (Canada): see Kaizen costing citation.

Lucent Technologies: Francesconi, "Transforming Lucent's CFO," *Management Accounting,* July 1998.

Multidimensional balanced benchmarking in the service sector: Sherman, "Generate Increased Service Profits with MBB," *Management Accounting,* January 1988.

Ritz-Carlton: "Quality: How to Make It Pay," *Business Week,* August 8, 1994.

Shionogi Pharmaceutical: see kaizen costing citation.

Tennant Company: see Carr and Tyson article (Automobile industry above) and Crosby, *Quality is Free* (New American Library), 1980, for his 14-step TQM program it used.

Texas Instruments: see COQ use survey.

Westinghouse: Albright and Roth, "The Measurement of Quality Costs: An Alternative Paradigm," *Accounting Horizons,* June 1992.

Xerox: (benchmarking) Camp, "A Bible for Benchmarking, by Xerox," *Financial Executive,* July–August 1993. (COQ) Carr, "How Xerox Sustains the Cost of Quality," *Management Accounting,* August 1995. (fishbones) Buehlmann and Stover, "How Xerox Solves Quality Problems," *Management Accounting,* September 1993.

*Alphabetic by topic, idea, or company referenced.

CHAPTER 12

Which Process Should We Improve First?

Decision-Focused Management Using the Theory of Constraints

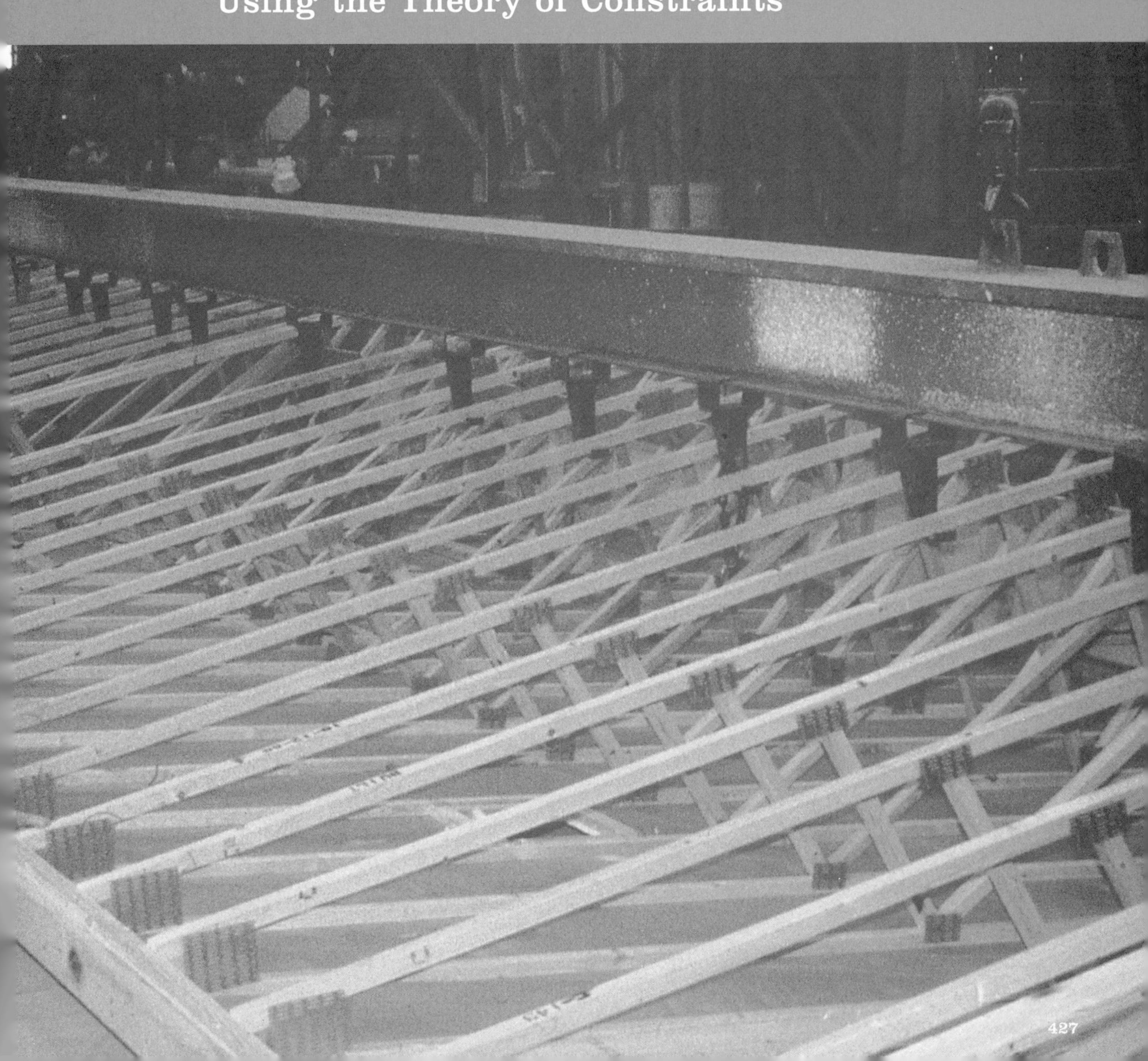

KEY OBJECTIVES:

1	*List TOC's continuous improvement steps and relate them to Pareto management using drum-buffer-rope scheduling.*
2	*Maximize profits by using throughput to schedule production.*
3	*Calculate the minimum sales price to break even when a constraint exists.*
4	*Show how to eliminate a constraint by using throughput with the payback period and make-buy analyses.*
5	*Demonstrate four ratios for continuous improvement management.*

After the last meeting on total quality management (TQM) and continuous improvement, Multree's halls burst with energy. Travel and new car brochures began to appear as the owners felt like all their problems were solved. Smiles and loud discussions contributed to the sun's power as it melted the spring snow and reawakened the landscape. Then a long cold spell struck, killing the budding roses. It seemed to spread to the conference room. The new owners slowly realized their enthusiasm was not shared by the rest of the company. To the workers, TQM and continuous improvement were daunting and confusing. Many had been doing the same things for so long they forgot why they did them that way. In storyboard sessions, the predominant comment was, "This is the way the Boss wanted it done." Again and again, the new owners became trapped in long debates about activities having little impact on value. Finally someone had to say the unspoken.

NANCY

"You know, TQM is pretty exciting until you actually have to do it. It seems awfully complex. Can't we find a simpler way to continually improve?"

TOMMY

"I agree! The level of detail is a little intimidating. And for many the ideas are radical, especially to those who have been here a long time and created our company's culture. If these radical ideas don't increase profits quickly, people won't support improvement programs. Too many companies have seen their TQM attempts fail.

"I'm also worried about TQM 'successes.' Too many firms, like ours, don't take the incentive to invest in improvement programs until they're in a crisis. The old American adage is, 'If it ain't broke, don't fix it.' Because we're in a financial crisis, the tendency is to first look for cost reductions. Activity-based management [ABM] and TQM focus on lowering costs through better activity management. Too often, this results in job reductions [downsizing, rightsizing, or outsourcing]. The plain fact is workers see TQM as a justification for cutting jobs. That's why the Japanese needed a lifetime employment guarantee to make continuous improvement work."

NANCY

"Well, we can do that, too! We can agree not to lay off workers. However, will we accomplish our TQM goals? Cutting excess labor is the major source of continuous improvement savings for many companies. Labor is over 60% of our nonvalue-adding costs!"

BILL

"You're right! To avoid layoffs, we have to use this new capacity [i.e., available labor time from TQM improvements] to increase cashflows and make more profits. The key to TQM success is to increase our sales and use this new 'free' labor capacity to make additional homes. If we can make more houses without incurring any new labor or overhead, I know I can sell them. *The magic formula really is to increase capacity through TQM improvements, sell more, and maintain our existing staffing levels!"*

"Now wait a minute! Why increase capacity? We have surplus capacity already. As is true with many American manufacturers, we're using only 80% to 85% of our capacity on average for all departments. I'll just increase production so you can increase sales. This simple solution will generate more contribution margin and cash, year after year."

"Let's not get carried away. This isn't as easy as it sounds. While we have excess capacity in *most* departments, we don't have it in *all* departments. To increase current output, we'll have to schedule overtime, invest in new machines, and retrain and move some people around. These are expensive decisions! For example, truss-making [making the frames for a roof] is always behind schedule as it is. They already generate the most unfavorable cost variances. TQM isn't working in truss-making because they just don't have enough time for the special training and analyses."

"If we can increase sales by simply increasing truss production, let's do it! If something is holding us back, let's fix it. *We may have a better way to create value if we focus on the one area influencing sales and value the most, instead of trying to control costs everywhere!"*

"So what you're saying is:

- Believing costs are more controllable and easier to change than revenues, we traditionally look for *cost-oriented answers.*
- Creating value, though, comes from making more money now and in the future.
- In reality, the easiest way for many organizations to make more money is by selling more products or services.
- Selling more products with the extra capacity created by continuous improvement programs means firms won't have to lay off workers. As a result, workers will support TQM.
- Thus we can discover simple, *value-oriented answers* if we focus on the one area increasing our revenues and contribution margins the most, instead of trying to control costs everywhere!"

"This makes a lot of sense. By focusing on the activities most affecting contribution margin, changes will have an immediate visible impact without threatening jobs. Does a management strategy exist for this idea?"

What Is the Theory of Constraints?

"When in school, I used the **theory of constraints [TOC]** to get better grades. TOC assumes every system has at least one bottleneck that limits value creation. We need to identify and eliminate that bottleneck. To identify it, I simply asked myself, 'Where do I get the most bang for the buck?' In other words, what's the most important activity for better grades? Obviously, it's study time. I never had enough time! So I prioritized my time based on the activities improving grades the most [e.g., exams, papers, homework, etc.]. Once I figured out how to make

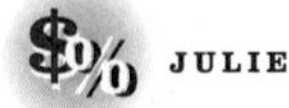

The **theory of constraints (TOC)** *believes one limiting factor always exists that keeps systems from doing more. TOC's goal is to optimally manage that "bottleneck" (constraint) until it can be eliminated.*

enough study time, I moved on to my next constraint, reading skills. After I improved my reading ability, I moved to my next constraint, computer skills. Using this approach, I continuously improved my grades. The short-run impact was immediate and obvious. Better grades lead to more financial support. By my senior year, I was able to trade in my Geo for a Mercedes!

"If Multree Homes didn't have any constraints, we'd be selling an infinite number of houses! Right now, our output is limited only by our production bottlenecks, like truss-making. Once we increase output, selling more is limited only by our pricing policy. Bill can sell more custom homes if he doesn't have to adhere to a 59% markup on manufacturing cost. TOC can attack both constraints."

The TOC foundation: Pareto management

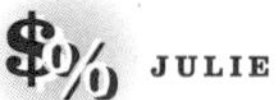

JULIE

"Fortunately, TOC attacks one bottleneck at a time. The idea is a few key factors ['the vital few'] drive the majority of activities ['the trivial many']. Centuries ago an Italian economist, Vilfredo Pareto, discovered about 80% of his city's wealth was held by about 20% of its citizens. This 80:20 rule is used in many business activities. For example, Toyota believes 80% of its revenues come from only 20% of its cars. A TQM guru, Juran, believes 80% of quality problems result from 20% of a system's activities. Using the 80:20 rule, we don't try to do everything. If we do, we'll spend too much time on trivial activities! *Let's first focus on the one activity influencing our money-making potential the most.*" [These ideas are summarized in Exhibit 12-1.]

The TOC Paradigm	
The problem:	Continuous improvement, *and* make it stick, *and* win general support for changes!
The solution:	Identify the constraint that will increase value the most when it is changed, *and* everyone agrees, *and* once fixed, it is not a problem next week, *so* we can go on to the next most important constraint, *and* start all over!

Exhibit 12-1

NANCY

"I see, it's like a softball game our company team is playing. If I'm up to bat, I don't pay much attention to the catcher or any other players. That old phrase 'keep your eye on the ball' means a lot to me. The goal is to win the ball game, but if you can't hit the ball, all the other activities don't count."

SID

"That's an interesting analogy, but there's more to winning. To increase long-run value, the coach, me, focuses on continuous improvement: winning more games and ultimately winning the championship. To improve the team, I look at the weakest area causing the most losses, and I don't necessarily concentrate on winning a single game.

"Our team already has good hitting but allows more runs than we can score. Improving hitting will have little effect on our long-term objective of winning the championship. On the other hand, improving pitching, while maintaining hitting ability, will immediately win more games, now and in the future!"

JULIE

"O.K. Let's be careful. We have two management issues: control day-to-day operations in order to win the game, and continually improve in order to win the championship. TOC says, 'Keep your eye on the ball!' It emphasizes winning the game today with the team we have, given our current pitching constraint. Then, it emphasizes winning tomorrow and the next day. If we win each game, day by day, we will win the championship. This won't happen, though, unless we first fix the pitching problem [eliminate the current bottleneck to winning more games]. After improving our pitching, will we still lose some games? Probably. Why? Because of defense [a new bottleneck]. So TOC will start again, trying to win more games by eliminating the new constraint [defense]."

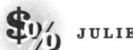

TOC's steps for continuous improvement

JULIE

"TOC is a five-step process [as shown in Exhibit 12-2].

TOC's Five Steps for Continuous Improvement

1. Identify the most important constraint.
2. Exploit it by optimally using the current constraint to maximize profits (drum-buffer-rope management).
3. Don't worry too much about the nonconstraints.
4. Eliminate the constraint.
5. A new constraint will exist, so start all over.

Exhibit 12-2

Good management's short-run continuous improvement goal is to identify the immediate bottleneck and fix it [e.g., managing our current pitching weakness]. Over the long run we need hitting, pitching, and defense to win consistently. At any specific time TOC doesn't necessarily monitor all the critical success factors [hitting, pitching, and defense]. Thus the long-run danger with TOC is permanently replacing too many good hitters with good pitchers, which will hurt our long-run value! So we have to be careful using TOC, although it is a powerful technique successfully used by many firms."

"I see. When we apply TOC to Multree Homes, focusing on the current constraint increases value, because improving it immediately will create more profits. While improvements in nonconstraints may save money, they do not add revenue, and often the savings are from cutting jobs. TOC focuses on increasing profits. We change continuous improvement programs from 'win for management and lose for workers' into 'win for management and win for workers.' Our people will support that!"

KEY OBJECTIVE 1

List TOC's continuous improvement steps and relate them to Pareto management using drum-buffer-rope scheduling.

Identify the constraint. "How to identify the constraint ranges from science to serendipity. Sometimes we can physically see it. A constraint, or bottleneck, usually has a lot of work-in-process inventory [WIP] in front of it waiting to be processed, while the next activity will be waiting for that constraint to finish whatever it does. Usually we just have to ask the people doing the job and they'll tell us where they have the most headaches."

As she reached for her aspirin, Doris hoped this would be a short meeting. Alas, she knew she'd be disappointed as she thought of all the work on her desk and the people waiting for her to do it. Suddenly she realized she was their constraint.

JULIE

"Here are some rough averages for our truss-making constraint [Exhibit 12-3]. To be more precise, we'll need more information."

Identifying the Constraint Activity in Truss-Making

Activity	Maximum capacity	Production quota	Surplus capacity
Sawing	100 trusses	80 trusses	20 trusses
Nailing	80 trusses	80 trusses	*none*
Moving	120 trusses	80 trusses	40 trusses

Production quota calculation:

Standard homes	100 homes ×	8 trusses per home =	800 trusses
Custom homes	10 homes ×	13 trusses per home =	130 trusses
Annual trusses needed			930 trusses
Average trusses needed per month			77.5
(round to 80 trusses per month for production quota)			

Exhibit 12-3

NANCY

"Pareto management, 80:20, right? Just enough of the right information to make the best decision. We don't need perfect information. Keep it simple."

JULIE

"Right! Truss-making has three activities: sawing the lumber [2 × 4 rails], nailing the 2 × 4's together into trusses, and moving trusses to assembly. We need to make 80 trusses a month. We can cut and move more than 80 [these activities have surplus capacity]. Given our current capacity, though, we can nail only 80 trusses a month. Nailing is the constraint, just like pitching is on our company's softball team. We can meet our sales forecast for the year, but we cannot increase sales. We just can't make any more trusses with its current capacity."

Exploit and manage the constraint to maximize profits. "Steps 2 and 3 focus on managing the current constraint until it's eliminated. If the nailing people are idle, trusses won't get made on time and sales will be delayed [on-time deliveries will decrease] or lost. We have to keep the constraint operating at full capacity all the time. Drum-buffer-rope scheduling does this. Bob will discuss this next after I finish explaining the five steps. Here's the trick, though. The nailing machine is our constraint. Increasing nailing capacity allows us to make more trusses, and thus sell more houses."

NANCY

"Of course it adds value. But is it more valuable than any of the other activities? For example, what will happen to profits if we lose 20% of our sawing capacity?"

JULIE

"Well, nothing really, at least in the short run. Look again at the truss-making capacity numbers [Exhibit 12-3]. Losing 20% of sawing capacity equals 20 trusses. Right now we don't need this extra capacity in order to satisfy sales. So why saw any more truss lumber? What will happen to the lumber after it's sawed? It will sit in front of the nailing machine as extra WIP. Even if we need the extra lumber because we can sell another house, we don't have the ability to nail this lumber into trusses. In other words, sawing is not our bottleneck. Losing surplus capacity in a nonconstraint activity will not reduce our sales.

"What about losing 20% of our capacity on the nailing machine, though? We lose 20% of our truss production. And every truss we make will be used on a house we can sell."

"But doesn't scientific management tell us to maximize sawing efficiency, that is, run the saw all the time? Don't we maximize profits by minimizing costs? We minimize the average cost per product by keeping everyone busy all the time."

"No! No, I mean 'yes.' I guess I can see how confusing this can be. Think back to our profit planning meeting [Chapter 3]. If we make more, and remain within our relevant range, *total* fixed costs will not change. In other words, we'll still be spending the same amount of cash [money]. The more we make, the lower our *average fixed costs per product*. However as both TOC and CVP tell us, to make more money, we have to sell those products!

"Look at it this way. We can saw enough lumber to make 100 trusses a month. But we can nail the lumber into trusses at a slower rate of only 80 per month. Sawing more lumber than can be nailed just results in it piling up in front of the nailing machine. WIP [sawed lumber] goes up, but the number of trusses made doesn't increase! So even though we can saw more lumber, it will not increase the number of houses we make and sell. Sawing is not our problem, it's nailing. *Focus on the constraint, make sure it runs at capacity, and don't worry too much about the non-constraints!*"

Eliminate this constraint and start all over on the next one. "Right now, the only way to increase sales is by nailing more trusses. We can buy another nailing machine, but before we consider an expensive alternative we should see what we can do cheaply. A number of policy changes can improve operations. Simple things can be effective. We might put an extra worker on nailing and stagger the break times. We can cross-train people so we never have to shut down for breaks or lunch. Nonvalue-added activities can be eliminated, and value-adding activities made more efficient. We might reschedule maintenance to times when the plant is closed, or keep running the constraint when the rest of the plant is closed. Another alternative is to purchase trusses [outsourcing]. We even may consider previously abandoned, less efficient ways to do the job because the value of the added capacity is greater than the extra cost of the less efficient methods.

"Sometimes the constraint is caused not by physical problems [like not enough machines or labor], but rather by policies and rules. Here are some examples:

- Saturn worked with their labor unions to change work classifications [the constraint], allowing people to move from surplus capacity activities into bottleneck areas. This increased the number of cars produced without increasing labor costs.
- The bottleneck at Stanley Furniture Company was in customer credit approval before jobs were scheduled. Of the normal 45 days lead time, 20 days were for administrative activities, including credit approval. The bottleneck was eliminated by streamlining the procedures for customers with good credit.
- Kent Moore Cabinets had a constraint at the other end of its value chain. Because of a lot of specialty work, modifications often are made after delivery, increasing the customer's price. The company had problems collecting the additional charges created by these changes. To solve this constraint on its cashflows, sales personnel were given a bonus if their customers' accounts were current. This reduced accounts receivable write-offs by 33% and average collection time from 43 to 35 days."

"This is very interesting. Eliminating the constraint is really obvious. Many decisions don't require any accounting information, not even a simple cost-benefit analysis."

TOMMY

"Yes! But we have to make sure our people are allowed the creativity to find good solutions. This is just good business ethics. We cannot allow them to justify what they do and how they do it with comments like, 'This is the way it's always been done' [therefore, it must be the best way], or, 'Why try to change? Somebody will have a silly rule somewhere keeping us from improving things!' The one lesson I learned from our strategic planning meeting is we can control our environment [see Chapter 2]. More often than not, improvement suggestions are squelched because of policies and procedures other people are unwilling to change. While a rule might have been needed a hundred years ago, it may actually impede improvement now! So why not change it?

"Too many answer, 'Why change it? The organization I work for doesn't really care about me, so why should I care about it?' Many people are not committed to their organizations. They just see their jobs as a way to get a paycheck. This is especially prevalent in the government sector. The policy constraint examples you just showed us convince me of the need to change our culture if we want to improve."

JULIE

"O.K. The final step is to look for the next constraint. We always will have some constraint to making more money and increasing our value. It may not be in our production process. It may move to support services and administrative activities within our value chain. Ultimately, it may even move into the market [how to increase market share]. No matter, TOC says we always will encounter another constraint. Simply identify it, optimize it until it can be eliminated, and move on."

NANCY

"All right, until the bottleneck is eliminated, we need to optimize it. This is your area, Bob. How do we manage the current constraint?"

Making the most of what we have: Drum-buffer-rope management

BOB

"TOC schedules production and manages raw materials and WIP inventories using **drum-buffer-rope** [DBR] scheduling. The idea is to maximize the bottleneck's output. TOC makes it the focus for day-to-day management [keeping your eye on the ball]. Technically speaking, usually at least two bottlenecks exist, the constraint we're focusing on and the shipping dock. Each sets the pace for the activities in front of it. Our bottleneck is the nailing machine. Just like the drummer in a marching band, the nailing machine's capacity is the 'drum' setting the pace of production. Why saw more lumber than can be nailed into trusses? That is, other activities preceding the bottleneck, like sawing, only work to the speed of nailing [i.e., they work 'to the beat of the drum']. Activities after nailing are paced by shipping dates.

Drum-buffer-rope *is a production scheduling and WIP management system to maximize the constraint's output. The drum is the constraint's production rate. The buffer is the WIP in front of the constraint. The rope is the production schedule to supply the constraint.*

"Some extra inventory is kept in front of the constraint, just in case the preceding departments have problems. These inventories are called the 'buffer.' We don't want the bottleneck to be idle because it is without work. DBR also uses the buffer to monitor prior activities. We scheduled what should be there. Any missing jobs that should be in the buffer [called 'holes'] are investigated. These holes exist because one of the nonconstraints failed.

"The 'rope' is simply the time scheduled for work to reach the constraint. For example, assume we always want one day's work [the buffer] available for nailing, and it takes two days to saw truss lumber. We'll schedule sawing to begin three days before the lumber is needed at the nailing machine.

"Consider traditional scientific management, in which departments are created for each specialization, like nailing or sawing. We keep sufficient WIP between every department so each can operate independently. The extra WIP allows a department to keep working even when the preceding departments have problems. Scientific management believes specialization minimizes costs. Each department should independently minimize its costs as the best way to create value.

"Under TOC, however, each department has a different objective. Rather than focusing on its own performance as compared to its budget, each department should work to maximize the constraint's performance. This is the right thing to do. Bottleneck performance determines value changes for the whole company. Thus our day-to-day control objective, what we want people to do, changes. We want each department to supply the constraint as needed and not to increase its costs. [Exhibit 12-4 compares these two management strategies.]

Control: What Do We Want People to Do?

Traditional management	**TOC**
◘ Minimize costs in each department	⌛ Maintain current expenses in every non-constraint (maintain hitting and defense)
◘ Don't have unfavorable cost variances	⌛ Focus on increasing constraint capacity to increase firm value (improve pitching)
◘ Maximize the output of every department to minimize the average cost per unit	⌛ Meet the production needs of the constraint (support pitching by using more defensive players in the game)

Note:

◘ means thinking within the box (Functional silo management: maximizing each department's output will optimize overall value)	⌛ means thinking outside the box (Constraint management: maximizing the constraint's output will optimize overall value)

Exhibit 12-4

"TOC lowers WIP throughout the plant while always keeping the bottleneck busy. Hundreds of companies have switched to drum-buffer-rope scheduling. Here's two examples. Baxter Corporation makes plastic bags and parts for the health care industry. Its Lessines, Belgium, plant used DBR to reduce lead times from 35 days to 3 days for one product, and from 5 days to ½ day for another. It also eliminated direct materials warehousing and reduced inventory from a 50-day to a 6-day supply. Wharton Manufacturing makes steel structures, including street light poles. DBR allows it to virtually guarantee lead times to customers. The rope [production time to the constraint] is 9 days long, the constraint needs 2 days, and post-constraint processing is 6 days, so lead time is 17 days. In its first year of TOC, Wharton improved on-time deliveries from 70% to 95%, lead times decreased 50%, finished goods inventories were eliminated, and profit rose 154%."

The TOC Accounting System

"Because TOC radically simplifies scheduling, coordination, and operational control, I expect we'll need radical changes in our accounting system, too."

JULIE

"Not really. People can handle only a limited amount of information. Optimizing the constraint until it can be eliminated should be our continuous improvement priority. The management accounting system primarily should monitor that key activity. So TOC accounting is much simpler than financial accounting. It has only three accounts and certainly does not account for revenues and costs in a way acceptable for GAAP. Let's leave our financial accounting system alone since it's required for external reporting. I'll just reorganize the data into information and reports supporting TOC."

NANCY

"I get it! Keep your eye on the ball. The Pareto principle, or 80:20 rule. Just enough of the right information. We want to keep it simple so everyone can understand it. This system is going to be very different from the one Grandfather Multree used!"

SID

"You're right! The Boss's management strategy was to keep everyone working all the time. He thought the most important and controllable cost variances involved efficiency [e.g., direct materials and labor usage]. Every department received its own cost variance report."

TOMMY

"Because cost variances were the only things used to evaluate performance, everyone was motivated to work, work, work. They never looked beyond their own departments, though. Make WIP and finished goods, even if we can't process the WIP because of a bottleneck or don't have a customer waiting for the home."

JULIE

"O.K. Keeping our eyes on the ball, I see three goals for the TOC accounting system [Exhibit 12-5]."

Goals for the TOC Accounting System (Keep your eye on the ball)

Measure how well we use the constraint
(management goal: maximize constraint output)
(accounting provides information for improving the constraint's value only)

Don't emphasize efficiency measures in the nonbottlenecks
(management goal: nonconstraints should work only to the beat of the drum, not at their own maximum rates)
(accounting provides overall budget-to-actual department costs only)

WIP information should be for the buffer inventory in front of the constraint
(management goal: monitor the buffer and minimize WIP at the nonconstraints)

Exhibit 12-5

Throughput

JULIE

"TOC has only three accounting categories: throughput, operating expenses, and investments. These are sufficient for most operating decisions. Throughput is the value of the constraint's output. The accounting question is how to value that output. By this I mean, 'What is the dollar amount we should use for the WIP leaving a constraint?' Which accounting numbers should be used to show us how well we are managing the constraint? Reporting on how well we optimize the bottleneck is our first accounting system goal."

JACKIE

"Why is this a problem? The nailing machine's output is trusses. The standard cost of $138.44 per truss is used to value WIP for the balance sheet and in the cost of each home for cost of goods sold on the income statement."

NANCY

"Wait a minute! Shouldn't we be using activity-based costing [ABC]? Where's the ABC standard cost card? [Exhibit 12-6 presents both standard costs.]

Traditional and ABC Truss Costs

Standard Cost Card for Trusses			
Resources	**Standard price**	**Standard quantity**	**Standard cost**
Direct materials:			
2" × 4" lumber	$0.10 per foot	500 feet/truss	$50.00/truss
Direct labor:			
Sawing	$10.00 per hour	1 DLhr/truss	$10.00/truss
Nailing	$10.00 per hour	5 DLhrs/truss	$50.00/truss
Variable overhead	$2.06 per DLhour	6 DLhrs/truss	$12.36/truss
Fixed overhead	$2.68 per DLhour	6 DLhrs/truss	$16.08/truss
Standard cost			***$138.44/truss***

ABC Standard Cost Card for Trusses			
Activities	**Standard price**	**Standard quantity**	**Standard cost**
Unit-level activities:			
Materials:			
2" × 4" lumber	$0.10 per foot	500 feet/truss	$50.00/truss
Nails	$0.01 each	100 nails/truss	$1.00/truss
Brackets	$0.25 each	8 brackets/truss	$2.00/truss
Labor:			
Sawing	$10.00 per hour	1 DLhr/truss	$10.00/truss
Nailing	$10.00 per hour	5 DLhrs/truss	$50.00/truss
Direct technology:			
Sawing machine	$3.00 per Machine hr	½ Mhr/truss	$1.50/truss
Nailing machine	$0.50 per Machine hr	1 Mhr/truss	$0.50/truss
Total unit-level costs			**$115.00/truss**
Unit-level costs for a batch of 5 standard homes (@ 8 trusses/house)			$4,600/batch
Batch-level activities:			
Purchasing			$5/batch
Forklift truck*	$15.00 per hour	1 hour/batch	$15/batch
Setups	$10.00 per labor hour	2 hours/batch	$20/batch
Total truss cost per batch			**$4,640/batch**
Average ABC standard cost per truss (@ 40 trusses per batch)			***$116.00/truss***
(*Truck and driver operating costs for delivering lumber and moving trusses to assembly.)			

Exhibit 12-6

"The variable and fixed overhead in the traditional standard cost card [the top panel in Exhibit 12-6] aren't all relevant to truss-making. Those predetermined overhead rates [PORs] include all indirect manufacturing costs for the entire plant.

Shouldn't we be looking only at a truss's relevant costs? Shouldn't the relevant costs include other costs like purchasing the lumber? And don't we have to identify batch-level costs? We make standard homes in batches of five, so trusses are made in batches of 40 [8 trusses per house]. The ABC standard cost [bottom panel in Exhibit 12-6] is $115 per truss plus $40 per batch. For a batch of 40, this averages $116.00 per truss."

$% JULIE

"Both of you just gave me a *cost-oriented* answer. Financial reporting rules [GAAP] require us to account for a truss at its absorptive manufacturing cost. ABC also allocates fixed costs to each product [absorption costing]. ABC, though, can include both manufacturing and nonmanufacturing costs. According to TOC advocates, neither of these approaches provides the short-run information necessary to maximize profits. Let me show you what I mean."

"Costing" throughput: a value-oriented approach. "TOC is a *value-oriented* approach. What is the value of making one more truss? This is similar to the special order pricing decision we discussed in our incremental CVP meeting [Chapter 7]. Think of it this way: every time we make 8 more trusses, we can *build and sell* one more house. The house's value is its contribution margin per unit [CMU]. CMU is sales price less variable costs. In calculating CMU, however, *TOC treats all labor as a fixed cost*. Many manufacturing and service firms have discovered when increasing productivity is the goal, materials are the only additional costs when squeezing one more product [or service] out of a constraint. So the value of incremental production is its revenue less direct materials. If significant, though, other variable costs should also be deducted from revenues in calculating CMU, as I have done for our truss constraint [Exhibit 12-7].

Throughput Calculation for Standard Homes

	Standard homes
Sales price	$50,000
Less: variable costs	
Direct materials	15,500
Indirect materials	1,000
Power usage	500
Sales commissions	2,500
Shipping fees	1,000
Total variable costs	($20,500)
CMU	$29,500
÷ Truss standard quantity	÷ 8
= **Throughput per truss**	$3,687.50

Exhibit 12-7

"**Throughput** is the incremental value of the constraint's output. Every time we make one more truss, it contributes $3,687.50 to a standard home's CMU, our total contribution margin, and profits. To be technically precise, every time we make 8 trusses, we can finish and sell one more house. The house generates a $29,500 CMU. The 8 trusses allow us to build this house and make $29,500 in extra [incremental] profit. From the opposite perspective, if we do not have another 8 trusses, we cannot make another house, and we lose the opportunity to have another $29,500. The $29,500 CMU is equal to 8 trusses, each creating $3,687.50 in throughput per truss."

Throughput *is the extra CMU we make with one more unit of output from a constraint. It's the product's contribution margin divided by the constraint's standard quantity.*

JACKIE

"Hold on a minute. Are you suggesting we 'cost' a truss at $3,687.50? That's outrageous! The Boss will turn over in his grave. Our auditors will shoot us, just like Slim the cowboy feared from his European lenders' auditor in *The Historical Development of Management Accounting* Nancy was reading after the Boss's funeral [Chapter 1]."

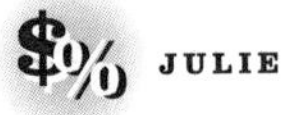

JULIE

"Hold on partner!" Chuckling to herself and gesturing like she was reining in her horse, Julie continued. "That's not what we're really doing. Throughput is what we earn from making that next truss. *If you want one accounting number for all uses, it can't be done.* Financial accounting serves external users by providing past average manufacturing costs. ABC expands and refines the average product cost calculation to include all costs, manufacturing as well as operating expenses. To the extent the past predicts the future, this information is useful in making long-range strategic decisions, such as expanding or dropping a product line. Throughput tells us the short-run incremental cashflow from one more constraint unit. *Remember, different decisions require different accounting information. Keep your eye on the ball!"*

TOMMY

Direct labor is a fixed cost. "Regardless of how we cost a product, I think the TOC treatment of direct labor is an improvement! If we really believe labor is a variable cost, shouldn't we hire only enough people for our budgeted sales volume this month? This isn't practical. If demand goes up by one house, we can't just go out and hire exactly enough people to build it, and then lay off those people when the house is done! Conversely, if demand decreases by one house, we simply can't lay off one house's worth of people and expect to hire them back when demand increases again. This is a major reason why most American firms operate at 80% to 85% of capacity. They need the flexibility to cope with short-run uncertainty, like fluctuations in weekly production volume. We don't continually hire and fire our people. We're committed to keeping them. We invested a lot of money in continuous improvement training. It's not like the traditional well-engineered system where just a few hours of job training would do." Tommy was thinking about the classic scientific management example of how management taught uneducated and inexpensive laborers to shovel coal into a blast furnace at the beginning of the 20th century.

"Direct labor really is a fixed cost for yet another reason, at least in TOC organizations. It relies upon nonconstraint workers' goodwill and motivation to sacrifice themselves for the constraint. Just imagine how threatening it is to be called a nonconstraint with excess capacity!

"I remember what happened at the Western Textile Products Greenville, South Carolina, plant. Some of the nonconstraint workers weren't comfortable with having idle time. They no longer could brag about output rates. Giving them meaningless work, like sweeping, caused resentment. Some constraint workers also resented those with idle time. Thus some nonbottleneck workers slowed down so they wouldn't be resented by their peers.

"To make TOC work, everybody has to have faith and believe our objective is to create value, not to reduce costs by firing nonconstraint labor. We have to commit to finding more profit-generating work for these employees. They also need significant cross-training. This is how Western Textile Products solved their behavioral problems. By moving workers to its bottleneck and training them to run those machines, nonconstraint workers felt they were again adding value to the company. TOC treats labor as a short-run fixed cost of day-to-day operations. Convincing workers to support TOC solutions now will be much easier because their employment is no longer threatened! But what happens to the nonconstraints' costs?"

Operating expenses

JULIE

"Since we have surplus capacity in our nonconstraints, we won't spend any more money in them on labor, new machinery, fixed overhead, or administrative costs if we build one more house. As these costs won't change in the short run, they are considered fixed costs. Exactly which costs will increase if we make one more house? According to the truss throughput calculation [in Exhibit 12-7], if we make one more house today, our costs will increase by only $20,500. All other costs are fixed costs and are called **operating expenses** in TOC."

> **Operating expenses** *include all costs of running the business except for the variable costs used in the throughput calculation.* **Investments (or inventories)** *are the costs of our assets.*

NANCY

"So you're saying these operating expenses don't affect the real profits from one more house, or in other words, our cashflows. *Even though TOC accounting changes our cost classifications, it is the same idea as the contribution margin approach we use in our cashflow analyses [Chapters 3 and 8].*"

JULIE

"You're right!"

Investments (inventories)

"**Investments** [sometimes called inventories] are the cost of assets, including raw materials, WIP, and finished goods. Usually, TOC companies just use the assets' costs shown on the balance sheet. So *TOC gives us a very simple perspective for increasing value. We have only three possibilities:*

- *Increase throughput.*
- *Reduce investments.*
- *Decrease operating expenses.*

Traditionally, scientific management organizes operations into separate specialized departments. Accounting systems classify these departments as cost, profit, or investment centers. The message we send our people is very clear: cost center managers [factory people] should focus on what they can control [operating expenses]. Thus, when continuous improvement is introduced, it usually leads to layoffs, and doesn't focus on increasing throughput. Confoundingly, reducing investments is not always considered by upper management because financial accounting systems classify them as good things [assets]. Focusing only on costs is what TOC advocates call 'cost world' thinking. Little or no attention is focused on increasing value by increasing throughput.

"Cost world thinking is what Jackie did when she answered the question, 'What does a truss really cost us?' Her answer was the $138.44 standard cost from our traditional cost accounting system [see Exhibit 12-6]. Nancy also was thinking in the cost world when she answered with the $116 ABC standard cost [Exhibit 12-6].

TOC says if the truss-making activity is our current constraint, the real cost of another truss is the contribution margin we cannot have because that truss is not available, in other words, $3,678.50! [Exhibit 12-7]

"Instead of taking a cost-oriented approach to continuous improvement, TOC focuses on value. Continuous improvement programs are prioritized in the following order: first focus on increasing throughput, then reduce investments, and finally work on operating expenses. Often, with just some simple scheduling changes and drum-buffer-rope scheduling, throughput can be increased and investments reduced."

Throughput Accounting to Exploit and Eliminate Constraints

JULIE

"Throughput accounting supports three types of decisions: production scheduling, pricing, and eliminating constraints. We exploit the constraint [TOC's step 2, Exhibit 12-2] with scheduling and pricing decisions to maximize throughput. We will continue making these short-run decisions until the constraint is eliminated [step 4]."

Production scheduling decisions

KEY OBJECTIVE 2

Maximize profits by using throughput to schedule production.

"Scheduling is simple: *make the most profitable products first!* The most profitable product has the highest throughput. Here are the standard and custom homes throughput calculations [Exhibit 12-8].

Throughput Calculation for Standard and Custom Homes

	Standard homes	Custom homes
Sales price	$50,000	$100,000
Less: variable costs		
Direct materials	15,500	26,250
Indirect materials	1,000	1,500
Power usage	500	1,250
Sales commissions	2,500	3,000
Shipping fees	1,000	1,000
Architectural fees		10,000
Total variable costs	($20,500)	($43,000)
CMU	$29,500	$57,000
÷ Truss standard quantity	÷ 8	÷ 13
= Throughput per truss	$3,687.50	$4,384.62

Exhibit 12-8

Whenever Bill gets a custom home order, schedule it as soon as possible. Building a custom home is a more profitable use of our trusses until we eliminate the constraint. We'll maximize throughput [CMU *per truss*], total contribution margin, and profits by making custom homes before standard homes."

TOMMY

"You know, ethically this bothers me. Are you suggesting we should delay promised delivery dates to our standard home customers so we can schedule a custom home whenever one is sold? Consider long-run value creation. This comes from standard home sales. Many of these customers have been buying from us for many years. We should not alienate them for the sake of short-run profit maximization!"

JULIE

"You're absolutely correct! Our standard home customers guarantee us long-run profits year after year. If we lose one, the company's value certainly will decrease."

NANCY

"Well then, why does TOC tell us to schedule custom homes first if it's the wrong decision? Is TOC focusing too much on the short run?"

BILL

"It's not always the wrong decision. TOC scheduling becomes a bad decision only when delaying standard homes delivery causes us to lose long-term customers. It's a good decision when we still can deliver the standard homes on time. I think we need some ABM information to help us here. Let's compare standard home manufacturing lead times and customer lead times. If we still can make a standard home within the customer's lead time, go ahead and schedule the custom home first.

"But why haven't we scheduled this way before? Why didn't ABC tell us this?"

JACKIE

Why don't our financial accounting or ABC systems tell us this? "Our financial statements show standard homes are more profitable than custom homes. Our ABC income statement also shows this. Why? Because both accounting systems are based on full costs. In other words, both assign long-term costs to products. We've always scheduled production based on the most profitable products first. Check out the numbers:

	Standard homes	Custom homes
Financial accounting income statement:		
Gross profit ratio	40%	37%
Net income ratio	17%	14%
ABC income statement: net income	$10,427	($4,273)

(See Exhibits 8-5 and 9-16 for the details.)

JULIE

"These numbers include a lot of fixed cost allocations, which are averaged into the costs of each product line. The income statement tells us how we averaged over the year. It's like my batting average in softball.

"ABC gives me some more specifics, like singles, doubles, triples, home runs, walks, and strikeouts. With this information, I can be strategically placed in the batting order, giving us a better picture of my relative value to the team. ABC reminds us of batch-level and product line costs. If we make a significant change in our sales mix—for example, we make only custom homes—this will change our total costs over the long run. Just like in baseball—if we acquire another home run hitter, our lineup [batting order] will change.

"We use TOC to win today's game. Today's constraint is our shortstop. She has to attend Slim the cowboy's funeral and the hanging of the auditor who shot him." Julie almost chuckled out loud this time. "Gee, I'm really having fun with TOC now!" Nancy, on the other hand, was frowning. She was beginning to feel sorry about starting the baseball analogy at the beginning of the meeting. "Will her absence change the lineup? Of course it will! But only for a day. Until we eliminate the constraint, TOC tells us how to set our lineup [organize our batters . . . or products]. It is information for a short-run, temporary constraint decision.

"Let's take a look at the income statement formats to get a better grip on this issue [see Exhibit 12-9]." Nancy continued to frown, and it was getting more pronounced with each subsequent baseball pun from Julie. Picking up on this, Julie became more serious.

"The TOC income statement uses the contribution margin approach. *Contribution margin is called throughput with direct and indirect labor classified as a fixed cost [operating expense]*. Remember, we're going to use this information in deciding which product to make first [scheduling]. This is a very short-run decision. We are not going to hire or fire anyone because we schedule a custom home before a batch of standard homes.

"Not all of the ABC costs are relevant, as most batch, product line, and facilities-level costs won't change. However, some of the unit variable costs are relevant. Detailed ABC information about the unit-level costs allow us to correctly identify which costs will change if we can make one more house. Using this information to calculate throughput, TOC supports short-run, 'What should I do next?' decisions."

"It looks like the TOC income statement and the contribution margin income statement are the same thing. If so, what new contribution is TOC making for us in learning how to run the business?"

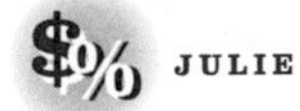

Merging TOC and ABC on the income statement. "TOC firms, like Northern Telcom of Canada, use an income statement format supporting their management strategy. And you're right, the contribution margin format is consistent with TOC. Some companies trying ABC abandoned it for TOC because of the cost of keeping information on each activity. Our cabinet supplier, Bertch Cabinet Manufacturing, was one. Its management accountant told me a single raised door panel requires 21 machining activities. She saw available cost accounting time as Bertch's constraint. It just wasn't possible to provide timely ABC information for management needs, like product pricing.

"A Wisconsin subsidiary of Illinois Tool Works also abandoned ABC. Its goal in setting up an ABC system was to attack nonvalue-added overhead activities. Through ABM and TOC, it accomplished this goal in a more simplified manner.

"Other companies, though, believe ABC and TOC can be merged into a hybrid income statement format. The logic is TOC tells us which costs are truly variable. ABC then can be used with all the other costs [batch, product line, and facilities-level costs now included in operating expenses] in charging them to product lines. In this way, management can have information about short-run profitability, as well as long-run product line profitability.

"Still other companies are experimenting with combined TOC-ABC income statements for measuring and allocating unused capacity [nonconstraint] costs to product lines. Ink Creations did this in measuring the profitability of T-shirts based on the number of silk screenings required.

"Think of it this way. We create monthly and annual income statements. The monthly income statement tells us how many games we won and lost this month. The annual income statement tells us if we won the championship. But is TOC primarily concerned with this? Or does TOC focus us on the correct lineup for today's softball game?"

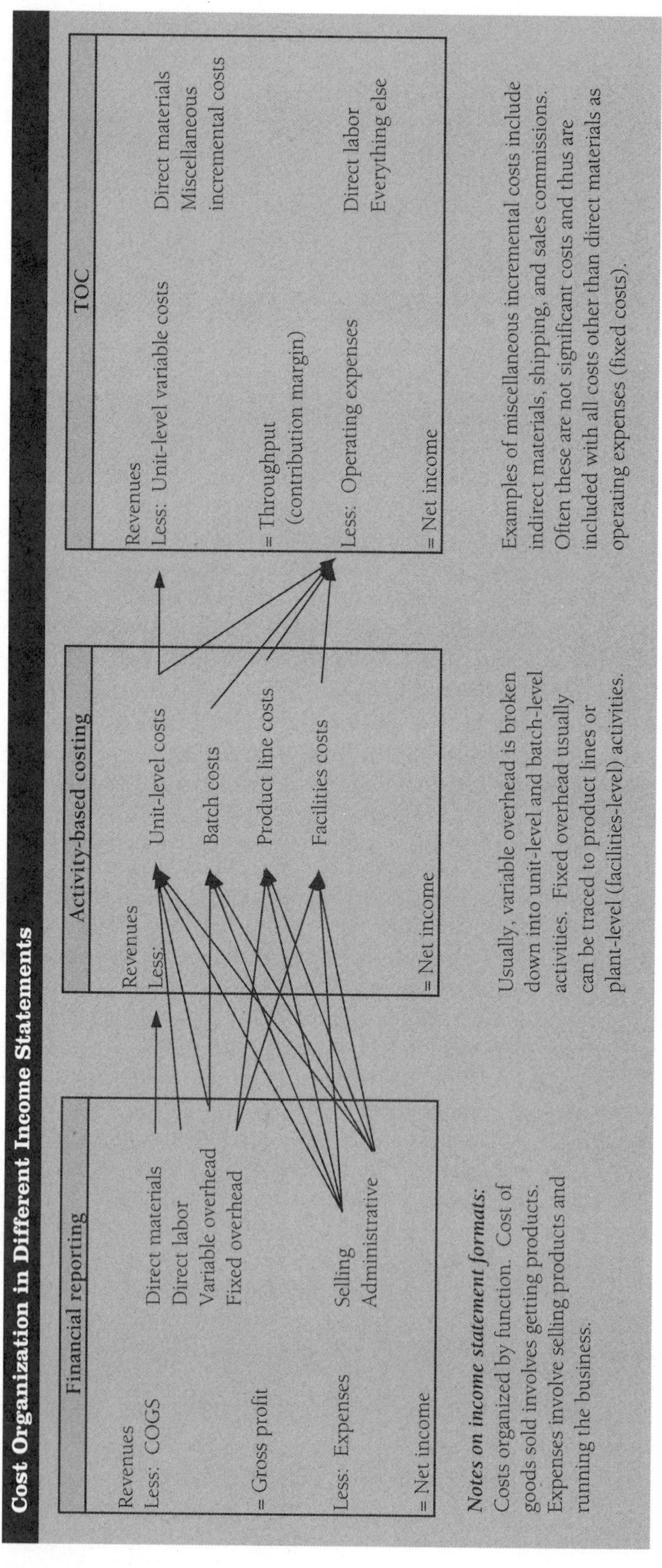
Cost Organization in Different Income Statements
Financial reporting
Revenues
Less: COGS
Direct materials
Direct labor
Variable overhead
Fixed overhead
= Gross profit
Less: Expenses
Selling
Administrative
= Net income
Activity-based costing
Revenues
Less:
Unit-level costs
Batch costs
Product line costs
Facilities costs
= Net income
TOC
Revenues
Less: Unit-level variable costs
Direct materials
Miscellaneous incremental costs
= Throughput (contribution margin)
Less: Operating expenses
Direct labor
Everything else
= Net income
Notes on income statement formats:
Costs organized by function. Cost of goods sold involves getting products. Expenses involve selling products and running the business.
Usually, variable overhead is broken down into unit-level and batch-level activities. Fixed overhead usually can be traced to product lines or plant-level (facilities-level) activities.
Examples of miscellaneous incremental costs include indirect materials, shipping, and sales commissions. Often these are not significant costs and thus are included with all costs other than direct materials as operating expenses (fixed costs).

Exhibit 12-9

NANCY

Maximizing the value of a scarce resource. "I see. Our short-run goal is winning the ball game, in other words, making more profit today given our current constraint. *A constraint is a scarce resource.* Throughput tells us how much profit we can make by better managing that scarce resource. For Multree Homes, a truss's throughput is the house's CMU *per unit of that scarce resource* [a truss in Exhibit 12-8]. I think I can provide some other examples:

- A computer manufacturer's constraint last month was memory chips. After improvements, the new constraint this month is burn-in [testing time]. Last month, computers yielding the highest CMU *per memory chip* were built first. This month, the company first builds computers with the highest CMU *per burn-in hour*.
- A hospital's Trauma Center [emergency room] constraint is nurses' time for filling out admissions forms.
- The Chicago post office's constraint is the letter-sorting machine. But in Shelter Cove [a very isolated area in northern California], it's the time necessary to receive mail from San Francisco.

This is what TOC is all about. *How can we best use a scarce resource? We use it on the product yielding the largest contribution margin per unit of that scarce resource.*"

Sales price decisions

BILL

"Somehow it seems we should be able to use throughput analysis in our pricing decisions, too. Is it possible to optimize a constraint through better pricing policies?"

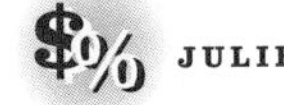

JULIE

KEY OBJECTIVE 3

Calculate the minimum sales price to break even when a constraint exists.

What's our break-even sales price? "Sure! Let me show you. Use cost-volume-profit [CVP] analysis and, specifically, our break-even point formula [from the Chapter 3 meeting]:

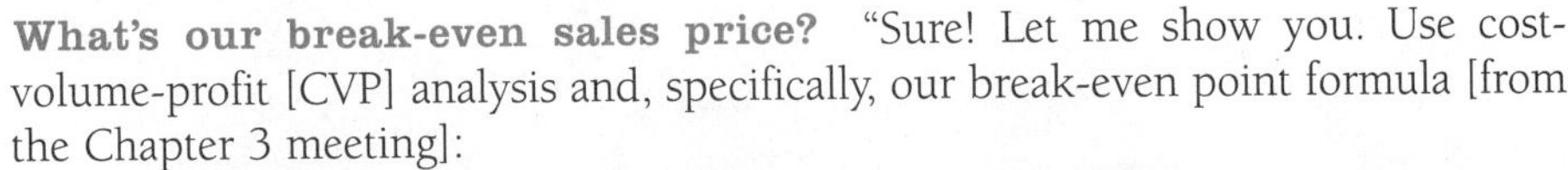

$$\textbf{Break-even volume} = \frac{\textbf{Fixed costs}}{\textbf{CMU}}$$

CMU is for an individual product and break-even volume is product volume. Just change CMU to throughput [i.e., CMU *per unit of the scarce resource*]. And remember, TOC treats labor as a fixed cost. This changes break-even volume from product volume to constraint volume. *Solve for the minimum throughput to cover fixed costs [i.e., operating expenses] given our bottleneck's capacity*. The equation becomes:

Break-Even Throughput

$$\textbf{Constraint capacity} = \frac{\textbf{Operating expenses}}{\textbf{Minimum throughput}}$$

Finally, convert minimum throughput into minimum sales price:

Product's Minimum Sales Price

	Minimum throughput
×	**Standard quantity of the constraint**
=	**Minimum CMU**
+	**Variable costs**
=	**Minimum sales price**

Let's look at a simple example. We have $2,000 in monthly operating expenses and 1,000 hours of constraint time. The minimum throughput to break even is $2.00 *per constraint hour*. If a product needs 5 constraint hours, its CMU must be $10.00 to break even. CMU equals sales price less variable costs. With variable costs of $5.00, the minimum sales price to break even is $15.00. Here's the calculations [Exhibit 12-10].

Calculating the Minimum Sales Price

Constraint capacity	=	Operating expenses / Minimum throughput	
1,000 hours	=	$2,000 / Minimum throughput	
Minimum throughput	=	**$2.00**	**per hour**
× Constraint's standard quantity		x 5	hours
Minimum CMU		**$10.00**	**per product**
+ Variable costs		5.00	per product
Minimum sales price	=	***$15.00***	***per product***

Exhibit 12-10

"Now try it with our custom homes. What's the minimum price we can accept to break even given our nailing constraint of 80 trusses per month? Operating expenses for the entire company are $210,000 per month, and a custom home uses 13 trusses. The variable costs [from Exhibit 12-8] are $43,000. The minimum sales price Bill can accept for a custom home is $77,125 [see Exhibit 12-11].

"I've made a critical assumption here. Custom homes are all we make, so they have to pay for all of Multree's operating expenses. Here's where ABC can help. Since we really make two products [standard and custom homes], ABC can provide us with a breakdown of the $210,000 between product lines."

BILL

"At $77,125 we will just break even. Since we want to make a profit, this average price must be higher. Our strategic plan and proforma income statement [Exhibit 3-5] include a $1 million profit goal for this year [which averages $83,333 per month]. The minimum average sales price to achieve our profit goal is $90,667 again assuming all we sell is custom homes [see Exhibit 12-12].

"This is really a sales management guideline, though. Obviously, the market sets sales prices. Of course, sales personnel are motivated to get the highest price possible. In negotiations, they can go as low as $90,667 and we will still realize our profit goal. I call this the TOC formula price. My salespeople can accept a lower price, but not all the time. I want to approve any price below the formula price, because if we do this too often we may not make our $1 million profit. In no situation will I accept a price below break even [$77,125 from Exhibit 12-11].

Custom Homes Minimum Sales Price

$$\text{Constraint capacity} = \frac{\text{Operating expenses}}{\text{Minimum throughput}}$$

$$80 \text{ trusses} = \frac{\$210{,}000}{\text{Minimum throughput}}$$

Minimum throughput	=	**$2,625**	**per truss**
× Constraint's standard quantity		x 13	trusses
Minimum CMU		**$34,125**	**per house**
+ Variable costs		43,000	per house
Minimum sales price	=	***$77,125***	***per house***

Exhibit 12-11

Custom Homes Formula Sales Price

$$\text{Constraint capacity} = \frac{\text{Operating expenses + Target profit}}{\text{Target throughput}}$$

$$80 \text{ trusses} = \frac{\$210{,}000 + \$83{,}333}{\text{Target throughput}}$$

Target throughput	=	**$3,667**	**per truss**
× Constraint's standard quantity		x 13	trusses
Target CMU		**$47,667**	**per house**
+ Variable costs		43,000	per house
Formula sales price	=	***$90,667***	***per house***

Note: Target CMU is correct. Cells are formatted to whole dollars.

Exhibit 12-12

"I also can use throughput to negotiate trade-offs between sales price and lead time with our customers. Consider the four homes we have scheduled for production this week:

Production order	Throughput
1. Alpine Meadows custom home	$5,000.00 per truss
2. Tahoe Chalet custom home	$4,000.00 per truss
3. Standard home	$3,687.50 per truss
4. Mountain View custom home	$3,000.00 per truss

The Tahoe Chalet has the highest sales price, but uses more trusses than the Alpine Meadows custom home. Even though the Alpine Meadows has a lower sales price, it should be scheduled ahead of the Tahoe Chalet because it generates more throughput. That 'hard sell' customer who negotiated a low sales price for the Mountain View will have to accept a longer lead time because of it. Knowing which jobs are in the queue [i.e., waiting to begin production] and their throughput and due dates, I can negotiate sales prices and delivery times in a way customers understand and appreciate. When Foldcraft Company switched to TOC and gave up emphasizing sales and cost variances in evaluating performance, its sales personnel were allowed the pricing flexibility to handle its seasonal business.

"Throughput accounting can give us a lot of pricing flexibility for our seasonal business. My constraint has always been the Boss's rigid pricing policy. Constraints don't have to be only in manufacturing! Our financial accounting proforma income statement shows a budgeted 37% gross profit for custom homes. This equates to a 59% markup on manufacturing cost. We've lost a lot of business because of not being able to accept a lower markup. Now, using throughput to set the minimum sales price, I can accept some very profitable orders, even though they do not provide a 59% markup.

"Foldcraft used to have a rigid markup policy. A lot of potentially profitable business was turned down even though workers didn't have enough to do. Switching to throughput pricing contributed to a 500% cashflow improvement in just one year! Wharton Manufacturing used throughput pricing in just the opposite way. TOC showed minimum throughput had to be $500 per constraint hour. Sometimes competition would not allow a sufficient price. While its pricing policy was to be competitive, orders for steel structures yielding less throughput would not be accepted."

But, what if the market is our constraint? "Wait a minute. I think we're losing our focus. *Why cut prices if our constraint is in production?* If anything, we should raise prices! Bill's already said he can sell more houses if Bob can make them. Our constraint is not in the market, that is, selling more homes."

JULIE

"If we start playing with sales prices, we're going to have long-run consequences with our major customers. Remember, TOC does not give us the information we need for long-term decisions. Our financial crisis is due to bad costing and pricing decisions that are changing our product mix. ABC helped us discover this problem. Our traditional cost system allocated too much overhead to standard homes [commodity products] and not enough to custom homes [specialty products]. ABC also showed us how and where we were miscosting some unit-level [directly traceable variable product costs] and product line costs. The miscosting affected our markups in pricing. As a result, we were pricing standard homes too high and losing business. We were pricing custom homes too low and getting too much unprofitable business. Now, should we use TOC to justify cutting custom home prices?"

"I get your point. *We can use TOC to make sure we're maximizing our profits today, as long as this approach doesn't cause a long-term sales mix change and we still achieve*

our target contribution margin and profit. To be safe, I shouldn't reduce prices unless we have surplus capacity in all value chain processes. This signals the market is the constraint, that is, when we can make more homes than we can sell. Right now, we can sell more houses than we can make. We have a production constraint.

"However, the market is our constraint during the winter. We can use TOC pricing to increase total sales if we had a winter market not affecting our existing customers. Our cabinet maker, Kent Moore, used TOC to solve this same problem. During the winter, it opened a sales office in Florida with lower TOC-based prices. Florida winter sales did not affect its normal Texas business. Another company using TOC offered price concessions on work done during Christmas, and on jobs with long lead times. The long lead-time work was done whenever an opportunity presented itself."

Eliminating the constraint

SID

"O.K., Bill. Go to work on finding a winter market. That will eliminate one constraint. But how can we eliminate the nailing constraint? I see two alternatives. Either we increase nailing capacity or we find another way to get trusses. How can throughput accounting help us make the best decision?"

JULIE

By increasing constraint capacity. "If a bottleneck is due to labor, we can cross-train nonconstraint people and move them into the constraint. Since we're already paying those laborers, the only incremental cost is training. That's what Saturn does. However, our constraint is nailing machine capacity. We could buy another nailing machine. I understand we can get a small one that improves capacity 10% and . . ."

BOB

"Stop right there, Julie! First, you told me I wasn't thinking right [not using Pareto management]. Next, I'm not scheduling right. Bill's not pricing right. And now you're telling me how to fix my problems! Besides, we've already done this analysis. It's way too expensive and takes up too much space. Besides, the machine increases sawing labor 5% and setup time 20%, while costing $350,000! The Boss chewed out all of us for suggesting an investment that actually increased labor cost! How can this be efficient? It just doesn't make any sense."

KEY OBJECTIVE 4

Show how to eliminate a constraint by using throughput with the payback period and make-buy analyses.

Everyone could see how Bob had taken the heat for this once before. Nancy felt a numbing chill again fill the room. All the TOC ideas sound good, but require a radical change in how people think. Even though it seemed pretty simple, radical changes are not easily accepted. She wondered if the others felt this way. She started tentatively. "Excuse me. I think I'm beginning to understand this TOC thinking. We have surplus labor for sawing and setups. Labor is not our constraint. We're paying these people anyway, so labor cost won't increase. Originally, we thought labor would increase because we believed it to be a variable cost. I think we should ask, 'How long will it take to get back the equipment's cost with the extra throughput it creates?'"

JULIE

"You're right! This calculation is called the **payback period** [see Exhibit 12-13].

"The greater capacity [10% = 8 trusses per month] increases throughput. The extra contribution margin will be a little less than normal, though, because this equipment increases variable costs $7.50 per truss for electricity. We'll also spend $440 in extra monthly operating expenses [e.g., insurance, maintenance, etc.]. Once we determine the additional net cashflow from the investment, simply divide it into

The **payback period** *is the time needed to recover an investment from the extra cashflows it generates.*

Payback Period for Nailing Machine Improvement

Throughput	$3,687.50	per truss
Less: incremental variable costs	(7.50)	
Throughput from investment	$3,680.00	per truss
x Increased capacity	x 8	trusses per month
Additional contribution margin	$29,440	per month
Less: incremental operating expenses	(440)	per month
Cashflow generated	**$29,000**	**per month**

$$\text{Payback period} = \frac{\textbf{Investment cost}}{\textbf{Cashflow generated}} = \frac{\$350{,}000}{\$29{,}000} = \mathbf{12.07\ months}$$

Exhibit 12-13

the investment's cost. This machine's payback period is just over one year. The extra cashflow from the increased throughput will pay for the machine in about a year!

"Sometimes the cashflow analysis is even simpler. We may not have any extra [incremental] variable or fixed costs. In any event, calculating the additional cashflow generated from eliminating a constraint just uses our basic CVP analysis:

CVP model	**TOC application**
Sales price	Throughput
Less: variable costs	Less: incremental variable costs
= CMU	= Throughput from investment
× Volume	× Increased capacity
= Contribution margin	= Additional contribution margin
Less: fixed costs	Less: incremental operating expenses
= Profit	= Cashflow generated

By outsourcing. "We also can purchase trusses as another way to eliminate the bottleneck. This is simply the make-or-buy analysis we did in our incremental CVP meeting [Chapter 7]. I've put together some numbers to demonstrate this [in Exhibit 12-14].

"Throughput tells us if we can make one more truss, it should be for a custom home [Exhibit 12-8]. So let's purchase trusses for standard homes. Which costs will we save? The $53.00 for materials is relevant since we won't need them if we don't make the truss. The labor, machinery, and other costs of the constraint will not change, though. We'll still be using these resources to make custom home trusses, so they aren't relevant. Outsourcing increases the incremental cost of a truss by $87.50, lowering the standard homes throughput to $3,600."

"Eliminating a bottleneck, that is, increasing the number of trusses we have, costs something. In this case, a standard home's CMU will go down $700 [$87.50 per truss × 8 trusses per house], from $29,500 [Exhibit 12-7] to $28,800. Still, as-

Eliminating the Constraint: Outsourcing Analysis		
Costs saved by not making a truss:		
Materials (from Exhibit 12-6, ABC costs)	$53.00	per truss
Less: purchase cost for a truss	(140.50)	
Change in cashflow if we purchase trusses	($87.50)	per truss
+ Throughput from additional truss (Exhibit 12-7)	3,687.50	
Contribution margin increase from outsourcing	**$3,600.00**	per truss

Exhibit 12-14

suming outsourcing is the only way to eliminate this bottleneck, I'd rather have $28,800 than not have it! And that's our choice. Either we buy trusses or we do not make another house which Bill can sell. I can live with this!"

Long-term problems created by throughput accounting. "Or can I? I'm keeping my eye on the ball, but it's not trusses anymore! We just eliminated this constraint. Our new constraint is framing. When truss-making was the constraint, framing had surplus capacity. Specifically, enough to make ½ home per month. Why is it our new constraint? With the new nailing machine, we just increased capacity by eight trusses, or one house per month. Framing can't complete another house per month with its current capacity. So we won't make any more than four extra trusses a month until we can eliminate the framing constraint.

"Now, how does this affect our original constraint elimination decision for trusses? We originally *assumed* we could use all new trusses to make houses we can sell now. In reality, it's going to take 2 months before we can sell that house. We will get the $28,800 CMU [averaging $3,600 per truss], but it will take twice as long. The new framing constraint doubled the payback period for the nailing machine!"

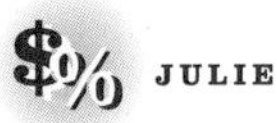

"I'm afraid it's worse than that! As soon as we eliminate the framing constraint, what's the next one? Remember, we will produce only enough trusses to supply the constraint, whatever it may be. *Every time a constraint is eliminated, its incremental profit analyses may no longer be valid! In the long run, we may be becoming less efficient. TQM is still important for nonconstraints. We will need to develop some measures to watch for this problem.* In the long run, we have to guard against destroying our profitability from inefficient cost increases that may be created in eliminating constraints."

"I knew I didn't like this TOC stuff! It's a short-run focus. Just like in baseball. To win today's game, we need to use our last pitcher. If we want to win the championship, though, we have to win tomorrow, too. And we may not if we use our last pitcher today! TOC focuses on winning today's game. Strategically, we still have to worry about the rest of the season!"

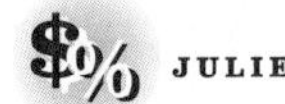

"You're right! We have to be very careful to use the right information for a particular decision. TOC is a continuous improvement system first, and a short-run decision system second. It's just the Pareto principle, the 80:20 rule. TOC information doesn't answer all of our questions, but it is very simple to understand and it's correct 80% of the time."

Operational Control Measures

BOB

Bob had had a very perplexed look on his face when he began again to question the Boss's traditional way of doing things. "I'm sorry for yelling at you, Julie. It's just TOC makes our planning decisions seem so simple. *I never realized how the wrong accounting information can lead to so many bad decisions.* Our operations are very complex, though. We have many departments with lots of workers to monitor and control. Jackie does an excellent job in producing all the WIP inventory reports and cost variances we need for this. But is it possible we're using the wrong information in monitoring day-to-day operations?"

JULIE

"Well, I think we're trying to use too much accounting information to control too many things simultaneously. Think again about our control and accounting system goals [in Exhibits 12-4 and 12-5]. *With our new TQM mentality, and drum-buffer-rope scheduling, our people take the initiative to control things. We don't need accounting information to initiate and enforce control.* It's simple. They know what to do. Thus we should be able to simplify our reports."

Managing the constraint

JULIE

"Remembering to keep our eyes on the ball, our first operational priority should be to maximize throughput. We should monitor constraint performance carefully [steps 2 and 3 in TOC's continuous improvement strategy, Exhibit 12-2]. For the people doing the work, graphical information at their location may be the most simple to understand. For upper management monitoring, some continuous improvement ratios provide simple and useful information."

Visual reports. "I've seen some interesting real-time monitoring systems on the shop floor at the constraint. Western Textile Products is a subcontractor in the apparel industry, making pockets, waistbands, and the like. Workers were delighted when the cost variance system was abandoned. About 20 minutes a day was needed just to fill out the labor productivity reports at the Columbus plant. Now, each day they update a big graph on the wall next to the constraint. It looks something like this [see Exhibit 12-15].

"The graph shows cumulative actual-to-budget throughput each day, so workers can track their progress toward the month's profit goal. Daily throughput also is plotted, which can be compared against the daily throughput goal to see if any money was made today. Both are similar to daily and average batting statistics in baseball.

"This graphic ABM report measures the output of a bottleneck. Monitoring the buffer inventory in front of it also is very important. Again, all we need is a simple report comparing job due date with actual arrival date. If a job does not arrive at the buffer on time, this signals a problem in a preceding nonconstraint. Immediately investigate this because we don't want the bottleneck running out of work."

NANCY

"The really neat thing about these reports is everybody in the plant can understand them and follow our progress, not just the accountants!"

JULIE

Continuous improvement ratios. "I've also created four ratios used to monitor continuous improvement in TOC shops. [These are illustrated in Exhibit 12-16 on p. 454.]

- *Constraint utilization rate* tells us whether the constraint is running at full capacity. Obviously, our goal is to get this to 100%. Right now, we're using only 88%

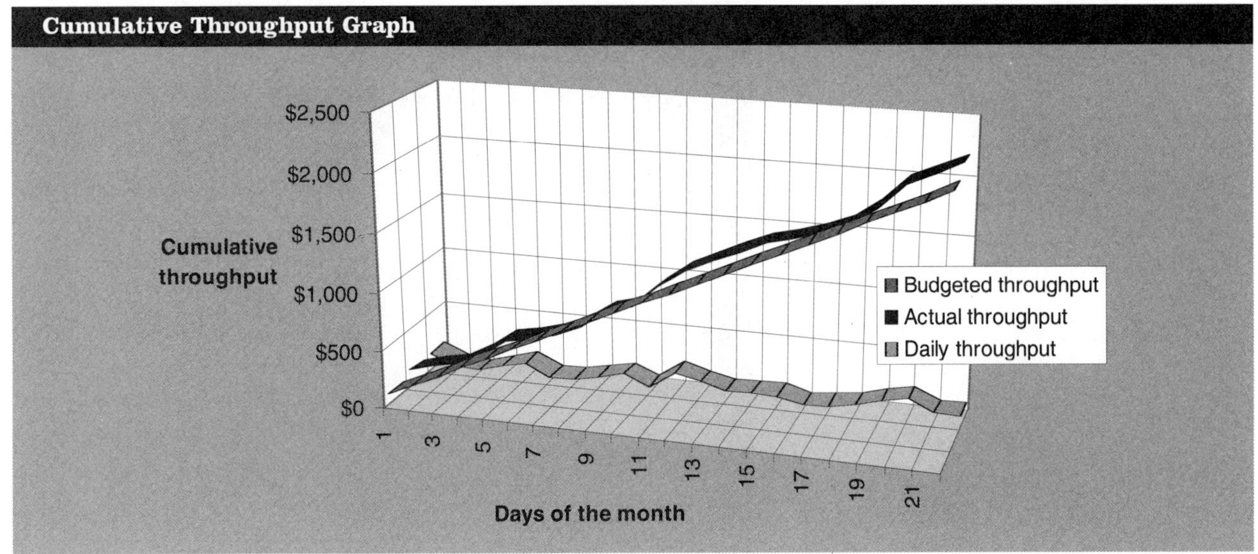

Exhibit 12-15

KEY OBJECTIVE 5

Demonstrate four ratios for continuous improvement management.

of the constraint's capacity. The continuous improvement question is, 'How can we get that last 12%?' Calculating this ratio daily helps explain the throughput plotted on the shop floor graph.

- *Throughput efficiency* is a rate to compare with budgeted and break-even throughput. While the bottleneck may be running most of the time [as measured by the utilization rate], is it producing the required throughput? To illustrate how these two ratios work together, assume our budgeted throughput is $75 per hour. We only worked 7 hours, but each hour actually generated $100 in throughput. Total throughput was $700 compared to our budget of $600 [8 hours × $75 per hour]. We didn't use the constraint as much as planned, but we got more throughput than budgeted for each hour worked.

- *Improvement efficiency* is a measure for comparing constraint elimination alternatives. We considered outsourcing trusses and buying a new nailing machine. Outsourcing increases our costs by $87.50 per truss [Exhibit 12-14]. Buying the machine increases operating costs $7.50 per truss plus $440 per month [Exhibit 12-13]. It increased monthly production capacity by 8 trusses. The average cost increase equals $62.50 per truss [the improvement efficiency ratio in Exhibit 12-16]. It appears outsourcing [$87.50 per truss] is a more expensive solution than buying the new nailing machine [$62.50 per truss].

  "More importantly, this measure also supports nonconstraint continuous improvement. As soon as we start using the new nailing machine, this activity is no longer a constraint. Should we now ignore it and focus our attention on the next constraint? Of course not! It costs an *extra* $62.50 per truss to eliminate the nailing constraint with the new machine. As we eliminate each constraint, our total costs change. If we do not initiate continuous improvement programs in our nonconstraints to reduce these extra costs, sooner or later the cumulative cost increases can drive us to bankruptcy!

- *Product mix* changes also should be monitored. TOC says whenever possible, make custom homes if we have a nailing constraint. Our cost and profit projections are based on a sales mix of 10 standard homes to each custom home.

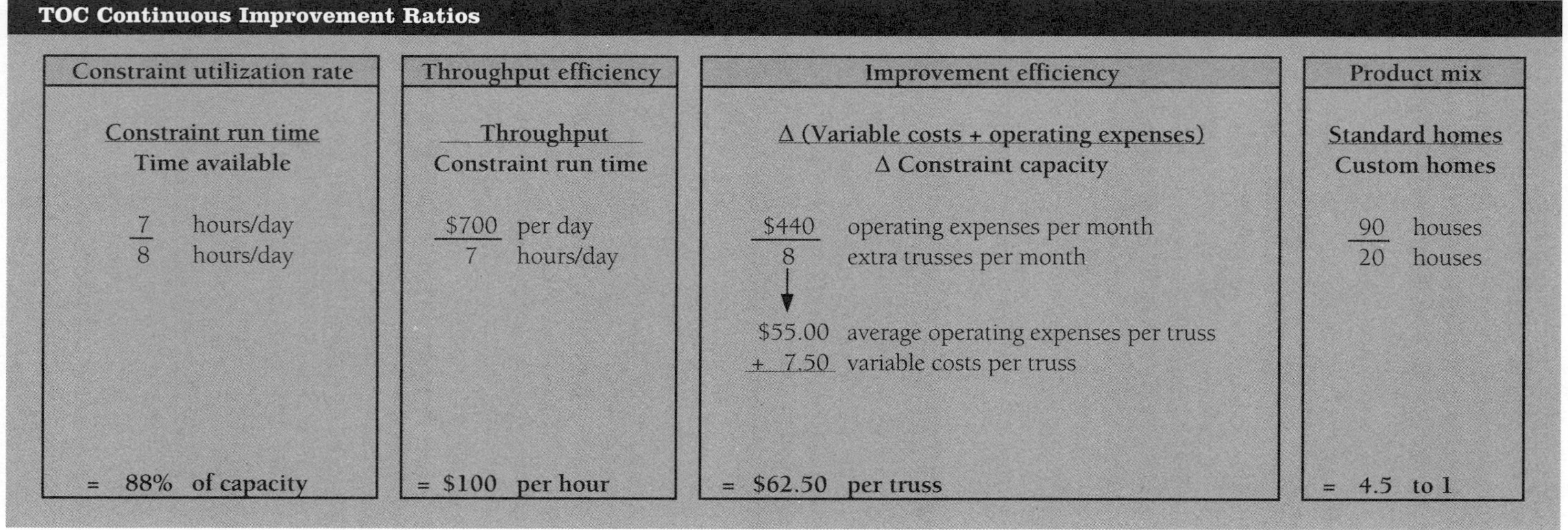

TOC Continuous Improvement Ratios

Constraint utilization rate	Throughput efficiency	Improvement efficiency	Product mix
Constraint run time / Time available	Throughput / Constraint run time	Δ (Variable costs + operating expenses) / Δ Constraint capacity	Standard homes / Custom homes
7 hours/day / 8 hours/day	$700 per day / 7 hours/day	$440 operating expenses per month / 8 extra trusses per month	90 houses / 20 houses
		$55.00 average operating expenses per truss + 7.50 variable costs per truss	
= 88% of capacity	= $100 per hour	= $62.50 per truss	= 4.5 to 1

Exhibit 12-16

Focusing on constraint decisions may change our product mix from the budgeted 10:1 ratio, so I calculated the actual ratio after emphasizing custom homes while our nailing constraint existed. As we move away from the 10:1 ratio, the need for new cost and profit projections becomes more important."

Managing nonconstraints

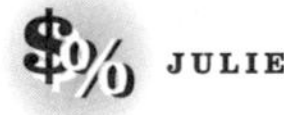

"Nonconstraint activities have surplus capacity. We don't want to encourage producing more than needed by the constraint. TOC considers nonconstraint costs as fixed. Any increases in nonconstraint spending need to be investigated because they aren't supposed to happen! A simple budget-to-actual monthly report may be sufficient for cost control.

"Also, nonfinancial information is useful, especially since we don't want WIP building up between the nonconstraints. For example, AlliedSignal's United Kingdom plant uses scheduled-to-actual output as the primary performance measure for nonbottleneck areas."

"I'm still nervous about ignoring TQM and continuous improvement programs in the nonconstraints. Are you suggesting we apply them only to constraints?"

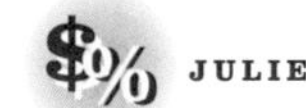

"Oh no! Everyone always should be improving. Nonconstraint TQM should result in significant savings through better quality, fewer rejects, and less rework. ABM and TQM measures still are important. By eliminating nonvalue-added activities, we should create resources [e.g., labor] to use elsewhere, like to eliminate a constraint. Thinking back to our motivation meeting [Chapter 8], we're changing our culture. As we move more toward shared values and beliefs [clan control], the less we need bureaucratic and accounting controls. TOC doesn't have the accounting controls we've had in our more traditionally designed organization, so we need to rely on our people. Of course, they must be motivated to do the right things.

"To change the culture and achieve this internal motivation within our people, TOC prefers finding new uses for increased surplus capacity in the nonconstraints, rather than the layoffs so frequently seen with TQM. Hofmans Forms Packing, in Rotterdam, was able to increase sales by expanding the market outside of Europe for one of its low volume products, wraparound labels. Labels are made in nonbottleneck operations. It's now one of Hofmans Forms' most high volume and profitable products.

"Remember, TOC is a value-oriented approach, not a cost-oriented one. Nonconstraint improvements are important, but our priority should be on optimizing and eliminating our constraints, and on increasing throughput and cashflows. To illustrate, a Hofmans Forms Packing TQM study showed some new equipment would significantly reduce setup time. An ABC study showed this to be very profitable, but the activity wasn't a constraint! The new machine would not increase throughput, and thus became a low priority instead of a high priority."

"O.K. Julie's showed us how TOC information can maximize short-run value and manage our TQM and continuous improvement programs. This seems like a good strategy. However, we cannot abandon our ABC system. It provides information we need to assure we're on target in the long run. For some reason, I feel like going to a baseball game. Let's adjourn this meeting!"

KEY OBJECTIVES SUMMARY

DORIS

"I'd like to review and summarize everything we discussed today before you go, Sid. Help me out here.

1. List TOC's continuous improvement steps and relate them to Pareto management using drum-buffer-rope scheduling.

- "*Identify the most important constraint.* Constraints [bottlenecks] are activities without surplus capacity [see Exhibit 12-3]. TOC management believes at least one constraint always exists, limiting the ability of a system to do more. So to make more money now and increase today's value, eliminate that constraint first. Even in the nonprofit and service sectors, organizations can benefit by systematically eliminating their constraints.
- *Exploit the constraint to maximize profit.* Drum-buffer-rope is a scheduling system designed to keep the constraint working at full capacity. The constraint's output rate is the drum that sets the work schedules for the other activities. Everyone works 'to the beat of the drum.' The buffer is the WIP in front of the constraint to make sure it is never idle due to lack of inputs. The rope is the time it takes for materials and WIP to reach the constraint. This determines when prior production should begin.
- *Focus on managing the constraint and don't worry too much about the nonconstraints.* Control the constraint by making sure it always has enough work to keep busy [the buffer] and by maximizing the value of its output [throughput]. Nonconstraints have surplus capacity, so when production volume fluctuates, the only cost changes are materials and perhaps machine power. The vast majority of nonconstraint costs are fixed capacity costs [including labor]. Cost control for nonconstraints is limited to staying within budget. Production control is limited to monitoring the output of these activities so only what is needed is produced and delivered on time.
- *Eliminate the constraint.* If labor is the problem, we can cross-train nonconstraint workers and move them into a constraint to increase its output. If machine time is our constraint, perhaps we should buy another machine. We might be able to buy more trusses whenever we need them [outsourcing]. Sometimes, though, the real constraint is a policy, for example, credit applications waiting for an unnecessary approval process.
- *A new constraint will exist, so start all over.* Continuous improvement is never done. We're always taking small steps to improve [e.g., identify constraints and eliminate them]. As soon as we eliminate one constraint, the next should be attacked because we always can make more money, or create more and better output if we are a nonprofit organization.

2. Maximize profits by using throughput to schedule production.

"As you know, I do word processing jobs at home in my spare [??] time. My constraint is the hours I have available. Right now I'm considering how to schedule three jobs. Here's the throughput numbers [Exhibit 12-17].

Throughput Calculation for Word Processing Jobs

	Job 1	Job 2	Job 3
Sales price	$50	$40	$60
Less: variable costs			
Paper	2	2	5
Pick up and delivery	12	6	15
Total variable costs	($14)	($8)	($20)
CMU	**$36**	**$32**	**$40**
÷ Budgeted labor hours	6	4	10
= Throughput per hour	**$6.00**	**$8.00**	**$4.00**

Exhibit 12-17

I had a schedule based on their apparent profitability. According to their CMUs, I was going to do Job 3 first, then Job 1, and finally Job 2. After I looked at the time each will take, I make the most money per hour on Job 2. I'll next do Job 1, and finally Job 3. What I did was divide each job's contribution margin by the time needed [i.e., the constraint's standard quantity]. I now will order the jobs according to which yields the highest CMU *per unit of my constraint*, that is, by each job's throughput. The job with the highest throughput gets done first!

"CMU tells me about the short-run profitability of a job. To maximize profits, I thought I should do the job with the highest CMU first. TOC taught me this is true only if I have no constraints, or each job uses the same amount of my constraint. ABC information is for strategic decisions. It's like a batting average. The higher my average, the higher I am in the batting order. But even though I have a high average, what if I'm not hitting today? Maybe I should consider trying to walk, bunt, or get hit by a pitch! TOC gives me the information for this type of short-run decision [e.g., the pitcher's wild and the third baseman is slow].

3. Calculate the minimum sales price to break even when a constraint exists.

"I always have more jobs than time available. The maximum time I can spare is 100 hours a month. I do have some fixed costs [operating expenses]. Most are minor [about $100], although my landlord charges me $400 a month to rent garage space she'd otherwise use for her workshop. I divided my $500 monthly operating expenses by my 100-hour constraint volume to determine the minimum CMU *per hour* to break even [minimum throughput = $5.00/hour]. If a job requires 5 hours, it better yield a minimum CMU of $25. If variable costs are $10, the minimum price I can accept is $35. I used this break-even and minimum sales price calculation on Job 3 [see Exhibit 12-18].

"That guy is only willing to pay me $60.00. If I accept jobs priced this low, I won't break even. I suspect I can find more profitable jobs, so I'm not going to do Job 3. However, if I have extra time with nothing else to do [i.e., I have surplus capacity—some free time], Job 3 does produce a positive contribution margin.

Calculating Job 3's Minimum Sales Price

Constraint capacity	=	Operating expenses / Minimum throughput
100 hours	=	\$500 / Minimum throughput
Minimum throughput	=	**\$5.00 per hour**
× Constraint time		× 10 hours
Minimum CMU		**\$50.00 for Job 3**
+ Variable costs		\$20.00 for Job 3
Minimum sales price	=	***\$70.00 for Job 3***

Exhibit 12-18

4. Show how to eliminate a constraint by using throughput with the payback period and make-buy analyses.

"I'm also thinking about investing in some new hardware and software for my computer. While this won't increase the real number of hours I have available, it will increase my efficiency 25%. The investment is equivalent to having an extra 25 hours a month available. Using my break-even throughput of \$5.00 per hour, the investment will create at least another \$125 per month. The stuff will cost \$1,000 and won't increase my variable or fixed costs. \$1,000 ÷ \$125 = 8 months to recover my investment if I earn only the \$5 break-even throughput rate. This is the payback period calculation Julie did for another nailing machine. I'll use her format to verify this [see Exhibit 12-19].

"You know, I could outsource some jobs. Albert is pretty good with word processing and spreadsheets, and he's always looking for ways to make extra money. Maybe he'd like Job 3! Let's see. I'll save the \$20 in variable costs. I'll still need one hour to coordinate things and proof his work. I think he'll do it for \$50. What's my throughput? [See Exhibit 12-20].

"Hey, I like this TOC analysis! I'll give Albert a call. We have to be careful to use the correct accounting numbers, though, in this make-or-buy decision. Often standard cost, whether traditionally calculated or by ABC, does not always identify the real relevant costs involved. Look back at my throughput calculations [see Key Objective 2's summary]. I'm assuming all the variable costs will be saved if I outsource this job. But what if I still have to pick up and deliver it? I'll have a negative \$5 CMU! Also consider the short-term nature of TOC analysis. If I outsource Job 3, I'll create 9 hours of surplus capacity. What if I can't find any new jobs for that 9 hours? Outsourcing becomes a bad decision. I'd rather do it myself and make \$40, than outsource it and make only \$10. Especially since I'll have to spend the surplus 9 hours watching football with my husband! [A very high opportunity cost, indeed!]

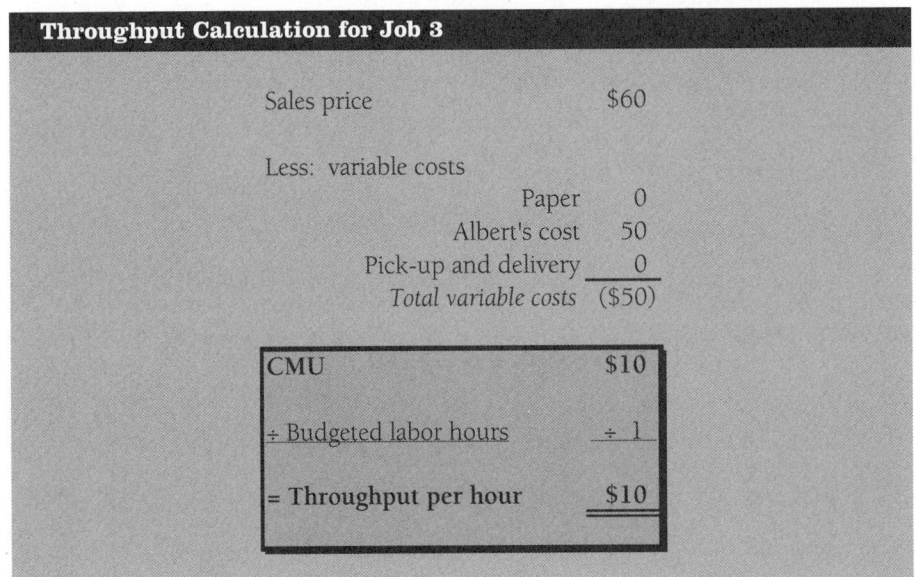

Payback Period for Hardware and Software Improvements

Break-even throughput		$5.00	per hour
Less: incremental variable costs		0.00	
Throughput with new computer		$5.00	per hour
x Increased capacity	x	25	hours per month
Additional contribution margin		$125	per month
Less: incremental operating expenses		0	per month
Cashflow generated		**$125**	**per month**

$$\text{Payback period} = \frac{\text{Investment cost}}{\text{Cashflow generated}} = \frac{\$1{,}000}{\$125} = 8.00 \text{ months}$$

Exhibit 12-19

Throughput Calculation for Job 3

Sales price		$60
Less: variable costs		
	Paper	0
	Albert's cost	50
	Pick-up and delivery	0
	Total variable costs	($50)
CMU		$10
÷ Budgeted labor hours		÷ 1
= Throughput per hour		**$10**

Exhibit 12-20

5. Demonstrate four ratios for continuous improvement management.

"These ratios complement shop floor information. For example, above my computer in the garage, I'll keep a graph like the one Julie showed us [Exhibit 12-15]. I will plot my throughput each day [did I make any money today?] and my cumulative throughput. I'll then compare cumulative throughput to cumulative break-even throughput [similar to the budgeted throughput line in Exhibit 12-15].

"I also will calculate a daily constraint utilization rate by dividing my budgeted work hours into my actual work hours. This helps me understand why I did not hit my break-even throughput. Yesterday, I budgeted 4 hours for word processing jobs, but I worked only 3 hours. No wonder I didn't break even. I worked my constraint only 75%. [The TOC continuous improvement ratios are presented in Exhibit 12-21.]

"Of course, I should consider my throughput efficiency ratio. This is throughput divided by actual hours worked. As you can see, I made an average of $10 per hour, twice my break-even rate.

Albert called me back and said he's willing to do some jobs, but only if I pay him $6.00 per hour. If I make the computer improvements for $1,000 [see Key Objective 4's summary], I'll have the equivalent of another 25 hours per month in surplus capacity. I'll have to borrow the money and pay it back at $100 a month. If I use these 25 hours to do the jobs I would have given to Albert, my *improvement efficiency ratio* shows the investment will cost me only $4.00 per hour [the $100 incremental operating expenses divided by the 25 extra constraint hours it creates]. I think I'll do the work myself.

"Finally, I'll calculate a weekly product mix ratio. My projected profits are based on accepting 10 word processing jobs for every 1 spreadsheet job. Spreadsheet jobs require a lot of time and wasted paper in reprinting them until they're just right. Last week, I accepted 8 word processing jobs and 2 spreadsheet jobs. I better be careful! If I maintain this 4-to-1 ratio [8 word processing jobs ÷ 2 spreadsheet jobs], my long-run costs and profits will significantly change from my proforma, and my bottleneck may shift to my printer!

"Throughput accounting does have its problems. It is based on maximizing short-term contribution margin. When used in pricing decisions, we have to be careful not to price products below the throughput-based break-even price [Exhibits 12-10 and 12-11]. However, if we price products below our average markup, will we achieve our profit goal?

"Because constraints are closely monitored while nonconstraints are not, we also have to guard against resentment among workers. Nonconstraint workers may slow down to avoid the problems created by idle time. This is another reason why TOC suggests building new products and markets. All in all, though, TOC provides many tools to support continuous improvement."

SID

"I think you've done an excellent job summarizing TOC. Here's a word processing job for you: go home and type up what you just told us! I'm going to the baseball game."

DORIS

"Thanks a lot! By the way, since your seat is right behind third base, keep your eye on the ball!"

TOC Continuous Improvement Ratios

Constraint utilization rate	Throughput efficiency	Improvement efficiency	Product mix
$\frac{\text{Constraint run time}}{\text{Time available}}$	$\frac{\text{Throughput}}{\text{Constraint run time}}$	$\frac{\Delta \text{ (Variable costs + operating expenses)}}{\Delta \text{ Constraint capacity}}$	$\frac{\text{Word processing jobs}}{\text{Spreadsheet jobs}}$
$\frac{3 \text{ hours/day}}{4 \text{ hours/day}}$	$\frac{\$30 \text{ per day}}{3 \text{ hours/day}}$	$\frac{\$100 \text{ per month}}{25 \text{ hours per month}}$	$\frac{8 \text{ word processing jobs}}{2 \text{ spreadsheet jobs}}$
= 75% of capacity	= $10 per hour	= $4 per hour	= 4 to 1

Exhibit 12-21

Kenco Engineering's Decision-Focused Accounting System

Kenco Engineering is a family-owned specialty blade edge manufacturer with annual sales of about $5 million. Blade edges are like gloves. They cover the edges of very expensive equipment. For example, construction road graders and snow plows have very large blades that scrape the ground surface. These blades can wear out rather quickly and cost between $50,000 and $200,000 to replace. Kenco's blade edges protect the blades, last longer, and cost between $500 and $2,000 to replace. The blade edges are made from steel which has been strengthened with tungsten carbide chips.

The production value chain contains three processes: tungsten crushing, blade cutting, and conversion (imbedding the tungsten into the steel "gloves" and finishing them to customer specifications). Tungsten can be purchased in crushed or uncrushed form, and Kenco constantly evaluates the short-term "make-or-buy" decision (crush it or buy already crushed tungsten). The accounting system focuses on this decision by dividing the operating expenses of this nonconstraint into avoidable versus facility-level costs. To illustrate, the avoidable costs of crushing equal $5,000 for a particular job. Buying pre-crushed tungsten is $4,000 more than uncrushed tungsten. For this job, buying pre-crushed tungsten will save Kenco $1,000.

Steel blade cutting used to be a labor-intensive process, and was physically demanding and dangerous. Workers had to manually position large plates of steel for cutting, causing many accidents. Fingers weren't just broken, they were crushed. Workman compensation costs were about $11,000 per month. TQM efforts resulted in an automated process reducing workman compensation to $4,000. Using strategic cost management, Kenco now contracts with only two steel mills that provide most of the steel plates precut to job sizes. The accounting system provides comparative information about purchasing and processing costs for steel from each supplier. This allows management to focus on annual contract negotiations with each supplier. Again, the accounting system is designed to provide the relevant information for the critical decisions made in each nonconstraint.

Tungsten imbedding is the constraint. The costs of imbedding, now done in a JIT cell, are calculated per inch of imbedded tungsten. Similar to Exhibit 12-15, a graphical report is prepared for profit analysis. Kenco updates the graph weekly (versus daily in the exhibit). On the shop floor, though, a daily graph reports inches of steel blades imbedded per day (a physical measure instead of a throughput dollar measure as in the exhibit).

Since most products are custom designed, the sales price bid sheet is based on activity cost tables (see Exhibit 11-12) for the value-adding activities. The bid price is itemized by setup costs, materials (crushed tungsten, steel, bolts, etc.), imbedding, and conversion. Customers now can see how different specifications impact cost and value. Once agreed to, bid prices reflect the product's value as perceived by the customer.

The results from strategic partnering, TQM and process value analysis, throughput accounting, and decision-focused accounting information have been quite impressive. Lead time dropped from eight weeks to eight days, and defects fell from 25% to one per week. Additionally, the savings in workman compensation premiums paid for the new equipment.

Source: James T. Mackey and Vernon H. Hughes, "Decision-focused Costing at Kenco," *Management Accounting*, May 1993. © The Institute of Management Accountants.

READING LIST*

ABC and TOC: Demmy and Talbott, "Improve Internal Reporting with ABC and TOC," *Management Accounting*, November 1998.

———-: Holmen, "ABC Vs. TOC: It's a Matter of Time," *Management Accounting*, January 1995.

AlliedSignal: Darlington, Innes, Mitchell, and Woodward, "Throughput Accounting: The Garrett Automotive Experience," *Management Accounting*, April 1992.

———-: Coughlan and Darlington, "As Fast as the Slowest Operation: The Theory of Constraints," *Management Accounting*, June 1993.

Baxter Corporation: Noreen, Smith, and Mackey, *The Theory of Constraints and its Implications for Management Accounting* (North River Press), IMA Foundation for Applied Research, 1995.

Bertch Cabinet Manufacturing: MacArthur, "From Activity-Based Costing to Throughput Accounting," *Management Accounting*, April 1996.

Foldcraft Company: Westra, Srikanth, and Kane, "Measuring Operational Performance in a Throughput World," *Management Accounting*, April 1996.

Hofmans Forms Packing: Noreen, Smith, and Mackey, *The Theory of Constraints and its Implications for Management Accounting* (North River Press), IMA Foundation for Applied Research, 1995.

Illinois Tool Works: Tatikonda, O'Brien, and Tatikonda, "Succeeding with 80/20," *Management Accounting*, February 1999.

Ink Creations: Baxendale and Gupta, "Aligning TOC & ABC for Silkscreen Printing," *Management Accounting*, April 1998.

Job costing and TOC: Koziol, "How the Constraint Theory Improved a Job-Shop Operation," *Management Accounting*, May 1988.

Kent Moore Cabinets: Noreen, Smith, and Mackey, *The Theory of Constraints and its Implications for Management Accounting* (North River Press), IMA Foundation for Applied Research, 1995.

Northern Telcom: Sharman, "Time to Re-examine the P&L," *CMA Magazine*, September 1991.

Pricing and TOC: Campbell, "Pricing Strategy in the Automotive Glass Industry," *Management Accounting*, July 1989.

Stanley Furniture: Spencer and Wathen, "Applying the Theory of Constraints Process Management Technique," *National Productivity Review*, Summer 1994.

Toyota: Pine, Victory, and Boynton, "Making Mass Customization Work," *Harvard Business Review*, September-October, 1993.

Western Textile Products: Noreen, Smith, and Mackey, *The Theory of Constraints and its Implications for Management Accounting* (North River Press), IMA Foundation for Applied Research, 1995.

Wharton Manufacturing: Mackey, *Cases From Management Accounting Practice* (Volume 8, Institute of Management Accountants and American Accounting Association), 1992.

*Alphabetic by topic, idea, or company referenced.

CHAPTER 13

Can't We Improve Them All?

Business Process Reengineering, Just-in-Time, and the Journey to Automation

KEY OBJECTIVES:

1	*Measure the opportunity costs of unused capacity.*
2	*Explain business process reengineering, just-in-time, and why organizations are changing to JIT.*
3	*Describe the role for management accounting information in JIT purchasing.*
4	*Calculate the cost of a product made in a JIT cell.*
5	*Prepare a machine uptime report and a continuous improvement productivity ratio.*
6	*Discuss how JIT can improve on-time delivery and complete order filling.*

It was time for another Monday morning meeting. Tommy and Nancy were the first to arrive at the conference room. As they waited for the others, Tommy sipped his hazelnut-flavored coffee and ate his favorite pastry: a large, hot, cinnamon-laced apple fritter.

"You know, I've got to admire Doris for her continuous improvement activities. I actually look forward to these meetings because we have my favorite coffee and pastries. This is a very good way to start the week! I wonder what new ideas we can learn today."

The Need for Business Process Reengineering (BPR)

Nancy gazed out the window at the beautiful spring morning as she ate her maple-iced donut, reflecting on her weekend at the beach and how hard getting into her swimming suit was. "Well, our morning treats are nice, but maybe we should completely change them. As part of my continuous improvement program, I've cut back to only two donuts. But tonight I'm having steak and baked potato smothered in sour cream and real bacon bits. *Sometimes, incremental improvement strategies don't give enough attention to the big picture. They also may not work fast enough in a competitive environment.* Instead of coffee with the fat-adding flavors, decaffeinated herb tea might be better. We also should replace the pastries with wheat germ and skim milk!"

"Yuck! I know you're right, but *radically changing what we've always done is not easy*. In the short run, I'd rather eat this donut than exercise! Of course, in the long run, I'd rather look like . . ."

"Actually, this is very similar to the problem I'm having with my dune buggy. *I've made all the incremental improvements I can*. But when I took it to the beach last weekend, something else always seemed to break down. Maybe it's time for a whole new engine."

BPR compared to continuous improvement

Bob walked into the room, poured his favorite coffee, grabbed a chocolate eclair, and patted his stomach. "I see you've already begun discussing today's topic: should we begin our journey to becoming a world-class organization by using a continuous improvement strategy or **business process reengineering [BPR]**? Employing a continuous improvement strategy, today you install a new carburetor, next week a new transmission, and following that a new radiator. Today I'll stop eating donuts. Next week I'll work on replacing baked potatoes with broccoli. I'm always making small improvements. In contrast, BPR is completely redesigning how work is done. It's like replacing your old engine with a completely new and different one. I suppose I can replace this eclair with dry wheat toast, or I can completely change my diet and start exercising every day. Do I continually make small changes, or do I radically change my lifestyle?

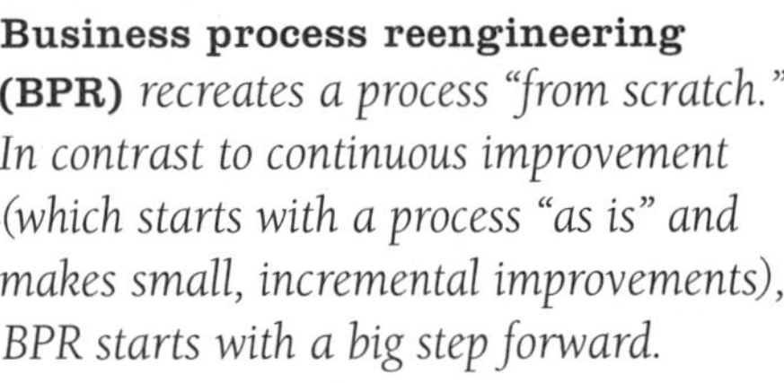
Business process reengineering (BPR) *recreates a process "from scratch." In contrast to continuous improvement (which starts with a process "as is" and makes small, incremental improvements), BPR starts with a big step forward.*

"The Boss would have replaced broken equipment with the same kind of equipment; a very traditional approach. *Now, shorter product life cycles, rapidly changing technologies, and global competition continually force us to consider radically different methods to do our work.* To remain competitive and increase long-term value, we may need a new kind of engine for our dune buggy. BPR doesn't replace an engine with another just like it. Instead, BPR looks for creative new ways to redesign a system."

"O.K. I agree I should get a new engine for my dune buggy. But how do I know what kind to get? I guess this is like the problems we had in our continuous improvement meetings. Our workers are the experts in how they are doing their jobs. However, they may not be experts in how to do their jobs in the best way possible. All too often they tell us, 'Well, this is the way I've always done it.' The implication is, 'So, this must be the best way.'"

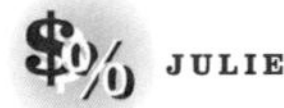

"You're right! We need to do some benchmarking, as discussed in our total quality management [TQM] meeting [Chapter 11]. We've been so involved with trying to improve our processes ourselves, we forgot to look to see if other organizations may be doing similar value chain processes in better ways. Not looking for companies that do the same processes in better ways [external benchmarking] and relying only on ourselves [internal benchmarking] is called 'naval gazing' by some management experts. We need to start thinking 'outside the box.' Johnson & Johnson benchmarked Wal-Mart and Federal Express in its BPR of accounts payable. J & J's average productivity was 7,700 vouchers per person compared to benchmarks of 30,000. By reengineering accounts payable, it projected a $5.9 million annual savings, mainly by reducing personnel from 220 to 76.

"This brings up another issue. BPR is not limited to manufacturing systems [the car's engine]. Cummins Engine [a Fortune 500 diesel engine manufacturer] reengineered its entire value chain, creating a 40% cost and sales price reduction. With BPR, Motorola's Accounting department was able to reduce the time needed to produce monthly financial statements from 40 days to 4 days. The U.S. Department of Defense used BPR to reduce costs by $35 billion. Of course, BPR is not as quick and inexpensive as individual continuous improvement programs. AT&T's global business communications system took about two years to redesign. Bayside

Controls spent $5 million on equipment just to replace a small assembly line of only 35 workers."

KEY OBJECTIVE 1

Measure the opportunity costs of unused capacity.

The opportunity cost of unused capacity

SID

By now, the rest of the grandchildren were seated with their morning treats and ready to work on today's new lesson about how to run the business and create long-term value. Sid interrupted Julie. "Our theory of constraints [TOC] strategy has created another problem which BPR may solve. I call this the 'creeping overhead' problem. Every time we eliminate a bottleneck, we create additional surplus capacity. In other words, we turn a constraint [which has no unused capacity] into a nonconstraint [having unused capacity]. The cost to do this for each constraint is captured in our improvement efficiency ratios [refer to Exhibit 12-16].

"An important benefit from TOC, though, is a change in our focus from cost control to value management. This value orientation raises a question about how to measure the unused [surplus] capacity's cost. Remember, the TQM and continuous improvement cost orientation too often leads to lost jobs and, therefore, TQM failures because workers oppose it. TOC, on the other hand, advocates using our surplus capacity to increase sales."

JULIE

"Through our TOC programs, we've eliminated some constraints in purchasing and production. In addition to a cash cost, this extra capacity also has an opportunity cost. By opportunity cost, I mean the lost contribution margin from not using our productive capacity to its full potential. Look at our three general processes [Purchasing, Production, and Sales in Exhibit 13-1].

Opportunity Cost of Unused Capacity

Processes: / Products:	Unused capacity		
	Purchasing	Production	Sales
Standard homes	25	**20**	30
Custom homes	**10**	15	12

Contribution margin lost	Standard homes	Custom homes
Sales price	$50,000	$100,000
Less: sales discount	(2,500)	0
Net sales price	$47,500	$100,000
Less: variable costs	(20,500)	(43,000)
Contribution margin per house	$27,000	$57,000
x Minimum unused capacity	x **20**	x **10**
Lost contribution margin	**$540,000**	**$570,000**

Exhibit 13-1

"The first step is to determine the unused capacity in each process. Since we make two products, the number of products that can be made with a process's unused capacity may be different. For example, with our current production facilities we can make another 20 standard homes or another 15 custom homes [top panel of Exhibit 13-1].

"Next, calculate the contribution margin for each house [CMU]. I considered two issues. First, think back to our activity-based costing [ABC] discussion [Chapter 9]. Because of overhead allocation problems, we have been overpricing our commodity product [standard homes] and underpricing our specialty product [custom homes]. To sell more standard homes, Bill tells me we will have to discount the sales price 5%. Since we're already underpricing custom homes, Bill does not believe we have to discount them in order to sell more. The other issue is determining which costs are really variable. In our last meeting, we concluded labor is really a fixed cost for us. Labor is a fixed cost because we are not going to continually hire and lay off workers. We've invested a lot of money in training them to make continuous improvements. So, I used the variable costs from our TOC analysis [Exhibit 12-8].

"Finally, multiply each product's CMU by the minimum unused capacity. Why minimum capacity? Look at the standard homes surplus capacity line [in Exhibit 13-1]. With our current sales force, we can sell another 30 homes. But it doesn't make sense to do this if, given our current purchasing staff, we can order materials for only 25. Production, on the other hand, can make only 20 homes with its surplus capacity. So why order materials for 25 homes? This is simply the TOC logic we discussed in our last meeting when we looked at production scheduling. We've eliminated the purchasing and production constraints and moved our current constraint to sales [which is a now a markup pricing policy constraint].

"What does this analysis [Exhibit 13-1] tell us? Without increasing fixed costs, we have enough unused capacity to increase profits $540,000 if we can sell more standard homes, or $570,000 if we can sell more custom homes. As many organizations are discovering, we should consider better management of our surplus capacity!"

SID

"*We cannot continue to create even more surplus capacity by systematically eliminating constraints. Instead of the TOC focus on one constraint at a time, maybe we should look at the entire system and use BPR.* I'm suggesting we redesign the entire production process first and then make continuous improvements to it, rather than accepting the system 'as is' and improving it through a long series of incremental changes."

NANCY

"So, BPR and continuous improvement can work together? It's not an 'either-or' decision?"

Just-in-Time Systems (JIT)

KEY OBJECTIVE 2

Explain business process reengineering, just-in-time, and why organizations are changing to JIT.

BOB

"Yes. It's just a matter of *how* we want to begin. Do we begin with continuous improvement of existing processes, or do we start all over with a newly designed process, and then continuously improve it? In our last two meetings, we looked at *what* to do [TQM] and *where* to begin [TOC]. TOC is a continuous improvement strategy [see Exhibits 12-1 and 12-2]. If we believe it's time to start all over, let's consider just-in-time systems, which is one BPR alternative receiving a lot of attention."

What is JIT?

"Before I explain what JIT is, how do we do things now? The Boss designed Multree Homes using good scientific management principles. Processes are organized into independent departments [functional silos], like sawing, truss-making, plumbing, framing, and painting. Each department is individually evaluated and people are rewarded for efficiency. Direct labor and direct materials usage variances measure this. To illustrate, compare the following information about two workers:

	Standard hours for one product (SQ)	Products made (actual output, AO)	Standard hours allowed (SQA = SQ × AO)	Actual hours worked (AQ)	Direct labor efficiency variance in hours (SQA – AQ)
Alice:	2	10	20	15	+5 (favorable)
John:	2	8	16	15	+1 (favorable)

Alice made 10 products in the same time John made only 8. Alice was more efficient than John. If efficiency is the only performance evaluation measure, people are motivated to maximize their output. The problem is if we don't coordinate processes carefully, people will make too much of the right things or will make the wrong things, just to avoid unfavorable efficiency variances."

"So inventories build up and components [WIP] get lost in the maze. Quality can go down in the quest to make more. Lead times increase and customer responsiveness declines because it gets more difficult to navigate work through all of the specialized departments and the WIP between them."

Push versus pull systems. "We've seen this happen too many times. People producing to meet a schedule is called a **push system**. People maximize their output and push it out of their department. If the next department is not ready for it, though, it's pushed into WIP. On the demand side, if we don't have a buyer for the next house off the line, it gets pushed into finished goods inventory. On the supply side, Purchasing is rewarded for favorable price variances, so they buy in large quantities to get purchase discounts. If production does not need it all now, it also gets pushed into raw materials inventory.

> **Just-in-time** *systems deliver goods or services when they are needed. Products are not made until requested by the customer (internal or external). This is called a* **pull system**. *In a* **push system**, *goods or services are made to meet a production schedule.*

"Compare this to a **pull system**. In a pull system, you cannot make something until the next process needs it. In other words, one goal is minimal inventories. You do not make anything until someone asks for it. **Just-in-time** systems are pull processes. Materials arrive just-in-time for assembly [JIT purchasing systems]. Assembly is completed just-in-time for shipment [JIT production], and the customer receives the product just-in-time [according to his lead time: JIT delivery]."

"This can't work! Fred over in Roofing can't simply ask Carol in Truss-making for another truss whenever he needs it. And Carol cannot go over to Sawing and ask for the 2 × 4's to be cut at that moment. Everyone's busy making something. They cannot stop what they're doing to fill Carol's order."

BOB

"You're right. So to make JIT work, the production process has to be reengineered. Usually, functional silos [welding, sawing, etc.] are replaced with cells. Cells contain all the equipment and people to make something from beginning to end. For example, think about truss-making. Instead of having all the saws in one department and all the nailing machines in another, let's create two cells. Each will be located next to Assembly and have its own saw and nailing machine. One cell makes trusses for standard homes, and the other makes trusses for custom homes. Now we won't have to continually move stock back and forth between departments and WIP storage areas. This will eliminate the nonvalue-added activities and costs associated with moving, storing, and waiting. Now, instead of functional silos, we've created production cells linked directly to our customers. Since we placed one machine from each of the operations into the cell, cell workers are cross-trained to run more than one machine. Let me draw you a picture [see Exhibit 13-2]."

Comparing Traditional and Cellular Manufacturing

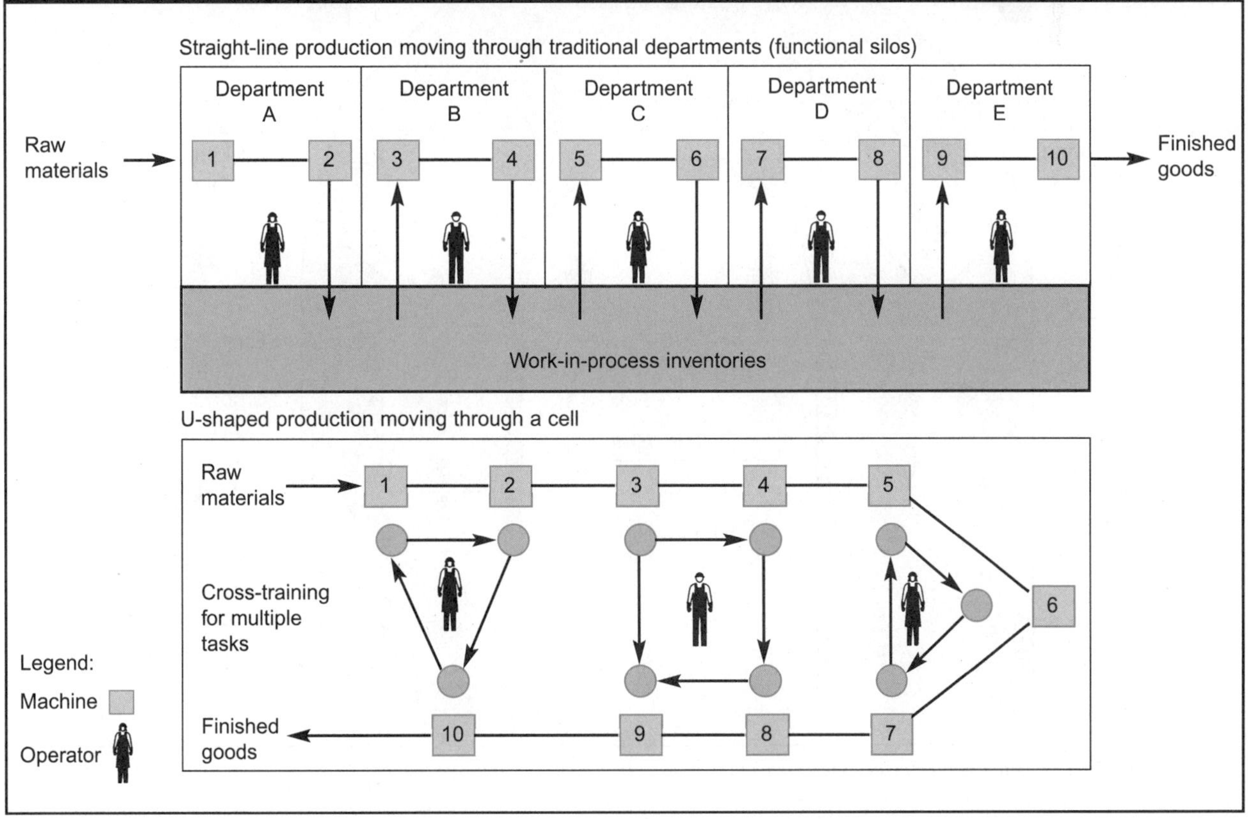

Straight-line production moving through traditional departments (functional silos)

Raw materials → Department A (1, 2) | Department B (3, 4) | Department C (5, 6) | Department D (7, 8) | Department E (9, 10) → Finished goods

Work-in-process inventories

U-shaped production moving through a cell

Raw materials → 1 — 2 — 3 — 4 — 5 — 6 — 7 — 8 — 9 — 10 → Finished goods

Cross-training for multiple tasks

Legend:
Machine
Operator

Source: Adapted from John G. Burch, *Cost and Management Accounting: A Modern Approach*. © 1994 West Publishing Co. Used with permission.

Exhibit 13-2

NANCY

"O.K. But how will I know when that 'just-in-time' moment is? How does the next process 'ask' a preceding process for a component or product? Does it just send the preceding department a card saying, 'Hello. How are you? Wish you were here. Please send me one of whatever you make so I can make whatever I make because my customer [internal or external] wants it now.'?" Everyone chuckled aloud.

"Surprisingly, this is how JIT works. The card is called a kanban. It's an order from the subsequent process or activity to the one preceding it. JIT starts with the customer. To use a TOC analogy, the customer [instead of the bottleneck] is the drum setting the pace for production. The customer buys a product, which signals production to make a replacement. Each process then requests what it needs from the preceding process, all the way back to raw materials suppliers. The amount requested is determined by the size of the kanban containers. Kanban containers allow us to minimize WIP everywhere, to the quantity necessary for the current order. Let me draw you another picture [Exhibit 13-3].

Using Kanban Containers to Control Production Quantities in a JIT Cell

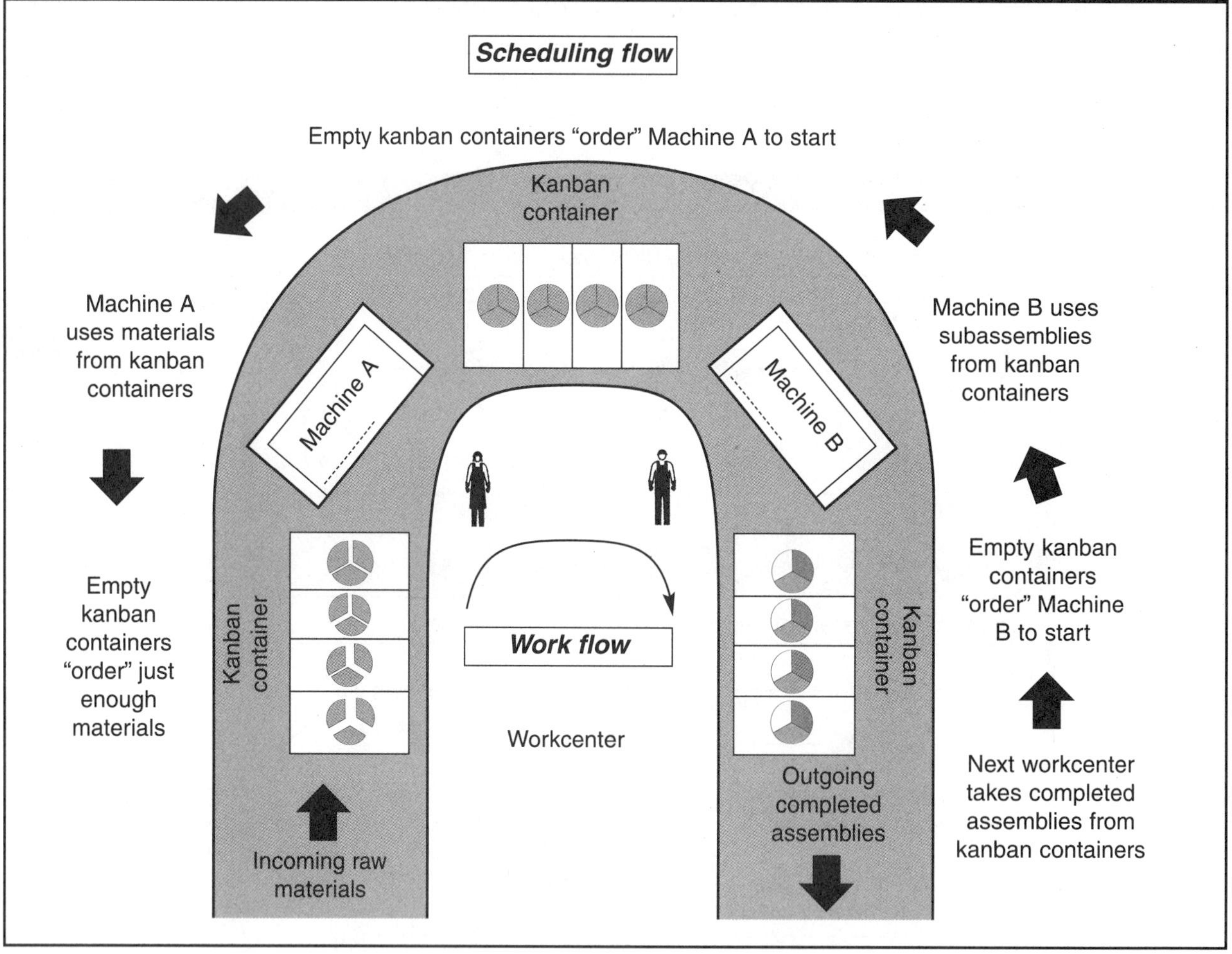

Scheduling flow

Empty kanban containers "order" Machine A to start

Kanban container

Machine A uses materials from kanban containers

Machine A

Machine B

Machine B uses subassemblies from kanban containers

Empty kanban containers "order" just enough materials

Kanban container

Work flow

Workcenter

Kanban container

Empty kanban containers "order" Machine B to start

Incoming raw materials

Outgoing completed assemblies

Next workcenter takes completed assemblies from kanban containers

Source: Adapted from Burch, *Cost and Management Accounting: A Modern Approach*. Used with permission.
Exhibit 13-3

Kanban containers can take many forms. For example, General Motors builds Cadillac front seats in a U-shaped cell. Workers build the seats on workbenches with wheels [their kanban containers], which they move around the ten-meter-long cell."

"I understand! It's like our box of donuts next to the coffee machine. We don't want too many sitting around. Either they'll sit too long in inventory and become stale, or I'll get fat [an unused and not needed inventory of potential energy] eating them all! We should have just enough. If the box becomes empty, that's the signal to Doris to get some more." Doris glanced over to the coffee table and saw the empty donut 'kanban container' Nancy was referring to. Excusing herself from the room, Doris understood Nancy's 'kanban' message.

"I understand the difference between push and pull systems, and how kanbans control production flows. But do we really need a JIT system? New home buyers are not in a big hurry to get their product. We have about a five-month total lead time, and our customers are willing to wait that long for a new home. I don't see how reengineering into a JIT will help us sell more houses and increase our value."

Customer responsiveness and the need for production flexibility. "Good observation! The answer lies in the post-World War II Japanese economic environment in which JIT arose. Japanese re-industrialization was very difficult. Its cities and factories were in ruins. Very little capital and natural resources existed. The Japanese needed to sell in the United States in order to raise large amounts of capital for rebuilding its economy. To sell in the United States, though, they had to understand the U.S. consumer. Marketing mistakes were extremely expensive. If consumer preferences changed, all of the products in American stores and in transit would become valueless.

"To reduce the penalty for product failures, Japanese manufacturers focused on short lead times and flexible processes. This allowed a more effective response to U.S. market changes while minimizing inventories. Toyota often has been credited with the development of JIT. Unlike the huge American automobile manufacturers, Toyota did not have the sales volume and wealth to exploit large-scale, specialized production. Toyota needed the economies of mass production without the volume. Short lead times were accomplished through cellular manufacturing, which eliminated nonvalue-added activities such as moving materials, storing WIP between departments, and waiting for it when needed. Flexibility was achieved by reducing machine setup times and using common parts for different car models. This allowed cells to make related products with only minimal changes in the process [as well as shortening lead times even more]. Toyota could respond quickly to consumer preference changes without the need for large inventories."

"So you're saying as our global economy grows and competition becomes more fierce, we'll have to decrease inventories, reduce lead time, and increase manufacturing flexibility. We can do this for both of our products because I see two types of JIT, one for mass production of commodity products like our standard homes and one for related products ['product families'] like our custom homes.

- For standard homes, we can create a series of linked JIT cells controlled by a kanban system. This will minimize raw materials and WIP throughout the entire process. Our lead time will go down dramatically because we can group activities in order to eliminate the move and wait time between departments.
- We also can create an independent cell for our custom homes. It will need specialized equipment requiring little setup time when changing from one type of custom home to another. This will give us flexibility in responding to changing customer preferences without disrupting standard home production."

JIT is more than a zero inventory system

BOB

"So, on the upside, JIT can reduce inventories by reorganizing work into cells controlled by a kanban-driven pull system. On the downside, JIT is very risky. With no inventories, if something goes wrong anywhere in the value chain the entire chain may shut down. Inventories are buffers between processes so a problem in one department will not cause work to stop in another department. As I see this, it may be more important to have inventories than to eliminate them. JIT may not be right for us!"

JULIE

"O.K. Let's take a look at these issues. You start with a reason for having large inventories. I'll present the JIT response."

BOB

- "We organize work into functional silos so people can specialize. This strategy maximizes their productivity. Because the time it takes to do each activity varies, departments work at different speeds. We need WIP so everyone can keep busy."

  JULIE

  "Look at the comparison of functional departments and JIT cells [Exhibit 13-2]. By putting tasks together into a JIT cell, we can see exactly where these differences are and their magnitude. Eliminating nonvalue-added activities reduces these differences and better coordinates the work flow. The comparison also shows cross-trained workers performing different activities. Keeping busy does not necessarily mean doing one task repeatedly for eight hours a day. In a JIT cell it means, 'When you're done making a part on machine A, go to machine C. If the kanban containers are all full, do maintenance on the equipment and/or learn new skills.'

  "Scientific management believes minimizing activity costs in each department minimizes total cost. If maximizing each department's output is the only 'critical success factor' measured by the accounting system [i.e., cost variances] and the only factor in rewarding performance, large inventories of good and bad products often result. JIT takes a more global perspective on cost management. Coordination and synchronization may provide lower total costs over the long run."

BOB

- "Traditionally, we have believed an acceptable amount of loss [bad products] minimizes total costs. It's just too expensive to eliminate all bad quality. We need large inventories because if some materials or WIP are bad, more good parts will be available to keep everyone working."

  JULIE

  "One lesson we learned from TQM is it's more expensive to make good and bad products than it is to make only good products. Strategic cost management showed us how to use certified vendors in our supply chain to reduce scrap. These are prerequisites for JIT. If we and our suppliers are committed to TQM, large inventories will not be needed. Besides, large amounts of WIP make it hard to identify why defective parts occur. For example, we usually have 10 days of sawed lumber in front of wall assembly. Suppose framers discover some 2 × 4's are cut wrong. When did this happen? Why did this happen? Will they find more bad lumber? Or has the problem already been identified and fixed?"

JACKIE

- "I've got one. Batch-level costs, such as machine setups, are very expensive, which is why we make standard homes in batches of five. The more products we make in a batch, the less our average batch cost per product. We're just spreading a fixed batch cost over more units. This is good because minimizing average product costs means we can lower their sales prices."

JULIE

"Assuming, of course, all the extra products can be sold! Think about TOC and our last meeting. Truss-making was our constraint. All other processes had surplus capacity [they were nonconstraints]. If the nonconstraints each work to capacity, where does all the extra output go? Not through the constraint and to our customers! The extra output ends up in inventory. We can't get back the money we spent until the products are sold. I prefer to keep the cash now and spend it on making products closer to the time they can be sold!

"Also remember, we're reengineering the process into a JIT cell. As part of BPR we want to minimize setup activities and costs. Our ultimate goal is to be able to make one product as cheaply per unit as ten. This will give us the flexibility to satisfy changing customer demands."

JACKIE

- "Let's talk raw materials. Obviously, one way to minimize our product's cost is through purchasing materials as cheaply as possible. Quantity purchase discounts are an important cost savings. We also avoid the risk of future price increases."

JULIE

"That's true. But think of all the nonvalue-added activities associated with large raw materials inventories: receiving, inspection, returns, moving to storage, warehousing, insurance, taxes, moving out of storage, re-inspection, scrap, all the accounting paperwork involved with each activity, and auditing, filing, and saving all that paperwork. You know, an ABC analysis probably will show us the cost of buying in large quantities is greater than having more frequent deliveries directly to the factory from a certified vendor paid through an EDI system [electronic data interchange]. With certified vendors, we also can negotiate long-term purchase contracts to avoid price increases."

BILL

- "Let's talk about finished goods inventories. We've got to have product available when our customers want it!"

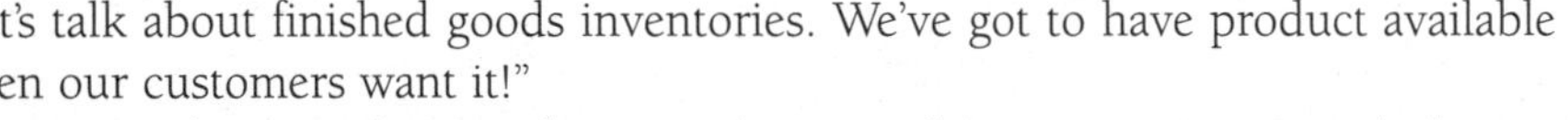

JULIE

"You're right, too! The JIT advocate asks a simple question, 'How much do you really need?' The real issue is customer lead time versus our lead time. In other words, how long does it take us to get a product to the customer? How long is she willing to wait? If the customer's lead time is greater than ours, we can make to order and maintain no inventories. The key is to reduce our lead time to match the customer's. Until we can do that, we'll need some finished goods inventory. How much? If a customer is willing to wait one month for a house, but it takes us five months to make and deliver it, we will need four months of inventory.

"We also need to consider the effects of WIP on our lead time. If we have four months of WIP sitting around, it takes even longer than the actual processing and delivery times to get a home to our customer. We have a new competitive disadvantage because our competitors have shorter lead times, around three months. Customers believe they can change things whenever they want during the first month after they have ordered a home from us! Other customers force us into meeting our competitors' three-month lead time. Both of these problems cause havoc due to all the expediting and rework needed."

As the grandchildren bantered back and forth, Doris summarized the arguments on the white board [see Exhibit 13-4].

Benefits from reengineering into a JIT

JULIE

"JIT is a customer-driven system. The customer pulls the product through the system. Nothing is made, or no service provided, until the customer places an order

The Pros and Cons of Inventories

Reasons for inventories	The JIT alternative
1. Departments are uncoordinated. WIP keeps everyone working.	1. Coordinate work with cells and a kanban system. Cross-train workers to do different tasks.
2. Defective materials and WIP exist. Large inventories provide enough good parts to keep working.	2. Use certified vendors and TQM techniques to eliminate scrap, rework, and defects.
3. We need long production runs (large batches) to minimize the per-unit product cost.	3. Why spend the money now when we can't sell the product? And, by minimizing batch-level costs, we can make one product for the same unit cost as ten.
4. To minimize our materials costs, we need to buy in large quantities.	4. The nonvalue-added costs from the extra inventories makes it more expensive than the more frequent JIT deliveries.
5. Our customers are not willing to wait for a house. We have to keep large finished goods inventories.	5. Instead of maintaining large inventories (which may or may not be exactly what they want), reduce lead time to match how long our customers are willing to wait.

Exhibit 13-4

that triggers kanbans backwards through production. To respond to that order, we need a simple but flexible production process, with short lead times and a commitment to TQM. I see these as JIT's objectives. This will provide the service and quality desired at the lowest cost. *We want to combine the economies of mass production with the benefits of specialty products.* To realize this vision and accomplish our objectives, we need a set of BPR goals. I've created what I call 'JIT's Strategic Planning Matrix' to relate JIT objectives and goals [Exhibit 13-5].

JIT's Strategic Planning Matrix

Vision statement:
Combine the economies of low-variety, high-volume production with the benefits of diversified product lines

Objectives: / Goals:	Short lead time	Flexibility	TQM and continuous improvement	Simplicity
Reengineer for high quality			×	
Reengineer to eliminate nonvalue-added activities	×	×		×
Cellular operations	×	×		×
Eliminate inventories (pull manufacturing)	×	×		×
Minimize setup time	×	×		×
Cross-train workers	×	×	×	
Certified vendors	×	×		×

Exhibit 13-5

Let's consider the benefits each goal has provided to other companies:

- *Reengineer for high quality:* Samsonite's Henin Beaumont plant in France makes hard and soft-sided luggage. Damage was considerable because of all the movement between functional departments. After creating JIT cells, soft-sided damaged luggage decreased from 5% to 1%, and hard-sided 'seconds' went from 2% to 1%. Inspection labor was virtually eliminated.

- *Reengineer to eliminate nonvalue-added activities:* Motorola's portable radio plant reduced lead time from 55 days to 15 days in 1990, and then to 7 days in 1991. Simplifying the process shortens the lead time and increases our ability to respond to changing customer desires. Motorola's pager plant in Boynton Beach, Florida, receives email orders from sales personnel all over the country. Pick-and-place robots provide parts for the special features ordered, and assemblers often complete the order in less than 1½ hours.
- *Cellular operations:* A 1994 survey reported over 40% of small plants [less than 100 employees] and over 75% of larger plants used cells in some phase of operations. Why? We eliminate nonvalue-added activities by bringing together the different activities into one place. Cells are basically a factory within a factory. No more 'send parts to WIP, wait, move to the next department, setup, move back to WIP' . . . [and then repeat this cycle with each department]. Cells simplify production and create available space [increase capacity]. For example, Compaq Computer's Scotland plant increased output per square foot by 16% while decreasing total plant size 23%.
- *Eliminate inventories:* Samsonite's French plant cut lead time from 6 weeks to 1 week. Because of this, only 2 weeks of WIP was needed instead of the original 6-week level. The shortened lead time meant lost sales due to stock-outs were reduced from 25% to 5%.
- *Minimize setup time:* In cells dedicated to making a single product, like a standard home truss cell, equipment does not have to be off-line for setup changes. Setup, or 'get ready,' time is not relevant just to machines. Employing JIT techniques, Motorola's lead time to file patents was reduced from 1½–3 years to 2 months. With nominal setup times in multi-product cells, such as a custom home truss cell, we quickly can change from making one product to another. For example, Ford makes Explorers and Aerostars in the same plant at a rate of 50 per hour in any mix.
- *Cross-train workers:* Anytime we attempt to change something, someone will be threatened. When making small, incremental changes, people may not be able to see where else they are needed in the value chain. All they see is losing their jobs. JIT brings the different activities together into a cell. People are cross-trained to perform multiple activities, including running other machines, and repairing and maintaining equipment. When Cummins Engine reengineered its Accounts Payable department, job security was one of the first issues addressed. JIT should not mean 'jobs-in-trouble.' Its reengineering team offered two pieces of advice: train, train, and train some more; and communication, inside and outside [with the people doing the work and their customers]. USAA insurance and financial services discovered cross-training can be expensive, but worth it, as its agents were more satisfied with their jobs and better able to suggest improvements. Also, by having cell workers trained in all aspects of providing a service or making a product, they are uniquely responsible for product quality.
- *Certified vendors:* Having a few certified vendors operating under long-term contracts and frequently delivering small amounts directly to JIT cells avoids much

of the purchasing, receiving, inspecting, warehousing, and moving activities. Firms realize huge overhead savings from eliminating these nonvalue-added activities. Also, many accounting and recordkeeping activities are eliminated, along with their costs. Lead times are reduced and flexibility increased because, as we change from making product A to product B, we can get the materials needed JIT. I'll say more about this when we talk about JIT purchasing."

"I think I can summarize. When we combine the higher quality from certified vendors with cross-trained and empowered workers, and with streamlined operations, we have a powerful synergy. Intuitively, we know it's less expensive to make commodity products like standard homes, than it is to make specialty products like custom homes. We needed to change how overhead is allocated in our financial accounting-based system to an ABC system in order to see this in our accounting reports. Specialty products increase the variety of activities needed. ABC showed us variety is an important cost driver. *JIT, though, allows us to produce as if we are making only commodity products, even though sales is delivering specialty products. JIT gives us the best of both worlds.* Here's my comparison of traditional systems and JIT characteristics [see Exhibit 13-6].

Process Characteristics Comparison

Traditional systems	JIT systems
◘ Functional departments performing a single activity on all products using single-skilled workers	↳ Cells performing multiple activities on a single product using multi-skilled, cross-trained workers
◘ Each department works at its own pace, maximizes output, and pushes it into WIP, creating large inventories to buffer against uncoordinated production	↳ Production is pulled through the cells with kanbans to coordinate cells and minimize WIP
◘ Acceptable levels of scrap, rework, and rejects (another reason for large inventories)	↳ Commitment to TQM, elimination of scrap and rework (nonvalue-added activities), and no rejects
◘ Uncommitted workers, not involved in continuous improvement, with formal worker-manager hierarchy	↳ Empowered employees involved and rewarded for continuous improvement, and performing many management activities
◘ Large inventories and uncoordinated production results in long lead times (too much moving, storage, waiting, and inspection)	↳ Cellular manufacturing, shorter setup times, and nonvalue-added activity elimination to minimize lead time
◘ Infrequent purchases in large lots from many suppliers to minimize purchase price	↳ Frequent (hourly or daily) JIT deliveries from a few certified vendors using long-term contracts

Note: ◘ means thinking within the box, ↳ means thinking outside the box (JIT is a cellular process flow).

Exhibit 13-6

I guess I've just solved my dune buggy problem. By replacing engine parts one at a time, I've been taking a TOC marketing focus: what improves value the most today? That is, what makes the car go faster? Maybe I should take a JIT engineering focus: what will make the entire engine run more smoothly?"

JIT begins the journey to automation

"I just applied for a new home loan. The bank's loan approval process used to take weeks. I received approval the same day. The whole process is now computerized and done at my local bank by one person. The need to mail documents to another office in a different state, wait for the loan officer to review it, etc., has been eliminated. Everything is transmitted electronically using email. Computerized communication and cross-training one bank employee to do all the activities at his desk [within his 'cell'] have resulted in higher quality, more flexibility, and better customer service."

"What you've experienced, Nancy, is the evolution of JIT into computer-integrated manufacturing [CIM] and a flexible manufacturing systems [FMS]. Of course, you experienced this in the service, not the manufacturing, sector of our economy. Let me briefly explain how JIT leads to CIM and FMS. The first industrial revolution introduced assembly-line production methods and scientific management. This changed our 'cottage industry' into mass production. The second industrial revolution was information-based, caused by the introduction of computers. We may be witnessing a third industrial revolution now with the movement toward CIM and FMS.

Computer-integrated manufacturing (CIM) and flexible manufacturing systems (FMS) are completely automated processes. With CIM, computers control robots, machines, and transportation equipment moving materials and WIP between operations. FMS cells make product families rather than only one product.

"CIM links computer-controlled machine [robotic] cells via automated material-handling equipment [e.g., tote vehicles, conveyor belts]. The entire operation is controlled with computers using local and wide area networks. Here's a picture [Exhibit 13-7].

"CIM can be used in 'long-line cells' mass producing a single product, or in customized FMS cells making a number of related products [a 'product family'] with the same equipment. Because CIM and FMS are entirely automated, they're often called 'lights out' factories. [No lights are needed because no people are in them.] JIT makes this possible because it brings together the different activities and processes in a value chain. Processes are no longer organizationally and physically separated.

"Ingersoll-Rand's Roanoke, Virginia, FMS provides a good example. It can assemble 500 parts into 16 products without any significant setup changes. Toshiba's FMS in Ome, Japan, can make 9 word processor varieties in one cell and 20 different laptop computers in the next one. When AT&T computerized its billing center, 19,000 service order paper copies were no longer needed. This saved $42,000 per month. Levi Strauss & Company's FMS makes custom jeans on demand for its Levi's® Only stores.

"CIM and FMS are responsible for much of the Japanese economic growth globally. As early as 1991, Japan had over 2,500 industrial robots per 100,000 workers, leading the world. The U.S. was 10th with about 200 robots per 100,000 workers. Japan had about 400,000 FMSs; but the United States had only 45,000. One of the largest FMS producers, Okuma Corporation, sells 14 FMSs in Japan for every one sold in the United States."

"Automating processes has been greatly enhanced by enterprise resource planning [ERP] software. In 1996, $7 billion was paid to software development companies like SAP, Oracle, and PeopleSoft for ERP programs. 1997 spending was projected to be $10 billion."

"So what you're saying is customers and technology are becoming more sophisticated every day. To remain competitive and maintain our long-term value,

Computer-Integrated Manufacturing (CIM) Cells

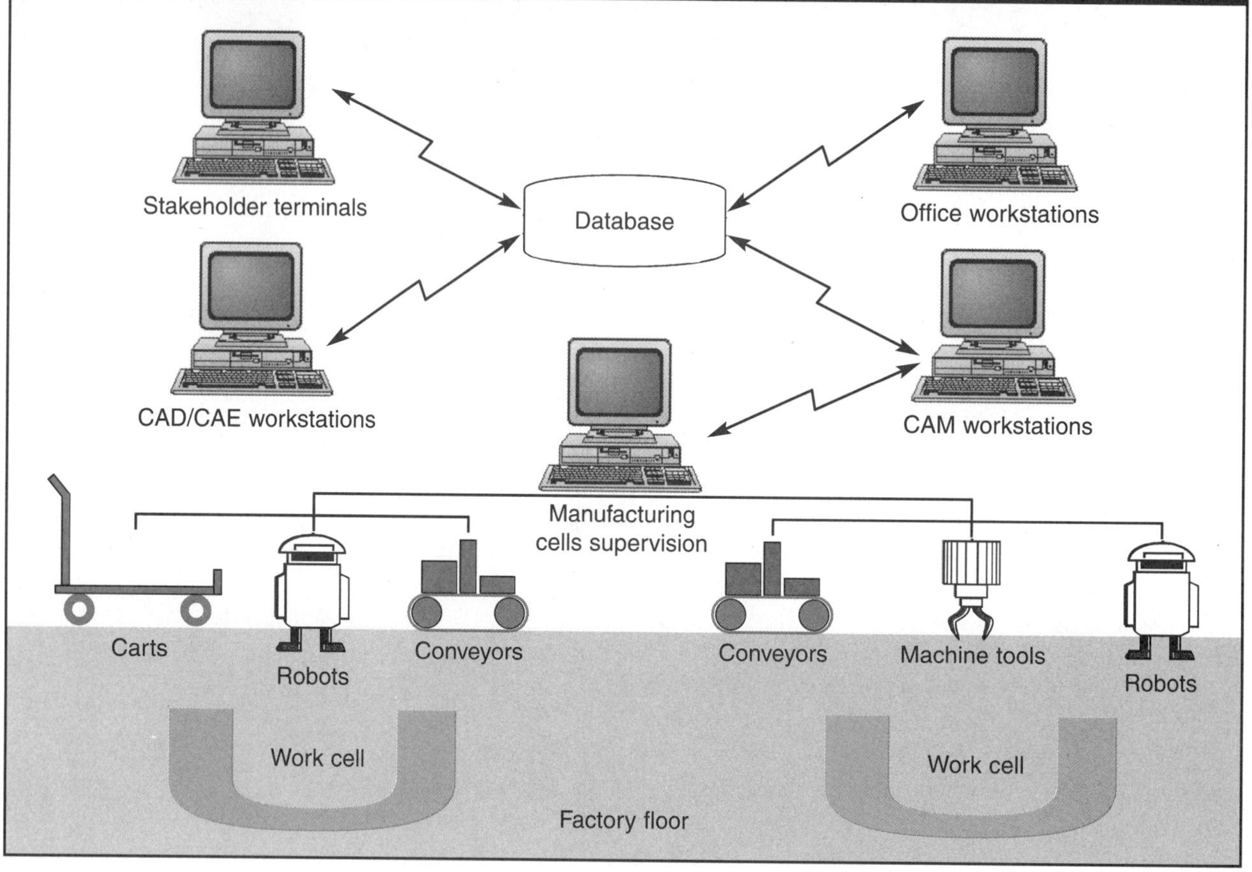

Stakeholder terminals
Database
Office workstations
CAD/CAE workstations
CAM workstations
Manufacturing cells supervision
Carts
Robots
Conveyors
Conveyors
Machine tools
Robots
Work cell
Work cell
Factory floor

Source: Adapted from Burch, *Cost and Management Accounting: A Modern Approach*. Used with permission.
Exhibit 13-7

we should consider reengineering how we do things and then continually improve them. *Starting our TQM quest with small continuous improvements, as advocated by TOC, may not be responsive enough to competitive and customer pressures.* This raises two issues. First, we need a better understanding of how JIT works in purchasing, production, and product delivery. Second, what management accounting information can we give our people to help them do their jobs better in a JIT environment?"

KEY OBJECTIVE 3

Describe the role for management accounting information in JIT purchasing.

JIT Purchasing

BOB

"Think of how we've evolved with our lumber suppliers. In the beginning, we inspected every piece of lumber. Developing a better working relationship with suppliers, we're now able to inspect only samples from each shipment, rather than everything. Ultimately, though, wouldn't it be nice not to have to do any materials inspection?"

How does it work?

"Many of the purchasing activities we now consider necessary are classified as nonvalue-adding in JIT. Thus, we reengineer this process to eliminate them. A JIT purchasing system has four characteristics [summarized in Exhibit 13-8].

Value Chain Process Activities for JIT Purchasing

1. Use only a few certified suppliers
2. Orders, deliveries, and payments are made under long-term contracts
3. Materials arrive JIT and are delivered directly to manufacturing cells
4. Suppliers are paid periodically and automatically

Exhibit 13-8

"First, we'll use only a few certified vendors, as we discussed in our strategic cost management meeting [Chapter 10, strategic partnering]. In our ABC meeting [Chapter 9], Tommy discussed the difficulties in getting technical support because we had so many suppliers. Having that support is one advantage of strategic partnering."

"Yes! Ford jointly designs car seats and interiors with suppliers such as Lear Seating. This strategic partnering has reduced vehicle costs over $700. And I've seen tech support work both ways. Toyota operates a supplier counseling program. When Garden State Tanning couldn't meet the delivery schedules for Lexus production, Toyota worked with them to improve operations, instead of replacing them with another leather seat supplier. Toyota staff spent about two years at Garden State Tanning."

"Second, to make it worth their while, we'll sign long-term supply contracts with vendors, as Toyota did with Garden State Tanning. We'll guarantee them our orders and a fixed price if they deliver according to our schedule [JIT] and guarantee their product's quality. Mercedes Benz cut its suppliers from 1,000 to 100 for its new sports utility vehicle being built in Vance, Alabama. It even got 5% price cuts by offering 5-year contracts.

"Third, we'll provide the kanban containers so vendors can deliver just what we need directly to the cells. So they know when to make deliveries, we'll set up a computer link with our scheduling system. When a kanban is initiated at the end of our process, vendors will know it along with the lead time to deliver the materials. Wal-Mart does this with its suppliers. Its suppliers have to install software linking to Wal-Mart's cash register ['point-of-sale'] and inventory systems. It's the suppliers' responsibility to keep Wal-Mart's shelves stocked."

"Our suppliers won't do this! We can't get them to cooperate now. All we do is negotiate for the lowest price. In return, we have to purchase in large quantities and allow them to make infrequent deliveries days early or late."

"Suppliers deliver on a JIT basis all the time in the food service industry. Both in retail grocery and restaurant businesses, baked goods, dairy, produce, and fish are received daily, and sometimes more frequently. Why do our purchasing agents spend all their time getting multiple bids and negotiating for the lowest price? Because they're evaluated primarily with a materials purchase price variance. Their only motivation is to get the lowest price. Realizing our traditional accounting system was a little narrow-sighted here, we developed some different ABM measures in our strategic cost management meeting [Chapter 10]. Now we have a vendor performance index, and ratios for on-time delivery and complete order filling.

"With certified vendors and long-term contracts, we can get JIT deliveries. The on-time delivery window at the Toyota plant in Georgetown, Kentucky, is one hour. The Marysville, Ohio, Honda plant receives parts every three hours.

"Fourth, we'll not only have computer links with our suppliers, we'll also link with freight carriers and banks. Using this EDI system, our initial production kanban triggers our cells, suppliers, freight carriers [for delivery scheduling] and the bank [for electronic funds transfer (EFT) payments]. With EDI, R.J. Reynolds lowered purchase order costs from $75–$100 per purchase order to under one dollar each! EDI allows Ryder Truck Systems to coordinate deliveries between 300 suppliers and the Saturn plant in Spring Hill, Tennessee. EDI and EFT are here to stay. In 1996, the U.S. government passed the Debt Collection Improvement Act. Now all government vendors have to be paid by EFT. The greatest push for this will come not from manufacturing, though, but rather from the banking service sector. Over 60 billion checks are written each year in the United States, costing banks more than $50 billion to process.

"Neat system, huh? Very simple, designed with the KISS principle in mind ['keep it simple, stupid']."

Management accounting for JIT purchasing

JACKIE

"This can't possibly work! We need purchase orders to verify suppliers are delivering the right materials at the correct prices. We need receiving memos verifying receipt of the correct amounts, inspection reports verifying the materials are good, and invoices so we have a bill to pay. Without this paperwork protection, how can I perform my stewardship role [protecting the firm's assets]? Our auditors will never go along with this. I'll be shot, just like Slim the cowboy thought he would be by his auditor!!"

JULIE

"You're missing the point, Jackie. JIT views all the financial accounting system paperwork for purchases as nonvalue-adding. We no longer need to negotiate a purchase order for each shipment. Nor do we need to solicit three bids for each purchase. Shipments are ordered by kanban with amounts limited by the size of the kanban containers. How do we know if we receive the correct materials at the right time, and if the materials are good quality? Simple—if we don't, the product does not get made! If the product doesn't get made, the supplier doesn't get paid. KISS! As products leave the cell, our EDI system can signal the bank to pay the supplier.

"*The critical point is accounting no longer is needed for activity control. JIT moves the responsibility for operational control to the shop floor, to the people doing the work* [clan and bureaucratic controls versus accounting controls]. We don't need the vendor performance measures [vendor performance index, on-time deliveries, complete order filling] we developed in our strategic cost management meeting [Chapter 10]. If materials are late, incomplete, or of poor quality, the cell cannot make its product. The line shuts down. Do we need cost variances? Not the traditional materials price variance. It always will be zero as suppliers automatically are paid at the long-term contract price.

"However, we may need our 2nd generation ABC system [see Chapter 9's Reality 101 and Chapter 11, Improving value-added activities]. Cost variances result from production problems. They translate the effect of production problems into dollars. To continuously improve, we need to know the cause of the variance. If a cell shuts down because of late or incomplete deliveries, or a product is rejected due to poor material quality, we want to know the cause and cost of that problem. Second generation ABC cost variances report this information. I'll show you how we can use this type of accounting information when we talk about JIT production."

JACKIE

"I guess I can go along with this. However, I'm still skeptical. We're talking about a truly radical change in how we do things. We have a lot to learn while reengineering and implementing this new JIT system. Until we have matured, it may be prudent to continue tracking the vendor performance measures."

JULIE

"O.K. I agree. *JIT offers the potential to eliminate much of the management accounting information used for day-to-day operations control.* However, this will not happen overnight. *Until we feel control adequately exists on the shop floor, it makes sense to continue monitoring key value chain activities such as vendor performance.*"

JIT Production

"Let's move on to manufacturing. We already know how a JIT cell works, whether staffed with people or robots. As we just saw with purchasing, *JIT significantly changes the role of management accounting information. Control is now on the shop floor. Accounting information does not drive operating decisions.* JIT also changes the cost accounting system. We should discuss this first."

Backflush cost accounting systems

"The cost accounting system supplies the costs of raw materials, WIP, and finished goods to value these inventories on the balance sheet, and to value cost of goods sold [COGS] on the income statement. This is its role in financial reporting. With JIT, we have no raw materials inventory. WIP is not significant because it's limited to the size of our kanban containers. So the only information the financial reporting system needs is the cost of finished goods."

NANCY

"Wow! If we have no unfinished production at the beginning of the year and no unfinished production at the end of the year, all of our costs went into completed products. If all our products have been sold, which is what JIT's pull system is all about, we simply can charge all production costs to COGS! Regardless of which resources we are paying for [materials, labor, or overhead], just debit COGS and credit cash."

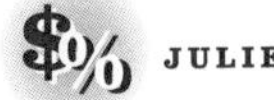
JULIE

"Basically, you're correct. It's a little more complicated, though, because we want monthly income statements. We'll need an average product cost. We can use our standard absorptive manufacturing cost for this and still keep the costing simple. *As we incur production costs, charge them to [debit] WIP. When we finish a product, take the standard cost out of WIP [credit] and move it to COGS [debit].* [Exhibit 13-9 illustrates the backflush system.]

"This is called a **backflush cost accounting system** because costs are flushed out of WIP when the product is completed. It works backwards, just like a pull system. The sale of a product trig-

Backflush cost accounting systems *can be as simple as a two-journal entry system. Charge (debit) costs into WIP when incurred, and remove (credit) costs from WIP (and debit into COGS) when products are completed (using the product's standard cost).*

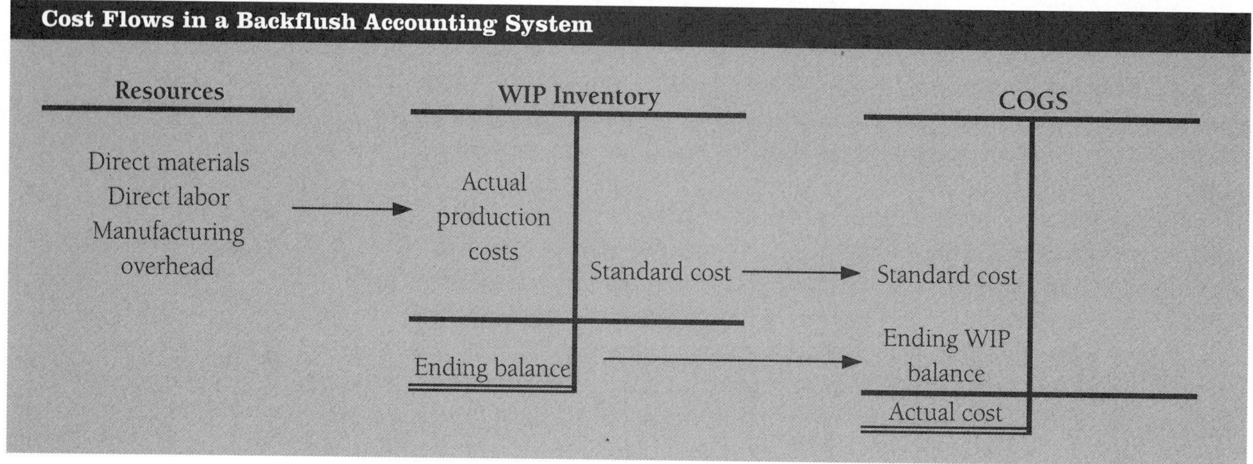

Exhibit 13-9

gers the making of a replacement product backwards through the cells [all the way to our suppliers]. Similarly, the completion of a product triggers the journal entry to take the costs of making that product [backwards] out of WIP. Whenever we want to create an income statement, we just multiply the number of completed products by their standard cost and make one journal entry moving the costs of completed products from WIP to COGS. KISS!

"At the end of the year, if everything was under control, the total actual costs charged into WIP [debited] should equal the sum of the standard costs taken out of WIP [credited]. The WIP account should have a zero balance. In reality, we probably will have some surplus debit or credit balance in WIP. Hopefully, this is an insignificant amount we can write off to COGS.

"I've just given you a very general and brief overview. At year-end we should not have a WIP balance, since a JIT system does not have unfinished production at the beginning or end of the year. Technically, we will have an ending balance, though, equal to the cost of WIP in the kanban containers and all production cost variances [if we have any]. We also may maintain some minimum levels of raw materials and finished goods just to be on the safe side. These are details we can leave to the accountants.

"Ron Turk, the controller for Harley-Davidson, popularized this system when it converted to JIT production in the 1980s. About 65% of the cost accounting activities involved labor accounting [including overhead allocations], but after JIT labor accounted for only 10% of total manufacturing costs. Using the Pareto principle [80:20 rule] from our TOC meeting, the KISS principle, and the TOC realization that labor is a fixed cost of the cells, Turk eliminated all the nonvalue-added accounting for labor. Hewlett-Packard also eliminated its labor reporting after converting to JIT and saved 100,000 journal entries every month!"

Planning (budgeting) for a JIT cell

NANCY

"What information do we need from the management accounting system to help people do their jobs better? How can it help our people make better planning, operational control, and evaluation decisions?"

Budgeting truss cell and standard homes truss costs. "What we've learned about TOC provides us with some interesting insights into JIT budgeting. Here's the budget I've created for the standard homes truss cell and the truss standard cost [Exhibit 13-10].

JULIE

Standard Homes Truss Cell Budget

Activities	Resources	Amounts	
Unit level:	Direct materials	$53	per truss
	Direct technology	2	per truss
Total unit-level costs		**$55**	**per truss**
Costs incurred in the cell			
Batch level:	none	$0	per year
Cell level:	Cell labor	62,400	
Allocated product line level:	none	0	
Allocated facilities level:	Supervision, factory administration	500	
	Building (landscaping, security, etc.)	1,100	
Total cell costs		$64,000	per year
÷ Production forecast		÷ 800	per year
Standard truss cell cost		**$80**	**per truss**
Standard absorptive truss cost		**$135**	***per truss***

Exhibit 13-10

KEY OBJECTIVE 4

Calculate the cost of a product made in a JIT cell.

TOC assumes the only significant variable unit-level costs are materials. This assumes we treat machinery operating costs as fixed. In our situation, though, we don't run the machinery all the time. ABC shows us the variable machinery cost, which is called direct technology. So we have two variable costs for a truss, totaling $55 per truss. I took these from the traditional costing comparison to TOC [see Exhibit 12-6].

"We have no batch costs. All we make in this cell is standard home trusses, so we don't have to continually set up the machines as we used to when we made some standard trusses and then some custom trusses. Remember, TOC said, 'Schedule truss production to maximize throughput.' With separate JIT cells for standard and custom home trusses, we don't have to switch back and forth.

"On the cell level, using our TOC thinking again, cell labor is a fixed cost. The total cell labor budget is $62,400.

"We have no product line manufacturing costs to allocate to the cell. On the facilities level, though, we have two. Supervision and administration are allocated based on the time these people spend on truss cell activities. Building costs are allocated based on the square footage of the truss cell to the whole factory. Here, again, I'm using some ABC ideas. The two facilities-level costs total $1,600 per year.

"We're planning to sell 100 standard homes. At 8 trusses per house, the cell should make 800 trusses. I divided this into the total fixed cell cost of $64,000 per year to get the average budgeted cell cost per truss [the standard truss cell cost = $80]. I then added the unit-level variable cost to the average fixed cost per truss to get the standard absorptive truss cost of $135 [$55 + $80]. Now we have a budgeted cost for the cell, and for its product."

Budgeting truss cell and custom homes truss costs. "Budgeting for the custom homes truss cell is a little trickier. In this cell, we make different truss sizes depending on the particular custom home being built. Different trusses need different amounts of time to make. *Thus, I use time in the cell as the cost driver for its fixed costs.* Here are the numbers for the custom homes truss cell [Exhibit 13-11].

Custom Homes Truss Cell Budget

Activities	Resources	Amounts	
Unit level:	Direct materials	$53	per truss
	Direct technology	2	per truss
Total unit-level costs		**$55**	**per truss**
Costs incurred in the cell			
Batch level:	none	$0	per year
Cell level:	Cell labor	62,400	
Allocated product line level:	none	0	
Allocated facilities level:	Supervision, factory administration	500	
	Building (landscaping, security, etc.)	1,100	
Total cell costs		$64,000	per year
÷ Cell operating time		÷ 1,600	hours per year
Standard truss cell cost		**$40**	**per hour**
Standard absorptive truss cost	*$55 per truss* +	*$40*	*per hour*

Exhibit 13-11

"To keep the numbers simple, let's assume all custom home trusses have the same unit-level variable costs as a standard home truss, and the cell costs are the same as the standard homes truss cell [$55 per truss and $64,000 per year from Exhibit 13-10]. To determine how much to charge a truss for cell costs, I divided the $64,000 annual cell costs by the cell's annual operating time [1,600 hours]. The factory is open 250 days a year, and 6.4 hours per day are available for making trusses. The other 1.6 hours per day is used for employee breaks, setup, cleanup, repairs and maintenance, and continuous improvements [learning new skills]. This creates an average cell cost of $40 per hour. The truss's cost becomes $55 per truss + $40 per hour in the cell. Because we make different products in this cell and they require different amounts of time, I need a cell rate per hour."

Operating decisions and performance evaluation

TOMMY "I like your idea of looking at individual cells. *In well-established, 'mature' JIT cells, activities are controlled by the cell workers.* They control production volume [keep the kanban containers full, but don't make any more], maintain and repair the cell's equipment, and learn new skills to continually improve. I've summarized what's expected of them on a day-to-day basis [see Exhibit 13-12]."

What Do We Want Cell Workers To Do?

1. Produce just enough at the right times (i.e., keep the kanban containers full)
2. Improve quality (eliminate rejects and rework)
3. Increase efficiency (reduce lead time—time in the cell—use surplus capacity profitably)
4. Reduce overhead support (learn how to do maintenance and repairs, quality control, etc.)
5. Become more flexible (cross-train to learn all jobs in cell, make different products)

Exhibit 13-12

NANCY

Controlling production volume. "Oh! We can run our traditional standard cost system [from the Chapter 6 meeting] and calculate materials and labor usage variances, and variable overhead efficiency [usage] variances, for each cell."

JACKIE

"No we can't! If we use a backflush system, we don't account for the costs of each cell separately. All costs go into one overall WIP account when incurred [when we begin production in the first cell] and come out of WIP when the product is finished [leaves the last cell]. If we don't have actual costs for each cell, we cannot calculate its cost variances!"

JULIE

"Well, we can modify the backflush system to trace costs up to the cell we want variance information about. To do this, set up two WIP accounts. The first will track costs up to cell 3. We'll charge [debit] actual costs through cell 3 into this account, and take out [credit] the standard cost through cell 3 when the product leaves it. This standard cost will be charged into [debit] the second WIP account for cell 4 through the end. When the product leaves the last cell, take out [credit] the product's total standard cost from the second WIP account.

"Cell 3 is called a trigger point. Each WIP account has actual costs going into it for that portion of the production process. Standard cost is taken out. The difference between actual and standard cost can be broken down into the cost variances for that part of the process. With two trigger points [cell 3 and the last cell] we can calculate two sets of variances: one set for the process through cell 3, and one set for the process from cell 4 to the end.

"I saw the Hewlett-Packard computer terminal plant in Roseville, California, do this. While touring the plant, I noticed three long racks about half-way through the process. A computer monitor displayed some production data. It had a sign attached with the words 'Trigger Point.' I jokingly asked my guide, 'Where's the gun?' She pointed to the Accounting department. Then she explained. They originally anticipated many problems in the second half of the production process. The racks were extra kanban containers half-way down the line. They allowed production in the first half to continue when problems occurred in the second half so the entire line would not shut down. I asked why the racks were empty. She replied they had solved the problems and the accountants removed this trigger point from the backflush system.

"We have another problem with trying to use traditional cost variances. Let's say we get monthly cost variance reports for each cell. By setting up a trigger point at the end of each cell, we create a process cost system. Instead of having a separate WIP account for each department, as in a traditional process system, we have one for each cell. *Traditional cost variance theory works like this.* The cell gets its monthly report. It investigates any unfavorable direct labor usage variance. It tries to prevent the underlying problem from happening again. Notice the assumption in this theory: *the accounting system [i.e., the cost variance report] initiates problem investigation [control].*

"How does control work in a JIT system? A customer wants a product, but can't get it. The kanban container at the end of the last cell is empty. So, we increase kanban container sizes to keep production going and immediately investigate the problem. Once the problem has been solved, which is a long time before a cost variance report is delivered, kanban container sizes are reduced to their original levels. *People initiate control when problems happen. They don't wait for a cost variance report to tell them about their problems.*

"A variation of this idea is used for continuous improvement. Once we have all the cells running smoothly, let's start reducing kanban container sizes until the line has a problem. Wherever a problem occurs is where our constraint is and where we should place our next continuous improvement program."

TQM and JIT. "The second set of control activities [in Exhibit 13-12] concerns TQM. Our first goal is to eliminate rejects and rework. For this goal, cost variance information is helpful. How serious is the quality control problem in our new truss cell? Here's the cost variance report for the first week [Exhibit 13-13].

Truss Cell Cost Variance Report

Cost variances: Problem	Cause	Materials	Labor	Direct technology	Total costs
Lumber cut wrong	Dull saw blade	$15	$12	$3	$30
Renail a truss	Nailing machine out of alignment	1	5	1	7
Rejected 8 trusses	Operator error—wrong size	436	400	12	848
Nailing machine breakdown	Lack of maintenance		20		20
Totals		$452	$437	$16	$905

Traditional cost variances reported for each resource.

2nd generation ABC cost variances reported for each problem.

Exhibit 13-13

"Instead of just reporting traditional variances, like the $452 unfavorable materials usage variance, cell workers coded what it cost them to correct problems according to problem type and cause. This is a 2nd generation ABC system, similar to the one designed for Ditch Witch's new cylinder cell [also see the CCSSCo example in Chapter 9's Reality 101]. We had four problems last week. Three weren't very important [$30 due to bad lumber cuts, $7 renailing a truss, and $20 fixing the nailing machine], but one problem was important. A kanban order for one standard home [8 trusses] had to be rejected because the trusses were the wrong size. To prevent this problem from recurring, we redesigned the kanban form so the workers can more easily [and correctly] read it."

"Now wait a minute! I thought we weren't going to keep detailed time records. It looks like cell workers are still going to be filling out time reports for accounting!"

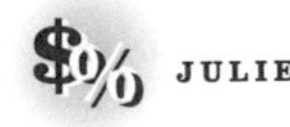

"I hope not! They don't have to track all their time, just the time on exceptional activities, like quality problems. And I hope this system will be needed only while we transition into JIT. In mature cells, I don't expect any serious problems. We shouldn't have significant cost variances, and a backflush system should work well. Very little time tracking should be needed. As workers are learning how to run the cell, though, we'll need to know where our problems are and their significance. As we discussed in our TQM meeting [Chapter 11], cost variances reported by quality problem will help us identify our TQM priorities."

Efficiency and surplus capacity usage. "The third item on our cell workers' 'to do' list [Exhibit 13-12] is to constantly improve efficiency. If efficiency is increasing, cell workers are making the product faster. This means lead time [cycle time] is going down. Lead time is time in the cell. We also should see the cell's lead time efficiency [LTE] ratio increasing as workers discover and eliminate other nonvalue-added activities. I'd like to install big-screen monitors in the cells that report the lead time on each kanban order. This way, the workers can continuously monitor their productivity. Accounting can prepare LTE ratios on demand for the cells."

"Coleman's [the camping products manufacturer] JIT conversion was prompted by the need to eliminate nonvalue-adding activities. In the early 1990s, it was losing market share to Rubbermaid and Igloo. Many of the constraints to improving were in its policies and incentive system. By eliminating those constraints, Coleman was able to motivate its workers to continuously improve. Now that our continuous improvement programs have created surplus cell capacity, how do we encourage cell workers to use it profitably?"

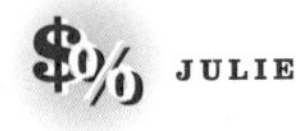

"The TOC throughput idea may help. Let's look again at the standard homes truss cell costs [Exhibit 13-10]. All the costs in the cell are fixed [$64,000 per year]. The only incremental cost of making another truss is $55. Now, if the cell has surplus capacity, selling trusses to other home builders for a price greater than $55 will create positive throughput. In other words, any price above the unit-level variable costs will generate additional contribution margin."

"To motivate cell workers and sales personnel to find new markets for our surplus capacity, let's offer them a percentage of the extra contribution margin they create [a profit-sharing bonus]!"

"Do we have any surplus capacity in the standard homes truss cell? How can it be calculated? We have to be careful because we don't want workers to create surplus capacity by not doing other activities like equipment maintenance and quality control."

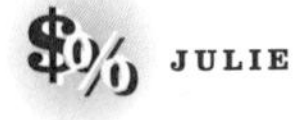

"I agree! We can measure surplus capacity for any time period. I'll do it for this year. The cell's capacity is limited by some constraint. First, what's our constraint?"

"Well, we can run the machines 24 hours a day, 365 days a year, less time for repairs and maintenance. But we're not working three shifts. We work only 8 hours a day, and we're not open on weekends or holidays. If we had more sales, we could use the equipment more to meet the extra demand. I think our real constraint is labor. We need three people in the cell to meet our sales forecast. Here's how I calculated our surplus capacity [Exhibit 13-14].

Truss Cell's Surplus Capacity			
Work days per year			
Days factory open*	(52 weeks x 5 days) - 10 holidays =	250	days per year
Less: vacation time	2 weeks per year =	(10)	
Work days per person per year		**240**	**days per year**
Work hours per day			
Hours per day cell is available to work		8.00	hours per day
Less: downtime	Setup and cleanup	(0.25)	
	Breaks	(0.50)	
	Repairs & maintenance, continuous improvements/new skill learning	(0.85)	
Production time available		**6.40**	**hours per day**
Surplus cell labor			
Total production time available (capacity)	3 people x 240 days x 6.4 hours per day =	4,608	hours per year
Less: production forecast	100 standard homes x 8 trusses x 5 hrs/truss =	(4,000)	
Surplus capacity		**608**	**hours per year**
Surplus cell capacity	608 hours ÷ 5 hours per truss =	***121***	***trusses per year***

*If the factory is open 52 weeks + 1 day, everyone gets an extra holiday.

Exhibit 13-14

"The cell can make another 121 trusses with the labor time available. This is enough for 15 standard homes. If we have no other constraints to making and selling 15 more homes, our first priority should be to make these trusses. Our second priority for using this surplus capacity should be eliminating constraints in other areas of the plant. For example, if framing labor is the constraint, truss cell workers can be cross-trained to do framing. Saturn negotiated with the United Auto Workers union to allow workers in one area to move to other bottleneck areas as needed. Our third priority should be finding outside markets for trusses. The market will set the maximum price we can charge other builders for our trusses. Our incremental costs [$55 in Exhibit 13-10] set the minimum price. This is simply the special order pricing analysis we did in our incremental CVP meeting [Chapter 7].

"Over time and as circumstances change, we can change these numbers. For example, we may not need as much time per day for repairs and maintenance or learning new skills in the future. Through continuous improvements, the standard labor hours needed [5 hours per truss] should decrease. Adjusting our standards as we continue to improve is called kaizen costing. We discussed this in our TQM meeting [Chapter 11]."

Reducing overhead. "We also want cell workers to eliminate the need for overhead departments such as Repairs & Maintenance and Quality Control. Cell workers should be trained in equipment maintenance and repairs, as well as process inspection. What role can our management accounting system play here?"

"If they do a good job on equipment repairs and maintenance, the machinery should be usable for 6.4 hours each day according to Bob's analysis [Exhibit 13-14]. One ABM measure we can use is the **machine uptime ratio**. Here's an example bar chart for last week [Exhibit 13-15].

JULIE

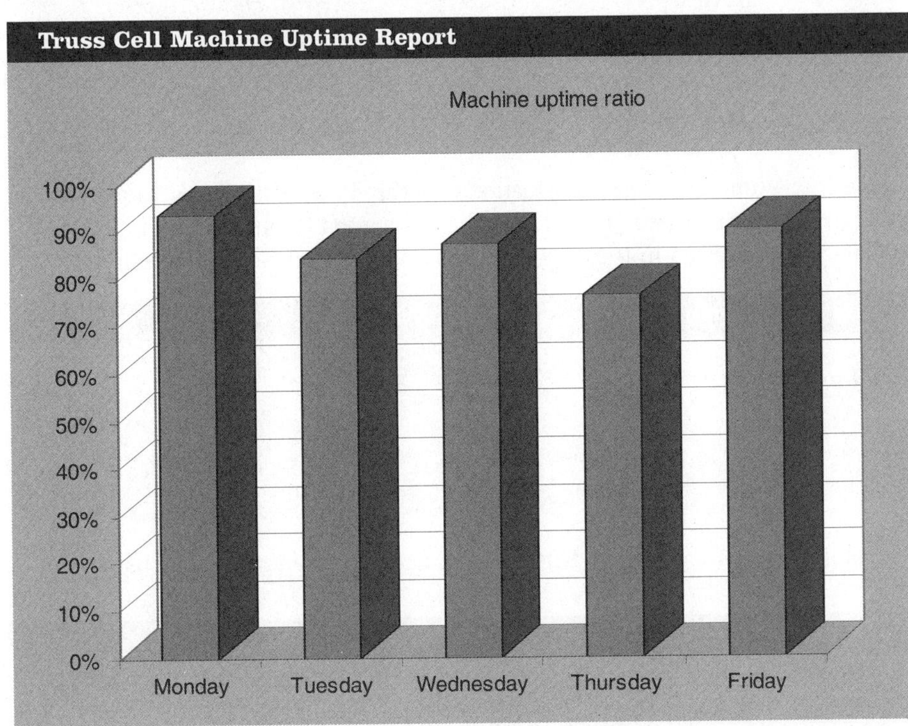

Exhibit 13-15

Machine uptime is simply the percentage of time the equipment is operational. To illustrate this, look at Thursday's ratio. The saw was 'down' [not usable] 1½ hours of the 6.4 hours it should have been available. It was down 23% of the day's work time. It was usable ['uptime'] only 77% of that day. Our goal is to have a 100% machine uptime ratio every day."

The ***machine uptime ratio*** *measures the percentage of time a machine is available to do work.*

Flexibility, cross-training, and continuous improvement. "I see how continuous improvements can be much easier in a JIT cell, as compared to other management and production environments we've considered. Until now, we've accepted the production process as it is and attempted small continuous improvements to it. In other words, we started by taking small steps. With JIT, though, we start with one huge step, business process reengineering. By redesigning how work is done, in one step we eliminated the nonvalue-added activities and created processes to improve quality. Levi Strauss, for example, cut lead time from 6 days to 7 hours while reducing defects through its BPR into cells.

TOMMY

KEY OBJECTIVE 5

Prepare a machine uptime report and a continuous improvement productivity ratio.

"We still want to continually improve, though. Motorola set some impressive continuous improvement goals after it implemented JIT. Every five years, lead time should be one-tenth of what it was. Defects should be reduced to one-tenth of beginning levels every two years. How can we motivate cell workers to continually improve?"

JULIE

"We can motivate them in two ways. First, let's place a big bulletin board in each cell that tracks who has learned which skills and the effect on the cell's kaizen standards. It could look something like this:

Person	Skill learned	Change in standard truss cost
Juanita	Saw blade replacement	$1.00 reduction
George	Nailing machine maintenance	$2.25 reduction
Chen Li	Improved setup techniques	$0.75 reduction

Second, I'll summarize this information monthly in a **continuous improvement [CI] productivity ratio**. This relates the reductions in our standard costs to the dollars we've invested in learning new skills. The formula looks like this:

Continuous Improvement Productivity Ratio

$$\textbf{CI productivity ratio} = \frac{\textbf{Savings created by CI}}{\textbf{CI program cost}}$$

$$= \frac{\Delta \textbf{ Standard cost allowed from improvements}}{\textbf{CI program cost}}$$

[Exhibit 13-16 uses our three truss cell workers information to demonstrate this.]

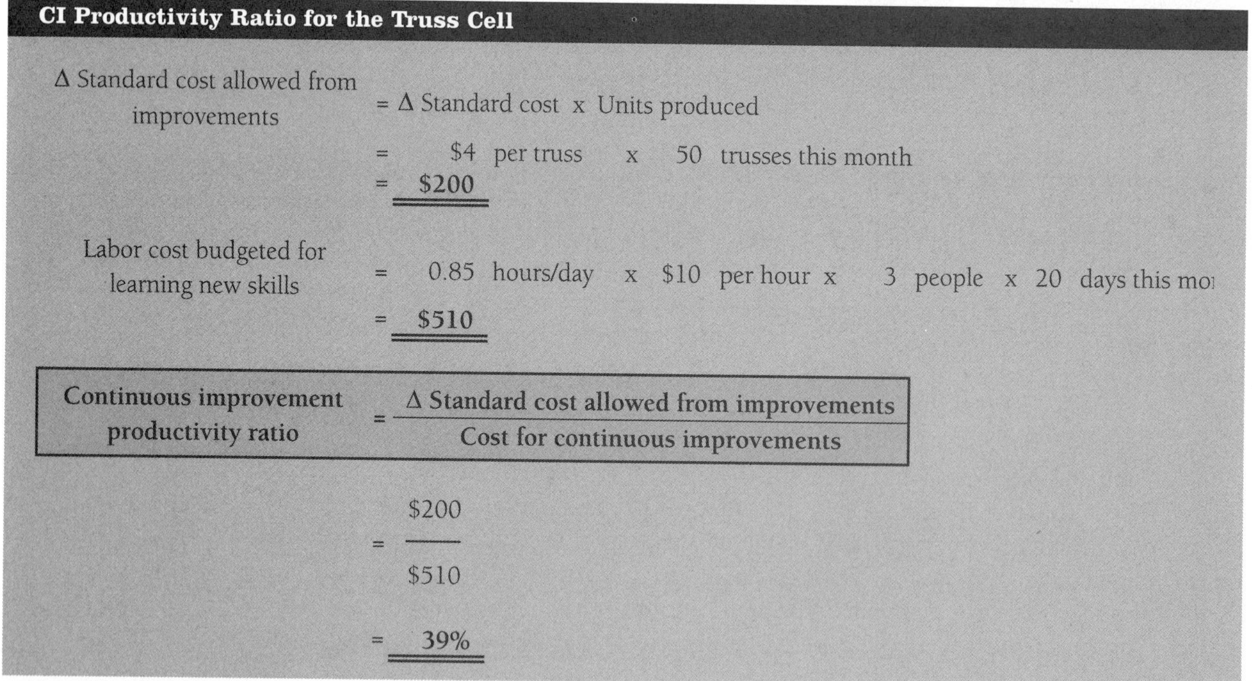

CI Productivity Ratio for the Truss Cell
Δ Standard cost allowed from improvements = Δ Standard cost x Units produced
= $4 per truss x 50 trusses this month
= $200
Labor cost budgeted for learning new skills = 0.85 hours/day x $10 per hour x 3 people x 20 days this mo
= $510
Continuous improvement productivity ratio = Δ Standard cost allowed from improvements / Cost for continuous improvements
= $200 / $510
= 39%

Exhibit 13-16

Our three cell workers learned new skills that reduced our truss cost by $4 per truss. We should change our standard cost to reflect this. This is how kaizen costing works. Of course, these improvements are not free. The cost of these improvements equals the labor time we allowed workers to learn these new skills. If any other incidental costs were incurred, such as going to a training seminar or purchasing manuals, these costs should also be added to the denominator.

*The **continuous improvement (CI) productivity ratio** is the savings created by continuous improvements as a percentage of the cost of those improvements.*

"The 39% CI productivity ratio tells us for every dollar we invested in truss cell continuous improvements this month, our profits increased by 39¢. It's kind of like a return on our investment, similar to the ROI measure we created for investment center performance evaluation [in Chapter 8]. It's better, though, because this savings lasts for many future time periods."

TOMMY

"As with giving workers a bonus for finding profitable ways to use the cell's surplus capacity, let's share some of this extra profit with them! This is called gainsharing. A 1997 IMA report stated companies with gainsharing programs average annual improvements of about 20%. The report also stated over 3,000 American firms have these incentive programs, including Champion International, Harley-Davidson, ITT, Kaiser Aluminum, and Rockwell International. Gainsharing motivates workers to learn skills that increase our value. And it avoids the problem of people learning skills just to get pay increases, even though the skills don't improve operations.

"From an ethical perspective, I think we have to do this. An important way to increase the firm's value is through increasing our workers' value. Cross-training and new skills development, coupled with employee empowerment, should improve worker satisfaction. Happy workers should be more productive. They also should be more motivated to continuously improve. This is what we want. So, if we reward it, they will want to do it. Remember, what gets measured gets done. Here's one way we can motivate goal-congruent behavior."

JIT Delivery

KEY OBJECTIVE 6

Discuss how JIT can improve on-time delivery and complete order filling.

SID

"Ultimately, we want everyone thinking about how they help improve total [global] company performance. We want to use JIT to break out of the pattern of focusing just on a particular task. People need to think 'outside the box.' Therefore, JIT does not organize work into a series of isolated tasks [functional departments or 'silos']. What's driving our evolution to JIT? It's the three objectives of quality, service, and cost."

BILL

"The one objective we haven't discussed yet is customer service, specifically product delivery. Thinking again about our strategic cost management meeting [Chapter 10], our goals should be 100% on-time delivery and 100% complete order filling. When we discussed these two ABM customer performance measures in that meeting, on-time means delivery the day we promised. I think we need to continue measuring these two ratios. But how can JIT help us to do this better and faster?"

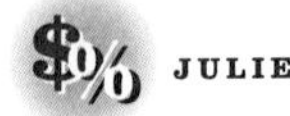
JULIE

"Well, Sid suggests we think strategically. Strategic partnering with our customers is critical to JIT delivery. Consider Procter & Gamble's partnering with Wal-Mart. P&G has a direct computer link to Wal-Mart's inventory system. It's P&G's responsibility to have the right merchandise delivered in the right quantities, just-in-time. And, what did one of my favorite rock groups, Aerosmith, do? They released their 1994 hit, 'Head First,' on CompuServe! Instead of buying a CD, I just downloaded it to my personal computer."

"Delivery speed is perhaps the most critical factor in long-term value, especially in multinational firms and markets. Obviously, delivering faster than our competition creates value. In the mid 1990s, Cadillac management believed 10% of its sales were lost because of long delivery lead times.

"Many companies have discovered speedier delivery also drives lead time reduction and better quality. Red Lobster used JIT principles in assigning a team of waiters to a specific dining area. They were responsible for all aspects of dealing with the customer. Besides eliminating cashiers [which saves $12 million a year], customer service speed increased, as did customer satisfaction."

"Sounds good! Can we summarize how JIT helps us create value throughout our value chain? Let's write down our ideas [Exhibit 13-17]."

JIT, Management Accounting, and Continuous Improvement

Value chain process	How JIT can help	How management accounting helps
Purchasing	1. Certified vendors 2. Guaranteed material quality 3. Guaranteed material prices 4. Kanban container-sized JIT deliveries to minimize inventories 5. EDI ordering, shipping, and payment	1. Strategic measures during early JIT life cycle development (on-time delivery, complete order filling, vendor performance index) 2. Problem costing with 2nd generation ABC cost variances
Production	1. Reengineer to eliminate nonvalue-added activities through cellular design 2. Reengineer for high quality by training cell workers for quality control 3. Kanban scheduling to minimize WIP 4. Minimize setup times for flexibility 5. Employee empowerment and training for equipment maintenance, multiple jobs, and continuous improvements	1. Lead time and LTE ratios 2. TQM information (defect rates, scrap rates, tracking quality-caused cost variances) 3. Kaizen standards for target costing achievement and continuous improvement measurement 4. Machine uptime ratio and CI productivity ratio
Delivery	1. EDI ordering, shipping, and payment 2. Minimize inventories to difference between customer lead time and our lead time	1. Customer performance measures: on-time delivery, complete order filling

Exhibit 13-17

KEY OBJECTIVES SUMMARY

"Let's see if I have good notes from this meeting.

1. Measure the opportunity costs of unused capacity.

"Since our last meeting, I've made some constraint-eliminating improvements to my word processing business. They have created extra capacity I can use to make more money. I can accept another 10 word processing jobs or another 5 spreadsheet jobs a month. Here's my calculation of the opportunity cost of not using this surplus capacity [Exhibit 13-18].

Opportunity Cost of Unused Capacity

	Word processing	Spreadsheet jobs
Net sales price	$25	$40
Less: variable costs	(15)	(15)
Contribution margin per job	$10	$25
x Surplus capacity	x 10	x 5
Lost contribution margin	**$100**	**$125**

Exhibit 13-18

Even though I hate spreadsheets, I should look for these jobs because they're more profitable than the word processing jobs.

2. Explain business process reengineering, just-in-time, and why organizations are changing to JIT.

"BPR is redesigning a system. It's like a complete engine overhaul versus replacing one part at a time as it breaks. Continuous improvement is a lot of continual small steps. BPR is one big step. It is not an 'either-or' decision. After starting with BPR, continuous improvement programs can be more focused, quicker, and less expensive.

"JIT is a system methodology. It begins with receiving materials only when needed. Thus, little raw materials inventory is necessary. Materials are delivered directly to work cells. If raw materials inventories are not needed, all the costs associated with them are nonvalue-adding. Eliminating these activities streamlines our system [reduces lead time and increases customer responsiveness] and decreases overall cost from the customer's point of view.

"By relocating different machines and activities from functional departments into a cell, all the nonvalue-added activities and costs of moving WIP from an activity, storing, waiting, moving to the next activity, inspecting, and continual setup changes are eliminated. Production becomes coordinated. Eliminating WIP inventories further reduces our costs and lead times, and increases customer responsiveness.

"Until our lead time is less than or equal to the customer's [time he or she is willing to wait for a house], we will need finished goods inventory. With JIT, however, we'll need only enough finished goods to cover this time difference. JIT is a pull system. Cells do not make products unless the next department [or customer] requests them. The request is called a kanban. The amount needed determines the size of the kanban container. Cells make only enough to fill up their kanban containers, thus controlling the amount of inventory.

"Not having extra inventory can cause the whole system to stop if a serious problem occurs. To avoid this, JIT emphasizes quality in materials, WIP, and equipment. Cell workers are trained to assure the quality of their work, and to maintain and repair their equipment. They also are cross-trained to do all the tasks within the cell [and possibly other cells].

"Why are so many firms reengineering to JIT? To simplify operations, shorten lead times, improve operations and product/service quality, and to be more flexible in response to the more international and sophisticated markets we all now must live within. The most important long-run, value-creating reason, however, is JIT facilitates the evolution to fully automated, computer-controlled systems [CIM and FMS].

3. Describe the role for management accounting information in JIT purchasing.

"One of our JIT objectives is simplicity. In purchasing, we'll reduce the number of suppliers to a few certified vendors. With guaranteed long-term contracts and fixed material prices, they will be motivated to make JIT deliveries and ensure material quality. We'll supply the kanban containers so they will deliver the right quantities. We'll even guarantee the most prompt payment possible, EFT through an EDI system. EDI will allow us to coordinate customer orders, kanbans, shippers, suppliers, and bankers. This evolution to a virtually paperless purchasing and accounting process will increase efficiency and effectiveness while reducing costs.

"What role does management accounting information play in JIT purchasing? As we're implementing JIT, we will be learning a lot! During this transition, it's probably prudent to continue reporting vendor performance, on-time deliveries, and complete order filling. We also may want to create a 2nd generation ABC cost variance system that reports variances according to their cause. Bad quality or missed deliveries can have serious consequences, and we will want to know the costs of these problems. Through time, supplier reliability will cease to be a concern. In mature JITs, management accounting information about purchasing activities may not be needed.

4. Calculate the cost of a product made in a JIT cell.

"While you were at lunch, I reengineered my word processing business. I now have two cells, one for word processing jobs and one for spreadsheet jobs. I did the computer upgrades based on my TOC analysis, so each cell has its own computer and printer. I hired Albert at $10 per hour to do the spreadsheets. I'm paying myself $10 per hour. We can each work 100 hours a month.

"Word processing jobs are all the same. I won't accept any jobs that are too small or too big. This allows me to use an estimated average variable cost in my job and cell cost analysis [see Exhibit 13-19].

"Spreadsheet jobs are completely different, however, so I've calculated a cell charge per hour for bidding and costing these jobs [see Exhibit 13-20].

"My minimum [break-even] price for a word processing job is $52. If I can get anything above this price, I'll make more than $10 per hour. I'll bid spreadsheet jobs at $4.00 each plus $12.50 per hour of Albert's time. If he thinks a job will take 2 hours, my break-even price will be $29.00. If I can get more, I'll make a profit from Albert's work!

Word Processing Cell Budget

Activities	Resources	Amounts	
Unit level:	Paper	$2	per job
	Pick-up and delivery	0	per job
Total unit-level costs		**$2**	**per job**
Costs incurred in the cell			
Batch level:	none	$0	per month
Cell level:	Cell labor	1,000	
Allocated product line level:	none	0	
Allocated facilities level:	Rent	200	
	Miscellaneous	50	
Total cell costs		$1,250	per month
÷ Anticipated number of jobs		÷ 25	per month
Standard cell cost		**$50**	**per job**
Standard absorptive job cost		***$52***	***per job***

Exhibit 13-19

Spreadsheet Cell Budget

Activities	Resources	Amounts	
Unit level:	Paper	$4	per job
	Pick-up and delivery	0	per job
Total unit-level costs		**$4**	**per job**
Costs incurred in the cell			
Batch level:	none	$0	per month
Cell level:	Cell labor	1,000	
Allocated product line level:	none	0	
Allocated facilities level:	Rent	200	
	Miscellaneous	50	
Total cell costs		$1,250	per month
÷ Cell operating time		÷ 100	hours per month
Standard cell cost		**$12.50**	**per hour**
Standard absorptive job cost	*$4 per job*	*+ $12.50*	*per hour*

Exhibit 13-20

5. Prepare a machine uptime report and a continuous improvement productivity ratio.

"The new spreadsheet program is giving us a lot of trouble. It's a shame it came installed on Albert's new computer as part of the operating system. To track the extent of our problems, I prepared a machine uptime report for this week [Exhibit 13-21].

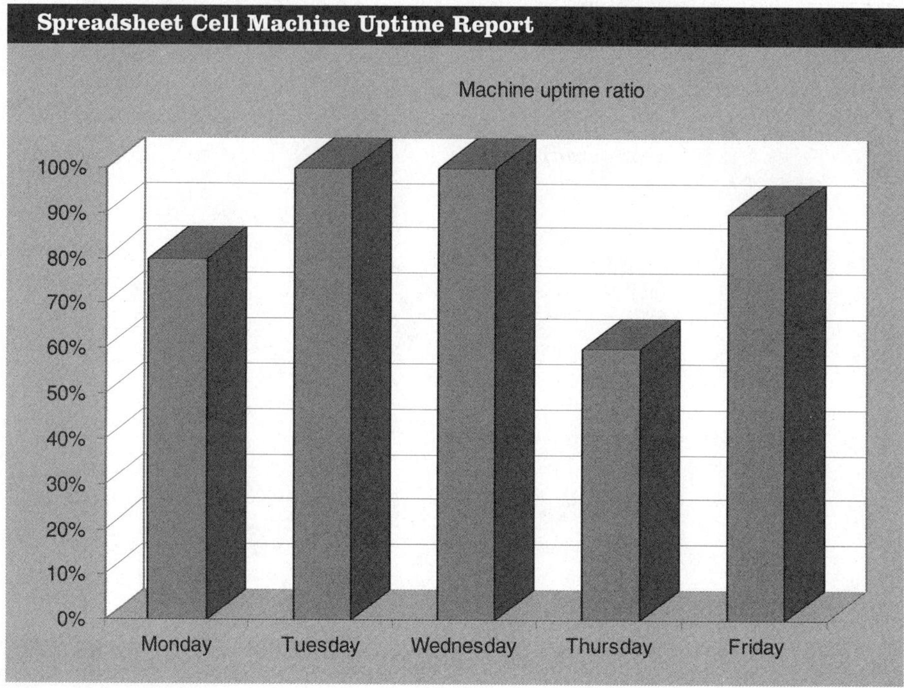

Exhibit 13-21

Albert works 5 hours a day, 5 days a week. On Monday, he was down 1 hour. Tuesday and Wednesday were O.K. Thursday, due to problems with a more complex job, he decided to reload the program. This took 2 hours [40% of his time: 60% uptime ratio]. Friday, he still had to tinker with the program, costing us another ½ hour.

"We discovered many problems could have been solved if Albert had a manual for the software. None came with the software, and the Help program isn't all that good. So, I spent $10 on one. We figure this will reduce each job's cost an average of $0.50. He should be able to finish another 10 jobs this month. Here's the return on this investment [the continuous improvement productivity ratio in Exhibit 13-22].

"The good news is I'll continue to realize this savings month after month with no additional investment!

6. Discuss how JIT can improve on-time delivery and complete order filling.

"Through strategic partnering, and especially EDI, suppliers can provide goods and services to manufacturers much faster. Similarly, manufacturers can supply merchandisers just-in-time. Albert is a great worker, but a little scatterbrained. Too often, he's forgotten to make copies of all the spreadsheets for a customer's job. He's also not very punctual in making deliveries. To fix these problems, I only accept jobs that can be transmitted electronically to the customers. Using email to receive

CI Productivity Ratio for the Spreadsheet Cell

$$\Delta \text{ Standard cost allowed from improvements} = \Delta \text{ Standard cost} \times \text{Units produced}$$
$$= \$0.50 \text{ per job} \times 10 \text{ jobs this month}$$
$$= \$5$$

$$\text{Computer manual cost} = \$10$$

$$\text{Continuous improvement productivity ratio} = \frac{\Delta \text{ Standard cost allowed from improvements}}{\text{Cost for continuous improvements}}$$

$$= \frac{\$5}{\$10}$$

$$= 50\%$$

Exhibit 13-22

their data and instructions, and to deliver the completed jobs, I've been able to eliminate late deliveries and incomplete output."

SID

"It looks to me like Doris has this JIT thing figured out! What do you think, Bob? Should we promote her to vice president of manufacturing?"

BOB

"I don't think you want to do that, Sid, until you reengineer our food supply for these meetings. You see, I won't bring the donuts!"

REALITY 101

Reengineering in Accounting and Finance

The Institute of Management Accountants (IMA) includes many member interest groups. In 1997, the Cost Management Group surveyed its members about reengineering projects in accounting and finance. Sixty percent had current reengineering projects, with over half having 2 to 5 projects in progress. Projects were in the planning stages for another 17% of the companies. The remainder believed reengineering should be done in their organizations.

When asked to rank their activities on a scale of 0 (intolerable service) to 10 (world-class service), overall averages were between 4.6 and 6.0, supporting a need for reengineering. These are shown in Exhibit 13-A1.

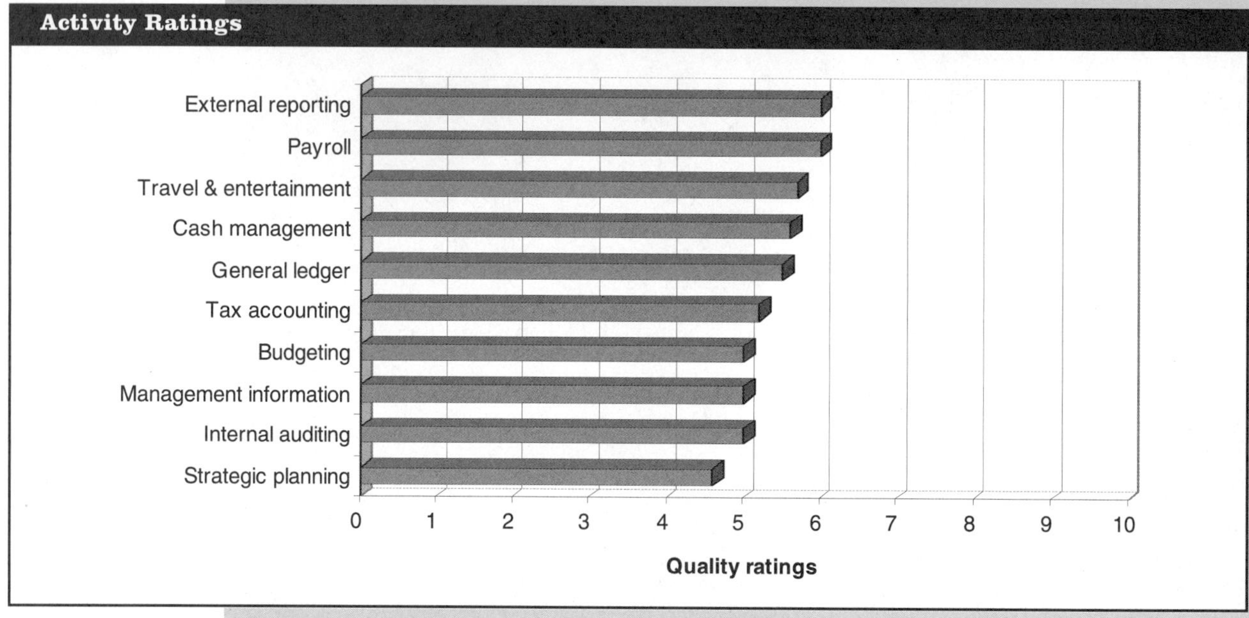

Exhibit 13-A1

The reasons given for reengineering projects included:

Productivity improvements	79%
Cost cutting	74%
Improving processes	65%
Customer satisfaction	57%
Competition	50%
Profit	49%
Quality	45%
Reducing headcount	25%
Ordered by top management	20%

The tools used in reengineering are shown in Exhibit 13-A2.

Reengineering projects were the second-most common improvement projects behind computer system upgrades (73% engaged in upgrade projects). Most members believed reengineering would be successful (66%), with 33% commenting that it was too soon to know. Were the projects successful to-date? Only 30% said "yes," while 60% said it was too early to say. Of the 10% classifying their programs as failures, the most important reason was lack of computer sophistication (83%). Employee resistance influenced 33% of the failures. Other reasons included lack of realistic goals, other higher priority projects, lack of staff, and lack of top management support.

In its 1998 survey, reengineering projects again declined (66% in 1996, 60% in 1997, 49% in 1998), although the number of companies planning new projects increased, as did those who believed their firms should do more reengineering.

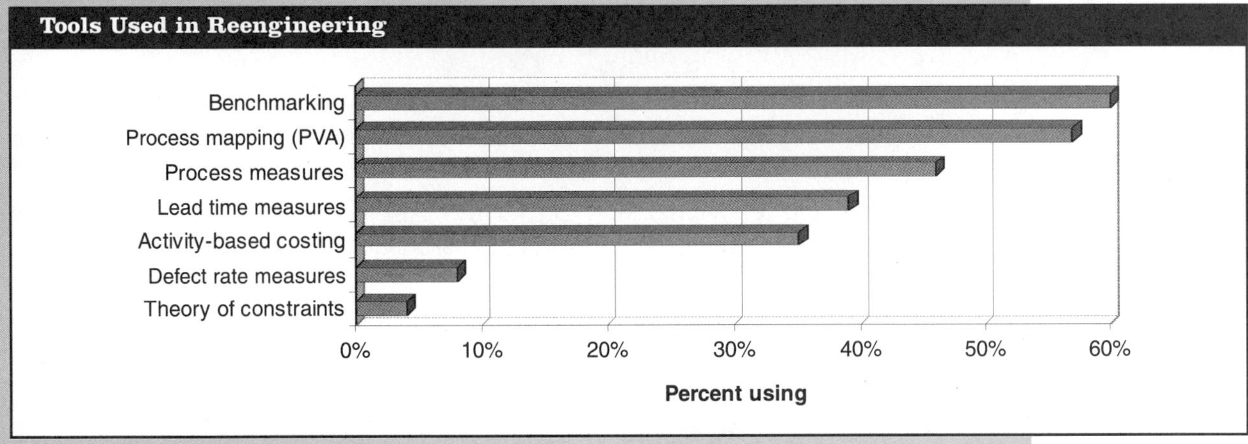

Exhibit 13-A2

Success rates also increased, as did the beliefs that ongoing projects would be successful. Interestingly, accounting reengineering priorities changed. Cost accounting system reengineering projects surpassed financial systems, accounts receivable and payable, and travel and entertainment.

Source: *Cost Management Update*, June 1997, July–August 1998. © Institute of Management Accountants.

READING LIST*

Aerosmith and CompuServe: Landis, "Aerosmith Jumps onto Info Highway 'Head First,'" *USA Today*, June 15, 1994.

AT&T's billing center automation: Hodby, Thomson, and Sharman, "Activity-Based Management at AT&T," *Management Accounting*, April 1994.

AT&T's Global Business Communication System reengineering: Steward, "Reengineering: The Hot New Managing Tool," *Fortune*, August 23, 1993.

Bayside Controls: Mehta, "Cell Manufacturing Gains Acceptance in Smaller Plants," *The Wall Street Journal*, September 15, 1994.

Cadillac: Stern, "Cadillac Will Test Distribution Method to Cut Delivery Time and Dealer Stock," *The Wall Street Journal*, August 16, 1994.

Cellular manufacturing survey: Mehta, "Cell Manufacturing Gains Acceptance in Smaller Plants," *The Wall Street Journal*, September 15, 1994.

Check processing vs. EFT: Bleakley, "Electronic Payments Now Supplant Checks at More Large Firms," *The Wall Street Journal*, April 13, 1994.

CIM and robots, international comparisons: Steward, "The Information Age in Charts," *Fortune,* April 14, 1994.

Coleman: Dumaine, "Earning More by Moving Faster," *Fortune,* October 7, 1991.

Cummins Engine: Klimas, "Reengineering in the Real World," *Management Accounting,* May 1997.

Department of Defense: Morevec and Yoemans, "Using ABC to Support Business Process Reengineering in the Department of Defense," *Journal of Cost Management,* Summer 1993.

Ditch Witch: Thomas and Mackey, "Activity-Based Cost Variances for Just-in-Times," *Management Accounting,* April 1994.

ERP: Brown, "The Best Software Business Bill Gates Doesn't Own," *Fortune,* December 29, 1997.

Gainsharing: Goodfellow, "Why Gainsharing is Growing in Popularity," *Cost Management Update,* Institute of Management Accountants, August 1997.

Harley-Davidson: Turk, "Management Accounting Revitalized: The Harley-Davidson Experience," Brinker, ed., *Emerging Practices in Cost Management* (Warren, Gorham & Lamont), 1990.

Honda: see Toyota citation.

Ingersoll-Rand: Dilts and Russell, "Accounting for the Factory of the Future," *Management Accounting,* April 1985.

Johnson & Johnson: Carr, *Cases in Management Accounting, Volumes 10 and 11,* Institute of Management Accountants, 1997.

Levi Strauss: "The Global Economy: Who Gets Hurt?" *Business Week,* August 10, 1992.

Lexus and Garden State Tanning: Bamford, "Driving America to Tiers," *Financial World,* November 8, 1994.

Mercedes-Benz: Woodruff and Miller, "Mercedes' Maverick in Alabama," *Business Week,* September 11, 1995.

Motorola: Main, "How to Win the Baldrige Award," *Fortune,* April 23, 1990. Henkoff, "Keeping Motorola on a Roll," *Fortune,* April 18, 1994. Bylinsky, "The Digital Factory," *Fortune,* November 14, 1994. Cherry, "Reengineering: Harnessing Creativity and Innovation," *Journal of Cost Management,* Summer 1995.

Oracle: see ERP citation.

PeopleSoft: see ERP citation.

R.J. Reynolds: Kessler, "Fire Your Purchasing Managers," *Forbes,* October 10, 1994.

Ryder Truck and Saturn: Henkoff, "Delivering the Goods," *Fortune,* November 28, 1994.

Samsonite: Noreen, Smith, and Mackey, *The Theory of Constraints Management and its Implications for Management Accounting* (The North River Press), Institute of Management Accountants, 1995.

SAP: see ERP citation.

Toshiba: Stewart, "Brace for Japan's Hot New Strategy," *Fortune,* September 21, 1992.

Toyota: Raia, "JIT Delivery: Redefining 'On-time,'" *Purchasing,* September 13, 1990.

*Alphabetic by topic, idea, or company referenced.

CHAPTER 14

How Can We Control the Change Process?

Capital Budgeting and the Balanced Scorecard

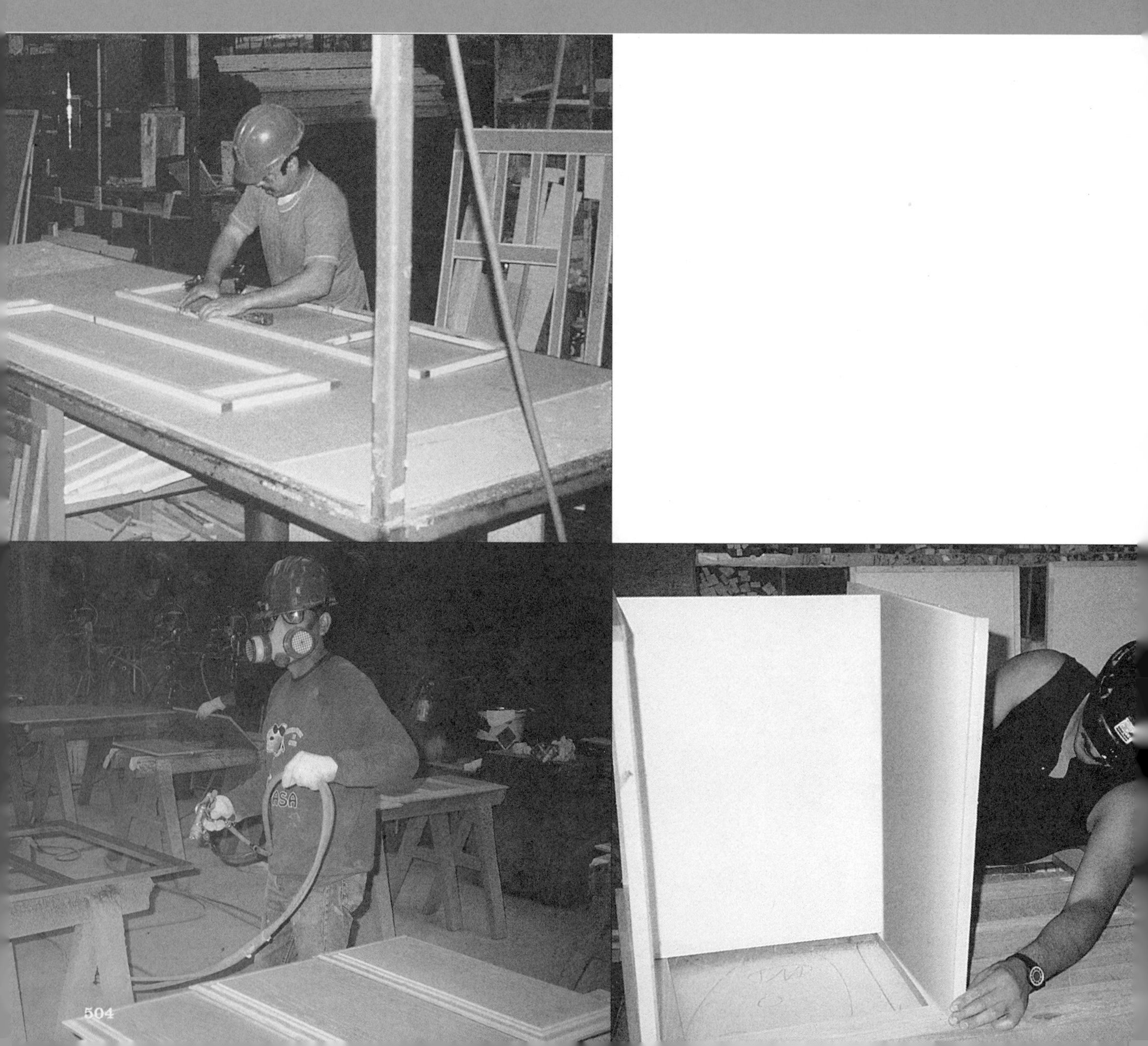

KEY OBJECTIVES:

1	*Define present value, and compute the present value of a lump sum and an annuity.*
2	*Calculate an investment's net present value and relate NPV to the investment's time-adjusted ROI.*
3	*Discuss how the timing of cashflows and risk affect capital budgeting decisions, and determine the payback period.*
4	*Explain the need for multiple capital budgeting methods, and calculate the accounting rate of return.*
5	*Describe four perspectives for long-run value and create a balanced scorecard.*
6	*[Appendix A] Incorporate taxes into NPV and time-adjusted ROI calculations.*

The morning meetings were reengineered. The grandchildren just returned from their pre-meeting group exercise. Instead of coffee and pastries, Doris served wheat germ and skim milk. Everyone was in a congratulatory mood. Love and self-confidence permeated the room. They had grown a lot since taking over the business. With their new strategic continuous improvement focus, everyone felt confident in their knowledge and skills for long-term value creation.

SID

"We all agree. We must be a continuous improvement organization. It's the only way to assure our long-run survival. Our reengineering into a just-in-time [JIT] system is ready to go."

"You know, though, I'm a little concerned. Creating a JIT system is more than just moving around some equipment. As we discovered in our TOC [theory of constraints] meeting [Chapter 12], eliminating constraints is not free. For the truss cell, we have to buy a new nailing machine. New tools and equipment are needed to reduce setup costs and prevent quality problems. We have to invest in employee training. We'll need a new management accounting system. This is going to be a very large investment!"

"So what? We've already justified reengineering into a JIT. Our people will have a 'big picture' perspective, an organizational focus rather than just thinking about their particular jobs. They also will assure quality in what they do. Continuous learning, lead-time reductions, and a customer focus [considering both internal customers and external customers] will guide their decisions. What more justification do we need?"

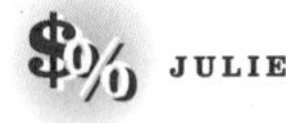

"If improvements are relatively inexpensive, we just go ahead and do them without any special analysis. For continuous improvement to work, we need to budget funds for these projects within our annual cash budget. Every part of the company now has a budget for short-run continuous improvement programs.

"But when improvements are very expensive and last over many years, we should do a special analysis, called capital budgeting. **Capital budgeting** involves investments lasting for multiple years. In other words, our returns from these investments—the cashflows they create—will be received over many time periods. Remember, an enterprise's economic value is the cash it generates. Our company is simply a multi-year cash machine. *Are these future cashflows worth the investment we have to make today?*

> **Capital budgeting** *decisions evaluate the current value of multi-year investments by comparing today's value of the future cashflows to the investment's cost.*

"U.S. companies invest trillions of dollars annually in capital investments. Phillips Petroleum spent $1.4 billion in one year. Coca-Cola spent almost $1 billion. BMW spent about $1 billion just on its South Carolina plant. Reengineering also is more than production process redesign. Think about our entire value chain and product life cycles, which we discussed in our strategic cost management meeting [Chapter 10]. Chrysler capital improvement projects have emphasized simultaneous engineering and quality function deployment [QFD]. New car development personnel have been reduced from 2,000 to 740, and new car development lead time is down to just over three years [from about 4½ years]. Ford's QFD investments have reduced its capital budget for new cars by $11 million. General Electric's capital improvement programs have lowered appliance lead times from 80 days to 20, saving $200 million in inventory."

NANCY

"I get it! The motivation for continuous improvements comes from the value-creating effects on our customer-driven critical success factors, like time to market, quality, on-time delivery, and customer service. However, we also need to justify these investments in terms of their financial costs and benefits. *We need to financially justify these decisions.*"

The Time Value of Money

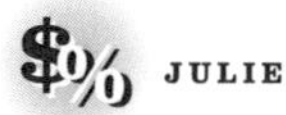
JULIE

"Because these cashflows last for many years, we need to consider the 'time value' of this money. For example, $100 dollars received today is not equal to $100 received in a year. Thus, our financial analysis must consider the investment's unique cashflows, when we will receive them, and their risk [i.e., the chances of actually receiving them]. Let's start with the time value of money."

Multi-year cashflows, compound interest, and the future value of money

"Waiting a year to receive $100 has an opportunity cost. If I had the $100 today, I could invest it and earn interest. That's just common sense. Assume I deposit $100 in a savings account earning 10% interest. In one year, I'll receive $110. The $100 today is worth $110 in one year. If I leave the $110 in my savings account for another year, earning 10% interest, it will be worth $121. The original investment of $100 has earned 10% interest for two years [$10 per year, $20 in total]. And the $10 interest from the first year also earns 10% interest during the second year—another $1—which is called 'compounding.' Compound interest results when we leave previously earned interest in our savings account [rather than withdrawing it at the end of each year and spending that interest on something]. Let me show you how this works [see Exhibit 14-1].

"This illustration shows us the future value of $100 invested at 10% is $110 in one year [$100 × 110% = $110]. In two years, the future value is $121 [$110 × 1.1 = $121]."

The present value of future cashflows

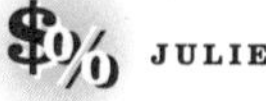
JULIE

"In capital budgeting decisions, we want to know just the opposite information. We estimate the benefits from an investment, that is, the future cashflows, and then ask, '*What are these future values worth today?*'"

Compound Interest and the Future Value of Money

	Deposit $100 today	In 1 year		In 2 years	
Savings account beginning balance	$100		$100		$110
+ Interest earned		Beginning balance × 10% =	+ 10	Beginning balance × 10% =	+ 11
Savings account ending balance			$110		$121

Exhibit 14-1

NANCY

"I know why this is important! I remember failing my calculus course the first time I took it. Dad would only pay my tuition the first time. If I had to repeat a course, I had to pay for it. I decided to wait two years to retake it. I estimated the tuition to be $121. I wanted to know how much to deposit into my 10% savings account so I would have $121 in two years. Mom was so impressed with my planning ability, she gave me the $100. I promptly deposited it, and two years later I repeated calculus successfully."

TOMMY

"Today's value of future cashflows can be quite enlightening. Remember when the Exxon Valdez oil tanker spilled 11 million gallons of crude oil in Alaska's Prince William Sound? The damage settlement was $1 billion to be paid over 10 years. How much did Exxon have to deposit in 1989 in order to make the payments? After taxes, Exxon's actual cost was only $486 million!"

JULIE

"That's very impressive! You determined the present value of future cashflows. The opposite of future value is **present value**. Starting with the future value and working backwards to the present value is called **discounting**. The present value of $121 received in two years is $100, assuming a 10% interest rate. When calculating present values, the interest rate is usually called a 'discount rate.' Alternative ways of saying this are:

> *Calculating the* **present value** *(today's worth or value) of future cashflows is called* **discounting**.

- $121 discounted at 10% for two years is worth $100 today.
- The present value of $121 in two years is $100, given a 10% return on investment [ROI].
- Assuming I can earn a 10% ROI, I'm indifferent between $100 today and $121 in two years.

How do we calculate the $100 present value if we know the $121 future value? We simply do the future value [compound interest] calculation backwards. [Exhibit 14-2 demonstrates this.]

KEY OBJECTIVE 1

Define present value, and compute the present value of a lump sum and an annuity.

"The present value [PV] factor of 0.82644 is the mathematical inverse, or reciprocal, of 1 + the compound interest rate [1 + 21% = 1.21; and 0.82644 = 1 ÷ 1.21]. Technically speaking, it is the *PV factor for a lump sum* received in two years discounted at 10%. We can look up the PV factor in a PV factor table for any number of years at any discount rate [e.g., 5 years at 18%, or 10 years at 7%]. A simple

	Comparing Future Values and Present Values		
	Present value	**x (1 + compound interest rate) =**	**Future value**
	$100	x 1.21 =	$121
	Future value	**÷ (1 + compound interest rate) =**	**Present value**
	$121	÷ 1.21 =	$100
or:	$121	x (1 ÷ 1.21) =	$100
or:	**Future value**	**x Present value (PV) factor =**	**Present value**
	$121	x 0.82644 =	$100

Exhibit 14-2

multiplication determines the present value." Julie thought about Nancy's calculus course comment. She noticed Nancy frowning at her. Nancy also was never very good at getting the right number from a long and complicated table.

"Do we really have to look up PV factors in a table? Don't we have calculators and spreadsheet programs to do this for us?"

"Of course. I think calculators and spreadsheets are easier than using those long, complicated tables we had to use in our high school and introductory college math courses. Pull out your calculator and try this."

Immediately after saying this, Julie's face turned crimson. As she looked around the boardroom table, no one had a calculator. They all had laptop computers, though. So Julie thought she'd show Nancy how a spreadsheet program does this without the need to look up PV factors [see Appendix A].

"Capital budgeting decisions are choices about how to invest our money in order to maximize future cashflows. Usually, investments create cashflows every year, rather than only one 'lump-sum' amount at the end of a time period. For example, if we invest $1 million to build the truss JIT cell, Bob estimates it will increase our cashflows by $200,000 a year for 7 years. By that time, the equipment will need to be replaced due to technological innovations. Receiving a cashflow every year is called an annuity.

"Tables also exist showing the *PV factor for an annuity* for any number of years and discount rate. Do you want to see it?" Julie was grinning while Nancy was grimacing. "No? O.K., I'll just show you how the PV factors for a lump sum are related to the PV factors for an annuity, and how we can compute the present value of an annuity [see Exhibit 14-3].

"The JIT cell will generate a $200,000 'annuity stream' for 7 years. Using the 10% PV factors for a lump sum, we can discount each year's cashflow separately and compute its present value. I did this in the first 7 rows of my spreadsheet program [Exhibit 14-3]. Then, sum the present values for each year to determine the present value of the investment. Adding the present values for each of the 7 years, the investment's present value is $973,680.

"Alternatively, we can use the PV factor for a 7-year annuity at 10%. Multiplying the annuity amount by the 10% annuity factor gives us the same answer [$200,000 × 4.8684 = $973,680]. I did this in the last row [Exhibit 14-3]. Notice, the PV factor for an annuity is simply the sum of the PV factors for a lump sum. If you like to use tables, it is easier to use the PV factor for an annuity."

"Ah ha! We can't use the PV factor for an annuity, though, if the annual cashflows are different. For example, if the first year's cash inflow is $200,000, the sec-

Comparing Present Value Factors for Lump Sums and Annuities

Year	Cashflow		PV factor for a lump sum at 10%		Present value
1	$200,000	x	0.9091	=	$181,820
2	200,000	x	0.8264	=	165,280
3	200,000	x	0.7513	=	150,260
4	200,000	x	0.6830	=	136,600
5	200,000	x	0.6209	=	124,180
6	200,000	x	0.5645	=	112,900
7	200,000	x	0.5132	=	102,640
	$200,000	x	4.8684	=	**$973,680**

10% PV factor for an annuity = the sum of the PV factors for a lump sum

Exhibit 14-3

ond year's cash inflow is $150,000, and each of the remaining years' cashflows are different, we have to discount each one separately using the PV factors for a lump sum. I knew I didn't like the idea of using tables!"

JULIE

"You're right. Nowadays, everyone's using spreadsheet programs to do discounting. But are the basic ideas [concepts and calculations] now clear?"

NANCY

"Oh yes. I understand what's going on and I see the importance of knowing how things should work when building a spreadsheet program [or doing this with my calculator]. What's next?"

In Which Projects Should We Invest Our Money?

KEY OBJECTIVE 2

Calculate an investment's net present value and relate NPV to the investment's time-adjusted ROI.

JULIE

"The first question we asked was, 'What's the present value of an investment's future cashflows?' Now we need to ask, 'Should we invest in this project?' Look again at my spreadsheet program [Exhibit 14-3]. The present value of the JIT cell's future cashflows is $973,680. What does this mean? If we deposit $973,680 in a 10% savings account today, we can withdraw $200,000 a year for 7 years before the account runs out of money. In other words, the 7-year $200,000 annuity is worth $973,680 today.

"Focus on the 10% interest rate. The JIT cell investment costs $1 million today. If we can have the same annuity stream by depositing less than $1 million in a savings account, is the savings accounts' interest rate greater than 10%? It must be! *If we can have the same annuity stream for a smaller investment [deposit], that investment must yield a higher interest rate.* To illustrate this, for a deposit of $500,000 to yield a 7-year $200,000 annuity, the interest rate has to be 35%!"

The net present value answer

"Now consider the opposite situation. You deposit $1 million today in order to get this annuity. Doesn't the interest rate have to be *less than 10%* on this investment?

At 10%, you only have to deposit $973,680 in order to receive $200,000 a year for 7 years. Which would you rather have: $1 million today, or $200,000 a year for 7 years?"

NANCY

"I'll take the $1 million today! It is worth more than the annuity stream if I can invest my money at 10%. I'll invest the $973,680 [so I can receive $200,000 a year for 7 years], and I'll take the difference of $26,320 and split it with my management accounting professor for showing me this!"

JULIE

"Use this same logic for the JIT cell decision. Assuming we can earn a 10% return on $1 million, should we invest it at 10% or should we build the JIT cell? If the JIT cell will generate only $200,000 additional cash for 7 years, we are better off investing. At 10%, the present value of this annuity [$973,680] is less than the $1 million investment required to get it. Subtracting the investment required today from the present value of the future cashflows it generates is called the **net present value [NPV]**. [Exhibit 14-4 presents the analysis for this decision.]

Net present value (NPV) *is the difference between the cash outflow today and the present value of the future cash inflows it creates. NPV is the change in today's value of the firm due to this investment.*

Net Present Value for the JIT Cell Investment

Year	Cashflow		PV factors at 10%		Present value
now	($1,000,000)	x	1	=	($1,000,000)
1-7	$200,000	x	4.8684	=	$973,680
Net present value (NPV)					($26,320)

Exhibit 14-4

"Nancy, take a dollar out of your wallet. What's it worth?"

NANCY

"It's worth one dollar." Nancy handed Julie the $1 bill. All of the sudden she realized it wasn't worth anything unless Julie gives back the dollar! Fat chance, Nancy thought, as she saw Julie put it in her pocket.

JULIE

"O.K. The present value of a cash outflow today, like the dollar Nancy just spent, is the amount of that cashflow. Thus, the PV factor for a cashflow today is always 1. To make this point, I placed the number 1 in the PV factor column for the cash-out today. Now, what does the JIT cell's NPV tell us [in Exhibit 14-4]?

- *The negative NPV means today's value of the future cashflows [the benefit] is less than the investment [the cost].*
- *Our investment does not yield a 10% return [ROI].*
- *The cost-benefit analysis says we should not build the JIT cell. The NPV decision rule is invest when the project yields a positive NPV [a return greater than the discount rate]."*

BOB

"Let's not reject the investment yet. What if I can trade in some old equipment when buying the new equipment for the JIT cell? This will reduce our initial investment to $950,000. How does this affect our cost-benefit analysis?"

JULIE

"I'll just change that amount and recalculate the NPV [see Exhibit 14-5]. Now, the NPV is positive [$23,680]. *This means the annuity's present value [benefit] is greater than today's investment [cost].* Relating this to our savings account analogy, depositing $950,000 today in a 10% savings account will not produce a $200,000 7-year annuity stream."

Net Present Value for the JIT Cell Investment

Year	Cashflow		PV factors at 10%		Present value
now	($950,000)	x	1	=	($950,000)
1-7	$200,000	x	4.8684	=	$973,680
Net present value (NPV)					$23,680

Exhibit 14-5

"Of course not! We already know we have to deposit $973,680 in a 10% savings account to have a $200,000 annuity [see Exhibit 14-3]. With a 10% savings account, we need to deposit another $23,680 [in addition to the $950,000] if we want a $200,000 annuity. *The return on this investment [the JIT 'savings account' interest rate] must be greater than 10% because we can deposit less than $973,680 and receive the same $200,000 annual annuity.*

"O.K. I understand. The best investment alternative we had yesterday was a 10% savings account. Today, however, we have the opportunity to invest in the JIT cell. Its ROI is greater than 10%. By investing in the JIT cell, we have just increased our company's value by $23,680. *NPV tells us the change in today's value of the firm if we make this investment.* A positive NPV is an important financial criterion for multi-year investments! The investment's ROI is greater than the discount rate, but how much greater? I also want to know the real ROI for the JIT cell."

The time-adjusted ROI (internal rate of return) answer

"That's a valid question. *The NPV discount rate represents the minimum ROI we require from an investment.* If we have to invest $1 million in the JIT cell, it is a 'no go' decision because we have another more profitable investment opportunity [the 10% savings account]. If the investment is only $950,000 though, it's a 'go' decision.

- Spending $1 million on the JIT cell, which results in a negative NPV [in Exhibit 14-4], means the investment will not yield a 10% time-adjusted ROI.
- However, the positive NPV from spending only $950,000 [in Exhibit 14-5] means the investment yields an ROI greater than 10%.

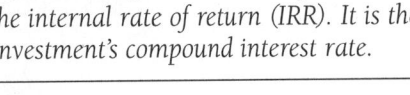

The ***time-adjusted ROI*** *is often called the internal rate of return (IRR). It is the investment's compound interest rate.*

"The **time-adjusted ROI** is the discount rate [interest rate] that makes the present value of an annuity stream equal to the investment amount. *It's the discount factor that results in a zero NPV.*"

"Time-adjusted ROI is like a break-even interest rate because it makes today's value of the future cashflows equal to today's investment cost."

"Well, that's not technically precise, but it is a good way to look at it. 'Break even' means zero profit. The NPV discount [interest] rate is the minimum rate of return [profit] we are willing to accept given our other investment opportunities. So when NPV is zero, the investment's time-adjusted ROI equals the NPV discount rate. In other words, the investment yields the minimum profit [rate of return] we want, with no residual income, or extra profit beyond that ROI [see Chapter 8].

"The JIT cell's ROI is the discount rate producing a $200,000 annuity over 7 years from an initial $1 million investment today. To find this discount rate, just solve the present value equation for the PV factor:

Discount rate	Annuity	×	PV factor	=	Present value
This is what we originally did (in Exhibit 14-3):					
Given a 10% discount rate, solve for PV:	$200,000	×	4.8684	=	$973,680
Now, do this:	**Present value**	÷	**Annuity**	=	**PV factor**
Solve for the discount rate (given the PV and annuity):	$1,000,000	÷	$200,000	=	5.00

What is the 7-year annuity discount rate [ROI] if the PV factor equals 5.00? We can look it up in an annuity table. The PV factor for 7 years at 9% is 5.03. So, with a 5.00 PV factor, the JIT cell investment will yield about a 9% ROI. Annuity tables only work, though, if the annuity stream is the same each year. We normally have to interpolate to find the time-adjusted ROI. The table gives us a 9% factor [5.03], but what is the ROI for a 5.00 factor?"

NANCY

"I always carry a calculator in my purse. I plugged in the numbers and solved for the ROI. I also see my spreadsheet program has a function command solving for NPV and IRR. Both gave me a 9.2% [rounded] time-adjusted ROI."

JULIE

"To use the time-adjusted ROI method, we must know the minimum ROI required for funding capital projects. *The decision rule is to accept projects yielding a time-adjusted ROI greater than the minimum ROI.* Therefore, do not invest in the JIT cell. Its 9% ROI is less than our required [or break even] 10% ROI. By the way, I just recalculated the NPV using a 9.2% discount rate [see Exhibit 14-6].

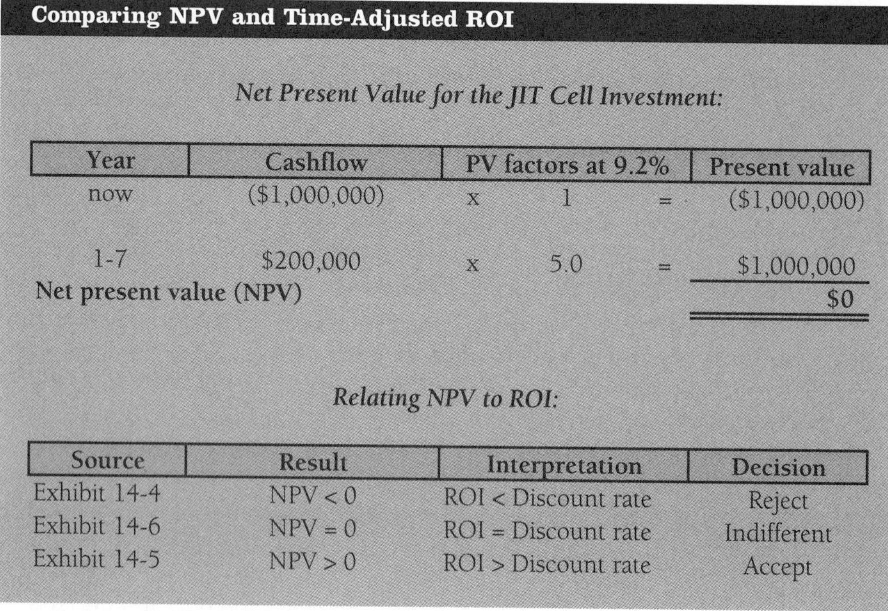
Comparing NPV and Time-Adjusted ROI

Net Present Value for the JIT Cell Investment:

Year	Cashflow	PV factors at 9.2%			Present value
now	($1,000,000)	x	1	=	($1,000,000)
1-7	$200,000	x	5.0	=	$1,000,000
Net present value (NPV)					**$0**

Relating NPV to ROI:

Source	Result	Interpretation	Decision
Exhibit 14-4	NPV < 0	ROI < Discount rate	Reject
Exhibit 14-6	NPV = 0	ROI = Discount rate	Indifferent
Exhibit 14-5	NPV > 0	ROI > Discount rate	Accept

Exhibit 14-6

By comparing these analyses [Exhibits 14-4 through 14-6] we can see the relationship between NPV and ROI.

- *A positive NPV means the project's ROI is greater than the discount rate [the minimum, or break-even, ROI for investing], so invest in this project.*
- *A negative NPV means the project's ROI is less than the discount rate, so do not invest in this project.*
- *A zero NPV means the project's ROI equals the discount rate, so we are indifferent between investing or not investing in this project.*

Because the discount rate used in NPV is the minimum ROI we require in order to invest, both methods tell us the same thing. Invest in the project if its ROI is greater than the minimum ROI [i.e., it has a positive NPV]. I've drawn a picture for these ideas [see Exhibit 14-7]."

The Effects of Time Value and Risk on NPV and ROI

NANCY

"What should we do when NPV equals zero, that is, when the project's ROI is the minimum we will accept? Will the decision have to be made with other criteria? What other decision criteria should we consider in capital budgeting?"

The timing of cashflows

JULIE

Julie pulled Nancy's one dollar bill out of her pocket. "Nancy, do you want your dollar back now? Or can I wait a year and then give it back?"

NANCY

"Common sense, Julie. I'll take the dollar now. It's worth more today than it is in one year. This is the time value idea we first discussed."

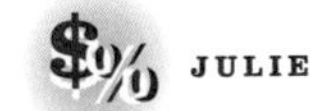
JULIE

"Right! The longer we have to wait for a cashflow, the less valuable it is. Here's two investments. Which investment should we choose? [See Exhibit 14-8 on p. 515.]

"Investment B should be worth more than Investment A because the cashflows are received sooner. To support this intuition, it has a higher ROI than Investment A [23% compared to 19%]. This also explains why PV factors decrease over time. The longer we wait, the less valuable a cashflow is. Compare the PV factors for 1 year and 4 years. A dollar in one year is worth 91¢ today [$1 × 0.9091]. The same dollar is worth only 68¢ today if we must wait four years to get it [$1 × 0.6830]."

NANCY

"Well, that makes sense. But, why does Investment A have a higher NPV? If my decision is based on NPV, I invest in A. If my decision is based on ROI, I choose B. Why do these methods lead to different decisions?"

JULIE

KEY OBJECTIVE 3

Discuss how the timing of cashflows and risk affect capital budgeting decisions, and determine the payback period.

"Two reasons. Investment A's cashflows total $1.5 million, while B's are only $1.3 million. Investment A should have a higher NPV than B. Each method also is based on a different assumption about how the returns are reinvested. NPV assumes cashflows are reinvested [earning compound interest] at the discount rate [10%]. ROI assumes cashflows are reinvested at the time-adjusted ROI [19% for A and 23% for B]. Technicalities aside, these methods can lead to different investment decisions because of their different reinvestment assumptions. So, most organizations use both measures. We also can create some other measures to use with NPV and ROI, but let's leave that for another meeting.

"This is my first answer to your question about decision criteria. *Use more than one technique.* The timing of cashflows [when cashflows are received] affects each method differently."

Using ROI and NPV in Capital Budgeting

ROI and discount rate	NPV	The cashflow teeter-totter	Investment decision
Project's ROI (IRR) = minimally acceptable ROI (discount rate)	0	Cost Investment amount = Benefit PV of cashflows 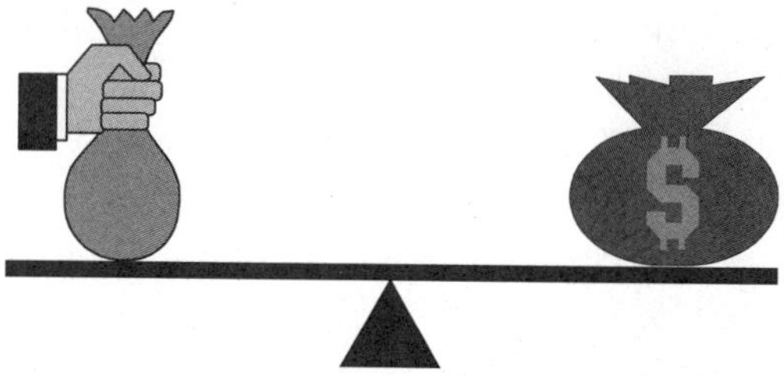 Discount rate	Indifferent
ROI > minimum	> 0	Cost < Benefit Discount rate 	Accept
ROI < minimum	< 0	Cost > Benefit 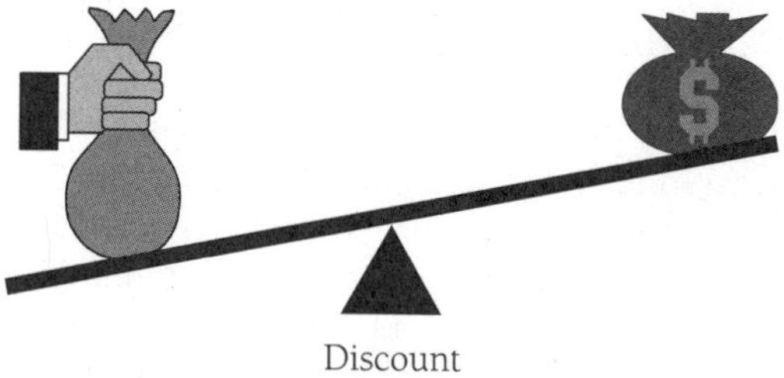 Discount rate	Reject

Exhibit 14-7

Incorporating environmental risk into the analysis

JULIE

"We should consider two types of risk involved in our investments as well. First, we may not get future cashflows when expected, or in the amounts estimated. Pacific Gas & Electric thought it could build its Diablo Canyon nuclear power plant

Cashflow Timing Effects on NPV and ROI

Investment A						
Year	Cashflow		PV factor for a lump sum at 10%		Present value
Cash outflow:					
now	($1,000,000)	x	1.0000	=	*($1,000,000)*
Cash inflows:					
1	$300,000	x	0.9091	=	$272,730
2	400,000	x	0.8264	=	330,560
3	700,000	x	0.7513	=	525,910
4	100,000	x	0.6830	=	68,300
Sum	$1,500,000				
PV of cash inflows (assumes cashflows are invested at 10%)					*$1,197,500*
NPV:					*$197,500*
Time-adjusted ROI (IRR): (assumes cashflows are invested at 19%)					*19%*

Investment B					
Year	Cashflow		PV factor for a lump sum at 10%		Present value
Cash outflow:					
now	($1,000,000)	x	1.0000	=	*($1,000,000)*
Cash inflows:					
1	$900,000	x	0.9091	=	$818,190
2	400,000	x	0.8264	=	330,560
3	0	x	0.7513	=	0
4	0	x	0.6830	=	0
Sum	$1,300,000				
PV of cash inflows (assumes cashflows are invested at 10%)					*$1,148,750*
NPV:					*$148,750*
Time-adjusted ROI (IRR): (assumes cashflows are invested at 23%)					*23%*

Exhibit 14-8

in central California and bring it on-line in just a few years. After it was complete, public resistance delayed the startup for many more years [until its useful life had almost expired!]. Secondly, it is very difficult to correct a bad capital investment. Hyundai abandoned its $300 million Canadian auto plant because of poor sales. Barnes and Noble changed its strategy over time, moving from small stores in shopping malls to large stand-alone stores. As a result, it closed many shopping mall stores at a loss. Anheuser-Busch believed its core competencies would support a profitable snack food market entry. After investing over $300 million, it sold that division at a $200 million loss. What a shame to have to disclose this in the annual stockholders reports, as these companies did!"

TOMMY

"These risks are really serious with multinational enterprises. Grandpa Multree told me a story about how he lost a plant in India because he crossed his legs when sitting on the speaker's platform at a reception dinner. The bottom of his shoe faced the speaker, a government official. This is a cultural insult. It cost him millions in lost predevelopment costs when he was not allowed to build the plant. Other international investment risks include radical inflation, tax and tariff law changes, the ability to move cash out of a foreign country, a government seizure of the plant, and a lack of legal protection. Consider the problems the recording industry, and companies like Microsoft and Kellogg, have had in China."

SID

"How do you incorporate these types of risk into our capital budgeting analyses? Are these externalities that cannot be quantified, or can we formally include risk in our calculations?"

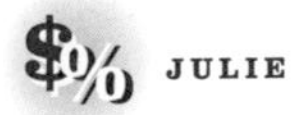
JULIE

"Many of these risk factors may not be quantifiable, but we have to consider them. Whenever possible, we should formally incorporate risk into our decision, even though we may not be able to place a dollar amount on specific risks. Quantitative decision models exist for this, but that discussion will have to wait for a future meeting.

"One way we can consider the differential risk associated with a specific investment is by changing our NPV discount rate. Right now, our minimum [breakeven] ROI is 10%. For riskier projects, like international projects, let's require a higher ROI, say 20%. Look at this comparison [Exhibit 14-9].

Comparing Present Value Factors for Different Discount Rates

Domestic investment						
Year	Cashflow		10% PV factors (10% for lower risk)		Present value
Cash outflow:					
now	($1,000,000)	x	1.0000	=	*($1,000,000)*
Cash inflows:					
1	$350,000	x	0.9091	=	$318,185
2	350,000	x	0.8264	=	289,240
3	350,000	x	0.7513	=	262,955
4	350,000	x	0.6830	=	239,050
PV of cash inflows					*$1,109,430*
NPV:					*$109,430*
Time-adjusted ROI (IRR):					*15%*

International investment					
Year	Cashflow		20% PV factors (20% for higher risk)		Present value
Cash outflow:					
now	($1,000,000)	x	1.0000	=	*($1,000,000)*
Cash inflows:					
1	$350,000	x	0.8333	=	$291,655
2	$350,000	x	0.6944	=	243,040
3	$350,000	x	0.5787	=	202,545
4	$350,000	x	0.4823	=	168,805
PV of cash inflows					*$906,045*
NPV:					*($93,955)*
Time-adjusted ROI (IRR):					*15%*

Exhibit 14-9

The domestic and international investments have identical cashflows, so both yield a 15% ROI. The international project is much riskier, though. By requiring a higher ROI for riskier investments, it is not acceptable, as shown in its negative NPV. A higher discount rate results in smaller PV factors [compare the 10% factors used with the domestic project to the 20% factors for the international project]. Smaller PV factors mean the future cashflows are less valuable. The riskier they are, the less valuable they should be because the likelihood we will not receive these cashflows as planned is higher."

"My teeter-totter analogy [Exhibit 14-7] also illustrates this. Let me show you [see Exhibit 14-10]. Using your numbers [from Exhibit 14-9], both investments have identical cashflows. As the discount rate increases, the teeter-totter's fulcrum moves to the right. Thus, it takes less 'weight' on the left side [the longer side] to tilt the teeter-totter down. In other words, we can invest less to get the same annuity as the interest rate increases. The same future cashflows as in the domestic investment are worth less in the international investment. Why? They are riskier." Nancy watched Julie place the dollar bill in her pocket again. The risk of not getting it back had just been resolved. Nancy knew she would never see it again!

Future Cashflows are Less Valuable with Higher Discount Rates

Domestic investment	The cashflow teeter-totter	Investment decision
ROI > discount rate NPV > 0	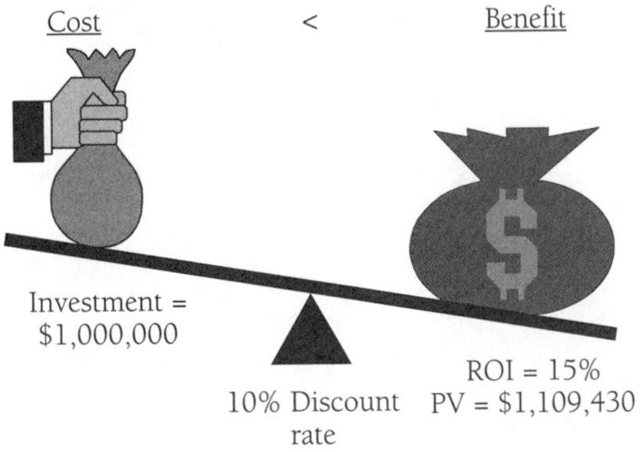 Cost < Benefit Investment = $1,000,000 10% Discount rate ROI = 15% PV = $1,109,430	Accept
International investment	**The cashflow teeter-totter**	**Investment decision**
ROI < discount rate NPV < 0	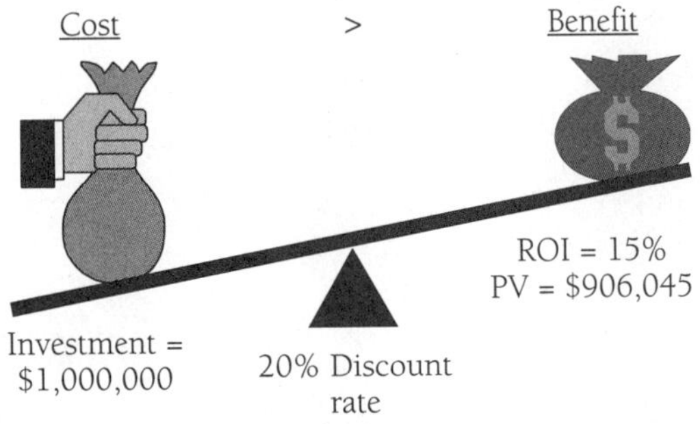 Cost > Benefit Investment = $1,000,000 20% Discount rate ROI = 15% PV = $906,045	Reject

Exhibit 14-10

The payback period

The payback period is the time needed to recover an investment from the cashflows it generates.

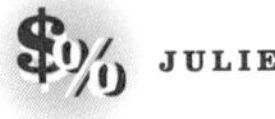

"We have another way to quantify risk. In our TOC meeting, [Chapter 12] we used the payback period as a method to financially justify eliminating a constraint. The payback period answers, 'How long before the cashflows received equal the original investment amount?' In capital budgeting decisions, this provides a simple measure of risk. The faster we get back our money, the less likely forecast errors will occur and the less risky the investment is. If we estimate a $400,000 annual annuity from a $1 million investment, the project will be paid back in 2½ years [$400,000 × 2½ years = $1 million]. With a constant annuity, the payback period formula is:

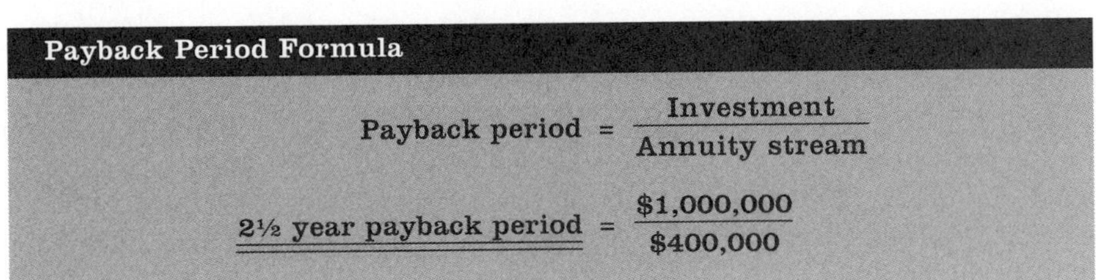

Payback Period Formula

$$\text{Payback period} = \frac{\text{Investment}}{\text{Annuity stream}}$$

$$\text{2½ year payback period} = \frac{\$1{,}000{,}000}{\$400{,}000}$$

The formula approach has to be modified if the annual cash inflows are different each year, though. [Exhibit 14-11 demonstrates the calculation.]

Payback Period for a Variable Annuity Stream

Illustration for a constant annuity:

Year	Investment	Annuity received	Net cashflow
now	$1,000,000		($1,000,000)
1		$400,000	(600,000)
2		400,000	(200,000)
3		400,000	200,000
4		400,000	600,000

$$\text{Payback period} = 2 \text{ years} + \frac{\$200{,}000}{\$400{,}000}$$

Payback period = 2.5 years

Illustration for a variable annuity:

Year	Investment	Annuity received	Net cashflow
now	$1,000,000		($1,000,000)
1		$100,000	(900,000)
2		200,000	(700,000)
3		400,000	(300,000)
4		700,000	400,000

$$\text{Payback period} = 3 \text{ years} + \frac{\$300{,}000}{\$700{,}000}$$

Payback period = 3.5 years

Exhibit 14-11

The top of the exhibit shows how this calculation works with a constant annuity stream [the example above]. The bottom panel repeats the calculation with a variable annuity [different amounts each year]. The payback period is really 3.43 years, but I don't like this much precision. [When should we stop? My calculator stopped at 3.428571429.] Too much precision can be misleading. Remember, the cashflows are estimates. Also remember to always round up. We don't quite recover the investment in 3.4 years!"

Evaluating Capital Projects

"So far, we've discussed how to make investment decisions. I'm also concerned about an ethical issue in forecasting future cashflows. Executives can use capital projects to increase the size of their investment centers. As their divisions grow, so may their power. Thus, executives may want to bias their cashflow estimates to make projects look better than originally believed. For example, in the early 1990s leasing was one means for automobile companies to differentiate themselves. At Nissan, competitive pressures to lease its luxury car, the Infiniti, lead to overestimating its resale value at the end of the lease. Industry analysts estimated Nissan lost millions of dollars when the actual cashflows from selling Infinitis after the leases expired were significantly less than projected.

"Too often, investment center managers are evaluated with financial accounting numbers. We discussed this in our motivation meeting [Chapter 8]. Since the financial accounting system does not measure the benefits from specific investments, managers know once a project is accepted, it probably won't be evaluated upon completion. Thus, they may have little motivation to accurately budget or control the project's financial aspects. What can our management accounting system do to help us?"

External evaluations and the accounting rate of return

"I don't see the problem. Every time I prepare financial statements, an **accounting rate of return [ARR]** is included. ARR is an ROI measure using the financial accounting numbers. Return on investment is profit divided by investment. We discussed this performance evaluation method in our motivation meeting [Chapter 8]. For the life of an investment, ARR is the average annual profit it creates divided by the average investment. [Exhibit 14-12 illustrates the measure.]

Accounting rate of return (ARR) *is the average financial accounting profit from an investment expressed as a percentage of the average investment (financial accounting net book value).*

"These amounts come from an ARR analysis I just did for the city fire department. It was trying to justify a new alarm system costing $100,000. The system reduces operating costs $30,000 per year. Reducing expenses is equivalent to increasing profits. The system will last 5 years, so depreciation is $20,000 per year [straight line]. This asset's initial cost [book value] is $100,000. At the end of 5 years, after full depreciation, its book value [asset value on the balance sheet] will be zero. So over its 5-year life, the average investment is ($100,000 + $0) ÷ 2, or $50,000. It was easy to justify the investment because of its lifetime average 60% ARR.

KEY OBJECTIVE 4

Explain the need for multiple capital budgeting methods, and calculate the accounting rate of return.

"ARR is an important investment measure because it uses financial accounting numbers. These are the only financial numbers external users see [e.g., city officials, creditors, stockholders]."

"I understand the need to provide financial accounting information to outsiders. But ARR just doesn't make sense to me! Looking at the annual ARR calculations [in Exhibit 14-12], ARR increases over time as an asset gets older and loses its value! How can this represent economic value? While external users evaluate our performance with financial accounting information, using it to run the business may be disastrous! Because the book value is so high in the first years, ARR is understated. Using this to evaluate people I will bias them against making the investments! They will be punished in the early years for not achieving the 60% return used to justify the investment. Is this ethical?"

Accounting Rate of Return (ARR)

$$ARR = \frac{\text{Investment's average annual profit}}{\text{Investment's average book value}}$$

$$ARR = \frac{\$30,000}{\$100,000 \div 2}$$

$$ARR = 60\%$$

Annual ARR calculations

Depreciation and book value table:

Year	Beginning book value	Less depreciation	Ending book value	Average book value
1	$100,000	($20,000)	$80,000	$90,000
2	80,000	(20,000)	60,000	70,000
3	60,000	(20,000)	40,000	50,000
4	40,000	(20,000)	20,000	30,000
5	20,000	(20,000)	0	10,000

Annual ARR calculations:

Year	Profit	÷	Average book value	=	ARR
1	$30,000	÷	$90,000	=	33%
2	30,000	÷	70,000	=	43%
3	30,000	÷	50,000	=	60%
4	30,000	÷	30,000	=	100%
5	30,000	÷	10,000	=	300%

Exhibit 14-12

JULIE

"Well, what we are seeing is another example of the conflict between financial accounting measures of value and economic measures of value. *Economic value is cash. ARR does not measure cashflows.*"

Internal evaluations using post-implementation audits

TOMMY

"We need an evaluation method comparing the reasons for funding a capital project to its actual outcomes. If the City of Denver did this, maybe it would not have had as many problems in constructing its new airport. Didn't they decide to fund this capital project back in 1985? Three of the factors supporting it were an increase in annual passenger volume from 16 million to 26 million by 1995, a projected completion by 1993, and for a $1.2 billion cost. By 1993, the passenger volume had not changed, the airport was not finished, and projected cost increased to $3.1 billion. In 1994, the high-tech baggage system still was not working. Another $50 million was budgeted for a manual system conversion. Delays cost Denver more than $2 million a day, and the budget surpassed $4 billion."

JULIE

"I agree! To properly evaluate the successfulness of multi-year investments, we should be conducting post-implementation audits. Recognizing economic value is cash creation, let's do some cash comparisons. We also should evaluate other factors justifying capital budgeting decisions, such as feasibility and benefit factors. A **post-implementation audit** compares:

- Predicted cashflows to actual cashflows,
- Projected feasibility with the actual implementation, and
- Anticipated benefits against benefits realized.

Basically, each report is a variance analysis."

> **Post-implementation audits** *evaluate a project's success and identify activities to improve the capital budgeting and implementation process.*

TOMMY

"Post-implementation audits may be dangerous if used to evaluate and reward people, though. Capital projects are multi-year investments. The world is too dynamic and radically changing over this long of a time to hold individuals responsible for the estimates used years ago to justify a project. Holding them accountable raises some serious ethical issues. The most important issue is what this will do to our long-term value. Employees may become risk averse, making ultra-conservative cashflow projections to avoid unfavorable variances. They also may down-grade feasibility and underplay the potential benefits. *While not evaluating capital project success may lead to riskier investments, evaluating people [versus project] performance will bias against many profitable, long-term, value-creating projects!*"

BOB

"I agree! Why should I assume the risk of a project not working out as planned [achieving the goals originally justifying its investment many years ago]? Why conduct post-implementation audits?"

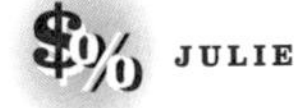
JULIE

"Simple. Don't use them to evaluate and reward people. Use them to improve our long-term, value-creating processes. In other words, use them to learn. Post-implementation audit goals should be to:

- Analyze the project's success.
- Determine activities still required [e.g., additional investments, change in focus, abandonment].
- Identify the strengths and weaknesses of our capital budgeting and implementation process.
- Avoid past mistakes.
- Suggest process changes for continuous improvement in capital budgeting."

The need for multiple methods

TOMMY

"I think one conclusion is obvious. *We need multiple methods for capital budgeting, and these methods cannot be restricted to financial criteria.* We also must consider qualitative factors [externalities]."

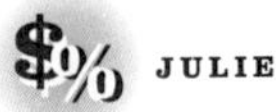
JULIE

Financial methods. "The key management issue with financial methods is each provides different information, and it's all important. Here's a summary of the major differences [Exhibit 14-13].

"This helps us realize why multiple methods are used in practice. To illustrate, in deciding which military bases to close, the Federal Base Closure and Realignment Commission requires NPV. Colgate specifically emphasizes rapid payback in its decisions, according to its 1994 annual report. Many firms require 2- to 3-year paybacks, and use 15% to 20% discount rates in NPV, reflecting the technological risk currently existing in our economy. Over 85% of the Fortune 1000

Management Considerations in Using Capital Budgeting Methods	
Capital budgeting method	**Differentiating features**
Net present value (NPV):	Reinvests cashflows at the discount rate.
Time-adjusted ROI (IRR):	Reinvests cashflows at the project's ROI.
Payback period:	Measures the length of time our investment is at risk, but does not consider the time value of money (the interest we can earn from the returns).
Accounting rate of return (ARR):	How the outside world sees us. How investments affect our financial statements (again, without considering the time value of money).

Exhibit 14-13

companies use NPV, while 77% use IRR. Their third most frequently used method is the payback period.

"The forest products industry gives us some further insight into why multiple methods are used. In timber investments, which cover a very long time period, NPV and IRR are used by 76% of these companies. NPV and IRR are used by only 55% of firms in shorter time period investments, like for equipment purchases. The payback period is a secondary measure for timber purchases, but much more important in shorter time period investments. Not surprisingly, the use of multiple methods is prevalent internationally." [Consider Exhibit 14-14.]

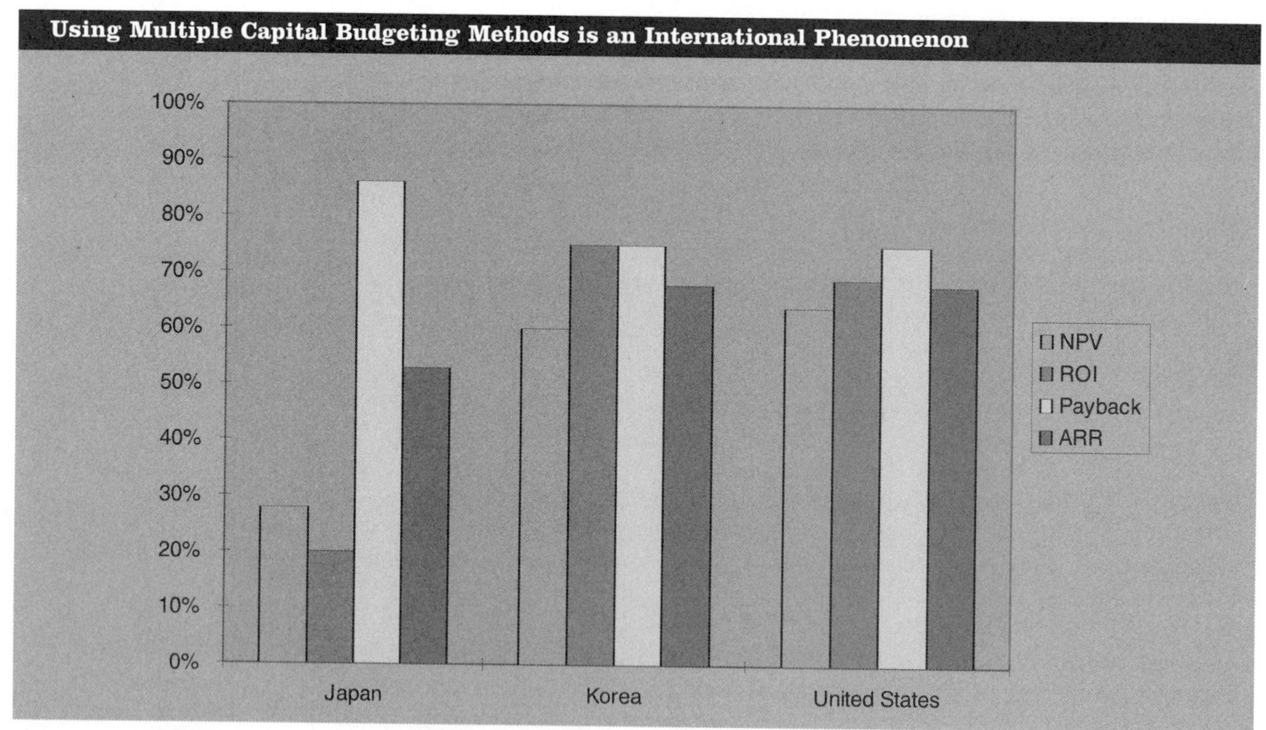

Exhibit 14-14

Nonfinancial decision criteria. "In identifying future benefits, not all are simply cashflows. Long-term value may be better estimated by nonfinancial measures. What other criteria should we consider?"

TOMMY

"Well, Sears differentiates its products and services on quality rather than cost. General Motors' $5 billion investment in Saturn was driven by the desire to pioneer affordable, ecologically engineered cars. Toyota believes its projects must improve the quality of working life for its employees. Each of these companies believes improving nonfinancial measures increases long-term value.

"Especially in the government sector, social welfare concerns [long-term nonfinancial value to citizens] are often the dominate criteria. Cities and states often offer investment 'carrots' such as free land and/or improvements, lower [or no] property taxes, and relocation allowances in order to entice firms to relocate. The immediate benefits usually involve better employment opportunities for their citizens. Large capital investments often are justified by environmental and safety concerns. How do we measure the effects of cleaner air? How do we justify subsidizing a hospital with tax dollars? New and growing areas for management accounting systems include health care management and environmental accounting."

Four Perspectives on Value Measurement: The Balanced Scorecard

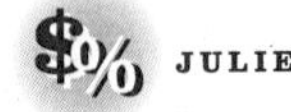
JULIE

"I don't think any of us question the need for multiple financial and nonfinancial measures to determine value. We're certainly not alone in this belief. Over 80% of large American organizations want to change their performance evaluation systems. Instead of relying solely on financial accounting numbers, many organizations are developing a new formal performance report. It's called a **balanced scorecard**. According to a 1998 IMA survey, 51% of responding companies are in some stage of implementing a balanced scorecard, and 22% have fully implemented it and use it in performance evaluations. Another study reported over 60% of the Fortune 1000 firms are experimenting with it.

A **balanced scorecard** *reports the change in critical success factors from four perspectives: the customer, business process improvements, innovation and learning, and financial.*

"The growing popularity of balanced scorecards is not limited to the manufacturing sector, either. In addition to manufacturers like AMD [Advanced Micro Devices], Arco, Apple Computers, and Tenneco, service sector firms are switching to balanced scorecards, for example: Allstate, AT&T, the Bank of Montreal, Cigna, IBM Consulting, KPMG-Peat Marwick, and Sears. Even nonprofits and governmental organizations are using it, like the West Mercia Constabulary, which services over 1 million citizens of Herefordshire, Shropshire, Telford & Wrekin, and Worchestershire [the fourth largest police area in the United Kingdom].

"What's a balanced scorecard? It's a report combining financial and nonfinancial measures critical to long-term value creation. It's kind of like an income statement in that it shows us how we have changed [increased value] during the year. It's more than an income statement, though, because it includes all of our critical success factors, not just net income.

"Our financial accounting system, like the summary statistics from last night's baseball game, cannot provide all the information we need for good management. Our management accounting system must provide the other statistics. The World Series champion probably is not the best in every category. It may not even be the best in any category. But it probably will be among the leaders in most categories."

NANCY

"I see! The World Series champion may be the team winning most of its games during the season. But to predict which team will win the most games next year, is last year's won-loss record sufficient information? No! We need information on how teams have improved or changed on each critical success factor, like hitting, pitching, and defense."

SID

"O.K. We may not be able to measure the exact change in value from any one activity, decision, or investment. However, in baseball's three broad categories of pitching, hitting, and defense, a team should be able to measure if it is improving. What are the value creation categories we want to monitor?"

Focusing on value creation

JULIE

"First and foremost, we're concerned with economic value; our ability to generate cash. To do this, we have to satisfy our customers. This requires business processes that are customer focused [quality, service, and cost]. To sustain these processes, we need continuous improvement and learning measures.

"I structure my thoughts using a value chain perspective. The financial numbers look at past cashflows resulting from how we have been doing things [our past strategy and activities]. Using only the financial numbers, we cannot see inside the value chain. It is a black box.

"Supplementing the financial measures with the activity-based management measures we've developed over the past four meetings [Chapters 10–13], we can look inside the value chain at its components. I work the value chain backwards. So I start with how customers view our goods and services. This determines our ultimate value. Next, I look inside the value chain at our internal processes. Finally, we want to see if processes and activities are improving sufficiently. So, we should measure four perspectives on value:

- The customer focus,
- The internal processes focus,
- The innovation and learning focus, and ultimately
- The financial focus.

What should each perspective tell us? Here's the general model [Exhibit 14-15].

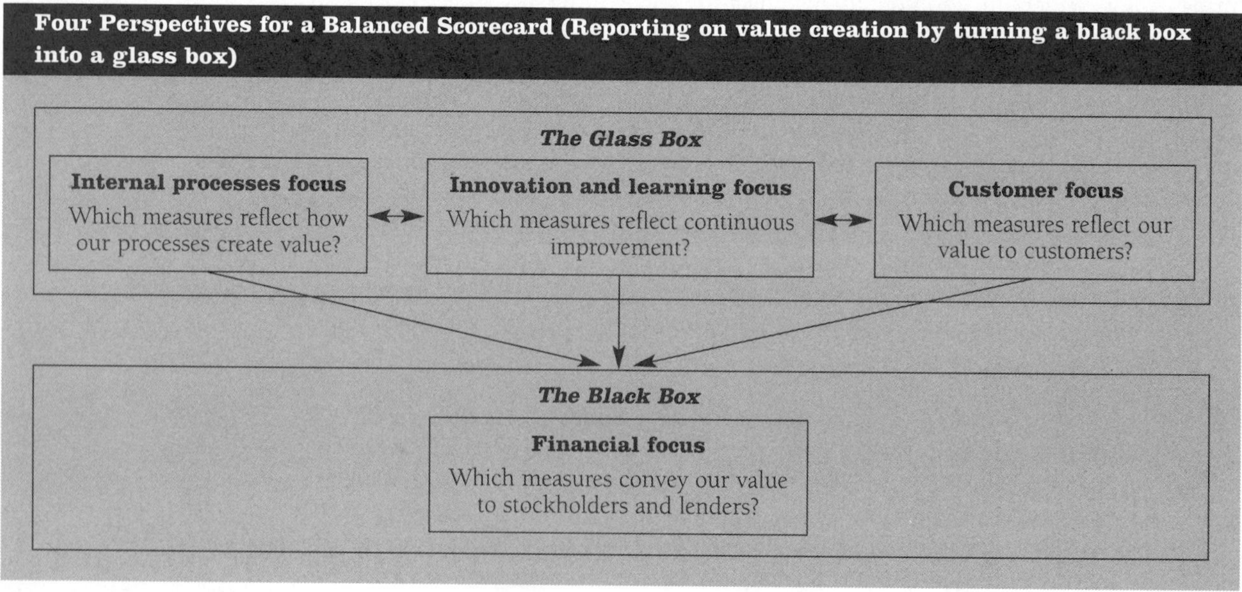
Four Perspectives for a Balanced Scorecard (Reporting on value creation by turning a black box into a glass box)
The Glass Box
Internal processes focus
Which measures reflect how our processes create value?
Innovation and learning focus
Which measures reflect continuous improvement?
Customer focus
Which measures reflect our value to customers?
The Black Box
Financial focus
Which measures convey our value to stockholders and lenders?

Exhibit 14-15

"Let's examine each in turn. I'd like to illustrate the measures other firms are using in each category before we decide which measures best reflect value creation for Multree Homes. It's kind of like a benchmarking approach. Once we understand what others are doing, we'll be in a better position to choose the best measures for us. This is especially important because specific measures are not right or wrong. We have no rules, such as GAAP for financial reporting, to tell us what our reporting constraints and options are. From everything I've seen, each firm defines its own perspectives and measures based on its unique strategic plan and goal set."

KEY OBJECTIVE 5

Describe four perspectives for long-run value and create a balanced scorecard.

The customer focus. "The **customer focus** asks, 'What's important to our customers?' Obviously, this depends on who our customers are, the competitive environment we are in, and what goods or services we provide them. Here's how some firms in different economic sectors have answered this question [Exhibit 14-16]."

The **customer focus** *identifies measures reflecting how we create value for our customers.*

Examples of Customer Focus Goals and Measures

Company	Goals	Measures
Underwater engineering and construction	1. Value for the money 2. Hassle-free relationships 3. Innovation	1. Competitive price comparisons 2. Customer satisfaction surveys 3. Market share
Electronics firm	1. Customer support 2. Delivery 3. Quality	1. Response time 2. On-time delivery ratio 3. Number of defects, number of visits to customers
Food company	1. Customize products for local customers 2. Lowest cost supplier 3. Product expansion	1. Cross-sell ratio 2. Total cost comparison with competition 3. Percentage of R&D products being test marketed by customers
Commercial bank	1. Personalized service 2. Pricing 3. Competitive products	1. Number of complaints 2. Competitive comparisons 3. Number of products offered per year
Biotechnology firm	1. New products 2. Accurate invoices 3. Early payment	1. Percentage of sales from new products 2. Percentage of error-free invoices 3. Percentage of customers paying early

Exhibit 14-16

NANCY

"Wow! *We see a real mix of financial and nonfinancial measures, as well as hard and soft data.* What do these firms have in common when they determine the factors that create value to their customers?"

TOMMY

"It seems *they consider the three critical success factors we identified in our strategic cost management meeting [Chapter 10]: quality, service, and cost.* We should do this, too, by starting with our snake chart [Exhibit 10-10]. They also seem to be 'backwards-looking' measures, much like financial statements. Each company is reporting on what already happened. But this is the nature of performance evaluation; comparing what we have done against our plans.

"In setting customer satisfaction goals, much of the information we need may come from industry sources. For example, a computer company wanting to be the best in customer satisfaction had a marketing firm benchmark it against the competition. In the automobile industry, J.D. Powers conducts independent quality surveys. The airline industry often relies on U.S. Department of Transportation reports about on-time departures and arrivals, baggage handling, safety factors, and passenger complaints.

"Information also can be internally generated. Rockwater Construction, a Scottish subsidiary of Halliburton, tracked time with customers on new projects. This type of strategic partnering drives future sales. My point is we need both forward- and backward-looking information so we can focus our future improvement projects. It's one thing to know what we did last year. It's quite another, however, to know what we have to do next! In other words, *if we're going to use measures like these, they better be part of our strategic plan.*"

We create value for our customers through our value chain processes. The **internal processes focus** *addresses how we do this.*

JULIE

The internal processes focus. "Before we get involved in determining our own measures, let's see what these firms did in analyzing the other perspectives. Next, we should focus on our internal value chain processes. This **internal processes focus** recognizes *what's important to our customers should drive the processes we seek to improve.* So, this focus should help us evaluate our core competencies." [Exhibit 14-17 looks at this focus.]

Examples of Internal Processes Focus Goals and Measures

Company	Goals	Measures
Underwater engineering and construction	1. Workplace safety 2. Project success 3. Project quality	1. Safety incident index 2. Project performance index 3. Rework
Electronics firm	1. Manufacturing efficiency 2. Innovation 3. New businesses	1. Lead time 2. Rate of new product introduction per quarter 3. Number of new business starts per year
Food company	1. Predictable production 2. Lowest cost base 3. Distribution efficiency	1. First pass success rate 2. Comparison against lowest cost competitor 3. Percent of perfect orders
Commercial bank	Incorporated in customer focus	Incorporated in customer focus
Biotechnology firm	1. Low-cost producer 2. Inventory reduction 3. New products	1. Per unit cost versus competition 2. Inventory as a percent of sales 3. Budget versus actual number introduced

Exhibit 14-17

"Again, we see how each firm viewed this perspective differently. Some measures here are used also for the customer focus [e.g., lowest cost, quality, and new product introduction]. Perhaps these firms realized summary measures can tell us more than one thing. *One problem I want to avoid is having too many measures.* We easily can overload people by asking them to look at too much."

The innovation and learning focus. "Next, we should consider *how improving internal processes can happen*. The **innovation and learning focus** addresses the motivation for long-run improvements, which lead to process changes. We have to empower our people through training programs, and then motivate them to continuously improve by tying process improvements to rewards. For example, Motorola spent $150 million, which increased productivity 139% over the next 5 years. One survey reported creativity programs resulted in 300% increases in ROI, compared to 100% from TQM programs and 50% increases from research and development." [Exhibit 14-18 provides some insights into what other companies are measuring for this focus.]

JULIE

How does continuous improvement happen? The **innovation and learning focus** *addresses this management question.*

Examples of Innovation and Learning Focus Goals and Measures

Company	Goals	Measures
Underwater engineering and construction	1. Employee motivation 2. Revenue generation 3. Employee morale	1. Number of suggestions per employee 2. Revenue per employee 3. Staff attitude survey
Electronics firm	1. Research and development 2. Market leadership 3. Technology leadership	1. Number of patents 2. Market share in all major markets 3. Product performance compared to competition
Food company	1. Culture supports innovation 2. Linking strategies to rewards 3. Develop core competencies	1. Annual preparedness assessment 2. Net income per dollar of payroll 3. Percent competency deployment matrix filled
Commercial bank	1. Enhanced job skills 2. Participation in firm's success 3. Competitive wages and benefits	1. Training, schooling 2. Bonuses based on corporate and personal performance 3. Annual market survey
Biotechnology firm	1. New active ingredients 2. Proprietary position	1. Number of new ingredients identified 2. Number of new patents

Exhibit 14-18

The financial focus. "You know, the more we study the balanced scorecard approach, the better I like it. One problem we've been wrestling with throughout this first year of business ownership is relying on financial statements to run the business. 'Management by the numbers' is 'risky business.'"

"Yes, I now agree. But we cannot ignore the importance of financial accounting information. It tells external users [stockholders/owners, creditors] whether continuous improvements are improving the 'bottom line.' Financial success [cash and profits] is the logical result from improving our value chain processes."

"So if we focus on process improvements, should the financial numbers take care of themselves? I still don't see why we need to consider the financial focus."

"We have no guarantee that process improvements translate into long-term financial value. For example, the major long-run problem we discovered with TOC is the continuing unused capacity created by eliminating constraints. If we do not use that extra capacity to generate additional profits, it is wasted. We continue incurring an extra cost to maintain surplus capacity, without receiving any extra

> The **financial focus** *assures our continuous improvement programs result in better financial performance.*

benefit. The **financial focus** tells us whether our nonfinancial balanced scorecard measures lead to improved financial performance. If not, we need to adjust our strategic plan. The financial measures are the ultimate umpire!" Julie looked around the room for the other baseball fans. "What measures are companies using here?" [See Exhibit 14-19.]

Examples of Financial Focus Goals and Measures

Company	Goals	Measures
Underwater engineering and construction	1. Investor value 2. Liquidity 3. Project success	1. ROI 2. Cashflow 3. Project profitability
Electronics firm	1. Sales growth 2. Profitability 3. Prosperity	1. Annual change in sales and profits 2. ROI 3. Cashflow
Food company	1. Aggressive global expansion 2. Remain the preferred supplier 3. Increasing share of market growth	1. Ratio of U.S. to international sales 2. Volume and revenue trends by line of business 3. Company growth versus industry growth
Commercial bank	1. Efficiency 2. Loan loss minimization 3. Loan delinquencies	1. Overhead expense ratios 2. Number of problem loans, early detection 3. Number of bad loan underwritings
Biotechnology firm	1. Growth 2. Profitability 3. Industry leadership	1. Revenue percentage increase 2. ROI, earnings per share 3. Market share

Exhibit 14-19

Multree's balanced scorecard

"Now that we've seen what others are doing, how do we choose our measures?"

Criteria for choosing measures. "We've identified four criteria:

> **Stakeholders** *determine (influence) our value. External stakeholders sustain our existence. Internal stakeholders provide our value-adding activities, products, and services.*

- The measures should reflect long-term value.
- 'We are creating value' should be communicated to external stakeholders.
- 'You are creating value' should be communicated to internal stakeholders.
- Don't have too many measures."

NANCY

"What do you mean when using the term 'stakeholders'? Is this just another fancy word for information users? Why is it important to consider stakeholders?"

"**Stakeholders** are very important people. They influence our long-run value. However, this is true only if we, as an organization, create value for them. We need to provide value to our external stakeholders. These are owners, investors, creditors, customers, and society. They ultimately measure our worth through financing what we do, buying our goods and services, and supporting our existence.

"Internal stakeholders are the people within our organization. If we create an environment adding value to our internal stakeholders, they will do the things that make our organization valuable."

"Only by taking care of our 'family' of Multree workers can our company provide value to others. I think in choosing performance measures, we should consider three criteria:

- Is this what we want our people to do? [Can we see how this measure increases long-term value?]
- Does this measure correctly motivate our people? [To make decisions in the organization's best interest.]
- Do our people understand the measure? [Is the measure just common sense to those evaluated with it?]"

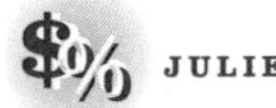

"Those are good ideas, Tommy. We have two perspectives for choosing performance measures [summarized in Exhibit 14-20]."

Criteria for Choosing Performance Measures

The communication focus	The behavioral focus
Measures should reflect long-term value creation	Is this what we want our people to do?
Communicate to external stakeholders that *we* are creating long-term value	Does this measure correctly motivate them?
Communicate to internal stakeholders that *they* are creating long-term value	Is this measure understandable and common sense to those being evaluated by it?

Exhibit 14-20

Our measures. "The types and number of measures we have are limited only by our imagination and creativity. However, we do not want too many. Therefore, the measures we choose should evaluate activities having the greatest effect on value. Let's go to lunch and develop the most important measures from each perspective. I'll buy!"

Nancy's stomach was growling, but she was grinning from ear-to-ear. She now knew she was going to get her 'money's worth' from the one dollar 'investment' she made in Julie at the beginning of the meeting. Little did Nancy realize she was focusing on only one short-run financial factor. Julie intends to charge lunch on the corporate credit card, which means all the owners ultimately share its cost.

After returning from lunch, Julie summarized what they had decided. "We thought of a lot of measures during lunch. Here's the ones we decided to include in our balanced scorecard. From our *customer's perspective*, we have three critical success factors: quality, service, and cost.

- Customers should never have to deal with quality problems. Therefore, compare budgeted and actual external failure costs. Did we achieve our TQM goal? We justified this measure because warranty service received an importance rating of 9 [on a scale to 10] in our snake chart.
- Customers should never unduly wait for our product or service. Therefore, compare year-end on-time deliveries and complete order filling ratios to our strategic plan goals. By the end of the year, did we achieve these goals? [On-time delivery had a snake chart importance rating of 10, and complete order filling was 8.]

- To better serve our business customers, we should be forming strategic partnerships with them. Therefore, compare the number of strategic partnerships we have, and sales revenues from them, with our strategic plan.
- Customers should pay a fair price for our products and services. Therefore, compare our sales prices at the end of the year to our competition.

From an *internal processes perspective*:

- Our processes should provide high-quality products and services. Therefore, report the total costs of quality [COQ]. We already have a COQ variance report for the year [Exhibit 11-3]. What other COQ information do we think is important in signaling value? Our products and services will be more valuable when we eliminate nonconformance costs [internal and external failure costs]. Our COQ report showed us how actual total COQ costs were less than budget [a favorable variance]. This was not good news, however, because the distribution of quality costs between conformance and nonconformance was very unfavorable. Bob and I developed a COQ failure index to capture this information:

Costs of Quality Failure Index

$$\text{COQ failure index} = \frac{\text{Nonconformance costs}}{\text{Conformance costs}}$$

$$\textit{Budget:} \quad \underline{\underline{1.57}} = \frac{\$550{,}000}{\$350{,}000}$$

$$\textit{Actual:} \quad \underline{\underline{3.63}} = \frac{\$635{,}000}{\$175{,}000}$$

I calculated this measure from our COQ report [Exhibit 11-3]. Our long-range objective is to drive nonconformance costs to zero. Each year we should have a goal to reduce this ratio until we ultimately achieve our target. Each year's COQ failure index should reflect the mix we wish to achieve between these costs. Our budget doesn't look good and our actual results look even worse! This should be a high-priority item in next year's strategic plan.

- In servicing both our internal and external customers, our processes should be as efficient as possible. Therefore, compare our actual year-end lead time and lead-time efficiency ratio to our year-end goal in the strategic plan.
- The cost of providing products and services should be decreasing. We want to focus on standard homes. Did we reach our year-end kaizen standard cost? Therefore, compare our year-end actual cost to our kaizen goal. We decided to focus only on the unit and batch-level costs. [Exhibit 9-16 provides our ABC pro-forma income statement.] The year-end kaizen goal is $30,000.

Focusing on *innovation and learning*:

- Learning new skills should lead to cost reductions from quality and efficiency improvements. Therefore, compare our actual continuous improvement [CI] productivity ratio for the year with our strategic plan's goal. [The CI productivity ratio for the truss JIT cell was presented in Exhibit 13-16.]
- Our people should be gaining job satisfaction through the new skills they are learning and a higher quality of working life. This should lead to greater loyalty and retention, which in turn should reduce long-run employee costs. Therefore,

compare our employee turnover goal to the actual number of people leaving Multree due to job dissatisfaction, a better opportunity with a competitor, and the like.

- Better maintained equipment and employee training should result in a safer work environment. A safer environment will reduce future employee-related costs from accidents. Therefore, compare actual time lost due to accidents this year against our strategic plan goal.

In addition to the financial statements external stakeholders receive, we also want to report the following *financial information*:

- If our strategy for creating long-term value is successful, our budgeted and actual profits should be increasing year after year. Therefore, compare budgeted profit increase from last year, and whether we actually accomplished this goal.
- Economic value is cash-generating potential. Therefore, report on whether we achieved our budgeted ending cash balance for the year.

Now let's look at our balanced scorecard for this year [presented in Exhibit 14-21]."

Nonfinancial measures provide strategic links in our value chain

"I know our people will be very happy and highly motivated by our new management accounting information. All they ever used to see was summary dollar-and-cent numbers which were hard to interpret, difficult to relate to their day-to-day activities, and irrelevant to their self-worth [how they create value for the company]."

"One thing we didn't discuss at lunch concerns our new JIT strategy. Control in a JIT environment is initiated by the people in real time. It is not initiated after the fact by accounting information. Do we need a balanced scorecard if we are a JIT company?"

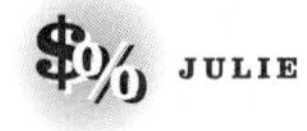

"American companies, unlike the Japanese, have had problems with JIT. One reason is due to not changing the performance evaluation system and measures to reflect the new culture. Remember, the traditional performance measures were developed for scientific managements' functional silos. Even with JIT, we still need to link process controls and people controls. The balanced scorecard can help us achieve this goal."

"Well, I still don't like some of these measures. It's just not financial data. Value is measured in dollars and cents. We journalize financial transactions because they represent value changes. Transactions and their journal entries are auditable. By placing nonfinancial measures in a formal performance evaluation report, we're implying that they, too, are auditable, and both external and internal stakeholders can rely upon all of the reported information. In fact, the cause-effect linkage between nonfinancial measures and financial value is not clear. The auditors will not touch it! They'd rather shoot us dead, just like Slim the cowboy's fear back in our first meeting."

Linking to internal stakeholders: the employee turnover example. "I have to disagree. Look at employee turnover. Even though this is a nonfinancial measure, it is a critical driver of Multree's future value. In a learning organization, employee skills and motivation drive innovation and process improvements. We're making a significant investment in our employees. We don't have 'managers' versus 'workers' anymore. Everyone is empowered and responsible for good 'management'

Multree Homes Balanced Scorecard

Critical success factors	Strategic plan and budget	Actual	Variance* Amount	Variance* %**
Customer measures:				
External failure costs	$350,000	$418,000	($68,000)	(19%)
On-time deliveries	85%	90%	5%	6%
Complete order filling	75%	70%	(5%)	(7%)
Number of strategic partnerships	3	2	(1)	(33%)
Sales revenues from strategic partners	$3,000,000	$3,000,000	$0	0%
	Competition	**Multree**		
Standard homes sales price comparison	$48,000	$50,000	($2,000)	(4%)
Custom homes sales price comparison	$110,000	$100,000	$10,000	9%
	Budget	**Actual**		
Internal process measures:				
COQ failure index	157%	363%	(206%)	(131%)
Year-end total lead time (months)	3	5	(2)	(67%)
Year-end lead-time efficiency ratio	50%	55%	5%	10%
Year-end kaizen cost: standard homes	$30,000	$29,500	$500	2%
Innovation and learning measures				
Continuous improvement productivity ratio	20%	21%	1%	5%
Employee turnover	1	3	(2)	(200%)
Lost workdays due to accidents	50	45	5	10%
Financial measures				
Change in budgeted profit from last year	$100,000	$85,000	($15,000)	(15%)
Ending cash balance	$100,000	$120,000	$20,000	20%

Notes:
*Positive is favorable, negative is unfavorable
**Variance amount as a percentage of plan

Exhibit 14-21

[decision making, learning, continuous improvement]. Our people are expensive and valuable assets. We can't afford to lose them. The cause-effect linkage between employee turnover and long-run value is very clear to me! Our ability to make cash is our economic value. Multree Homes is a cash machine. Every time we lose an employee, our cashflow suffers, today and in the future. Yes, we spend a lot on our employees. But we'll spend even more whenever we have to replace one."

TOMMY

"Today is not the same as when the Boss just hopped into his pickup truck, drove down to the county employment office, and hired the guys standing around looking for a day's work. Labor is no longer a variable cost. We don't hire a few more people on a busy day, teach them how to nail pieces of wood together, and then fire them the next day. In many industries, scientific management methods the Boss followed may still work fine. Any fast food franchise demonstrates this. However, in our new highly competitive markets, where other firms are eliminating nonvalue-added activities, continuously improving value chain processes, and striving for zero defects, we have to operate under a new 'learning organization' strategy.

"Now our people truly are assets, even though the income statement still treats them as expenses. Having always focused on the income statement, I understand why our employee investments were so pathetic in the past, and why our employee turnover was so high. Employees were just an expense of doing business. Every dollar we spent on them reduced net income by a dollar. Today, that short-run focus really can hurt our competitive position and long-run value."

Linking to external stakeholders: the customer quality and service examples. "Bob's absolutely right! From my marketing perspective, our customers determine our value through the volume of products bought and the prices they are willing to pay. O.K., so some of the customer measures are nonfinancial. But I have to look at it this way: customers with no quality complaints or service problems will buy more of our products, today and tomorrow. And they will bring new customers to us. In contrast, if we treat our customers poorly, Multree Homes will go down the toilet. I think the cause-effect relationship between value creation and nonfinancial measures of quality and service is obvious. This is what gives our management accounting system value. It supports good judgment. Nonfinancial measures are useful because they predict future cashflows."

Closing the control loop: the balanced scorecard, strategic planning, and performance evaluation

"O.K. We seem to have some consensus here. But we are not finished yet. Just because this is the year-end, and we've issued our financial statements, doesn't mean the world has come to an end. Won't we all be coming back to work tomorrow? We're going to start a new year. We need a new strategic plan. This time, let's do it right. Our next strategic plan should be based on the balanced scorecard measures we just created."

"This is not a new thought. Over 20 years ago, a now classic article was written, 'On the Folly of Rewarding A, While Hoping for B.' The author, Steven Kerr, is now vice-president and chief learning officer at General Electric. His point was simple. We cannot ask people to do one thing but then reward them for something else. We should look at how Conair-Franklin rewards its people. They can earn up to 6% in extra wages each month by achieving its financial and nonfinancial goals.

"What gets measured, gets done! Most companies still base top management compensation on financial performance as measured by financial accounting's rules [GAAP]. Look at the ethical issue this creates. Top management answers to external stakeholders, who receive only financial statements. Thus, strategic decisions are partly motivated by their effects on financial statements. Where's the motivation to invest in research and development? While this is a critical driver of long-term value, it is an expense on the income statement. Furthermore, paying for it drains cash, adversely affecting the balance sheet. By not investing in research and development, managers improve their 'performance' by making the financial statements look better. Doing this at year-end to positively affect evaluations often is called 'window dressing' the financial statements.

"I talked to a friend yesterday. She said her company used monthly balanced scorecards, until the first time they failed to achieve a monthly financial goal. After that, they did not talk about the balanced scorecard anymore. In the mid-1990s, Apple Computers used balanced scorecards for planning, but not for control. This may have been a strategic mistake contributing to their long-run financial problems! Apple is not an isolated case. A recent survey of U.S. Fortune 500 and Canadian Post 300 firms reported some interesting statistics. While 76% rated employee empowerment as highly important, only 38% measured it. With innovation, it was 63% versus 22%. For customer service, the statistics were 84% of firms rated it highly, but only 71% used it. What we're seeing is a huge gap between importance and use.

"From an ethical perspective, we should use balanced scorecards to link planning, operational control, and performance evaluation. Companies like Campbell Soup, DuPont, IBM, and Johnson & Johnson do this by formally incorporating ethics in their internal control systems. To make this work, balanced scorecards cannot be restricted to firm-wide reporting. They need to be part of the planning, control, and evaluation process of departments and individuals. Applying balanced scorecard to departments, like Information Systems, has already been done. And, when riding back from lunch, Doris showed me how she can apply it to herself [see key objective 5 summary]."

$% JULIE

"Maybe we can learn something from the French. French companies have been using a 'Tableau de Bord' for over 50 years. Much like a balanced scorecard, it links goals and measures. It goes much farther, though, through tying the strategic plan to performance evaluation criteria. [Exhibit 14-22 shows this linkage.]

"To help us, the IMA recently published a statement providing step-by-step guidance in developing balanced scorecard measures and linking them through the strategic plan to performance evaluation. Balanced scorecard software programs also are now available. Motorola reports performance using its balanced scorecard through its intranet. Its graphical report uses colors mimicking a stop light [red, yellow, green]."

NANCY

"When I think about everything we've talked about today, as well as in all of our previous meetings, two *strategic conclusions* seem obvious:

- We need to consider multiple decision criteria to assure long-term value creation.
- We exist in a dynamic environment. As technology and markets change, our processes must change to remain competitive [responsive to our customers].

What is good management? In order to create long-term value, we must:

- Identify our customers' needs [both internal and external].
- Determine our core competencies [where we fit in the value chain].
- Create a strategic plan to exploit our core competencies for the firm's benefit [owners and employees].
- Monitor and control day-to-day operations in order to keep on-track toward our goals.
- Evaluate performance, rewarding our people and motivating them to continually improve product and service quality, customer service, and to reduce cost.

What are the implications for management accounting systems?

- The key characteristic of high-quality management accounting information is relevance, information to support value-increasing decisions.

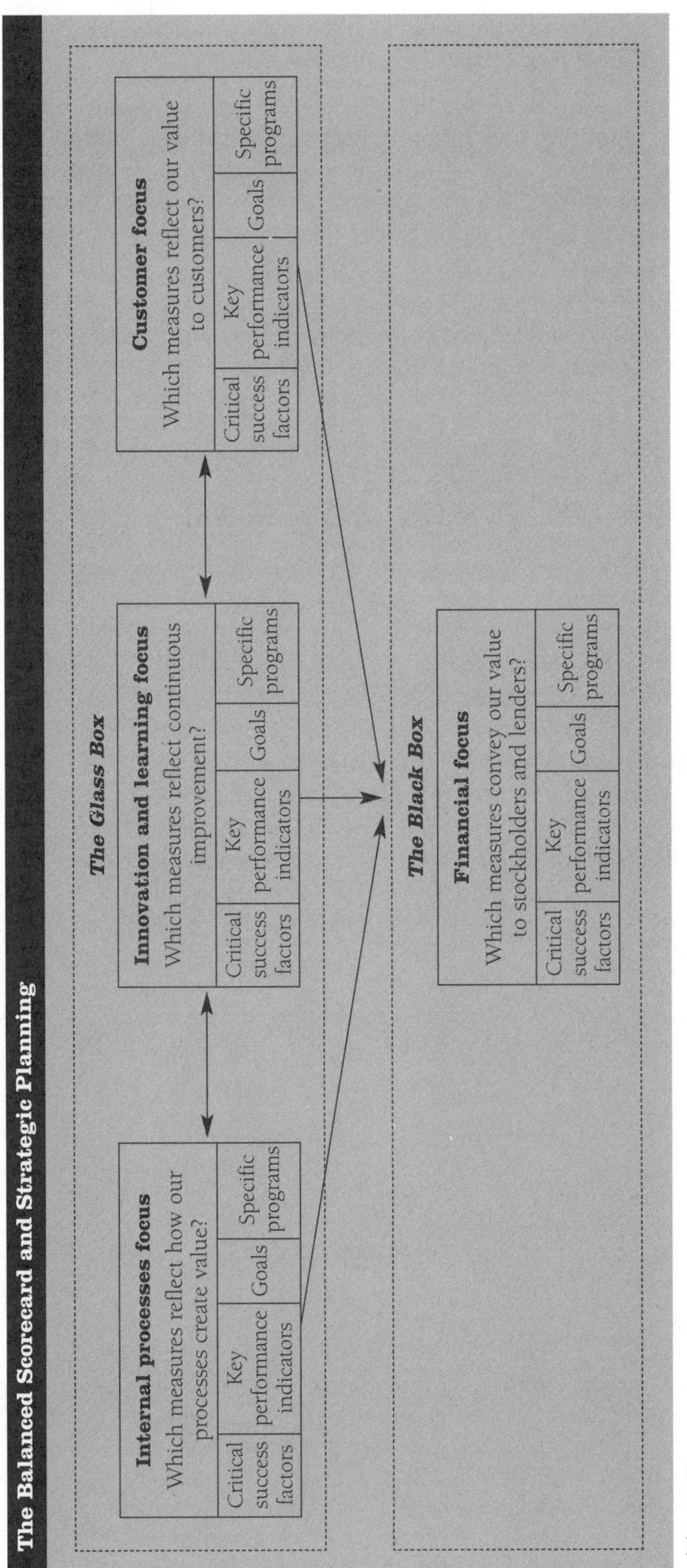
The Balanced Scorecard and Strategic Planning
The Glass Box
Internal processes focus
Which measures reflect how our processes create value?
Critical success factors
Key performance indicators
Goals
Specific programs
Innovation and learning focus
Which measures reflect continuous improvement?
Critical success factors
Key performance indicators
Goals
Specific programs
Customer focus
Which measures reflect our value to customers?
Critical success factors
Key performance indicators
Goals
Specific programs
The Black Box
Financial focus
Which measures convey our value to stockholders and lenders?
Critical success factors
Key performance indicators
Goals
Specific programs
Exhibit 14-22

- Relevant information can include financial as well as nonfinancial information. Data can be either hard or soft [factual or estimated].
- The appropriateness of accounting systems depends on the environment we are in. In other words, we need different types of information for different situations. No one accounting system will work in all environments. To understand which information is relevant, we must identify the activities adding value to our customers.
- What gets measured gets done. So, make sure management accounting information specifically links strategic plans to operational budgets, develops relevant measures to monitor day-to-day operations, appropriately motivates our people, and is used consistently in performance evaluation."

KEY OBJECTIVES SUMMARY

DORIS

"Here are the notes I've taken from this last meeting of the year. Let's see if I've grasped the major concepts and important calculations.

1. Define present value, and compute the present value of a lump sum and an annuity.

"Capital budgeting decisions concern multi-year investments. We invest in assets today that create future cashflows. Capital budgeting analysis compares today's cost to the benefits received in future years. These benefits are called an annuity stream. The difficulty with this cost-benefit analysis is we cannot directly compare a dollar today with a dollar in the future. The future dollar is not worth as much as the dollar today. This is called the time value of money. Today's dollar can be invested and earn interest. If I deposit a dollar today in my 5% savings account, it will be worth $1.05 in a year. So, one dollar in a year is worth less than a dollar today. In fact, you have to offer me $1.05 in a year in order to get my dollar today. Today's dollar has a future value of $1.05.

"One difference between future value and present value is interest [technically, compound interest]. Another difference is risk. As risk increases, I'll need a higher return in order to justify the investment. Unlike Nancy, I will not give a dollar to Julie, not even if she offers me more than $1.05 in a year. The risk of never getting back the dollar is too great." Julie just smiled as she put her hand in her pocket and felt the dollar bill Nancy had 'given' her earlier.

"Today's dollar is like an apple. The future dollar is like an orange. We can translate that future dollar [the orange] into the equivalent of today's dollar [an apple]. Then we can compare apples to apples. This is called discounting." Doris was exceptionally proud of herself. She always hears accountants saying, "You can't compare apples to oranges," but it never made sense to her until just now. Besides, the grandchildren were all into a fitness and health craze. Half empty bowls of wheat germ and skim milk still were in the corner of the conference room.

"Today's worth of the future cashflows is called present value. Present value tables provide PV factors for discounting. Alternatively, we can use a calculator or build a spreadsheet program to do this. To illustrate, I'll deposit one dollar in my 5% savings account. We already know its future value is $1.05 in one year.

Compute future value: Multiply present value by the interest rate
The future value of $1.00 = $1.00 × 1.05 = $1.05

Now, compute present value:

Present value = Future value divided by the interest rate
The present value of $1.05 = $1.05 ÷ 1.05 = $1.00
Or: The present value of $1.05 = $1.05 × .9524 = $1.00

Dividing by 1.05 is the same as multiplying by [1 ÷ 1.05]. The PV factor for 1 year at 5% is .9524 [1 ÷ 1.05].

"Now let's discount an annuity stream to its present value. How much do I have to deposit in my 5% savings account so I can withdraw $1.00 every year for 10 years? Again, just multiply the future value by the PV factor.

The present value of a $1.00 10-year annuity at 5% = $1.00 × 7.7217 = $7.73 [always round up]

I have to deposit $7.73 today in a 5% savings account so I can withdraw $1.00 a year for 10 years.

2. Calculate an investment's net present value and relate NPV to the investment's time-adjusted ROI.

"I want to work as a 'candy-striper' in our local hospital. While I want to do this volunteer work because we should all help our community, it does have some financial costs and benefits I need to consider. I can take the bus or my friend will sell me his car for $5,000. The car will last 4 more years. Having a car will save bus fare. Of course, I'll incur some operating costs [gasoline, insurance, license plates, repairs and maintenance]. It will also save time, which has an opportunity cost because I can use that extra time in my word processing business and make more money. As a volunteer, I get free medical insurance. Adding up these annual cashflows, I can discount them to their present value. Then I'll compare the present value of these future cashflows [benefits] against today's cost. Here's my analysis [Exhibit 14-23].

"I multiplied each annual cashflow by its PV factor for a lump sum. If the annuity stream is the same each year, I can do one multiplication instead of a separate calculation for each year [multiply the annuity amount by the PV factor for a 4-year 5% annuity]. Net present value is the difference between the present value of the annuity and today's cost. A positive NPV means the investment yields a time-adjusted return on investment [ROI] greater than the discount rate. A common name for the time-adjusted ROI is internal rate of return [IRR]. IRR is less than the discount factor when a negative NPV results. An NPV equal to zero means IRR equals the discount rate. IRR can be manually calculated if we have a constant annuity stream [the same amount every year], but I don't want to do it!! It's really best to let a spreadsheet program do the work.

NPV and ROI Calculations for Doris

Year	Cashflow		PV factor for a lump sum at 5%		Present value
Cash outflow:					
now	($5,000)	x	1.0000	=	*($5,000)*
Cash inflows:					
1	$1,700	x	0.9524	=	$1,619
2	1,400	x	0.9070	=	1,270
3	1,300	x	0.8638	=	1,123
4	1,200	x	0.8227	=	987
PV of cash inflows					*$4,999*
NPV:					*($1)*
Time-adjusted ROI (IRR):					*5%*

Exhibit 14-23

"As far as the financial analysis is concerned, I'm indifferent between leaving the $5,000 in my 5% savings account or buying the car. I used 5% for the discount rate because it is my opportunity cost for the $5,000 investment with the same risk. The negative $1.00 NPV means I'm not quite earning a 5% return. The IRR is 4.992%. This level of precision affects only my ulcers. O.K. I'm getting a 5% return on my investment, which is what I'd earn in my savings account.

"I probably should consider the tax effects of this decision, too. The extra money I make is taxable income. The costs of charitable work are tax deductible. If I only use the car for charity work, I can deduct its depreciation, so I'll depreciate the car over 4 years at $1,250 per year. Here's the NPV and ROI analysis [Exhibit 14-24, using the spreadsheet program in Appendix A].

"I have two cashflows each year, the cost savings and the change in income taxes from those savings. I could have done a lot of manual discounting calculations to get NPV and IRR. Instead, I let the spreadsheet program do it [these are financial functions available on all spreadsheet programs].

"After taxes, I am not getting a 5% ROI. If financial factors are the only decision criteria, I will not buy the car and not work at the hospital. But considering qualitative factors [externalities], like the value to my community from charitable work, I'll do this even though the NPV is negative [in other words, the IRR is less than 5%]. This charitable work is more important to me than the interest income I will lose.

3. Discuss how the timing of cashflows and risk affect capital budgeting decisions, and determine the payback period.

"Who's crystal ball is perfectly clear? Who can predict the future with total accuracy? I wish I could! Because capital budgeting decisions look a long way into the future, we need to consider when we will receive the benefits [future cashflows], as well as the risk of not receiving them as originally estimated.

"PV factors decrease as the time before receiving a cashflow increases. Look again at my first analysis [Exhibit 14-23]. The smaller PV factor for 4 years

Capital Budgeting Spreadsheet Program and Income Taxes

Year	Cashflows Investment	Change in profit	Less depreciation	Change in taxable income	Change in taxes (25% tax rate)	Cashflows Net change after taxes*
now	($5,000)					($5,000)
1		$1,700	($1,250)	$450	($113)	1,588
2		1,400	(1,250)	150	(38)	1,363
3		1,300	(1,250)	50	(13)	1,288
4		1,200	(1,250)	(50)	13	1,213
Totals		$5,600	($5,000)	$600	($150)	$450

Net present value =	*($143)*
Time-adjusted ROI (IRR) =	*4%*

**Note:* Net change after taxes = Cashflow change in profit - Change in taxes. All amounts formatted to zero decimal places.

Exhibit 14-24

[0.8227], compared to the one-year factor [0.9524], means a dollar in 4 years is less valuable than a dollar in one year. This simply tells us the longer we have to wait to receive cash, the less valuable it is to us today. Looking at this from the present value point of view, investing $1.00 will result in more money in 4 years than in one year. I can earn 4 years' worth of compound interest. So, I have to deposit less money today to receive $1.00 in 4 years than I have to deposit if I want that $1.00 in only one year.

"The sooner we receive a cashflow, the less risky it is, and the more valuable it becomes. One decision criterion is how long it takes to get back my investment. This is called the payback period. Again, let's use my original analysis for the hospital volunteer work [see Exhibit 14-25].

"In 3 years, I'll recover all but $600 of my investment. How long into the fourth year do I have to wait before I recover the last $600? I'm projecting a $1,200 cashflow in year 4. It will take a half-year to get $600. Thus, I'm projecting a 3½ year payback period for this investment.

4. Explain the need for multiple capital budgeting methods, and calculate the accounting rate of return.

"Different methods can lead to different decisions. Why? NPV assumes cashflows are invested at the discount rate. ROI assumes cashflows are invested at the time-adjusted rate of return. If the discount rate and the ROI are very different, and most of the cashflows are received early or late in the investment's life, NPV and ROI can yield conflicting results. Obviously, they will assume significantly different amounts of interest are earned throughout the project's life. And the cashflows at the end of the project will have very different present values because of the large

Hospital Volunteer Work Payback Period

Year	Investment	Annuity received	Investment balance remaining
now	$5,000		$5,000
1		$1,700	3,300
2		1,400	1,900
3		1,300	600
4		1,200	(600)

$$\text{Payback period} = 3 \text{ years} + \frac{\$600}{\$1{,}200}$$

Payback period = 3.5 years

Exhibit 14-25

difference between the NPV discount rate and the ROI. Thus it is important to do both analyses.

"We've also seen the importance of the payback period analysis. Now let's consider how external stakeholders evaluate our capital budgeting decisions. They have only financial statement information. The best they can do is calculate an accounting rate of return [ARR] in evaluating our ability to increase long-term value. Here's the ARR for my decision [Exhibit 14-26].

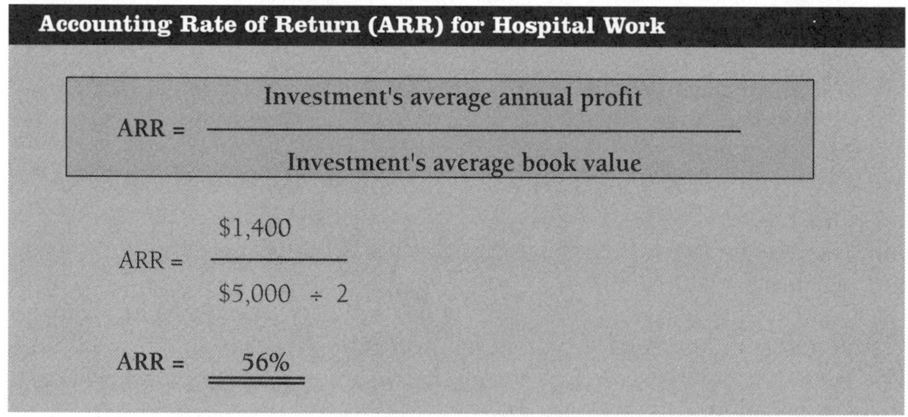
Accounting Rate of Return (ARR) for Hospital Work

$$\text{ARR} = \frac{\text{Investment's average annual profit}}{\text{Investment's average book value}}$$

$$\text{ARR} = \frac{\$1{,}400}{\$5{,}000 \div 2}$$

$$\text{ARR} = 56\%$$

Exhibit 14-26

In the ARR numerator, the average annual profit is the sum of the annuity stream divided by its life [($1,700 + $1,400 + $1,300 + $1,200) ÷ 4 years = $1,400 average cashflow per year. I'm ignoring taxes]. For the ARR denominator, the average investment is $2,500. I invest $5,000 now. After fully depreciating the car over 4 years, its financial accounting value will be zero [($5,000 + $0) ÷ 2 = $2,500]. The ARR is 56%. This easily justifies a car for me!

"Capital budgeting decisions and performance evaluation are not simple activities. Because these methods provide different information and are used by different stakeholders, it makes sense to use multiple decision criteria. In other words, the more information we have, the better our decision will be.

5. Describe four perspectives for long-run value and create a balanced scorecard.

"Multree Homes is a cash machine. Our primary criterion for long-run value is our ability to make money, now and in the future. As with all organizations, though, cash is not our only concern. However, I do not know of any organization that does not have to be concerned with its ability to get cash! So let's start with a financial perspective. This perspective emphasizes creating value for the owners. Usually they are external stockholders, but they can be taxpayers [for a governmental organization], a government [for a nonprofit organization], or even creditors.

"How do we succeed financially? By creating value for our customers. Thus we also need measures reflecting our value from a customer perspective. Our value chain processes must assure continuing customer satisfaction through their effectiveness and efficiency. Next we need value measures from an internal processes perspective. Finally, how can we sustain our value-creating processes? Only through learning and innovation. Therefore, we need measures for this perspective as well.

"The one lesson I've learned is long-term value does not result from a formula we follow blindly. It comes from good management: good judgment, common sense, and good information. Many organizations create different perspectives unique to how they create value. For example, some add a perspective for society and their community. I have four perspectives on my value as a hospital volunteer. Here's my balanced scorecard [Exhibit 14-27].

Balanced Scorecard for Hospital Volunteer Work

Critical success factors	My goals	Actual	Variance* Amount	Variance* %**
Patient measures:				
Time to answer calls for assistance (minutes)	5	4	1	20%
Overall satisfaction with my service***	8	9	1	13%
Administration measures:				
Total volunteer hours per month	15	10	(5)	(33%)
Number of complaints received per month	2	3	(1)	(50%)
Community measures:				
Meals-on-wheels deliveries per week	10	10	0	0%
Other in-home visits per week	4	3	(1)	(25%)
Innovation and learning measures				
New services I can provide per month	1	0	(1)	(100%)
New entertaining activities learned for children	2	1	(1)	(50%)

Notes:
*Positive is favorable, negative is unfavorable
**Variance amount as a percentage of plan
***Measured on a 10-point scale from a snake chart

Exhibit 14-27

Balanced scorecards are not restricted to organizations. Individuals should create balanced scorecards for the roles they serve.

Postscript

"Since this is our last meeting, I just want to thank you all. I've really learned a lot I've been able to apply to my personal life. I never realized management accounting is not just for manufacturing organizations. *Everything we've learned applies equally as well to services, nonprofit, and governmental organizations, as well as to our personal lives.*"

"Well, Doris, you are mistaken about one thing. This won't be our last meeting. Remember, management accounting is truly a road of discovery!"

TO BE CONTINUED . . .

REALITY 101

Financial and Nonfinancial Information Used in Performance Evaluation

Many companies are realizing the need to tie balanced scorecard measures to rewards. MBNA Bank, one of the largest credit card providers, bases bonuses of up to 20% on customer measures. Cigna Insurance and the Bank of Montreal also use balanced scorecards to determine compensation. In a 1996 survey, the IMA's Cost Management Group reported a growing dissatisfaction with financially-based performance evaluations. While 66% reported using nonfinancial measures, 92% said they should be used more extensively. Over 60% are either doing a major overhaul or replacing their performance evaluation systems.

The area of greatest concern seems to be with the linkage between shareholder value and process measures as shown below (see Exhibit 14-A1).

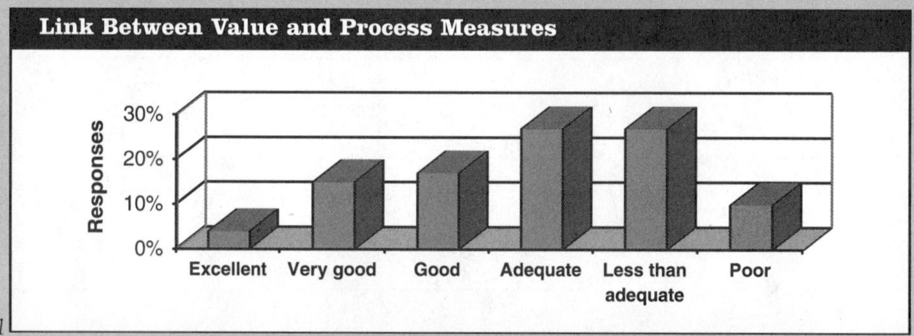

Exhibit 14-A1

We also see a deteriorating linkage between top management objectives and performance measures as shown on the following page (see Exhibit 14-A2).

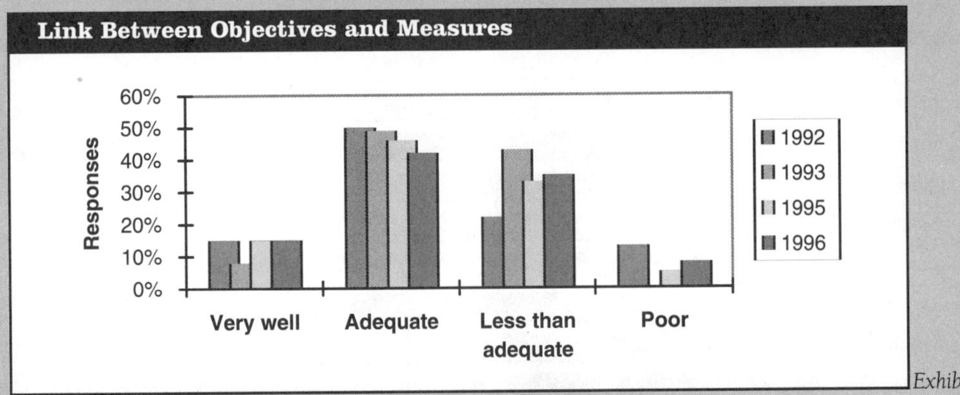

Exhibit 14-A2

The 1997 Compensation and Benefits survey shows some interesting changes:

- 51% were evaluated only with qualitative measures,
- 45% with a combination of qualitative and quantitative measures, and
- only 4% evaluated solely with quantitative measures.

Surprisingly, qualitative measures were more important than quantitative ones 80% of the time. Both were equally important in 20% of performance evaluations. Note, quantitative measures were never more important. This change in emphasis is highlighted by what has happened to one of the most popular new financial performance measures, economic value added (EVA). (See Exhibit 14-A3.)

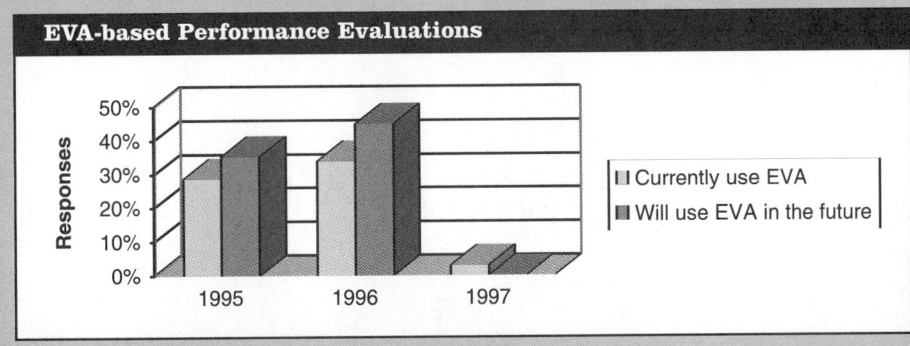

Exhibit 14-A3

(1997 information on future EVA use was not reported.)

Key qualitative measures used are shown on the following page (see Exhibit 14-A4).

Over 67% also reported profit-based bonuses averaging 10%. Nonfinancial measures affect 66% of these bonuses.

Source: *Cost Management Update*, June 1996 and September 1997. © Institute of Management Accountants.

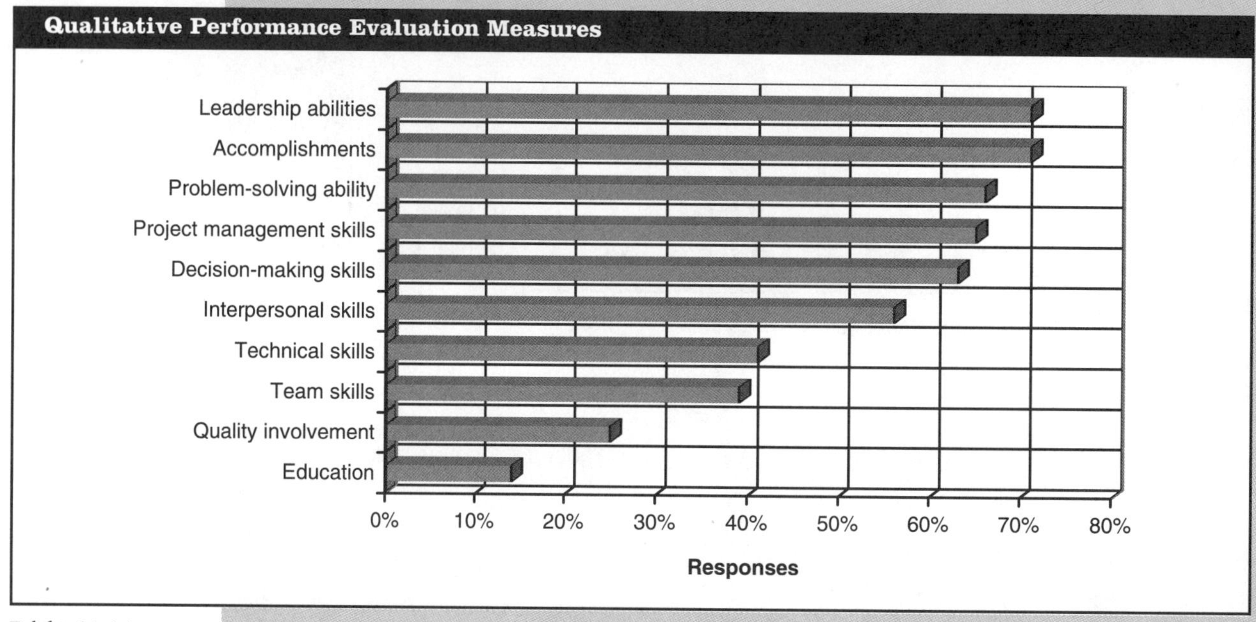

Exhibit 14-A4

APPENDIX A

KEY OBJECTIVE 6

Incorporate taxes into NPV and time-adjusted ROI calculations.

CAPITAL BUDGETING, INCOME TAXES, AND SPREADSHEET PROGRAMS

Creating a spreadsheet program to calculate the NPV and time-adjusted ROI (IRR) is not difficult. This program also will incorporate the effects of depreciation and income taxes on the cashflows. Most capital investments involve the purchase of depreciable assets (e.g., machinery). The asset's purchase occurs now, but it is not used up in making profits right away. An "asset" means we have acquired something that will create profits in the future. As these profits are realized in subsequent years, the amount of the asset "used up" becomes a cost of making those profits. This cost is called depreciation expense. We do not write a check for depreciation each year. It is just an allocation of the asset's original cost when calculating each year's profits. Over all the years, depreciation will equal the asset's cost (this is called accumulated depreciation).

Depreciation expense each year does affect the net profit from the investment, however, and thus the income taxes a firm must pay. So, an investment creates three cashflows:

- The cash-out now for the investment,
- The cash-in in future years from the investment (the annuity stream), and
- The change in income taxes owed due to the extra profits created each year (another annuity stream).

The first two cashflows are shown in columns C and D of Exhibit 14-A5.

Capital Budgeting Spreadsheet Program and Income Taxes

	B	C	D	E	F	G	H
5		Cashflows		Income tax effects			Cashflows
6	Year	Investment (c)	Change in pretax profit (d)	Less depreciation (e)	Change in taxable income (d - e)	Change in taxes (g)	Net change after taxes (c + d + g)
7	now	($1,000)					($1,000)
8	1		$200	($200)	$0	$0	200
9	2		300	(200)	100	(25)	275
10	3		500	(200)	300	(75)	425
11	4		700	(200)	500	(125)	575
12	5		300	(200)	100	(25)	275
13	Totals		$2,000	($1,000)	$1,000	($250)	$750
14							
15	*Net present value =*			$292			
16							
17	*Time-adjusted ROI (IRR) =*			20%			
18							

Exhibit 14-A5

- The initial investment is an asset and does not immediately affect income. Therefore, it does not affect income taxes.
- Each year's cashflow ("Change in pretax profit" in column D) does increase profits for that year.
- The depreciation for the year reduces that profit (column E).
- Column F is the change in pretax profit (column D minus E).
- The exhibit uses a 25% tax rate to calculate the income taxes owed (column G).

Look at year 2. The $300 cashflow (from operating expense savings or increased revenues, for example) increases profits. Deducting $200 in depreciation (using the straight-line method for 5 years with no salvage value, in column E), the net taxable income is $100 (column F). Income taxes go up $25 (column G). We received $300 (column D) less $25 in taxes we owe (column G). The net after-tax cashflow is $275 (column H). Column H contains the annuity stream we must use in NPV and ROI.

This example uses a 10% discount rate for NPV. Using the column H cashflows, the NPV is +$292. The NPV formula input into this cell is:

=NPV(discount rate, annuity stream) – Investment
=NPV(0.10,H8:H12)-H7

NPV is the spreadsheet function name for this calculation. Cells H8 through H12 contain the annuity stream ($200, $275, $425, $575, and $275). Cell H7 contains the $1,000 investment. It must be subtracted because it is a cash-out. The formula's logic goes like this: discount the annuity stream (H8 through H12) at 10% to get its present value and then subtract the investment amount [H7]. This is the same "formula" we used to manually calculate NPV.

The time-adjusted ROI is 20%. It is called the "IRR" in the spreadsheet program. This formula also is very simple:

=IRR(entire annuity stream including the original investment amount)
=IRR(H7:H12)

Here's a thought: If your professor assigns a lot of NPV and IRR homework problems, you'll save much time and frustration by building this program. If you're really a "high-quality management accountant wannabe" by now, you might add cell names and print out the cell formulas so you have a helpful study guide for exams! Good luck!

READING LIST*

Apple's use of the balanced scorecard: Kaplan and Norton, "Putting the Balanced Scorecard to Work," *Harvard Business Review,* September–October 1993.

Balanced scorecard IMA survey: Frigo and Krumwiede, "1998 Cost Management Group Survey on Performance Measurement," *Cost Management Update,* Institute of Management Accountants, April 1998, May 1998, and February 1999.

Balanced scorecard, seminal article: Kaplan and Norton, "The Balanced Scorecard—Measures That Drive Performance," *Harvard Business Review,* January–February 1992.

Balanced scorecard software: Silk, "Automating the Balanced Scorecard," *Management Accounting,* May 1998.

Balanced scorecards for the IS department: Edberg, "Creating and Implementing a Balanced Measurement Program," *Information Management: Strategy, Systems, and Technologies,* 1997.

Balanced scorecards for small organizations: Chow, Haddad, and Williamson, "Applying the Balanced Scorecard to Small Companies," *Management Accounting,* August 1997.

Capital budgeting methods survey: "Changes in the Capital Budgeting Practices of the Fortune 1000," *Controllers Update,* Institute of Management Accountants, November 1998.

Chrysler: Bulkeley, "The Latest Thing at Many Big Companies is Speed, Speed, Speed," *The Wall Street Journal,* December 23, 1994, p. A5.

Conair-Franklin: Downie and Pastoria, "Measuring Change at Conair-Franklin," *Management Accounting,* June 1997.

Denver airport: "Still Late for Arrival," *Newsweek,* August 22, 1994. "The Rocky Horror Airport Opening," *Business Week,* February 13, 1995.

Ethics and the balanced scorecard: Verschoor, "Principles Build Profits," *Management Accounting,* October 1997.

Ford: Suris, "Ford Slashes $11 Billion Out of Budget for New Products Over Next Five Years," *The Wall Street Journal,* February 29, 1996, p. A4.

Forest products industry use of capital budgeting techniques: Bailes, Nielsen, and Lawton, "How Forest Products Companies Analyze Capital Budgets," *Management Accounting,* October 1998.

Gap between identifying and using balanced scorecard measures: Stivers, Covin, Hall, and Smalt, "How Nonfinancial Measures Are Used," *Management Accounting,* February 1998.

General Electric: "Jack Welch's Lessons for Success," *Fortune,* January 25, 1993.

Innovation's effect on ROI: Tatikonda and Tatikonda, "We Need Dynamic Performance Measures," *Management Accounting,* September 1998.

International survey of capital budgeting: Kim and Song, "U.S., Korea, & Japan: Accounting Practices in Three Countries," *Management Accounting,* August 1990.

JIT and balanced scorecards: Clinton and Hsu, "JIT and the Balanced Scorecard: Linking Manufacturing Control to Management Control," *Management Accounting,* September 1997.

Linking the strategic plan to performance measures: *Tools and Techniques for Implementing Integrated Performance Measurement Systems,* SMA 4DD, Institute of Management Accountants, 1998.

Motorola: Tatikonda and Tatikonda, "We Need Dynamic Performance Measures," *Management Accounting,* September 1998.

Motorola's intranet balanced scorecard: Frigo and Krumwiede, "Tips on Implementing the Balanced Scorecard Approach," *Cost Management Update,* May 1998.

Nissan: Woodruff and Armstrong, "A High-Stakes Spin of the Wheel," *Business Week,* December 16, 1994.

Rockwater: Kaplan and Norton, "Putting the Balanced Scorecard to Work," *Harvard Business Review,* September–October 1993.

Saturn: Stern, "Saturn Experiment Is Deemed Successful Enough to Expand," *The Wall Street Journal,* April, 15, 1995, pp. B1–2.

Tableau de Bord: Epstein and Manzoni, "The Balanced Scorecard and Tableau de Bord: Translating Strategy Into Action," *Management Accounting,* August 1997.

Toyota: Taylor, "How Toyota Copes with Hard Times," *Fortune,* January 28, 1993.

West Mercia Constabulary: Silk, "Automating the Balanced Scorecard," *Management Accounting,* May 1998.

*Alphabetic by topic, idea, or company referenced.

KEY TERMS

Absorption costing includes an allocation of fixed overhead in the product's manufacturing cost. It is required for tax and financial reporting in the United States. (Chapter 6)

Accounting rate of return (ARR) is the average financial accounting profit from an investment expressed as a percentage of the average investment (financial accounting net book value). (Chapter 14)

Activities represent the work done in providing a service or making a product. (Chapter 9)

Activity-based costing (ABC) systems directly trace resources to activities, and then activities to products and services. (Chapter 9)

Activity-based management (ABM) is a strategy to maximize value by focusing on the quality, service, and cost of processes and activities. (Chapter 10)

Applied overhead is the overhead cost (indirect manufacturing cost) charged (allocated) to a department or product. (Chapter 5)

Appraisal costs are one of the four costs of quality categories representing the costs of testing product quality. Appraisal and prevention are conformance costs. (Chapter 11)

Asset turnover is a short-run measure of how well assets are used in generating sales. It is the ratio of sales revenues to the investment in assets generating those revenues. (Chapter 8)

Authoritative budgeting involves top management dictating the budget to the rest of the organization. (Chapter 4)

Backflush cost accounting systems can be as simple as a two-journal entry system. Charge (debit) costs into WIP when incurred, and remove (credit) costs from WIP (and debit into COGS) when products are completed (using the product's standard cost). (Chapter 13)

Balanced scorecards report the change in a firm's critical success factors from four perspectives: the customer, business process improvements, innovation and learning, and financial. (Chapter 14)

Batch-level activities are step costs. Every time another batch of products is made, another level of these costs is incurred. (Chapter 9)

Benchmarking is studying the best practices of other firms to learn how they perform activities similar to ours. (Chapter 11)

Break-even revenues are the sales revenues for zero profit. Revenues just equal costs. (Chapter 3)

Break-even volume (break-even point) is the sales volume for zero profit. Revenues just equal costs. (Chapter 3)

Budgetary slack is the reduction in budgeted revenues, or the increase in budgeted costs, above reasonable estimates. (Chapter 4)

Business process reengineering (BPR) recreates a process 'from scratch.' In contrast to continuous improvement (which starts with a process 'as is' and makes small, incremental improvements), BPR starts with a big step forward. (Chapter 13)

Capital budgeting decisions evaluate the current value of multi-year investments by comparing today's value of the future cashflows to the investment's cost. (Chapter 14)

A **cash budget** is the output from the cash management planning stage. It presents the cashflows expected for a future time period (e.g., a year) and the their timing within that period (e.g., each month). (Chapter 4)

Cashflows are the deposits made (**cash inflows** or "cash-ins") and withdrawals from (**cash outflows** or "cash-outs") our bank account. (Chapter 4)

Cash inflows are deposits to the bank account. (Chapter 4)

Cash outflows are withdrawals from the bank account. (Chapter 4)

Certified Management Accountant (CMA) is the professional designation for management and cost accountants passing the **Institute of Management Accountants'** professional licensing exam. (Chapter 1)

Complete order filling ratio is an ABM vendor performance measure relating the number of complete orders received to the total orders received. (Chapter 10)

Conformance costs are incurred to make sure our products (services) perform as expected. They include **prevention costs** and **appraisal costs**. Together with nonconformance costs, they make up the costs of quality. (Chapter 11)

Continuous budgeting adds a new month (or whatever time period is used in the budget) on to the end of the budget each month so an organization always has a current 12-month budget. (Chapter 4)

Continuous improvement programs are part of a TQM strategy focusing on gradual improvements over time. CI often is contrasted with business process reengineering (BPR), a strategy of radical redesign Chapter 13). (Chapter 11)

Continuous improvement (CI) productivity ratio is the savings created by continuous improvements as a percentage of the cost of those improvements. (Chapter 13)

Contribution margin-based income statements organize costs as variable and fixed to aid in management decision making. (Chapter 3)

Contribution margin per unit (CMU) is the extra profit from selling one more product, which can be used to help pay for fixed costs, or kept if total fixed costs are already covered. (Chapter 3)

Contribution margin ratio is the percentage of a sales dollar that remains after paying for variable costs. It is contribution margin divided by revenues. (Chapter 3)

Control role: management accounting information is used to promote decisions in the best interest of the organization. In other words, it influences people's behavior because it's used to evaluate and reward them. (Chapter 1)

Controllable segment margin reports the profit resulting from activities under the segment manager's control. It is used in evaluating the segment manager's performance (contrast this subtotal with segment margin). (Chapter 8)

Core competencies are those processes and activities a firm does best. They result in products or services yielding long-run value to the firm. (Chapter 10)

Cost accounting systems measure a product's manufacturing costs for financial reporting. To support decision making and motivation (its role in management accounting), the cost accounting system also should provide cost information on all activities of the product or service. (Chapter 1)

Cost allocation is the process of dividing up a cost, or averaging it, over the products made, or some other measure of its use. For example, nails costing $100 might be divided over the 10 houses made, yielding an average cost of $10 per house. Or, nail cost could be divided over the 1,000 carpenter hours worked, yielding an average cost of 10¢ per hour. Allocation is one of two methods for cost assignment. The other method is direct tracing. (Chapters 2 and 5)

Cost assignment is attaching resource costs to something of interest (a "cost object," e.g., a specific product, a batch of products, a department, a product line, a geographic sales territory, etc.). (Chapter 5)

Cost behavior patterns identify how costs change with changes in volume. Costs usually are classified as **variable** (constant per unit) or **fixed** (constant in total). (Chapter 3)

Cost centers are responsible for controlling the costs of their activities. They do not have profit or investment responsibilities. Cost variance reports often are used in evaluating their performance. (Chapter 8)

A **cost driver** is the activity causing a specific cost. In labor-intensive departments, for example, labor hours worked may cause overhead. But, in automated processes, machine usage may cause overhead. (Chapter 5)

Cost of goods manufactured is the production cost of completed products made by a manufacturer. (Chapter 2)

A **cost-plus pricing strategy** begins with a product's or service's cost and then adds an amount to cost (a **markup**) in determining its sales price. (Chapter 7)

Cost pools are subsets of overhead having their own unique causes (cost drivers). (Chapter 9)

Costs of quality (COQ) include all costs of preventing, correcting, and detecting quality problems, as well as the opportunity costs of not correcting problems before they reach our customers. (Chapter 11)

A **credit collection pattern** shows the percentage of a month's credit sales to be collected in that month and each subsequent month. (Chapter 4)

The **customer focus** identifies **balanced scorecard** measures reflecting how we create value for our customers. (Chapter 14)

Decision support role: management accounting information is used in long-run strategic planning, short-run operational planning, monitoring and controlling operations, and evaluating performance. (Chapter 1)

Direct labor is physically and easily traced to products. Time cards, computer touch screens, and bar code scanners can track an individual's time to the products he/she works on. Usually, direct laborers physically work on the products. (Chapter 2)

Direct materials are the raw materials physically and easily traced to a product. Examples for building a house include lumber, appliances, carpeting, and windows. (Chapter 2)

Direct tracing specifically identifies a resource's cost with a cost object. It is one of two methods for cost assignment. Direct tracing is accomplished by using source documents such as: purchase orders and material requisition forms for direct materials; and time cards, touch screens, or bar code scanners for direct labor. (Chapter 5)

Discounting is calculating the **present value** (today's worth or value) of future cashflows. (Chapter 14)

Drum-buffer-rope is a TOC production scheduling and WIP management system to maximize the constraint's output. The drum is the constraint's production rate. The buffer is the WIP in front of the constraint. The rope is the production schedule to supply the constraint. (Chapter 12)

Economic value is the ability to make more money, now and in the future, subject to acceptable risk and effort. (Chapter 2)

Economic value added (EVA) modifies residual income by adjusting profits and investments from the accounting system values to measures better reflecting long-term shareholder value. (Chapter 8)

Employee empowerment is giving traditional management decision-making responsibility to workers. For this to work, they need to be properly trained and provided with good accounting information. (Chapter 1)

Equivalent units is a measure of the work done in terms of how many products (units of output from a department) could have been started, fully processed, and completed (made "from scratch") with the resources used in a time period (e.g., a month). (Chapter 5)

External failure costs result from customers discovering quality problems. These are one of the four costs of quality, and are reported with internal failure costs as nonconformance costs. (Chapter 11)

Externalities are hard-to-quantify effects from choosing an alternative. (Chapter 7)

Facilities-level activities include common costs for the entire company. They cannot be traced directly to any product line. When costing products and services, these are fixed costs. (Chapter 9)

The **financial focus** in **balanced scorecards** assures our continuous improvement programs result in better financial performance. (Chapter 14)

Finished goods inventory is the cost of completed products waiting to be sold. (Chapter 2)

Fishbone diagrams organize problem causes into the four ABC resource groups (people, materials, direct technology, and facilities) and links them to a quality problem. (Chapter 11)

Fixed costs are constant in total. Total fixed costs do not vary with changes in production or sales volume, so fixed costs do not change during a time period (e.g., a month or year). When expressed as amounts per product, fixed costs vary inversely with volume. (Chapter 3)

A **flexible budget** is a revised budget prepared at the end of a reporting period, which is based on actual sales volume. It is compared to actual revenues and costs within **profit variance reports**. The original budget cannot be used for variance calculations because they may be misleading. For example, favorable spending variances may result simply because actual sales are less than budgeted sales. But, when spending is compared to what it should have been for the actual sales made, it really may be unfavorable. (Chapter 6)

A **functional form income statement** organizes costs according to the functions they serve: getting products (product costs), and getting rid of products (selling expenses) and running the business (administrative expenses). Expenses are period costs. This format is used for external financial reporting. (Chapter 3)

Goal congruent behavior is when people are motivated to make decisions accomplishing the organization's goals and objectives. (Chapter 1)

An **ideal standard quantity** is the minimum amount of a resource needed given our current operating conditions, and does not allow for any waste or loss in the use of our resources. (Chapter 6)

Incremental budgeting increases (decreases) everyone's budget by the same percentage. (Chapter 4)

An **incremental pricing policy** determines the minimum, or break-even, price just covering the product's or service's incremental cost. (Chapter 7)

The **innovation and learning focus** of **balanced scorecards** looks at how a firm supports continuous improvement. (Chapter 14)

The **Institute of Management Accountants** is the world-wide professional organization for management and cost accountants. It offers professional certifications as a **Certified Management Accountant (CMA)** and Certified in Financial Management (CFM). (Chapter 1)

Intermediate products can be sold as is, or processed further into a final product. (Chapter 7)

Internal failure costs are the costs of fixing or rejecting bad products before customers receive them. Internal and external failure costs make up the costs of nonconformance (one of the two costs of quality categories). (Chapter 11)

The **internal processes focus** in **balanced scorecards** addresses how we create value for our customers through our value chain processes. (Chapter 14)

Investment centers are responsible for decisions involving asset investments and financing, and generating profits (revenues and costs). (Chapter 8)

Investments (or inventories), according to TOC, are the costs of all assets. (Chapter 12)

Job order cost accounting systems account for production costs by individual product or batch (a "job"). Each job has a subsidiary ledger account in WIP. Job costing is used in organizations providing many different types of products or services. (Chapter 5)

Just-In-Time (JIT) is a management system to eliminate inventories while delivering materials, manufactured components, and finished products only when needed. This is done by emphasizing total quality management and doing only those activities that create value. (Chapters 1 and 13)

Kaizen costing supports continuous improvements through frequent revisions to (lowering of) standard costs as improvements are made. (Chapter 11)

Lead time efficiency (LTE) ratios compare value-added time to lead time. Lead, or cycle, time is the total time to perform an activity. (Chapter 11)

Life cycle costing projects whether target costs for a new product or service can be obtained by budgeting value chain process costs across all stages of a product's life cycle. (Chapter 10)

A **line-of-credit** is a short-term loan arrangement with the bank in which money will be placed into a firm's checking account when needed, and repaid when it has a surplus. (Chapter 4)

Machine uptime ratios measure the percentage of time machines are available to do work. (Chapter 13)

Management by exception is focusing on management's attention on its problems. Variance reporting identifies and communicates profit and/or cashflow problems in support of the management by exception philosophy. (Chapter 6)

Manufacturing overhead includes all the indirect manufacturing costs that cannot be traced directly to a product. Examples include factory utilities, insurance, property taxes, indirect materials, and indirect labor. (Chapter 2)

Margin of safety is the difference between the sales forecast and break-even point, which is usually expressed as a percentage of the sales forecast. (Chapter 3)

A **markup** is the amount added to cost for setting a sales price. Since "cost" can be defined to include different activities, such as direct manufacturing costs versus indirect costs (overhead) or manufacturing cost versus expenses, the markup (the difference between the base cost and sales price) includes costs not in the base cost, as well as a desired profit. (Chapter 7)

Materials requisitions track the movement of materials from raw materials inventory to production departments, and allow direct tracing of material costs to products (or other cost objects such as a department). (Chapter 5)

Mixed costs are partly variable and partly fixed. For profit planning, mixed costs are separated into their variable and fixed portions. (Chapter 3)

Net present value (NPV) is the difference between the cash outflow today and the present value of the future cash inflows it creates.

NPV is the change in today's value of the firm due to this investment. (Chapter 14)

Nonconformance costs result from product failures. They include **internal** and **external failure costs**. Together with conformance costs, they make up the costs of quality. (Chapter 11)

Nonvalue-added activities do not create an extra benefit for our customers. (Chapter 11)

On-time delivery ratio is an ABM measure of vendor performance relating the number of deliveries received on time to the total deliveries made. (Chapter 10)

Operating expenses, according to TOC, include all costs of running the business except for the product's variable costs used in the throughput calculation. (Chapter 12)

An **opportunity cost** is the net cashflow given-up by not choosing the most profitable alternative. (Chapter 7)

Outsourcing is a long-run strategic decision to stop making a component (or providing a service), and instead obtain it from an outside source. (Chapter 1)

Pareto charts are bar graphs of quality problems expressed in terms of each problem's cost and the cumulative costs for all problems. (Chapter 11)

Participative budgeting involves everyone jointly working together to prepare the budget. (Chapter 4)

Payback period is the time needed to recover an investment from the extra cashflows it generates. (Chapter 12)

Period costs are assigned to time periods as expenses, but not to individual products. (Chapter 2)

Post-implementation audits evaluate a project's success and identify activities to improve the capital budgeting and implementation process. (Chapter 14)

Practical standard quantities include realistic expectations for problems like poor quality materials, equipment breakdowns, and labor downtime. (Chapter 6)

A **predetermined overhead rate (POR)** is the estimated amount of overhead cost per unit of its **cost driver**, that is, the activity that causes overhead cost. For example, if labor causes overhead, a POR of $2.00 per labor hour means we estimate $2.00 of overhead, on average, will be incurred for each labor hour worked. (Chapter 5)

Present value is today's worth of future cashflows. (Chapter 14)

Prevention costs are one of the four costs of quality categories representing the costs of problem prevention programs and controls. Appraisal and prevention are conformance costs. (Chapter 11)

A **process cost accounting system** accounts for production costs by department, and provides an average cost per product for each department. It is used in mass (continuous) production processes. (Chapter 5)

Process value analysis (PVA) is a method to identify value-added and nonvalue-added activities and their costs. Its objective is to identify opportunities for quality, service, and cost improvements. (Chapter 11)

Product costs are assigned to specific products through direct tracing (direct materials and direct labor) or through allocation (of overhead). (Chapter 2)

Product (or unit)-level activities happen each time another product is made. These are direct variable costs. (Chapter 9)

Product line-level activity costs are direct fixed costs of a product line. (Chapter 9)

Production departments make products, in contrast to **service departments** which provide support to the production departments. (Chapter 5)

A **production quota** is the number of products to make in order to satisfy the sales forecast. (Chapter 4)

A **production schedule** is the operating budget which calculates production quotas for each period (e.g., a month). (Chapter 4)

Profit centers are responsible for costs and revenues. They do not have the responsibility for investment decisions. Segmented income statements and variances often are used in evaluating their performance. (Chapter 8)

Profit margin is a short-run measure of operating efficiency, which expresses profit as a percentage of sales. (Chapter 8)

A **profit variance report** reconciles budgeted to actual profit. If budgeted and actual sales volume differ, and variable costs exist, the original budget is converted into a **flexible budget** showing expected profit for the actual sales volume. (Chapter 6)

A **proforma income statement** is a projected, or budgeted, income statement for next year (or some other future time period). (Chapter 3)

Program budgeting does not require annual justification, but does contain a termination date. (Chapter 4)

Pull systems do not provide goods or services until requested by their internal or external customers. JITs are pull systems. (Chapter 13)

Purchase orders are formal source documents authorizing a specific purchase of certain resources at a specified price. (Chapter 5)

Push systems seek to minimize average production costs by maximizing output. Production schedules control to workflows. Output not currently needed by the next process is pushed into inventory. (Chapter 13)

Quality function deployment (QFD) assures the product's characteristics (functions) are what the customers want. (Chapter 10)

Raw materials inventory is the cost of materials waiting to be used in making a product. (Chapter 2)

Receiving reports document we have received the materials ordered on a purchase order, and authorize payment. (Chapter 5)

Relevant cashflows are the differences between the incremental cashflows of each alternative being considered in a decision (choosing between the alternatives). (Chapter 7)

Relevant information improves decisions. It helps people do their jobs better. (Chapter 1)

The **relevant range** is that range of production volumes where variable costs are constant per product and total fixed costs do not change. Outside the relevant range, variable costs per product and total fixed costs may not be the same as within the range. (Chapter 3)

Residual income is the remaining profit after deducting the cost of financing an investment. (Chapter 8)

Resources are assets needed to perform activities. (Chapter 9)

Return on investment (ROI) is the profit earned on money invested, expressed as a ratio of profit to the investment amount. ROI is the mathematical product of two ratios: **profit margin** (profit as a percentage of sales), and **asset turnover** (how many sales dollars result from a $1 investment). (Chapter 8)

Sales price variances measure the difference between budgeted and actual profit because of unplanned sales prices. (Chapter 6)

Sales volume variances measure the difference in budgeted and actual profit due to an unplanned sales volume. (Chapter 6)

2nd generation ABC systems identify cause-effect relationships in quality problems, and report cost variances in terms of problems and their causes. (Chapter 11)

Segment margin is the profit contributed directly by a segment to the company. The sum of all segment margins is used to pay for the company's common costs, with anything left over being profit. Segment margin is used to evaluate the profit contribution of the segment (versus evaluating its manager, see controllable segment margin). (Chapter 8)

A **segmented income statement** includes 'mini-income statements' for each profit center. (Chapter 8)

Service departments provide support to **production departments**, which actually make a product. Examples of service departments include: the cafeteria, building and grounds maintenance, machine repairs and maintenance, janitorial, IS Department, and Cost Accounting Department. (Chapter 5)

Simultaneous engineering includes people from all the value chain processes in the initial design of a product or service. (Chapter 10)

Slack resources are extra people (time), materials, machinery, or other resources available to protect against uncertainties. (Chapter 5)

Snake charts graphically display product or service attributes customers think are important along with how well the provider performs on each attribute. (Chapter 10)

Spending variances measure the difference between expected and actual costs due to unplanned acquisition price changes. (Chapter 6)

Stakeholders determine (influence) our value. External stakeholders sustain our existence. Internal stakeholders provide our value-adding activities, products, and services. (Chapter 14)

A **standard cost** is the budgeted cost to make one product or service *for a particular resource item*. (Chapter 6)

A **standard cost card** itemizes the resources used in making a product, and shows their budgeted costs *per product*. (Chapter 6)

Standard price is the budgeted price for one unit of a resource. (Chapter 6)

A **standard quantity** is the amount of each resource we plan on using *to make one product*. (Chapter 6)

Standard quantity allowed is the total amount of a resource that should be used for the actual number of products made. (Chapter 6)

Step costs are fixed costs over a limited volume range. Small step costs usually are budgeted as variable costs. Large step costs usually are budgeted as fixed costs. (Chapter 3)

Stewardship is: (1) developing records and controls to safeguard assets, and (2) reporting on the firm's financial condition and how it has changed. (Chapter 1)

Strategic cost management evaluates industry-wide value chain processes to identify how and where a firm can create a sustainable competitive advantage and long-term value. (Chapter 10)

Strategic partnering builds long-run relationships with a few suppliers to eliminate activities not adding value, increase vendor quality, and reduce costs across the value chain. (Chapter 10)

A **strategic plan** begins with a firm's vision statement: what it ultimately wants to be. The vision statement identifies critical success factors which include objectives (where it wants to be for each factor). Measurable goals are attached to each objective. To accomplish each goal, the environment is evaluated, specific plans are made, and performance measures are created. (Chapter 2)

A **sunk cost** has already been incurred. The money has been spent. Since decisions can only affect the future, a sunk cost is irrelevant to any decision we are now considering. (Chapter 7)

Target costing is a market-based approach to determine the total allowable lifetime cost of a product by subtracting a profit goal from estimated lifetime revenues. (Chapter 10)

The **theory of constraints (TOC)** believes one limiting factor always exists which keeps systems from doing more. TOC's goal is to optimally manage that "bottleneck" (constraint) until it can be eliminated. (Chapter 12)

Throughput is the extra CMU we make with one more unit of output from a constraint. It's the product's contribution margin divided by the constraint's standard quantity. (Chapter 12)

Time-adjusted ROI is often called the internal rate of return (IRR). It is an investment's compound interest rate. (Chapter 14)

Time cards directly trace labor costs to products, departments, or other cost objects. (Chapter 5)

Total quality management (TQM) is simply knowing how to delight our customers, and then doing it. (Chapter 1) It is a strategic and operational commitment to increasing value through improving product (service) quality and customer service, while decreasing cost. (Chapter 11)

A **transfer** is the "sale" of a product or service from a profit center to another division within the company. (Chapter 7)

A **transfer price** is the sales price attached to a good or service transferred from a profit center to another division within the company. (Chapter 7)

Usage, or efficiency, variances report the difference between budgeted and actual profit or cash due to using more or less of a resource. (Chapter 6)

Value-added activities increase the worth (sales price, value) of products and services to customers. (Chapter 11)

Value chain: a listing of the processes involved in providing goods and services. Value chains can be created for industries or for specific firms within an industry. (Chapter 2)

Variable costs are constant per unit. They remain the same amount for each product. Because variable costs are always the same for each product, total variable costs increase proportionately with volume. (Chapter 3)

A **variance** is the difference between budgeted and actual profits or cashflows. (Chapter 6)

Vendor performance index (VPI) is an ABM measure relating the cost of extra work created by a supplier to the cost of materials purchased. (Chapter 10)

Virtual companies are created by sharing information between them so they behave as one large organization. (Chapter 1)

Work-in-process inventory is the cost of making the product while it is being manufactured. (Chapter 2)

Zero-based budgeting requires each project to be justified before it's included in the budget. (Chapter 4)

INDEX

C

D

E

F

G

H

O

P

Q

R

S

T

U

V

W

X

Z